BEGINNING JAVA® PROGRAMMING

BEGINNING

Java® Programming

BEGINNING

Java® Programming

THE OBJECT-ORIENTED APPROACH

Bart Baesens

Aimée Backiel

Seppe vanden Broucke

A Wiley Brand

Beginning Java® Programming: The Object-Oriented Approach

Published by
John Wiley & Sons, Inc.
10475 Crosspoint Boulevard
Indianapolis, IN 46256
www.wiley.com

Copyright © 2015 by John Wiley & Sons, Inc., Indianapolis, Indiana

Published simultaneously in Canada

ISBN: 978-1-118-73949-5

ISBN: 978-1-118-73951-8 (ebk)

ISBN: 978-1-118-73935-8 (ebk)

Manufactured in the United States of America

10 9 8 7 6 5 4 3 2 1

For general information on our other products and services please contact our Customer Care Department within the United States at (877) 762-2974, outside the United States at (317) 572-3993 or fax (317) 572-4002.

Wiley publishes in a variety of print and electronic formats and by print-on-demand. Some material included with standard print versions of this book may not be included in e-books or in print-on-demand. If this book refers to media such as a CD or DVD that is not included in the version you purchased, you may download this material at http://booksupport.wiley.com. For more information about Wiley products, visit www.wiley.com.

Library of Congress Control Number: 2013948012

ABOUT THE AUTHORS

PROFESSOR BART BAESENS is a professor at KU Leuven (Belgium) and a lecturer at the University of Southampton (United Kingdom). He has been teaching courses on programming for more than 10 years. His research focuses on big data and analytics, customer relationship management, web analytics, fraud detection, and credit risk management. His findings have been published in well-known international journals and presented at top international conferences. He is also the author of the books *Credit Risk Management: Basic Concepts* (Oxford University Press, 2008) and *Analytics in a Big Data World* (Wiley, 2014). His research is summarized at www.dataminingapps.com. He also regularly tutors, advises, and provides consulting support to international firms.

AIMÉE BACKIEL is a PhD researcher in applied economics at KU Leuven in Belgium. Her focus of research is survival analysis, a statistical modeling technique. She was first introduced to Java in 2003 while studying mathematics at the University of Southern Maine. After working some years in data analysis and assessment, she followed up with an Object-Oriented Programming course at KU Leuven, earning a perfect 20/20 for the electronic agenda system she pair-programmed with a partner. Currently, she incorporates Java daily in her own research. In addition, she leads basic programming exercise sessions for students of various disciplines, giving her insight into teaching and learning Java from the ground up and providing a multitude of practical examples for learners who may or may not be technically oriented. Her background provides a balance between a theoretical foundation and an applied business-oriented approach.

SEPPE VANDEN BROUCKE is a PhD researcher in the Department of Decision Sciences and Information Management at KU Leuven. His interest in programming began when he was six years old, starting with languages such as BASIC and Logo. Throughout the following years, Seppe gained experience in a large number of languages, including PHP, Python, Ruby, and Java. He is applying the latter extensively in his day-to-day research activities in order to extract knowledge and insights from business-process-oriented data. His research interests include business process management, process mining, data mining, and machine learning. His work has been published in well-known international journals and presented at top conferences. Seppe has also contributed to and participated in a number of open-source projects. His research is summarized at www.dataminingapps.com, and his personal page is located at www.seppe.net.

CREDITS

Project Editor
Kelly Talbot

Technical Editors
Andres Almiray
Alan Williamson
Christian Ullenboom

Production Manager
Kathleen Wisor

Copy Editor
Kezia Endsley

**Manager of Content Development &
Assembly**
Mary Beth Wakefield

Marketing Director
David Mayhew

Marketing Manager
Carrie Sherill

**Professional Technology & Strategy
Director**
Barry Pruett

Business Manager
Amy Knies

Associate Publisher
Jim Minatel

Project Coordinator, Cover
Patrick Redmond

Proofreader
Kathy Pope, Word One

Indexer
John Sleeva

Cover Designer
Wiley

Cover Image
©istockphoto.com/rrocio

ACKNOWLEDGMENTS

THIS BOOK WOULD NOT HAVE BEEN POSSIBLE without the support and assistance of many dedicated, helpful, bright, and supportive individuals. Therefore, the authors wish to acknowledge the contributions and assistance of various colleagues, friends, and fellow Java lovers to the writing of this book.

This book is the result of many years of teaching programming courses and working with Java in a research context. We first would like to thank our publisher, Wiley, for accepting our book proposal less than one year ago. Next, we would like to thank our editor, Kelly Talbot, for the excellent collaboration, close follow-up, and timely replies to the many email exchanges we had, as well as the copy, technical, and other assistant editors for the many comments and positive feedback relayed to us, which immensely improved the quality of this book. We are also grateful to the active and lively Java community for providing various user fora, blogs, online lectures, and tutorials, which proved very helpful.

We would also like to acknowledge the direct and indirect contributions of the many colleagues, fellow professors, students, researchers, and friends with whom we have collaborated during the past 10 years.

Last but not least, we are grateful to our partners, parents, and families for their love, support, and encouragement. We hope the readers will enjoy the book and welcome any feedback or suggestions for improvement.

Bart Baesens

Aimée Backiel

Seppe vanden Broucke

January 2015

CONTENTS

INTRODUCTION

CONGRATULATIONS! By picking up this book you have made the first step in your voyage toward learning Java. Java is a programming language with a long history, starting with its inception in 1991, when it was still named "Oak," through the first public release (Java 1.0) in 1995 and the newly released Java 8. Its "write once, run anywhere" approach, together with robust language features and numerous libraries led to a spectacular adoption rate. Java is one of the most popular languages in use today, and has been especially successful in enterprise and business environments.

Note, however, that Java is not without its criticism (no programming language is). You might have picked upon the often-repeated criticism that Java is verbose, unsecure, suffering from a slow release cycle, and that it is fading in popularity compared to the interest in new, more exciting languages (Ruby, Erlang, and Haskell, to name a few) by the computer science and programmer communities. The reality, however, tells a different story. Java remains widely taught in schools and universities and is regarded as the language of choice in many organizations. The introduction of Java 7 in 2011 made many tasks simpler, and the availability of many seasoned and stable libraries, tools, and feature-complete IDEs is unmatched by the ecosystem found around other languages. In 2014, Java 8 introduced lambda expressions to streamline code and a reengineered date and time interface that simplifies and improves the internationalization of applications. Java's strong architectural foundations make the language ideally suited for both newcomers and experienced programmers who want to expand their knowledge of Object-Oriented Programming.

Before reaching the end of this book, you will agree that being proficient in Java is a strong skill to possess indeed. We aim to get you started and up to speed as quickly as possible, without making sacrifices in terms of depth and breadth of topics. The goal is not to guide you in simply adding yet another (or first) language to your repertoire, but also to familiarize you with Java's underlying approach toward robust and structured Object-Oriented Programming. As you will see, Java's "verbosity" makes it ideally suited to teach programming best practices in an explicit manner. Providing step-by-step explanations together with many examples—inspired by real-life environments rather than toy exercises—will help you quickly appreciate Java's design and usefulness, and learn that programming in Java can even be great fun!

WHO THIS BOOK IS FOR

Java is a great language to learn for both new and experienced programmers. As such, this book is geared towards a broad audience, including practitioners, analysts, programmers, and students wanting to apply Java in a pragmatic context. It doesn't matter whether you are new to programming and have chosen Java as a place to start or whether you come in from another programming language; Java is a great choice. Many books exist on the topic of Java (just look at the shelf where you found this book!), but we feel that existing offerings reuse the same approach to demonstrate concepts. Therefore, you will not find the archetypical (and honestly, completely useless) "Hello World" example in this book. Instead, we delve into concrete, thought-out examples that illustrate how Java can be useful and used in real life. Whether you are an analyst struggling with spreadsheet formulas to perform a somewhat advanced calculation (there has to be a smarter way, right?), a student wondering how your future employer is using Java, or a hobbyist programmer trying to keep track of stock quotes or a book database, this book aims to familiarize you with all the necessary concepts.

TOPICS COVERED IN THIS BOOK

The topics discussed in this book can, broadly speaking, be outlined in the following three categories. First is a general introduction to programming and Java. The first chapters briefly discuss programming in general, before moving on to a high-level description of Java's history and language features. We also make sure to set up everything you need to get started with Java.

The second part deals with Object-Oriented Programming in Java. The goal is to help readers acquire a strong knowledge of how Object-Oriented Programming works and how Java programs are structured.

The third part is more focused and practical, and shows how you can leverage Java to talk to data sources (such as files, databases, and even web services) and how you can create a graphical user interface around your program logic.

Note that we have not structured the book around the aforementioned three parts. Instead of splitting the book into "theoretical" and "practical" parts, we chose to introduce new concepts step-by-step as they are needed so that you can quickly move on to examples and exercises. The best way to learn is by doing, and this saying particularly holds true when learning to program.

In Chapter 1, we provide a brief general introduction to programming geared toward newcomers and novice programmers. In Chapter 2, we start introducing Java by providing an overview of the language's history, the different technological components that make up the language, the general language structure, and data types. At that point, you will know enough to get started, so that in Chapter 3, we will guide you toward setting up your development environment and trying out some basic examples and exercises. In Chapter 4, we introduce Object-Oriented Programming basics; flow-control statements are covered in Chapter 5. At that point, you will be able to create simple but functional programs. Chapter 6 explains how to catch errors and debug your programs, which will come in handy as you start using resources and coding more advanced programs. At this point, you will have all the necessary components to start looking at some more advanced Object-Oriented Programming concepts in Chapter 7. After this, you'll be ready to tackle more complex interactions with files, external sources, and users. In Chapter 8 you will look at dealing with file-based input and output, including how to load files, perform basic operations, and save the results back to disk. Chapters 9 and 10 build on this by explaining how to interact with databases and web sources. At this point, you will be itching to move away from command-line based applications, and Chapter 11 explains in-depth how to build graphical user interfaces. Chapter 12 concludes the theory by providing an overview of some common architectural patterns (best practices, if you will) used by seasoned Java developers.

By the end of this book, you will have gained a strong knowledge of Java's internals, you will know what is meant by Object-Oriented Programming, know how to debug and deal with errors in your programs, know how to handle file-based input and output, talk to databases, talk to web services, make a full-fledged graphical application, and be familiar with some common and well-known programming "patterns," which are best practices to structure and organize a program's architectural setup.

TOPICS NOT COVERED IN THIS BOOK

This book is not a reference manual. The goal is to get readers acquainted with the basics of Java and Object-Oriented Programming to use within practical applications, not to provide a full overview of Java's API. As such, given the scope of this book, there are some concepts that are not discussed in detail. However, we have taken care to avoid elements you can live without at this point in your Java career.

Working with generics in Java, for example, is not discussed explicitly, but instead explained briefly where needed (when we talk about collections in Java, such as lists or sets, for example). Working with generic classes can be daunting for novice Java programmers, and the Object-Oriented Programming concepts discussed suffice to cover the multitude of use cases. That said, familiarizing yourself with generic types after going through this book should not prove difficult.

Other topics that are not discussed in-depth include networking in Java (socket programming), multithreaded and concurrent programming, reflection, and the lambda expressions introduced with Java 8. Networking aspects, however, are dealt with from a "higher-level" view. We discuss how to interact with web services, which provides a great starting point for practitioners to load data coming from the web. Concurrent, multi-threaded programming is a beneficial practice when performance and speed becomes an issue in applications, but for most use cases in a practical context, Java performs just fine without having to deal with multi-threading. Additionally, programming in a concurrent fashion introduces some particular challenges and "gotchas" that are unfit for beginning Java programmers to deal with. Reflection is a part of the Java API that allows programmers to examine and "reflect" on Java programs while they are running and perform changes to programs while they are being executed. While very helpful in some cases, it also is out of scope for a beginner's book on Java. Finally, the recently released Java 8 introduces some new concepts, most notably lambda expressions. Java 7 also provides functionality to work with so-called "anonymous classes," which are ad hoc implementations of a base class without a specific name or definition. Other than the fact that these classes can appear somewhat verbose, they are perfectly fine to use instead of lambda expressions (which provide the same functionality in a more concise manner) and are still widely used. We do, however, provide short notes on developments within Java 8 whenever appropriate.

Finally, Java is composed of a certain number of "technologies" (also called platform components). The "standard" Java is denoted as "Standard Edition" (SE), and is the one we tackle here. An Enterprise Edition (EE) also exists, as well as a number of extensions to develop embedded and mobile applications (Embedded Java and Java ME), applications for smart TVs (Java TV), and graphic-intensive applications (Java FX and Java 2D). We do not discuss these extensions in this book, as they have no place in a beginner's book on Java. Readers wanting to apply Java in these specific areas should, however, be ready to move on to these more focused topics after reading this book.

CONVENTIONS

This book applies a number of styles and layout conventions to differentiate between the different types of information.

TRY IT OUTS   What Are They?

This book comes with many code examples and exercises that introduce and explain new concepts step-by-step. These are called "Try It Outs" and can be executed directly while reading the chapters or revisited at a later time. Each Try It Out is followed by a How It Works, which is designed to help you understand exactly what's happening in the Try It Out exercise.

In addition to providing extensive examples in the form of Try It Outs, you will also encounter frequent tips, hints, advice, and background information, which are formatted like this:

> **NOTE** *Tips, hints, advice, and background information are formatted like this. Reading these segments can help to make concepts clearer. You may also notice a Warning or Common Mistakes heading on these boxes to bring your attention to particular things you should avoid.*

Discussions that extend beyond a short tip or note will look a little bit different.

> ### SIDEBAR
>
> We use this format to explain concepts that require more than a simple note. The details are not necessary to the understanding of the book but offer a more complete discussion on a particular topic.

Finally, program code within this book is formatted in two ways. The first way is as code type: (/* Like this comment */). Variables (like *iAmAVariable*) appear in italic code type.

Larger code blocks look like the following:

```java
public class NoHelloWorld {
    public static void main(String[] args) {
        System.out.println("This is not an Hello World program...");
    }
}
```

> **NOTE** *Eclipse is the Integrated Development Environment (IDE) we will be using throughout this book. Don't worry what this means for now. Everything you need to set up in order to follow along is explained in Chapter 3.*

All these styles are designed to make sure it's easy for you to know what you're looking at while you read.

SOURCE CODE

As you work through the examples in this book, you may choose either to type in all the code manually or to use the source-code files that accompany the book. All of the source code used in this book is available for download at www.wrox.com. Once at the site, simply locate the book's title (either by using the Search box or by using one of the title lists) and click the Download Code link on the book's detail page to obtain all the source code for the book.

> **NOTE** *Because many books have similar titles, you may find it easiest to search by ISBN; this book's ISBN is 978-1-118-73949-5.*

Once you download the code, just decompress it with your favorite compression tool. Alternately, you can go to the main Wrox code download page at www.wrox.com/dynamic/books/download .aspx to see the code available for this book and all other Wrox books.

ERRATA

We make every effort to ensure that there are no errors in the text or in the code. However, no one is perfect, and mistakes do occur. If you find an error in one of our books, like a spelling mistake or faulty piece of code, we would be very grateful for your feedback. By sending in errata, you may save another reader hours of frustration, and at the same time you will be helping us provide even higher-quality information.

To find the errata page for this book, go to www.wrox.com and locate the title using the Search box or one of the title lists. Then, on the book details page, click the Book Errata link. On this page you can view all errata that have been submitted for this book and posted by Wrox editors. A complete book list, including links to each book's errata, is also available at www.wrox.com/misc-pages/ booklist.shtml.

If you don't spot "your" error on the Book Errata page, go to www.wrox.com/contact/ techsupport.shtml and complete the form there to send us the error you have found. We'll check the information and, if appropriate, post a message to the book's errata page and fix the problem in subsequent editions of the book.

P2P.WROX.COM

For author and peer discussion, join the P2P forums at p2p.wrox.com. The forums are a web-based system on which you can post messages relating to Wrox books and related technologies and interact with other readers and technology users. The forums offer a subscription feature to e-mail you topics of interest of your choosing when new posts are made to the forums. Wrox authors, editors, other industry experts, and your fellow readers are present on these forums.

At http://p2p.wrox.com you will find a number of different forums that will help you not only as you read this book, but also as you develop your own applications. To join the forums, just follow these steps:

1. Go to p2p.wrox.com and click the Register link.

2. Read the terms of use and click Agree.

3. Complete the required information to join as well as any optional information you wish to provide, and click Submit.

4. You will receive an e-mail with information describing how to verify your account and complete the joining process.

> **NOTE** *You can read messages in the forums without joining P2P, but in order to post your own messages, you must join.*

Once you join, you can post new messages and respond to messages other users post. You can read messages at any time on the Web. If you would like to have new messages from a particular forum e-mailed to you, click the Subscribe to this Forum icon by the forum name in the forum listing.

For more information about how to use the Wrox P2P, be sure to read the P2P FAQs for answers to questions about how the forum software works, as well as many common questions specific to P2P and Wrox books. To read the FAQs, click the FAQ link on any P2P page.

HOW TO READ THIS BOOK

This book is mostly designed as a hands-on tutorial and tries to keep you practicing and trying out new concepts as quickly and often as possible. As mentioned before, you will find Try It Outs throughout this book where you will find step-by-step instructions for working with Java.

You will notice that we alternate between chapters that are more theoretical in nature (such as what Object-Oriented Programming is) and chapters that are more practical (such as how to read in a file and do something with it). As such, the preferred way to go through this book when you're reading it the first time is to work your way from beginning to end. Think of this book as a tour through Java. We do not visit every nook and cranny—you don't need to examine each and every small detail—but you do want to get the big picture, enabling you to get proficient with Java as quickly as possible without taking dangerous shortcuts by explaining concepts in a haphazardly manner. Whenever you encounter a practical chapter that seems less useful, however, you are free to skip it and return to it later. That said, we have clearly separated the chapters to match a specific set of topics, so readers revisiting this book will have no trouble immediately navigating to the right spot.

Given the nature of programming, it is unavoidable that you will run across some examples in earlier chapters that includes a concept that will be explained in a later section. We always indicate these forward references in a clear manner and tell you "not to worry about this until Chapter X." Trust us on this; these elements will be covered later.

As you proceed, remember the best way to learn is to try out things on your own, extend projects, and create new ones. The Try It Out exercises provide examples throughout the text for you to start programming with a lot of guidance. As your knowledge and confidence build, try creating your own simple programs to complete tasks that are interesting for you. This way, you will put the concepts you've learned to use and start to see how Java can work for you.

GET IN TOUCH

We have tried to make this book as complete, accurate, and enjoyable as possible. Of course, what really matters is what you, as the reader, think of it. Please let us know your views by getting in touch. The authors welcome all feedback and comments.

Bart Baesens

Aimée Backiel

Seppe vanden Broucke

January, 2015

BEGINNING

Java® Programming

1

A General Introduction to Programming

WHAT YOU WILL LEARN IN THIS CHAPTER:

➤ The key steps in a programming process

➤ The different types of programming errors

➤ The key principles of software testing

➤ The different types of software maintenance

➤ The key principles of structured programming

WROX.COM CODE DOWNLOADS FOR THIS CHAPTER

The wrox.com code downloads for this chapter are found at www.wrox.com/go/
beginningjavaprogramming on the Download Code tab. The code is in the Chapter 1
download and individually named according to the names throughout the chapter.

Developing good and correct software is a very important challenge in today's business
environment. Given the ubiquity and pervasiveness of software programs into our daily
lives, the impact of faulty software is now bigger than ever. Software errors have caused
flight crashes, rocket launch errors, and power blackouts, to name a few examples. Hence,
it is important to design high-quality, error-free software programs. This chapter covers the
fundamental concepts of programming. First, it elaborates on the programming process. The
next section provides a sneak preview of object-oriented programming. This is followed by a
short discussion on programming errors. The basic principles of software testing and software
maintenance are also discussed. The chapter concludes by giving some recommendations
relating to structured programming. You will revisit many of these ideas in future chapters,
with a more hands-on approach.

THE PROGRAMMING PROCESS

A *program* (also referred to as an application) is a set of instructions targeted to solve a particular problem that can be unambiguously understood by a computer. To this end, the computer will translate the program to the language it understands, which is machine language consisting of 0s and 1s. Computers execute a program literally as it was programmed, nothing more and nothing less. Programming is the activity of writing or coding a program in a particular programming language. This is a language that has strict grammar and syntax rules, symbols, and special keywords. People who write programs are commonly referred to as programmers or application developers. The term software then refers to a set of programs within a particular business context.

An example of a programming exercise is a program that calculates the body mass index (BMI) of a person. The BMI is calculated by dividing a person's weight in kilograms by the square of his or her height in meters. A person is considered overweight if his or her BMI is over 25. A BMI calculator program then requires the weight and height as inputs and calculates the associated BMI as the output. This is illustrated in Figure 1-1. This BMI example is used to demonstrate the steps in the software development cycle.

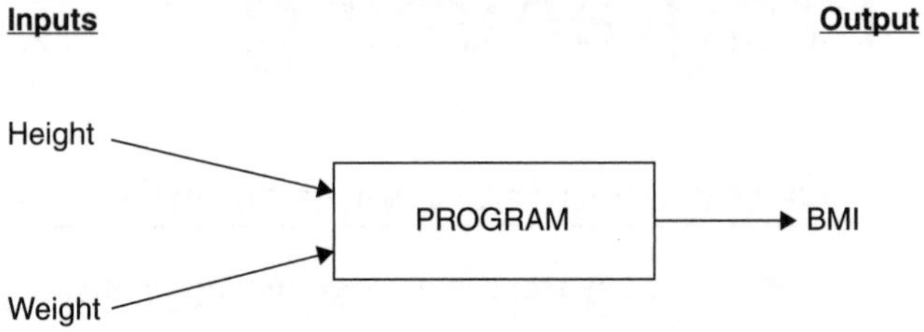

Inputs   **Output**

Height

Weight

PROGRAM → BMI

FIGURE 1-1

Programs are typically written using a step-by-step approach, as follows:

1. Requirements gathering and analysis
2. Program design
3. Program coding
4. Translation to machine language
5. Testing and debugging
6. Deployment
7. Maintenance

Because our environment is continuously evolving, software, too, is often continually reviewed and adapted. Therefore, these steps are often represented as a cycle, as shown in Figure 1-2, rather than as a ladder.

The first step is to make sure you understand the problem in sufficient detail. This means analyzing the problem statement carefully so you fully grasp all the requirements that need to be fulfilled by the software program. This may involve Q&A sessions, interviews, and surveys

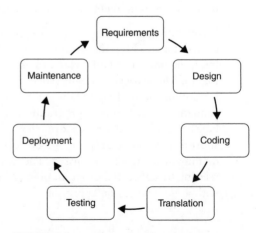

FIGURE 1-2

with business experts who have the necessary subject matter expertise. Even if you are programming for yourself, taking the time upfront to consider all the demands you want your program to meet will limit the amount of changes required later in the process. At the end of this step, it is important to know what the input to the program will receive and what output it should give. In the BMI example, you will need to know whether the height will be measured in meters or feet and the weight in kilos or pounds. You would also want to determine whether the output should be just the BMI results or also a message stating whether or not the person is overweight.

Once you have a thorough understanding of the business problem, you can start thinking about ways to solve it using a computer program. In other words, which processing steps should take place on the input(s) in order to give the desired output(s)? The procedure needed to solve the problem is also often referred to as the *algorithm*. When working out an algorithm, common sense and creativity both play an important role. A first useful step in designing an algorithm is planning the application logic using pseudo-code or flowcharts. Pseudo-code is a type of structured English but without strict grammar rules. It is a user-friendly way of representing application logic in a sequential, readable format. It allows the problem statement to be broken into manageable pieces in order to reduce its complexity. Following is an example of pseudo-code for the BMI case. A flowchart represents the application in a diagram, whereby the boxes show the activities and the arrows the sequences between them. Table 1-1 presents an overview of the most important flowchart construction concepts. Figure 1-3 then gives an example of a flowchart for the BMI case. Both pseudo-code and flowcharts can be used concurrently to facilitate the programming exercise. A key advantage of flowcharts when compared to pseudo-code is that they are visual and thus easier to interpret.

```
ask user: height
ask user: weight
if height = 0 or weight = 0:
error: "Incorrect input values"
return to beginning (ask height and weight)
end if
x = weight / (height * height)
message: "Your BMI is ",x
```

Table 1-1 is an overview of the most important flowchart modeling concepts.

TABLE 1-1: Key Flowchart Modeling Concepts

FLOWCHART SYMBOL	MEANING
(terminator symbol)	A terminator shows the start and stopping points of the program.
(arrow symbol)	An arrow shows the direction of the process flow.
(rectangle symbol)	A rectangle represents a process step or activity.

continues

TABLE 1-1: *(continued)*

FLOWCHART SYMBOL	MEANING
◇	A diamond indicates a decision point in the process.
▱	This symbol represents a document or report.
▱	This rhombus represents data used as inputs/outputs to/from a process.
⌷	This cylinder represents a database.

A next step is to code the program in a particular programming language. The choice of the language will depend on the programming paradigm and the platform adopted (such as hardware, operating system, or network).

Once the source code of the program has been written, it will be given to a translator to translate it to machine language (0s and 1s) so that it can be executed and solve the business problem.

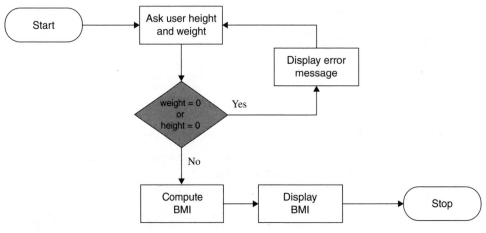

FIGURE 1-3

During application development, it is important that every program is intensively tested to avoid any errors. Often, in programming, errors are called *bugs*. Various types of errors exist and an entire chapter is devoted to this topic. Programming tools frequently have debugging facilities built in to easily track bugs down and correct them. It is possible to debug your program without the use of such tools, but in either case, you should follow a structured and systematic review to be sure you've identified any bugs before your program is deployed.

Once a program has been thoroughly tested, it can be deployed. This means that the program will be brought into production and actively used to solve the business problem. Remember, users of your software don't usually understand as much about programming as you. Try to keep them in mind throughout the process to make this deployment step as seamless as possible.

Finally, programs should be maintained on an ongoing basis. There are many reasons for regular maintenance, namely correcting newly discovered bugs, accommodating changing user needs, preventing erroneous user input, or adding new features to existing programs.

It is important to note that programming is not a strict, sequential, step-by-step process. Quite to the contrary, it often occurs as an iterative process, whereby the original business problem is refined or even reformulated during the coding process.

OBJECT-ORIENTED PROGRAMMING: A SNEAK PREVIEW

In object-oriented (OO) programming, an application consists of a series of objects that ask services from each other. Each object is an instance of a class that contains a blueprint description of all the object's characteristics. Contrary to procedural programming, an object bundles both its data (which determines its state) and its procedures (which determines its behavior) in a coherent way. An example of this could be a student object having data elements such as ID, name, date of birth, email address, and so on, and procedures such as registerForCourse, isPassed, and so on. A key difference between OO and procedural programming is that OO uses local data stored in objects, whereas procedural programming uses global shared data that the various procedures can access directly. This has substantial implications from a maintenance viewpoint. Imagine that you want to change a particular data element (rename it or remove it). In a procedural programming environment, you would have to look up all procedures that make use of the data element and adapt them accordingly. For huge programs, this can be a very tedious maintenance exercise. When you're using an OO programming paradigm, you only need to change the data element in the object's definition and the other objects can keep on interacting with it like they did before, minimizing the maintenance.

OO programming is the most popular programming paradigm currently in use. Some examples of object-oriented programming languages are Eiffel, Smalltalk, C++, and Java.

The following code example demonstrates how to implement the BMI example in Java. Contrary to the procedural programming example, it can be clearly seen that the data (weight, height, and BMI) is bundled together with the procedures (BMICalculator, calculate, and isOverweight) into one coherent class definition.

```java
public class BMICalculator {
  private double weight, height, BMI;

  public BMICalculator( double weight, double height ){
    this.weight = weight;
    this.height = height;
  }
```

```
public void calculate(){
  BMI = weight / (height*height);
}

public boolean isOverweight(){
  return (BMI > 25);
}
}
```

PROGRAMMING ERRORS

A programming error is also referred to as a *bug*, and the procedure for removing programming errors is called *debugging*. Debugging usually has the following three steps:

1. Detect that there is an error.
2. Locate the error. This can be quite time consuming for big programs.
3. Solve the error.

Different types of programming errors exist and are explored in the following sections.

Syntax/Compilation Errors

A syntax or compilation error refers to a grammatical mistake in the program. Examples are a punctuation error or misspelling of a keyword. These types of errors are typically caught by the compiler or interpreter, which will generate an error message. Consider the following Java example:

```
public void calculate(){
  BMI = weight / (height*height),
}
```

The statement that calculates the BMI should end with a semicolon (;) instead of a comma (,), according to the Java syntax rules. Hence, a syntax error will be generated and displayed. Syntax errors are usually easy to detect and solve.

Runtime Errors

A runtime error is an error that occurs during the execution of the program. Consider the following piece of Java code to calculate the BMI:

```
public void calculate(){
  BMI = weight / (height*height);
}
```

If the user enters a value of 0 for height, a division by zero occurs. This creates a runtime error and will likely crash during execution. Another example of a runtime error is an infinite loop into which the program enters at execution. During the design of the program, it is important to think about possible runtime errors that might occur due to bad user input, which is where the majority of bugs will originate. These errors should be anticipated as much as possible using appropriate error-handling routines, as we will discuss later.

Logic/Semantic Errors

Logic or semantic errors are the hardest to detect since the program will give an output and not generate an error. However, the output that is given is incorrect due to a formula being incorrectly programmed. Consider the BMI example again:

```
public void calculate(){
  BMI = (weight*weight) / height;
}
```

This routine is clearly erroneous since it calculates the BMI as (weight*weight)/height instead of weight/(height*height). These errors cannot be detected by compilers or interpreters.

PRINCIPLES OF SOFTWARE TESTING

In order to avoid software errors (and their impact), a program should be thoroughly tested for any remaining errors before it is brought into production. The main purpose of testing is verification and validation of the software build. Verification aims at answering the question as to whether the system was built correctly, whereas validation tries to determine whether the right system was built. The quicker an error is found during development, the cheaper it is to correct it. As illustrated in Figure 1-4, the cost of testing typically increases exponentially, whereas the cost of missed bugs decreases exponentially with the amount of testing conducted. The optimum testing resources can then be found where both curves intersect.

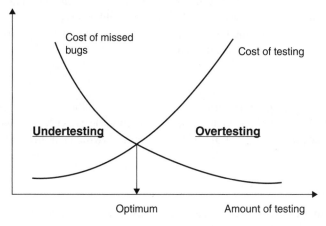

FIGURE 1-4

A first basic way of testing is to desk-check the program by using paper and pencil. The manual calculations and output can then be contrasted with the program calculations and output. It is especially important to consider extreme cases and see how the program behaves. Of course, this only works for small-scale programs; more sophisticated procedures might be needed for bigger programs.

Static testing procedures test the program not by executing it, but by inspecting and reviewing the code and performing detailed walk-throughs. It is aimed at verification. On the other hand, dynamic testing procedures test the program by executing it with carefully selected test cases. It is thus more related to validation. The test cases can be chosen according to a *white box* or *black box* strategy. In white box testing, they are selected by thorough inspection of the source code of the program; for example, by making sure all the branches in an `if-then-else` selection are covered, boundary conditions for loops are verified, and so on. One popular approach is to intentionally inject faults in the source code, which then need to be tracked down in a follow-up step. Black box testing considers the program as a black box and does not inspect its internal source code. One example is a procedure that tries to test all possible input parameter combinations. It is especially important to also test what happens when impossible values are entered (such as a negative value for weight and height, value of 0 for height, missing value for gender, and so on). Obviously, this becomes computationally infeasible in case many inputs are present and intelligent sampling procedures could be adopted to test as many useful input combinations as possible.

Software development typically has two phases of testing. *Alpha testing* is done internally by the application developers before the software is brought to the market. In *beta testing,* the software is given to a selected target audience and errors are reported back to the development team.

SOFTWARE MAINTENANCE

Software is always dynamically evolving, even after delivery. Maintenance is the activity of adjusting the program after it has been taken into production. This is done to boost its performance, solve any remaining errors, and/or accommodate new user requirements. Maintenance typically consumes a large part of the overall software development costs (up to 70% or more according to some estimates). This can be partly explained by the fact that much of the software people work with today is relatively old (legacy software) and has been maintained on an ongoing basis. This section covers the four main types of maintenance. They are categorized according to their intended goals.

Adaptive Maintenance

Adaptive software maintenance refers to modifying a program to accommodate changes in the environment (both hardware and software). An example of this is a new Windows release with new features added (which can also be used by the program) and old features removed (which can no longer be used by the program).

Perfective Maintenance

This refers to enhancing a program to support new or changed user requirements. Consider again the BMI example. When the user wants to be able to enter height in feet units and weight in pound units, this is a perfective maintenance operation.

Corrective Maintenance

Corrective maintenance aims at finding errors during runtime and fixing them. A further distinction can be made here between emergency fixes (which need to be solved as quickly as possible due to their critical relevance) and routine debugging (which is less urgent).

Preventive Maintenance

Preventive maintenance aims at increasing software maintainability in order to prevent future errors. A popular example here was the Y2K problem, where companies massively anticipated date calculation errors in their software programs at the end of the previous century. Another example concerns the transition of many countries from their own independent currency toward the Euro. One important activity to facilitate preventive maintenance is documentation. This means that the application is extended with various comments that are not executed by the compiler, but that indicate the meaning of the various data elements, procedures, and operations in order to facilitate future maintenance.

Among the four types of maintenance, perfective maintenance typically takes the main share of all maintenance efforts (it can even be more than 50%), followed by adaptive, corrective, and preventive maintenance.

The major causes of maintenance problems are unstructured code, lack of documentation, excessive user demand for changes, lack of user training and understanding, and high user turnover. Many organizations have standard procedures for maintenance, which typically start with the formal filing of a change request specifying the modifications needed to the software. Depending on the severity of the request and the change management strategy adopted by the organization, these change requests can be grouped and dealt with at fixed time stamps, or treated immediately.

PRINCIPLES OF STRUCTURED PROGRAMMING

To finish this introductory chapter, this section discusses some of the basic principles of structured programming.

A first important concept is *stepwise refinement*. Programs should be designed using a top-down strategy where the problem statement is subdivided into smaller, more manageable subproblems. These subproblems can be further broken down into smaller subproblems until each piece becomes easy to solve. This strategy should decrease the program development time and its maintenance cost.

Documentation is another important concept. It provides invaluable clarification for complex programming statements, which will again facilitate future maintenance operations. Every programming language offers facilities to include documentation lines that are ignored by the compiler or interpreter but can be easily read and understood by programmers.

Also of key importance is to assign meaningful names to programming concepts such as variables. Instead of naming a variable `i` or `j` without any explicit interpretation, it is much better to use `student` or `course`, which immediately indicate their meanings.

By incorporating these principles into your programs, you will improve your own work and at the same time make it possible for others (or even yourself—it's not always easy to remember what you meant by `varX` months later) to update and continue using your software. After all, the goal is to create something useful that people will want to keep using.

That being said, let's immerse ourselves further into the wonderful world of Java programming and continue with the next chapter!

2

Getting to Know Java

WHAT YOU WILL LEARN IN THIS CHAPTER:

➤ The history of Java

➤ The key features of Java

➤ How the Java technology works

➤ The key components of the Java Runtime Environment (JRE) and how they collaborate

➤ The different types of Java platforms and applications

➤ The relationship between Java and JavaScript

➤ The basic concepts of the Java language structure

➤ The primitive Java data types and how they are used

WROX.COM CODE DOWNLOADS FOR THIS CHAPTER

The wrox.com code downloads for this chapter are found at www.wrox.com/go/
beginningjavaprogramming on the Download Code tab. The code is in the Chapter 2
download and individually named according to the names throughout the chapter.

Before you get your hands wet trying your first Java program, you need to learn some basic
concepts relating to the Java architecture and language semantics. The chapter starts by providing a bird's eye overview of Java's history, its key features, and the underlying technology.
The chapter then zooms into the Java Runtime Environment (JRE), which is the software
environment in which Java programs are executed. This will be followed by a discussion of
various types of Java applications, such as standalone applications, applets, servlets, and
Java beans.

The chapter then covers the basic concepts of the Java language structure. You will read about various concepts such as classes, identifiers, Java keywords, variables, methods, comments, and naming conventions in depth. After that, you'll learn about Java data types. First, the various primitive data types will be covered, followed by a discussion of literals, operators, arrays, and type casting. The BMI example introduced in Chapter 1 is used to demonstrate and clarify the new concepts. This chapter is a very important one because it lays the foundation for all subsequent chapters. Many of the concepts that are introduced here will be elaborated on in later chapters.

A SHORT JAVA HISTORY

In 1991, Sun Microsystems funded the research project called "Green" to design a programming language to be used in intelligent consumer electronic devices, like televisions, VCRs, and washing machines. Since home appliance processor chips change on a continuous basis, the programming language used needed to be extremely portable. Existing programming languages such as C++ were clearly not suitable. Often, the embedded language was tied closely to the appliance processor, and a new language needed to be developed. This new language was originally termed Oak (referring to the tree that was outside the main developer's, James Gosling's, window), but was quickly renamed Java. The use of Java for home appliance applications turned out to be initially unsuccessful, but the emergence of the Web gave it a new future. In 1994, the first Java-enabled web browser HotJava was developed. A year later, Netscape incorporated Java support into its web browser. Other companies quickly followed and Java's popularity rapidly rose. Sun released Java 1.0 to the public in 1995. In 2007, Sun made Java's core code available as open source under the terms of the GNU General Public License (GPL). In 2009, Sun was acquired by Oracle, which is currently continuing the development of Java. Table 2-1 gives an overview of the major releases, together with some key characteristics. Note that the versions were originally referred to as JDKs (Java Development Kits) and later rebranded into J2SE (Java 2 Platform, Standard Edition).

TABLE 2-1: Characteristics of Major Java Releases

MAJOR RELEASE	DATE	KEY CHARACTERISTICS
JDK 1.0	1996	First stable version of Java
JDK 1.1	1997	Inner classes; Java beans; JDBC; RMI; Just in Time (JIT) compiler for Windows platforms
J2SE 1.2	1998	Swing classes; Java IDL; Collections
J2SE 1.3	2000	Java platform debugger architecture (JPDA); JavaSound; HotSpot JVM
J2SE 1.4	2002	Regular expressions; IPv6 support; image I/O API; non-blocking I/O (nio); XML parser and XSLT processor
J2SE 5.0	2004	Generics; annotations; autoboxing; enumerations; varargs; for each loop
Java SE 6	2006	Improved GUI support; improved web service support

Java SE 7	2011	New file I/O capabilities; support for new network protocols
Java SE 8	2014	Lambda expressions; new date and time API
Java SE 9	2016 (expected)	Money and currency API

FEATURES OF JAVA

The key characteristics of the Java programming language that have made it so popular include the following:

➤ **Simple:** Java omits some of the vaguely defined features of C++. It has facilities for automatic garbage collection to automatically release unused memory while a program is running. It also includes a rich predefined set of packages (such as for mathematics, statistics, database access, GUI design, and so on) that can be easily reused by application developers. Its syntax looks very similar to C/C++, making it easy for experienced programmers to learn and use.

➤ **Platform independent and portable:** By using a hybrid compilation/interpretation approach, Java programs can be executed in a networked environment with different hardware platforms and architectures. This also makes Java applications extremely portable, effectively realizing the "write once, run everywhere" philosophy.

➤ **Object-oriented:** Java implements the object-oriented programming paradigm by grouping data and operations into classes and/or objects.

➤ **Secure:** Java has many facilities to guarantee security in a networked environment. It imposes various types of access restrictions to (networked) resources and carefully supervises memory allocation. It allows code to be downloaded over a network and executed safely in the confined spaces of memory. It also foresees extensive capabilities for configuring security levels.

➤ **Multi-threaded:** Java delivers the power of advanced multi-threaded capabilities to the developer in an environment without complexity. More specifically, Java code can be run concurrently as multiple threads in a process, in order to improve its execution performance.

➤ **Dynamic:** Java allows code to be added to libraries dynamically and then can determine which code should run at execution time. It also foresees a strict separation between interface and implementation.

The remainder of this book explores each of these features in much greater detail.

LOOKING UNDER THE HOOD

In this section, we will take a look under the hood of Java. We will discuss Java bytecode, the Java Runtime Environment (JRE), and Java platforms and applications.

Bytecode

Given the proliferation of hardware platforms and/or machine architectures available in today's net-worked environment, the Java developers aimed at coming up with a cross-platform solution that would not require developing expensive compilers to compile Java source code to machine code for every possible target platform. In order to accomplish this goal, Java introduced a hybrid approach to run programs by combining both compiler and interpreter technology. First, every Java source program (BMI.java) is compiled into an intermediate language called *bytecode* (BMI.class), which is platform independent. During this compilation step, errors in the code can be reported. Java bytecode is not native machine code, so it cannot be run as such on a host computer. Instead, the bytecode will be parsed by a platform-specific interpreter in order to run it on a particular architecture, such as on Windows, Linux, Mac OS, Sun Solaris, and so on. Interpreters have been developed for various platforms. All of them are implementations of the Java virtual machine (JVM). The bytecode can then be considered as machine code for the JVM. The JVM is basically a virtual CPU complete with its own operation codes. Irrespective of which platform you are on, the bytecode is the exact same. The JVM is then a separate process that runs on top of a native processor. Figure 2-1 illustrates the byte-code for a Windows 8 platform generated for a Java program based on the BMI calculator example.

```
static double BMI;

public BMIcalculator();
  Code:
    0: aload_0
    1: invokespecial #12          // Method java/lang/Object."<init>":()V
    4: return

public static void main(java.lang.String[]);
  Code:
    0: ldc2_w      #20        // double 60.0d
    3: putstatic   #22        // Field weight:D
    6: ldc2_w      #24        // double 1.7d
    9: putstatic   #26        // Field height:D
   12: invokestatic #28       // Method calculateBMI:()V
   15: getstatic   #31        // Field java/lang/System.out:Ljava/io/PrintStream;
   18: new         #37        // class java/lang/StringBuilder
   21: dup
   22: ldc         #39        // String Your BMI is
   24: invokespecial #41      // Method java/lang/
                              // StringBuilder.
                              // "<init>":(Ljava/lang/String;)V
   27: getstatic   #44        // Field BMI:D
   30: invokevirtual #46      // Method java/lang/StringBuilder.append:
      (D)Ljava/lang/StringBuilder;
   33: ldc         #50        // String .
   35: invokevirtual #52      // Method java/lang/StringBuilder.append:
      (Ljava/lang/String;)Ljava/lang/StringBuilder;
   38: invokevirtual #55      // Method java/lang/StringBuilder.toString:
      ()Ljava/lang/String;
   41: invokevirtual #59      // Method java/io/PrintStream.println:
      (Ljava/lang/String;)V
   44: return
```

```
public static void calculateBMI();
  Code:
    0: getstatic    #22       // Field weight:D
    3: getstatic    #26       // Field height:D
    6: getstatic    #26       // Field height:D
    9: dmul
   10: ddiv
   11: putstatic    #44       // Field BMI:D
   14: return
}
```

When compared to a pure interpreter technology, errors are detected during compilation time instead of during execution time. When compared to a pure compiler technology, the portability is better since this setup essentially implements a "write once, compile, run everywhere" strategy so that every platform with a Java Virtual Machine can run Java bytecode. This is especially relevant in a networked (Internet) environment with many host systems having their own specific platform.

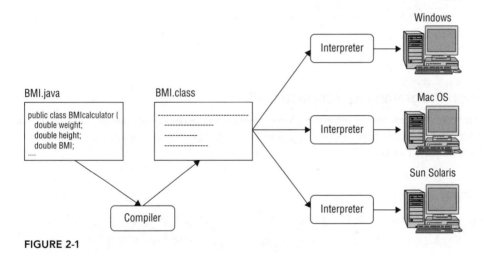

FIGURE 2-1

Java Runtime Environment (JRE)

The Java Runtime Environment (JRE) is the software environment in which Java programs run. It consists of various components, as depicted in Figure 2-2.

The next subsections elaborate on the following components:

➤ Java API (Application Programming Interface)

➤ Class loader

➤ Bytecode verifier

➤ Java Virtual Machine (JVM)

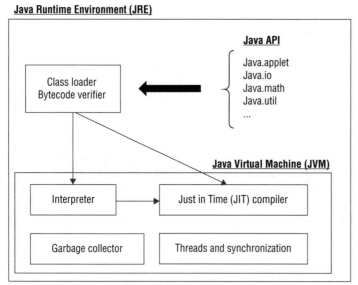

Java Runtime Environment (JRE)

Java API

Java.applet
Java.io
Java.math
Java.util
...

Class loader
Bytecode verifier

Java Virtual Machine (JVM)

Interpreter

Just in Time (JIT) compiler

Garbage collector

Threads and synchronization

FIGURE 2-2

Java Application Programming Interface (API)

The Java Application Programming Interface (API) is the set of prepackaged, ready-made Java components grouped into libraries. It provides programmers with many useful capabilities. Some popular API libraries are listed in Table 2-2.

TABLE 2-2: Example Libraries from the Java API

JAVA LIBRARY	FUNCTIONALITY
Java.awt; Java.swing	Support for creating graphical user interfaces (GUIs)
Java.applet	Functionality to create applets
Java.beans	Functionality to create Java beans
Java.io	Support for I/O through files, keyboard, network, and so on
Java.lang	Functionality fundamental to the Java programming language
Java.math	Mathematical routines
Java.security	Security functions
Java.sql	Support for accessing relational databases by means of SQL
Java.text	Text support
Java.util	Various programming utilities
Javax.imageIO	Support for image I/O
Javax.xml	Support for XML handling

Many of these libraries are discussed and used in later chapters of this book. When developing new Java applications, it is important to consider the API to see if you can use some of the functionalities that are already implemented. This saves you from having to program every aspect yourself, and it can also make your program more recognizable and usable to other programmers. The API is flexible and open, which means that new packages or libraries can be added to it on an ongoing basis.

Class Loader

The class loader locates and reads the *.class files needed to execute the Java program and loads the bytecodes into memory. To safeguard a secure execution, it can assign different portions (namespaces) of memory to locally versus remotely obtained classes. Classes are typically assembled into libraries that are stored physically in JAR (Java Archive) files. The libraries may have been written by the user or obtained externally. In order to locate the classes, the class loader will first find the corresponding libraries and then load the classes as they are needed by the program (called on-demand loading). The class loader basically has three subcomponents:

➤ Bootstrap class loader

➤ Extensions class loader

➤ System class loader

The bootstrap class loader loads the core Java libraries located in `<JAVA_HOME>/jre/lib`. The contents of this directory in the JRE7 environment are shown in Figure 2-3.

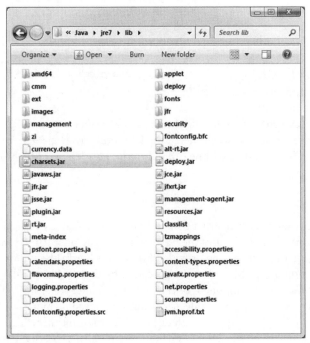

FIGURE 2-3

You can clearly see the different *.jar files that will be considered (charsets.jar, deploy.jar, and so on).

The extensions class loader loads the classes from the extensions directory <JAVA_HOME>/jre/lib/ext. Figure 2-4 shows the contents of the extensions directory in a JRE7 environment.

Again, you can clearly see the different JAR files available: access-bridge-64.jar, localedata.jar, and so on.

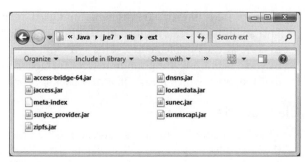

FIGURE 2-4

Finally, the system class loader loads the code from the locations specified in the CLASSPATH environment variable, which is defined by the operating system. The latter provides the path to all physical directories where the system class loader can look for Java files. It can be found in Windows 7 and Windows 8 by going to the Control Panel ➤ System and Security ➤ System, Advanced System Settings ➤ Advanced tab ➤ Environment Variables. Figure 2-5 shows the window from a Windows 7 operating system, but Windows 8 looks very much the same.

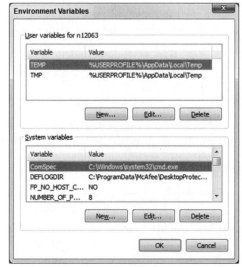

FIGURE 2-5

Bytecode Verifier

The bytecode verifier checks to make sure the byte-codes are valid without breaching any of Java's security rules. It pays special attention to type checking all the variables and expressions in the code and ensures that there is no unauthorized access to memory. Note that when a Java program is invoked, you can choose to disable the bytecode verifier (which will make it run slightly faster), enable it only for code that was downloaded remotely from the network, or enable it for all the code. Once the code is verified, it will be offered to the Java Virtual Machine (JVM) for interpretation.

Java Virtual Machine (JVM)

The Java Virtual Machine (JVM) can be considered an abstract computer machine capable of executing bytecode on a particular hardware platform. It constitutes the heart of the "write once, run everywhere" philosophy. Various JVM implementations have been provided for various hardware and/or operating system environments. The most popular JVM is HotSpot produced by Oracle. It is available for Windows, Linux, Solaris, and Mac OS X. A key component of the JVM is the interpreter responsible for interpreting the bytecode instructions. The garbage collector cleans up unused memory to improve the efficiency of the program. The JVM typically also includes facilities for multithreading and synchronization, whereby a Java program can be executed in one or more parallel execution paths (threads) scheduled on one or more CPUs, hereby significantly accelerating its execution time.

The interpreter may monitor how often each bytecode instruction is executed and hand over the frequently executed instructions (also called *hot spots*) to the Just in Time (JIT) compiler, which is also an environment-specific component. The JIT compiler will then compile the bytecode of these hot spots into native, more efficient machine code so they can be executed by the JVM directly (just in time) instead of having to interpret them. In this way, frequent code will be compiled and less frequent code will be interpreted. The user can set the threshold to determine whether a piece of code is considered frequent or not. This feature substantially improves the execution time of the program at runtime, especially when it is executed multiple times. Although this is not recommended, the JIT compiler option can also be turned off.

Java Platforms

A Java platform or edition consists of a JRE with a specific set of libraries for a specific application environment. Table 2-3 gives an overview of the most important Java platforms.

TABLE 2-3: Java Platforms

PLATFORM	KEY CHARACTERISTICS
J2SE (Java 2 Platform, Standard Edition)	Core Java platform designed for applications running on desktop PCs
J2EE (Java 2 Platform, Enterprise Edition)	Design, development, assembly, and deployment of business applications
J2ME (Java 2 Platform, Micro Edition)	Design of small, embedded applications in consumer devices (such as mobile phones)
Java Card	Design of small Java applications that run on smart cards
JavaFX	Design of Rich Internet Applications (RIAs)

As discussed, this book predominantly focuses on the J2SE platform.

Java Applications

In this section, we will discuss various types of Java applications such as standalone applications, Java applets, Java servlets, and Java beans.

Standalone Applications

A *standalone* application is one that can run on its own without needing to be embedded in a particular host environment (such as a web browser). Standalone applications only need a JVM to execute. They can be command-line applications or graphical user interface (GUI) applications. A command-line application uses the command prompt for the input and output. This is illustrated in Figure 2-6.

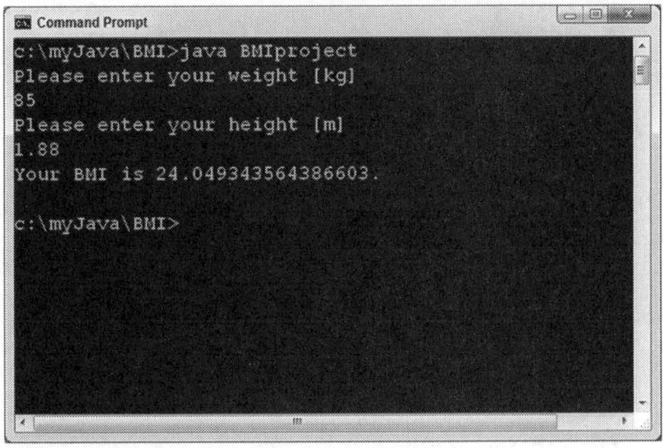

FIGURE 2-6

A GUI application uses graphical components to facilitate the input and output of the program. An example GUI for calculating BMI is shown in Figure 2-7.

Java Applets

An *applet* is a Java application that's typically embedded in an HTML page and run by the client web browser. Applets run in a *sandbox*, which is a confined space in memory that guarantees their execution is secure. Applets can make use of the full expressive power of the Java language. They are defined in HTML by means of the `<applet>` tag, as follows:

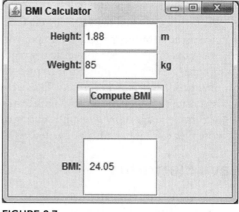

FIGURE 2-7

```
<Applet>

</Applet)
```

They were typically used for graphics and rich interfaces but are not that popular anymore due to some recent security exploits. Their functionality has been replaced more and more by JavaScript and HTML 5. In fact, applets are no longer supported by many tablets or other mobile devices.

Java Servlets

Servlets are part of the J2EE platform and are small Java applications that run on a Java-enabled Application server. Servlets can read and process data (originated from, for example, an HTML form) sent by the client browser through HTTP. They can interact with a server database, invoke web services, or call other servlets or server-side functionality. The results can then be communicated back to the client browser in a variety of formats (such as in HTML, XML, Word, and so on). Servlets are used in an environment where they may process multiple requests simultaneously. This is visualized in Figure 2-8.

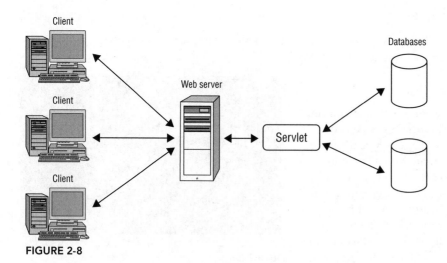

FIGURE 2-8

Java Beans

A Java bean is a reusable software component that can be visually manipulated in a builder tool. These tools allow beans to be customized by setting their properties and specifying how they react to events.

JAVA LANGUAGE STRUCTURE

This section provides a brief overview of the Java language structure. Many of the concepts addressed will then be further elaborated on in subsequent chapters. Let's consider the following running example of a Java program calculating BMI to illustrate the discussion.

```java
public class BMICalculator {

    // declare variables
    double weight;
    double height;
    double BMI;

    public BMICalculator(double w, double h) {
        weight = w;
        height = h;
    }

    public double calculateBMI() {
        return weight / (height * height);

    }

    // This is our main method.
        public static void main(String[] args) {
            BMICalculator calculator = new BMICalculator(60, 1.70);
            double bmi = calculator.calculateBMI();

            // print BMI to screen
            System.out.println("Your BMI is " + bmi + ".");
        }

}
```

Before you start discussing this example in more detail, let's quickly note a few things. First, note that Java is a form-free language and does not require special indentation. Any statement can start at any place of indentation. Also, extra whitespace, tabs, and new lines are ignored by the compiler. The program can thus be formatted in many ways. To improve the readability of your code, it is highly recommended that you use a consistent formatting style. This book always formats the code according to convention. This makes it easy to read and also helps you get used to a standard formatting style.

The program contains several statements, each ending with a semicolon (;). A statement performs a specific action and can span multiple lines. The bytecode corresponding to this program was presented earlier in the "Bytecode" section of this chapter. Figure 2-9 shows the output after executing this program in Java.

Classes

In Java, all code is grouped into classes. A class is thus a code container. The definition of the class starts with an access modifier (public in this case), which specifies which classes have access to it (you will learn about this later more extensively). This is followed by the keyword class and the name of the class (BMICalculator). Every class defini-

FIGURE 2-9

tion is enclosed within brackets { }. It has both variables (*weight*, *height*, and *BMI*) and methods (BMICalculator, calculateBMI, and main). The main method is a special method since it is the entry point of program execution. In other words, when the class BMICalculator is run by the Java Runtime Environment, it will start by executing the main method. Note that not every Java class should have a main method.

Identifiers

An *identifier* is a name of a language element. This can be a class, variable, or method. In the BMI example, the following are identifiers: BMICalculator, *weight*, *height*, *BMI*, main, and calculateBMI. Use these naming conventions when defining identifiers:

➤   In theory, an identifier can have an unlimited length, although practically it needs to be less than 64k of Unicode characters and digits, but it cannot begin with a digit. Although technically it is possible to start an identifier with a currency sign ($) or punctuation character (such as _), it is highly discouraged since it will decrease the readability of the code.

➤   An identifier cannot be equal to a reserved keyword, null literal, or boolean literal.

Just like C, Java is case sensitive. So the identifiers *bmi*, *Bmi*, and *BMI* are all different according to Java. Hence, it is important to carefully check your spelling and capitalization. When creating identifiers, make sure to use full words instead of abbreviations as much as possible, unless the abbreviations can be unambiguously interpreted. This will facilitate the understanding and future maintenance of the code. In the BMI example, it's more intuitive to work with *height*, *weight*, and *BMI*, rather than *h*, *w*, and *b*. Imagine if you added new functionality to the calculator that accepted the measurement of a person's waist. It would be even more difficult to keep track of what *w* meant.

Java Keywords

Table 2-4 lists the 50 keywords of Java. All these keywords have a special reserved meaning in Java and thus cannot be used as identifiers. The BMI example uses the following keywords: public, class, static, void, and double.

TABLE 2-4: Java Keywords

abstract	continue	for	new	switch
assert	default	goto	package	synchronized
boolean	do	if	private	this
break	double	implements	protected	throw
byte	else	import	public	throws
case	enum	instanceof	return	transient
catch	extends	int	short	try
char	final	interface	static	void
class	finally	long	strictfp	volatile
const	float	native	super	while

Variables

As stated earlier, every class definition consists of both variables and methods. A variable is a name for a memory location that stores a specific value. This value may change during program execution, which is why it's called a "variable." The BMICalculator class starts by defining the following variables:

```
// declare variables
double weight;
double height;
double BMI;
```

The *weight*, *height*, and *BMI* variables are defined using the data type double, which represents a floating point number. Other data types exist in Java and will be covered in a subsequent section. In Java, variables must always be defined in a class.

Methods

As discussed earlier, a method is a piece of code within a class definition, and it performs a specific kind of functionality. Just as with a class, every method definition is enclosed within brackets { ... }. In the BMICalculator example, three methods have been defined—BMICalculator, CalculateBMI, and main. Consider the main method:

```
public static void main(String[] args) {
        BMICalculator calculator = new BMICalculator(60, 1.70);
        double bmi = calculator.calculateBMI();

        // print BMI to screen
        System.out.println("Your BMI is " + bmi + ".");
}
```

As stated earlier, the `main` method is the main entry point of program execution. So, it is the first method that runs when executing the class `BMICalculator`. The first line, called the method declaration, contains several keywords. We'll discuss these in much greater length in later chapters, but for now, we will briefly introduce those you see here.

➤ `public`: This method can be accessed by other classes and/or methods without restriction.

➤ `static`: This method does not need an object.

➤ `void`: This method does not return any value.

➤ `(String[] args)`: This is a conventional way to refer to the arguments of the method. In this case, the method takes an array of strings as its input parameter.

Now you will investigate what is actually happening inside the `main` method. The method starts by assigning the values of `60` and `1.70` to the variables of *weight* and *height*, respectively. In later chapters, you will allow the user to interactively enter the weight and height using either the console or a graphical user interface. It then continues by calculating the *BMI* by calling another method called `calculateBMI`. The `calculateBMI` method then looks as follows:

```
// method calculating BMI
public static void calculateBMI(){
    BMI = weight/(height*height);
}
```

It calculates the *BMI* as *BMI = weight/(height*height)*. The `main` method then prints the *BMI* to the screen using the following statement:

```
System.out.println("Your BMI is " + BMI +".");
```

You will learn the exact meaning of this statement later. To conclude this subsection, remember that all methods in Java must be defined in a class.

Comments

Java has several ways of adding comments to program code. Remember, comments are needed to improve code readability and facilitate future maintenance operations. They are not executed when the Java program runs. One way of including comments is as follows:

```
// This is our main method.
```

Using `//`, you create a line comment that runs until the end of the line. Block comments span multiple lines and can be defined using the delimiters `/* ... */`, as follows:

```
/* Here, we call the method calculateBMI which will
 *  calculate the BMI
 */
```

A very handy feature is the Javadoc tool, which is a documentation generator developed by Oracle and comes as part of the core JDK. It produces HTML documentation from Java source code and allows for various pieces of documentation to be hyperlinked together. Reconsider the BMI example as follows:

```java
/** This class allows you to calculate the <b> <u> BMI </u></b> using the inputs:
 * <ul>
 * <li> weight; </li>
 * <li> height. </li>
 * </ul>
 * See <a href="http://en.wikipedia.org/wiki/Body_mass_index">Wikipedia</a> for
 * more information.
 * @author Bart Baesens
 */
public class BMICalculator {

    // declare variables
    static double weight;
    static double height;
    static double BMI;

    // This is our main method.
    public static void main(String[] args){
        weight=60;
        height=1.70;

    /* Here, we call the method calculateBMI which will
     * calculate the BMI
     */
    calculateBMI();

    // print BMI to screen
    System.out.println("Your BMI is " + BMI +".");

    }

    // method calculating BMI
    public static void calculateBMI(){
        BMI = weight/(height*height);
    }
}
```

This is essentially the same code as before, except that a header has been added, as follows:

```java
/** This class allows you to calculate the <b> <u> BMI </u></b> using the inputs:
 * <ul>
 * <li> weight; </li>
 * <li> height. </li>
 * </ul>
 * See <a href="http://en.wikipedia.org/wiki/Body_mass_index">Wikipedia</a> for
 * more information.
 * @author Bart Baesens
 */
```

This header adds Javadoc HTML documentation to the class definition. Javadoc comments are enclosed between /** ... and */. Remember the HTML tags ... , and <ul>... </ul>

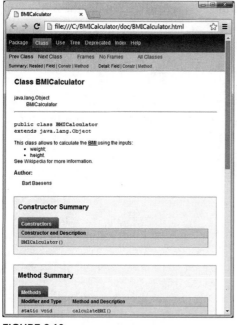

FIGURE 2-10

represent text in bold face and underlined, respectively. The HTML tag `<ul>`... `</ul>` defines an unordered list with the items specified as `<li>` ... `</li>`. You can add a link to the Wikipedia page with BMI information using the HTML tag `<a href="...">`... `</a>`. You can then use the `@author` tag to credit the programmer. Part of the Javadoc generated from this program is shown in Figure 2-10.

Note that at the top of the page, you will find the information included in the program. Next to the information we added, Javadoc will also generate some documentation by default, like the fields (variables) and methods of the class defined. As you will see later, some integrated development environments (IDEs) such as Eclipse generate Javadoc HTML documentation code by default.

It is highly recommended that you use a consistent documentation style. Consider providing comments at the top of the class, explaining what the class does and naming the author, and also adding comments to each variable and method definition to clarify their meaning. This is especially important with large-scale projects, where many Java classes are simultaneously being programmed by multiple developers.

Naming Conventions

Various Java communities have introduced naming conventions for identifiers. These are not strictly enforced, so your code will compile successfully even if you don't comply. However, you will improve the readability and future maintenance of your Java programs if you follow these conventions. A very popular naming convention originally suggested by Sun Microsystems is explained in Table 2-5.

TABLE 2-5: Java Naming Convention

IDENTIFIER	CONVENTION	GOOD EXAMPLES	BAD EXAMPLES

Class	UpperCamelCase: The first letter of each word is capitalized.	`BMICalculator`
		`Student`
		`MyProgram`
			`bmiCalculator`
			`STUDENT`
			`myProgram`

Variable	lowerCamelCase: The first letter is lowercase and the first letters of all following words are capitalized.	`myHeight;`
		`myWeight;`
		`height;`
		`weight;`
			`MyHeight;`
			`myheight;`
			`Height;`
			`WEIGHT;`

Method	lowerCamelCase: The first letter is lowercase and the first letters of all following words are capitalized.	`main` `calculateMyBMI`	`Main` `CalculateBMI`

JAVA DATA TYPES

Java is a strongly typed language. This means that every variable should first be carefully declared upfront before it can be used. You already saw examples of this in the `BMIConstructor` class, as follows:

```
// declare variables
double weight;
double height;
double BMI;
```

The data type of a variable specifies the kind of values it can be assigned. For example, the `weight`, `height`, and `BMI` variables are declared as double variables, so they can only be assigned floating-point numbers from a specific range. A data type tells the compiler how much memory to allocate to a variable, the format in which it will be stored, and the operations that can run on it. Although a variable can change value during program execution, its type always remains fixed. A distinction can be made between primitive and composite data types. A *primitive* data type is a basic building block supported by Java. On the other hand, a *composite* data type is composed of primitive data types using a composition construct. The following sections elaborate on both of these data types.

Primitive Data Types

Java supports eight built-in primitive data types. Table 2-6 defines each of these and specifies the range and default value. If the user has not initialized a variable, the compiler will automatically assign the default value. Note that the ranges and default values are uniform and do not depend on the underlying machine architecture on which the Java program runs.

TABLE 2-6: Java Primitive Data Types

TYPE	DEFINITION	MINIMUM	MAXIMUM	DEFAULT
byte	8-bit signed integer	-128	127	0
short	18-bit signed integer	32,768	32,767	0
int	32-bit signed integer	-2^{31}	2^{31}	0
long	64-bit signed integer	-2^{63}	$2^{63}-1$	0L
float	Single-precision 32-bit IEEE 754 floating point number	$1.40239846 \times 10^{-45}$	$3.40282347 \times 10^{38}$	0.0f
double	Double-precision 64-bit IEEE 754 floating point number	$4.9406564581246544 \times 10^{-324}$	$1.79769313486231570 \times 10^{-308}$	0.0d
boolean	One bit of information; flag indicator	false	true	false
char	Single 16-bit Unicode character	'\u0000' (or 0)	'\uffff' (or 65,535)	'\u0000'

> **NOTE** *Beginning with Java 8, some changes have been introduced. The data type* int *can also be used to define an unsigned integer from 0 to 2^{32}-1. The data type* long *can be used to define an unsigned integer between 0 and 2^{64}-1. If your application doesn't require negative values, this will offer you a larger range of valid positive numbers.*

You may think that strings (such as `name = "Bart Baesens"`) are lacking in Table 2-6. In fact, as we will discuss later, Java does not have a built-in string type. It offers special facilities to work with strings. Note that the default value for the `long` data type is `0L`. The L stands for long and is capitalized to avoid confusion with the number one (`1` versus `l`). Likewise, the default values for float and double end with `f` and `d`, respectively.

It is important to define each variable using the appropriate data type. In fact, limiting the range of a variable can serve as very useful documentation to better understand its meaning during code inspection and/or maintenance. Furthermore, it can also help save memory if a variable is defined as `byte` instead of `int` (since `byte` is four times smaller than `int`).

Literals

A *literal* is a value assigned to a variable of a specific type. An example of this is:

```
weight = 60;
height = 1.70;
```

In this example, the equals sign (=) is used as an assignment operator to assign the literals `60` and `1.70` to the variables *weight* and *height*, respectively.

Here are some other examples of literals:

```
boolean overweight = true;
short age = 38;
character initial = 'B';
```

Note that literals of type `long`, `float`, and `double` can end with the letters `L/l`, `F/f`, and `D/d`, respectively. Floating point literals can also be expressed in scientific notation using `E` or `e`. This is illustrated here:

```
Double bmi = 24.2;
Double bmi = 24.2d;
Float bmi = 0.242e2;
```

Character literals (`char`) are always enclosed in single quotes and may contain any Unicode character (see www.unicode.org for more details). An example of this is as follows:

```
char gbPoundUniSymbol = '\u00A3';
char gbPoundSymbol = '£';
char dollarUniSymbol = '\u0024';
char dollarSymbol = '$';
```

There are also some characters, called *escape* characters, that have a special meaning. They are used for displaying text in specific ways, either for inserting tabs or enters where desired, or by displaying a character that's normally reserved for code syntax. For example, we just discussed that the single quote (') indicates the beginning and end of a char literal. But what if you want to use the (') character in your code? You can do so by putting a backslash (\) before it. Some of the more common escape characters are listed in Table 2-7.

TABLE 2-7: Escape Characters in Java

SHORTCUT NOTATION	MEANING	UNICODE
\b	Backspace	\u0008
\t	Tab	\u0009
\n	Linefeed	\u000A
\r	Carriage return	\u000D
\''	Quote mark	\u0022
\'	Apostrophe	\u0027
\\	Backslash	\u005C

In order to improve code readability, you can use underscores (_) anywhere within literals of a numeric data type. Just like a space in a sentence, they break up a number into smaller parts to make it easier to read and verify it. Consider this example:

```
long creditCardNumber = 1234_4567_8901L;
```

Operators

Operators perform data manipulations on one or more input variables (called *operands*). For example, in the expression 2+3, the operands are 2 and 3, and the operator is +. In terms of the number of operands, a distinction can be made among *unary* operators (one operand), *binary* operators (two operands), and *ternary* operators (three operands). In terms of the operations performed, a distinction can be made among the following:

➤ Arithmetic operators

➤ Assignment operators

➤ Bitwise operators

➤ Logical operators

➤ Relational operators

Arithmetic Operators

Arithmetic operators perform basic mathematical operations on numerical values. The most popular ones are listed in Table 2-8.

TABLE 2-8: Arithmetic Operators

ARITHMETIC OPERATOR	EXAMPLE	MEANING	RESULT
+	4+2	Addition	6
-	4-2	Subtraction	2
*	4*2	Multiplication	8
/	4/2	Division	2
%	8%3	Modulo (remainder after integer division)	2

Most of these operators are probably very familiar to you already. Addition, subtraction, multiplication, and division are used in everyday calculations. It is worth noting at this point that while they operate in the way you understand and expect, the answer is not always exactly what you're looking for. In other cases, the way data is stored as binary numbers cannot accurately represent non-whole numbers. For this reason, operations on floating point numbers often result in a number that's very close to what you expect, but with several digits after the decimal point. This is simply due to the fact that these decimals are approximations. For example, if you multiply 1.3 times 0.01, the answer would be 0.013. However, when you ask Java to calculate 1.3f*0.01f, the result is 0.12999999. Of course, this rounds to the 0.013 you are expecting, so the operation is the same.

Sometimes the problem is not with rounding, but due to the data type being used. To illustrate this, imagine you have two integers, 5 and 2. If you add them together, you expect 7 (and this is what Java will return as well). However, if you divide 5 by 2, you already know the answer is 2.5. However, Java is using integers, so the result of integer operations must be an integer. Therefore, Java evaluates 5/2 = 2. The remainder is not included in the result.

This is where the modulo operator comes in. It will calculate the remainder in division. So, while 5/2 = 2 (and the remainder of 1 was ignored), 5%2 = 1 (here is that remainder of 1). Between the two operators, you have the complete solution. It's interesting to note that the modulo operator is often used to check whether a number is even or odd. For an even number, %2 will result in 0, whereas for an odd number, %2 will result in 1.

In Java, expressions are evaluated following the usual mathematical order of operations. This means in terms of precedence, the operators (*), (/), and (%) are processed before the operators (+) and (-). For example, the expression 4+6*2 will be evaluated to 16. To change the order of processing, you can use parentheses to indicate which operations should be evaluated first. The expression (4+6)*2 will consequently be evaluated to 20. When you use more than one operator with the same level of precedence, the expression will be evaluated from left to right. The expression 6+2+4+5*6 will thus be equivalent to (((6+2) +4)+(5*6)), or 42.

Assignment Operators

The assignment operator assigns values to a variable. In previous examples, you read about the (=) operator, which assigns a value to a variable. Table 2-9 lists some important assignment operators.

TABLE 2-9: Assignment Operators

ASSIGNMENT OPERATOR	EXAMPLE	MEANING	RESULT
=	weight = 85;	Assign the value 85 to the variable *weight*	85
+=	weight += 2;	Same as weight = weight + 2;	87
-=	weight -= 2;	Same as weight = weight - 2;	85
*=	weight *= 2;	Same as weight = weight * 2;	170
/=	weight /= 2;	Same as weight = weight / 2;	85
%=	weight %= 2;	Same as weight = weight % 2;	1
++	weight++;	Same as weight = weight + 1;	2
--	weight--;	Same as weight = weight - 1;	1

Bitwise Operators

Bitwise operators work on bits and perform bit-by-bit operations on the operands. The operands can be of type long, int, short, char, or byte. To illustrate these operators, consider the following Java integer variables and their bitwise representation. Note the preceding 1 in int c indicates that it is a negative number:

➤ int a = 40;   //binary a: 0010 1000

➤ int b = 122;   //binary b: 0111 1010

➤ int c = -12;   //binary c: 1111 0100

Table 2-10 shows the bitwise operators and some examples of how they are used.

TABLE 2-10: Bitwise Operators

BITWISE OPERATOR	MEANING	EXAMPLES	RESULT
&	Bitwise AND operator: Puts a 1 bit in the result if both input operands have a 1 bit at the given position.	a&b;	a: 0010 1000 b: 0111 1010 r: 0010 1000
|	Bitwise OR operator: Puts a 1 bit in the result if one of both input operands have a 1 bit at the given position.	a|b;	a: 0010 1000 b: 0111 1010 r: 0111 1010

continues

TABLE 2-10 *(continued)*

BITWISE OPERATOR	MEANING	EXAMPLES	RESULT
^	Bitwise exclusive OR (XOR) operator: Puts a 1 bit in the result if one of the operands, but not both, has a 1 bit at the given position.	a^b;	a: 0010 1000 b: 0111 1010 r: 0101 0010
~	Unary bitwise inverse operator: Changes every 1 bit to 0 and every 0 bit to 1.	~a	a: 0010 1000 r: 1101 0111
>>	Signed right shift operator: Shifts the left operand to the right by the number of bits specified. The left digits of a positive number are then filled with 0s, while the left digits of a negative number are filled with 1s. This preserves the original sign of the number, hence the name "signed right shift."	a>>2 c>>2	a: 0010 1000 r: 0000 1010 c: 1111 0100 r: 1111 1101
>>>	Unsigned right shift operator: Shifts the left operand to the right by the specified number of bits. The left digits are always filled with 0s, regardless of the sign, hence the name "unsigned right shift."	a>>>3 c>>>3	a: 0010 1000 r: 0000 0101 c: 1111 0100 r: 0001 1110
<<	Left shift operator: Shifts the left operand to the left by the number of bits indicated. The right digits are then filled with 0s. Since only the right side is filled, it is not possible to fill with 1s or 0s to ensure a positive or negative number. Therefore there is no distinction between a "signed left shift" and an "unsigned left shift."	a<<2 c<<2	a: 0010 1000 r: 1010 0000 c: 1111 0100 r: 1101 0000

Logical Operators

A logical operator returns a Boolean result based on the Boolean result of one or more expressions. For this reason, they may also be called Boolean operators. Logical or Boolean operators are always evaluated from left to right. Consider, for example, the following expressions and their Boolean results. Table 2-11 then illustrates the evaluation of the logical operators that can be used in Java on these expressions.

➤ A: 3 > 2 (True)

➤ B: 2 < 1 (False)

TABLE 2-11: Logical Operators

LOGICAL OPERATOR	MEANING		
&&	Conditional AND operator: True if both operands are true.		
||	Conditional OR operator: True if at le... one operand is true.		
^	Bitwise and Logical XOR operator: T... one, and only one, operand is true.		
!	Unary NOT operator: True if the operand is false.	!A	False

The truth tables for these Boolean operators are illustrated in Table 2-12. Table 2-12 assumes two operands that may be either true or false, as indicated by the first and second column.

TABLE 2-12: Truth Table for Logical Operators

OPERAND 1	OPERAND 2	AND	OR	XOR	NOT (OPERAND 1)
True	True	True	True	False	False
True	False	False	True	True	False
False	True	False	False ?	True	True
False	False	False	False	False	True

The bitwise AND (&) and OR (|) operators can also be used with Boolean operands. However, there is a difference between the conditional and bitwise operators. If the first operand evaluates to false, the conditional AND operator (&&) will not consider the second operand, since it already knows the outcome will be false. This is often referred to as short-circuiting behavior. The bitwise AND operator (&) always evaluates both operands. Similarly, if the first operand evaluates to true, the conditional OR operator (||) will no longer evaluate the second operand, since it already knows that the outcome will be true. The bitwise OR operator (|) always evaluates both operands.

This means that using the conditional (&&) and (||) operators can lead to more efficient program executions. But that is not the only reason to use the conditional operators. If evaluating an expression may lead to an error, taking advantage of the short-circuiting feature can prevent this by ignoring the error-prone expression in cases where the error would occur. For example, trying to divide a number by 0 will cause an error. So you could use the conditional AND (&&) to first check if the number is not zero and then check the result of dividing by it only if it is, in fact, not zero. If it is zero, the second expression will not be evaluated.

erators

operators are usually binary operators. They check the relationship between two oper-
are usually numbers or at least can be represented as numbers. They typically return a
value. Consider the following variables:

```
int a=4;
int b=9;
int c=4;
```

Table 2-13 illustrates the relational operators that can be used in Java.

TABLE 2-13: Relational Operators

RELATIONAL OPERATOR	MEANING	EXAMPLES	RESULT
>	Greater than: Verifies whether operand 1 is strictly bigger than operand 2.	a > b	False
>=	Greater than or equals: Verifies whether operand 1 is strictly bigger than or equal to operand 2.	b > a	True
<	Less than: Verifies whether operand 1 is strictly lesser than operand 2.	c < b	True
<=	Less than or equals: Verifies whether operand 1 is strictly lesser than or equal to operand 2.	b < a	False
==	Equal: Verifies whether operand 1 is equal to operand 2.	a == c	True
!=	Not equal: Verifies whether operand 1 is not equal to operand 2.	a != b	True

Arrays

An array is a composite variable holding a fixed amount of values of a specific type (such as int, long, char, float, double, and so on). When an array is declared, the data type it will contain is set. When it is initialized, the number of elements must be set as well. An array has a fixed number of elements that are accessed by an index, which points to the nth element of the array. It's important to note that the first element of the array has an index of 0. To begin working with arrays, consider the following statement:

```
float [] weightArray;
```

This defines a variable called weightArray, which is an array of floating point numbers. Note the square brackets ([]), which denote that the variable is an array. Although not recommended, an array can also be declared as follows:

```
float weightArray[];
```

The array can then be initialized using the `new` operator, as follows:

```
weightArray = new float[5];
```

The array now has space to store five floating numbers—the first number is stored at index position 0 and the last number is stored at index position 4. The values stored initially will be the default values for the data type, which is 0.0 for float. Figure 2-11 gives a visual representation of the array in this initialized state.

weightArray

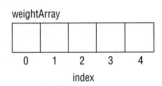

FIGURE 2-11

You can now populate the array as follows:

```
weightArray[0] = 85f;
weightArray[1] = 72f;
weightArray[2] = 68f;
weightArray[3] = 94f;
weightArray[4] = 78f;
```

Remember the letter `f` is added at the end of each of the numbers to indicate that they are floating point numbers. The `weightArray` populated with the specified floats is visualized in Figure 2-12.

weightArray

85	72	68	94	78
0	1	2	3	4

index

FIGURE 2-12

Initializing and populating the array can both be done more concisely, as follows:

```
float[] weightArray = {85f, 72f, 68f, 94f, 78f};
```

This way, the data type is given, the array is indicated with the square brackets (`[]`), the name is given as `weightArray`, and the size is set based on the number of elements given between the brackets (`{}`).

The following Java program illustrates how arrays can be used to calculate the BMI for a set of five people.

```
public class BMIcalculator {

    // This is our main method.
    public static void main(String[] args){

        // initialize the three arrays as each having 5 elements

        float[] weightArray = new float[5];
        float[] heightArray = new float[5];
        float[] BMIArray = new float[5];

        // assign the values to the weight array
        weightArray[0] = 85f;
        weightArray[1] = 72f;
        weightArray[2] = 68f;
        weightArray[3] = 94f;
        weightArray[4] = 78f;

        //assign the values to the height array
        heightArray[0] = 1.74f;
```

```
            heightArray[1] = 1.80f;
            heightArray[2] = 1.90f;
            heightArray[3] = 1.84f;
            heightArray[4] = 1.88f;

            //compute the BMIs and store in the BMIArray
            BMIArray[0] = weightArray[0]/(heightArray[0]*heightArray[0]);
            BMIArray[1] = weightArray[1]/(heightArray[1]*heightArray[1]);
            BMIArray[2] = weightArray[2]/(heightArray[2]*heightArray[2]);
            BMIArray[3] = weightArray[3]/(heightArray[3]*heightArray[3]);
            BMIArray[4] = weightArray[4]/(heightArray[4]*heightArray[4]);

            // print the BMIs to the screen
            System.out.println("The BMI of person 1 is: " + BMIArray[0] + ".");
            System.out.println("The BMI of person 2 is: " + BMIArray[1] + ".");
            System.out.println("The BMI of person 3 is: " + BMIArray[2] + ".");
            System.out.println("The BMI of person 4 is: " + BMIArray[3] + ".");
            System.out.println("The BMI of person 5 is: " + BMIArray[4] + ".");
        }
    }
```

The output of the Java program is:

```
The BMI of person 1 is: 28.075043.
The BMI of person 2 is: 22.222223.
The BMI of person 3 is: 18.836565.
The BMI of person 4 is: 27.76465.
The BMI of person 5 is: 22.06881.
```

Multidimensional arrays are arrays where the elements are arrays themselves. A popular example of this is a matrix. Consider the following Java class:

```
public class MatrixExample {

// declare and initialize the matrix


// This is our main method.
public static void main(String[] args){
    int[][] matrix={{1, 2, 4},{2, 6, 8},{10, 20, 30}};
    // print some of the matrix numbers to the screen
    System.out.println("Element at row 0 and column 1 is: " + matrix[0][1] + ".");
    System.out.println("Element at row 2 and column 2 is: " + matrix[2][2] + ".");
    System.out.println("Element at row 2 and column 1 is: " + matrix[2][1] + ".");
    System.out.println("Element at row 1 and column 0 is: " + matrix[1][0] + ".");
    }
}
```

The matrix variable is an array of an array of integer numbers. It is immediately initialized during declaration. The output of this program will be as follows:

```
Element at row 0 and column 1 is: 2.
Element at row 2 and column 2 is: 30.
```

```
Element at row 2 and column 1 is: 20.
Element at row 1 and column 0 is: 2.
```

Note that the matrix variable is an array of equal size arrays, each having three elements. This does not necessarily need to be the case. You can also create arrays of unequal sized arrays, as follows:

```
public class MatrixExample {

    // declare and initialize the matrix
    static int[][] weirdMatrix={{1, 2},{2, 6, 8},{10}};

    // This is our main method.
    public static void main(String[] args){

        // print some of the matrix numbers to the screen
        System.out.println("Element at row 0 and column 1 is: " +
            weirdMatrix[0][1] + ".");
        System.out.println("Element at row 2 and column 2 is: " +
            weirdMatrix[2][0] + ".");
        System.out.println("Element at row 2 and column 1 is: " +
            weirdMatrix[1][2] + ".");
    }
}
```

The output of this program is now:

```
Element at row 0 and column 1 is: 2.
Element at row 2 and column 2 is: 10.
Element at row 2 and column 1 is: 8.
```

Here, you are accessing each element directly using the *weirdMatrix*[1][2] notation, but there are also loop structures that are often used to iterate through the elements of an array somewhat automatically. These are discussed in Chapter 5, and arrays will be revisited there.

Type Casting

Type casting refers to converting a value from a specific type to a variable of another type. Booleans cannot be converted to numeric types. For the other data types, two types of conversion can be considered: widening conversion (implicit casting) and narrowing conversion (explicit casting). Before we discuss these further, remember the hierarchy of primitive data types as follows (from high precision to low precision): double, float, long, int, short, and byte.

A widening conversion is when a value of a narrower (lower precision) data type is converted to a value of a broader (higher precision) data type. This causes no loss of information and will be performed by the JVM implicitly. An example is as follows:

```
static int a = 4;
double x = a;
```

In this example, an integer variable *a* with value 4 is promoted to a higher-order double data type without loss of information. Although this code will successfully compile, it is good programming practice to explicitly mention the casting as follows:

```
static int a = 4;
double x = (double) a;
```

In Java, the following widening conversions are possible:

> ➤ From a `byte` to a `short`, an `int`, a `long`, a `float`, or a `double`

> ➤ From a `short` to an `int`, a `long`, a `float`, or a `double`

> ➤ From a `char` to an `int`, a `long`, a `float`, or a `double`

> ➤ From an `int` to a `long`, a `float`, or a `double`

> ➤ From a `long` to a `float` or a `double`

> ➤ From a `float` to a `double`

A narrowing conversion is when a value of a broader (higher precision) data type is converted to a value of a narrower (lower precision) data type. This will typically involve loss of information. An example of this is as follows:

```
static float b = 6.82f;
int y = b;
```

Because of Java's strict type checking, this code will not compile and an error will be generated, as follows:

```
Type mismatch: cannot convert from float to int
```

Here, the casting is not done implicitly by the JVM and should be made explicit by the programmer using the following statement:

```
int y = (int) b;
```

In Java, the following narrowing conversions are possible:

> ➤ From a `byte` to a `char`

> ➤ From a `short` to a `byte` or a `char`

> ➤ From a `char` to a `byte` or a `short`

> ➤ From an `int` to a `byte`, a `short`, or a `char`

> ➤ From a `long` to a `byte`, a `short`, a `char`, or an `int`

> ➤ From a `float` to a `byte`, a `short`, a `char`, an `int`, or a `long`

> ➤ From a `double` to a `byte`, a `short`, a `char`, an `int`, a `long`, or a `float`

To conclude, consider the following `TypeCastingExample` class in Java:

```
public class TypeCastingExample {

    // This is our main method.
    public static void main(String[] args){
        int intA = 4;
```

```
        float floatB = 6.82f;
        //Widening conversion
        double doubleX = (double) intA;

        //Narrowing conversion
        int intY = (int) floatB;

        // print out the values
        System.out.println("The value of intA is: " + intA +".");
        System.out.println("The value of floatB is: " + floatB +".");
        System.out.println("The value of doubleX is: " + doubleX +".");
        System.out.println("The value of intY is: " + intY +".");
    }
}
```

The output of this program is:

```
The value of intA is: 4.
The value of floatB is: 6.82.
The value of doubleX is: 4.0.
The value of intY is: 6.
```

Observe how narrowing the conversion of the floating point number 6.82 caused the floating point to be dismissed. Consider the following example:

```
public class AnotherTypeCastingExample {

    public static void main(String[] args){

        float x = 3/9;
        float y = (float) 3/(float) 9;
        float z = (float) 3/9;

        System.out.println("The value of x is: " + x +".");
        System.out.println("The value of y is: " + y +".");
        System.out.println("The value of z is: " + z +".");
    }
}
```

The output of this program is:

```
The value of x is: 0.0.
The value of y is: 0.33333334.
The value of z is: 0.33333334.
```

Let's now discuss why Java gives this output. For the first expression, float x = 3/9;, Java considers both operands as integers and thus uses integer division. The result of this is zero, and Java will then do the widening conversion to float, yielding a zero floating number. For the second expression, float y = (float) 3/(float) 9;, Java will first perform the widening conversion for the values 3 and 9, and then do the floating point division and assign the result to the floating point variable y. For the third expression, float z = (float) 3/9;, Java will first do a widening conversion to the value 3, and then do an (implicit) widening conversion to the value 9. It will then perform the floating point division and assign the desired value to the floating point variable z.

SUMMARY

This finishes this introductory chapter on getting to know Java. Remember, we started by discussing the history of Java, its key features, and how the Java technology works. This was followed by an overview of the key components of the Java Runtime Environment (JRE) and how they collaborate. Also the different types of Java platforms and applications were highlighted. The chapter was concluded by discussing the basic concepts of the Java language structure, together with the primitive data types.

3

Setting Up Your Development Environment

WHAT YOU WILL LEARN IN THIS CHAPTER:

➤ How and where to start programming

➤ What Integrated Development Environments are

➤ How to install Eclipse IDE for your own use

➤ How to begin using Eclipse for Java programming

WROX.COM CODE DOWNLOADS FOR THIS CHAPTER

The wrox.com code downloads for this chapter are found at www.wrox.com/go/ beginningjavaprogramming on the Download Code tab. The code is in the Chapter 3 download and individually named according to the names throughout the chapter.

The first two chapters provided you with some background and a theoretical foundation for basic programming in Java. So that you can get started programming right away, this third chapter takes a short detour from Java concepts to give you a development environment to start coding. In this book, Eclipse is the development environment used. However, it is by no means the only or even the best environment. This chapter covers some of the most commonly used development platforms, so you'll be familiar with them if you encounter a different environment in use on a project you join in the future. You may also like to try the different options to see which is most comfortable for your personal use. In order to provide consistency throughout this book, the following chapters assume you are using Eclipse when giving directions related to the environment. There is no reason the concepts you read in the later chapters cannot be implemented in the environment of your choice.

Because of the focus, this chapter is more technical, as it includes download and installation instructions and far less concept or theory about Java or basic programming. If you have been programming in Java or another language, you probably already have a preferred development environment. It should not be difficult for you to continue using that while following the exercises in this book, even if it is not Eclipse. Just note that the figures and instructions are based on how Eclipse looks and functions.

This chapter is organized in two main sections: introduction to Integrated Development Environments and installing Eclipse. In the introduction, you'll look at programming in basic text editors and command-line execution and in more advanced Integrated Development Environments (IDE), such as Eclipse, NetBeans, and IntelliJ IDEA. The second section focuses on one commonly used IDE, Eclipse, including how to download and install it and set it up for the first time. At the end of the installation section, you will practice using Eclipse by creating a small program, so you can compare programming in an IDE to programming with text editors and the command line. If you already have a development environment, and do not need or want to investigate others, you can skip this chapter. If you are brand new to programming, this chapter should help you get started with your first coding experience.

INTEGRATED DEVELOPMENT ENVIRONMENTS

Integrated Development Environments (IDEs) are applications that offer programmers facilities for developing software. IDEs include tools that support all aspects of software development, including creating, debugging, compiling, and running the code. Typically, IDEs check your code for syntax errors, as you type not so different from how spelling and grammar check works in word processing programs. Debugging support allows you to move slowly and methodically through your program to find errors. IDEs also keep track of your many projects and programs, and the files associated with them, so you can easily organize your work.

Most of the features provided by IDEs are available as stand-alone tools, but IDEs integrate several programming components into one user-friendly interface. An Integrated Development Environment is not required for programming. However, in order to create and compile Java programs of your own, you need the Java Development Kit (JDK). If you don't have it already, you can download the latest version from Oracle's website at `http://www.oracle.com/technetwork/java/javase/downloads/index.html`. Make sure you choose the most recent release of the JDK that is appropriate for your operating system. Oracle offers the JDK for Linux (32 or 64 bit), Mac OS, Solaris, and Windows (32- or 64-bit). If you're using a Windows machine and aren't sure if it's 32-bit or 64-bit, you can right-click on My Computer and check Properties (or go to Control Panel ➤ System and Security ➤ System). You should see the system type listed there. The Windows JDK you download from Oracle includes an installer, which will lead you through the installation step-by-step. If you need more instructions for another system or want a more detailed explanation, installation guides are available on the Oracle website.

Coding in Text Editors

Once you have installed the Java Development Kit, you can begin coding with simple text editors, like Notepad, which you already have on your computer. You will try this as your first exercise, before learning about the different IDEs available. You learned in Chapter 1 about source code and byte code. When you think of programming or coding, you are thinking about writing source code. Since you're learning basic programming in Java, you must type statements using the specific language and structure that Java prescribes. Source code doesn't look exactly like writing you'd read in a newspaper, but it's relatively readable to humans, particularly those who have learned Java basics. It's essentially text, and for that reason, you can write it in a text editor like Notepad or any similar program.

After you've written the source code, a Java compiler can translate what you've written into machine-readable byte code. That's one of the features that your newly installed JDK offers. Once your code has been compiled, you can run the program. In the first exercise, you'll go through these three steps to create, compile, and run your first Java application.

TRY IT OUT Creating Your First Java Application in Notepad

In this exercise, you code a very simple Java program in a text editor, then compile and run it from the command window of your computer.

1. Open Notepad or a similar text editor and start a new text file. On Windows 7 and earlier, you can open Notepad by opening the Start menu. Then under All Programs, find the Accessories folder. In Windows 8, you can access the Apps screen by clicking the down arrow at the bottom of your screen.

2. Enter the following code in your text file:

```
/**
* This is a simple Java application.
* It prints a short statement to the standard output.
*/

class MyFirstApplication {
    public static void main(String[] args){
        System.out.println("I've coded, compiled, and run my first Java program!");
    }
}
```

    Be aware that Java code is case-sensitive, so pay attention to upper- and lowercase letters as you type. MyFirstApplication, myfirstapplication, MyFIRSTApplication, and so on are all different names.

3. Save the file as MyFirstApplication.java (as before, watch for capitalization and be consistent between the name of your class and the filename). Save your file as a text document with the *.txt extension. If you do not specify the encoding, the platform default converter is used. For this exercise, save the file in a location that you can easily find. You should end up with something like Figure 3-1 when you go to save.

4. Close Notepad and open a command window. In Windows 7 and earlier, you can click Start ➤ Run, then type cmd and press Enter. On a Windows 8 machine, you can go back to the Apps screen and scroll to the Windows System section where you will find the command prompt.

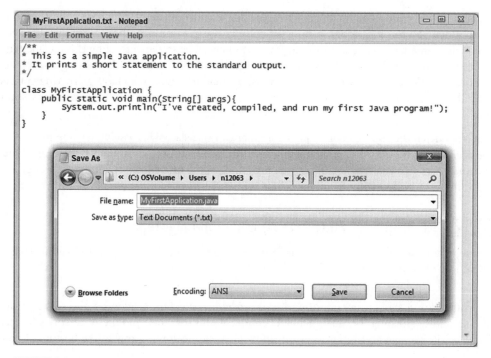

FIGURE 3-1

5. Note the drive that is shown when the command window opens; this is your current directory. You can move your new Java file to this location or change your current directory to the location where you saved your file. To change the current directory, type **cd** followed by the location path (the example shown here will not be identical to your own path), and then press Enter:

    ```
    cd C:\Users\n12063\MyFiles
    ```

6. You can verify that your file is in the current directory by typing **dir** and pressing Enter. This will show you the contents of the current directory. If you can see MyFirstApplication.java in the list, you're ready to proceed.

7. Next, you want to instruct your Java compiler to compile your program. To do so, you need to point to the compiler's location and then instruct it to compile your Java file. Your Java compiler is called javac and is located in the bin folder of your JDK; it depends on where you first installed the JDK. Navigate to the right folder and find the location path, then enter it exactly in the command prompt to tell Windows where to find your Java compiler. Start with a quotation mark, enter the location of the bin folder, then type \javac and another quotation mark. Finally, add a space and the name of your java file. Press Enter. It should look something like this:

    ```
    "C:\Program Files\Java\jdk1.8.0_25\bin\javac" MyFirstApplication.java
    ```

8. You can type **dir** again to see if the newly compiled MyFirstApplication.class file is there. If you see both MyFirstApplication.java and MyFirstApplication.class, you're ready to continue.

9. You're ready to run your program now. Enter the following prompt and press Enter:

```
java -cp . MyFirstApplication
```

10. You should end up with something like Figure 3-2 in the end.

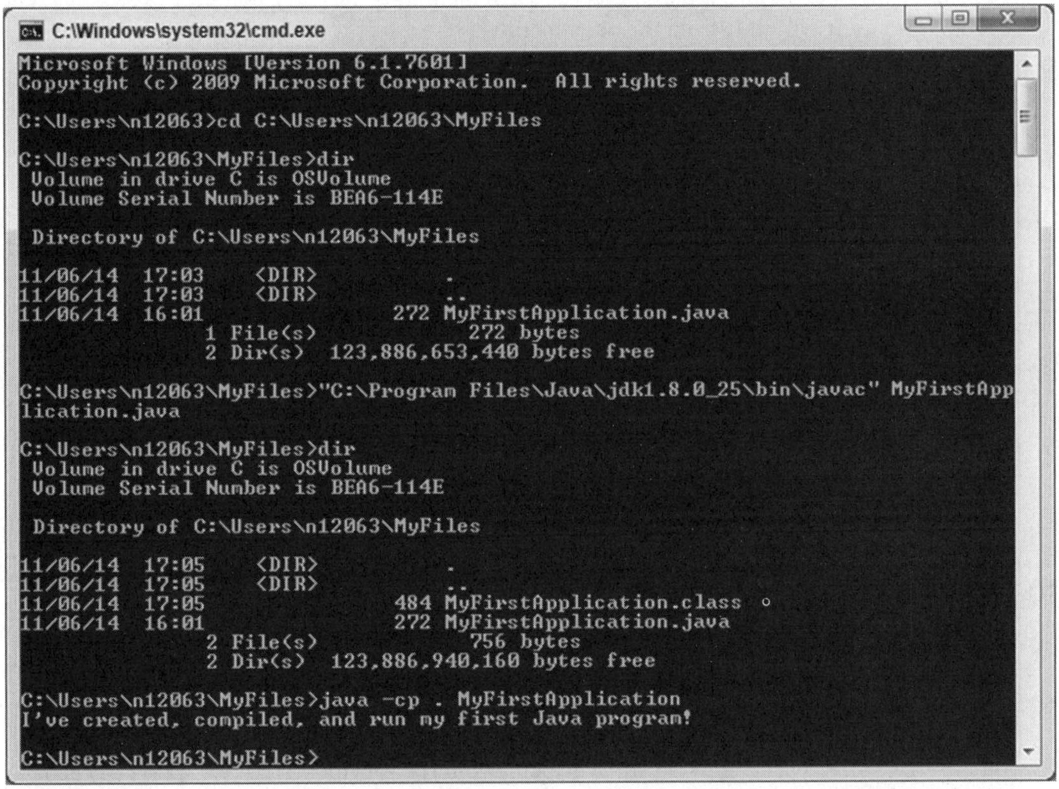

```
C:\Windows\system32\cmd.exe

Microsoft Windows [Version 6.1.7601]
Copyright (c) 2009 Microsoft Corporation.  All rights reserved.

C:\Users\n12063>cd C:\Users\n12063\MyFiles

C:\Users\n12063\MyFiles>dir
 Volume in drive C is OSVolume
 Volume Serial Number is BEA6-114E

 Directory of C:\Users\n12063\MyFiles

11/06/14  17:03    <DIR>          .
11/06/14  17:03    <DIR>          ..
11/06/14  16:01               272 MyFirstApplication.java
               1 File(s)            272 bytes
               2 Dir(s)  123,886,653,440 bytes free

C:\Users\n12063\MyFiles>"C:\Program Files\Java\jdk1.8.0_25\bin\javac" MyFirstApp
lication.java

C:\Users\n12063\MyFiles>dir
 Volume in drive C is OSVolume
 Volume Serial Number is BEA6-114E

 Directory of C:\Users\n12063\MyFiles

11/06/14  17:05    <DIR>          .
11/06/14  17:05    <DIR>          ..
11/06/14  17:05               484 MyFirstApplication.class
11/06/14  16:01               272 MyFirstApplication.java
               2 File(s)            756 bytes
               2 Dir(s)  123,886,940,160 bytes free

C:\Users\n12063\MyFiles>java -cp . MyFirstApplication
I've created, compiled, and run my first Java program!

C:\Users\n12063\MyFiles>
```

FIGURE 3-2

How It Works

Here's how it works:

1. In Java, source code is saved in .java files that may contain one or more classes or other types that you will learn more about later in this book, such as interfaces, enums, and annotations. Each source code file can contain at most one public access type and any number of non-public types. When your compilation unit contains a public access type, like the public class in this exercise, both the type and the .java file must have the same name. You declared a public type with the name MyFirstApplication and stored it in a .java source code file called MyFirstApplication.java.

2. The first few lines of code start with /** and end with */. These are special symbols that indicate a block comment. Comments are not compiled or executed, so they allow you to provide

information to humans that can be ignored by the computer. Here, a comment is used to indicate the purpose of the class. Single-line comments begin with `//` and function the same way.

3. Next, you have a class declaration class `MyFirstApplication`, and you'll find the body of the class between curly brackets: { and }.

4. First in your class is the declaration of your `main` method: `public static void main (String[] args)`. Remember from Chapter 2 that the `main` method is the entry point for execution. When a program runs, it will start from the `main` method.

5. Inside the `main` method, between an inner set of curly brackets, you find the statements to be executed. In this small example, there is only one statement: `System.out.println("I've coded, compiled, and run my first Java program!");`. This statement prints the text you see between parentheses to the standard output.

6. The last two lines contain the closing bracket of the `main` method and the closing bracket of the class.

7. Now, the command prompts need to be explained. First, the `cd` prompt changes the current directory so the `.java` file can be located.

8. The `dir` prompt simply displays the current contents of the directory. You used it to check if the `.java` and `.class` files were located in the current directory.

9. Then you pointed Windows to your Java compiler, called `javac`, and instructed it to compile your `.java` file. This may be confusing, because you need to first locate your compiler. However, if the compiler was located in the current directory, you could have just typed `javac MyFirstApplication.java`, and it would find both without needing the whole path.

10. Finally, you used the `java -cp` prompt to run your program. This executes the program as explained in Steps 1–6. You should have seen the text `I've created, compiled, and run my first Java program!` printed to the command window after you pressed Enter.

You may have already encountered some difficulties in the previous Try It Out. If you typed the program yourself, it's possible you introduced some small typos that prevented your code from properly compiling or running. You may have had trouble accessing the correct directory for reading or writing your files. Integrated Development Environments can make this easier as they allow you to write, compile, and run in the same place. They also check for errors as you type and remind you when you misspell something or forget a punctuation mark. In the next sections, you learn about some different IDEs and what they offer you as a developer.

Choosing an IDE

IDEs offer many tools and conveniences compared to coding in text editors and compiling from the command line. Due to the popularity of Java, you can choose from dozens of IDEs. This book introduces three: Eclipse, NetBeans, and IntelliJ IDEA. Why these three? First, they are very popular, which means it's easier to find support from online communities. Second, they are all available as open source software, so you can download and use them for free. (IntelliJ IDEA does have a paid Ultimate Edition, which offers enhanced support for some more advanced features.) Finally, all three are available on Windows, Mac OS, Linux, and Solaris, so most readers should be able to use any of them. In fact, they offer very similar functionality, so your choice may come down to personal preference or what the people around you are using. In the rest of this section, you look a little closer at each IDE.

Eclipse

Eclipse Foundation (`https://eclipse.org/home/`) offers an online cloud-based platform and the more common desktop version, referred to as a workbench. The workbench contains several perspectives, each of which offers multiple views and tools to the developer. Eclipse Platform 4.4, called Luna, was released in 2014 and includes support for Java 8. Platform 4.8 (Mars) is planned to be released in mid-2015. Eclipse is offered under the open source Eclipse Public License. Eclipse is associated with IBM, so it was adopted early by a huge IBM community and had the resources of the computing giant behind its development. These early advantages made it one of the most popular IDEs available, but others are gaining popularity. Orion is the cloud-based platform that allows developers access and to edit their code from any browser. Because it is web-based, initial support is focused on web client languages like JavaScript, CSS, and HTML. Java development is possible, but you will find better features in Eclipse's desktop workbench.

NetBeans

NetBeans (`https://netbeans.org/`) is a modular environment where each module provides some functionality for the developer. In this way, the environment can be expanded to meet the demands of each project. Because NetBeans is a part of Oracle, the owner of the Java platform, it is considered the official IDE for Java 8. NetBeans IDE 8.0 was released in 2014, and the 9.0 release is not yet scheduled, as of the writing of this book. NetBeans is offered under a dual license of Sun's Common Development and Distribution License and the GNU General Public License. Because of its start as an open source Sun project, NetBeans was more slowly adopted in the beginning; however, that is changing.

IntelliJ IDEA

IntelliJ IDEA (`https://www.jetbrains.com/idea/`), offered by JetBrains, was developed more recently than Eclipse or NetBeans, first appearing in 2001. The most current IntelliJ IDEA 14 was released in November 2014. One difference with this IDE is they sell an Ultimate Edition in addition to the open source Community Edition. It is available at varying prices for different categories of users (you can see the different licensing options at `https://www.jetbrains.com/idea/buy/license-matrix.jsp`). For programming beginners, the premium features are probably not necessary; the Community Edition should be more than sufficient to get you started.

Continuing with One IDE

It's probably not easy to choose an IDE right now. After all, you've only been briefly introduced to three popular choices, and if you've never programmed before, you probably don't even know what you're looking for in a development environment. However, for cohesiveness in this book, from this point forward only one IDE will be used. All the exercises, figures, and instructions you'll find in the other chapters are based on the Eclipse IDE. This is not to say that Eclipse is better than the others, but it will be easier for you to follow if everything in this book remains consistent.

If you have a preference for one of the other IDEs, already have one installed on your computer, or work in a company or group that expects you to use their choice, you can still follow along with the exercises on another platform. Some of the images and instructions won't entirely match what you see on your screen, but the code will be the same and the process will be quite similar.

On the other hand, if you proceed with Eclipse now and want to try the others later, they all offer facilities to transfer projects from one platform to the other. There are many help resources devoted to assisting users of other environments to quickly learn their way around a new environment. The skills you develop programming in Eclipse are transferable to other environments.

INSTALLING ECLIPSE ON YOUR COMPUTER

In this second section of this chapter, you learn how to download and install Eclipse. Before finishing, you'll have a chance to try out the Eclipse environment and compare the experience to coding in a plain text editor. If you already have Eclipse or another IDE running on your machine, this may be redundant. In that case, you may want to proceed to the next chapter, where you can start right away with Object-Oriented Programming.

Earlier in this chapter, there were instructions for downloading and installing the Java Development Kit (JDK) from Oracle. In order to program in Java, whether compiling code from your text editor or using an IDE, you need the JDK. Be sure you have installed it before you continue. You need it to develop Java programs in Eclipse.

Downloading and Installing Eclipse

If you do not have Eclipse on your computer, you can follow these instructions to download and install it. Eclipse 4.4.1 (Luna release) includes support for Java 8, so it's recommended that you use this or a later version. If you have an older version of Eclipse, you can update to Luna by following these instructions. If you must continue using Eclipse 4.3.2 (Kepler), you can find a Java 8 patch that offers preliminary Java 8 support. You can download the standard Eclipse platform from Eclipse packages that bundle some additional components.

The standard Eclipse platform is sufficient to complete the exercises in this book and offers enough functionality for most beginner programmers. You can download it from `http://download.eclipse.org/eclipse/downloads/`. Make sure you choose the most recent build date under Latest Release. Click on the build name, and you should see a list of Eclipse SDK options, as shown in Figure 3-3. As with the JDK, you'll have to choose the version that matches your operating system. Click on the corresponding (http) under the column heading Download to access the download site. Your download may begin automatically, or you may need to press the green arrow to download the compressed file.

If you prefer to download a package, Eclipse IDE for Java Developers offers some extra tools for developers. You can download a package from `http://eclipse.org/downloads/`. Figure 3-4 shows you where to look for the Java Developer package. There is a drop-down to select your operating system. Once you choose the correct platform, click on the link for the correct version.

Once you have downloaded the ZIP (compressed) file, you need to unzip (decompress) it. Inside the decompressed folder, you should see the icon for starting Eclipse. The icon from the Luna release is shown in Figure 3-5.

Eclipse SDK				
Platform	Download	Size	File	Checksum
Windows	(http)	197 MB	eclipse-SDK-4.4.1-win32.zip	[SHA512]
Windows (x86_64)	(http)	197 MB	eclipse-SDK-4.4.1-win32-x86_64.zip	[SHA512]
Linux (x86/GTK+)	(http)	195 MB	eclipse-SDK-4.4.1-linux-gtk.tar.gz	[SHA512]
Linux (x86_64/GTK+)	(http)	195 MB	eclipse-SDK-4.4.1-linux-gtk-x86_64.tar.gz	[SHA512]
Linux (PPC/GTK+)	(http)	195 MB	eclipse-SDK-4.4.1-linux-gtk-ppc.tar.gz	[SHA512]
Linux (PPC64/GTK+)	(http)	195 MB	eclipse-SDK-4.4.1-linux-gtk-ppc64.tar.gz	[SHA512]
Linux (s390x/GTK+)	(http)	195 MB	eclipse-SDK-4.4.1-linux-gtk-s390x.tar.gz	[SHA512]
Linux (s390/GTK+)	(http)	195 MB	eclipse-SDK-4.4.1-linux-gtk-s390.tar.gz	[SHA512]
Linux (PPC64LE/GTK+) (Early Access)	(http)	195 MB	eclipse-SDK-4.4.1-linux-gtk-ppc64le.tar.gz	[SHA512]
Solaris 10 (SPARC/GTK+)	(http)	196 MB	eclipse-SDK-4.4.1-solaris-gtk.zip	[SHA512]
Solaris 10 (x86/GTK+)	(http)	196 MB	eclipse-SDK-4.4.1-solaris-gtk-x86.zip	[SHA512]
HP-UX (ia64/GTK+)	(http)	196 MB	eclipse-SDK-4.4.1-hpux-gtk-ia64.zip	[SHA512]
AIX (PPC/GTK+)	(http)	196 MB	eclipse-SDK-4.4.1-aix-gtk-ppc.zip	[SHA512]
AIX (PPC64/GTK+)	(http)	197 MB	eclipse-SDK-4.4.1-aix-gtk-ppc64.zip	[SHA512]
Mac OSX (Mac/Cocoa)	(http)	195 MB	eclipse-SDK-4.4.1-macosx-cocoa.tar.gz	[SHA512]
Mac OSX (Mac/Cocoa/x86_64)	(http)	195 MB	eclipse-SDK-4.4.1-macosx-cocoa-x86_64.tar.gz	[SHA512]

FIGURE 3-3

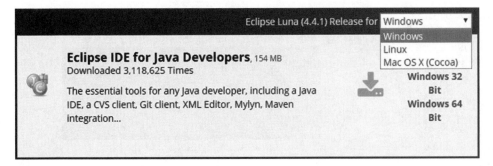

FIGURE 3-4

FIGURE 3-5

You can create a shortcut to this file on your desktop or in your Start Menu to make it easier to find and open Eclipse. When you're ready to proceed, open the eclipse.exe file to start the program. When you open Eclipse, it will ask you where you want to store your workspace. This is a folder where all your projects are stored. You can check a box to save that location as the default and not have to confirm the location every time you open Eclipse. If you work with different workspaces, such as one for work and one for personal use, you might want to leave this box unchecked and select the appropriate workspace each time you open Eclipse.

Using Eclipse

After you choose your workspace, Eclipse opens to the Welcome screen, shown in Figure 3-6, by default. From here you can link to some introductory materials for Eclipse, including tutorials, samples, and an overview of features and updates. Take your time exploring. When you're ready, you can close the Welcome screen by pressing the white "x" next to the Welcome tab or by clicking the arrow in the top-right corner to proceed to your workbench.

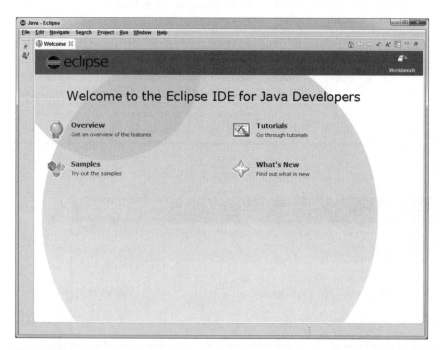

FIGURE 3-6

Your workbench should look similar to the workbench shown in Figure 3-7, from the Eclipse IDE for Java Developers of the Luna release. It is divided into several views, which give you access to different information and tools. The views can be thought of as sub-windows, where one activity or display is contained. A *perspective* groups together a particular set of views necessary or helpful for a particular task. By default, you are shown the Java perspective, which is a collection of views used when programming in Java. In this perspective, you'll see the Package Explorer on the left, the Code Editor in the center, the outline of the current class on the right (with the task list above it if you're using the Java developer package), and a series of tabs at the bottom.

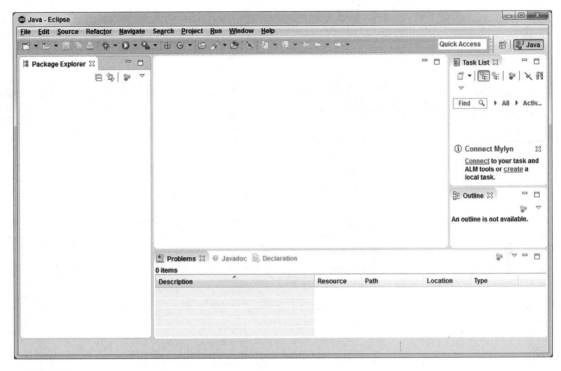

FIGURE 3-7

In the Window menu, you can change the perspective, for instance the Debug perspective includes the views linked to the debugging facilities in Eclipse. You can close or minimize views by clicking the x or - in the top-right corner of each view, similar to how you close and minimize windows in the Windows operating system. You can add other views by selecting Show View from the Window menu (see Figure 3-8). You can rearrange the views in your workbench by clicking and dragging on the title bar of the view.

One recommendation for customizing your Java perspective is to remove the Package Explorer and replace it with a Project Explorer. The two look very similar in that they show you a list of your projects and the packages and classes included in them. However, the Project Explorer will display a red "x" on classes that have unresolved errors. This makes it much easier to spot code that needs your attention, especially when you start working with multiple classes in the same project.

To close the Package Explorer, you can just click the white "x" in the top-right corner of the Package Explorer tab. You'll notice when you close it, your Code Editor will stretch to fill the space. To add the Project Explorer, click Window and choose Show View. If Project Explorer is displayed there, you can select it. If not, click Other and you'll find it in the General folder. When you open the Project Explorer, it will take the place of the Package Explorer, and the Code Editor will shrink back to the center again.

Java programs are organized in a project hierarchy in Eclipse, as depicted in Figure 3-9. Projects are the top-level folder. You should use one project for each program you are working on. Projects are divided into packages that keep related Java classes together. Packages are a Java construct that serves not only to organize your class files, but also allows you to specify a specific class based on its package location. You can have several classes with the same name, but by referring to its package, you can distinctly identify one class. Projects can also contain folders that can be used to store other non-class files, such as text or image files associated with your program.

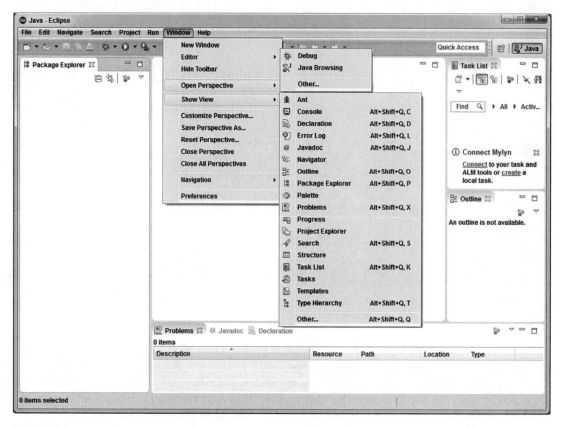

FIGURE 3-8

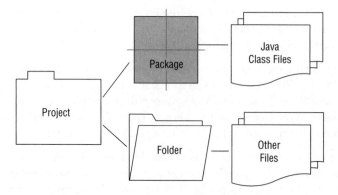

FIGURE 3-9

You are now ready to start your first project in Eclipse. The following exercise takes you through the process step-by-step, to help you get acquainted with Eclipse and how its projects are organized. You'll follow very similar steps in every exercise that follows in this book.

TRY IT OUT   Creating Your First Java Application in Eclipse

In this exercise, you create a very simple Java program. You will code, compile, and run it all within the Eclipse development environment.

1. Open Eclipse and select the workspace you want to use. This is where your project will be saved by default.

2. Go to File ➤ New ➤ Java Project to create a new project. You will see a New Java Project window, like the one shown in Figure 3-10, to input information about the project.

FIGURE 3-10

3. Type **MyFirstJavaProject** for the project name.

4. Leave the default settings for the remaining fields. Check that the execution environment is the most recent Java. JavaSE-1.8 is the most recent as of the printing of this book.

5. Click Finish to create your project. You should see the project appear in your Project Explorer (or Package Explorer if you did not change the view).

6. If you double-click on the project name or press the small arrow to the left of the project, you will see the contents of the project folder. Right now, it contains a folder called `src`, which stands for source, and the JRE System Library for the Java release attached to this project, JavaSE-1.8, in the book examples. The `src` folder is still empty since you have not created any source files yet.

7. Create a package to organize your source files. This step is not necessary, as putting class files directly into the `src` folder will place them in a default package. However, using this default package is discouraged. As you develop larger programs, it will become more important to use packages. Add a package by right-clicking on the project or `src` folder, as shown in Figure 3-11, or choosing File ➤ New ➤ Package.

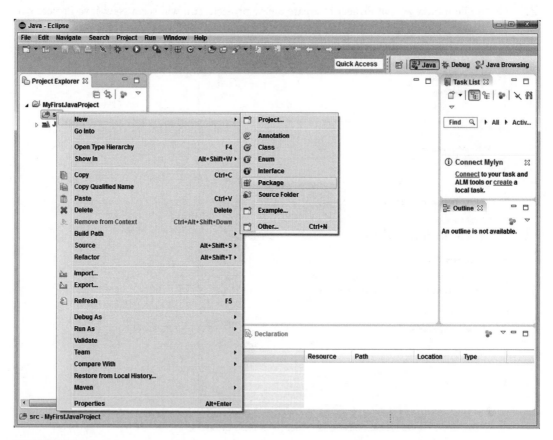

FIGURE 3-11

8. A New Java Package window, like the one shown in Figure 3-12, will appear. Indicate which project this package belongs to and the name of the package. The source folder should say `MyFirstProject/src`; it may automatically enter this or you may need to enter it yourself. You can also find the correct project location using the Browse button. Name the package `myPackage` and press Finish. You should see the package appear under the `src` folder in your project. The square package icon will be white, indicating that it is empty.

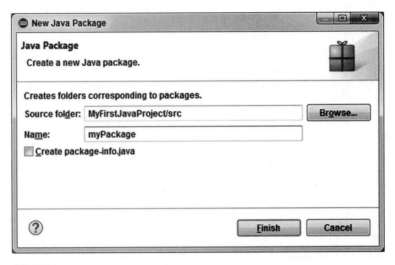

FIGURE 3-12

9. Now you need to create a new class. As with the package, you can do this multiple ways. You can right-click on the project name, the `src` folder, or package and select New ➤ Class, as shown in Figure 3-13. You can also choose File ➤ New ➤ Class. In either case, a New Java Class window will appear, where you enter information about your class, as shown in Figure 3-14.

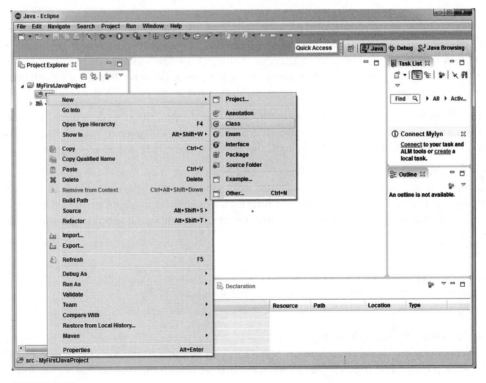

FIGURE 3-13

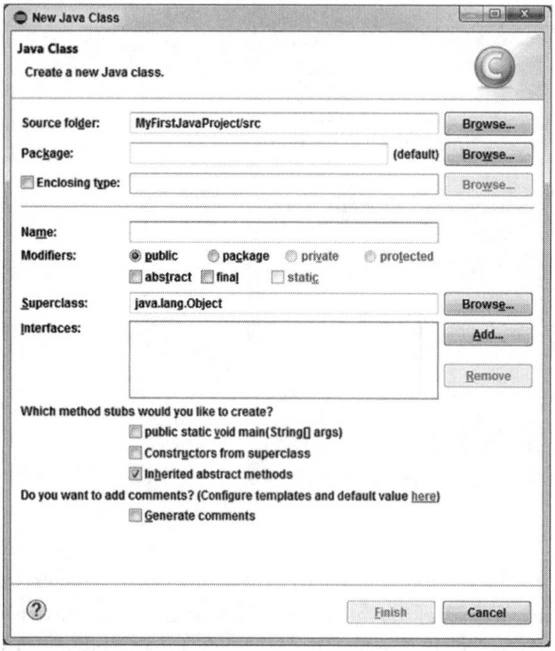

FIGURE 3-14

10. Enter **MyFirstApplication** as the class name. Make sure the source folder refers to the correct project and the package refers to the correct package. You can leave the Modifier set to Public and the Superclass set to java.lang.Object. None of the checkboxes need to be checked. You will learn much more about these concepts as you continue through the book. Press Finish to create your class.

11. You should see some code already written in the Code Editor. Also, the view should now include the tab MyFirstApplication.java, the source file for your first class. If some of your checkboxes were checked, you might have more code automatically provided than what is shown in Figure 3-15.

12. Below the package myPackage; line, type /** and press Enter. You should see a blue comment block appear with space for you to enter comments about your class. It may include the @author information if your computer has some user information saved. You can delete or edit this if you like. Add a comment describing your class after one of the * symbols. It should look something like this:

```
/**
 * This is a simple Java application.
 * It prints a short statement to the standard output.
 */
```

13. Below this comment, you will see public class MyFirstApplication {, then a blank line and }. In between the two curly brackets, where the blank line is, you can add the code for your class. This is a very small program, so you only need a main method. Add it so the class looks like the following:

```
public class MyFirstApplication {
    public static void main(String[] args){
        System.out.println("I've coded, compiled, and run my first Java program!");
    }
}
```

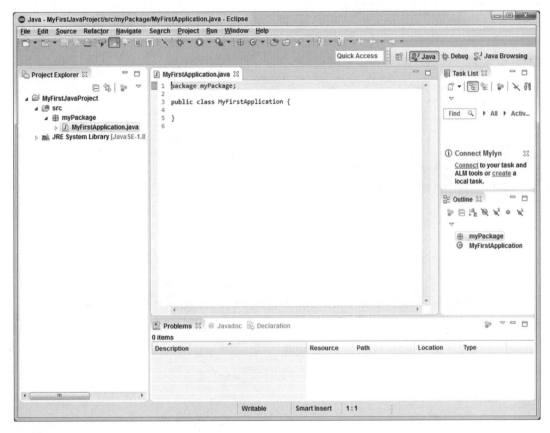

FIGURE 3-15

14. Save your files. Again, there are multiple ways of doing this. Choose File ➤ Save or press Ctrl+S to save the class you are currently working on. Choose File ➤ Save All or press Ctrl+Shift+S to save all the open classes. Notice that unsaved files have an asterisk (*) next to their name in the Code Editor tab. Once they are saved, this * will disappear. You can see an example of this in the top-left corner of Figure 3-16.

15. You're ready to run your program now. Go to Run ➤ Run to compile and run your application. If you have not saved your files, Eclipse will warn you and offer to save them for you. You can check the box to instruct Eclipse to always save your files before running. After the program runs, you should see a new Console tab displayed in the bottom view. This is where standard output is printed in Eclipse. The bottom view will look something like Figure 3-17.

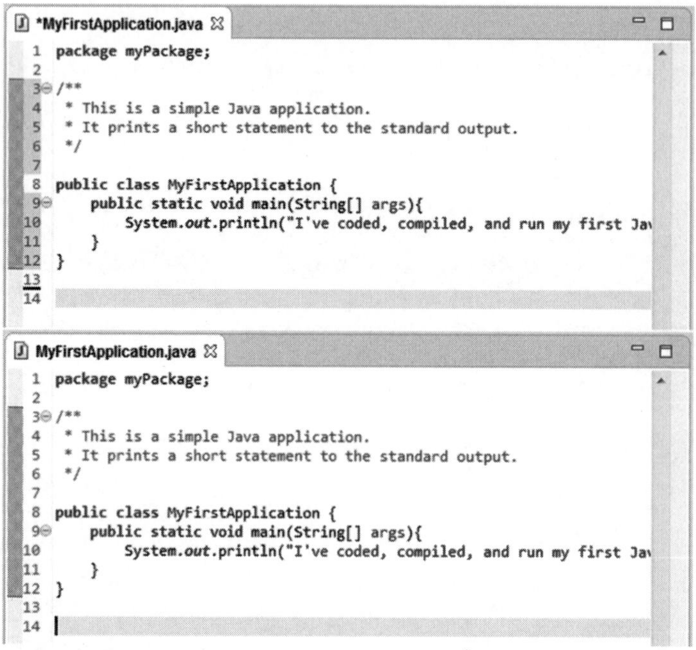

```
*MyFirstApplication.java ⊠
  1  package myPackage;
  2
  3⊝ /**
  4   * This is a simple Java application.
  5   * It prints a short statement to the standard output.
  6   */
  7
  8  public class MyFirstApplication {
  9⊝     public static void main(String[] args){
 10         System.out.println("I've coded, compiled, and run my first Ja
 11     }
 12  }
 13
 14
```

```
MyFirstApplication.java ⊠
  1  package myPackage;
  2
  3⊝ /**
  4   * This is a simple Java application.
  5   * It prints a short statement to the standard output.
  6   */
  7
  8  public class MyFirstApplication {
  9⊝     public static void main(String[] args){
 10         System.out.println("I've coded, compiled, and run my first Ja
 11     }
 12  }
 13
 14  |
```

FIGURE 3-16

```
Problems  @ Javadoc  Declaration  Console ⊠
<terminated> MyFirstApplication [Java Application] C:\Program Files\Java\jre1.8.0_25\bin\javaw.exe (Nov 21, 2014, 2:22:48 PM)
I've coded, compiled, and run my first Java program!
```

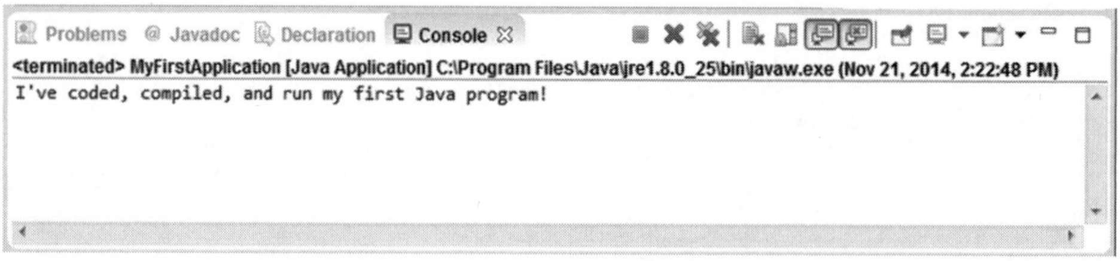

FIGURE 3-17

How It Works

Here's how it works:

1. In Eclipse, every Java project is stored in its own location, referred to conveniently as a *project*. You created your first project called MyFirstJavaProject to store all the components required for the project in this exercise.

2. Next, you created a package. A package acts as a folder for related class files.

3. You created a class and placed it inside this package. The first line of your class reads package myPackage; and indicates where the class is located. The word package is a keyword in Java, so it is shown in a bold purple font to highlight it.

4. After the package declaration, there are a few lines of code that start with /** and end with */. These are special symbols that indicate a block comment. Comments are not compiled or executed,

so they allow you to provide information to humans that can be ignored by the computer. Here, comments are used to indicate the purpose of the class. Single-line comments begin with // and function the same way. In Eclipse, unlike in very basic text editors, comments are colored to set them apart from other parts of the code. Block comments are displayed in blue while single-line comments are displayed in green.

5. Next you have a class declaration `public class MyFirstApplication`, and you'll find the body of the class between curly brackets { and }. The `public` modifier indicates that classes outside the package can access this class. This concept was introduced in Chapter 2 but will be covered in more detail in Chapter 4.

6. The first statement in your class is the declaration of your `main` method: `public static void main (String[] args)`. Remember from Chapter 2 that the `main` method is the entry point for execution. When a program runs, it will start from the `main` method. Sometimes you will see a notification from Eclipse that it is searching for the `main` method before it can run a program. You may also see an error if the `main` method cannot be found. You should always check to be sure that your program has a `main` method (if you want to run it) and that the declaration is correct and complete. It should always start: `public static void main (String[] args){`.

7. Inside the `main` method, between an inner set of curly brackets, you find the statements to be executed. In this small example, there is only one statement: `System.out.println("I've coded, compiled, and run my first Java program!");`. This prints the text you see between the parentheses to the standard output. In Eclipse, the standard output is the console.

8. The last two lines contain the closing bracket of the `main` method and the closing bracket of the class.

9. Unlike the exercise using the command window, Eclipse manages the compilation and execution of your program for you. When you click Run, the `.java` source file is compiled to a `.class` machine-readable file. After compilation, the program is executed.

10. After execution, you should have seen the text `I've created, compiled, and run my first Java program!` printed to the Console tab in the bottom view of your workbench.

11. If there were any errors, you can simply edit the class file in the Code Editor view and re-run the program. Also, if there were typos or other mistakes, Eclipse can often highlight these the way a word processing program will show you misspellings and grammatical errors. The code checker and the seamless integration of coding, compiling, and executing are some of the many benefits a new programmer will enjoy when using an IDE compared to command-line programming.

In addition to the menu bar and right-click options, Eclipse has a row of buttons you can use for many common operations. Some of the buttons are shown in the next few figures with a short description of what they do. The first set of buttons on the far left are from the File menu. The first, an icon of a window with a yellow plus sign, allows you to create new projects, packages, classes, and so on. The next looks similar but shows some details inside the window icon; this is for creating new graphical components. The icon of a single floppy disk is the equivalent of choosing File ➤ Save. The icon of a stack of three floppy disks is the equivalent of choosing File ➤ Save All. The last one in this panel, an icon of a printer, is for printing. These icons are shown in Figure 3-18.

FIGURE 3-18

The second button panel includes some different display options for the Code Editor view. The third panel includes a bug icon for debugging your programs, a green play button for running your programs, and one other button for running external tools. The first two, debug and run, are most useful at this point. This panel is shown in Figure 3-19.

FIGURE 3-19

Five more buttons that you might find useful are in the next two panels, shown in Figure 3-20. The new package button has an icon that matches the package icon in the Project Explorer, which is a small brown square with a cross through it. Next to it is a green circle with a C and a plus sign; this is a shortcut to create a new class. You can change it from a class to another type with the drop-down arrow beside it. The yellow folder with a blue ball and a green ball is for opening classes (or other types). If you are using the IDE for Java Developers, there's a yellow folder with a white box in it; this is for opening a task. Finally, there is an icon of a yellow flashlight, which opens the search window.

FIGURE 3-20

Now that you've had a tour of Eclipse, you're prepared to continue with the rest of this book. In the following chapters, there will be many exercises to demonstrate Object-Oriented Programming concepts in Java. They are written with the Eclipse IDE in mind, so you can refer back to this chapter if you need a refresher on some of the basic technical aspects of creating programs in Eclipse. You can also find a wealth of resources online from Eclipse if you're having trouble with something. Also, as stated earlier, if you prefer to use another development environment, you will still be able to follow along, but the instructions intended for Eclipse won't exactly match your IDE. The many platforms available, including NetBeans and IntelliJ IDEA as well as many others, are often similar enough that you can easily adapt from one to the other.

Moving Toward Object-Oriented Programming

WHAT YOU WILL LEARN IN THIS CHAPTER:

➤ What is Object-Oriented Programming and why it is useful

➤ How to work with classes and objects and the differences between them

➤ How variables are defined and what is meant by their scope

➤ How methods are defined and what is meant by their scope

➤ Some of the frequently used standard classes

WROX.COM CODE DOWNLOADS FOR THIS CHAPTER

The wrox.com code downloads for this chapter are found at www.wrox.com/go/ beginningjavaprogramming on the Download Code tab. The code is in the Chapter 4 download and individually named according to the names throughout the chapter.

Now that you're familiar with programming in general, understand Java's general concepts, and have set up your development environment, it's time you delve into Java for real. Chapter 2 highlighted the fact that Java is an object-oriented programming language, meaning that objects, with their data variables and methods, are first-class citizens in Java and that defining a well-thought-out class architecture is the foundation of any solid program or application you will develop.

This chapter is organized as follows. The first section provides a general overview of the basic concepts of the object-oriented programming paradigm. Next, it discusses how to work with classes and objects in Java. This is then further explored in the following sections, which explain in more detail how to define data (variables) and behaviors (methods) for classes. The final section in this chapter provides an overview of helpful built-in classes in Java SE, which will be used throughout this book as well.

BASIC CONCEPTS OF OBJECT-ORIENTED PROGRAMMING

As you saw in Chapter 1, object-oriented programming is a programming paradigm where concepts in the program are represented by "objects." Each object is an instance of a class, which can be seen as a "blueprint" or template of the object's characteristics. Contrary to procedural programming, these characteristics include data—attributes or variables describing the object's *state*—and behaviors—methods or procedures describing the *actions* an object can perform.

A simple example can help explain this. Imagine you are developing an application to keep track of courses and student registrations. In procedural programming, your first task would be to come up with an appropriate data structure to represent the concepts you are dealing with. You thus might define two lists—one for holding the students and one for holding the courses. Each list would contain a dictionary of values representing a single student or course. This might look as follows:

```
STUDENTS = [
    {id : 'S0001', last: 'Demmick', first: 'Larry', birthdate: '1989-05-13'},
    {id : 'S0002', last: 'Newandyke', first: 'Freddy', birthdate: '1991-01-05'},
    ...
]

COURSES = [
    {id : 'C00A', name: 'Introduction to Java'},
    {id : 'C00B', name: 'Advanced Data Base Management'},
    ...
]
```

Pay no attention to the syntax being used here—it's just pseudo-code to illustrate the point. The following step defines a series of operations—procedures—that you want to perform on your concepts. For example, you'll need a procedure to add a student:

```
procedure add_student(i, n, fn, bd) {
    STUDENTS += {id : i, name: n, firstname: fn, birthdate: bd}
}
```

Similar procedures can be created to add courses and to remove or modify students and courses. You also might want to keep track of which students registered for which courses. Multiple possibilities exist as to how to approach this: you can either add a list of course IDs to each student (representing the courses the student registered for), or a list of student IDs to each course (representing the students registered for this course). Another way to do this is to create an additional data structure—REGISTRATIONS—to keep track of registrations.

Procedural programming has substantial drawbacks from a maintenance viewpoint. For one, when the definition of a data structure changes, all procedures using this structure need to be reviewed and updated accordingly. Second, when data structures are linked, care needs to be taken that the state of the program is kept valid at all times. When deleting a course in this example, for instance, you'll also need to ensure that all registrations for this course are removed as well. The greatest drawback comes from the fact that all data is stored in global structures, which are accessible to all procedures. For large programs, it becomes unwieldy to keep track of which procedures are using which structures, how they modify them, and what effect a change in one procedure or data structure will have in other parts of the program.

When using an object-oriented programming paradigm, objects encapsulate only local data, which is by default accessible only by the object itself. Rather than having to think about data and code as two separate concepts, an object-oriented program merges the two in the concept of an *object*. This increases understanding (analysts and programmers can consider objects of interest without internalizing the workings of the complete program) and ease of maintenance.

To realize the latter, object-oriented programming applies two concepts known as *encapsulation* and *information hiding*. One of the greatest sources of errors in programs is when some parts of the program are interfering with other parts. Indeed, it is easy to see that, in this course administration example, the addition of more procedures and data will quickly lead to so-called spaghetti code, where it becomes very complex to follow the trace of execution as data can jump from one part to another in the program. Object-oriented programming resolves this issue by *encapsulating* both data and behavior within an object.

However, this in itself is not sufficient to guarantee maintainable programs, as you also need to prevent an object's data from being directly accessible by other objects. Therefore, object-oriented programming also emphasizes the concept of *information hiding*, where an object's data can by default be accessed only by methods contained in the same object. When data elements of one object need to be used by another object, the latter must call a publicly accessible method of the former, basically requesting the "owning object" to perform a change to its data. As such, object-oriented programming encourages programmers to place data where it is *not* directly accessible or modifiable by the rest of the system. Instead, the data is accessible through methods, which can also include checks and safeguards to make sure the requested change is permitted by the owning object.

Object-oriented programming also defines concepts to help with structuring programs so that they can be easily extended and evolved. These concepts are *polymorphism*, which is the ability to treat objects of different types in a similar manner, and *inheritance*, which is a concept to allow for extending objects and enabling code reuse. You will revisit these concepts in more detail in Chapter 8, when you delve deeper into object-oriented concepts. For now, you'll see how the object-oriented concepts you have seen so far—the classes, objects, variables (data), and methods (behavior)—are used in Java.

CLASSES AND OBJECTS IN JAVA

Now that you have gained knowledge on the basics of Java, it is time to move on to the topics that make Java an object-oriented language: classes and objects. The following sections will guide you through the concept of a class, which serves as a declaration, or blueprint, for objects, which can be instantiated from classes.

Defining Classes in Java

As discussed in Chapter 2, Java is a "pure" object-oriented programming language, meaning that there are no standalone constants, variables, or functions. It is not possible to define such standalone elements, and everything is thus accessed through classes and objects. Before version 5 of Java, primitive types (such as `int` and `double`) were not represented as objects, a decision made by Java's designers for performance reasons. Due to this, Java was not considered to be a pure object-oriented programming language. However, Java 5 introduced a concept called *autoboxing*, where programmers can access primitive types as if they were instances of their wrapper class.

AUTOBOXING

Autoboxing is an automatic conversion made by the Java compiler between primitive types and their corresponding wrapper classes. For example, converting a `double` to a `Double` is called boxing, and converting a `Double` back to a `double` is called unboxing.

For each primitive type, there is an associated wrapper class available:

➤ `boolean` wrapper class: `Boolean`

➤ `byte` wrapper class: `Byte`

➤ `char` wrapper class: `Character`

➤ `float` wrapper class: `Float`

➤ `int` wrapper class: `Integer`

➤ `long` wrapper class: `Long`

➤ `short` wrapper class: `Short`

➤ `double` wrapper class: `Double`

➤ `void` wrapper class: `Void`

The `void` wrapper class does not actually hold a value but is a representation for the `void` return type.

The mechanism of autoboxing entails that it is perfectly fine to write code like this:

```
Double d1 = 5.4;
double d2 = new Double(3.3);
```

You might be wondering if it makes sense to use the primitive types' wrapper classes instead of the default keywords. The best practice, however, is simply to use the primitive keywords and the wrapper classes only when you need to, that is, when you want to access a primitive variable as an object. Later in this chapter, when you read about Java's collection types, you will see a typical use case where this is necessary.

In Chapter 2, you read an overview on Java's language structure, including the syntax for classes, methods, and variables, and the different types in Java. Don't worry if you don't recall all the details, as you will revisit these concepts again in the following sections and learn about them step-by-step.

You'll now convert the example of the course administration system to an object-oriented Java program. The first thing you need to do is define the concepts—the blueprints, templates, and types—that will be used in your application. These are the *classes*. In this example, you can introduce two class definitions: one for a `Course` and one for a `Student`.

TRY IT OUT   Course and Student Classes

To create some simple Java classes representing students and courses, follow these steps:

1. If you haven't opened a project in Eclipse, or just prefer to follow along and create a new one, you should do so by navigating to File ➤ New and then selecting Java Project in Eclipse. A dialog window will open asking you to fill in a project name. Choose `CourseAdministration`. You can then press Finish to create the project.

2. You will create two classes within the `src` folder: `Course.java` and `Student.java`. You do so by right-clicking the `src` folder in the package explorer in Eclipse and then selecting New ➤ Class. A window will pop up asking you to fill in some details. The number of options offered might seem a bit daunting at first, but remember that the only necessary element you need to provide is the class name. All other aspects can be modified directly in the class' source code, or changed by moving the class around. Let's start with the `Student` class. In the wizard screen, you should enter the class name without the `.java` suffix, as Eclipse will add this for you (you will receive a warning when you do add the file suffix). Do not pay attention for now to the `"The use of the default package is discouraged"` warning. You're just starting out, and can thus afford to be a bit sloppy. You will learn about packages later.

3. The `Student.java` file is created and opened in the Eclipse code editor (if it is not, you can double-click the file to open it in the Eclipse editor), showing a bare-bones class definition:

```java
public class Student {

}
```

4. Edit `Student.java` to look like the following:

```java
class Student {
    int id;
    String firstName;
    String lastName;
    int birthYear, birthMonth, birthDay;
}
```

5. Save your file. You have now created a bare-bones class definition for the `Student` concept, containing variables for the ID, first name, last name, and date of birth. (For now, you'll use a combination of three integers to represent the date of birth. There is also a `Date` class that will be discussed later.)

6. Similarly, create a `Course.java` class with the following source code:

```java
class Course {
    int id;
    String name;
}
```

How It Works

Now take a look at how it works.

1. In Java, classes are stored in `.java` files, which should bear the same name as the class that is defined in them. In the first two steps, you initiate a new Java project in Eclipse and add two class source files using the wizard: `Course.java` and `Student.java`.

2. The student and course classes are defined by declaring some variables, such as `id`, `firstName`, and `birthYear`. You remove the `public` declaration Eclipse has automatically added to the class source, as you will learn about access modifiers (such as `public`) later.

3. This is all you do for now. You're not actually running or executing anything yet. Feel free to experiment, however, by adding more variables you can think of using the primitive types you saw in Chapter 2 to familiarize yourself with the syntax (Eclipse will provide errors or warnings when you make a mistake).

If you've followed along with the Try It Out, you will have noticed that a class definition looks pretty straightforward at this point:

```
class CLASSNAME {
    // VARIABLE DEFINITIONS
}
```

That is, class definitions start with the keyword `class`, followed by the class name. Java imposes almost no restrictions on which characters or names you can use for class names, except for the fact that class names should start with a letter, the underscore character ("_") or a dollar sign ("$"). The following names can all be valid class names:

➤ Course

➤ Student

➤ _

➤ abcde

➤ Number0

➤ $DOLLAR$

➤ 学生

➤ หลักสูตร

Remember, as discussed in Chapter 2, keywords are not valid class names, meaning that `class`, `true`, `null`, and so on are not accepted as class names.

In general, however, it is a very good idea not to go overboard when defining classes and to stick to (western) alphabetical characters only. If you recall the section on naming conventions in Chapter 2, you will remember that you format class names in `UpperCamelCase` (meaning that each word in the class name starts with a capital letter). This is the widely accepted convention in the Java community, and one this book follows as well.

NOTE *By the way, you might have tried to create a class named "学生" in Eclipse, only to have it show up as an empty file with Eclipse throwing a warning about character encodings. The reason for this is that Eclipse by default uses a subset of all possible characters for source code, called* Cp1252. *While this subset contains most Western characters, it does not contain Chinese, Japanese, Thai, or other characters found in non-Western languages. This implies that it is also not possible to include code such as this:*

```
System.out.println("The word for student in " +
    "Chinese and Japanese is written in the " +
    "same way: 学生");
```

If you want to use all characters in Eclipse source code, you will need to open the Preferences window, navigate to General ➤ Workspace, and then select Other: UTF-8 under Text File Encoding. This will ensure that Eclipse saves your source files with Unicode encoding, and will thus allow you to use Unicode class names and output. (Unicode is a gigantic character set supporting and containing almost all character glyphs in use by humanity today; see www.unicode.org *for more details.)*

Before you rush off to the preferences to change this setting, keep in mind, however, that changing the source file encoding is generally a bad idea. The reason for this mainly stems from portability and compatibility. Not all operating systems and Java versions support Unicode equally well, meaning that Unicode characters that look and open fine on your workstation (with your version of Eclipse) might not show up correctly on other people's machines.

But what if you just came up with a killer application and want to target the Chinese market? Surely, it should be possible to translate your program? When that happens, you have two ways to make this work. The first is to change your source file encoding (and deal with portability issues as they pop up). The second way is to use "escape" Unicode characters, like so:

```
System.out.println("The word for student in " +
    "Chinese and Japanese is written in the " +
    "same way: \u5B66\u751F");
```

To escape a Unicode character, you write a backslash (\), followed by the lowercase letter u, followed by four hexadecimal (0-9, A-F) characters representing the code point of the character. You can find tables and websites helping out with this task online. One such example that allows you to look up characters is: http://www.fileformat.info/info/unicode/char/search.htm

As a final note, you might have tried one of these code samples in Eclipse to see if the text appears in the output, only to see two question marks (??) or garbled text appearing where the Unicode characters should be. The reason behind this is that not only does your editor need to enable support for saving Unicode files, your console—which runs the program—must also be able to

continues

> *continued*
>
> *show them. By default, neither the Eclipse console nor the Windows console offers support for this (showing Unicode code characters in GUI applications, however, will work). On Linux—another operating system—the console does support Unicode character output.*
>
> *This all being said, I'm sure you will agree that character encodings, Internationalization, and Unicode is a complex affair. In fact, this is not a problem with Java itself. Java actually provides very solid Unicode support compared to most other programming languages. This problem plagues all aspects of computing, programming, and software engineering. Computers in the 80s did not deal with languages other than English and thus supported only a very small, basic set of characters, the effects of which still have an impact on programming languages today. As such, I will keep things simple throughout this book and work with basic Western characters only.*

The class' body is surrounded by curly brackets, { and }. Within this body, you define the variables (the data) and the methods (the behaviors) of the class. Variable definitions start with a variable type, followed by one or more variable names, followed by a semicolon (used at the end of each statement in Java). Here are some examples:

➤ `int id;`

➤ `String firstName, lastName;`

➤ `double discountPercentage;`

Observe the use of the comma (,) as a shorthand to define variables of the same type. That is, you could also write `String firstName, lastName;` as:

```
String firstName;
String lastName;
```

Recall the naming convention of writing variable names in `lowerCamelCase`, whereby each word in the variable name is capitalized, except for the first one, which starts with a lowercase letter. This convention helps to distinguish variables from class names. Note that this convention is not as widely adhered to as `CamelCase` for class names. That is, you might find code that uses `snake_case` (using underscores) as well.

You will learn about variable definitions in a little more detail later. For now, you'll continue looking into the basic class definition, and seeing how you extend it to add method definitions:

```
class CLASSNAME {
    // VARIABLE DEFINITIONS
    // METHOD DEFINITIONS
}
```

The following Try It Out shows you how to add some simple methods to the `Student` and `Course` classes.

TRY IT OUT Adding Methods to the Course and Student Classes

You will use the `Student` class definition to add a number of methods.

1. Open the `Student.java` class you defined in the previous Try It Out in Eclipse, or create a blank class if you haven't done so already.

2. Modify the class definition so that it looks as follows:

```java
class Student {
    int id;
    String firstName;
    String lastName;
    int birthYear, birthMonth, birthDay;

    boolean isBirthday() {
        // Return true if it's the student's birthday today.
        return false;
    }

    void giveWarning(boolean isFinalWarning) {
        // You should study harder!
    }

    int numberOfFriends() {
        // Return the number of friends the student has.
        return 0;
    }
}
```

How It Works

Now take a look at how it works.

1. In the source code of this class, you have now added three method definitions: for `isBirthday`, `giveWarning`, and `numberOfFriends`, respectively.

2. Each of these methods starts with a return type (`boolean`, `int`, or `void` when no return type is expected), the name of the method, and a number of arguments the method takes as inputs.

3. The method bodies do not look particularly interesting as of now, and just return a value immediately or do nothing.

4. Again, you're not running this code yet, but feel free to add more method definitions for the `Student` and `Course` classes. If you're up to it, you can also try adding some code to the method bodies.

Again, if you've followed along with the Try It Out, you'll recognize the same pattern showing up for each method definition. That is, methods start with a return type, followed by the name of the method, and then a number of arguments the method takes as inputs (for example, the `isFinal-Warning` argument for the `giveWarning` method). Just as with variables, recall that method names are written in `lowerCamelCase`. The method's "body" is surrounded by curly brackets, { and }, just as for classes. Note that this creates a hierarchy: methods are defined within the class body, and the code for the method itself is defined within the method body.

Methods can return any kind of type, meaning that the following can all be valid method definitions:

➤   `String nickname(){ /* ... */ }`

➤   `int numberOfPartiesWentTo(){ /* ... */ }`

➤   `Student bestFriend(){ /* ... */ }`

➤   `String[] listOfFavoriteCountries(){ /* ... */ }`

When a method returns something, you need to specify the return value by using a `return` state-ment in the method's body. Even when a method does not return anything, you need to explicitly specify this fact by using the `void` keyword in the method's definition, as shown, for example, in the `giveWarning` method in the Try It Out.

A method takes an arbitrary number of arguments. Arguments are separated by commas (,), and for each argument, the type needs to be specified. Even when a method takes no arguments, the paren-theses () need to be added to the method name. Some examples:

➤   `void drinkBeer(int nrOfGlasses){ /*...*/ }`

➤   `int numberOfCoursesPassed(boolean onlyIncludeFirstTry) { /*...*/ }`

Take some time to get acquainted with these concepts and familiarize yourself with basic class defi-nitions. Feel free to add more classes (`Teacher` and `CourseRoom` are fine examples) and come up with some variables and methods for them.

Schematically, a class definition with a variable and methods can be represented as shown in Figure 4-1.

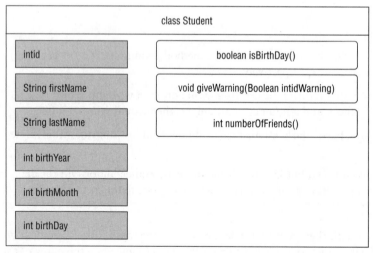

FIGURE 4-1

You now know how to define the "blueprints" for these concepts, but you haven't seen yet how to instantiate these blueprints. That is, how do you create objects from the blueprints you defined? The next section explains how to do so.

> **NOTE** *Recall that the basic class definition, for now, looks as follows:*
>
> ```
> class CLASSNAME {
>     // VARIABLE DEFINITIONS
>     // METHOD DEFINITIONS
> }
> ```
>
> *You might be wondering if this ordering is strict, meaning whether the classes really have to start with variable definitions first, followed by method definitions. The answer is no. For example, it is perfectly okay (syntactically) to write a class like the following:*
>
> ```
> class Student {
>     boolean isBirthday() {
>         // Return true if it's the student's birthday today.
>         return false;
>     }
>
>     int id;
>
>     void giveWarning(boolean isFinalWarning) {
>         // You should study harder!
>     }
>
>     String firstName;
>
>     int numberOfFriends() {
>         // Return the number of friends the student has.
>         return 0;
>     }
>
>     int birthYear, birthMonth, birthDay;
>     String lastName;
> }
> ```
>
> *While neither Eclipse nor Java will care about this, you—the programmer—should. Stylistically, this code scores badly. It's hard to follow and will only serve to confuse you and others later. Therefore, it's best to stick to the convention of "variables first, methods next." In addition, keep in mind that code is read more often than written, no matter the language it is written in. Therefore, it is always a good idea to keep program code as clean, organized, structured, and readable as possible, as well as to follow common conventions and commenting where necessary.*

Creating Objects

You have seen how to define simple classes in Java. Remember that classes are like blueprints or prototypes from which objects are created. For example, you defined the class Student as a concept having a name, an ID, and some methods describing its behavior, but you have not yet created an actual student. Now that you have defined the class, however, you can create, or instantiate, hundreds of students, each with their own properties. In object-oriented programming terms, you say that you want to create a student object that's an *instance* of the *class of objects* known as Student.

Objects are created using the new keyword. For example, to create a new student, you would simply write the following statement:

```
new Student();
```

Of course, just creating a student in itself does not help you much, as you need to have a way to access this particular object later on. How do you do so? By simply assigning the newly created student to a variable, of course:

```
Student myFirstStudent = new Student();
```

Now you can use the myFirstStudent variable to access the first student later. You might be wondering why the parentheses appear at the end of student. It's not a method definition, right? So, why not just write:

```
Student myFirstStudent = new Student; // Incorrect!
```

The reason is that when you instantiate a class, you are in fact actually calling a special method of the class called a *constructor*. Since it is a method, it can take a number of arguments. For example, you might have defined the class so that you immediately need to pass a name for the new student:

```
Student myFirstStudent = new Student("Sophie", "Last Name");
```

In fact, this is a better way to define the class, as it doesn't make much sense to allow programmers to define students who do not have a name. Since you are just getting started with classes and objects, however, you can be a bit sloppy in the name of learning. Don't worry, you will return to *constructors* later in this chapter. For now, the classes can be instantiated without any arguments.

NOTE *Observant readers might wonder why the* Student *class definition does not contain a constructor method to create a new* Student, *even when this method does not take any arguments. For all the other methods, you see that you have written, for example:*

```
int numberOfFriends() {
    // Return the number of friends the student has.
    return 0;
}
```

So where is the constructor method? The answer is that you do not have to define it. When you do not supply any constructor method, Java will be smart enough to know that it should just create a new Student *object with all its variables set to the default values when you write:*

```
Student myFirstStudent = new Student();
```

You will explore constructors in more detail later in this chapter.

Now that I am talking about constructors and `Student` objects being created without a name, it's a good time to emphasize another important aspect, namely the fact that the name you give your `Student` *variable* has nothing to do with the *variables of the Student*. An example will help to illustrate this. Say you define a student as follows:

```
Student marc = new Student();
```

Even though the variable is named `marc`, this does not mean that the `firstName` variable of this object must be equal to `marc`. Of course, it makes sense to use `marc` as a variable name for the student named Marc, and no one in their right mind would use `sophie` as a variable name for the student named Marc, but there is nothing prohibiting you from doing so. The name of the `Student` variable is just a handle to refer to the `Student` object itself, and has nothing to do with the internals of that object.

The following Try It Out will show you how to create some students in the example course administration program.

TRY IT OUT   Creating Student Objects

You will use the `Student` class definition as a blueprint to create a number of `Student` objects. If you have not followed along with the previous Try It Outs, you should create a `Student` class now with the following content:

```java
class Student {
    int id;
    String firstName;
    String lastName;
    int birthYear, birthMonth, birthDay;

    boolean isBirthday() {
        // Return true if it's the student's birthday today.
        return false;
    }

    void giveWarning(boolean isFinalWarning) {
        // You should study harder!
    }

    int numberOfFriends() {
        // Return the number of friends the student has.
        return 0;
    }
}
```

1. Add the following `main` method to the `Student` class definition as follows. Note the use of the `new` keyword to create objects:

```java
public static void main(String[] args) {
    Student firstStudent = new Student();
    Student secondStudent = new Student();
    firstStudent.id = 1;
    firstStudent.firstName = "Marc";
```

```
        secondStudent.id = 2;
        secondStudent.firstName = "Sophie";

        System.out.println("The student object referred to "+
                "by the variable secondStudent has the first "+
                "name: "+secondStudent);
    }
```

2. You should now be able to run the Student class from Eclipse and observe the output given on the console.

How It Works

Now take a look at how it works.

1. The new keyword is used to create objects, which you will use to create a bunch of students. Note the use of the dot (.) operator in this code to access (read and write) the Student objects' variables.

2. As Java is a fully object-oriented program, however, you need to find an appropriate place to create the students. Loose scripts cannot exist in Java, meaning that you have to create the students inside a method definition of a class.

3. To actually execute, that is, run the program, you add a so-called main method to the Student class. As Java has no way of knowing which particular method you want to use as the entry point of the program, a special method exists—the so-called main method—that serves exactly this purpose.

4. When running this program from Eclipse, Java will call the class' main method. The main method will create some students, set their variables, and print some information to Eclipse's console.

5. You might be wondering what the public and static keywords are doing before the main method definition. Don't worry about these too much for now. You will see what static does later on in this chapter and learn about the role of public in Chapter 8. For now, just keep in mind that the main method must be public, static, return nothing (void), and take a single argument: an array of strings, String[]. The name of the argument can be changed, but by convention, args is used. The reason for this is that this method argument will contain the list of arguments that was passed to Java.

6. Note that, generally speaking, mixing in this main method with the student class definition is not a good idea. Ask yourself the following: is a student responsible for creating some students? The answer is, of course, no.

7. As such, you can also put this program logic somewhere else. The question is then, of course, where? Think about this, which *class of objects* should *be responsible for the behavior* of creating some students? You might come up with different answers. For example, you might say, "I just want my program to create some students." So what you can do is add a class, called MyProgram, to hold a single main method:

```
class MyProgram {
    // I am the program managing your Student and Course objects.

    public static void main(String[] args) {
        Student firstStudent = new Student();
        Student secondStudent = new Student();
        firstStudent.id = 1;
        firstStudent.firstName = "Marc";
```

```
        secondStudent.id = 2;
        secondStudent.firstName = "Sophie";

        System.out.println("The student object referred to "+
                "by the variable secondStudent has the first "+
                "name: "+secondStudent.firstName);
    }
}
```

8. The behavior of managing students is now cleanly separated from the behavior a student itself exposes. Later, you might want to create an `Administrator` class to perform this sort of management, but for now, all you want to do is run this simple example program, so the current way of doing things is fine to illustrate the idea.

Figure 4-2 represents the creation of objects from classes, schematically.

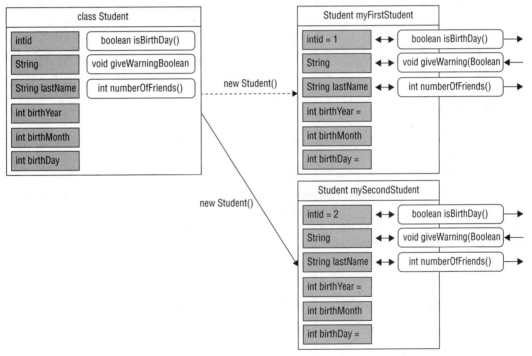

FIGURE 4-2

You have now seen how to create simple class definitions in Java, containing variables and methods. By now, you should grasp the differences between classes and objects, and should be able to define classes and to instantiate them. You've been taken on a quick tour through the concepts of classes and objects in Java, so now that you get the bigger picture, you can take a step back and learn more about variables and methods, with all their intricacies, which is exactly what you will do in the following sections.

STORING DATA: VARIABLES

In the previous section, I defined the simple class outline as follows. A class contains a block of variable definitions (data) and methods (behaviors), like so:

```
class CLASSNAME {
    // VARIABLE DEFINITIONS
    // METHOD DEFINITIONS
}
```

You will now zoom in further on the aspect of defining variables within a class. Specifically, this section discusses:

➤ **Instance variables:** Variables that will be used to hold data of objects.

➤ **Class variables:** Variables that are not bound to an object but instead belong to the class as such, that is, to the blueprint of the object.

➤ **Final variables:** Variables that—after their initial assignment—cannot be modified.

Finally, I will also devote some words to the topic of variable *scope*. A scope of a variable is the context in which it's defined. This means that, depending on how you define a variable, it will affect where and how this variable can be accessed.

Instance Variables

In object-oriented programming, an *instance variable* is a variable that's defined in a class (as you have done before for `firstName` and `lastName` in the `Student` class, for instance). Instance variables are also commonly referred to as *member variables* or *fields* of a class.

Instance variables belong to objects, meaning that each object of the class keeps a separate copy of this variable. Let's illustrate this idea with an example: instance variables can be introduced by simply defining them in the class body. Let's say you want to create a class for the concept of a book. The bare-bones class then looks like this:

```
class Book {

}
```

(Feel free to follow along in Eclipse.) An empty class it not much fun to work with, so you need to think of some data. Well, since books have a title and an author, you might want to define some variables to represent this. Since a book can have multiple authors, you might even want to define this data aspect as a composite data type. Perhaps something like the following:

```
class Book {
    String title;
    String[] authors;
}
```

> **NOTE** If you were thinking, "Wouldn't it be a good idea to abstract authors away into a separate class, say, Author?", you would be absolutely right, although it depends on the complexity you foresee your program having to deal with. Can you imagine keeping author information nicely separated with authors having their own data (first name, last name, and birth date) and behaviors? Then yes, it makes sense to create an Author class. If you are planning on keeping a simple string to represent author information for books (like you are doing here), the simple solution is fine.
>
> To paraphrase the famous quote from Einstein, "Everything should be made as simple as possible, but no simpler."

Now, you have already seen how to create some `Book` objects, that is, some books. For example, you might write a piece of code doing something like the following:

```
Book book1 = new Book();
book1.title = "Beginning Java";
book1.authors = new String[]{
    "Bart Baesens",
    "Aimee Backiel",
    "Seppe vanden Broucke"
};

Book book2 = new Book();
book2.title = "Catcher in the Rye";
book2.authors = new String[]{"J. D. Salinger"};
```

This code creates two book objects—`book1` and `book2`—and sets their `title` and `author` variables. As you can observe, each book object keeps its own copy of the `title` and `author` variables, which can be accessed and modified independently.

That is all you need to know to get the idea about what instance variables are all about. They are basically just a part of the class blueprint, and get instantiated for each object you define belonging to that class.

As a reminder, however, recall that you can define multiple variables of the same type by separating them with commas, like so:

```
int a, b, c;
```

In fact, this not only works for instance variables, but works for any variable you define no matter where and no matter of which type (it does not have to be a primitive type). For example, the code sample to create the two books could also be rewritten like so:

```
Book book1, book2; // Define two empty Book objects

book1 = new Book(); // Set first book
book1.title = "Beginning Java";
book1.authors = new String[]{
```

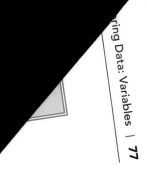

```
cke"

Set second book
in the Rye";
ng[]{"J. D. Salinger"};
```

variable you define defaults to a particular value, depending on the variable type. For instance, you might wonder what happens if you ask for the title of a book, without specifying a title first:

```
Book book3 = new Book();
// Oops, forgot to set title...
System.out.println("Title equals: "+book3.title);
```

The answer is that "Title equals: null". For variables with a class type, the default value is a special keyword representing emptiness, null. Since String is a non-primitive class, its default value is thus null. Remember, as discussed in Chapter 2, the default values, per data type, are:

➤ For boolean: false

➤ For byte: 0

➤ For short: 0

➤ For int: 0

➤ For long: 0L

➤ For float: 0.0f

➤ For double: 0.0d

➤ For char: \u0000 (the null character)

➤ For String or any object: null

Note that these default values apply only to fields (instance variables). That means if you try to be clever and add the following to the code snippet:

```
Book book;
System.out.println("Now, book equals: "+book);
book = new Book();
System.out.println("And now, book equals: "+book);
```

Eclipse will complain about the book variable not being initialized. This can be fixed like so:

```
Book book = null;
System.out.println("Now, book equals: "+book);
book = new Book();
System.out.println("And now, book equals: "+book);
```

The same applies for other variables you define that are not instance variables:

```
int a = 0;
System.out.println("int a equals"+a);
```

NOTE *You might have tried to execute this code snippet to see something like the following appearing on-screen:*

```
Now, book equals: null
And now, book equals: Book@709fa12f
```

What's going on with this `Book@709fa12f` *(your output will differ and return a different part after the* `@`*)? The reason for this is that all Java objects have a built-in method to return their so-called "String representation," which can be extended by programmers to provide a friendly output for an object, that is, a* `String` *that textually represents the object (don't worry about the specifics of this too much for now; you will get back to this later). The key aspect to know here is that, when no extension is provided by the programmer, Java will just resort to showing the class name (*`Book`*), followed by an* `@`*, followed by the hexadecimal representation of the object's hashcode.*

Hashcodes are an advanced Java concept and are used to provide a quick integer representation for an object, which can be used as a quick check to see if two objects are equal (they have the same hashcode). Again, the way a hashcode is calculated can be extended by the programmer. If this is not done, then the hashcode corresponds to the internal address of the object in memory, although the particular default behavior may vary from one JVM implementation to another.

Finally, you might be wondering what happens when you try to access an object's field (instance variable) when an object was not created first, such as done here:

```
Book book = null;
System.out.println("Now, book title equals: "+book.title);
```

Eclipse will allow you to execute this code, but the program will quickly crash with the following message:

```
Exception in thread "main" java.lang.NullPointerException
    at Book.main(Book.java:XX)
```

Not surprising, because accessing a variable of something that doesn't exist is sure to give problems. In this code sample, it's easy to see where the problem lies (Eclipse will even put up a warning regarding this foolish behavior), but in larger programs, it is a common pattern for methods to create objects, or return `null` *in case something failed. When this object is then accessed (or passed on to another method, perhaps) without explicitly checking for* `null`*, a* `NullPointerException` *error will pop up as soon as you try to access a variable or method of this object, as the following code sample illustrates:*

```
Book giveMeABook() {
    //return new Book();  --> Sorry, no books available for now
    return null; // Return null instead
}
```

continues

continued

```
        Book myNewbook = giveMeABook();

        // Forgot the check for null?
        System.out.println("Title equals: "+myNewBook.title);
        // This will give an error
```

`NullPointerException` *errors are a prevalent problem when programming in Java, and oftentimes it is hard to track down the root cause behind them as you have to track down where and why a particular object has not been instantiated (i.e., the variable equals* `null`*). Therefore, it is a good idea either to program defensively and always check for* `null` *when retrieving an object and before moving on with using the object, or to program in such a way that only in a limited number of cases a null variable is passed from one part of your program to another.*

This code also immediately illustrates that you are not forced to use the default values for instance variables. For example, you can modify the `Book` class to assign defaults to the `title` and `author` variables:

```
class Book {
    String title = "Unknown Title";
    String[] authors = new String[]{"Anonymous"};
}
```

And, combining this with the knowledge on how to define multiple variables of the same type in one go, you can add:

```
class Book {
    String title = "Unknown Title";
    String[] authors = new String[]{"Anonymous"};
    int yearReleased = 2014, copiesSold = 0;
}
```

With this knowledge under your belt, you might be wondering, as each object keeps its own copy of instance variables, is there also a way to define a common variable, something that's shared between all objects belonging to the same class? Indeed there is . . .

Class Variables

In object-oriented programming, a *class variable*, also denoted as a *static variable*, is a variable that's been allocated "statically"—meaning that this variable is shared between all objects (instances) belonging to this class. Further, since class variables belong to the class blueprint, it is not necessary to create objects to be able to access and modify class variables. It is sometimes argued that class variables do not really adhere to "pure" object-oriented programming principles. Other, stricter programming languages, such as Scala, do not allow them, for instance. That said, this is not to be regarded as a shortcoming of Java, as we will see that class variables can come in handy in many cases. However, it is best not to overuse them.

I'll explain this by providing an example. Let's modify the Book class so it looks as follows:

```
class Book {
    static int maxAmountOfPages = 500;

    String title = "Unknown Title";
    String[] authors = new String[]{"Anonymous"};
    int yearReleased = 2014, copiesSold = 0, nrOfPages = 1400;
}
```

Note the static keyword in front of the maxAmountOfPages *class* variable. This variable denotes the maximum amount of pages you currently support for books, which could be used in combination with the nrOfPages *instance* variable to check whether you can publish a given book, for instance. Although the number of pages is different for each book you define, the maximum amount of pages the printers support is a global property throughout all Book objects, is defined as a class variable, and is thus accessible by all Book objects.

A code sample illustrating this concept might look like this:

```
Book superLargeBook = new Book();
superLargeBook.title = "Super Large Boring Book";

System.out.println("I have a book here with the title: "+superLargeBook.title);
System.out.println("Written by: "+superLargeBook.authors);
System.out.println("Released in: "+superLargeBook.yearReleased);
System.out.println("With number of pages: "+superLargeBook.nrOfPages);

System.out.println("However, we only support books with max. pages: "
    +superLargeBook.maxAmountOfPages);
```

Running this code outputs:

```
I have a book here with the title: Super Large Boring Book
Written by: [Ljava.lang.String;@1271ba
Released in: 2014
With number of pages: 1400
However, we only support books with max. pages: 500
```

> **NOTE** *You might have spotted the following line:*
>
> ```
> Written by: [Ljava.lang.String;@1271ba
> ```
>
> *And wondered what's up with this. This isn't the default* Anonymous *author you set! The reason for this behavior is again due to the way Java derives a* String *representation of composite types, which is not very user friendly in this case. There are two ways to resolve this issue. The first is to loop through the array and show each element one by one (you will look at looping constructs in the next chapter). The second way is to use so-called "Collection" classes, which are similar to arrays in the sense that they hold a bunch of information, but are also much more flexible and efficient. In addition, their* String *representation looks much friendlier. You will learn about collections later in this chapter.*

However, for the last line, when accessing the static variable, Eclipse complains about the fact that `"The static field superLargeBook.maxAmountOfPages should be accessed in a static way"`. What is meant by this? Well, it means that it's generally preferred to access and modify static variables not by accessing them through an object variable, but by using the class name directly, like so:

```
Book.maxAmountOfPages = 2000; // Let's increase the max amount of pages
System.out.println("We now support books with max. pages: "
    +Book.maxAmountOfPages);
```

Accessing and modifying static variables in this manner has two benefits. First, you do not need to create an object in order to access the `static` variable. Second, this way makes it clear to readers that the variable being accessed is a static one, without them needing to read the class definition. Finally, speaking of class definitions, it's generally a good idea to define class variables before defining instance variables when you write classes, just to keep things clean and readable.

Static variables are oftentimes used to define so-called constants: variables whose values will never change during the execution of a program. However, as you have seen, it is perfectly okay to change the maximum amount of pages by setting a new value to `Book.maxAmountOfPages`. If you want to keep variables fixed during the program's execution, you need to consider another concept: final variables.

Final Variables

In Java, final variables are variables that can be initialized only once, either directly when defining the variable, or later in one of the class methods. Once a value has been given to the variable, however, it cannot be modified any longer.

You can see an example of a final variable by returning to the book class and modifying it a little, so the complete class looks as follows:

```
class Book {
    final String title = "Unknown Title";
    String[] authors = new String[]{"Anonymous"};

    int yearReleased = 2014, copiesSold = 0, nrOfPages;

    public static void main(String[] args) {
        Book superLargeBook = new Book();
        superLargeBook.title = "Super Large Boring Book";
        superLargeBook.nrOfPages = 1400;
    }
}
```

Note the change to the `title` variable, as it now has the `final` property. To keep things simple for now, I have also removed the `static` variable and have put some testing code in a `main` method, so you can execute this class.

> **NOTE** The previous testing code snippets can also be placed in the `main` method of `Book`, but remember that it is generally not a good idea to "pollute" classes representing real-world concepts with `main` methods. Alternatively, you may also create a `MyProgram` class and put the code snippets in its `main` method, similar to what you did in the course administration example earlier in this chapter.

However, Eclipse will refuse to compile this code, as it complains that you cannot give the `title` variable a new value ("Super Large Boring Book"), as it has already received its value at the time of creating the object ("Unknown Title"). To get this code to work, you might be inclined to make `title` a *blank final* variable, like so:

```
class Book {
    final String title;
    final String[] authors;

    final int yearReleased, nrOfPages;

    int copiesSold = 0;

    public static void main(String[] args) {
        Book superLargeBook = new Book();
        superLargeBook.title = "Super Large Boring Book";
        superLargeBook.nrOfPages = 1400;
    }
}
```

Note that I have also reworked some other variables, as it makes sense that the title, authors, number of pages, and the release date never change for a book (not taking into account reprints and other such intricacies at the moment). Hence, it makes sense to set these to read-only.

However, you will notice that Java will still complain about the `title` and `nrOfPages` assignments and refuse to compile this code fragment. Why? Especially when the following code (you can put this somewhere in the `main` method) does in fact work:

```
final int a;
a = 5;
```

The reason lies in the fact that `title`, `authors`, `yearReleased`, and so on are class variables, whereas the a integer is just a local variable. Remember that when you initialize an object, Java will assign default values to the instance and class variables for which no value was set. For final variables, on the other hand, Java will not set an initial value and will force you, the programmer, to explicitly provide an initial value. For local variables inside our `main` method, we can define a blank variable and initialize it later (before using it), as seen above, but for instance and class variables, this remark entails that we cannot do the following:

```
class Book {
    final String title;
}
```

If we try to do this, Java will warn that we have not initialized the `title` variable.

Given this point, it might occur to you that final class variables are, for now, pretty useless. You have found no way to create books with a given initial title that's kept as a read-only variable. To resolve this, you need to understand another concept: object *constructors*. Don't worry, you will learn about these a few pages later, and you will revisit final class variables there as well.

There is, however, another way that final variables come in handy, and that is when you use them in combination with static variables. Change the `Book` class again to look like the following:

```
class Book {
    final static int MAX_AMOUNT_OF_PAGES = 500;
    final static int MIN_AMOUNT_OF_PAGES = 50;

    String title;
    String[] authors;

    int yearReleased, nrOfPages;
    int copiesSold = 0;

    public static void main(String[] args) {
        Book superLargeBook = new Book();
        superLargeBook.title = "Super Large Boring Book";
        superLargeBook.nrOfPages = 1400;

        System.out.println("Check if your book has a correct amount of pages...");
        System.out.println("- Minimum amount: "+Book.MIN_AMOUNT_OF_PAGES);
        System.out.println("- Maximum amount: "+Book.MAX_AMOUNT_OF_PAGES);
        System.out.println("- Your book: "+superLargeBook.nrOfPages);
    }
}
```

Note the two `final static` variables at the top of the class body. This pattern is very heavily used by Java programmers to define constants, meaning that you desire to set the maximum and minimum amount of pages only once (they are final), and also to keep them shared by all objects (they are part of the class blueprint). Note by the way that Java has a `const` keyword, but it currently remains unused.

Also observe the change in naming convention when declaring constants with `final static` variables. Instead of writing in `lowerCamelCase`, you name them using `CAPITALIZED_UNDERSCORE_SEPARATED` form. Again, this is not required, but it's a widely followed convention by Java programmers to indicate constant variables.

There is one final (no pun intended) important remark I need to make regarding final variables. Remember that I have stated that final variables can only be initialized once, and then keep their value. For primitive types, the effects of this are easy to grasp—a final integer set to the number five remains five for the remainder of its life. However, for more complex types, such as objects, the story is a little more complicated. Consider the following example:

```
class Book {
    final static int MAX_AMOUNT_OF_PAGES = 500;
    final static int MIN_AMOUNT_OF_PAGES = 50;
```

```
        String title;
        String[] authors;

        int yearReleased, nrOfPages;
        int copiesSold = 0;

        public static void main(String[] args) {
            final Book superLargeBook = new Book();
            superLargeBook.title = "Super Large Boring Book";
            superLargeBook.nrOfPages = 1400;

            // Change the amount of copies sold
            superLargeBook.copiesSold += 1000;
        }
    }
```

Note how `superLargeBook` is final. However, later on, you have to modify the number of copies sold for this object. How is this possible when the code declared this object as final? After all, you should not be able to change it, right? The reasoning here is that final affects the number of times a variable may be initialized, or set. It does not mean that all the fields of an object (when the variable represents an object) will become "frozen" as well.

To illustrate the difference, the following code shows what you cannot do:

```
class Book {
    final static int MAX_AMOUNT_OF_PAGES = 500;
    final static int MIN_AMOUNT_OF_PAGES = 50;

    String title;
    String[] authors;

    int yearReleased, nrOfPages;
    int copiesSold = 0;

    public static void main(String[] args) {
        final Book superLargeBook = new Book();
        superLargeBook.title = "Super Large Boring Book";
        superLargeBook.nrOfPages = 1400;

        // Change the amount of copies sold

        superLargeBook.copiesSold += 1000;

        // Assign a new book
        superLargeBook = new Book(); // EEK!
    }
}
```

Eclipse throws an error, telling you that you are not allowed to assign a new book (or any other existing book) to the `superLargeBook` variable.

The same reasoning holds for composite types (arrays). The following code again shows an example:

```
final int[] numbers = new int[]{1,2,3};
```

```
numbers[0] = 10; // This is okay

int[] newNumbers = new int[]{10,20,30};
numbers = newNumbers; // This is not okay
```

There is one case, however, that's a little bit special, namely *Strings*. As you have seen, Strings are not a primitive type in Java, and are, in fact, objects like any other. You might thus try something like the following:

```
final String myString = "Hi there";
myString = "bye";
```

However, this approach will not work, as this is actually a shorthand notation for the following:

```
final String myString = new String("Hi there");
myString = new String("bye");
```

When writing this piece of code, it becomes clear why you cannot do it this way. However, when you are particularly observant, you might say, since `String` is a class and I create `String` objects, surely the actual *value* of the `String` object must be stored somewhere, probably as an array of `char`'s. The answer is that, indeed, a `String` object keeps an internal representation of the actual textual value, but it cannot be publicly accessed or modified. This is done for performance reasons. But wait—why then can you execute the following:

```
String myString = "a";

myString = "b";
myString += "cde";
```

Again, the reason is that this is shorthand and Java helps you out. In fact, this code actually corresponds to:

```
String myString = new String("a");
myString = new String("b");
myString = new String(myString + "cde");
```

This immediately provides you with the reasoning behind the fact that changing Strings in Java are an intensive, relatively slow operation. For a few modifications, this does not matter, but when you have to modify a String many thousands of times, it is advisable to look at other text-representing classes, such as `StringBuilder`—more about this later.

> **NOTE** Variables are not the only elements that can be defined as being final. Methods can also be set as being final—meaning that they cannot be overridden or hidden by subclasses. Classes can also be set to final, meaning that they cannot be subclassed at all.
>
> Don't worry about what subclassing and subclasses mean at this point, as I will explain them when we talk about advanced object-oriented concepts in Chapter 8. Just remember for now that "final" can serve as a way to allow for
>
> *continues*

continued

stricter and more secure coding (in fact, many of Java's built-in classes are final so they cannot be tampered with).

A common misconception exists that says that declaring classes or methods as final helps to speed up execution. The explanation behind this oftentimes follows a reasoning such as, "Well, since the compiler knows this method will never be modified or extended by subclasses, it must be able to optimize on this." This perception, however, is incorrect, as the Java JIT compiler does no such thing. In fact, declaring classes and methods final can be a great burden when programming, as they limit the options for code reuse and extending functionality of existing classes. Of course, there are good reasons to declare a class or method final, when you want to guarantee that classes and methods remain immutable (meaning that they cannot be extended or modified by other classes).

For instance variables, however (as seen here), the reasoning is so dissimilar that it's almost confusing that we use the same `final` keyword. Not only is setting a variable to final a great way to enforce a read-only variable, which occurs more often than you might think (many variables are read-only), it also does help the compiler to optimize your program. As a final variable keeps the same value after initialization, the compiler is able to cache (store) this value to perform quick checks on this variable whenever it's asked to.

Variable Scope

A very important aspect when working with variables in Java—and, in fact, other programming languages as well—is their scope. Without knowing anything about variable scope, trying to access variables can get confusing once the compiler starts yelling at you for making a mistake. Consider the following simple class with two methods:

```
class ScopeTest {
    void makeA() {
        int a = 5;
    }

    void readA() {
        System.out.println("The value of a is: "+a);
    }
}
```

If you try to enter this in Eclipse, you'll get an error telling you that the variable a cannot be resolved. The reason for this is scope. A variable's scope is basically the context in which the variable is known. Depending on where a variable is declared, you will be able or unable to access this variable. The following "levels" of scope can be defined:

➤ **Local variables:** Variables that are declared inside a method or block.

➤ **Parameter variables:** Variables that are declared as a method argument or a loop variable.

➤ **Instance variables:** Variables that are declared in the class definition.

These levels of scope are ordered so that variables that are defined in a higher level can be accessed from lower-level locations. To give the simplest example, instance variables (highest level) can be accessed by all methods inside the class. Method arguments (a parameter variable) can only be accessed by that method, but not by other methods. This is exactly why the previous example doesn't work.

Figure 4-3 graphically illustrates the scope of an instance variable (`instanceVar`), a parameter variable (`paramVar`), and a local variable (`localVarA`).

```
class ScopeTest {

    int instanceVar;

    void makA(int paramVar) {
        int localVarA = 5;
        System.out.println("The value of instanceVar is: " + instanceVar);
        System.out.println("The value of paramVar is: " + paramVar);
        System.out.println("The value of localVarA is: " + localVarA);
    }

    void makeB(int paramVar) {
        System.out.println("The value of instanceVar is: " + instanceVar);
        System.out.println("The value of paramVar is: " + paramVar);
    }
}
```

FIGURE 4-3

As the example in Figure 4-3 shows, the instance variable (`instanceVar`) is accessible by each method in the class. Parameter variables are accessible only within their methods, and can thus reuse the same name throughout different method definitions. Finally, locally declared variables (such as `localVarA`) are accessible only within their method, meaning that method `makeB` will not be able to access `localVarA`.

Note that parameter variables are accessible only within their method or loop. What do I mean by their loop? I will leave the main explanation regarding loops for the next chapter, but the following example provides a sneak preview:

```
class ScopeTest {
    void doTheLoop() {
        String[] names = new String[]{"Alice", "Bob", "Mia", "Marcus"};
        for (int i = 0; i < names.length; i++) {
            System.out.println("Name number "+i+" equals: "+names[i]);
        }
        System.out.println("The value of i is now: "+i); // Will not work
    }
}
```

Again, you have one class definition, with one method, taking no arguments this time. Inside the method, you have one local variable (`names`) followed by a so-called `for` loop. Don't concern yourself with the specifics of this construct for now, just understand that this code basically says, "For an integer `i` going from 0 but not including the number of names. That is, for `i` equal to 0, 1, 2, and 3, do whatever's inside this block." What is important to know, however, is that the variable `i` is only available within the `for` block, which is why the last `println` statement in the previous code snippet will throw an error in Eclipse, as `i` is no longer accessible at this point. Another point to note is that the `names` variable is also accessible from within the loop block. Again, this illustrates the basic rule saying that variables that are declared at a higher level (locally in the method) can be accessed by a lower level (a loop block within the method).

I close this section on variable scope—and variables in general—with a number of important remarks. First, you might be wondering what happens whenever variables defined in different locations (that is, at a different level of scope) clash in terms of naming. For example, consider the following example:

```
class ScopeTest {
    int a = 5;
    void printA() {
        int a = 10;
        System.out.println("The value of a is now: "+a);
    }
}
```

What will show up when the method `printA` is called? Again, remembering that rule that higher-level variables can be accessed from lower-level locations provides some guidance here, as accessing a variable will "bubble up" from the current scope. This means that Java will first try to access the variable locally, and then move outward until looking for instance variables or static class variables bearing the requested name. This means that in the previous example, the local variable gets precedence and the result displaying on the screen will thus be 10. This concept is known as "variable shadowing" (consider the local variable to overshadow the higher-level ones). Keep this in mind when naming variables. Note also that Eclipse will provide subtle formatting and coloring hints to indicate which variable is being accessed.

> **NOTE** *What if you really wanted to access the instance variable and not the local variable in this example, without renaming one of them? In that case, you have to explicitly tell Java you want the instance variable, using the keyword* `this`, *like so:*
>
> ```
> class ScopeTest {
>     int a = 5;
>     void printA() {
>         int a = 10;
>         System.out.println("The value of INSTANCE VARIABLE " +
>             "a is now: "+this.a);
>     }
> }
> ```
>
> *And when* `a` *is a class variable, remember to use the class name:*
>
> ```
> class ScopeTest {
>     static int a = 5;
>     void printA() {
>         int a = 10;
>         System.out.println("The value of INSTANCE VARIABLE " +
>             "a is now: "+ScopeTest.a);
>     }
> }
> ```
>
> *For now, it is best to stick to clear, unambiguous naming; you will return to learn about the keyword* `this` *in-depth in a later chapter.*

Another important remark concerns the fact that local and parameter variables are forgotten once their scope is exited, meaning that method arguments will disappear once you exit the method (this allows you to use the same variable name for arguments throughout different methods), just as local variables will be discarded once the compiler steps out of its block (a method or loop body). To illustrate this once more, consider the following:

```java
class ScopeTest {
    void scopeTest(int a) {
        int b = a + 10;
        for (int c = 0; c < 10; c++) {
            int d = c + 3;
            b = b + 1;
        }
    }
}
```

Try to work out what is happening here. Variable d (local variable) is only accessible within the loop block. Variable c (parameter variable) is initialized for each iteration of the loop and is only accessible within the loop body. Variable b (local variable) is discarded after the method is exited but is accessible in the whole method. Variable a (parameter variable) is also discarded after the method is exited and is accessible in the whole method, but it's passed as a method argument.

> **NOTE** If you want to do so, note that you can also arbitrarily create your own scope blocks, different from class, method, or loop bodies. This is done simply by wrapping a piece—a block—of code in curly brackets: { and }. For example, the previous code snippet can be extended as such:
>
> ```java
> class ScopeTest {
>     void scopeTest(int a) {
>         int b = a + 10;
>         for (int c = 0; c < 10; c++) {
>             int d = c + 3;
>             {
>                 int e = d + 3;
>             }
>             // e not accessible here
>             b = b + 1;
>         }
>         // c not accessible here
>         {
>             int c = 3;
>         }
>         // c also not accessible here
>     }
> }
> ```
>
> While this is an often forgotten tidbit of Java that can come in handy to structure complex pieces of code, it's best not to rely on this feature too much. When you find yourself putting large amounts of code in blocks like this, it is probably a good idea to try to separate some behavior into multiple methods or classes to split things up.

This concludes the discussion of scope and the overview of different types of variables. You now know how to declare instance variables (member variables or fields), class (static) variables, and final variables, and are aware that variables are defined within a specific scope or context, which determines how they can be accessed.

The next section turns your attention to the other big part of classes: behavior as defined through methods. Just as with variables, there are different types of methods, but many of the aspects you learned here will return.

DEFINING BEHAVIOR: METHODS

Recall once more the simple class outline as follows. A class contains a block of variable definitions (data) and methods (behavior), like so:

```
class CLASSNAME {
    // VARIABLE DEFINITIONS
    // METHOD DEFINITIONS
}
```

Or, to be more specific:

```
class CLASSNAME {
    // FINAL CLASS VARIABLE DEFINITIONS
    // CLASS VARIABLE DEFINITIONS
    // FINAL INSTANCE VARIABLE DEFINITIONS
    // INSTANCE VARIABLE DEFINITIONS

    // METHOD DEFINITIONS
}
```

This section discusses in full the concept of class behavior, as defined through its methods. Specifically, you will see:

➤ **Instance methods:** Methods that are accessible by objects.

➤ **Class methods:** Methods that are not bound to an object but instead belong to the class as such, that is, to the blueprint of the object.

➤ **Constructors:** A special method that governs how a class is instantiated; you have already read about this method.

➤ **The main method:** A special method definition that can be used to run your application.

Finally, you will also learn about *argument passing*. You have seen how methods can take argument variables to use within the method's body. The way variables are passed to methods can be a little bit daunting in Java at first—and can introduce subtle bugs when you're not aware—so it makes sense to learn about this in a separate section.

Instance Methods

Just as with instance variables, an instance method (or a member method) is a method that's accessible only through objects belonging to that class—meaning that they can be accessed only through an initialized object.

A simple example can help to explain this. Suppose you create a Dog class with one method, bark, like so:

```
class Dog {
    void bark() { // Instance method
        System.out.println("Woof!");
    }
}
```

Since bark is an instance method, you first need to create an object to call it, like so:

```
Dog myDog = new Dog();
// Call the instance method on the object myDog:
myDog.bark();
```

That's all there is to defining instance methods. As a reminder, however, recall that methods always return a type or void if they don't return anything. The following example modifies the Dog class to illustrate this once again:

```
class Dog {
    boolean isSitting;

    String getBarkSound() {
        return "Woof!";
    }

    boolean isSitting() {
        return isSitting;
    }

    void sit() {
        isSitting = true;
    }

    void stand() {
        isSitting = false;
    }
}
```

> **NOTE** Note that the sit, stand, and isSitting methods neatly illustrate the concept of encapsulation, meaning that data in a class (the isSitting variable) should be accessed through instance methods (myDog.sit()), instead of directly accessing its variables (myDog.isSitting = true). When you learn about advanced object-oriented programming concepts in Chapter 8, you will see how to effectively block accessing instance variables directly, forcing the use of methods.

Recall that methods returning something (that is, methods that do not return void) always need to include a reachable return statement in their body. Note that you can also place return statements in void methods. In this case, the return statement does not actually return something, but just exits the method. For example, if you want to exit out of the `sit` method before sitting down, you can change this method as follows:

```
void sit() {
    if (isSitting)
            return; // Exit out method if already sitting
    isSitting = true;
}
```

This will especially come in handy for governing the control flow of your program. This aspect will be discussed in detail in the next chapter.

Recall that methods can also take one or more arguments. Consider, for example, the following method declarations:

➤ `void giveCookie(Cookie cookie) { /*...*/ }`

➤ `void chaseDog(Dog dog) { /*...*/ }`

➤ `void lickPerson(Person person, int nrLicks) { /*...*/ }`

➤ `void giveNickNames(String[] nickNames) { /*...*/ }`

➤ `void giveNickNames(String... nickNames) { /*...*/ }`

The last example in this listing will look unfamiliar to you, and it uses a construct called *varargs* (variable arguments). Basically, the last two methods are equivalent in the sense that the `nickNames` variable will be available as an array of strings in the method body, for instance:

```
void giveNickNames(String... nickNames) {
    System.out.println("You have given me "+nickNames.length+" names");
}
```

The way these two methods are called, however, differs. In the first case (`String[] nickNames`), the method is called using an array of strings as an argument, as you'd expect:

```
String[] newNames = new String[] {"Puppers", "Droopy"};
myDog.giveNickNames(newNames);
```

In the second case, however (`String... nickNames`), you can just supply an arbitrary number of strings (including none at all), like so:

```
myDog.giveNickNames("Puppers", "Droopy");
// Or any other amount of strings:
myDog.giveNickNames("Puppers", "Droopy", "Tissues", "Clifford");
myDog.giveNickNames();
```

Varargs can provide a handy way of avoiding having to pass an array explicitly. However, keep in mind that the varargs argument (the one with the three dots, ...) must always be the last method argument, and only one varargs argument can be defined for a method. With arrays, on the other hand, you are free to define any number of arguments in any order you want. To illustrate:

➤ `method(String... s1)`: Allowed

➤ `method(String... s1, String s2)`: Not allowed

➤ `method(String... s1, int s2)`: Not allowed

➤ `method(String... s1, String... s2)`: Not allowed

➤ `method(String... s1, Dog... dogs)`: Not allowed

➤ `method(String[] s1)`: Allowed

➤ `method(String[] s1, String s2)`: Allowed

➤ `method(String[] s1, String[] s2)`: Allowed

➤ `method(String[] s1, String[] s2, Dog[] dogs)`: Allowed

➤ `method(int i1, String[] s1, int i2)`: Allowed

➤ `method(int i1, String[] s1, String... s2)`: Allowed

➤ `method(int i1, String... s1, String[] s2)`: Not allowed

You don't have to memorize this list (or these rules), as Eclipse will simply warn you when you define a method incorrectly.

Class Methods

Just as you've seen for class variables, a *class method*, also denoted as a *static method,* is a method that has been defined statically, meaning that this method is shared between all objects (instances) belonging to the class. Again, as class methods belong to the class blueprint, it is not even necessary to create objects to be able to use them.

I'll illustrate this concept with another example from the realm of pets. This time, let's define a `Cat` class as follows:

```
class Cat {
    static String preferredFood() {
        return "Fish";
    }
}
```

Note the static modifier in front of the method declaration is similar to what you've seen with static variables. `preferredFood` is defined as a blueprint method, returning the preferred food for all cats. Just as for instance methods, it is possible to call class methods through an object:

```
Cat myCat = new Cat();
System.out.println("A cat's preferred food is: "+myCat.preferredFood());
```

However, just as for class variables, this is not good practice, and Eclipse will warn you about such behavior. Again, you should clearly indicate that you're accessing a `static` method by using the class name, instead of the object variable:

```
System.out.println("A cat's preferred food is: "+Cat.preferredFood());
```

This also clearly illustrates that you do not have to create an object to use `static` methods.

It is important to note that, since class methods operate on the class as a whole (as a blueprint), they are not able to access instance variables. For example, the following is not allowed:

```
class Cat {
    String name;

    static void changeName() {
        name = "ANONYMOUS CAT";
    }
}
```

What you can do, however, is the following:

```
class Cat {
    static String preferredFood = "fish";

    static String getPreferredFood() {
        return preferredFood;
    }

    static void setPreferredFood(String newFood) {
        preferredFood = newFood;
    }
}
```

And call this code as follows:

```
System.out.println("A cat's preferred food is: "+Cat.getPreferredFood());
Cat.setPreferredFood("milk");
System.out.println("A cat's preferred food is now: "+Cat.getPreferredFood());
```

This last example illustrates the power of combining class variables with class methods, as they allow you to create class-global variables that can be changed if necessary.

> **NOTE** *Again, you are seeing the concept of encapsulation in practice here. Whereas earlier you would have accessed the class variable* preferredFood *by writing* Cat.preferredFood *directly, you now neatly use the* getPreferredFood *and* setPreferredFood *methods to do so. Does this mean you can no longer write* Cat.preferredFood = "milk"*? The answer is that— for now—you can, but again, you will see later how you can effectively block accessing instance variables directly, forcing the use of methods (and preventing tampering of variables outside their owning class).*

Constructors

Constructors are special class methods that are used to initialize objects of that class. If you recall the discussion on final variables, you might remember that you had—at the time—no way to create

`Book` objects with an initial title that's kept as a read-only variable (using `final`). You might also recall that when you do the following:

```
Book myBook = new Book();
```

You are writing `()` as if you are invoking a method, because, in fact, you are—namely the constructor method for the class. Constructor methods are defined similarly as instance methods, with the following differences:

➤ Constructors bear the same name as the class in which they are defined.

➤ Constructors have no return type, not even `void`.

In all the classes you have seen so far, you will notice that you did not define a constructor method. The reason for this is that Java will automatically assume a "blank" constructor when you do not define one, meaning that defining a class like:

```
Class Book {

}
```

Is exactly the same as writing:

```
class Book {
    Book() {

    }
}
```

So far, this constructor does not really do much. What can they be used for? A constructor is invoked each time you instantiate (that is, "construct") a new object using the `new` keyword. Most commonly, constructors will initialize default values for the object being created. To illustrate this, let's return to the earlier issue: you aim to define a variable to hold the title of a book, but you want to define this variable so it can be set only once. As such, the following solution does not suffice:

```
class Book {
    String title;
}
```

As there is nothing preventing multiple assignments to title in this case. You have seen that you can use the `final` keyword like so:

```
class Book {
    final String title = "Initial Title";
}
```

But of course, you would like to make the initial title user-specified and different for each book. The previous solution does not allow you to write:

```
Book myBook = new Book();
myBook.title = "The Real Title";
```

Finally, you have seen that you can remove the initialization of the variable to make it a so-called *blank final* variable:

```
class Book {
    final String title;
}
```

Recall, however, from our discussion regarding final variables that Java will complain about the fact that the `title` instance variable might not be initialized, as you need to explicitly assign a value. You have seen before that you can solve this by doing something like:

```
class Book {
    final String title = "";
}
```

But again, we have no way to change the `title` variable to the title we actually want to give to a particular book. That is, Java will complain about doing something like:

```
Book myBook = new Book();
myBook.title = "The Real Title";
```

This happens because we have already initialized the `title` variable to `""`, preventing it from being changed again. So how do you deal with this problem? Well, by initializing final variables inside your own constructor, like so:

```
class Book {
    final String title;

    Book() {
        title = "Initial Title";
    }
}
```

To supply a user-specific title, you now can just modify the constructor method so that it takes an argument. Watch out when naming your constructor arguments. Remember that using local or parameter variables with the same name as instance variables will take precedence. Hence, you should modify the constructor like so:

```
class Book {
    final String title;

    Book(String t) {
        title = t;
    }
}
```

Now how do you call this constructor? Easily, by providing an argument when creating an object:

```
Book myBook = new Book("Title of the Book");
```

Note that you have seen how Java will assume the presence of a blank constructor taking no arguments when you do not define one in the class. If you do define a constructor with arguments—like you've just seen—the constructor taking no arguments will not be available any longer, unless you also explicitly define it. Meaning that for this example, you can no longer write:

```
Book myBook = new Book("Title of the Book"); // This works
Book myBook = new Book(); // This no longer works
```

You might be confused by the wording of "unless you *also* explicitly define it." Is it possible to define multiple constructor methods? Indeed it is; consider, for example, the following class definition:

```
class Book {
    final static int DEFAULT_YEAR = 2014;
    final String title;
    final int releaseYear;
    int copiesSold;

    Book(String t) {
        title = t;
        releaseYear = DEFAULT_YEAR;
        // copiesSold will default to 0
    }

    Book(String t, int r) {
        title = t;
        releaseYear = r;
        // copiesSold will default to 0
    }

    Book(String t, int r, int s) {
        title = t;
        releaseYear = r;
        copiesSold = s;
    }
}
```

Given everything you've seen so far, you should be able to understand this class. Take some time to figure out what is happening here, and make sure to note the following:

➤ Three constructors are available for this class, each taking a different number of arguments.

➤ One final static variable is acting as a constant that will be used as a default initializing value in one of the constructors.

➤ The two other blank final variables (non-static) *need* to be initialized by every constructor.

➤ Constructors can also initialize nonfinal variables.

> **NOTE** *Using methods with the same name—but taking different arguments—is provided by a feature called method overriding. As the name suggests, this feature is not only available for constructors, but in fact for every method. Method overriding provides advanced capabilities, so it's covered in-depth in Chapter 8.*

You might be annoyed by the fact that some statements, such as `title = t;`, are duplicated across different constructors, while in fact the constructors are forming a hierarchy. Luckily, it is possible for constructors to call other constructors to perform a piece of the requested initialization, as the following code snippet shows:

```java
class Book {
    final static int DEFAULT_YEAR = 2014;
    final String title;
    final int releaseYear;
    int copiesSold;

    Book(String t) {
        // Call other constructor:
        this(t, DEFAULT_YEAR, 0);
    }

    Book(String t, int r) {
        // Call other constructor:
        this(t, r, 0);
    }

    Book(String t, int r, int s) {
        title = t;
        releaseYear = r;
        copiesSold = s;
    }
}
```

Note the use of the keyword `this` here. I've briefly mentioned this keyword before when illustrating how you can use it to refer to the current object (`this.title`), but here it acts as a way to call another constructor. Again, don't worry if this is still a bit overwhelming, as the `this` keyword will be revisited later. In fact, for now, I will avoid defining multiple constructors until you are ready to move a step further, so that you will not run into the intricacies relating to defining more than one constructor. So for now, just keep in mind that it is possible to create multiple constructors within a class.

NOTE *When you think about the concept of constructors—or if you're coming from other programming languages such as C++—you might wonder if the counterpart of destructors also exists. In Java, it does not, as the JVM itself will keep an eye out for objects that are no longer accessible and should thus be removed automatically. Consider for example:*

```java
Book myBook = new Book("My first book");
myBook = new Book("My second book");
myBook = null;
```

What happens with the `"My first book"` *object stored in the* `myBook` *variable once you assign the second book (a new object) to this variable? Since*

continues

---

continued

you have no way to refer to this object anymore (which is now floating around nameless somewhere in the computer memory), the JVM will automatically clean up this piece of memory (this is performed by a mechanism called garbage collection) to remove (destroy) the object. The same happens when assigning `null` to the variable with the second object. The variable now refers to nothing, and the second object can also no longer be referenced, and is thus removed as well.

Whenever the JVM cleans up objects in this manner, it will call a special built-in method, `finalize()`, on them. Programmers can implement their own finalization method if they desire, which comes in handy when objects are utilizing resources that need to be cleanly closed when they are removed (think, for example, about open network connections). In practice, however, there is rarely a need to override the default behavior.

Again, you need to learn how to walk before you can run, so for now, just be glad about the fact that Java takes care of these cleanup aspects for you. You do not need to concern yourself with writing destructors.

The Main Method

Earlier in this chapter, you learned that there exists one special method used as an entry point to actually execute (run) your program—the so-called `main` method.

The `main` method can be defined in any class, but is *always* defined as:

```
public static void main(String[] args) {

}
```

Meaning that the `main` method:

➤ Is publicly accessible. (`public` is an access modifier. I have ignored access modifiers for now, but for the `main` method, you *have* to define it.)

➤ Is a `static` class method, as no objects exist yet when a program is started.

➤ Returns nothing (`void`).

➤ Takes one argument, the arguments passed to the program.

Let's have a closer look at the `main` method. Suppose you once more define a simple `Book` class to look as follows:

```
class Book {
    final String title;
    final int releaseYear;
    int copiesSold;
```

```
        Book(String t, int r) {
            title = t;
            releaseYear = r;
        }

        void sell(int nrCopies) {
            copiesSold += nrCopies;
        }

        int nrCopiesSold() {
            return copiesSold;
        }
    }
```

If you now want to create an actual program that can be executed, the simplest way to do so is by creating a main method within this class, like so:

```
class Book {
    final String title;
    final int releaseYear;
    int copiesSold;

    Book(String t, int r) {
        title = t;
        releaseYear = r;
    }

    void sell(int nrCopies) {
        copiesSold += nrCopies;
    }

    int nrCopiesSold() {
        return copiesSold;
    }

    public static void main(String[] args) {
        Book firstBook = new Book("First Book", 2004);
        Book secondBook = new Book("Another Book", 2014);
        firstBook.sell(200);
        System.out.println("Number of copies sold of first book is now: "
            +firstBook);
        System.out.println("Title of the second book is: "+secondBook.title);
    }
}
```

In general, however, it is not good practice to mix a main method with a class definition relating to a real-world concept. As such, it is better to create a separate "controller" class to separate program logic from class concepts, like so:

```
// File Book.java:
class Book {
    final String title;
    final int releaseYear;
    int copiesSold;
```

```java
    Book(String t, int r) {
        title = t;
        releaseYear = r;
    }

    void sell(int nrCopies) {
        copiesSold += nrCopies;
    }

    int nrCopiesSold() {
        return copiesSold;
    }
}

// File Program.java:
class Program {
    public static void main(String[] args) {
        Book firstBook = new Book("First Book", 2004);
        Book secondBook = new Book("Another Book", 2014);
        firstBook.sell(200);
        System.out.println("Number of copies sold of first book is now: "
            +firstBook);
        System.out.println("Title of the second book is: "+secondBook.title);
    }
}
```

Some developers like to supply `main` methods in their class definitions in larger programs as a quick way to test if the class is working correctly, without having to run the complete program and go through a series of steps. This is fine, so long as you keep these "test" `main`s small and short, for testing purposes only, and remember that there exist better ways to perform thorough code tests. This remark does illustrate another aspect, though, namely the fact that a Java project can contain multiple `main` methods. In fact, it's possible to provide a `main` method in every class you define. So how does Eclipse or Java know how to execute which one? To figure this out, you'll return to the very first example context you saw at the beginning of this chapter: the course administration program. The following Try It Out will guide you from beginning to end to re-create the course administration example, using all of the knowledge you've gained so far.

TRY IT OUT Course and Student Administration Revisited

Let's revisit the course and student administration example you saw earlier, now applying all of the knowledge you've gained so far.

1. It's best to create a new project in Eclipse. Remember you can do so by navigating to File ➤ New and then selecting Java Project in Eclipse. A dialog window will open asking you to fill in a project name, such as `CourseAdministrationDoneWell`. You can then press Finish to create the project.

2. Create the `Course.java` class by right-clicking the `src` folder in the package explorer in Eclipse and then selecting New ➤ Class. Define this class as follows:

```java
import java.util.HashSet;

class Course {
    static int nextId = 0;
```

```
    final int id;
    final String name;
    final HashSet<Student> registeredStudents =
            new HashSet<Student>();

    Course(String n) {
        id = nextId;
        nextId++;

        name = n;
    }

    String getName() {
        return name;
    }

    void registerStudent(Student s) {
        registeredStudents.add(s);
    }

    void unregisterStudent(Student s) {
        registeredStudents.remove(s);
    }

    HashSet<Student> registeredStudents() {
        return registeredStudents;
    }

    int nrOfRegisteredStudents() {
        return registeredStudents.size();
    }
}
```

3. Similarly, create a Student class with the following content:

```
class Student {
    static int nextId = 0;

    final int id;
    final String firstName, lastName;

    Student(String fn, String ln) {
        id = nextId;
        nextId++;

        firstName = fn;
        lastName = ln;
    }

    String getFirstName() {
        return firstName;
    }

    String getLastName() {
        return lastName;
    }
```

```
    void registerForCourse(Course c) {
        c.registerStudent(this);
    }

    void unregisterForCourse(Course c) {
        c.unregisterStudent(this);
    }
}
```

4. Create a `Program` class containing the `main` method:

```
class Program {
    public static void main(String[] args) {
        p("Welcome to the course administration program");
        p("---------------------------------------------");
        p("");

        p("Creating two courses...");
        Course courseA = new Course("First Course");
        Course courseB = new Course("Second Course");

        p("- courseA ID is: "+courseA.id);
        p("- courseA name is: "+courseA.getName());
        p("- courseB ID is: "+courseB.id);
        p("- courseB name is: "+courseB.getName());
        p("");

        p("Creating two students...");
        Student student1 = new Student("Alice", "The Student");
        Student student2 = new Student("Bob", "McStudent");

        p("- student1 ID is: "+student1.id);
        p("- student1 name is: "+student1.getFirstName()+", "+
                student1.getLastName());
        p("- student2 ID is: "+student2.id);
        p("- student1 name is: "+student2.getFirstName()+", "+
                student2.getLastName());
        p("");

        p("Registering for courses...");
        student1.registerForCourse(courseA);
        student1.registerForCourse(courseB);
        courseA.registerStudent(student2);

        p("- courseA number of students: "+courseA.nrOfRegisteredStudents());
        p("- courseB number of students: "+courseB.nrOfRegisteredStudents());
    }

    static void p(String l) {
        System.out.println(l);
    }
}
```

5. To run this program from Eclipse, make sure the `Program` class is open and the `main` method is active (by putting your cursor inside the method body), and then press the Run button. Eclipse will show you the name of the class that contains the `main` method that will be run.

How It Works

Now take a look at how it works.

1. You're creating two new `Student` and `Course` classes in a new Eclipse project.

2. For the `Course` class, note the use of the `nextId` variable to automatically use an incrementing counter to provide IDs for courses. This is a well-known pattern that you will see show up commonly in Java code. Also note the use of the `HashSet` object. A `HashSet` is a set, storing a bunch of objects (`Student` objects, in this case). The `HashSet` class is built-in by default in Java, but to enable its use, you first have to import it, hence the `import` statement before defining the class itself. Don't concern yourself too much with its usage for now, but make sure you understand the `registerStudent` and `unregisterStudent` methods, which add and remove students to and from the set.

3. For the `Student` class, you're using the keyword `this` to pass the current student object (meaning the object the method was called on) to the course object to register or unregister a student, as it is the course object that keeps a list of registered students.

4. The `Program` class contains the `main` method, and it creates two courses, gives some information about them, creates two students, and registers them in the courses. The `p` method just serves as a shorthand to avoid having to write `System.out.println` all the time.

5. You then run this program from Eclipse by invoking the `main` method in the `Program` class. Note that it is possible at this point to create another class containing a `main` method and run that one in Eclipse by just making sure the `main` method you want to run is open in the code editor.

ACCESS MODIFIERS

You might have noticed that this code uses `courseA.id` (directly accessing a variable) and `courseA.getName()` (accessing a variable through a method) in the Try It Out. In other examples, you read that it's generally better to access variables through methods whenever possible instead of directly accessing variables.

If it is generally recommended to go through methods, then why does Java allow you to access `courseA.id` directly? The reason for this is due to the access modifier being used. Classes, variables, and methods can all take access modifiers. In Java, four access modifiers exist:

`public`: For classes, methods, and member variables (class or instance)

`protected`: Methods and member variables (class or instance) (not for classes)

no modifier: For classes, methods, and member variables (class or instance)

`private`: Methods and member variables (class or instance) (not for classes)

You have seen one of these (`public`) already, namely in the `main` method, where the inclusion of this access modifier was mandatory:

```
public static void main(String[] args)
```

continues

continued

For all the other classes, methods, and variables you've seen so far, however, I've avoided talking about access modifiers and just supplied no modifier. So what do these modifiers actually do? You will read an in-depth discussion about them in Chapter 8, but for now, just be aware that access-level modifiers determine which other classes can use the class, method, or variable the modifier relates to. When no modifier is supplied, as with these examples, Java will make the class, method, or variable accessible to the class itself (luckily, this should always be the case, otherwise the method or variable would not be of much use), and also to classes living in the same *package*. So far, you have not dealt with packages, so that each class you created in Eclipse lives in the so-called "default package," and each class can access the variables from another class.

This default behavior goes against the *encapsulation* ideology of object-oriented programming, and it is a little bit of a pity that this is chosen as the default behavior in Java. For now, you can afford to be a little sloppy, but you will notice that you start to encapsulate more and more data by wrapping methods around them when you define classes, until you arrive at Chapter 7, where you will be introduced to access modifiers for real—as to prevent direct variable access. One question you might have at this point is whether it ever makes sense to make a member variable directly accessible (by supplying no modifier or by making it `public`). The answer is very rarely. In most cases, it pays off to keep data hidden within the object and use methods as guards around it. Only for very simple "data structure" classes (such as a `Point` class with `x` and `y` variables) is it okay to allow direct access.

The previous Try It Out mentioned that it is possible to add more than one `main` method to your Java projects (although they should be contained in different classes, of course). You might be wondering how Java decides which `main` method to run when running your programs directly (without going through Eclipse). The answer is that Java will either rely on a special description file, or on the users passing the class name they want to run the `main` method from explicitly. If you're interested in knowing more, you can explore the following Try It Out. The Try It Out will also show you how to utilize the `main` method's single `String[]` argument, which we've ignored so far.

TRY IT OUT   Working with Program Arguments

This exercise demonstrates how to use program arguments.

1. Create a new Eclipse project and add a single `Program` class with the following `main` method:

```
class Program {
    public static void main(String[] args) {
        p("You have supplied "+args.length+" arguments...");
```

```
        for (int i = 0; i < args.length; i++) {
            p("Argument "+i+" equals: "+args[i]);
        }
        p("");
    }

    static void p(String l) {
        System.out.println(l);
    }
}
```

2. When running this code from Eclipse, you will notice that the `args` variable is empty (the array has a length of zero).

3. You're going to create a so-called "runnable JAR" file. JAR stands for Java ARchive, which is basically the same as a compressed folder (a ZIP file) containing compiled classes. A *runnable* JAR file is a JAR file that can be executed. To execute it, right-click your project folder in Eclipse and choose Export. Next, navigate to Java and select Runnable JAR File. A wizard will pop up asking you to select a launch configuration and an export destination. In the launch configuration, you can select the class Java should use to run the `main` method. In this case, select `Program` - `YOURPROJECT` (of course, `YOURPROJECT` represents the name you've chosen). If this option does not appear in the drop down, you might have forgotten to run the `main` method in Eclipse first (see Step 2). As the export destination, you will create a JAR file somewhere in the desktop (`C:\Users\USERNAME\Desktop\YOURPROJECT.jar`, replacing `USERNAME` with your actual username).

4. Press Finish to create the runnable JAR, which should then appear on your desktop. Normally, it is possible to just double-click this file to run it (like with normal programs), but since you have not created a GUI application, you need to run this JAR from the command line. Open a command window (run `cmd.exe` in Windows) and execute the following:

```
cd "C:\Users\USERNAME\Desktop\"
java -jar courseadministration.jar
```

5. You should get back the same output as the Eclipse console gave you earlier. Now let's take a look at the `args` variable. Keeping the command-line window open, execute the following:

```
java -jar courseadministration.jar Argument1 Argument_2 Argument-3 Argument 4
```

6. Take note of the output now. The program will report that you have supplied five arguments: `Argument1`, `Argument_2`, `Argument-3`, `Argent`, and `4`. This immediately shows you that arguments are just strings (hence the `String` array) coming from what you pass in the program call (split based on spaces, ' '). What if you want to include a space in your argument? Then you just enclose your arguments in double quotes, like so:

```
java -jar courseadministration.jar "first argument" "second argument"
```

7. The final question that remains is how Java knows which `main` method to run in a given JAR file. This information is stored in a special `META-INF` folder inside the JAR file. This folder contains a `MANIFEST.MF` file, which will in this case contain the following information (you can hunt down

this file yourself by opening YOURPROJECT.jar in an archive manager, such as WinZIP, WinRAR, or 7-Zip, but this is by no means required):

```
Manifest-Version: 1.0
Class-Path: .
Main-Class: Program
```

8. Finally, if you want to run a main method from a JAR file not containing a MANIFEST.MF file (not exported as a runnable JAR file in Eclipse) or want to run another main method, you can do so by executing the following command:

```
java -classpath courseadministration.jar Program
```

How It Works

Now take a look at how it works.

1. When running programs from Eclipse, the args variable will be empty by default. It is also possible to supply arguments to programs from Eclipse, but this is a bit involved and generally not required.

2. In the next steps, you create the runnable JAR. Eclipse will compile your classes, compress them, and store them in the JAR file together with a MANIFEST.MF file.

3. Next, you run the program from the command line:

```
cd "C:\Users\USERNAME\Desktop\"
java -jar courseadministration.jar
```

You should get back the same output as the Eclipse console gave you earlier. The first command (cd) navigates to the desktop directory where you saved your JAR. The second command (java) calls Java and tells it to execute your JAR in the command line. JAR files can be distributed to others and run on all platforms where a Java Runtime Environment (JRE) is available.

4. The next command does the same, but passes in some arguments from the command line to the program:

```
java -jar courseadministration.jar Argument1 Argument_2 Argument-3 Argument 4
```

Why are arguments useful? In most cases—especially for command-line programs—they supply configuration parameters to the program at hand, for example, an argument can indicate the filename that should be read in by a program, or an argument can specify an image-conversion program indicating the desired quality of the resulting image, and so on. In most cases, however, you will not need to use program arguments in day-to-day programming, as it is oftentimes easier (and cleaner) to either let your program read in a configuration file (you will see how to deal with file input and output in a later chapter) or create a GUI to provide configuration options to users (GUIs will be dealt with later as well).

5. The next steps show how Java determines which main method to run from a JAR file, either by using a MANIFEST.MF file (created by Eclipse), or by passing this manually:

```
java -classpath courseadministration.jar Program
```

This command will add your JAR file to the Java classpath (the locations in which Java will look to find classes) and then supplies the class name (Program) from which to run the main method.

Method Argument Passing

There is one final point I want to make in regard to the way parameter variables are passed to methods. *Argument passing* can be daunting and tricky in Java at first sight, so I've devoted a section to this concept to get the point across.

To start the discussion, consider the following code:

```
class Test {
    int a = 4;

    static void increaseInt(int anInt) {
        anInt++;
    }

    public static void main(String[] args) {
        Test t = new Test();
        System.out.println("Instance var a is: "+t.a);
        Test.increaseInt(t.a);
        System.out.println("Instance var a is now: "+t.a);
    }
}
```

What will this code output?

```
Instance var a is: 4
Instance var a is now: 4
```

Even though you have supplied the instance variable to the method, after the method finishes, the value of this variable remains unchanged. This might lead you to believe that the anInt variable will be considered as a *copy* of t.a. In programming jargon, this behavior is called "pass by value."

This is easy enough to understand until you try the same trick with a non-primitive data type, such as arrays:

```
class Test {
    int[] array = new int[]{1,2,3};

    static void increaseFirstInt(int[] anIntArray) {
        anIntArray[0]++;
    }

    public static void main(String[] args) {
        Test t = new Test();
        System.out.println("First element in array is: "+t.array[0]);
        Test.increaseFirstInt(t.array);
        System.out.println("First element in array is now: "+t.array[0]);
    }
}
```

The output given now? Completely different:

```
First element in array is: 1
First element in array is now: 2
```

Is Java going haywire? Not really. . . Some sources might explain this behavior by telling you that primitive types in Java are passed by value (as seen before), but all other types are passed by reference, meaning that the argument variable will refer to the same location in memory as the original variable, and thus, any changes you make in the argument variable will be reflected in the original variable (as they both reference the same location). This explanation, however, is wrong.

To see why, consider the following slight modification of this example:

```java
class Test {
    int[] array = new int[]{1,2,3};

    static void increaseFirstInt(int[] anIntArray) {
        anIntArray[0]++;
    }

    static void changeIntArray(int[] anIntArray) {
        anIntArray = new int[] {100,200,300};
    }

    public static void main(String[] args) {
        Test t = new Test();
        System.out.println("First element in array is: "+t.array[0]);
        Test.increaseFirstInt(t.array);
        System.out.println("First element in array is now: "+t.array[0]);
        Test.changeIntArray(t.array);
        System.out.println("First element in array is now: "+t.array[0]);
    }
}
```

The output is probably different than what you would expect:

```
First element in array is: 1
First element in array is now: 2
First element in array is now: 2
```

If Java indeed passes non-primitive types by reference, the changeIntArray would effectively put a new integer array in the same memory address the old array was stored in, and the final line of code would output 100 instead of 2, but this is not what is happening here. The truth is that *all arguments in Java are passed by value*. The key thing to understand as well, however, is that Java objects are internally represented as a reference to a location in memory, and this reference is passed as a value. That is, the memory address of objects is passed by value.

At first sight, it seems like this should make no difference, but it does in fact help to figure out what is happening in this example. Step through the code line by line. First, you create a new variable, called t, as such:

```java
Test t = new Test();
```

Try not to think of this variable as containing all information and behavior stored in the Test object (this helps you understand the difference between classes and objects, but is not the way Java uses object variables), but just as a piece of paper holding an address in memory, as shown in Figure 4-4.

FIGURE 4-4

Next, you call the following method:

```
Test.increaseFirstInt(t.array);
```

t.array is also a non-primitive type, so once again, try to imagine this variable as a piece of paper holding an address. When you write t.array, think of Java first going to the address in memory written on the piece of paper for t, then retrieving the array variable there, which contains another address pointing toward the location in memory where the actual data can be found. When you write t.array[0], you would thus traverse two memory addresses to eventually find the actual integer data. Figure 4-5 shows a simplified view of the basic idea.

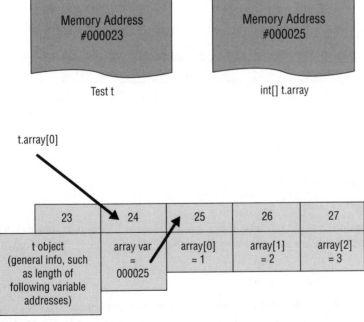

FIGURE 4-5

The address written on the t.array piece of paper is passed to the increaseFirstInt method by value (!). This means that you do not pass the piece of paper itself, but instead take another sheet of paper, write down the same address, and use that piece within the method (a copy of the address is made).

However, when this method executes the following:

```
anIntArray[0]++;
```

It will, of course, point to the same address in memory, as you have created a copy of the piece of paper, but both contain the same address. This is why the changes are reflected in the member variable, even though your second piece of paper (`anIntArray`) is thrown away once the method exits. Figure 4-6 depicts this in the simplified view you've been following.

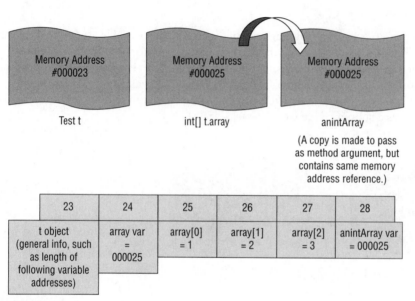

FIGURE 4-6

Now let's take a look at what happens next:

```
Test.changeIntArray(t.array);
```

Again, there is the same reasoning. You do not pass the `t.array` piece of paper itself, but again make a copy to pass to the `changeIntArray` method, which is named `anIntArray`. However, this method calls:

```
anIntArray = new int[] {100,200,300};
```

Meaning that you create a new object and scribble down its address on the copied `anIntArray` sheet of paper, overriding the old one, which is different from the one written in `t.array`. This means that all the changes you then make to `anIntArray` will not be reflected in the member variable (as the addresses differ). Even more, the object stored in the location referred to by `anIntArray` will cease to exist when the method exits, as the piece of paper is discarded, and Java will detect that the object living at that address can no longer be accessed through any variable, as shown in Figure 4-7.

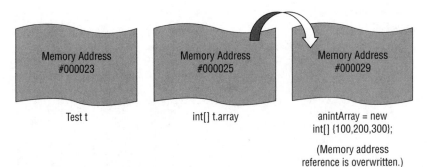

23	24	25	26	27	28	29	30	31
t object (general info, such as length of following variable addresses)	array var = 000025	array[0] = 1	array[1] = 2	array[2] = 3	anintArr ay var = 000029	anintArr ay[0] = 100	anintArray ay[1] = 200	anintArray ay[2] = 300

FIGURE 4-7

> **NOTE** *Again, it's important to take special care when dealing with Strings. Strings are a non-primitive type, meaning that you might try to write the following code:*
>
> ```
> class Test {
>     String a = "a";
>
>     static void changeString(String s) {
>         s = "b";
>     }
>
>     public static void main(String[] args) {
>         Test t = new Test();
>         System.out.println("a is: "+t.a);
>         Test.changeString(t.a);
>         System.out.println("a is now: "+t.a);
>     }
> }
> ```
>
> *But see that the changes you make to the String are not reflected in the member variable. The reason for this is simple. Remember that assigning (new) values to a String will always create a new* `String` *object. This code is thus equal to writing:*
>
> ```
> class Test {
>     String a = new String("a");
> ```
>
> *continues*

continued

```
        static void changeString(String s) {
            s = new String("b");
        }

        public static void main(String[] args) {
            Test t = new Test();
            System.out.println("a is: "+t.a);
            Test.changeString(t.a);
            System.out.println("a is now: "+t.a);
        }
    }
```

As such, modifying the argument variable s *will cause a new* String *object to be created, which will also cause the address referenced to by that variable to change, and be different from the original address in* t.a.

One interesting remark to make in this context is about final variables. As you have seen, instance variables and local variables can be declared as being final to prevent multiple initializations. Parameter variables can also be final, meaning that it's possible to write a method like so:

```
class Test {
    void editNames(final String[] argNames) {
        // Will not work due to final modifier:
        // argNames = new String[]{"Caesar"};

        // This will work:
        argNames[0] = "Caesar";
    }
}
```

This completely corresponds with the definition of final variables as explained before, keeping in mind that finalizing a variable is not the same as "freezing" it completely, but it does prevent new initializations. However, since argNames will be discarded once the method is exited, why would you even bother to declare a parameter variable as final? One particularly straightforward reason is to prevent you from accidentally re-initializing the variable, to prevent you from overwriting the address stored on a variable's piece of paper with a new one. When you actually *want* methods to directly modify an object, you in fact want to avoid creating a new object, as the address referenced by the argument will then change and be discarded once you exit the method. Using final helps prevent such mistakes.

This concludes the overview on beginning object-oriented programming in Java. You have covered a lot of ground. You have seen how to define classes, with data being represented by instance and class variables—final or not—and behavior being represented by instance and class methods. You have also seen how to define class constructors, and read about the special main method to execute your programs.

The complete class definition "template" now looks like this:

```
class CLASSNAME {
    // FINAL CLASS VARIABLE DEFINITIONS
    // CLASS VARIABLE DEFINITIONS
    // FINAL INSTANCE VARIABLE DEFINITIONS
    // INSTANCE VARIABLE DEFINITIONS

    // CONSTRUCTOR METHOD DEFINITIONS
    // INSTANCE METHOD DEFINITIONS
    // CLASS METHOD DEFINITIONS

    // MAIN METHOD DEFINITION (OPTIONAL)
}
```

The final section of this chapter guides you through Java's standard edition built-in classes and highlights some particularly useful ones that will return in many of the following chapters.

JAVA SE BUILT-IN CLASSES

Recall from the introduction to Java in Chapter 2 that there are multiple "editions" of Java. The most widely used edition—the one used here as well—is aptly named Java SE, Standard Edition. This edition comes with class libraries containing a number of built-in classes that meet most of your needs you will encounter while programming. One of them—the HashSet—was already briefly discussed in the last Try It Out, as a simple way to keep a set of objects. This class is part of the so-called "collections" class library, which contains a number of other helpful "array alternatives" as well.

The following subsections provide a short tour through all of Java SE's frequently used built-in classes. I've organized them by their packages. I still need to discuss packages in-depth, but for now, just think of them as a way to organize classes using a naming scheme that looks a bit like web URLs. For example, both the Java HashSet and ArrayList classes are found in the package java.util. Their full canonical names are java.util.HashSet and java.util.ArrayList, which is all you need to know for now.

Classes in the java.lang Package

The java.lang package contains core classes related to the Java language, including:

➤ java.lang.Object: Every class you define silently inherits all the behavior defined in this class. This class contains methods such as equals (to perform object equality checks), clone (to make a copy of an object), and toString (to retrieve a textual representation of an object), which can be overridden and customized by programmers. Chapter 8 will tell you more about this.

➤ java.lang.Exception and all its subclasses: Classes representing errors. Chapter 6 talks more about exceptions, errors, debugging, and testing.

➤ java.lang.String, as well as wrapper classes for all primitive types (java.lang.Integer, java.lang.Double, and so on).

➤ java.lang.StringBuilder: An alternative class for dealing with strings that's especially helpful if you need to perform a lot of modifications to a String.

➤ `java.lang.System`: Class providing system operations.

➤ `java.lang.Math`: Class providing methods to perform basic mathematics.

Other than this, this package also provides a number of classes to deal with complex Java aspects such as reference management, reflection, and process spawning and control. All advanced concepts which you can safely ignore for now.

The two classes that jump out, however, and that can be very useful are the `Math` and `StringBuilder` classes.

`Math` contains two static constants (`E`, the base of natural logarithms, and `PI`, the ratio of the circumference of a circle to its diameter), as well as a number of methods—`abs`, `max`, `min`, `ceil`, `floor`, `sin`, `cos`, `tan`, `pow`, and `sqrt`—to help out with mathematics when programming.

TRY IT OUT   Mathematics in Java

Here is a short exercise to begin using mathematics in Java.

1. Create a `MathTester` class in Eclipse with the following content:

```
class MathTester {
    public static void main(String[] args) {
        double num1 = 2.34;
        double num2 = 1.56;

        System.out.println(Math.max(num1, num2));
        System.out.println(Math.min(num1, num2));
        System.out.println(Math.sqrt(num1));
        System.out.println(Math.pow(num1, num2));
    }
}
```

2. Run the `main` method and observe the output.

How It Works

Now take a look at how it works.

1. The `Math` class contains a number of methods to help out with mathematics when programming. Take your time to explore other methods using Eclipse's context menu.

2. Since the `Math` class belongs to the `java.lang` package, you do not need to write an `import` statement but can use this class directly.

3. All of `Math`'s methods are `static`, meaning that you do not have to create a `Math` object to be able to use its methods. This is a common pattern for "utility" classes in Java, which are classes containing a set of helpful grouped methods that can be statically accessed.

The `StringBuilder` class represents a mutable sequence of characters, compared to a normal String that represents an immutable sequence of characters (which is why Java creates a new `String` object every time you modify a String). The following Try It Out shows where the `StringBuilder` can be useful.

TRY IT OUT StringBuilder versus String

Different classes can be used for working with strings. This exercise will help you differentiate two common classes: `String` and `StringBuilder`.

1. Create a `StringTester` class in Eclipse with the following content:

```java
class StringTester {
    public static void main(String[] args) {
        String string = "";
        long startTime1 = System.currentTimeMillis();
        for (int i = 0; i < 100000; i++) {
            string += "a";
        }
        long endTime1 = System.currentTimeMillis();

        StringBuilder stringBuilder = new StringBuilder();
        long startTime2 = System.currentTimeMillis();
        for (int i = 0; i < 100000; i++) {
            stringBuilder.append("b");
        }
        long endTime2 = System.currentTimeMillis();

        System.out.println("String took: "+(endTime1-startTime1)+"ms");
        System.out.println("StringBuilder took: "+(endTime2-startTime2)+"ms");
    }
}
```

2. Run this piece of code to benchmark the performance of `String` (100,000 times adding a character) with `StringBuilder`.

How It Works

Now take a look at how it works.

1. This code benchmarks the performance of the `StringBuilder` class against normal strings, by performing 100,000 single character concatenations. The example uses a `for` loop here, which I've not discussed in-depth yet, but the meaning is clear—you simply count from 0 to 100,000.

2. When running the benchmark, you should get something like the following output. Observe the drastic difference:

```
String took: 3231ms
StringBuilder took: 5ms
```

Classes in the java.io and java.nio Packages

The `java.io` package provides classes to deal with input and output, for instance to deal with reading and writing files. In Java SE 1.4, New IO (`java.nio`) was added to optimize performance and to include a number of new features. Chapter 7 discusses how to deal with files in detail, and you will revisit these classes there.

Classes in the java.math Package

The `java.math` package provides classes supporting multi-precision arithmetic, such as `BigDecimal` and `BigInteger`. These classes come in helpful in cases where rounding errors, which can occur when working with normal float or double types, are unacceptable, e.g., in financial and scientific applications.

Contrary to what logical thinking would imply, the main `Math` class is found in `java.lang` and not in `java.math` (and is also not duplicated there).

Classes in the java.net, java.rmi, javax.rmi, and org.omg. CORBA Packages

The classes contained in `java.net` allow functionality for networking, talking to web servers, and other transactions. `java.rmi` and `javax.rmi` contain classes dealing with Remote Method Invocation (RMI), the object-oriented counterpart of RPC (Remote Procedure Calls). The `org.omg.` `CORBA` package provides a number of complex classes supporting remote communication between applications using the CORBA RMI protocol, but is not widely used anymore.

The keyword to remember here is "communication." Providing an in-depth discussion on network programming is out of scope for this book, but you will see in Chapter 10 how to access web sources with Java, where these packages and their classes show up again.

Classes in the java.awt and javax.swing Packages

The classes contained in `java.awt` (Abstract Window Toolkit) provide access to a basic set of GUI (graphical user interface) widgets, as well as classes to provide support for clipboard operations (copying and pasting) and input devices (mice, keyboards, and the like). `Swing` —`java.swing`—provides a collection of classes that builds on top of the Abstract Window Toolkit to extend GUI support with more advanced routines.

You will learn about building graphical user interfaces in Java in Chapter 11, where these packages and their classes are covered in full.

Note that Java 8 also introduces a large update for the so-called JavaFX technology. JavaFX describes a series of packages aiming to bring rich, graphical applications to a number of devices and web browsers, and is intended to replace Swing in the future, although both Swing and JavaFX will remain in the JRE for some time. Main features of JavaFX include support for modern 3D graphics and web technologies. On the other hand, building applications with JavaFX has a steeper learning curve than Swing, so the latter remains the preferred option in most cases for beginners, and for the development of applications that do not require advanced graphical capabilities.

Classes in the java.util Package

The `java.util` built-in classes in Java contain a large number of classes to deal with various data structures. You will heavily utilize these classes throughout the rest of the book, and as they will no doubt be the built-in classes in Java SE you will use the most, it makes sense to discuss them in more detail.

Collections

A large part of the classes contained in the `java.util` package belong to the Java's collections framework (the JCF). The Collections API provides a number of general-purpose data structures, which generally can be described as "better alternatives for arrays." One of these, the `HashSet`, you briefly encountered in the last Try It Out, as a simple way to keep a set of objects.

To illustrate why Java's Collections API is so useful, consider this example of how to implement a set of `Strings`, using only arrays:

```java
class SetAsArray {
    String[] items;

    SetAsArray() {
        items = new String[] {};
    }

    int indexOf(String item) {
        // Check if item is already present
        for (int i = 0; i < items.length; i++) {
            if (items[i].equals(item)) {
                return i;
            }
        }
        return -1;
    }

    boolean hasItem(String item) {
        return indexOf(item) > -1;
    }

    void addItem(String item) {
        if (hasItem(item)) {
            // Item already present
            return;
        }

        // Make new array
        String[] newItems = new String[items.length + 1];

        // Add existing items
        System.arraycopy(items, 0, newItems, 0, items.length);

        // Add item to new array
        newItems[newItems.length - 1] = item;

        // Set new array
        items = newItems;
    }

    void removeItem(String item) {
        if (!hasItem(item)) {
            // Item not present
            return;
        }
```

```
        // Make new array
        String[] newItems = new String[items.length - 1];

        // Add existing items except item to be removed
        System.arraycopy(items, 0, newItems, 0, indexOf(item)); // First half
        System.arraycopy(items, indexOf(item) + 1, newItems, indexOf(item),
                items.length - indexOf(item) - 1); // Second half

        // Set new array
        items = newItems;
    }

    void showContents() {
        System.out.println("Set contains " + items.length + " elements");
        for (int i = 0; i < items.length; i++) {
            System.out.println(" - Element " + i + ": " + items[i]);
        }
    }

    int size() {
        return items.length;
    }

    public static void main(String[] args) {
        SetAsArray mySet = new SetAsArray();
        mySet.addItem("A");
        mySet.addItem("B");
        mySet.addItem("C");
        mySet.addItem("A");
        mySet.showContents();
        mySet.removeItem("B");
        mySet.showContents();
        mySet.addItem("D");
        mySet.showContents();

    }
}
```

As shown, the SetAsArray class provides functionality for adding, removing, and looking up items, as well as for returning the size of the set. This example might look a bit daunting (it uses a for loop to iterate over the array and the if construct to govern program flow, which you'll read about in-depth in the following chapter), but the point is that rolling data structures such as sets by hand is frustrating, difficult, and time-consuming. Here is the same main method, using a HashSet:

```
import java.util.HashSet;

public class HashSetTester {
    public static void main(String[] args) {
        HashSet<String> mySet = new HashSet<String>();
        mySet.add("A");
        mySet.add("B");
        mySet.add("C");
        mySet.add("A");
```

```
            System.out.println(mySet);
            mySet.remove("B");
            System.out.println(mySet);
            mySet.add("D");
            System.out.println(mySet);
        }
    }
```

Clearly, using Java collections is much more straightforward. Notice again the `import` statement at the top, before the class definition. Contrary to classes located in `java.lang`, you need to specify which classes to use in your code when they are outside your current package. You will read about packages and importing classes in Chapter 8, and Eclipse will help you to figure out which `import` statement to include, but the basic idea should be clear from this example.

So which data structures does Java provide out of the box? These are:

➤ Lists (classes implementing `java.util.List`), such as `ArrayList` and `LinkedList`, that provide a user-friendly alternative to arrays.

➤ Stacks (classes implementing `java.util.Stack`) that keep a stack of objects. A stack is a last-in-first-out (LIFO) data structure that allows you to add (push) new objects on top of the stack and retrieve (pop) objects back out from the stack. As a metaphor, you can compare a stack to a pile of papers on your desk. New papers (objects) are placed on top of the pile, and every paper (object) can be taken from the top of the pile as well.

➤ Queues (classes implementing `java.util.Queue`) provide a data structure similar to a stack, but with the difference that objects are taken from the beginning of the queue (first-in-first-out, FIFO). Double-ended queues (`java.util.Dequeue`) are also provided and allow you to insert and remove objects both at the front and the back.

➤ Sets (classes implementing `java.util.Set`), such as the `HashSet` and `TreeSet`, store a set of objects (that is, a group of objects without duplicates).

➤ Maps (classes implementing `java.util.Map`) provide a simple data structure that associates values (objects) with a key. That is, it *maps* keys to values. Think of a map as a dictionary (in other programming languages, this is the term used for this data structure): the word being looked up is the key, whereas the description is the value. Just as a real-life dictionary organizes words according to the alphabet, maps in Java organize their keys in an efficient manner, so retrieving values is generally very fast.

Maps, lists, and sets are by far the most commonly used collection types in Java. The following Try It Out shows how they work.

TRY IT OUT Collections in Java

This Try It Out shows how collection types work in Java.

1. Create a class called `CollectionsTester` in Eclipse.

2. Add a `main` method. Create an `ArrayList`, `HashSet`, and `HashMap` variable and store some items, so that the class looks like this:

```
class CollectionsTester {
    public static void main(String[] args) {
        ArrayList<String> listOfStrings = new ArrayList<String>();
        listOfStrings.add("first item");
        listOfStrings.add("second item");
        listOfStrings.add("third item");
        listOfStrings.add("fourth item");
        listOfStrings.remove(0); // Remove the first item

        HashSet<Integer> setOfIntegers = new HashSet<Integer>();
        setOfIntegers.add(2);
        setOfIntegers.add(4);
        setOfIntegers.add(2);
        setOfIntegers.remove(2);

        HashMap<String, Integer> mapOfStringToInteger =
            new HashMap<String, Integer>();
        mapOfStringToInteger.put("Alice", 4);
        mapOfStringToInteger.put("Bob", 3);
        mapOfStringToInteger.remove("Alice");

    }
}
```

3. Eclipse will complain about the fact that it does not recognize the `ArrayList`, `HashSet`, and `HashMap` classes. If you mouse over the error, you will see that Eclipse automatically provides a way to import these classes. The first option is `Import 'ArrayList' (java.util)`.

4. Another handy way to automatically resolve missing imports in Eclipse is by navigating to Source and then selecting Organize Imports. You can also use the helpful keyboard shortcut Ctrl+Shift+O. After fixing all the errors, the following imports should appear at the beginning of your code:

```
import java.util.ArrayList;
import java.util.HashMap;
import java.util.HashSet;
```

How It Works

Now take a look at how it works.

1. The `CollectionsTester` class shows the use of `ArrayList`, `HashSet`, and `HashMap` classes, that is, lists, sets, and maps. These are the three collection types you'll use the most.

2. The program returns no output, but you can use the `get()` method to retrieve and show items from the collections. Take some time to play around with this code fragment to get a feel for the different methods provided by the collection types. You can use Eclipse's context menu to browse around by typing `listOfStrings` and then looking through the possible methods offered.

You will be using collection types extensively throughout the remainder of this book, and you will become more familiar with them as you move on. For now, I leave you with two remarks. First, note that most collection types (sets and lists) in Java implement the Collection interface. You have not seen interfaces yet, but what this means is that all of the following methods are available for each of these classes (as illustrated in the last Try It Out):

➤ `boolean add(E e)`: Adds an element; returns `true` if the collection changed.

➤ `boolean addAll(Collection<? extends E> c)`: Adds all elements from the given collection to this collection; returns `true` if the collection changed.

➤ `void clear()`: Removes all elements from the collection.

➤ `boolean contains(Object o)`: Returns `true` if the collection contains the given object, `false` otherwise.

➤ `boolean containsAll(Collection<?> c)`: Returns `true` if this collection contains all of the elements in the given collection, `false` otherwise.

➤ `boolean equals(Object o)`: Performs an equality comparison.

➤ `boolean isEmpty()`: Returns `true` if the collection is empty (contains no elements).

➤ `boolean remove(Object o)`: Removes the given element from the collection; returns `true` if the collection changed.

➤ `boolean removeAll(Collection<?> c)`: Removes all elements in the given collection from this collection; returns `true` if the collection changed.

➤ `boolean retainAll(Collection<?> c)`: Keeps only the elements in this collection that are contained in the given collection; returns `true` if the collection changed.

➤ `int size()`: Returns the number of elements in the collection.

➤ `Object[] toArray()`: Returns an array containing all the elements in the collection.

➤ `<T> T[] toArray(T[] a)`: Returns an array containing all the elements in the collection; the type of the array will be that of the specified array.

Note that maps use a different set of methods:

➤ `void clear()`: Removes all mappings from the map.

➤ `boolean containsKey(Object key)`: Returns `true` if the map contains the specified key, `false` otherwise.

➤ `boolean containsValue(Object value)`: Returns `true` if the map contains the specified value, `false` otherwise.

➤ `Set<Map.Entry<K,V>> entrySet()`: Returns a set containing `Entry` objects. Each `Entry` object models a key and value pair.

➤ `boolean equals(Object o)`: Performs an equality comparison.

➤ `V get(Object key)`: Returns the value mapped to the key, or `null` if the key is not present.

➤ `boolean isEmpty()`: Returns `true` if the map contains no mappings, `false` otherwise.

➤ `Set<K> keySet()`: Returns a set containing all the keys contained in this map.

➤ `V put(K key, V value)`: Inserts a key/value pair; if the key exists, the value will be overridden.

➤ `void putAll(Map<? extends K,? extends V> m)`: Inserts all mappings contained in the given map in this map.

➤ `V remove(Object key)`: Removes a mapping for the given key.

➤ `int size()`: Returns the number of mappings in this map.

➤ `Collection<V> values()`: Returns a collection of all values in the map; note that this function does not return a set (like `keyset()` does), as duplicate values may exist in the map.

A second point I want to make at this point is related to so-called "generics" in Java. When glancing over the code and method lists, you might be wondering what the use of `<T>`, `<? extends T>`, and `<String>` in `ArrayList<String>` indicates. Generics was added to Java in 2004, in Java SE 5 to be precise. Put briefly, generics allow classes and methods to work with objects of various classes, without declaring up front what these classes should be while still retaining compiler safety checks. To illustrate this, try writing the following in Eclipse:

```
ArrayList aList = new ArrayList();
aList.add(2);
aList.add("Alice");
```

This will work, but Eclipse will throw up warnings complaining about the fact that `ArrayList` should be parameterized. To explain what this means, try to think about what a list should represent. Basically, a list class should be able to store a list of objects that all belong to a specific type. Which type? Well, when rolling the custom `SetAsArray` before, you enforced all items to be `Strings`, but ideally, you would like to keep this *generic*, as lists, sets, and maps should be able to contain objects of any type. This is exactly why the example provides this type when instantiating collection types, like so:

```
ArrayList<String> aList = new ArrayList<String>();
aList.add(2);
aList.add("Alice");
```

Initializing collections in this way allows the Java compiler to perform an additional number of type checks. If you're following along, you'll note that Eclipse now displays an error when trying to add an integer (2) to this list, as the list is only allowed to hold `Strings`.

Now what if you want your list to hold any kind of object? Then you can just write:

```
ArrayList<Object> aList = new ArrayList<Object>();
aList.add(2);
aList.add("Alice");
```

In general, however, it's best to be as precise as possible when instantiating collections (and other classes using generics). Not only does this allow Java to perform safety checks for you, but another reason is that Java will use the class you provided when instantiating the collection to return objects stored in the collection when retrieving them, for instance:

```
ArrayList<Object> aList = new ArrayList<Object>();
aList.add(new Dog("Puppers")); // Add a Dog object as the first item
aList.add(2);
aList.add("Alice");

Object item = aList.get(0); // Get first item
```

As you can observe, when you want to fetch an item from the list and assign it to a variable, this variable must be declared as an `Object`. Even though you know that your first element belongs to the `Dog` class, you will be unable to execute the following code:

```
//...
Object item = aList.get(0); // Get first item
item.bark();
```

Java will complain about the fact that there is no `bark()` method for the `Object` class. Is there a way to specify that the item you retrieved is really of the class `Dog`? The answer is yes, using *type casting*, as mentioned in Chapter 2:

```
//...
Dog item = (Dog) aList.get(0); // Get first item and type cast it
item.bark();
```

Keep in mind, however, that type casting is generally an unsafe operation and should be avoided. As such, it's best to keep your collections as specific as possible, and use multiple collections to hold different items whenever necessary. Finally, in case you were wondering, it's also possible to define your own classes using generics in Java, but this is a more advanced aspect of programming in Java I will not cover in full.

AUTOBOXING ONCE AGAIN

In the beginning of this chapter, you read about the concept of Autoboxing, which is an automatic conversion made by the Java compiler between primitive types and their corresponding wrapper classes. For example, converting a `double` to a `Double` is called boxing, and converting a `Double` back to a `double` is called unboxing.

Back then, I stated that there was one typical use case where you should know about autoboxing, and now—as I've discussed collections and generics—is the time to mention this. Generics in Java are always provided as classes. This means that primitive types cannot be used as generic types and you cannot declare a list as follows:

```
ArrayList<int> aList = new ArrayList<int>();
```

Luckily, using the mechanism of autoboxing, you can just replace the primitive type with its wrapper class, `Integer`, like so:

```
ArrayList<Integer> aList = new ArrayList<Integer>();
```

Other than keeping this in mind, you do not have to worry about the differences between `int`—the primitive type—and `Integer`—its wrapper class, as Java will handle all the rest for you. What about an array of integers? Then you just write:

```
ArrayList<int[]> aList = new ArrayList<int[]>();
```

continues

continued

This declares a list of integer arrays. As arrays are proper, non-primitive classes, it's fine to use them as generic parameters. It's even possible to define a list that's holding lists of integers, like so:

```
ArrayList<ArrayList<Integer>> aList =
    new ArrayList<ArrayList<Integer>>();
```

By combining collections in this manner, it's easy to define complex custom data structures to hold complex information. Don't go overboard with this however. When you find yourself declaring maps of lists of sets, it might be better to abstract some of this hierarchical complexity by creating some additional classes instead.

Other Utility Classes

Besides collection classes, the `java.util` package also contains a number of other helpful classes to provide a great deal of functionality. These include:

➤ `java.util.Arrays`: This class contains a large number of `static` helper methods to sort and search arrays. Note, however, that the `arraycopy` method is part of the `java.lang.System` class (you saw this method in the `SetAsArray` class). The reason for this is that this method directly performs a memory operation and is thus closer to a "system operation" than what the methods provided by arrays do. Another reason is the fact that `java.util.Arrays` was introduced in Java 1.2, whereas the `arraycopy` method existed before that point.

➤ `java.util.Date`: A class to deal with dates and time. While this class provides solid support for working with dates and time, proper date and time support has been the thorn in the eye of many Java developers, as this class rapidly ceases to be useful once complex aspects such as multiple time zones come into play. The class is also not very well designed. For example, years start counting at 1990, months at 1, and days at 0 (!), which is not very intuitive. This is exactly why Java SE 8 introduced a new Date and Time API, which is located in its proper package: `java.time`. Whenever possible, it is highly advisable to use this class instead of the older ones.

➤ `java.util.Calendar`: A class that provides methods to convert between a point in time and a set of calendar fields. This can be helpful to retrieve the year, month, day, and so on for a given `Date` object. This class has been updated in Java SE 8 as well, with better support for internalization.

➤ `java.util.Currency`: A class to represent a currency.

➤ `java.util.Locale`: A class to represent a geographical, political, or cultural region. This class has been updated in Java SE 8 as well.

➤ `java.util.Random`: A class providing a random number generator.

➤ `java.util.Scanner`: A class providing a text scanner that can parse texts. You will utilize this class to parse text files in Chapter 7.

Other Classes and Custom Libraries

There are a number of other built-in classes in Java SE that I do not cover in-depth here. For instance, there is `java.text`, which contains a number of classes to provide parsing routines for text; `java.security`, which provides encryption services; and classes to work with sound and images.

Finally, it is also good to keep in mind that Java has a rich ecosystem of third-party libraries you can easily incorporate in your own projects whenever you find that the built-in classes do not suffice. Many of these libraries in fact provide alternatives for some of these built-in classes, providing better support to deal with dates and times, for instance, or providing alternatives or extensions for Java's collection classes. Chapter 12 provides an overview of some of these libraries and shows you how to include them in your projects.

For now, however, the built-in classes will guide you through the rest of this book. You have seen how to get started with object-oriented programming in Java. You now know how to define classes, variables, and methods, and are aware of Java's built-in classes, most notably of which being Java's collection types. You still have a lot of ground to cover, however. In some of the examples discussed in this chapter, I already hinted at the `for` and `if` constructs to govern the control flow of your program. In the next chapter, this topic will become your focus of attention.

5

Controlling the Flow of Your Program

WHAT YOU WILL LEARN IN THIS CHAPTER:

➤ How to determine if a certain condition is met

➤ How to control what a Java program does and when it should do it

➤ How to use loops in Java to repeat an action

➤ How to determine which control structure to use

WROX.COM CODE DOWNLOADS FOR THIS CHAPTER

The wrox.com code downloads for this chapter are found at www.wrox.com/go/ beginningjavaprogramming on the Download Code tab. The code is in the Chapter 5 download and individually named according to the names throughout the chapter.

Control structures allow a programmer to define how and when certain statements will be executed. In other words, if certain conditions are met, specified behaviors will result. Several structures exist in Java and other languages, such as loops and if-then statements, which allow this control to be implemented. This chapter begins by introducing (or re-introducing) some operators that will be used extensively in control structures. The operators, essentially, allow you to compare values. In order to make similar comparisons on different data types, some comparative methods will also be introduced. Once you can make these comparisons and assessments, you can start using them to make decisions. That is where the if-then statement comes in. In its simplest form, this structure can be read as follows: if some condition is true, then do something. Next, you will look at `for` and `while` loops, and some extensions of these, which allow sections of code to be repeated based on the conditions you define. A `switch` is an alternative structure that's similar to an if-then statement, but offers a list of cases that can be defined so each is handled differently or so groups of cases can be handled the same. Finally, you'll learn about some keywords that have specific uses in guiding the execution of a program.

COMPARISONS USING OPERATORS AND METHODS

You have already seen operators, such as arithmetic operators, in Chapter 2. Operators are based on mathematical concepts and many will look familiar, even to those unfamiliar with programming. This chapter discusses two types of control operators, *comparative* and *logical*, that are used frequently in control structures. The syntax for operators will differ whether the data type is primitive or composite. Recall that primitive types include `char`, `boolean`, and many numeric representations, like `int`, `double`, and `float`. Arrays, strings, and other defined classes are composite data types.

Comparing Primitive Data Types with Comparison Operators

Given the importance of operators when defining control structures, this section briefly revisits some of the underlying concepts covered in Chapter 2.

For primitive data types, there are well-defined operators, as outlined in Table 5-1, which can be used to compare the values of two variables. Equality and relational comparison operators compare the values of two operands for equality, inequality, greater than, or less than. The result of these expressions is a Boolean `true` or `false`. With primitive types, the following expressions are used for comparison:

➤ Equal: `==`

➤ Not equal: `!=`

➤ Greater than: `>`

➤ Greater than or equal: `>=`

➤ Less than: `<`

➤ Less than or equal: `<=`

Note that the `!` indicates negation. While these operators are used for most primitive data types, there is an exception; Boolean operands can only be compared with equality operators and not with relational operators. That is, `true` cannot be greater than or less than `false`; however, `true` can be equal to `true`. Other primitive data types can be compared with both equality and relational operators.

It is important to distinguish a single equal sign (`=`) from a double equal sign (`==`). The first is used for variable assignment. The variable on the left is assigned the value on the right. For example, `balance = 5000`; assigns the value of `5000` to the variable `balance`. The second is a comparison operator to test whether two things are equal. For example, `balance == 5000`; will return `true` if the value of the variable `balance` is `5000` and `false` otherwise.

TABLE 5-1: Control Operators for Primitive Data Types

OPERATOR	JAVA SYNTAX	ENGLISH EQUIVALENT
Equality	x == y x != y	Is x equal to y? Is x not equal to y?
Relational	x < y x <= y x > y x >= y	Is x less than y? Is x less than or equal to y? Is x greater than y? Is x greater than or equal to y?
Logical	x && y x || y !x	Are x and y both true? Is x, y, or both true? Is x false?

Logical operators, on the other hand, are specific to Booleans, and are used to combine or negate one or more conditions. There are three logical operators: AND (&&), OR (||), and NOT (!). If two or more Boolean operands are joined using the AND operator, all must evaluate to `true` for the overall expression to evaluate to `true`. If they are joined using the OR operator, at least one of them must evaluate to `true` in order for the overall expression to evaluate to `true`. Finally, if the NOT operator precedes a Boolean operand that evaluates to `true`, the overall expression will evaluate to `false` and vice versa. It evaluates as the opposite of the original expression.

Truth tables are used in logic to show the outcome of Boolean operators on pairs of statements. In the first two columns are two statements that can be `true` or `false`. In the columns that follow, operators are listed with their results based on whether the statements are `true` or `false`. Table 5-2 is a truth table demonstrating the Boolean operators discussed here—namely NOT, AND, and OR.

TABLE 5-2: Boolean Operator Truth Table

P	Q	!P NOT P	P && Q P AND Q	P || Q P OR Q
TRUE	TRUE	! TRUE =FALSE	True AND True = TRUE	True OR True = TRUE
TRUE	FALSE		True AND False = FALSE	True OR False = TRUE
FALSE	TRUE	! FALSE =TRUE	False AND True = FALSE	False OR True = TRUE
FALSE	FALSE		False AND False = FALSE	False OR False = FALSE

In fact, you probably encounter these kinds of logical operators in your everyday life. For example, a public transit system might follow a certain schedule if the day is Saturday OR a holiday and another schedule otherwise. In other words, if (day == Saturday || day == holiday), then follow the weekend schedule. Then it is understood that if it is Saturday or a public holiday or both, the entire statement is `true`. On the other hand, you might have a rule that states if a person is over 60 years old AND they possess a bus card, then their fare is reduced, or if (age > 60 && busCard == true), then charge a reduced bus fare. Then you require both conditions—a person must be over 60 AND they must have a bus card—for the entire statement to be true. Regardless of whether a person is 50 years old with a bus card or if they are 62 years old without a bus card, their fare will not be reduced.

& AND | VERSUS && AND ||

This section covered && and ||, the AND and OR operators. There are also bit-wise operators called & and |, which behave similarly on Boolean operands. The main difference is that the double symbols && and || will first check the left side operand and will only check the right side if necessary. So for &&, if the left side is true, it will check if the right side is also true. If the left side is false, then you already know the outcome will be false and the right side will not be evaluated. This is called short circuiting, because like electricity will take the shortest path (sometimes causing a short circuit if there is another shorter route), these operators will stop the evaluation early if the answer is already known. This is particularly useful in avoiding exceptions or errors, when the first operator must be true in order to evaluate the second operator. A common example is (x != 0 && 1/x > 1). If you use & here, and x equals 0, then 1/x will be evaluated, but of course, zero cannot be a divisor so this would cause an error. Java's inclusion of the && operator with short circuiting will prevent this kind of error.

Similarly, for ||, if the left side is true, there is no need to check if the right side is true, so the result will be true without evaluating the right operand. If, however, the left operand is false, it will check the right operand. You could use a very similar example (x == 0 || 1/x < 1) to see how the short circuiting can prevent the same errors when using the OR operand.

Comparing Composite Data Types with Comparison Methods

When you think of the differences between primitive data types, like int, and composite date types, like String, it should not be surprising that you will need to compare them in different ways. If asked the question, "Is 5 less than 10?" almost everyone will compare the two numbers in the same way and respond affirmatively. Although the comparison of char variables is not as immediately apparent, all possible char values have been assigned a numeric value, allowing them to be ordered similarly to integers. However, the question, "Is order less than delivery?" is not at all apparent. Therefore, comparison methods for composite data types must be defined in the class, rather than using the comparison operators discussed in the previous section.

This early chapter, in addition to the primitive types, includes a discussion on strings and arrays, since you will encounter both these composite data types frequently. Many more classes will be covered in later chapters. These classes are well-defined and include comparison methods. It often makes sense to compare strings relationally, such as putting a list into alphabetical order. For other composite data types, including pre-existing classes and classes you will create on your own, comparison methods can be implemented in different ways. You will read about some of these possibilities later in the book.

The `String` class includes an equality comparison method in the `equals()` method. This method will return `true` for any two strings with a matching sequence of characters and `false` if there is any difference in the characters. Consider the following code:

```
String myString = "I'm a string.";
String anotherString = "I'm a string, too.";
String oneMoreString = "I'm a string.";
myString.equals(oneMoreString); //this will evaluate as TRUE
myString.equals(anotherString); //this will evaluate as FALSE
```

EQUALS VERSUS ==

At this point, you might have tried to do something like the following:

```
String abc = "the letters a, b and c";
if (abc == "the letters a, b and c"){
    System.out.println("Strings are equal");
}
```

Notice that Java actually prints out that the string `abc` equals "the letters a, b and c". So why do you need to use the `equals()` method?

The reasoning behind this is a bit tricky. For objects, it is perfectly fine to use `==` and `!=` to compare them, but note that Java will not check whether the two objects are equal in the sense that they contain the same contents, but rather whether they reference the same position in memory.

The following code sample shows this in a clearer way:

```
String abc = "the letters a, b and c";
String xyz = abc;
if(abc == xyz)
    System.out.println("Both refer to the same memory address");
```

However, in some cases the use of `==` actually leads to the expected result when checking the contents of a string. The reason behind this is due to the way the Java Virtual Machine handles strings. Java makes use of a concept called "interning" to reduce memory overhead when working with strings. This is particularly tricky if you try to outsmart the JVM optimizer by instantiating two strings like this:

```
String abc = "the letters a, b and c";
String xyz = "the letters a, b and c";

if(abc == xyz){
    System.out.println("Refers to same string");
} else {
    System.out.println("Refers to different strings");
}
```

continues

continued

```java
if(abc.equals(xyz)){
    System.out.println("Contents of both strings are same");
} else {
    System.out.println("Contents of strings are different");
}
```

The interning mechanism in Java is smart enough to detect that these two strings have the same value and can thus be represented by only one object. Hence, both == and `equals()` will evaluate as being `true`. However, the JVM has its limits in terms of how smart it is, so the following code sample will not work with ==:

```java
String abc = "the letters a, b and c";
String xyz = "the letters a, b";
xyz = xyz + " and c";

if(abc == xyz) {
    System.out.println("Refers to same string");
} else {
    System.out.println("Refers to different strings");
}
if(abc.equals(xyz)) {
    System.out.println("Contents of both strings are same");
} else {
    System.out.println("Contents of strings are different");
}
```

In practice, there exist few cases where you want to check whether two objects (and strings in particular) refer to the same in-memory address compared to checking its contents. The best practice is thus to make sure to always use `equals()` when comparing string contents.

Similarly, the `Arrays` class implements a static `equals()` method. However, the syntax is different, and if you use the same format as for strings, the result will not be as you expect. When comparing the equality of two arrays, you want to test whether the sequence of elements matches in both arrays. For that, use this construct: `Arrays.equals(array1,array2)`.

```java
int[] myIntArray = {1,2,3};
int[] anotherIntArray = {1,2,3};
int[] oneMoreIntArray = {2,4,6};
int[] andAnother = {2,1,3};

Arrays.equals(myIntArray, anotherIntArray); //evaluates TRUE
Arrays.equals(myIntArray, oneMoreIntArray); //evaluates FALSE
Arrays.equals(myIntArray, andAnother); //evaluates FALSE
```

For relational comparisons, the `String` class implements a `compareTo()` method from the `Comparable` interface. Interfaces are discussed in Chapter 6, but essentially, interfaces are like class outlines that specify what a class should do, but not how to do it. `Comparable` is one such outline that offers methods to compare objects. String's `compareTo()` method compares two strings lexicographically, similar to how words or phrases would be sorted alphabetically. If the first string comes first alphabetically, the method will return a negative integer, indicating the first is less than the second. If the first operand comes last alphabetically, the method will return a positive integer, indicating the first is greater than the second. If the two strings are equal, the method will return 0. If *myString*.equals(anotherString) evaluates to true, then *myString*.compareTo(anotherString) will return 0. An example using the compareTo() method follows:

```
String employee1 = "Addams";
String employee2 = "Brown";
String employee3 = "O'Connor";
String manager = "Brown";

employee1.compareTo(employee2); //evaluates to -1 (negative)
employee3.compareTo(employee2); //evaluates to 13 (positive)
employee2.compareTo(manager); //evaluates to 0
```

There is not a similarly straightforward approach to comparing arrays relationally, partially because there is not one single way to rank one set of elements against another. Also, the elements of an array can be any type of object. You can think of many criteria that might determine which int array is greater than another: the greatest length, the greatest sum of all elements, the greatest single element, and so on, and that is only for int arrays. Arrays of more complex objects require even more unique criteria. Relational comparisons of arrays, like many other objects, must be defined according to the needs of the program.

UNDERSTANDING LANGUAGE CONTROL

This section explores how comparison operators and methods can be used in Java control structures. These structures include for and while loops, if-then statements, and switches. While each situation may be better suited to one type of structure, in fact, they are usually interchangeable as they function much the same way using different constructs. The following sections explain each of these structures independently and also compare and contrast them.

Creating if-then Statements

The most fundamental control structure is an if-then statement. Simply put, if a condition is met, then execute a piece of code. It may also be called branching, since different branches of code are executed according to the conditional statements. Often a control operator will be used as the condition in an if-then statement. The most basic syntax is as follows:

```
if (/*condition*/) {
    /*then execute these statements*/
}
```

In this case, if the conditions inside the parentheses are evaluated as true, then the statements between curly brackets will be executed. Otherwise, the program will not execute the statements and continue just after the last curly bracket, indicating the end of the block.

> **NOTE** *If there is only a single statement following the if condition, the curly brackets are optional. It is recommended to use the brackets, even when unnecessary, both to make it more clear to someone reading the code and also to improve maintainability. For instance, if you (or another programmer) later add additional statements to the if-then statement, you will not risk forgetting to place brackets around the entire block at that time.*

For a concrete example of if-then statements, imagine a banking program that prints a short notification at the bottom of each ATM transaction receipt according to the remaining balance on the account. This example prints to the console for simplicity's sake.

```
if (accountBalance > 100) {
    System.out.println("Safe balance.");
}
```

If the value of the variable *accountBalance* is greater than 100, then output a notification of "Safe balance." to the console. If *accountBalance* is not greater than 100, nothing will happen.

The basic if-then statement can also be extended with the keyword else. This provides an alternative set of statements to be executed if the condition is not true.

```
if (accountBalance > 100) {
    System.out.println("Safe balance.");
} else {
    System.out.println("Warning: Low balance.");
}
```

Now, if *accountBalance* is greater than 100, the same notification will be printed. However, if *accountBalance* is less than or equal to 100, a different notification will be printed.

The else keyword can also be followed by a second if statement, which is then evaluated only if the first condition is false.

```
if (accountBalance > 100) {
    System.out.println("Safe balance.");
} else if (accountBalance < 0){
    System.out.println("ALERT: Negative balance!");
} else {
    System.out.println("Warning: Low balance.");
}
```

The first if condition is evaluated if *accountBalance* is greater than 100, at which point the "Safe balance." notification will print and nothing further is executed. If *accountBalance* is not greater than 100, the second if condition is evaluated. If *accountBalance* is less than 0, the ALERT will be printed and nothing further will be executed. If *accountBalance* is not less than 0, that is, if *accountBalance* is between 0 and 100, the warning will be printed, and the end of the statement is reached.

Nesting if-then Statements

Control structures, such as if-then statements, can also be nested. This means that one if-then statement is inside another if-then statement, as if the outer statement formed a nest for the inner statement. This concept looks something like the following:

```
if (accountBalance > 0) {
    System.out.println("Safe balance.");
    if (accountDays > 90) {
        System.out.println(savingsAccountOffer);
    }
} else {
    System.out.println("ALERT: Negative balance!");
}
```

This is an example of nested if-then statements because the `if (accountDays > 90)` statement is nested inside the `if (accountBalance > 0)` statement. This program will first check if the account balance is greater than zero. If it is greater than zero, it will print a safe balance notification and then check if the account has been active more than 90 days. If this is also true, then an offer to open a savings account will also be printed. However, if the account balance is not greater than zero, the negative balance alert will be printed and the *accountDays* variable will never be evaluated.

This could also be accomplished using the Boolean operators discussed earlier in this chapter. That approach would look like this:

```
if (accountBalance > 0 && accountDays <= 90) {
    System.out.println("Safe balance.");
} else if (accountBalance > 0 && accountDays > 90) {
    System.out.println("Safe balance.");
    System.out.println(savingsAccountOffer);
} else {
    System.out.println("ALERT: Negative balance!");
}
```

You will notice that the `"Safe balance"` print command is repeated for the first two if-then statements. That means if you want to adjust the statement that is printed whenever a balance is over zero, or if you want to add and change any other actions to perform when the balance is greater than zero, you would have to make those changes in both places.

If you have more than two conditions to evaluate, you can nest deeper than two levels. To maintain readability, the closing bracket (`}`) should be lined up vertically with the `if` keyword it closes.

```
if (accountBalance > 0) {
    System.out.println("Safe balance.");
    if (accountDays > 90) {
        System.out.println(savingsAccountOffer);
        if (creditAccounts > 1) {
            balanceTransferPossible = true;
        } else {
            sendCreditApplication();
        }
    }
}
```

```
    } else {
        System.out.println("ALERT: Negative balance!");
    }
```

If you wanted to accomplish the same with Boolean operators, it would require an if-then statement for every combination of conditions.

```
if (accountBalance > 0 && accountDays <= 90) {
    System.out.println("Safe balance.");
} else if (accountBalance > 0 && accountDays > 90 && creditAccounts > 1) {
    System.out.println("Safe balance.");
    System.out.println(savingsAccountOffer);
    balanceTransferPossible = true;
} else if (accountBalance > 0 && accountDays > 90) {
    System.out.println("Safe balance.");
    System.out.println(savingsAccountOffer);
    sendCreditApplication();
}
} else {
    System.out.println("ALERT: Negative balance!");
}
```

This can quickly become unwieldy, first to program and even more so for maintenance later. For these reasons, a set of nested if-then statements can often be a better alternative.

Creating for Loops

Loops, as the name suggests, are structures that cycle through a section of code as long as some condition is met. This allows for repetitive execution without repetitive coding. It reduces redundancy, which improves the maintainability of code, but perhaps more importantly, it allows for flexibility since the number of times a program loops can change according to the specific conditions present during a certain execution. Imagine you run a small business and have last year's sales figures and staff numbers for each month stored in int arrays. You would like to calculate the average sales per staff member for each month and the total annual sales for the year.

```
int[] sales2014 = {500,720,515,377,400,435,510,1010,894,765,992,1125};
int[] staff2014 = {7,5,5,5,5,6,6,7,7,8,9,9};
int[] salesPerStaff = new int[12];
int totalSales2014 = 0;

salesPerStaff[0] = sales2014[0]/staff2014[0];
salesPerStaff[1] = sales2014[1]/staff2014[1];
salesPerStaff[2] = sales2014[2]/staff2014[2];
salesPerStaff[3] = sales2014[3]/staff2014[3];
salesPerStaff[4] = sales2014[4]/staff2014[4];
salesPerStaff[5] = sales2014[5]/staff2014[5];
salesPerStaff[6] = sales2014[6]/staff2014[6];
salesPerStaff[7] = sales2014[7]/staff2014[7];
salesPerStaff[8] = sales2014[8]/staff2014[8];
salesPerStaff[9] = sales2014[9]/staff2014[9];
salesPerStaff[10] = sales2014[10]/staff2014[10];
salesPerStaff[11] = sales2014[11]/staff2014[11];

totalSales2014 = sales2014[0]+sales2014[1]+sales2014[2]+sales2014[3]
```

```
+sales2014[4]+sales2014[5]+sales2014[6]+sales2014[7]+sales2014[8]+sales2014[9]
+sales2014[10]+sales2014[11];
```

You can immediately spot the redundancy in this code. To find a better solution, simply describe what it is you would like to do. For every month of the year, divide the sales by the staff and sum the sales. In order to implement this in Java, you can use a for loop. A for loop executes a block of code over a range of values. An index variable keeps track of the loop. The standard syntax for a for loop is as follows:

```
for (/*Initialization*/; /*Termination*/; /*Increment*/){
    /*execute these statements*/
}
```

Rather than just a condition as you saw in the if-then statement, for loops require three parts. *Initialization* declares the index variable for the loop and its starting value; commonly this is int i = 0. *Termination* specifies a stopping criterion, or maximum value for the index variable. *Increment* indicates how the index variable should change after each iteration, commonly this is i++, meaning that the value of i will increase by one after each loop. Alternatively, you can use i- for the increment and a minimum value in the termination; in this way your looping will count down, rather than up. Finally, all the statements that should be executed during each loop are placed between the curly brackets.

You can implement the previous example in the following for loop:

```
int[] sales2014 = {500,720,515,377,400,435,510,1010,894,765,992,1125};
int[] staff2014 = {7,5,5,5,5,6,6,7,7,8,9,9};
int[] salesPerStaff = new int[12];
int totalSales2014 = 0;

for (int i=0; i<sales2014.length; i++){
    salesPerStaff[i] = sales2014[i]/staff2014[i];
    totalSales2014 = totalSales2014 + sales2014[i];
}
```

This for loop starts with an index value of 0 and evaluates *salesPerStaff* at month 0 and *total-Sales2014* at month 0. At the end of this iteration of the loop, the index increments to 1, and those same variables are evaluated for month 1 and so on, until month 11. The value of *sales2014.*length is the number of elements in the *sales2014* array, which is 12. So when the index increments to 12, it will evaluate *i<sales2014.*length as false, and the looping will terminate.

There are several benefits to this improved loop implementation. You might notice it is easier to read and less prone to typing errors than the longer and more tedious version. Recall that loops improve maintainability and flexibility. Now that you have an example, it might be easier to visualize the impact of these factors. Easier maintenance means that future changes to the application are easier to implement. If you needed to change how *SalesPerStaff* is calculated, you would have to make 12 changes in the first version versus only one in the for loop. The flexibility of loops is based on the self-determined termination criteria. In the example, the loop iterates 12 times, because the array has 12 elements. Now imagine your company begins recording weekly sales instead of monthly sales, increasing the elements of the sales array from 12 to 52 per year. In the first version of the program, the number of statements would increase by the same amount, also increasing the chance of errors. However, the for loop in the second version would accommodate arrays of any length without need for manual modification.

You can also leave either the initialization or increment blank in a `for` loop. In this case, you would need to specify the variable before the `for` loop or the increment during the `for` loop. Following are two examples that function the same as the previous example, but with a slightly different syntax.

```
int[] sales2014 = {500,720,515,377,400,435,510,1010,894,765,992,1125};
int[] staff2014 = {7,5,5,5,5,6,6,7,7,8,9,9};
int[] salesPerStaff = new int[12];
int totalSales2014 = 0;

int i = 0; //specify initialization variable here, not before termination
for (  ; i<sales2014.length; i++){
    salesPerStaff[i] = sales2014[i]/staff2014[i];
    totalSales2014 = totalSales2014 + sales2014[i];
}
```

```
int[] sales2014 = {500,720,515,377,400,435,510,1010,894,765,992,1125};
int[] staff2014 = {7,5,5,5,5,6,6,7,7,8,9,9};
int[] salesPerStaff = new int[12];
int totalSales2014 = 0;

for (int i=0; i<sales2014.length;  ){
    salesPerStaff[i] = sales2014[i]/staff2014[i];
    totalSales2014 = totalSales2014 + sales2014[i];
    i = i + 1; //specify increment here, not after termination
}
```

It is important to keep your termination condition and increment direction in mind when you are setting up a `for` loop. You could unintentionally create an infinite loop by having these misaligned. For example, imagine the following `for` loop: `for (int i = 5; i > 0; i++)`. Your loop will continue to repeat indefinitely. The starting value for i is 5, which is greater than 0, and the value of i will continue increasing as you loop, so it will always remain greater than 0. In general, a termination condition using > will have an increment using --, and a termination condition using < will have an increment using ++.

Another consideration is how your iterator may be altered within the `for` loop. It is possible to reassign the value of your iterator as part of the loop, instead of or in addition to the increment expression. Consider adding a line to the example.

```
int[] sales2014 = {500,720,515,377,400,435,510,1010,894,765,992,1125};
int[] staff2014 = {7,5,5,5,5,6,6,7,7,8,9,9};
int[] salesPerStaff = new int[12];
int totalSales2014 = 0;

for (int i=0; i<sales2014.length; i++){
    i = i*2; //this line is added
    salesPerStaff[i] = sales2014[i]/staff2014[i];
    totalSales2014 = totalSales2014 + sales2014[i];
}
```

Here, the value of i is changed as part of the increment and also within the loop. So the loop will be processed in the following way:

1. Start at the beginning of the `for` loop. $i=0$ and $0 < 12$, so the loop is entered.

2. $i=i*2$ or $i = 0*2 = 0$, so the statements are evaluated on the 0 (first) element of each array.

3. At the end of the `for` loop, *i* is incremented to `i++` or `i=1`.

4. Return to the start of the `for` loop. `i=1` and 1 < 12, so the loop is entered a second time.

5. `i=i*2` or $i = 1*2 = 2$, so the statements are evaluated on the 2 (third) element of each array.

6. At the end of the `for` loop, *i* is incremented to `i++` or `i=3`.

7. Return to the start of the loop. `i=3` and 3 < 12, so the loop is entered a third time.

8. `i=i*2` or $i = 3*2 = 6$, so the statements are evaluated on the 6 (seventh) element of each array.

9. At the end of the `for` loop, *i* is incremented to `i++` or `i=7`.

10. Return to the start of the loop. `i=7` and 7 < 12, so the loop is entered a fourth time.

11. `i=i*2` or $i = 7*2 = 14$, so the statements *should be* evaluated on the 14 (fifteenth) element of each array. However, there are only twelve elements in each array. Here you will run into an error and the program will be terminated.

In short, a `for` loop is a control structure that lets you repeat a certain block of code a specified number of times. The amount of times can be determined in advance or dynamically, depending on the situation. When creating a `for` loop, pay attention to the initialization, termination, and increment specified to be sure you are not creating infinite loops or errors at execution.

TRY IT OUT   Your First for Loop

To create a simple `for` loop, follow these steps:

1. Create a new project in Eclipse. Perhaps call it `Chapter5` to keep the exercises organized according to the chapters in this book.

2. Create a new class by right-clicking on the `src` folder in your new project. Select New and then Class.

3. In the Name field, enter the name of your class, `ForLoop`, beginning with a capital letter by Java convention. In the bottom portion of the New Java Class window, there is a section that reads: "Which method stubs would you like to create?" You may choose to check the box next to "`public static void main(String[] args)`" to automatically create a `main` method.

4. You should automatically have the basis for the class body shown here:

```
public class ForLoop {
    /**
    * @param args
    */
    public static void main(String[] args) {
        // TODO Auto-generated method stub

    }
}
```

If not, you can type it yourself. You do not need the comments denoted with /** or //. In Eclipse, they appear as blue or green text. Comments are useful for explaining what the code is doing, but are never compiled or executed by Java.

```
public class ForLoop {
    public static void main(String[] args){

        }
}
```

5. Recall that the `main` method provides the starting point and ordering for the execution of your program. Inside the `main` method, create a `for` loop as follows:

```
for (int i = 1; i <= 10 ; i++){

}
```

It should be placed after `(String[] args) {` and before the next `}`.

6. Now insert the statements that will be executed during each loop. On each iteration, you will multiply the value of `i` by 2 (doubling it) and then print a string containing the resulting value to the console. Use the following statements to do so:

```
int doubled = i * 2;
System.out.println(i + " times two equals " + doubled);
```

Place these between the { } of the `for` loop.

7. Finally, add a print statement to indicate the end of the program. Use the following statement:

```
System.out.println("End of program");
```

This time, make sure it is placed after the closing bracket (}) of the `for` loop, but before the closing bracket (}) of the `main` method. This ensures that it will not be repeated on each iteration, but it will be executed once before the `main` method concludes.

8. Your class body should now look like this:

```
public class ForLoop {

    public static void main(String[] args){
        for (int i = 1; i <= 10; i++){
            int doubled = i * 2;
            System.out.println(i + " times two equals " + doubled);
        }
        System.out.println("End of program");
    }
}
```

9. Save the class by clicking the disk icon or selecting File, then Save.

10. Run the application by clicking the green play icon or selecting Run, and then Run.

How It Works

Now take a look at how it works.

1. The application begins by executing the `main` method, which in this case is the only method.

2. The first statement begins with a `for` loop.

3. The iterator, named *i*, begins at value 1 and checks the termination condition. 1 is less than or equal to 10, so you enter the loop.

4. In the first statement inside the loop, a second `int`, named *doubled*, is assigned the value of $i*2$. In this first iteration, $i = 1$, so *doubled* = 2.

5. In the next statement of the loop, there is a `println` command. A line is output to the console that reads: 1 times two equals 2. Because the command is `println` instead of `print`, you can imagine pressing Enter or Return at the end of the string to create a new line.

6. The program reaches the end of the loop, and because the iteration of the loop is `i++`, 1 is added to the value of *i*. The iterator *i* is reassigned the value of 1+1 or 2.

7. The termination condition is evaluated again. Because 2 is still less than or equal to 10, you will go through the loop again.

8. The variable `doubled` is 2*2 or 4 this time.

9. Another line will be output to the console, this time reading: 2 times two equals 4.

10. This will continue until `i++` = 11 , when the termination condition will evaluate to `false` and the loop will not be entered anymore. At that time, the loop will be skipped over and the program will proceed with the final statement. One final line will be output to the console, indicating the end of the program.

What Is an Enhanced for Loop?

There is an alternate form, called an enhanced `for` loop, that was introduced specifically for arrays and other iterable objects. Instead of the index initialized as part of the standard `for` loop, enhanced `for` loops use an iterator. Unlike the index of a standard `for` loop, the iterator does not require initialization, termination, or increment, as it will automatically iterate through all elements in the array. Note that rather than an integer index, the iterator is the same type as the elements in the array or other Iterable object. From the previous example, this second form would be coded as follows:

```
for (int i: sales2014){
    salesPerStaff[i] = sales2014[i]/staff2014[i];
    totalSales2014 = totalSales2014 + sales2014[i];
}
```

This can be read in English as, "For each `int` in the *sales2014* array, do the following. . ." The array can contain other data types or objects.

> **NOTE** Enhanced `for` loops allow automatic iteration over arrays and other iterable objects.

Here's a second example using strings instead of ints. It follows the same pattern as before, "For each string in the *nameList* array, print that string."

```
String[] nameList = {"Adam Brown","Betsy Dudley","Carl Frank"};

for (String name: nameList){
    System.out.println(name);
}
```

Enhanced `for` loops offer the same functionality of regular `for` loops with a format that's easier to code and read. They do require a data structure that's iterable, but if you are working with arrays, they may provide a handy solution for you.

TRY IT OUT   Try It Out: An Enhanced for Loop

To create an enhanced `for` loop, follow these steps:

1. Create a new class named *EnhancedForLoop*, following the process you learned about earlier. You can continue to use the same *Chapter5* project. Create a new class by right-clicking on the src folder in your project. Select New and then Class.

2. In the Name field, enter the name of your class, *EnhancedForLoop*, beginning with a capital letter by Java convention. In the bottom portion of the New Java Class window, there is a section that reads: "Which method stubs would you like to create?" You may choose to check the box next to "`public static void main(String[] args)`" to automatically create a `main` method.

3. You should automatically have the basis for the class body shown here:

```
public class EnhancedForLoop {
    /**
     * @param args
     */
    public static void main(String[] args) {
        // TODO Auto-generated method stub

    }
}
```

If not, you can type it yourself. You do not need the comments, which are denoted with `/**` or `//`. In Eclipse, they will appear as blue or green text. Comments are useful for explaining what the code is doing, but are never compiled or executed by Java.

```
public class EnhancedForLoop {
    public static void main(String[] args){

    }
}
```

4. Recall that the `main` method provides the starting point and ordering for the execution of your program. An enhanced `for` loop will iterate through the elements of an array, but first you must declare an array for this:

```
int[] tenIntegers = {1,2,3,4,5,6,7,8,9,10};
```

It should be placed after `(String[] args) {` and before the next `}`.

5. Now add the following enhanced `for` loop immediately after the array declaration.

```
for (int i : tenIntegers){

}
```

6. Now insert the statements that will be executed during each loop. On each iteration, you will multiply the value of the current array entry by 2 (doubling it) and then print a string containing the resulting value to the console. Use the following statements to do so:

```
int doubled = i * 2;
System.out.println(i + " times two equals " + doubled);
```

Place these statements between the `{ }` of the `for` loop.

7. Finally, add a print statement to indicate the end of the program. Use the following statement:

```
System.out.println("End of program");
```

This time, make sure it is placed after the closing bracket (`}`) of the `for` loop, but before the closing bracket (`}`) of the `main` method. This ensures that it will not be repeated on each iteration, but it will be executed once before the `main` method concludes.

8. Your class body should now look like this:

```
public class EnhancedForLoop {

    public static void main(String[] args){
        for (int i : tenIntegers){
            int doubled = i * 2;
            System.out.println(i + " times two equals " + doubled);
        }
        System.out.println("End of program");
    }
}
```

9. Save the class by clicking the disk icon or selecting File, then Save.

10. Run the application by clicking the green play icon or selecting Run, and then Run.

How It Works

Now take a look at how it works.

1. The application begins by executing the `main` method, which in this case is the only method.

2. The first statement creates a new integer array with ten entries.

3. The next statement opens an enhanced `for` loop, which will iterate through all the entries of the array. In a regular `for` loop, the iterator is generally an integer. In an enhanced `for` loop, it takes the same type as the array entries. In this case, it is an integer because the array is an `int [ ]`. You use the name of the iterator to refer to the current entry within the loop. In the first iteration, `i` takes the value of the first entry of the array, in this case 1. On the next iteration, it will take the value of the next entry, 2.

4. In the first statement inside the loop, a second `int`, named `doubled`, is assigned the value of `i*2`. In this first iteration, `i = 1`, so `doubled = 2`.

5. In the next statement of the loop, there is a `println` command. A line is output to the console that reads: `1 times two equals 2`. Because the command is `println` instead of `print`, you can imagine pressing Enter or Return at the end of the string to create a new line.

6. When the program reaches the end of the loop, it will restart the loop with the next entry in the array. The iterator `i` is reassigned the value of the second array entry, in this case 2.

7. The variable `doubled` is 2*2 or 4 in this iteration of the loop.

8. Another line will be output to the console, this time reading: `2 times two equals 4`.

9. This will continue until every entry in the array has been used. Then, the program will proceed with the final statement. One final line will be output to the console indicating the end of the program.

10. If you executed the `for` loop in the previous Try It Out exercise, you'll notice that they produce the same output. The two types of `for` loops work in much the same way, but in some situations one will be preferable to the other. In this enhanced `for` loop exercise, it was probably unnecessary to create an array just to list the integers between 1 and 10; a standard `for` loop does this simply by incrementing the iterator by 1 on each loop. For an array of strings or other objects, iterating through the array in an enhanced `for` loop may be simpler to code and easier to read.

Nesting for Loops

As you saw with if-then statements, `for` loops can also be nested. The format is very similar, where one inner `for` loop is contained within another outer `for` loop. The general appearance is as follows:

```
for (/*Initialization*/; /*Termination*/; /*Increment*/){ //outer loop
    /*execute these statements*/
    for (/*Initialization2*/; /*Termination2*/; /*Increment2*/){ //inner loop
        /*execute these statements*/
    } //close inner loop
} //close outer loop
```

Because the statements inside the inner `for` loop can refer to the iterator of both the inner loop and outer loop, it's necessary to use different variable names in the initialization of each loop. You've probably noticed that many of the standard `for` loops shown in this chapter use x as the index name (and $x = 0$ as the initialization); this is by no means required, but is often used in practice.

Similarly, *x* and *y* are often used as index names in nested `for` loops. You will often encounter the use of nested `for` loops to iterate through a matrix of values. Here is an example of that type to demonstrate the use of nested `for` loops.

Suppose you run a small business with three employees. You store the hours worked by each employee in a matrix like the one shown in Table 5-3.

TABLE 5-3: Weekly Hours Worked by Employee

EMPLOYEE	MONDAY	TUESDAY	WEDNESDAY	THURSDAY	FRIDAY
Chris	3	2	8	2	3
Danielle	4	4	4	4	4
Michael	5	5	0	5	5

By using nested `for` loops, you can iterate through all the entries of this matrix, where the position (0,0), first row and first column, refers to the hours worked by Chris on Monday, and position (1,3), second row and fourth column, refers to the hours Danielle worked on Thursday. One `for` loop will refer to the column and the other will refer to the row.

```
int[][] hoursWorked = {{3,2,8,2,3},{4,4,4,4,4},{5,5,0,5,5}};
String[] employees = {"Chris", "Danielle", "Michael"};
double wage = 8.30;

for (int x = 0; x < hoursWorked.length; x++){ //outer for loop
    System.out.print(employees[x] + " worked ");
    int weeklyHours = 0;

    for (int y = 0; y < hoursWorked[0].length; y++){ //inner for loop
        weeklyHours += hoursWorked[x][y];
    } //close inner for loop

    System.out.println(weeklyHours + " hours at " + wage + " per hour.");
    double weeklyPay = weeklyHours * wage;
    System.out.println("Weekly Pay: " + weeklyPay);
} //close outer for loop
```

The two-dimensional `int` array *hoursWorked* represents the matrix shown in Table 5.3. Each row is a one-dimensional `int` array with five elements. A string array *employees* stores the names of the three employees. A `double` represents the hourly wage paid to employees. Here all employees receive the same pay, but if they are different, there could be a `double` array set up similarly to the array for names.

The outer loop iterates three times, one for each row in the matrix, in other words, once for each employee. When *x* = 0, this refers to the first row of the matrix and the first element in all the arrays. Remember, in *hoursWorked*, the first element is itself an array. First, you print the employee's name to the console. Note, this is a `print` command, rather than `println`, so whatever is printed next will continue on the same line. Then you initialize *weeklyHours* to zero. This is an important step to do inside the outer `for` loop; this "resets" the value to zero each time you change employee by incrementing the outer `for` loop. If you initialize this variable outside of the `for` loops, like the `wage` variable, it will continue adding all the employees' hours together.

Then the inner `for` loop begins. One important difference here is the termination condition. In the outer `for` loop, you stop when the iterator exceeds the length of the `hoursWorked` array, that is, the number of elements or number of employees, which is 3. In the inner `for` loop, you stop when the iterator exceeds the length of the first element of the `hoursWorked` array, that is the number of elements in the array, which is the first element or the number of days in the week (which is 5).

Inside the inner `for` loop, you simply add each day's hours to the total `weeklyHours` for the current employee. After the five iterations for each day of the week, you exit the inner `for` loop.

Now, you are still inside the outer `for` loop, but have calculated the hours from the inner `for` loop. The `weeklyHours` value is printed as well as the `wage`. Since that was a `println` command, the next print statement will begin on a new line. The weekly pay is calculated by multiplying the hours by the wage and this is printed on a new line. This concludes the outer loop, so the program will increment the value of x by 1 and return to the start of the outer loop. After three iterations, one for each employee, this part of the program will be done. If you put all of this inside the `main` method of a class, it is executable.

Creating while Loops

A `while` loop is an alternative loop structure that's based on meeting a certain condition, rather than iterating a set number of times. The standard syntax of a `while` loop is as follows:

```
while (/*conditional expression*/) {
    /*execute these statements*/
}
```

Remember the difference between a `for` loop and an enhanced `for` loop: the `for` loop iterator is initialized in the loop expression, but in an enhanced `for` loop, an array must be declared somewhere prior to entering the `for` loop. A `while` loop is similar to the enhanced `for` loop in this way. You will need to initialize some variable before the `while` loop that will be evaluated as part of the conditional expression.

When the execution of a program reaches a `while` loop, it will first check to see if the conditional expression evaluates to `true`. If so, it will enter the loop and execute the statements inside the loop. When the end of loop is reached, it will return to the conditional expression and check if it still evaluates to `true`. If so, the loop will be repeated. It should be clear, then, that evaluation of the conditional statement should change at some point during the looping process. Otherwise, the loop iterations will never end. Consider the following code example:

```
int i = 10;

while (i > 0){
    System.out.println(i);
}
```

Here, the integer i is given the value of 10. When the while loop is first encountered, the conditional expression $i > 0$ is evaluated: 10 is greater than 0, so the expression is true. The program outputs "10" to the console, then returns to the start of the while loop again. The conditional expression $i > 0$ is evaluated again, but i is still equal to 10 and 10 is greater than 0 so the expression is still true. Again, you'll see an output of "10" to the console. This will continue indefinitely, creating an infinite loop. To prevent this, you can add a statement inside the while loop to alter the value of the variable i.

```
int i = 10;

while (i > 0){
    System.out.println(i);
    i = i - 1;
}
```

This time, the conditional expression $10 > 0$ is still true when the while loop is first encountered. During the first iteration, the output "10" will be printed to the console, then int i will be reassigned the value $i-1$ or 9. The conditional expression will be evaluated again to true, so the loop will be repeated. Now 9 will be output to the console and int i will be reassigned the value 8. This will continue until $i = 0$, when the expression will evaluate to false.

It's possible that your conditional expression is not a variable at all. You will see some classic examples of while loops in Chapter 7 when dealing with inputs and outputs. For now, it's enough to understand that the Scanner class has two methods, hasNextLine() and nextLine(), that can be used when scanning files, to determine if a file still has more lines to be scanned, and to actually scan the next line, respectively.

```
int lines = 0;
while (myScanner.hasNextLine()){
    lines++;
}
```

This code might look like it will count the number of lines in the file being scanned by myScanner. However, this will actually create an infinite loop like the first while loop you saw. That's because the program never moves past the first line of the file. When the loop is first encountered, assuming the file has at least one line in it, the conditional expression hasNextLine() will evaluate to true. The variable lines will be reassigned the value 0+1 or 1 and the conditional expression will remain true. In order to ensure that the loop will end and the correct number of lines will be counted, you have to progress through the lines of the file using the nextLine() method.

```
int lines = 0;
while (myScanner.hasNextLine()){
myScanner.nextLine(); //scan the next line
    lines++;
}
```

In this way, in each iteration of the while loop, the scanner will scan another line of the file until the end of the file is reached. Then, the conditional expression hasNextLine() will evaluate to false and the program will not enter the loop again.

TRY IT OUT Your First while Loop

To create a while loop, follow these steps:

1. Create a new class named WhileLoop, following the same process. You can continue to use the same Chapter5 project. Create a new class by right-clicking on the src folder in your project. Select New and then Class.

2. In the Name field, enter the name of your class, WhileLoop, beginning with a capital letter by Java convention. In the bottom portion of the New Java Class window, there is a section that reads: "Which method stubs would you like to create?" You may choose to check the box next to "public static void main(String[] args)" to automatically create a main method.

3. You should automatically have the basis for the class body shown here:

```
public class WhileLoop {
    /**
     * @param args
     */
    public static void main(String[] args) {
        // TODO Auto-generated method stub

    }
}
```

If not, you can type it yourself. You do not need the comments, which are denoted with /** or //. In Eclipse, they will appear as blue or green text. Comments are useful for explaining what the code is doing, but are never compiled or executed by Java.

```
public class WhileLoop {
    public static void main(String[] args){

    }
}
```

4. Recall that the main method provides the starting point and ordering for the execution of your program. A while loop requires a variable to be initialized before the loop so that it can be evaluated as part of the conditional expression. Initialize an integer with the following statement:

```
int i = 1;
```

It should be placed after (String[] args){ and before the next }.

5. Now add the following while loop immediately following the int declaration.

```
while (i <= 10){
}
```

6. Now insert the statements that will be executed during each loop. In each iteration, you multiply the value of the current array entry by 2 (doubling it) and then print a string containing the resulting value to the console. Use the following statements to do so:

```
int doubled = i * 2;
System.out.println(i + " times two equals " + doubled);
```

Place these statements between the { } of the while loop.

7. Remember, you must alter the value of the variable used in the conditional expression during the loop to avoid infinite looping. You may add it anywhere within the loop, but keep in mind that the statements are executed from top to bottom, so if you change the value of *i* before doubling and printing, you will double and print the new value. Add the following line after the `System.out.println()` line, but before the next }.

```
i++;
```

8. Finally, add a print statement to indicate the end of the program. Use the following statement:

```
System.out.println("End of program");
```

This time, make sure it is placed after the closing bracket (}) of the while loop, but before the closing bracket (}) of the main method. This ensures that it will not be repeated in each iteration, but it will be executed once before the main method concludes.

9. Your class body should now look like this:

```
public class WhileLoop {
    public static void main(String[] args) {
        int i = 1;
        while (i <= 10){
            int doubled = i * 2;
            System.out.println(i + " times two equals " + doubled);
            i++;
        }
        System.out.println("End of program");
    }
}
```

10. Save the class by clicking the disk icon or selecting File, then Save.

11. Run the application by clicking the green play icon or selecting Run, and then Run.

How It Works

Now take a look at how it works.

1. The application begins by executing the main method, which in this case is the only method.

2. The first statement initializes an integer, named *i*, with the value of 1.

3. The next statement opens a while loop, which will loop based on the value of the integer *i* initialized in the previous statement.

4. In the first statement inside the loop, a second int, named *doubled*, is assigned the value of *i*2*. In this first iteration, *i=1*, so *doubled=2*.

5. In the next statement of the loop, there is a println command. A line is output to the console which reads: 1 times two equals 2. Because the command is println instead of print, you can imagine pressing Enter or Return at the end of the string to create a new line.

6. The last statement inside the while loop reassigns the value of *i* to *i+1* or *i=2*.

7. When the program reaches the end of the loop, it will return to the conditional expression to see if it will enter the loop again. Since 2 is still less than 10, it will loop again.

8. The variable `doubled` is 2*2 or 4 in this iteration of the loop.

9. Another line will be output to the console, this time reading: `2 times two equals 4`.

10. The integer `i` will be reassigned the value of `i+1` or `i=3`.

11. This will continue until `i=11` and then the conditional expression will evaluate to `false`. The `while` loop will be skipped on this last iteration and the program will continue below the loop.

12. One final line will be output to the console indicating the end of the program.

13. If you executed the `for` loops in the other Try It Out exercises in this chapter, you'll notice that they all produce the same output. For these simple examples, the loops can be used somewhat interchangeably, with some small adaptations. You will encounter situations in the later chapters that are more suited to one type of loop over others.

What Is a do while Loop?

There is also an alternate form of a `while` loop that's useful in some circumstances. It is called a `do while` loop and is very similar to the `while` loop. As you'll recall, a `while` loop starts by evaluating a conditional statement, much like a `for` loop begins by checking the termination condition. A `do while` loop is different because it will first execute ("do") the statements within the loop and then check the conditional expression ("while") to see if it should repeat the loop. A standard `do while` loop uses the following syntax:

```
do {
    /*execute these statements*/
} while (/*conditional expression*/);
```

To demonstrate the difference, consider the small example from the previous section of a `while` loop.

```
int i = 10;

while (i > 0){
    System.out.println(i);
    i = i - 1;
}
```

Now the same example is presented as a `do while` loop.

```
int i = 10;

do {
    System.out.println(i);
    i = i - 1;
} while (i > 0);
```

Now imagine you changed the conditional expression from `i>0` to `i<0`. In the example with the `while` loop, you would first check the condition `10<0`, which evaluates to `false`. The loop would be skipped and the program would continue below the `while` loop. In the second example with the `do while` loop, it would first execute the loop with `i=10`, then evaluate the condition `9<0` and find it to be `false`. The `do while` loop would not be repeated at this point.

A `do while` loop is useful when you want to ensure statements in the loop are executed at least the first time. It can be troublesome if it is possible to cause an error by executing the statements before checking the conditional expression. Consider the following example, which was used in the `for` loop section earlier:

```
int[] sales2014 = {500,720,515,377,400,435,510,1010,894,765,992,1125};
int[] staff2014 = {7,5,5,5,5,6,6,7,7,8,9,9};
int[] salesPerStaff = new int[12];
int totalSales2014 = 0;

for (int i=0; i<sales2014.length; i++){
    salesPerStaff[i] = sales2014[i]/staff2014[i];
    totalSales2014 = totalSales2014 + sales2014[i];
}
```

It is possible to implement this with a `do while` loop instead:

```
int[] sales2014 = {500,720,515,377,400,435,510,1010,894,765,992,1125};
int[] staff2014 = {7,5,5,5,5,6,6,7,7,8,9,9};
int[] salesPerStaff = new int[12];
int totalSales2014 = 0;
int i = -1;
do {
    salesPerStaff[i] = sales2014[i]/staff2014[i];
    totalSales2014 = totalSales2014 + sales2014[i];
    i++;
} while (i<sales2014.length);
```

You must ensure that the variable `i` is initialized with a value that will refer to an element in the array. In the example, `i=-1` will cause an error, as would `i=12`, because the arrays only have elements between 0 and 11.

TRY IT OUT A do while Loop

To create a `do while` loop, follow these steps:

1. Create a new class named `DoWhileLoop`, following the same process. You can continue to use the same `Chapter5` project. Create a new class by right-clicking on the `src` folder in your project. Select New and then Class.

2. In the Name field, enter the name of your class, `DoWhileLoop`, beginning with a capital letter by Java convention. In the bottom portion of the New Java Class window, there is a section that reads: "Which method stubs would you like to create?" You may choose to check the box next to `"public static void main(String[] args)"` to automatically create a `main` method.

3. You should automatically have the basis for the class body shown here:

```
public class DoWhileLoop {
    /**
     * @param args
     */
    public static void main(String[] args) {
        // TODO Auto-generated method stub

    }
}
```

If not, you can type it yourself. You do not need the comments, which are denoted with /** or //. In Eclipse, they will appear as blue or green text. Comments are useful for explaining what the code is doing, but are never compiled or executed by Java.

```
public class DoWhileLoop {
    public static void main(String[] args){

    }
}
```

4. Recall that the main method provides the starting point and ordering for the execution of your program. A do while loop requires a variable to be initialized before the loop so that it can be evaluated as part of the conditional expression. Initialize an integer with the following statement:

```
int i = 1;
```

It should be placed after (String[] args){ and before the next }.

5. Now add the following do while loop immediately following the int declaration.

```
do {
} while (i <= 10);
```

6. Now insert the statements that will be executed during each loop. On each iteration, you multiply the value of the current array entry by 2 (doubling it) and then print a string containing the resulting value to the console. Use the following statements to do so:

```
int doubled = i * 2;
System.out.println(i + " times two equals " + doubled);
```

Place these statements between the { } of the do while loop.

7. Remember, you must alter the value of the variable used in the conditional expression during the loop to avoid infinite looping. You may add it anywhere within the loop, but keep in mind that the statements are executed from top to bottom, so if you change the value of *i* before doubling and printing, you will double and print the new value. Add the following line after the System.out. println() line, but before the next }.

```
i++;
```

8. Finally, add a print statement to indicate the end of the program. Use the following statement:

```
System.out.println("End of program");
```

This time, make sure it is placed after the closing bracket (}) of the while loop, but before the closing bracket (}) of the main method. This ensures that it will not be repeated on each iteration, but it will be executed once before the main method concludes.

9. Your class body should now look like this:

```
public class DoWhileLoop {
    public static void main(String[] args) {
        int i = 1;
        do {
            int doubled = i * 2;
            System.out.println(i + " times two equals " + doubled);
            i++;
        } while (i <= 10)
        System.out.println("End of program");
    }
}
```

10. Save the class by clicking the disk icon or selecting File, then Save.

11. Run the application by clicking the green play icon or selecting Run, and then Run.

How It Works

Now take a look at how it works.

1. The application begins by executing the main method, which in this case is the only method.

2. The first statement initializes an integer named *i* with the value of 1.

3. The next statement opens a do while loop and enters the loop.

4. In the first statement inside the loop, a second int, named *doubled*, is assigned the value of *i*2. In this first iteration, *i*=1, so *doubled*=2.

5. In the next statement of the loop, there is a println command. A line is output to the console which reads: 1 times two equals 2. Because the command is println instead of print, you can imagine pressing Enter or Return at the end of the string to create a new line.

6. The last statement inside the do while loop reassigns the value of *i* to *i*+1 or *i*=2.

7. When the program reaches the end of the loop, it will evaluate the conditional expression to see if it will return to the start of the loop again. Since 2 is still less than 10, it will loop again.

8. The variable *doubled* is 2*2 or 4 in this iteration of the loop.

9. Another line will be output to the console, this time reading: 2 times two equals 4.

10. The integer *i* will be reassigned the value of *i*+1 or *i*=3.

11. This will continue until *i*=11, and then the conditional expression will evaluate to false and it will not return to the start of the loop. Instead, the program will continue below the loop.

12. One final line will be output to the console indicating the end of the program.

13. If you executed the `for` loops in the other Try It Out exercises in this chapter, you'll notice that they all produce the same output. For these simple examples, the loops can be used somewhat interchangeably, with some small adaptations. You will encounter situations in the later chapters that are more suited to one type of loop over others.

Comparing for and while Loops

As you've seen through the examples and exercises in the previous sections, `for` and `while` loops can both be used to obtain the same outcome. So how do you know which one to use?

For some problems, this will simply be a matter of preference. Some programmers tend to use `for` loops, except when a situation really demands a `while` loop. Others prefer `while` loops and include `for` loops only when needed. Many programmers, through practice and experience, learn a certain feeling for which one is best suited for the problem at hand, and you will too.

In general, keep in mind the following points:

➤ If you are iterating over a collection, consider a `for` loop first.

➤ If you know the number of loops in advance, consider a `for` loop first.

➤ If you don't know the number of iterations, but the number will depend on a certain condition, consider a `while` loop first.

When making your decision, simplicity and clarity are important considerations. You want a solution that's the simplest to code, for your own sake, and clearest to read and understand, for yourself and others who will have to maintain or reuse your code later.

Creating Switches

Earlier in this chapter, you learned that if-then statements are one of the basic control structures. Now you will see `switch` statements, which function in a similar way to if-then statements, but with a different syntax. They are particularly useful when you have several `else` clauses. A `switch` statement evaluates a single variable and, depending on its value, executes a certain block of code. The general syntax of a basic `switch` statement is as follows:

```
switch (/*variable*/ {
    case 1: /*execute these statements*/; break;
    case 2: /*execute these statements*/; break;
    default: /*execute these statements*/;
}
```

The variable that's evaluated can be a primitive `byte`, `short`, `char`, or `int`, as well as enumerated types and `String`. The `switch` checks the value of the variable for a match in one of the cases. If they are equal, the statements in that `case` will be executed.

NOTE *Switches were extended in Java 7 to allow the use of strings as switch variables. To use a string as your variable and label, just include the label in quotation marks so it is recognized as a string. For example:*

```
char initial;
String myName = "Bob";
switch (myName) {
case "Ann": initial = 'A'; break;
case "Bob": initial = 'B'; break;
case "Claire": initial = 'C'; break;
default: initial = '?'; break;
}
```

Notice the three new keywords in the syntax: `case`, `break`, and `default`. Cases are similar to the `if()` and `else if()` parts of an if-then statement. Each case is labeled with one possible value the variable might take. If the label matches the value of the variable, the statements that follow the `:` for that `case` will be executed. Cases are evaluated sequentially, from top to bottom. Once a match is found, all the statements to follow will be executed, even those intended for the other cases that follow. In order to prevent this from happening, the `break` keyword is used. The `break` keyword is discussed more in detail in the next section, but its purpose is to break out of the `switch` and continue with the rest of the program. `default` is the `switch` equivalent of the `else` clause in an if-then statement. If none of the explicit cases apply to the variable, `default` will still apply. Every value will match the `default` case, so this can be useful to handle unexpected situations.

Because a `switch` is organized into cases, it makes sense to use it when you have a finite number of expected values. Twelve months in a year, for example, could be represented by twelve cases. If the situation calls for a large range of values, it's more suited to an if-then statement. Recall the example concerning bank account alerts, where depending on if *accountBalance* was less than 0, greater than 100, or somewhere in between, a message was displayed.

Imagine you want to include a `switch` in a bookkeeping program that determines the last day of each month for recording monthly income and expenses. It might look something like this:

```
int month = 4; // here 4 represents April
int lastDay;
boolean leapYear = false;

switch (month) {
    case 1: lastDay = 31; break;
    case 2: if (leapYear == true) {
            lastDay = 29;
        } else {
            lastDay = 28;
        } break;
    case 3: lastDay = 31; break;
    case 4: lastDay = 30; break;
```

```
        case 5: lastDay = 31; break;
        case 6: lastDay = 30; break;
        case 7: lastDay = 31; break;
        case 8: lastDay = 31; break;
        case 9: lastDay = 30; break;
        case 10: lastDay = 31; break;
        case 11: lastDay = 30; break;
        case 12: lastDay = 31; break;
        default: lastDay = 0;
}
```

This can even be simplified because many of the cases result in the same outcome. As mentioned, cases are evaluated from top to bottom, and until the execution reaches a break keyword, the statements will continue to be executed. Notice how you can lump the months or cases together to treat a series of cases identically:

```
int month = 4; // here 4 represents April
int lastDay;
boolean leapYear = false;

switch (month) {
    case 1:
    case 3:
    case 5:
    case 7:
    case 8:
    case 10:
    case 12:
        lastDay = 31; break;
    case 2:
        if (leapYear == true) {
            lastDay = 29;
        } else {
            lastDay = 28;
        } break;
    case 4:
    case 6:
    case 9:
    case 11:
        lastDay = 30; break;
    default: lastDay = 0;
}
```

TRY IT OUT Creating a switch

To create a switch, follow these steps:

1. Create a new class named SwitchClass, following the same process. You can continue to use the same Chapter5 project. Create a new class by right-clicking on the src folder in your project. Select New and then Class.

2. In the Name field, enter the name of your class, SwitchClass, beginning with a capital letter by Java convention. In the bottom portion of the New Java Class window, there is a section that

reads: "Which method stubs would you like to create?" You may choose to check the box next to `"public static void main(String[] args)"` to automatically create a `main` method.

3. You should automatically have the basis for the class body shown here:

```
public class SwitchClass {
    /**
    * @param args
    */
    public static void main(String[] args) {
        // TODO Auto-generated method stub

    }
}
```

If not, you can type it yourself. You do not need the comments, which are denoted with `/**` or `//`. In Eclipse, they will appear as blue or green text. Comments are useful for explaining what the code is doing, but are never compiled or executed by Java.

```
public class SwitchClass {
    public static void main(String[] args){

    }
}
```

4. Recall that the `main` method provides the starting point and ordering for the execution of your program. A `switch` statement requires a variable to be initialized before the statement so that it can be evaluated for each of the cases. Initialize a string with the following statement:

```
String loanType = "Commercial";
```

It should be placed after `(String[] args){` and before the next `}`.

5. In this example, you will use the value of the string to determine how to set the value of a double variable. In the next line, declare a double variable *interestRate*. It does not need its value initialized here.

```
double interestRate;
```

6. Now add the `switch` statement. Remember to use the `loanType` variable as the conditional expression.

```
switch(loanType){

}
```

7. Now add your cases inside the `switch` statement.

```
case "Residential":
    interestRate = 0.055;
    break;
case "Commercial":
    interestRate = 0.062;
```

```
    break;
case "Investment":
    interestRate = 0.059;
    break;
default:
    interestRate = 0;
```

Place these statements between the { } of the `switch` statement.

8. Next, add a print statement to show the outcome of the `switch` cases. Use the following statement:

```
System.out.println (loanType + " loans have an annual interest rate of "
    + interestRate*100 + "%.");
```

This time, make sure it is placed after the closing bracket (}) of the `switch` statement, but before the closing bracket (}) of the `main` method.

9. Your class body should now look like this:

```
public class SwitchClass {

    public static void main(String[] args) {
        String loanType = "Commercial";
        double interestRate;

        switch (loanType) {
        case "Residential":
            interestRate = 0.055;
            break;
        case "Commercial":
            interestRate = 0.062;
            break;
        case "Investment":
            interestRate = 0.059;
            break;
        default:
            interestRate = 0;
        }

    System.out.println(loanType + " loans have an annual interest rate of "
        + interestRate * 100 + "%.");
    }
}
```

10. Save the class by clicking the disk icon or selecting File, then Save.

11. Run the application by clicking the green play icon or selecting Run, and then Run.

How It Works

Now take a look at how it works.

1. The application begins by executing the `main` method, which in this case is the only method.

2. The first statement initializes a `String`, named *loanType*, with the value of "Commercial".

3. The next statement declares a `double`, named *interestRate*, but does not initialize it with any value.

4. Next, a `switch` statement is opened, using the variable *loanType* as the conditional expression. This means it will try to match the value of *loanType* to the values listed in each of the cases.

5. Next, the program will evaluate a series of cases, each in the same way. In the first `case`, it will compare `"Commercial"` to `"Residential"`. Because they are unequal, it will move to the next `case`.

6. In the second `case`, it will compare `"Commercial"` to `"Commercial"`. This time, because the two strings are equal, it will evaluate the statements associated with this case.

7. Inside the `"Commercial"` case, the value of *interestRate* will be set to 0.062. Then, the `break` statement will indicate that the `switch` statement should be interrupted and no further cases or statements will be evaluated. Without the `break` statement, the value of *interestRate* will be reassigned to 0.059 and again to 0 following all the statements in the rest of the `switch` statement.

8. After leaving the `switch` statement, the print statement will output a line of text to the console. The string that will be printed is composed of four parts:

```
String loanType: Commercial
String: loans have an annual interest rate of
double interestRate*100: 0.062*100 = 6.2
String: %.
```

Altogether, the output will be: "`Commercial loans have an annual interest rate of 6.2%.`"

Comparing Switches and if-then Statements

Just like `for` and `while` loops are similar structures, switches and if-then statements are also easy to compare. When you are using a `switch`, you read it the same way as an if-then statement: if the value matches the case, then do something. So how do you know when to use each one?

As with the other control structures, there will be situations when either one is appropriate and you can choose according to your own preference. As you continue coding, your experience will tell you if a problem would be better solved with a `switch` or not.

In general, you might consider the following criteria:

➤ If you have a single variable that can take multiple values, a `switch` might be suitable.

➤ If you have multiple variables or conditions to consider, you will probably need an if-then statement.

➤ If the value you are considering can have a finite number of values, consider using a `switch`.

➤ If the variable can take any value within a continuous range of numbers, consider an if-then statement.

As before, try to keep simplicity and clarity in mind whenever you make decisions about how to code. You want a solution that's simple for you to code, but also as clear to read and understand as possible, for yourself and others who will have to maintain or reuse your code later.

Reviewing Keywords for Control

Chapter 2 briefly covered Java keywords in a more general way. This section reviews keywords used in control structures. Many of these keywords have already been featured in this chapter, as they are specific to the types of control structures you've been reading about. Table 5.4 lists the control keywords and their associated control structures. This section focuses on break, continue, and return, which are more general and can be found in different kinds of structures.

TABLE 5.4: Control Keywords

KEYWORD	ASSOCIATED CONTROL STRUCTURE
for	for loop Enhanced for loop
while	while loop do while loop
do	do while loop
if	if-then statement
else	if-then statement
switch	switch statement
case	switch statement
default	switch statement
break	General use
continue	General use
return	General use

The last three keywords—break, continue, and return—all interrupt the execution of the current block of code. The differences among them is found in what happens after the interruption.

Controlling with the return Keyword

You have seen the return keyword as part of a return statement already, so it may seem strange to think of it as part of a control structure. You know that a return statement of a method completes the execution of that method by returning a value. So, whenever a return statement is executed, that method is stopped, regardless of where in the list of statements it is placed. To imagine how this can be used for control, take the following example:

```
//array of employee ID numbers, stored as Strings
static String[] employees;

//method to search for a specified employee ID
static boolean findEmployee(String employeeID){
    for (String emp : employees){
```

```
        if (emp.equals(employeeID)){
            return true;
        }
    }
    return false;
}
```

As soon as the specified *employeeID* is found, the Boolean `true` will be returned. This will interrupt the search, whether it is the first string in the array, the last string, or anywhere in between. In this way, the flow of the program is controlled by the `return` statement.

It is also possible to use the `return` statement in the same way, but with a `void` method. In this case, the method will be interrupted, but no value will be returned.

```
import java.util.ArrayList;

static ArrayList<String> employeeList = new ArrayList< >();

//a method to add new Employees to the Employee array
static void addNewEmployee(String employeeID){
    if (employeeList.contains(employeeID)){
        return; //employee already exists
    }
    employeeList.add(employeeID);
}
```

In this example, if the employee is found in the `ArrayList`, then there is no need to put her into it. Therefore, the code returns nothing as soon as the employee is found and then exits the method.

Controlling with the break Keyword

The `break` keyword also interrupts the execution of the current block of code. You already saw this keyword used as part of the `switch` statement. It can also be used, in a similar way, with loop structures. A `break` could be thought of as a softer interruption than `return`, as the method continues to execute, just in a different place after breaking out of the current block. If `break` occurs as part of an iterative loop, the loop containing the `break` statement will be stopped and it will not complete any further iterations. In the following example, the use of the `break` keyword to exit a loop is shown.

```
//array of employee ID numbers, stored as Strings
static String[] employees;

//method to search for a specified employee ID
static void findEmployee(String employeeID){
    String myString = employeeID + " was not found.";
    for (String emp : employees){
        if (emp.equals(employeeID)){
            myString = employeeID + " was found.";
            break;
        }
    }
    System.out.println(myString);
}
```

Similar to the last example, as soon as the string is found in the array, if it is found, *myString* will be reassigned to indicate the *employeeID* was found. At that point, the enhanced `for` loop containing the `break` statement will stop looping and the program will resume after the curly bracket, which closes the `for` loop block. Then, the final print statement will be executed. If *myString* is never found in the array, the `for` loop will iterate through all elements of the array, exit the block in the same place, and then execute the same print statement, but the value of *myString* will be different.

Controlling with the continue Keyword

The `continue` keyword is the softest interruption, because only this particular iteration of the loop is stopped and the next iteration begins immediately. This is useful if there are statements you want to execute for only certain elements of an array or in specific iterations of the loop. To demonstrate, assume you have an array of `Employee` objects. Each `Employee` object has a method `isManagedBy()` to check if an ID value refers to the manager of that employee.

```
static Employee[] allEmployees;
static void printManagedBy(String managerID){
    for (Employee emp : allEmployees){
        if (!emp.isManagedBy(managerID)){
            continue;
        }
        System.out.println(emp.getName());
    }
}
```

Then the method `printManagedBy()` will loop through all `Employee` objects. If the current `Employee` is not managed by the ID specified, the current iteration will stop and the next `Employee` will be checked. If the current `Employee` is managed by the ID, the loop will continue to the print statement before proceeding to the next iteration.

Specifying a Label for break or continue Control

Both the `break` and `continue` keywords can be combined with a label in order to control the flow even more directly. Recall that using the `break` keyword without a label automatically interrupts the loop that most closely contains the `break` statement. If there are two nested `for` loops, the `break` statement would interrupt the inner `for` loop and resume at the outer `for` loop. By placing a label before the outer `for` loop and including that label in the `break` statement, you can force the `break` to apply to both loops at once.

To include a label in your program, simply choose a name for your label and insert it, followed by a colon (:), before the section of code you would like to break out of. For example, if you have a nested `for` loop and you would like a break in the inner `for` loop to break out of both `for` loops, your label would go before the first `for` keyword and the label name would follow the `break` keyword. Here's the syntax for this:

```
outer: //label to break both for loops
    for (/*Initialization*/; /*Termination*/; /*Increment*/){
        for (/*Initialization*/; /*Termination*/; /*Increment*/){
```

```
        /*execute these statements*/
        break outer; //break with label
    }
}
```

The following Try It Out exercise gives you some practice with the break keyword, both with and without labels.

TRY IT OUT   Breaking a for Loop

Follow these steps to create three sets of nested for loops. The first is a standard for loop, the second has a break statement added, and the last one includes the break statement with a label.

1. Create a new class named *BreakLoop*, following the same process. You can continue to use the same Chapter5 project. Create a new class by right-clicking on the src folder in your project. Select New and then Class.

2. In the Name field, enter the name of your class, *BreakLoop*, beginning with a capital letter by Java convention. In the bottom portion of the New Java Class window, there is a section that reads: "Which method stubs would you like to create?" You may choose to check the box next to "public static void main(String[] args)" to automatically create a main method.

3. You should automatically have the basis for the class body shown here:

```
public class BreakLoop {
    /**
    * @param args
    */
    public static void main(String[] args) {
        // TODO Auto-generated method stub

    }
}
```

If not, you can type it yourself. You do not need the comments, which are denoted with /** or //. In Eclipse, they will appear as blue or green text. Comments are useful for explaining what the code is doing, but are never compiled or executed by Java.

```
public class BreakLoop {
    public static void main(String[] args){

    }
}
```

4. Recall that the main method provides the starting point and ordering for the execution of your program. For this exercise, all the statements you want to execute will be inside the main method.

5. For the first nested for loop section, you use the standard syntax you saw earlier in the chapter. Begin with a print statement to display the area of the program that's being executed. In each iteration of the nested loops, you will simply print the values for x and y, the variables you are using as iterators. Type the first nested for loop as follows:

```
System.out.println("\nLooping with No Break:");
for (int x = 0; x < 3; x++){ //outer loop (x loop)
    for (int y = 0; y < 3; y++){ //inner for loop (y loop)
        System.out.println("x = " + x + " and y = " + y);
    }
}
```

6. Now add the second nested `for` loop section. This will include a `break` statement, which is executed whenever *x* and *y* have the same value. Type the second nested `for` loop as follows:

```
System.out.println("\nBreak with No Label:");
for (int x = 0; x < 3; x++){//outer loop (x loop)
    for (int y = 0; y < 3; y++){ //inner loop (y loop)
        System.out.println("x = " + x + " and y = " + y);
        if (x == y) { //new conditional expression
            System.out.println("Break out of y loop.\n");
            break; //new break statement
        }
    }
}
```

7. Finally, add a third nested `for` loop section. This time, include both a `break` statement and a label. It will be executed under the same condition as the previous section. Type the third nested `for` loop as follows:

```
System.out.println("\nBreak with No Label:");
outer: // new label
for (int x = 0; x < 3; x++) {// outer loop (x loop)
    for (int y = 0; y < 3; y++) { // inner loop (y loop)
        System.out.println("x = " + x + " and y = " + y);
        if (x == y) { // same conditional expression
            System.out.println("Break out of both loops.\n");
            break outer; // new break statement with label
        }
    }
}
```

8. All of the preceding `for` loops should be between the { } of the `main` method. Your class body should now look like this:

```
public class BreakLoop {
    public static void main(String[] args) {
        System.out.println("\nLooping with No Break:");
        for (int x = 0; x < 3; x++) { // outer loop (x loop)
            for (int y = 0; y < 3; y++) { // inner for loop (y loop)
                System.out.println("x = " + x + " and y = " + y);
            }
        }

        System.out.println("\nBreak with No Label:");
        for (int x = 0; x < 3; x++) {// outer loop (x loop)
            for (int y = 0; y < 3; y++) { // inner loop (y loop)
                System.out.println("x = " + x + " and y = " + y);
                if (x == y) { // new conditional expression
```

```
                    System.out.println("Break out of y loop.\n");
                    break; // new break statement
                }
            }
        }

        System.out.println("\nBreak with No Label:");
        outer: // new label
        for (int x = 0; x < 3; x++) {// outer loop (x loop)
            for (int y = 0; y < 3; y++) { // inner loop (y loop)
                System.out.println("x = " + x + " and y = " + y);
                if (x == y) { // same conditional expression
                    System.out.println("Break out of both loops.\n");
                    break outer; // new break statement with label
                }
            }
        }
    }
}
```

9. Save the class by clicking the disk icon or selecting File, then Save.

10. Run the application by clicking the green play icon or selecting Run, and then Run.

How It Works

Now take a look at how it works.

1. The application begins by executing the `main` method, which in this case is the only method.

2. The first statement outputs a line of text to the console indicating that the first set of `for` loops are being executed. They do not include any `break` statements.

3. The nested `for` loops iterate through nine times. During each iteration, the current values for x and y are printed to the console. This is how a standard nested `for` loop iterates: First, in the outer loop, $x = 0$ and the inner loop will iterate for $y = 0$, $y = 1$, and $y = 2$. When $y = 3$, the conditional expression on the inner `for` loop (3 < 3) will evaluate to `false`, so the inner `for` loop ends and the outer `for` loop iterates to $x = 1$. Again, the inner `for` loop will iterate for $y = 0$, $y = 1$, and $y = 2$. When $y = 3$, the conditional expression is `false` again and the inner loop ends. The outer `for` loop iterates again to $x = 2$, and the inner `for` loop cycles through three values for y again. Finally, when $x = 3$, the conditional expression on the outer `for` loop will be evaluated as `false` and both `for` loops will end. You can see each of these iterations printed to the console.

4. Another statement is then printed to the console, indicating that the second set of `for` loops will be executed with a `break` statement. The program proceeds to the next nested `for` loops.

5. The second set of nested `for` loops iterates through only six times. During each iteration, the current values for x and y are printed to the console. When the `break` statement is encountered, another line is output to the console indicating the break. This is how nested `for` loops with a `break` statement iterate: First, in the outer loop $x = 0$ and in the inner loop $y = 0$. These values are printed to the console and then the program checks if x equals y. Since $0 == 0$ is true, there is a line printed to the console and the `break` occurs. This breaks from the inner loop and proceeds to the next outer loop iteration. In the outer loop $x = 1$ and in the inner loop $y = 0$ again; these are printed to the console. The program again determines if x and y are equal, and because $0 == 1$ is `false`, the inner loop iterates to $y = 1$ and the values are printed to the console again. Checking again if x equals y, $1 == 1$ is now `true`, so the print statement and `break` occur a second time. This breaks from the inner loop and proceeds to the next outer loop iteration. This time, in the outer loop $x = 2$ and in the inner loop $y = 0$. The inner loop will iterate from $y = 0$ to $y = 1$ to $y = 2$, printing the values each time. At this point, $x == y$ or $2 == 2$ is `true` and the `break` occurs again. When the outer loop iterates to $x = 3$, the conditional statement $x < 3$ becomes `false` and the outer loop is ended. You can see all of these iterations and breaks printed to the console.

6. Another statement is then printed to the console, indicating that the third set of `for` loops will be executed with a `break` statement and label. The program proceeds to the next set of nested `for` loops.

7. The third set of nested `for` loops iterates through only once. During the iteration, the current values for x and y are printed to the console. When the `break` statement is encountered, another line is output to the console indicating the `break`. This is how nested `for` loops with a `break` statement and label iterate: First, in the outer loop $x = 0$ and in the inner loop $y = 0$. These values are printed to the console in the first iteration. Then the program checks if x and y are equal and evaluates $0 == 0$ as `true`. Therefore, a line is output to the console indicating a `break` will occur and the `break` with label is executed. The program will link the `break outer;` statement with the `outer:` label, and both the inner and outer `for` loops will be broken. The program then proceeds to the end of the `main` method, which has no further statements to execute, so the program terminates.

Reviewing Control Structures

By now, I hope you have a basic understanding of the most common structures you can use to control the flow of your program. This chapter covered control operators, if-then statements, `for` loops, `while` loops, switches, and keywords that can be used for control.

Recall that Java, like most other programming languages, includes operators, which are based on mathematical concepts and used to compare values. With Boolean operators, Java offers the double symbols `&&` and `||` in addition to the single symbols `&` and `|`. These double symbols offer short circuiting to prevent certain types of errors from occurring. It's advisable to make use of `&&` for AND and `||` for OR in Boolean logic.

The if-then statement is a basic control structure that simply tests a condition, and if it's `true`, executes some statements. It can be expanded with `else` or `else if` to allow for executing different statements based on various conditions. Switches operate as sort of a special kind of if-then statement. A single variable is considered, and its value is matched to cases. If they match, then some statements will be executed. You read about how to decide between if-then statements and switches.

Both `for` and `while` loops are structures that allow repetition or iteration of some statements. Because they use different syntax, they are each more or less suitable in different circumstances. You read about some considerations to make when choosing the loop structure for a particular problem.

Enhanced `for` loops allow for automatic iteration over iterable objects like arrays. On the other hand, `do while` loops offer an alternative syntax to `while` loops and can allow the first iteration to occur before testing the condition.

Finally, you looked at some keywords and how they can also be used to control the flow of a program. Any method will be interrupted and exited when the `return` keyword is encountered. In this way, you can influence how much of a method is evaluated and executed. The `break` keyword, with and without a label, can also control how loops and other structures are evaluated by exiting a loop immediately. The `continue` keyword works similarly, but by jumping to the next iteration of a loop.

Because these structures are so common, they will be used throughout the remainder of this book. This will give you a chance to continue practicing, but it also means it's important that you feel comfortable with the ideas in this chapter before continuing. If you can follow the execution of the programs from the Try It Out and How It Works exercises, you're probably ready to move on to the later chapters.

6

Handling Exceptions and Debugging

WHAT YOU WILL LEARN IN THIS CHAPTER:

➤ What kinds of errors can occur in programming

➤ How to find errors in your program

➤ How to handle exceptions that could crash your program

➤ How to test your program

WROX.COM CODE DOWNLOADS FOR THIS CHAPTER

The wrox.com code downloads for this chapter are found at www.wrox.com/go/ beginningjavaprogramming on the Download Code tab. The code is in the Chapter 6 download and individually named according to the names throughout the chapter.

You are now midway through this book. You've learned the basics of Java and programming already. In the following chapters, you'll be going more in depth with object-oriented programming and interacting with users and data sources outside your Java program. This chapter is placed in between to offer you the tools and techniques needed to handle many of the errors that might begin to pop up as your programs start to become more complex. The chapter is divided into three main sections: types of errors, testing options, and programming styles. You saw the concepts introduced as early as Chapter 1, but here you will see actual solutions put into practice with a chance to try them out on your own. By the end of this chapter, you should have developed the skills to avoid errors while you program and to find and fix the errors that will still inevitably occur.

RECOGNIZING ERROR TYPES

Errors are almost unavoidable when programming. Just as when you are writing an essay and sometimes make typos or misuse words, you will make occasional mistakes when programming in Java. These mistakes can be referred to as bugs, errors, or exceptions. Here you will find them classified into three main categories: syntax errors, runtime errors, and logical errors. In general, syntax errors are the easiest to find and correct while logical errors are the most difficult.

Identifying Syntax Errors

Syntax errors are the programming equivalent of spelling and grammar mistakes in natural languages. Syntax errors include the following examples:

➤   Misspelled class, variable, or method names

➤   Misspelled keywords

➤   Missing semicolons

➤   Missing return type for methods

➤   Out of place or mismatched parentheses and brackets

➤   Undeclared or uninitialized variables

➤   Incorrect format of loops, methods, or other structures

In the following code example, see how many syntax errors you can spot:

```java
public class errors {

    public static vod main(String[] args) {
        age = 30;
        int retirementFund = 10000;
        int yearsInRetirement = 0;
        String name = "David Johnson",
        for (int i = age; <= 65; ++) {
            recalculate(retirementFund,0.1);
        }
        int monthlyPension = retirementFund/yearsInRetirement/12
        System.out.println(name + " will have $" + monthlyPension
                + " per month for retirement."];
    }

    public static recalculate(fundAmount, rate) {
        fundAmount = fundAmount*(1+rate);
    }
  }
}
```

You probably can spot several just by reading the code. The keyword `void` is misspelled, the declaration of the string name should end with a semicolon instead of a comma, and the `print` statement should close with a parenthesis followed by a semicolon. If you have a good eye for it, you could see several others, too. Now, look at what Eclipse shows you when you enter the code exactly as it's typed. If you try to run the program now, Eclipse will warn you that there are errors and ask if you would still like to proceed. See Figure 6-1.

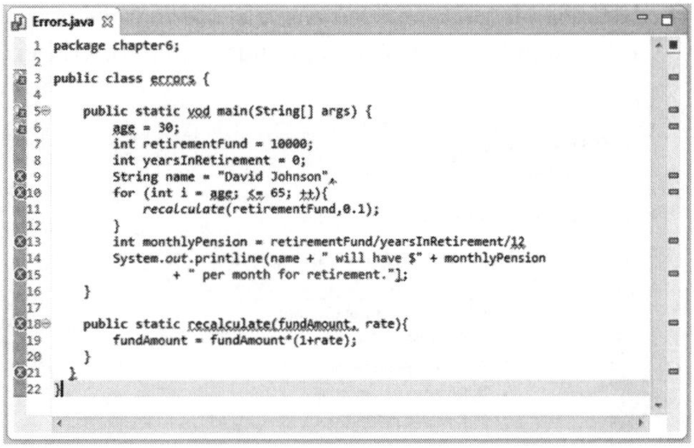

You can see that Eclipse points out syntax errors as you type, so you can more easily find them and fix them immediately. Errors are indicated in the code itself by a red underline, and also noted to the left of the line number as a red X. If you hover your mouse over the red X, you will see a pop-up note indicating what Eclipse thinks the problem is, as shown in Figure 6-2.

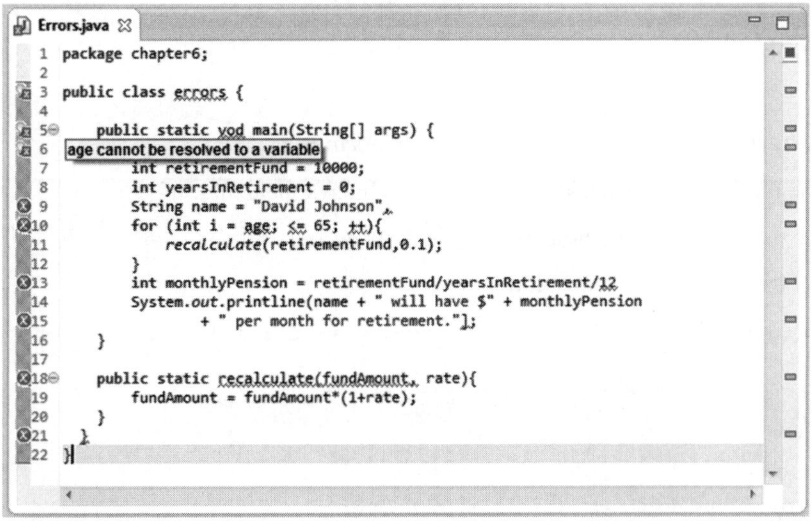

FIGURE 6-1

FIGURE 6-2

The note `age cannot be resolved to a variable` indicates that a variable called `age` has not been declared yet. Therefore, you cannot assign it a value. If you click on the red X, a new popup window appears with possible solutions for the error, if Eclipse has one or more solutions to propose. See Figure 6-3.

By double-clicking on the first solution, `Create local variable 'age'`, the code is automatically edited to include the variable declaration. You can see that it becomes an `int` variable, because Eclipse assumes a value of 30 belongs to an `int` data type. Also, the red X now shows as a faint white X, so you can see that the error was resolved. See Figure 6-4. When you save the file, this white X will disappear. It's important to note already that the proposed solution will not always be the correct one, so be careful that you read and understand both the error and the solution before applying it.

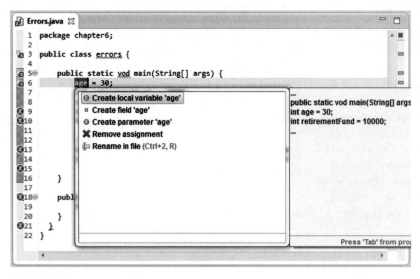

FIGURE 6-3

Following this approach, you can resolve all of the syntax errors in this code.

- ➤ Line 3: Rename type to `Errors` (class name must match .java filename).
- ➤ Line 5: Change to `void` (`main` method return type is always `void`).
- ➤ Line 9: Change the comma to a semicolon.
- ➤ Line 10: Change the `for` loop to `for (int i = age; i <= 65; i++)`.

```
Errors.java ⊠
 1  package chapter6;
 2
 3  public class errors {
 4
 5⊖     public static vod main(String[] args) {
 6         int age = 30;
 7         int retirementFund = 10000;
 8         int yearsInRetirement = 0;
 9         String name = "David Johnson",
10         for (int i = age; <= 65; ++){
11             recalculate(retirementFund,0.1);
12         }
13         int monthlyPension = retirementFund/yearsInRetirement/12
14         System.out.printline(name + " will have $" + monthlyPension
15             + " per month for retirement."];
16     }
17
18⊖     public static recalculate(fundAmount, rate){
19         fundAmount = fundAmount*(1+rate);
20     }
21   }
22  }
```

FIGURE 6-4

➤ Line 18: Set the method return type to `void` (recalculate method doesn't return any value).

➤ Line 18: Add the parameter data types to `double fundAmount, double rate` (this also solves the bug indicated at line 10).

➤ Line 13: Add a semicolon at the end.

➤ Line 14: Change to `println` (`printline` is not correct syntax).

➤ Line 15: Change the square bracket to a parenthesis.

➤ Line 22: Delete the last closing curly bracket (there was one too many).

After all of these corrections, the syntax errors are resolved and your program can be executed. The resulting code looks like this:

```java
public class Errors {

    public static void main(String[] args) {
        int age = 30;
        int retirementFund = 10000;
        int yearsInRetirement = 0;
        String name = "David Johnson";
        for (int i = age; i <= 65; i++){
            recalculate(retirementFund,0.1);
        }
        int monthlyPension = retirementFund/yearsInRetirement/12;
        System.out.println(name + " will have $" + monthlyPension
                + " per month for retirement.");
    }

    public static void recalculate(double fundAmount, double rate){
        fundAmount = fundAmount*(1+rate);
    }
}
```

Identifying Runtime Errors

If you tried running the program after fixing all the syntax errors, you probably already found your first runtime error. In the console you'll find red text indicating there was an exception in the thread `main`. See Figure 6-5. Exception is a Java class including many types of runtime problems. Java distinguishes exceptions and errors: exceptions can—and should—be managed by the programmer, while errors are serious problems that reasonable programs are not expected to handle. Here, the word error is more generally applied.

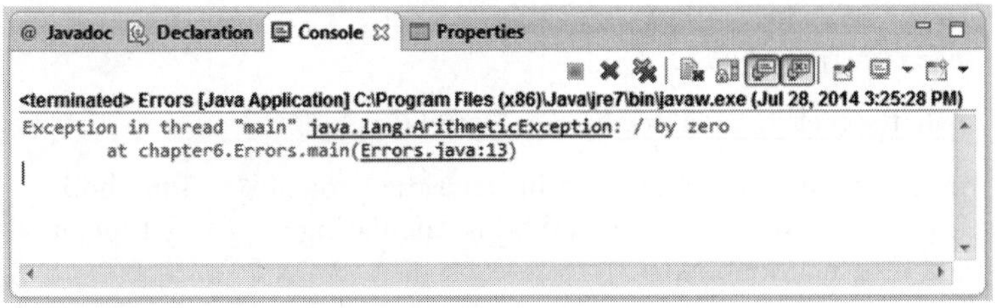

FIGURE 6-5

Luckily, there are clues in the error message that can help you sort out where and why it happened. First note the type of exception: `java.lang.ArithmeticException`. Already from the name, you can see it must be something related to the calculations. Then, specifically it states "/ by zero," so somewhere your program has tried to divide by zero, an operation that's undefined and therefore cannot be computed by Java. In such a small program, you can probably easily locate where the division is occurring, but in case you need some direction, the error message also shows where the error occurred: `chapter6.Errors.main(Errors.java:13)`. In other words, line 13 in the main thread of the `Errors` class in the `chapter6` package. If you go to line 13, you'll see the program is trying to divide `retirementFund` by `yearsInRetirement`. If you refer back to the initializations of these two variables, you'll find `retirementFund = 10000` and `yearsInRetirement = 0`. There's the problem! If you set `yearsInRetirement` to some other value, say 20 years, for a person retiring at 65 and living to age 85, you will no longer have a division by zero exception.

Division by zero is a classic runtime error example, because the syntax is correct and it is only during runtime that a problem occurs. Other typical examples that you will no doubt encounter, if you haven't already, include `null pointer exception`, index out of bounds exception, and file not found exception. In the next section, you'll see explanations of the most common exceptions beginners see.

Identifying Logical Errors

If you've run the code that you just fixed, did you notice anything strange? There shouldn't be any syntax or runtime errors, so your program should run normally. You should see `David Johnson will have $41 per month for retirement.` printed to the console. At first glance, this seems fine, but on further inspection, the number is lower than you would expect. In fact, 10,000 divided by 20 years divided by 12 months is 41 dollars per month. But the program is supposed to be calculating an annual return rate of 10% for all the years between age 30 and age 65. So what's going on here?

This is an example of a logical error. The code compiles and executes without error, but logically produces the wrong result. Logical errors are perhaps the most difficult to spot, because there's nothing to suggest there's an error unless you know what to expect and compare the actual results to the expected results. If you are not careful to review what is happening, you may easily miss logical errors lurking in your code.

So first try to sort out where this program went wrong. We know the return rate is not being calculated correctly; this could be a problem in the `for` loop that is iterating each year or in the recalculate method itself. You can start by testing one recalculate method call and see if it's working. Add the following print statement to the `main` method to check this: `System.out.println("100 at 10% annual interest is: " + recalculate(100,0.1));`

But now, there's already a hint that something isn't right. See Figure 6-6.

The error hint tells you that you cannot add a `void` to a string. But the `recalculate` method returns a `void`. You will have to change this. Since the method is calculating a `double` type, it makes sense to make the method return a `double`.

```
public static double recalculate(double fundAmount, double rate){
    return fundAmount*(1+rate);
}
```

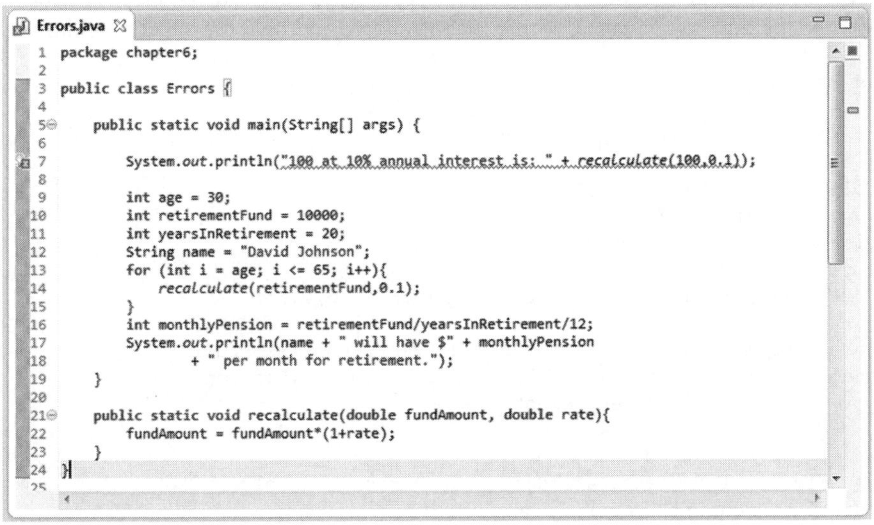

```
Errors.java ⊠
 1  package chapter6;
 2
 3  public class Errors {
 4
 5⊖     public static void main(String[] args) {
 6
 7          System.out.println("100 at 10% annual interest is: " + recalculate(100,0.1));
 8
 9          int age = 30;
10          int retirementFund = 10000;
11          int yearsInRetirement = 20;
12          String name = "David Johnson";
13          for (int i = age; i <= 65; i++){
14              recalculate(retirementFund,0.1);
15          }
16          int monthlyPension = retirementFund/yearsInRetirement/12;
17          System.out.println(name + " will have $" + monthlyPension
18                  + " per month for retirement.");
19      }
20
21⊖     public static void recalculate(double fundAmount, double rate){
22          fundAmount = fundAmount*(1+rate);
23      }
24  }
25
```

FIGURE 6-6

That corrects the syntax error, so you can try running the program now. The output should now read:

```
100 at 10% annual interest is: 110.00000000000001
David Johnson will have $41 per month for retirement.
```

So the method seems to be calculating correctly now, since 100 + 10% return is 110.

> **NOTE** It's worth mentioning the rounding error you see here. Doubles are not appropriate data types for dealing with things where precision is important, including money. `BigDecimal` would be a much more appropriate choice because it allows the developer control over the rounding of floating point values. An example of how this program could use `BigDecimal` is included at the end of this section.

So you now know the error is in the `for` loop. You might first check the initialization and termination conditions of the loop, just to be sure it's iterating properly. It should repeat for each year between age 30 and 65 (presumably retirement age). That shouldn't be a problem. Therefore, it must be in the body of the `for` loop. In fact, the change you made to the return type is already a hint as to what needs to be edited here, too. The method now returns a `double`, but that `double` is not used in any way during the loop. Therefore, every time the loop is executed, the same `retirementFund = 10000` is used in the calculation again. What you need to do is assign the newly calculated `double` value to the retirementFund variable, so the new amount is used in the next calculation. Because the fundAmount is a double, you also need to change the type of retirementFund to a double as well. If you do this, you'll also see an error pop up for the monthlyPension variable, since it uses retirementFund in its calculation. Change this to a double type also. You can, of course, remove the first print statement now that you know the method is calculating correctly. You should end up with something like this.

```java
public class Errors {

    public static void main(String[] args) {
        int age = 30;
        double retirementFund = 10000;
        int yearsInRetirement = 20;
        String name = "David Johnson";
        for (int i = age; i <= 65; i++){
            retirementFund = recalculate(retirementFund,0.1);
        }
        double monthlyPension = retirementFund/yearsInRetirement/12;
        System.out.println(name + " will have $" + monthlyPension
            + " per month for retirement.");
    }

    public static double recalculate(double fundAmount, double rate){
        return fundAmount*(1+rate);
    }
}
```

The output now, which should make you feel a little more optimistic about potential retirement, is David Johnson will have $1288.0283555362819 per month for retirement. It is also possible to reformat the string representation of that double to a more common two-decimal place number using a DecimalFormat class. That implementation isn't important for this chapter, but you might find it interesting.

```java
import java.text.DecimalFormat;

public class Errors {

    public static void main(String[] args) {
        int age = 30;
        double retirementFund = 10000;
        int yearsInRetirement = 20;
        String name = "David Johnson";
        for (int i = age; i <= 65; i++){
            retirementFund = recalculate(retirementFund,0.1);
        }

        double monthlyPension = retirementFund/yearsInRetirement/12;

        // create a decimal format with two decimal points
        DecimalFormat df = new DecimalFormat ("0.##");

        // use the df.format() method to format the double
        System.out.println(name + " will have $" + df.format(monthlyPension)
            + " per month for retirement.");
```

```
    }

    public static double recalculate(double fundAmount, double rate){
        return fundAmount*(1+rate);
    }
}
```

PRECISION ROUNDING: BIGDECIMAL VS. DOUBLE

You've seen in this small example that the way doubles are rounded makes them inaccurate, especially when representing important decimal values, such as money. There are other classes that will not result in these rounding errors and should be used in real applications. BigDecimal would be a much better choice because it offers the developer complete control over how values are rounded. BigDecimal allows you to specify a scale, or a number of digits after the decimal point, and the rounding method to use to accomplish this scaling. To illustrate this, have a look at the same program written with BigDecimal instead of doubles. Remember how you needed to specify a decimal format to display your double value nicely. With BigDecimal, you can control the rounding at each calculation, so not only is it displayed nicely, but the actual value matches the nice string representation as well.

```java
import java.math.BigDecimal;

public class Errors {

    public static void main(String[] args) {
        int age = 30;
        BigDecimal retirementFund = new BigDecimal("10000.00");
        // set the scale to 2 decimal points
        // and the rounding to round up when the next digit is >= 5
        retirementFund.setScale(2,BigDecimal.ROUND_HALF_UP);
        BigDecimal yearsInRetirement = new BigDecimal("20.00");
        String name = "David Johnson";
        for (int i = age; i <= 65; i++){
            retirementFund = recalculate(retirementFund,new
            BigDecimal("0.10"));
        }

        BigDecimal monthlyPension = retirementFund.divide(
                yearsInRetirement.multiply(new BigDecimal("12")));
        System.out.println(name + " will have $" + monthlyPension
                + " per month for retirement.");
    }

    public static BigDecimal recalculate(BigDecimal fundAmount,
        BigDecimal rate){
        // use BigDecimal methods for arithmetic operations
        return fundAmount.multiply(rate.add(new
        BigDecimal("1.00")));
    }
}
```

continues

continued

Actually, because `BigDecimal` is a class and its value is stored in an instance of the class, some of the problems with the method return type also disappear. You could change the `recalculate()` method so that it updates the value of the `BigDecimal` `retirementFund` instead of returning a `BigDecimal`.

```java
import java.math.BigDecimal;

public class Errors {

    public static void main(String[] args) {
        int age = 30;
        BigDecimal retirementFund = new BigDecimal("10000.00");
        // set the scale to 2 decimal points
        // and the rounding to round up when the next digit is >= 5
        retirementFund.setScale(2,BigDecimal.ROUND_HALF_UP);
        BigDecimal yearsInRetirement = new BigDecimal("20.00");
        String name = "David Johnson";
        for (int i = age; i <= 65; i++){
            recalculate(retirementFund,new BigDecimal("0.10"));
        }

        BigDecimal monthlyPension = retirementFund.divide
                (yearsInRetirement.multiply(new BigDecimal("12")));
        System.out.println(name + " will have $" + monthlyPension
                + " per month for retirement.");
    }

    public static void recalculate(BigDecimal fundAmount,
        BigDecimal rate){
        // use BigDecimal methods for arithmetic operations
        fundAmount.multiply(rate.add(new BigDecimal("1.00")));
    }

}
```

EXCEPTIONS

In the previous section, three kinds of errors were discussed: syntax errors, runtime errors, and logical errors. These types have been discussed in a more general way as they occur in many settings outside of Java programming, though as you saw in the examples, they certainly apply to Java as well. Exceptions are more specific to programming as they are events that disrupt the execution of a program. Exceptions can be indications that something went wrong, and they can happen automatically as a result of something Java is unable to complete or can be explicitly thrown when certain conditions are met. In the following sections, you'll be introduced to some common exceptions, and you'll get to see how to handle them in your own programs.

Common Exceptions

There are some exceptions that occur often enough, not just with new programmers, but even with experienced developers. In this short section, you'll get to see two in particular that come up all the time: `null pointer exceptions` and index out of bounds exceptions. There are explanations and examples that will help you recognize when, where, and why these exceptions might pop up in your programs.

`Null pointer exceptions` indicate that the program is trying to access an object that doesn't exist yet. Before you can reference a primitive data type, like `int`, you need to initialize it, which is setting the value. If you forget to do this, Eclipse will warn you, like it did for other syntax errors. When you declare a variable of a composite data type, you are actually creating a pointer to an object. Now, if you declare a variable without assigning an object to point to, you are left with a pointer to null or, in other words, you are pointing at nothing. Then trying to access that variable's object will likely result in a `null pointer exception`. Usually, if it's obvious, Eclipse will complain about this, too. But it is possible that the references are not so straightforward and the problem is not a syntax error. In that case, you will encounter a `null pointer exception`. Consider the following examples, which illustrate these concepts.

```java
public class ExceptionExamples {

    public static void main(String[] args) {
        Person employee;
        printPerson(employee);
    }

    public static void printPerson(Person myPerson){
        System.out.println(myPerson.name + " is " + myPerson.age + " years old.");
    }
}

class Person{
    String name;
    int age;

    Person (){

    }
}
```

> **NOTE** In some of these examples, you'll notice that instance variables, name and age, of a `Person` object are accessed directly through the `myPerson` instance. In Chapter 4, encapsulation and information hiding principles were introduced, but you'll see this in much more detail in Chapter 9. It is discouraged to access variables directly, but instead you should use accessor methods like `getName()` to return the person's name. To keep the examples in this chapter simple, getter and setter methods are not included in every code example, but it is good practice to get in the habit of creating these methods to access fields.

When you try to reference `employee` in line 7, Eclipse displays an error reminding you that the variable `employee` has not been initialized. See Figure 6-7.

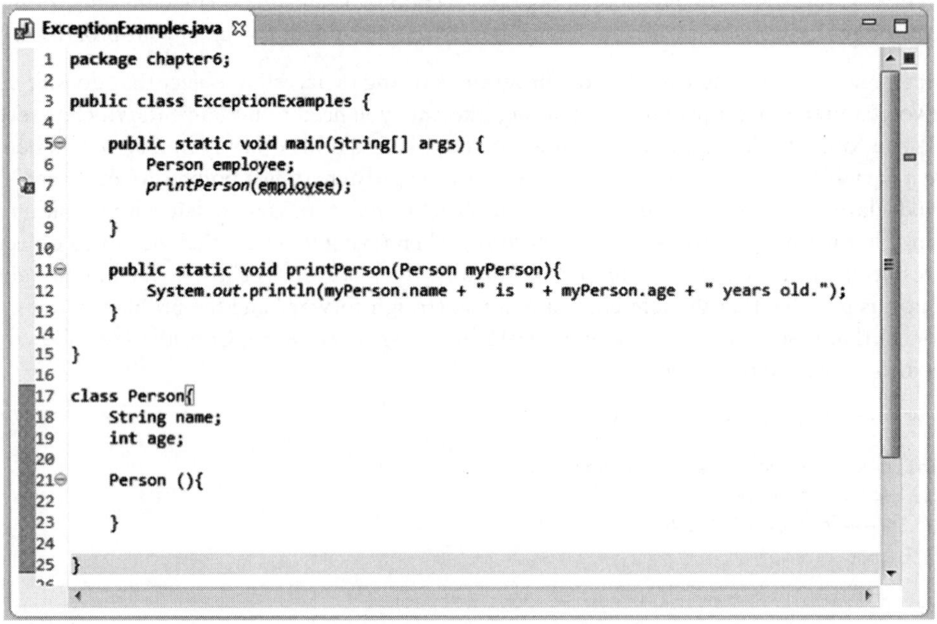

```
ExceptionExamples.java ✕
  1  package chapter6;
  2
  3  public class ExceptionExamples {
  4
  5      public static void main(String[] args) {
  6          Person employee;
  7          printPerson(employee);
  8
  9      }
 10
 11      public static void printPerson(Person myPerson){
 12          System.out.println(myPerson.name + " is " + myPerson.age + " years old.");
 13      }
 14
 15  }
 16
 17  class Person{
 18      String name;
 19      int age;
 20
 21      Person (){
 22
 23      }
 24
 25  }
```

FIGURE 6-7

The suggestion offered to initialize the variable will change line 6 to `Person employee = null;` Of course, this will lead to a `null pointer exception`; you can see that just by reading the code. You can correct it by initializing a new `Person` object referenced by the `employee` variable.

```
public class ExceptionExamples {

    public static void main(String[] args) {
        Person employee = new Person();
        printPerson(employee);
    }

    public static void printPerson(Person myPerson){
        System.out.println(myPerson.name + " is " + myPerson.age + " years old.");
    }
}

class Person{
    String name;
```

```
    int age;

    Person (){

    }
}
```

You probably expect this to lead to a null pointer exception at line 12 now, because you never initialized the name or age of the Person object referenced by employee. However, if you run this code, the following line is output to the console: null is 0 years old. This is because Java will automatically initialize fields of an object to a default value, null for objects and 0 for int, and it is possible to print these values.

You might be wondering then, how a null pointer exception comes up, aside from actually initializing a variable to null. One way this can happen, shown in the following code, is when a second object type JobType is added and a Person object is assigned a JobType object.

```
public class ExceptionExamples {

    public static void main(String[] args) {
        Person employee = new Person();
        printPerson(employee);

    }

    public static void printPerson(Person myPerson){
        System.out.println(myPerson.name + " is " + myPerson.age +
            " years old and works as a " + myPerson.job.JobName);
    }

}

class Person{
    String name;
    int age;
    JobType job;

    Person (){

    }

}

class JobType{
    String JobName;
    int salaryBand;

    JobType (){

    }
}
```

Now when you try to run this code, you will receive a null pointer exception, as shown in Figure 6-8.

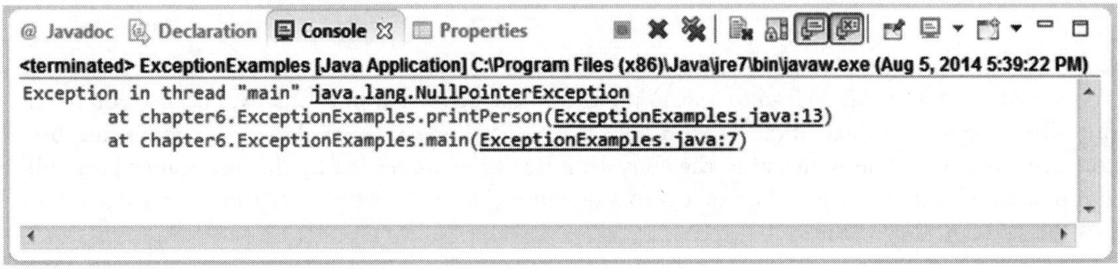

FIGURE 6-8

This looks very similar to the ArithmeticException you saw in the retirement fund examples. However, here, because you have more than just the main method, there is some further information about the location where the exception occurred. You can see from the first line the type of exception and that it occurred during the execution of the main method. After that, it's easier to read from the bottom up to try to find the exact cause of the error. During the execution, there was an error at line 7, when the printPerson() method was called. The execution then jumps to the body of that method and the exception occurred during line 13 of the printPerson() method. In that line, the only reference was to myPerson.job.JobName, so you know that the job or JobName was never initialized for the Person object referenced by myPerson. myPerson references employee from line 7.

One way to avoid this kind of situation is by requiring initialization as part of the constructor. Previously, you saw empty constructors for Person and JobType. This means that when you create a Person object, you do not specify a name, age, or job type. Depending on the system you are creating, there may be reasons to leave some of these empty when you create a new person. For example, if you create a Person object as soon as you start a job search, you may only know the job type. On the other hand, if you create a Person object as soon as someone applies to work at your company, you may only know their name and age, but not which job you will hire them for (if you hire them at all). However, if you create a Person object precisely when you hire a person for a specific job, you'll have all three pieces of information at creation. This last situation is implemented here, where all the information is known and can be initialized in the constructor. In real applications, you may need more than one constructor to handle different cases, but if you leave some fields null, you will need to handle null pointer exceptions in other ways. To avoid this, you might decide to create a JobType for every case, including Interviewee for people who have not yet been hired or NewHire for new employees who have not been given a specific JobType. Alternatively, you could have a Boolean method hasJobType() check whether the Person already has a JobType assigned and handle these cases as needed.

```java
public class ExceptionExamples {

    public static void main(String[] args) {
        JobType manager = new JobType("Manager", 6);
        Person employee = new Person("Bob Little", 47, manager);
```

```
            printPerson(employee);

    }

    public static void printPerson(Person myPerson){
        System.out.println(myPerson.name + " is " + myPerson.age +
            " years old and works as a " + myPerson.job.JobName);
    }

}

class Person{
    String name;
    int age;
    JobType job;

    Person (String name, int age, JobType job){
        this.name = name;
        this.age = age;
        this.job = job;
    }

}

class JobType{
    String JobName;
    int salaryBand;

    JobType (String name, int band){
        JobName = name;
        salaryBand = band;
    }
}
```

Another common exception is index out of bounds. This occurs when you have an indexed object, such as an array, and you try to access an element outside the limits of the array. As you've already seen, arrays are indexed starting from 0, so the last element is one less than the size of the array. For example, an array of size 5 has elements indexed at 0, 1, 2, 3, and 4. It is important to consider this, for example, when looping through the elements of an array.

```
public class IndexExceptionExample {

    public static void main(String[] args) {
        int[] hoursWorked = {7,8,7,9,5};
        int totalHours = 0;

        for (int i = 0; i <= hoursWorked.length; i++){
            totalHours += hoursWorked[i];
        }

        System.out.println("Total Hours = " + totalHours);
    }
}
```

This simple program iterates through an array and adds the total number of hours from each element together. Then, the total is output to the console. If you try to run it, though, you will encounter an exception, as shown in Figure 6-9.

```
@ Javadoc  Declaration  Console ✕  Properties                    ■ ✖ ✖ | ▤ ▥ ▦ ▧  ▨ ▨ ▼ ▨ ▼ ▭ ▢
<terminated> IndexExceptionExample [Java Application] C:\Program Files (x86)\Java\jre7\bin\javaw.exe (Aug 6, 2014 11:11:15 AM)
Exception in thread "main" java.lang.ArrayIndexOutOfBoundsException: 5
        at chapter6.IndexExceptionExample.main(IndexExceptionExample.java:10)
```

FIGURE 6-9

As before, you can track down the exception by the information shown in the error message. First, you can see that it is an `ArrayIndexOutOfBoundsException`. The index that's out of bounds is 5, and it occurred in line 10 of the program. If you look at line 10, it is the last line of the `for` loop, so you know to check the iterator of the `for` loop. In the code, it was set to start from 0, the lower limit of the array's index, and stop at `hoursWorked.length`, but the length is 5 and the index only goes to 4. Simply changing the termination condition to `i < hoursWorked.length` will stop the loop at 4 (since 4 is less than 5) and avoid an out of bounds exception.

```java
public class IndexExceptionExample {

    public static void main(String[] args) {
        int[] hoursWorked = {7,8,7,9,5};
        int totalHours = 0;

        for (int i = 0; i < hoursWorked.length; i++){
            totalHours += hoursWorked[i];
        }

        System.out.println("Total Hours = " + totalHours);
    }
}
```

Two other common exceptions you might encounter are `StackOverFlowError` and `OutOfMemoryError`. These occur when the program you are running demands more memory than your machine allows for Java or your IDE. The stack is the part of your memory allocated for parameters and local variables. This can overflow when you are calling a method recursively or when two methods call each other. The heap is where objects are allocated in memory. Creating too many objects, often within an infinite loop, can quickly consume all the available memory. To see these kinds of errors for yourself, try running the following small applications.

```java
import java.util.ArrayList;

public class EndlessLoop {
    static ArrayList<String> myStrings = new ArrayList<String>();
```

```java
    public static void main(String[] args) {
        for (int i = 0; i >= 0; i++) {
            myStrings.add("String number: " + i);
        }
    }
}
```

Depending on your machine and settings, this will sooner or later throw a `java.lang.OutOfMemoryError`. The problem is the termination condition of the `for` loop. The iterator, `int i`, is initialized with a value of 0 and increments by 1 with each loop. The loop is supposed to terminate when the value of `i` goes below 0, but it will never reach this condition because it is increasing, not decreasing. This might be easy to spot here, but if your termination condition is dependent on a variable or method result, you might not immediately see where infinite looping is possible. If you encounter an `OutOfMemoryError`, take a look at object creation events, especially inside loops or recursive method calls.

```java
public class EndlessMethodCall {

    public static void main(String[] args) {
        printMe();
    }

    public static void displayMe(){
        printMe();
    }

    public static void printMe(){
        displayMe();
    }
}
```

Running this program will almost immediately cause a `java.lang.StackOverflowError` exception to be thrown. The two methods call each other back and forth without end. If you experience this kind of error, you should first look into method calls to see whether you've unintentionally created an infinite loop. A related problem occurs when a method calls itself, something referred to as recursion. Recursion is often a valuable tool, as long as there is an appropriate stopping condition to keep it from calling itself infinitely, or until an exception is thrown, of course.

It is impossible to cover every possible exception in this book, but with this foundation, you should be able to begin to deal with them appropriately. If you encounter other exceptions as you are programming, searching online for the name of the exception will help you understand why it is occurring. The techniques demonstrated in the next section will help you deal with all kinds of exceptions.

Catching Exceptions

Now that you've been introduced to the three main error categories and some common exceptions, it's time to start learning how to handle them when you do encounter them. The first step is a new structure called a `try/catch` block. This essentially allows you to *try* executing a piece of code to see if an exception is thrown. If none is thrown, the program will proceed normally, but if one is thrown, you can *catch* it and specifically indicate what should be done next. This prevents your program from crashing and at least allows you to recover some information before it terminates.

The general form of a `try/catch` block looks like this:

```
try {
    // execute some statements
} catch (Exception exc){
    // statements to handle the exception
} finally {
    // no matter what, do this
}
```

> **NOTE** While this book refers to these as `try/catch` blocks, there are in fact three separate components: `try`, `catch`, and `finally` blocks. You may encounter any of the following: a `try` block with (one or more) `catch` blocks; a `try` block with (one or more) `catch` blocks and a `finally` block; or, less commonly, a `try` block with only a `finally` block.

Now you can see how they are used by looking again at the retirement fund examples. Recall how you got a division by zero exception when you tried to divide an `int retirementFund` by another `int yearsInRetirement`, if the latter was given the value 0.

```
public class Errors {

    public static void main(String[] args) {
        int age = 30;
        int retirementFund = 10000;
        int yearsInRetirement = 0;
        String name = "David Johnson";
        for (int i = age; i <= 65; i++){
            recalculate(retirementFund,0.1);
        }
        double monthlyPension = retirementFund/yearsInRetirement/12;
        System.out.println(name + " will have $" + monthlyPension
                + " per month for retirement.");
    }

    public static void recalculate(double fundAmount, double rate){
        fundAmount = fundAmount*(1+rate);
    }

}
```

You could enclose the division and print statements inside a `try` block and add a `catch` block, like this:

```
try {
    double monthlyPension = retirementFund/yearsInRetirement/12;
    System.out.println(name + " will have $" + monthlyPension
        + " per month for retirement.");
```

```
    } catch (ArithmeticException ae){
        System.out.println(ae);
        System.exit(0);
    }
```

The division and print statements will be attempted, but if an `ArithmeticException` is thrown, the `catch` block will catch it. Then the exception will be printed and the program will be terminated. Of course, you may prefer that the program not be terminated, but continue. You can change the statements inside the `catch` block to accomplish this.

```
    try {
        double monthlyPension = retirementFund/yearsInRetirement/12;
        System.out.println(name + " will have $" + monthlyPension
            + " per month for retirement.");
    } catch (ArithmeticException ae){
        System.out.println("Years in retirement should not be 0." +
            "Default value is 20 years.");
        double monthlyPension = retirementFund/20/12;
        System.out.println(name + " will have $" + monthlyPension
            + " per month for retirement.");
    }
```

Now if you run the program, it will try the original calculation, throw a division by 0 exception, catch the exception in the `catch` block, and calculate the monthly pension using another non-zero value. This way, the program can execute fully.

You'll notice though, that the `catch` block was designed here to catch only exceptions of the `ArithmeticException` type. You might have more than one exception type that must be handled. In older versions of Java, you had two choices: create a separate `catch` block for each type of exception or catch all exceptions (or even all *throwables*, which include errors and exceptions, though this is not advised) in one generic `catch` block. Since Java 7, you can catch more than one specific type of exception in a single `catch` block.

```
    try {
        double monthlyPension = retirementFund/yearsInRetirement/12;
        System.out.println(name + " will have $" + monthlyPension
            + " per month for retirement.");
    } catch (ArithmeticException|NullPointerException exc){
        System.out.println("Fields should not be null.");
        System.out.println("Years in retirement should not be 0." +
            "Default value is 20 years.");
        double monthlyPension = retirementFund/20/12;
        System.out.println(name + " will have $" + monthlyPension
            + " per month for retirement.");
    }
```

You can see that if either of the specified exceptions is caught, the response in the `catch` block is the same. In this particular case, you probably would prefer not to do this, since a `null pointer exception` does not mean that the `yearsInRetirement` needs to be overwritten by the default value. Therefore, it makes more sense to separate the two exceptions into two separate `catch` blocks.

```
try {
    double monthlyPension = retirementFund/yearsInRetirement/12;
    System.out.println(name + " will have $" + monthlyPension
        + " per month for retirement.");
} catch (ArithmeticException ae){
    System.out.println("Years in retirement should not be 0." +
        "Default value is 20 years.");
    double monthlyPension = retirementFund/20/12;
    System.out.println(name + " will have $" + monthlyPension
        + " per month for retirement.");
} catch (NullPointerException np){
    System.out.println("Fields should not be null.");
    System.exit(0);
}
```

Alternatively, you can also use a very generic `catch` block to catch all throwables, both errors and exceptions. In practice, it is better to be as specific as possible, so that you have the best chance at properly handling any foreseeable exceptions.

```
try {
    double monthlyPension = retirementFund/yearsInRetirement/12;
    System.out.println(name + " will have $" + monthlyPension
        + " per month for retirement.");
} catch (Throwable thrown){
    System.out.println(thrown);
    System.exit(0);
}
```

Thus far, you haven't seen the `finally` block in action. A `finally` block includes the statements you want to execute regardless of the outcome of the `try` block. When you try something, if it throws an exception or not, you still want to make sure certain things are done. You could do this by adding these statements to both the `try` and `catch` blocks, because that would mean they are executed in either case. However, as you've seen so far, it's best to avoid duplicate code for readability and maintainability later. Therefore, it's better to use a `finally` block for this. You should note that a `System.exit()` call will always immediately terminate the program and, in this case, the `finally` block, or anything after the `exit` call, would not be executed.

```
try {
    double monthlyPension = retirementFund/yearsInRetirement/12;
    System.out.println(name + " will have $" + monthlyPension
        + " per month for retirement.");
} catch (ArithmeticException ae){
    System.out.println("Years in retirement should not be 0." +
        "Default value is 20 years.");
    double monthlyPension = retirementFund/20/12;
    System.out.println(name + " will have $" + monthlyPension
        + " per month for retirement.");
} catch (NullPointerException np){
    System.out.println("Fields should not be null.");
    System.exit(0);
} finally {
    System.out.println("Finally was reached. ");
}
```

In this example, if the `monthlyPension` calculation succeeds without any exception, then `Finally was reached.` will be printed to the console. If the `monthlyPension` calculation throws an `ArithmeticExeption`, the `Finally was reached.` will still be printed to the console. If the calculation throws a `NullPointerException`, the program will terminate and `Finally was reached.` will not be printed. The last case, which perhaps was not considered, is if an exception is thrown but not one of the ones in the `catch` blocks, say an `IndexOutOfBoundsException`. Then the exception will be thrown, `Finally was reached.` will be printed to the console, and the unhandled exception will cause the program to crash.

You will see `finally` blocks commonly used to ensure that resources, like databases, are closed whether the update was successful or not. A feature added in Java 7, however, makes this even easier. The so-called try-with-resources block automatically ensures the resources are closed without the need for a `finally` block. You will see more in-depth examples in the chapter on input and output, but a short example is provided here to demonstrate the similarities and differences with more traditional try-catch-finally blocks.

Some concepts haven't been covered quite yet, but it is sufficient to know that `Scanner` objects can be used to scan simple text and parse primitive types or strings. Here it is scanning `System.in`, which includes user input to the console. The `nextInt()` and `nextDouble()` methods parse ints and doubles from the text entered by the user. If a user enters the character 5, the `nextInt()` method will parse an `int` with value 5. If a user enters the word `employee`, this cannot be parsed using the `nextInt()` method and an `InputMismatchException` will be thrown.

First, look at how this was done using `try` and `finally` blocks.

```java
import java.text.DecimalFormat;
import java.util.Scanner;

public class Resources {
    Scanner scan = new Scanner(System.in);

    public static void main(String[] args) {
        try {
            System.out.print("Enter the loan amount: ");
            double principle = scan.nextDouble();
            System.out.print("Enter the interest rate: ");
            double rate = scan.nextDouble();
            System.out.print("Enter the loan term (in years): ");
            double years = scan.nextInt();

            double interest = principle*rate*years;
            double total = principle + interest;
            double payment = total/years/12;

            DecimalFormat df = new DecimalFormat ("0.##");
            System.out.println("Monthly payment: $"
                    + df.format(payment));
        } catch (Exception exc){
            System.out.println(exc);
        } finally {
```

```
            scan.close();
        }
    }
}
```

Note that in order for the scan object to be accessible in both the `try` and `finally` blocks, it must be declared outside either block. Now look at the try-with-resources block.

```java
import java.text.DecimalFormat;
import java.util.Scanner;

public class Resources {

    public static void main(String[] args) {
        try (Scanner scan = new Scanner(System.in)){
            System.out.print("Enter the loan amount: ");
            double principle = scan.nextDouble();
            System.out.print("Enter the interest rate: ");
            double rate = scan.nextDouble();
            System.out.print("Enter the loan term (in years): ");
            double years = scan.nextInt();

            double interest = principle*rate*years;
            double total = principle + interest;
            double payment = total/years/12;

            DecimalFormat df = new DecimalFormat ("0.##");
            System.out.println("Monthly payment: $"
                + df.format(payment));
        } catch (Exception exc){
            System.out.println(exc);
        }
    }
}
```

By adding the declaration and initialization directly to the `try` block, the resource will automatically be closed no matter how the rest of the `try` block completes (with or without exception). Imagine you come back to this code later and decide to change the `System.in` scanner to some other user interface. Simply by changing the resource in the `try` clause, you are assured that it will be closed correctly. You can also declare more than one resource, if necessary, simply by separating the resources with a semicolon. You will see many more examples of this in Chapter 8, where the different tools available for reading and writing will be explained fully.

In Java, there are two types of exceptions: checked and unchecked. Specifically, the `Exception` class has a subclass called runtime exceptions. Runtime exceptions and any subclasses are unchecked, while all other types of exceptions are checked. Java requires that checked exceptions be handled, and you will see this indicated with an error alert in Eclipse or other compilers. Eclipse offers two possible solutions: declare that the method might throw a particular type of exception or enclose particular statements in a `try/catch` designed to handle those exceptions. If you simply add a `throws` declaration, you are not handling the exception in any way; you are simply alerting anyone who might call this method that an exception is possible. In order to handle the exceptions, you should use a `try/catch` block. In your `main` method, the `try/catch` solution is certainly appropriate. In other methods, it might be suitable to add the throws declaration and then handle the exception (with a try/catch block) in the main or other method that calls this method.

In order to demonstrate how this works, consider the next example.

```java
import java.text.DecimalFormat;
import java.util.InputMismatchException;
import java.util.Scanner;

public class ThrowsExceptions {

    public static void main(String[] args) {
        try {
            // store the double[] returned by the scanValues() method
            double[] userValues = scanValues();

            // store the double returned by the calculatePayment() method
            double payment = calculatePayment(userValues);

            // create a decimal format with two places after the decimal point
            DecimalFormat df = new DecimalFormat("0.##");

            // print the calculated payment according to the format above
            System.out.println("Monthly payment: $" + df.format(payment));
        } catch (InputMismatchException ime) {
            // scanValues() method throws InputMismatchException
            // if user's entry cannot be parsed into a double
            System.out.println("You must enter double values. "
                    + "Please restart program.");
            // terminate the program
            System.exit(0);
        } catch (ArithmeticException ae) {
            // calculatePayment() method throws ArithmeticException
            // if years == 0
            System.out.println("Years must be greater than 0. "
                    + "Please restart program.");
            // terminate the program
            System.exit(0);
        } catch (IndexOutOfBoundsException ioob) {
            // calculatePayment() method throws IndexOutOfBoundsException
            // if double[] has less than 3 elements
            System.out.println("Three doubles are required. "
                    + "Please restart program.");
            // terminate the program
            System.exit(0);
        }
    }

    // method asks for and scans three doubles:
    // principle, interest rate, and loan years
    public static double[] scanValues() throws InputMismatchException {
        double[] values = new double[3];
        try (Scanner scan = new Scanner(System.in)) {
            System.out.print("Enter the loan amount: ");
            values[0] = scan.nextDouble();
```

```
            System.out.print("Enter the interest rate: ");
            values[1] = scan.nextDouble();
            System.out.print("Enter the loan term (in years): ");
            values[2] = scan.nextInt();
        }
        return values;
    }


    // method takes a double[] with three elements
    // and calculates a monthly payment
    public static double calculatePayment(double[] values)
            throws ArithmeticException, IndexOutOfBoundsException {
        double principle = values[0];
        double rate = values[1];
        double years = values[2];
        double interest = principle * rate * years;
        double total = principle + interest;
        return total / years / 12;
    }
}
```

In this example, there are three methods: main(), scanValues(), and calculatePayment(), but together they accomplish the same goal as the previous example. You can see how the throws declaration in the "lower" methods warns that there are possible exceptions, but any exception is not handled directly there in the method. An exception will be thrown and caught "higher up" the chain, in the main method, where it is handled by the appropriate catch block.

This is also where you might encounter try blocks without catch blocks. When a method throws an exception (to be caught higher up), it will interrupt the execution of the method. Therefore, you may need a finally block to take care of things, like open resources, before exiting the method. Consider just the previous scanValues() method. You can see that there are no catch blocks, so you might use a try/finally here instead of the try with resources. Any exception will be thrown up, but the scanner will be closed in the finally block before exiting.

```
    // method asks for and scans three doubles:
    // principle, interest rate, and loan years
    public static double[] scanValues() throws InputMismatchException {
        double[] values = new double[3];
        Scanner scan = new Scanner(System.in);
        try {
            System.out.print("Enter the loan amount: ");
            values[0] = scan.nextDouble();
            System.out.print("Enter the interest rate: ");
            values[1] = scan.nextDouble();
            System.out.print("Enter the loan term (in years): ");
            values[2] = scan.nextInt();
        } finally {
            scan.close();
        }
        return values;
    }
```

DEBUGGING YOUR APPLICATIONS

In the previous section, you debugged a small program while you learned about the kinds of errors, or bugs, that you will encounter. One technique you saw was using `System.out.println()` messages to see what was happening at different points in your program. This is still used a lot, as a quick-and-dirty approach to debugging. But it is not ideal for a number of reasons. For one, it's not particularly elegant to fill up your code with print statements. It can be messy and you will not only have to add them in all the places you want to investigate, but you'll also have to carefully remove them afterward. Other debugging approaches offer more flexibility and functionality. In this section, you'll see and use debugger and logger tools to debug better.

Using a Debugger Tool

In the first part of this chapter, you learned about different kinds of errors or bugs. Because the example problems were small, it was relatively easy to spot the bugs yourself. As your applications grow, it may become difficult to track down each bug just by looking through the code and outputs, and even the error messages may not shed sufficient light on the problem. Eclipse and other development environments offer debugging tools to support this process. Essentially, a debugger allows you, the programmer, to execute a program step-by-step to see exactly what's happening at each line.

In order to control the debugging process, you need to set breakpoints on particular lines of code. When the program hits a breakpoint while running in debug mode, the execution will pause so you can review the current state of the program and the value of the variables at this point in time. You can then continue to the next breakpoint. This allows you to see exactly where something goes wrong.

To illustrate the process of debugging using the debugger tool, start from the small retirement fund program you saw earlier:

```java
public class Errors {

    public static void main(String[] args) {
        int age = 30;
        double retirementFund = 10000;
        int yearsInRetirement = 20;
        String name = "David Johnson";
        for (int i = age; i <= 65; i++){
            recalculate(retirementFund, 0.1);
        }
        double monthlyPension = retirementFund/yearsInRetirement/12;
        System.out.println(name + " will have $" + monthlyPension
                + " per month for retirement.");
    }

    public static void recalculate(double fundAmount, double rate){
        fundAmount = fundAmount*(1+rate);
    }

}
```

Recall that when running the program at this stage, the result was much lower than expected. You would like to find the bug and you've narrowed it down to two possibilities. The actual `recalculate` method might be programmed wrong or the `for` loop might not be using the method correctly. Therefore, you can place a breakpoint in each place to see what's happening there.

To place a breakpoint, move your cursor to the left of the line number you're interested in. You can either double-click there or right-click and select Toggle Breakpoint. You should see a small dot appear next to the line number, as shown in Figure 6-10.

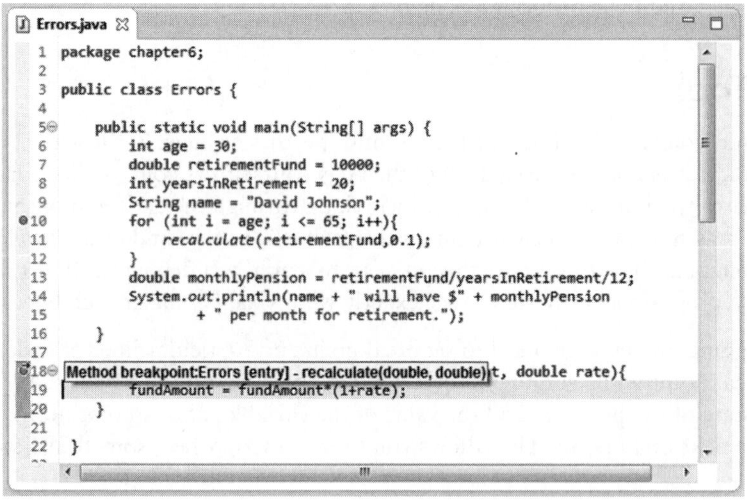

```java
1  package chapter6;
2
3  public class Errors {
4
5    public static void main(String[] args) {
6      int age = 30;
7      double retirementFund = 10000;
8      int yearsInRetirement = 20;
9      String name = "David Johnson";
10      for (int i = age; i <= 65; i++){
11        recalculate(retirementFund,0.1);
12      }
13      double monthlyPension = retirementFund/yearsInRetirement/12;
14      System.out.println(name + " will have $" + monthlyPension
15          + " per month for retirement.");
16    }
17
18    Method breakpoint:Errors [entry] - recalculate(double, double) t, double rate){
19        fundAmount = fundAmount*(1+rate);
20    }
21
22  }
```

FIGURE 6-10

Once your breakpoints are set, all you need to do is open the debug perspective. There are several ways to do this:

1. Click the Bug icon.

2. Click Run and then select Debug.

3. Right-click on the .java file in the navigator, select Debug As, then Java application.

4. Press F11 on your keyboard.

Eclipse will ask if you would like to switch to the Debug perspective. Select Yes and your layout will change. See Figure 6-11.

You will still see the `Errors` class and the outline and console look the same as the normal Java perspective. In addition, you will see at the top the Debug window and the names and values of the variables in your program. One thing to keep in mind is that the variables displayed depend on the method your program is currently inside and how much of that method has already been executed, so you can see the variables from the `main` method until just before the `for` loop, since this is your first breakpoint.

The program is paused here, waiting for your instructions. To control the execution, you can use the buttons built into Eclipse or the F5–F8 keys on your keyboard.

FIGURE 6-11

➤ **Step Into (F5):** Executes the current line and moves to the next line. Moves through the program step-by-step.

➤ **Step Over (F6):** Executes the current method without showing each step in the debugger tool. Lets the subroutines run in the background, but keeps the debugger in the main routine.

➤ **Step Return (F7):** Finishes executing the current method in the background and returns to the main routine.

➤ **Resume (F8):** Executes everything until the next breakpoint or the end of the program if there are no further breakpoints. Does not show everything step-by-step.

All of these have buttons in the program as well. You can find them at the top of the screen. See Figure 6-12.

FIGURE 6-12

For this small example, Step Into (F5) is fine to move through each step and check what is happening to the variables. Watch the variables change as you step into the `for` loop. First, the variable `i` (the iterator of the `for` loop) is added to the list and takes the value `30` (from the `age` variable). This is exactly what you should expect. See Figure 6-13.

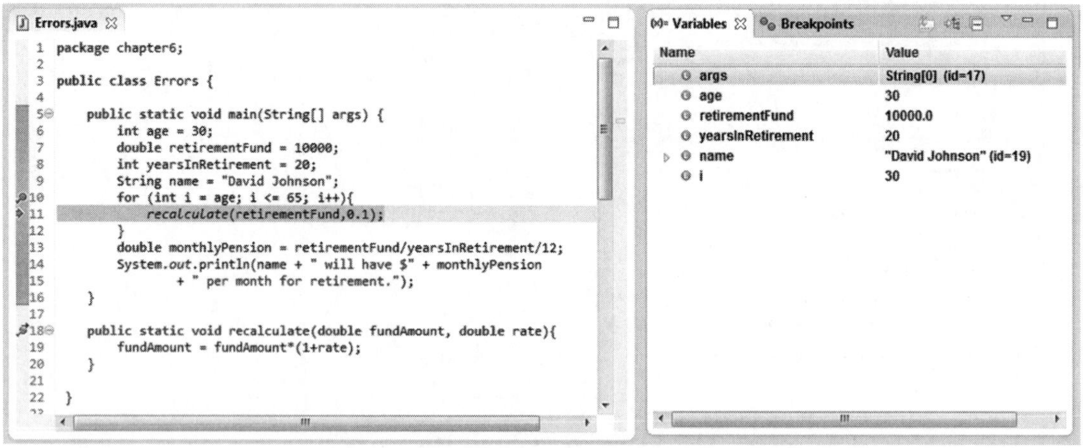

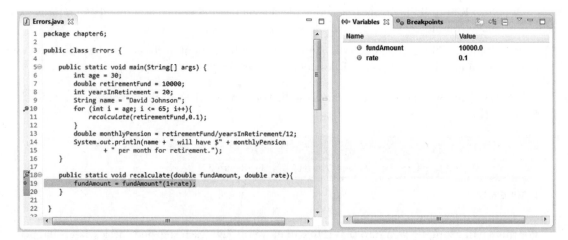

FIGURE 6-13

Next, the program steps into the `recalculate` method and the variables associated with the method are displayed: `fundAmount = 10000` and `rate = 0.1`. See Figure 6-14.

Notice in Figure 6-15 how a variable is highlighted in yellow when its value changes. After the method body is executed, the result is `fundAmount = 11000`, just as you would expect for a 10% increase.

Next, the program returns to the `for` loop and you can watch the iterator `i` increase to `31`. See Figure 6-16.

FIGURE 6-14

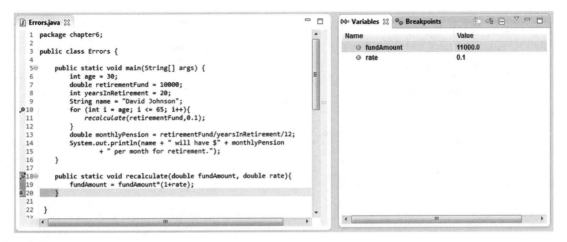

FIGURE 6-15

When you step into the `recalculate` method again, `fundAmount` is back to its original `10000`, as shown in Figure 6-17.

So now you can see that the newly calculated `fundAmount` is not being stored anywhere after the `recalculate` method is exited. This leads to the same conclusion as before, that the method should return a value, and the `main` method should reuse the returned value.

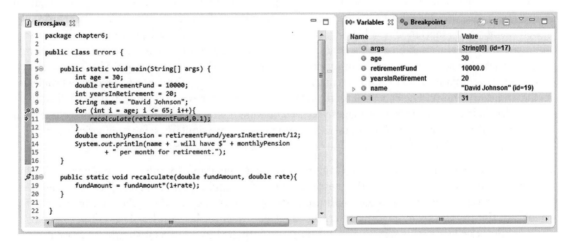

FIGURE 6-16

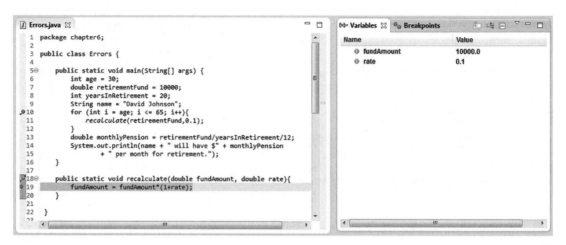

FIGURE 6-17

Using a Logging API

An alternative approach to debugging is using a *logger* to create log messages about the execution of your program. There is a built-in logging API in the `java.util.logging` package, which you will see here, but there are also several popular external APIs built for logging that you can try on your own. Logging allows you to check what's happening while you're developing, but it also offers a way to continue to monitor a program that's in use. You can configure your logger to log on different levels, to output to places other than the console, and to customize the output to whatever is most useful for the application.

There are eight predefined logging levels: Off, Finest, Finer, Fine, Config, Info, Warning, and Severe. As the name suggests, the Off level indicates no logging at all. The Finest level is designed for development and testing and logs the most messages. This is not appropriate for live applications, as the speed slows considerably with this amount of logging. As you move up through the levels, fewer and fewer messages are logged. The Finer and Fine levels offer less detailed messages. Info logs messages that give information about what is happening in the program, including connections and messages. The Warning level logs messages that indicate problems, while the Severe level only logs those most concerning problems that indicate a failure. The benefit of all these levels is that you can set up logging and then adjust the level depending on the types of messages you need or want to see, without making any changes to your program. The levels are organized numerically and messages are similarly scored numerically. In this way, a message with an importance value of 3 will be logged in any level 3 or higher.

There are two main components to a logging system: a logger and a handler. The *logger* picks up messages and checks the level of the message against the logging level in place. If the message seems to fit the level (or above), the logger will use a filter to determine for sure if the message should be logged. If it passes this more strict filter, the message is sent to the handler. The *handler* may also use a filter to check the message and a formatter to format the record as it should be written.

The process of logging is designed to offer flexibility, and for that reason, there are a lot of possibilities in how you set up and use your logger. This section only begins to scratch the surface, so that you can add a basic logger to your program and access the log messages. To begin logging, you should create a logger instance, using the `getLogger()` method, in each class you wish to log. Typically, this should be static and final, indicating that one single logger will be used for all instances of the class and it will remain unchanged. The logger will automatically include a default console handler that will print messages to the console. You can create additional handlers yourself. If you want your log files to be saved to a text file somewhere, you can create your own file handler.

Once your logger and handlers are created, you should create a special method that will essentially set them up for use. In the example, this is called method `logIt()`, but you can change the name. Inside this method, you should instantiate the file handlers with the path and name of the file where you would like to save the log messages. Because `IOExceptions` are checked exceptions, you need to put these in a `try/catch` block to handle the error. Next, you can set the formatter and level for each handler, attach the handlers to the logger, and set the level of the logger. Both the logger and the handlers can be independently set to their own level. However, if the logger is higher than the handler level, the handler level will effectively be at the logger's level, because no lower level messages will be generated by the logger. In the example, you see two handlers for the same logger. This allows more messages to be output to one file while fewer (more important) messages are output to another file.

Now you are ready to use the logger in your `main` and other methods. You can call methods from the `Logger` class to log the information you're interested in. The entire list of methods can be found in the `Logger` class documentation, but some of the methods you will see are listed here. Each method also has several parameter choices you can make that impact the results of the log.

➤ `entering()`: Log a method entry.

➤ `exiting()`: Log a method return.

➤ `log()`: Log a custom message.

The example is based on the retirement fund program you've been working with. There are now log messages indicating when the `recalculate` method is entered and exited, as well as the value of the `fundAmount` variable each time it is calculated. Finally, a log message is created if the value is extremely low, indicating something is wrong with the calculation. And at the end of the `main` method, several messages are logged at each level to demonstrate which ones are written by each handler.

```java
import java.io.IOException;
import java.util.logging.*;

public class LoggerExample {
    // create a Logger instance
    private final static Logger logger =
        Logger.getLogger(LoggerExample.class.getName());

    // create a file handler for fine messages and above
    private static FileHandler finerhandler = null;
    // create a file handler only for config messages and above
    private static FileHandler warninghandler = null;

    public static void logIt() {
        try {
            finerhandler = new FileHandler("src/loggerExample_finer.log", false);
            warninghandler = new FileHandler("src/loggerExample_config.log",false);
        } catch (SecurityException | IOException e) {
```

```java
            e.printStackTrace();
        }

        // attach a basic formatter and set the level
        finerhandler.setFormatter(new SimpleFormatter());
        //this handler will print all messages to its log
        finerhandler.setLevel(Level.FINER);

        // attach a basic formatter and set the level
        warninghandler.setFormatter(new SimpleFormatter());
        //this handler will only print warning and severe messages to its log
        warninghandler.setLevel(Level.CONFIG);

        // attach the handler
        logger.addHandler(finerhandler);
        logger.addHandler(warninghandler);

        // set the level to FINEST
        // (log ALL messages)
        logger.setLevel(Level.FINER);

    }

    public static void main(String[] args) {
        // set up the logger using the logIt() static method above
        // without this, only the default console handler will log
        // with this, the handlers created above will log
        LoggerExample.logIt();

        int age = 60;
        double retirementFund = 10000;
        int yearsInRetirement = 20;
        String name = "David Johnson";
        for (int i = age; i <= 65; i++) {
            recalculate(retirementFund, 0.1);
        }
        double monthlyPension = retirementFund / yearsInRetirement / 12;
        System.out.println(name + " will have $" + monthlyPension
                + " per month for retirement.");
        if (monthlyPension < 100) {
            // create a log entry (level: SEVERE) indicating a
            // problem with the calculation
            logger.log(Level.SEVERE, "monthlyPension is too low.");
        }

        // create a series of log entries to show which
        // levels are printed to which handler's log
        logger.log(Level.FINEST, "finest detailed message");
        logger.log(Level.FINER, "finer detailed message");
        logger.log(Level.FINE, "fine detailed message");
        logger.log(Level.CONFIG, "configuration message");
        logger.log(Level.INFO, "informational message");
        logger.log(Level.WARNING, "warning message");
        logger.log(Level.SEVERE, "severe message");
    }
```

```java
    public static void recalculate(double fundAmount, double rate) {
        // create a log entry (level: FINER) indicating the method entry
        logger.entering("LoggerExample","recalculate");

        fundAmount = fundAmount * (1 + rate);

        // create a log entry (level: INFO) indicating
        // the current value of fundAmount
        logger.log(Level.INFO, "fundAmount = " + fundAmount);

        // create a log entry (level: FINER) indicating the method return
        logger.exiting("LoggerExample", "recalculate");
    }
}
```

The contents of the finer log file look like this:

```
Aug 12, 2014 5:54:43 PM LoggerExample recalculate
FINER: ENTRY
Aug 12, 2014 5:54:43 PM chapter6.LoggerExample recalculate
INFO: fundAmount = 11000.0
Aug 12, 2014 5:54:43 PM LoggerExample recalculate
FINER: RETURN
Aug 12, 2014 5:54:43 PM LoggerExample recalculate
FINER: ENTRY
Aug 12, 2014 5:54:43 PM chapter6.LoggerExample recalculate
INFO: fundAmount = 11000.0
Aug 12, 2014 5:54:43 PM LoggerExample recalculate
FINER: RETURN
Aug 12, 2014 5:54:43 PM LoggerExample recalculate
FINER: ENTRY
Aug 12, 2014 5:54:43 PM chapter6.LoggerExample recalculate
INFO: fundAmount = 11000.0
Aug 12, 2014 5:54:43 PM LoggerExample recalculate
FINER: RETURN
Aug 12, 2014 5:54:43 PM LoggerExample recalculate
FINER: ENTRY
Aug 12, 2014 5:54:43 PM chapter6.LoggerExample recalculate
INFO: fundAmount = 11000.0
Aug 12, 2014 5:54:43 PM LoggerExample recalculate
FINER: RETURN
Aug 12, 2014 5:54:43 PM LoggerExample recalculate
FINER: ENTRY
Aug 12, 2014 5:54:43 PM chapter6.LoggerExample recalculate
INFO: fundAmount = 11000.0
Aug 12, 2014 5:54:43 PM LoggerExample recalculate
FINER: RETURN
Aug 12, 2014 5:54:43 PM LoggerExample recalculate
FINER: ENTRY
Aug 12, 2014 5:54:43 PM chapter6.LoggerExample recalculate
INFO: fundAmount = 11000.0
Aug 12, 2014 5:54:43 PM LoggerExample recalculate
FINER: RETURN
Aug 12, 2014 5:54:43 PM chapter6.LoggerExample main
SEVERE: monthlyPension is too low.
```

```
Aug 12, 2014 5:54:43 PM chapter6.LoggerExample main
FINER: finer detailed message
Aug 12, 2014 5:54:43 PM chapter6.LoggerExample main
FINE: fine detailed message
Aug 12, 2014 5:54:43 PM chapter6.LoggerExample main
CONFIG: configuration message
Aug 12, 2014 5:54:43 PM chapter6.LoggerExample main
INFO: informational message
Aug 12, 2014 5:54:43 PM chapter6.LoggerExample main
WARNING: warning message
Aug 12, 2014 5:54:43 PM chapter6.LoggerExample main
SEVERE: severe message
```

The contents of the config log file look like this:

```
Aug 12, 2014 5:54:43 PM chapter6.LoggerExample recalculate
INFO: fundAmount = 11000.0
Aug 12, 2014 5:54:43 PM chapter6.LoggerExample recalculate
INFO: fundAmount = 11000.0
Aug 12, 2014 5:54:43 PM chapter6.LoggerExample recalculate
INFO: fundAmount = 11000.0
Aug 12, 2014 5:54:43 PM chapter6.LoggerExample recalculate
INFO: fundAmount = 11000.0
Aug 12, 2014 5:54:43 PM chapter6.LoggerExample recalculate
INFO: fundAmount = 11000.0
Aug 12, 2014 5:54:43 PM chapter6.LoggerExample recalculate
INFO: fundAmount = 11000.0
Aug 12, 2014 5:54:43 PM chapter6.LoggerExample main
SEVERE: monthlyPension is too low.
Aug 12, 2014 5:54:43 PM chapter6.LoggerExample main
CONFIG: configuration message
Aug 12, 2014 5:54:43 PM chapter6.LoggerExample main
INFO: informational message
Aug 12, 2014 5:54:43 PM chapter6.LoggerExample main
WARNING: warning message
Aug 12, 2014 5:54:43 PM chapter6.LoggerExample main
SEVERE: severe message
```

Naturally, there are many more messages in the finer log file, because it includes more levels (particularly, the entering and exiting messages, which are defined as finer level messages). Also, note that neither log contains the "finest detailed message" from the main method. This is too low level for the finer logger to log. You can see again here that the fundAmount is 11000 every time the method is called, again suggesting that the value is not being stored and used in future calculations. But you can see for sure that the method is being entered and exited as expected. This leads to the same conclusion (and fix) as before, but logging allows ongoing monitoring of live applications. Simply by increasing the level of the logger, you can control how many and what types of messages are logged.

So far, you've only seen the built-in logger, but Log4j is a popular alternative logger. The Log4j utility has been in use for 15 years, but Apache Log4j 2 was released in 2014. It offers high performance, flexibility, and usability, and is well worth your consideration when deciding on a logging utility. You can download Log4j 2 at http://logging.apache.org/log4j/2.x/index.html.

Log4j has different levels defined than the ones used by the built-in logger. TRACE is the most detailed level, followed by DEBUG, INFO, WARN, ERROR, and FATAL, which is the least detailed level. There is also OFF to turn off logging. The methods differ from the built-in logger as well. In the previous example, you saw:

```
logger.log(Level.INFO, "informational message");
```

With Log4j, you would write:

```
logger.info("informational message");
```

To demonstrate the use of Log4j and compare it to the built-in logger, this next Try It Out repeats the previous example.

TRY IT OUT Logging with Apache Log4j 2

In this exercise, you'll set up logging in a small program using Apache's Log4j 2 logging utility.

1. Download the Apache Log4j 2 from the Apache website.

2. Attach two .jar files to the build path of the project you're working in: log4j-api-2.0.1.jar and log4j-core-2.0.1.jar.

3. Create a new class called ApacheLogging.

4. Import the logger and LogManager from Log4j and create a new logger object for the class.

```
import org.apache.logging.log4j.Logger;
import org.apache.logging.log4j.LogManager;

public class ApacheLogging {

    static final Logger log = LogManager.getLogger(ApacheLogging.class.getName());

}
```

5. Add two methods, main and recalculate, similar to the previous example, but without the logging for now.

```
public static void main(String[] args) {
    int age = 60;
    double retirementFund = 10000;
    int yearsInRetirement = 20;
    String name = "David Johnson";
    for (int i = age; i <= 65; i++) {
        recalculate(retirementFund, 0.1);
    }
    double monthlyPension = retirementFund / yearsInRetirement / 12;
    System.out.println(name + " will have $" + monthlyPension
            + " per month for retirement.");
    if (monthlyPension < 100) {
        System.out.println("monthlyPension is too low.");
    }
```

```
    }

    public static void recalculate(double fundAmount, double rate) {
        fundAmount = fundAmount * (1 + rate);
    }
```

6. Now, replace the `System.out.println()` statement with a log message: `logger.fatal("monthlyPension is too low.");`

7. Next, add some messages to test the different levels of the logger at the end of the `main` method.

```
    log.trace("finely detailed TRACE message");
    log.debug("detailed DEBUG message");
    log.info("informational message");
    log.warn("warning message");
    log.error("error message");
    log.fatal("fatal message");
```

8. Finally, add log messages to the `recalculate()` method.

```
    log.entry();
    fundAmount = fundAmount * (1 + rate);
    log.info("fundAmount = " + fundAmount);
    log.exit();
```

9. Your class should now look like this:

```
import org.apache.logging.log4j.Logger;
import org.apache.logging.log4j.LogManager;

public class ApacheLogging {

    static final Logger log = LogManager.getLogger(ApacheLogging.class.getName());

    public static void main(String[] args) {
        int age = 60;
        double retirementFund = 10000;
        int yearsInRetirement = 20;
        String name = "David Johnson";
        for (int i = age; i <= 65; i++) {
            recalculate(retirementFund, 0.1);
        }
        double monthlyPension = retirementFund / yearsInRetirement / 12;
        System.out.println(name + " will have $" + monthlyPension
                + " per month for retirement.");
        if (monthlyPension < 100) {
            log.fatal("monthlyPension is too low");
        }

        // create a series of log entries to show which
        // levels are printed to which handler's log
        log.trace("finely detailed TRACE message");
        log.debug("detailed DEBUG message");
        log.info("informational message");
```

```
            log.warn("warning message");
            log.error("error message");
            log.fatal("fatal message");
        }

        public static void recalculate(double fundAmount, double rate) {
            log.entry();
            fundAmount = fundAmount * (1 + rate);
            log.info("fundAmount = " + fundAmount);
            log.exit();
        }
    }
```

10. Run your program. Your output should look like this:

```
David Johnson will have $41.666666666666664 per month for retirement.
13:39:10.511 [main] FATAL chapter6.ApacheLogging - monthlyPension is too low
13:39:10.514 [main] ERROR chapter6.ApacheLogging - error message
13:39:10.514 [main] FATAL chapter6.ApacheLogging - fatal message
```

11. You only see these log messages because the default log level is set to `Error`. You can of course adjust this, and many other settings. In Log4j, this is done using an `.xml` configuration file.

12. Create your configuration file by opening a new text file and copying the following `.xml` code into it:

```xml
<?xml version="1.0" encoding="UTF-8"?>
<Configuration status="WARN">
  <Appenders>
    <Console name="Console" target="SYSTEM_OUT">
      <PatternLayout pattern="%d{HH:mm:ss.SSS} [%t] %-5level %logger{36} - %msg%n"/>
    </Console>
  </Appenders>
  <Loggers>
    <Root level="error">
      <AppenderRef ref="Console"/>
    </Root>
  </Loggers>
</Configuration>
```

13. This code essentially sets the configuration file according to the default configuration. Save the file as `:Log4j2.xml` and place it in the `src` folder for your project. Here you can change the root level and output destination.

14. First, change `<Root level="error">` to `<Root level="trace">`. Run your program and you'll see all the error messages output to the console.

```
14:18:30.719 [main] TRACE chapter6.ApacheLogging - entry
14:18:30.720 [main] INFO  chapter6.ApacheLogging - fundAmount = 11000.0
14:18:30.720 [main] TRACE chapter6.ApacheLogging - exit
14:18:30.720 [main] TRACE chapter6.ApacheLogging - entry
14:18:30.720 [main] INFO  chapter6.ApacheLogging - fundAmount = 11000.0
14:18:30.720 [main] TRACE chapter6.ApacheLogging - exit
14:18:30.720 [main] TRACE chapter6.ApacheLogging - entry
```

```
14:18:30.720 [main] INFO  chapter6.ApacheLogging - fundAmount = 11000.0
14:18:30.720 [main] TRACE chapter6.ApacheLogging - exit
14:18:30.720 [main] TRACE chapter6.ApacheLogging - entry
14:18:30.720 [main] INFO  chapter6.ApacheLogging - fundAmount = 11000.0
14:18:30.720 [main] TRACE chapter6.ApacheLogging - exit
14:18:30.720 [main] TRACE chapter6.ApacheLogging - entry
14:18:30.720 [main] INFO  chapter6.ApacheLogging - fundAmount = 11000.0
14:18:30.720 [main] TRACE chapter6.ApacheLogging - exit
14:18:30.720 [main] TRACE chapter6.ApacheLogging - entry
14:18:30.720 [main] INFO  chapter6.ApacheLogging - fundAmount = 11000.0
14:18:30.720 [main] TRACE chapter6.ApacheLogging - exit
David Johnson will have $41.666666666666664 per month for retirement.
14:18:30.720 [main] FATAL chapter6.ApacheLogging - monthlyPension is too low
14:18:30.720 [main] TRACE chapter6.ApacheLogging - finely detailed TRACE message
14:18:30.721 [main] DEBUG chapter6.ApacheLogging - detailed DEBUG message
14:18:30.721 [main] INFO  chapter6.ApacheLogging - informational message
14:18:30.721 [main] WARN  chapter6.ApacheLogging - warning message
14:18:30.721 [main] ERROR chapter6.ApacheLogging - error message
14:18:30.721 [main] FATAL chapter6.ApacheLogging - fatal message
```

15. Remember how you set up file handlers at different levels and with different output files in the previous example? You can do the same thing here, in the configuration file, by adding and editing appenders, files, and loggers. In the configuration file, under `</Console>`, add two new files to the appenders section. In the code here, `ApacheLog-Warn` is stored at `c:/users/n12063/ApacheLogging_Warn.log`. Make sure you use a filename that indicates a usable location on your own computer.

```
<Appenders>
    <Console name="Console" target="SYSTEM_OUT">
        <PatternLayout pattern="%d{HH:mm:ss.SSS} [%t] %-5level %logger{36}
                - %msg%n"/>
    </Console>
    <File name="ApacheLog-Info" filename=
            "c:/users/n12063/ApacheLogging_Info.log">
        <PatternLayout>
            <pattern>[%-5level] %d{yyyy-MM-dd HH:mm:ss.SSS} [%t] %c{1}
                    - %msg%n</pattern>
        </PatternLayout>
    </File>
    <File name="ApacheLog-Warn" filename="src/ApacheLogging_Warn.log">
        <PatternLayout>
            <pattern>[%-5level] %d{yyyy-MM-dd HH:mm:ss.SSS} [%t] %c{1}
                    - %msg%n</pattern>
        </PatternLayout>
    </File>
</Appenders>
```

16. Next, adjust the loggers section to add these new appenders to the root logger.

```
<Loggers>
    <Root level="debug">
        <AppenderRef ref="Console" level="fatal"/>
        <AppenderRef ref="ApacheLog-Info" level="info"/>
        <AppenderRef ref="ApacheLog-Warn" level="warn"/>
    </Root>
</Loggers>
```

17. The full configuration file should resemble this:

```xml
<?xml version="1.0" encoding="UTF-8"?>
<Configuration status="WARN">
    <Properties>
        <Property name="log-path">logs</Property>
    </Properties>
    <Appenders>
        <Console name="Console" target="SYSTEM_OUT">
            <PatternLayout pattern="%d{HH:mm:ss.SSS} [%t] %-5level %logger{36}
                    - %msg%n"/>
        </Console>
        <File name="ApacheLog-Info" filename=
                "c:/users/n12063/ApacheLogging_Info.log">
            <PatternLayout>
                <pattern>[%-5level] %d{yyyy-MM-dd HH:mm:ss.SSS} [%t] %c{1}
                        - %msg%n</pattern>
            </PatternLayout>
        </File>
        <File name="ApacheLog-Warn" filename="src/ApacheLogging_Warn.log">
            <PatternLayout>
                <pattern>[%-5level] %d{yyyy-MM-dd HH:mm:ss.SSS} [%t] %c{1}
                        - %msg%n</pattern>
            </PatternLayout>
        </File>
    </Appenders>
    <Loggers>
        <Root level="debug">
            <AppenderRef ref="Console" level="fatal"/>
            <AppenderRef ref="ApacheLog-Info" level="info"/>
            <AppenderRef ref="ApacheLog-Warn" level="warn"/>
        </Root>
    </Loggers>
</Configuration>
```

18. Now, you can run your program again. This time you should get a console output like this:

```
David Johnson will have $41.666666666666664 per month for retirement.
15:59:15.846 [main] FATAL chapter6.ApacheLogging - monthlyPension is too low
15:59:15.847 [main] FATAL chapter6.ApacheLogging - fatal message
```

19. Your log files should be stored in the designated folders on your computer. If you cannot locate them, try searching for the names `ApacheLogging_Info` and `ApacheLogging_Warn` using your computer's search function. You'll notice that files created in the `src` folder don't automatically show up in Eclipse. If you place the file there in Eclipse yourself, your program will write to it during execution and you'll be able to view it from Eclipse.

How It Works

Here's how it works:

1. By attaching and importing the Log4j 2 API, you're allowing your program to use these resources.

2. Very similarly to the example using the built-in logger, you created a single static logger object for use in this class.

3. Using the methods included in Log4j 2, you can create log messages of various importance levels.

4. Without creating any configuration file, there is a default logger that prints messages at the Error level or higher to the console.

5. By editing this configuration file, you can control which level of messages get printed and where they will be printed.

6. In the appenders section, you added two files. These create log files in which log messages can be written. Files require name and filename fields. In the filename file, you should include the path to the file. They should also be given a `PatternLayout`, which specifies how the messages will be formatted. In this exercise, they are named according to the level they will be assigned. One of the log files is stored in the `src` folder of the project you are working in. The other will be stored on the hard drive of the machine, as indicated in the filename.

7. In the loggers section, you can add new loggers or you can attach appenders to the root logger. This is similar to the approach with the built-in logger, where handlers were added to the logger.

8. You can control the level of the logger separately from the level of the appenders. Both of these are set in the loggers section. Here, you have to set the root level to debug, meaning that all log messages will be accepted by the logger. However, the three appender levels are set to fatal, info, and warn, so only those set to info and above will be used in the output. Only fatal messages will be printed to the console. Info level and above will be printed to the `ApacheLog_Info.log` file, and warn level and above will be printed to the `ApacheLog_Warn.log` file.

You've seen two types of logging utilities, a built-in version from Java and an open source API from Apache. Although they function similarly, there may be reasons to choose one over the other. Many developers are choosing Log4j over the built-in tool, not only because of its functionality, but because there are some criticisms of the implementation of the built-in logger. There are also several other well-known loggers that you may want to investigate further. Hopefully, the examples in this section have provided you with a foundation to begin logging your programs, as well as a basic understanding from which you can investigate other tools and the other options within the two tools presented here.

TESTING YOUR APPLICATIONS

Unit testing is another way you can ensure the completeness and correctness of your applications. It allows you to develop small test scenarios to check each aspect of your program. This offers some benefits over debugging from the `main` method. First, you can begin testing even when only small parts of your application are written. In fact, some development styles start from test cases and then write code that will satisfy the test. Compared to debugging from the `main` method, you can start testing much earlier in the process and may be able to find and fix problems early and before they impact many other areas of the development. Once your test cases are prepared, then any changes you make to the program later can be checked quickly by running the tests again to see if you've accidentally introduced new errors. Also, professional developers are not usually creating an entire program; they are working on pieces that will be integrated later. In this case, a `main` method doesn't really make much sense, but test units can provide confidence that the units themselves are functioning properly before trying to fit them together in the end. JUnit is a commonly used testing framework, which is also included in Eclipse.

To begin, you can create a JUnit test case the same way you create a new class. Eventually, you will create a test case for a class you've already developed, but practice with a standalone test case first. You create a new JUnit test case under File ➤ New ➤ JUnit Test Case or by right-clicking in the Navigator and selecting New ➤ JUnit Test Case. Name your test case JUnitTest. There are checkboxes next to several methods; select setUpBeforClass(), setUp(), tearDownAfterClass(), and tearDown() to create auto stubs. Finally, make sure the "Class Under Test" field is blank, since you are not testing a class right now. Press Finish to create your test case. You should have a class that looks like this:

```java
import static org.junit.Assert.*;

import org.junit.Before;
import org.junit.BeforeClass;
import org.junit.Test;

public class JUnitTest {

    @BeforeClass
    public static void setUpBeforeClass() throws Exception {
    }

    @AfterClass
    public static void tearDownAfterClass() throws Exception {
    }

    @Before
    public void setUp() throws Exception {
    }

    @After
    public void tearDown() throws Exception {
    }

    @Test
    public void test() {
        fail("Not yet implemented");
    }
}
```

The text beginning with the @ symbol are called *annotations*, and these indicate the purpose of specific methods. You will see more annotations as you move through later chapters in the book. The difference between comments and annotations is that annotations can be processed during compilation. Therefore, you should be careful to use the annotations correctly. There are five annotations you will see in JUnit tests: @Test, @BeforeClass, @AfterClass, @Before, and @After. The first, @Test, annotates each test method. There is no universally accepted naming convention for test methods, but it makes sense to name them in a way that makes it clear what you are testing and under what conditions.

The other four annotations allow you to prepare some objects and resources for use before your tests begin and to close out things appropriately after your tests are finished. The two setup methods, annotated @BeforeClass and @Before, are used to create necessary objects for testing. The first type, @ BeforeClass, is run once before anything else, and the results will be shared by all the tests. This is helpful for timely processes like logging into a database. The second type, annotated @Before, runs once before each test, so multiple times in a series of tests. Annotating computationally expensive processes as @Before will slow your overall testing down. The tear-down methods actually function similarly to the finally block of a try-catch-finally statement. If you allocate resources using a @Before method, you will need to release them using an @After method. If you allocate resources using a @BeforeClass method, you need to release them using an @AfterClass method. Just as the @BeforeClass runs once before everything else starts, @AfterClass runs exactly once after everything else finishes. Similarly, @After methods will run after each test. These @After and @AfterClass methods will run even if there is an exception thrown, just like the finally block.

Assertions are the main component you will use in your JUnit tests. There are several assert methods that allow you to state what you expect and the tests will check if it's correct. Any incorrect assert statement will result in a test failure. Here is a list of some assert methods you might find useful in your tests:

➤ assertEquals(a, b): Expect a and b to be equal.

➤ assertArrayEquals(arrayA, arrayB): Expect all elements in A and B to be equal.

➤ assertTrue(a): Expect a to be true.

➤ assertFalse(b): Expect b to be false.

➤ assertNull(a): Expect a to be null.

➤ assertNotNull(b): Expect b to not be null.

➤ assertSame(a,b): Expect a and b to reference the same object.

➤ assertNotSame(a,b): Expect a and b not to reference the same object.

> **NOTE** The assertEquals() method is slightly different for different data types. As you have seen previously, some number types like doubles are not precise due to rounding. To accommodate these shortcomings, the assertEquals() method for doubles or floats has an additional parameter, called epsilon, which allows you to choose how different two doubles can be and still be considered equal values. The format is then: assertEquals(double a, double b, double epsilon) or assertEquals(1.51, 1.52, 0.01), for example.

With these concepts, you're ready to start testing. You can start by declaring some objects that you will use for the tests. A static Scanner object is used just to symbolize the resources that you might need for your tests; it is initialized in the setUpBeforeClass() method and closed in the tearDownAfterClass() method. Some integers, an array, and an object are also added to compare values using the assert methods. The ints are initialized in the setup() method. Then using these (and the other variables created in the test methods), each of the assert methods is demonstrated. The entire test class looks like this:

```
import static org.junit.Assert.*;

import java.util.Scanner;
```

```java
import org.junit.After;
import org.junit.AfterClass;
import org.junit.Before;
import org.junit.BeforeClass;
import org.junit.Test;

public class JUnitTest {
    static Scanner scan;
    int myIntA, myIntB, myIntC;
    int[] myArrayA = {0,1,2};
    Object myObject;

    @BeforeClass
    public static void setUpBeforeClass() throws Exception {
        // access resources for use in the tests
        scan = new Scanner(System.in);

    }

    @AfterClass
    public static void tearDownAfterClass() throws Exception {
        // close resources after all tests complete
        scan.close();
    }

    @Before
    public void setUp() throws Exception {
        // assign some values to the variables
        // before beginning each test
        myIntA = 5;
        myIntB = 6;
        myIntC = 7;
    }

    @After
    public void tearDown() throws Exception {
        //nothing needs to be torn down
    }

    @Test
    public void testAssertEquals() {
        // (5 + 1) equals 6
        assertEquals((myIntA + 1), myIntB);
    }

    @Test
    public void testAssertArrayEquals() {
        int[] myNewArray = {0,1,2};
        // the elements in both arrays are 0, 1, and 2
        // order matters: {0,1,2} != {0,2,1}
        assertArrayEquals(myArrayA, myNewArray);
    }

    @Test
    public void testAssertTrue() {
```

```
        // 7 > 5
        assertTrue(myIntC > myIntA);
    }

    @Test
    public void testAssertFalse() {
        // myArrayA.length == 3, 3 != 4
        assertFalse(myArrayA.length == 4);
    }

    @Test
    public void testAssertNull() {
        // myObject has not been intialized
        assertNull(myObject);
    }

    @Test
    public void testAssertNotNull() {
        String newString = "Hello";
        // newString is intialized
        assertNotNull(newString);
    }

    @Test
    public void testAssertSame() {
        myObject = new Object();
        Object pointerA = myObject;
        Object pointerB = myObject;
        // both pointerA and pointerB reference myObject
        assertSame(pointerA,pointerB);
    }

    @Test
    public void testAssertNotSame() {
        myObject = new Object();
        Object pointerA = new Object();
        Object pointerB = myObject;
        // pointerA is a new Object,
        // pointerB references myObject
        assertNotSame(pointerA,pointerB);
    }
}
```

Once your test methods are written, you can run the test class the same way you run a normal program. You can also specify "Run as JUnit Test" if Eclipse does not automatically recognize it as a JUnit test and run it appropriately. The JUnit panel will take the place of the Navigator, and you will see a report of how many tests have been run, the number of errors, and the number of failures. If there is a failure, you can also see more information about the failure in the Failure Trace. In Figure 6-18, you can see a comparison of two runs: one with a failure and the other without any failures. In the failure case, the test method that resulted in failure—testAssertArrayEquals—is highlighted. Figure 6-18 also shows why it failed: element [1] in the first array was 1, but in the second array it was 2.

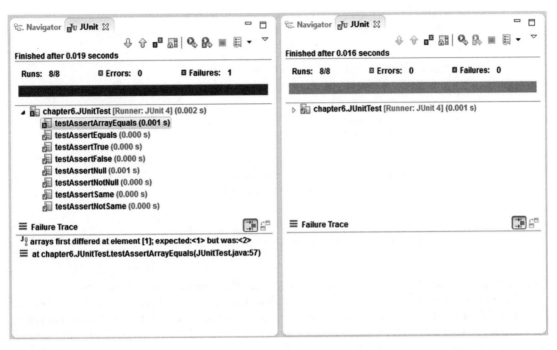

FIGURE 6-18

TRY IT OUT | Testing Programs with JUnit Test Cases

In this exercise, you develop a JUnit test case for a small program. This will show you how you can use JUnit testing to ensure your programs are operating as intended.

1. If you do not already have a project in Eclipse for Chapter 6, create one now.

2. Create a new class by right-clicking on the src folder in your new project. Select New and then Class. Name the class DistanceConverter. Uncheck the box that creates the main method for you. Click Finish to create the class.

3. Include the following methods in the body of the DistanceConverter class. Notice that there is no main method in this class. Therefore, it is not possible to test the methods simply by running the program.

```
public static double convertFeettoMeters(double feet){
      return feet * 0.3048;
   }

   public static double convertMeterstoFeet(double meters){
      return meters * 3.2808;
   }

   public static double convertFeettoInches(double feet){
      return feet * 12;
   }
```

```
public static double convertInchestoFeet(double inches){
    return inches / 12;
}

public static double convertCmtoFeet(double cm){
    return convertMeterstoFeet(cm / 100);
}

public static double convertFeettoCm(double feet){
    return convertFeettoMeters(feet) * 100;
}

public static double convertCmtoInches(double cm){
    return convertFeettoInches(convertCmtoFeet(cm));
}

public static double convertInchestoCm(double inches){
    return convertFeettoCm(convertInchestoFeet(inches));
}
```

4. Now create a JUnit test case by right-clicking on the `DistanceConverter.java` file in the Navigator. Select New, then JUnit Test Case. The name should be `DistanceConverterTest` and the class under test field should be `chapter6.DistanceConverter` (chapter6 is the package name; it may be different if you have used another package). You do not need any auto method stubs checked. Some of these fields may be filled in for you.

5. Click Next. If you place a check next to `DistanceConverter`, test method stubs will be created for all methods in the class. Click Finish.

6. Now you should have created a new testing class that looks like this:

```
import static org.junit.Assert.*;

import org.junit.Test;

public class DistanceConverterTest {

    @Test
    public void testConvertFeettoMeters() {
        fail("Not yet implemented");
    }

    @Test
    public void testConvertMeterstoFeet() {
        fail("Not yet implemented");
    }

    @Test
    public void testConvertFeettoInches() {
        fail("Not yet implemented");
    }

    @Test
    public void testConvertInchestoFeet() {
```

```
            fail("Not yet implemented");
        }

        @Test
        public void testConvertCmtoFeet() {
            fail("Not yet implemented");
        }

        @Test
        public void testConvertFeettoCm() {
            fail("Not yet implemented");
        }

        @Test
        public void testConvertCmtoInches() {
            fail("Not yet implemented");
        }

        @Test
        public void testConvertInchestoCm() {
            fail("Not yet implemented");
        }

    }
```

7. Add some class variables that you can use in the tests: `double feet`, `meters`, `inches`, and `cm`.

8. Fill in the body of your first test method, the `testConvertFeettoMeters()` method, like so:

```
        @Test
        public void testConvertFeettoMeters() {
            feet = 1;
            meters = DistanceConverter.convertFeettoMeters(feet);
            assertEquals(meters, 0.3048,0.001);
        }
```

To convert feet to meters, you should give a value for feet and the method will calculate the equivalent in meters. Therefore, in your test case, assign a value to the variable `feet`. Use the method to assign a value to the variable `meters`. Then calculate the equivalent in meters. Use the `assertEquals()` method to make sure the method calculation is equal to your own calculation. Because of the rounding issues with doubles, the `assertEquals()` method for doubles has an extra parameter, called `epsilon`, where you can indicate how close the two doubles should be to be considered equal. In this example, using 0.001 for `epsilon`, you are saying that if the calculated value for meters is within 0.001 of 0.3048, you should consider them equal.

9. Try to fill in the rest of the test methods in the same way. Give a value for the first variable. Use the method to calculate the second variable. Then compare the expected true conversion to the method's return value.

10. Your test case should resemble this after you've filled in all the test methods:

```
import static org.junit.Assert.*;

import org.junit.Test;
```

```java
public class DistanceConverterTest {
    double feet, meters, inches, cm;

    @Test
    public void testConvertFeettoMeters() {
        feet = 1;
        meters = DistanceConverter.convertFeettoMeters(feet);
        assertEquals(meters, 0.3048,0.001);
    }

    @Test
    public void testConvertMeterstoFeet() {
        meters = 1;
        feet = DistanceConverter.convertMeterstoFeet(meters);
        assertEquals(3.281,feet,0.001);
    }

    @Test
    public void testConvertFeettoInches() {
        feet = 1;
        inches = DistanceConverter.convertFeettoInches(feet);
        assertEquals(12,inches,0.001);
    }

    @Test
    public void testConvertInchestoFeet() {
        inches = 12;
        feet = DistanceConverter.convertInchestoFeet(inches);
        assertEquals(1,feet,0.001);
    }

    @Test
    public void testConvertCmtoFeet() {
        cm = 10;
        feet = DistanceConverter.convertCmtoFeet(cm);
        assertEquals(0.3281,feet,0.001);
    }

    @Test
    public void testConvertFeettoCm() {
        feet = 1;
        cm = DistanceConverter.convertFeettoCm(feet);
        assertEquals(30.48,cm,0.001);
    }

    @Test
    public void testConvertCmtoInches() {
        cm = 10;
        inches = DistanceConverter.convertCmtoInches(cm);
        assertEquals(3.9371,inches,0.001);
    }

    @Test
    public void testConvertInchestoCm() {
        inches = 10;
```

```
        cm = DistanceConverter.convertInchestoCm(inches);
        assertEquals(25.4,cm,0.001);
    }

}
```

11. Run the test case by clicking the green play icon or selecting Run, then Run. Ensure that no errors or failures occur.

How It Works

Here's how it works:

1. For each test method, a new method is being tested.

2. You have supplied one value and the method calculates the second method.

3. You find the expected value and enter this as one of the parameters in the assertEquals() method.

4. As long as the number you calculated and the number the method calculated are very close (+/- epsilon), the assertEquals() method will pass.

5. If all eight tests pass, the testing is complete and all methods function as they are designed to.

6. If there is a failure, you can use the Trace to find what went wrong. Is there a mistake in your method or in your own calculation? This is up to you to figure out.

SUMMARY

This concludes the chapter on exceptions and debugging. The techniques you've seen in this chapter should help you program with fewer errors and produce applications that function as expected. Debugging, logging, and testing alone or in combination will not only help you accomplish this for yourself, but will also demonstrate the correctness to others. When developing professionally, it is not enough to know that your code works and why, but you need to be able to convince others (colleagues, clients, managers, and so on) that it works. As your programs get larger and more complex, you will find these techniques more and more valuable.

Delving Further into Object-Oriented Concepts

- ➤ What annotations are

- ➤ What overloaded methods are

- ➤ How to use the `this` keyword

- ➤ What information hiding or encapsulation is

- ➤ What class inheritance and polymorphism mean

- ➤ What interfaces are and what they do

- ➤ How to organize your classes into packages

- ➤ How garbage is collected in Java

WROX.COM CODE DOWNLOADS FOR THIS CHAPTER

The wrox.com code downloads for this chapter are found at www.wrox.com/go/
beginningjavaprogramming on the Download Code tab. The code is in the Chapter 7
download and individually named according to the names throughout the chapter.

The first half of this book covered the basics of Java and Object-Oriented Programming.
Some of the chapters provided the tools or techniques needed to start building more complex
programs. Building on that foundation, you're ready to move on to these more advanced
concepts. This chapter expands on Chapter 4 to increase your knowledge of the principles of
Object-Oriented Programming. The three main topics covered here are information hiding,
inheritance, and interfaces. However, there are also several other ideas that are discussed,
including method overloading, packages, garbage collection, and annotations. After com-
pleting this chapter, you will have the tools you need to create organized and advanced Java

applications. The rest of the book helps you put object-oriented principles into practice with increasing functionality.

ANNOTATIONS

Annotations provide metadata about source code that's not part of the program itself. Unlike comments, which are ignored by the compiler, annotations can provide information for the compiler and can be processed by some tools to generate code, documentation, or other files.

Annotations always begin with the @ symbol. The compiler knows to expect an annotation following the @ symbol. You may have already seen some examples of annotations, such as @Test, @Before, and @After, from the unit testing section in Chapter 6.

Some annotations can replace comments, by providing a more structured format for metadata. This metadata can then be used to automatically generate documentation for your code. These annotations can be custom-designed for use by the programmer or for consistency across a department or company.

Other annotations are predefined in java.lang to be used in specific circumstances, such as @Deprecated, @Override, and @SuppressWarnings. @Deprecated indicates that the element, such as a method or class, has been replaced by an improved alternative and should no longer be used. Whenever an element marked @Deprecated is used in a program, the compiler will give a warning so the programmer knows to use an alternative. @Override indicates that a subclass is overriding an element from its superclass. You will learn more about this later in this chapter. By using the @Override annotation when you intend to override an element, the compiler will warn you if the method does not properly override a superclass element. @SuppressWarnings instructs the compiler to suppress specific warnings that it would normally generate. You may have seen this suggested as a solution for warnings appearing in your projects in Eclipse. Java 8 introduced a new annotation @FunctionalInterface to indicate that the programmer intends to create a functional interface according to the Java Language Specification.

Another change in Java 8 is the flexibility to use annotations anywhere a type is used, instead of only applying to declarations as previous Java versions required. This new flexibility allows better type-checking analysis, although Java 8 does not provide this type-checking framework itself. One example of a type annotation is if you were to write a piece of code to ensure that a particular variable is never null. Then you could annotate that variable @NonNull to indicate to the compiler that this variable will never be assigned to null. The compiler can then check for any discrepancies and warn you if something remains to be addressed.

OVERLOADING METHODS

As mentioned in the introduction to the chapter, there are several small topics covered here, aside from the main concepts. This first section covers the concept of overloading methods. Overloading simply refers to using the same name for more than one method in the same class. Java, and many other languages, can determine which method you're calling as long as the number or type of parameters is different in each method. This is illustrated with a few examples.

```
public class Book {
    String title;
    String author;
    boolean isRead;
    int numberOfReadings;

    public void read(){
        isRead = true;
    }

    public void read(){
        numberOfReadings++;
    }
}
```

If you try this first example in Eclipse, you'll see there are errors indicating the read() method is duplicated. The problem is you have two methods with the same name and neither has any parameters. Try the following instead:

```
public class Book {
    String title;
    String author;
    boolean isRead;
    int numberOfReadings;

    public void read(){
        isRead = true;
        numberOfReadings++;
    }

    public void read(int i){
        isRead = true;
        numberOfReadings += i;
    }
}
```

Now you have one method with the name read() and no parameters and another method with the name read() and one int parameter. To Java, these are two completely different methods, so you won't have any duplication errors. Of course, read(1) will have the same effect as read(), so you might not see much use for this concept. Alternatively, you could change the name of the methods to readOnce() and read(int i). You could easily avoid overloading methods at all in this example.

There is one type of method where overloading becomes very convenient: the constructor. This is because, as you learned in Chapter 4, the name of constructor methods is restricted to the class name. So if you want to create more than one constructor, you need to use the overloading principle. In the Book class, you would naturally want a constructor with two String parameters to set the title and author of the book.

```
public Book(String bookTitle, String authorName){
    title = bookTitle;
    author = authorName;
}
```

You might also need to create a book with an unknown author, perhaps for a publisher who has a particular book in mind but hasn't hired an author to write it.

```
public Book(String bookTitle){
    title = bookTitle;
    author = "Unknown";
}
```

On the other hand, you might have a book proposal from a known author, but you aren't yet sure what it will be named.

```
public Book(String authorName){
    title = "Unknown";
    author = authorName;
}
```

Now you have a problem. You have one kind of "method" called Book(), with one String parameter for the title, and another method called Book() with one String parameter for the author's name. Java cannot distinguish between these, so it will be considered a duplicate method. You will have to remove one of these and use one of the remaining constructors, for example, Book myBook = new Book("Unknown", "Bart Baesens"); to construct a book with unknown title and known author using the two String parameter constructor.

You could also add a constructor with no parameters if neither the title nor the author is known. Or you could add constructors with even more parameters:

```
public Book(String bookTitle, String authorName, boolean hasBeenRead){
    title = bookTitle;
    author = authorName;
    isRead = hasBeenRead;
}

public Book(String bTitle, String aName, boolean hasBeenRead, int read){
    title = bTitle;
    author = aName;
    isRead = hasBeenRead;
    numberOfReadings = read;
}
```

You might already notice quite a bit of repetition in these different constructors. You will see a way to reduce this in the next section by using the this keyword.

THE this KEYWORD

This section covers how and why to use the Java this keyword. The this keyword is placed inside an instance method or constructor in order to refer to the object whose method is being called. This is perhaps best explained with an example:

```
public class Person {
    String name;

    public Person(String personName){
```

```
            this.name = personName;
        }
    }
```

In this simple `Person` class, each `Person` has a name, which is stored as a `String` variable. The constructor has a `String` parameter that's assigned to the `Person`'s name variable when it is constructed. Here, you can read the constructor as "the name variable of *this* person object being constructed should be given the value of the `personName` `String` provided as a parameter."

```
        public void printName(){
            System.out.println(this.name);
        }
    }
```

If you add an instance method to print the name of a `Person` object, you can use the `this` keyword to identify which name should be printed: "the value assigned to the name variable of *this* `Person` object whose method is being called."

These examples should illustrate how the `this` keyword is used. You might be wondering why you would use it. After all, you could leave it out of the examples and they would function exactly the same way.

```
    public class Person {
        String name;

        public Person(String personName){
            name = personName;
        }

        public void printName(){
            System.out.println(name);
        }
    }
```

As you can see, the use of the `this` keyword is optional in this situation. It is recommended that you use it to be explicit and avoid ambiguity, but you could leave it out without impacting your program. However, there are cases where you must use the `this` keyword. This is usually when a local variable and an instance variable have the same name. Consider the following example:

```
    public class Person {
        String name;

        public Person(String name){
            name = name;
        }

        public void printName(){
            System.out.println(name);
        }
    }
```

If you try this in Eclipse, you'll see a warning: `The assignment to variable name has no effect`. In this case, because `name` is a local variable for the constructor method, you will be referring to this local variable if you refer to `name` inside the method. Essentially, you are saying the local `String name` should be assigned the value it already has, and you have done nothing with the instance variable name of the `Person` object. You must use the `this` keyword inside the constructor to refer to the instance variable name. You are not required to use it in the `printName()` method, but it is recommended to avoid ambiguity.

```java
public class Person {
    String name;

    public Person(String name){
        this.name = name;
    }

    public void printName(){
        System.out.println(name);
    }
}
```

Another case where you may need to use the `this` keyword is when you have overloaded the constructor method and want to explicitly call one constructor from within another constructor. Imagine, for instance, that sometimes you need to construct a `Person` object but you do not know their name. You could create another constructor with no parameters and use the `this` keyword to call the one `String` parameter constructor with a default name.

```java
public class Person {
    String name;

    public Person(){
        this("Unknown");
    }

    public Person(String name){
        this.name = name;
    }

    public void printName(){
        System.out.println(name);
    }
}
```

Again, you might think the `this` keyword is not necessary, as for this simple example, you could make a no-parameter constructor that assigns the name variable to "Unknown" itself, without using the `this` keyword. However, when your constructor is more complex, with several statements and perhaps some calculations, using the `this` keyword will limit redundancy, increase readability, and prevent discrepancies between what different constructors accomplish. The next exercise allows you to try method overloading using the `this` keyword.

TRY IT OUT   Method Overloading

In this exercise, you expand the `Person` class from the examples to demonstrate the use of method overloading and the `this` keyword.

1.   If you do not already have a project in Eclipse for Chapter 7, create one now.

2. Create a new class by right-clicking on the `src` folder in your new project. Select New ➤ and then Class. Name the new class `Person`. Uncheck the box to create a `main` method. This class should look like this:

```
public class Person {

}
```

3. Add the following instance variables to your class:

```
String name;
LocalDate birthdate;
```

4. In order to use `LocalDate`, you need to import the `java.time` package. Add the following statement above your class heading, or click the error notification and double-click the import suggestion.

5. Add a constructor method to set up new `Person` objects. Your constructor should accept the one String parameter for name and three `int` parameters for the year, month, and day of the birthdate. Include a statement inside the constructor to convert the `ints` to a `LocalDate` type. Assign the values to the instance variables. Your four-parameter constructor should look like this:

```
public Person (String name, int year, int month, int day) {
    LocalDate tempBD = LocalDate.of(year, month, day);
    this.name = name;
    this.birthdate = tempBD;
}
```

6. Overload the constructor by creating a second one with only `name`. Suppose this is used when you don't know someone's birthdate. Use the `this` keyword, with default values where needed.

7. Create a method to calculate someone's age. `LocalDate` has a method called `now()` that returns the current date. To calculate the period between two dates, use the following statements:

```
Period p = Period.between(date1, date2);
int age = p.getYears();
```

8. Overload the `calculateAge()` method by adding another method with the same name, but with a `LocalDate` parameter to calculate a person's age on a certain date. Make another one that accepts three `ints` for year, month, and day.

9. Your `Person` class should look something like this:

```
import java.time.*;

public class Person {
    String name;
    LocalDate birthdate;

    public Person(String name, int year, int month, int day) {
        this.name = name;
        this.birthdate = LocalDate.of(year, month, day);
```

```
    }

    public Person(String name) {
        this(name, 1900, 1, 1);
    }

    public int calculateAge() {
        Period p = Period.between(this.birthdate, LocalDate.now());
        return p.getYears();
    }

    public int calculateAge(LocalDate date) {
        Period p = Period.between(this.birthdate, date);
        return p.getYears();
    }

    public int calculateAge(int year, int month, int day) {
        Period p = Period.between(this.birthdate,
                LocalDate.of(year, month, day));
        return p.getYears();
    }
}
```

How It Works

Here's how this example works:

1. In the first constructor method, you used the `this` keyword to initialize the variables of "this" object being created. You also used the `LocalDate.of()` method to assign a date variable from three `int` values.

2. In the second constructor, you used the `this` keyword to use the first constructor of "this" class, but you filled in default values for year, month, and day.

3. In the first `calculateAge()` method, you used the `LocalDate.now()` method to compare a person's birthdate (using the `this` keyword) to the current date. `Period` and `Period.getYears()` handled the calculation for you, as they are defined as part of the date and time facilities added to Java 8.

4. In the second `calculateAge()` method, with a `LocalDate` parameter, you used a similar format to the first, but you used a specified date instead of the current date. You could change the first `calculateAge()` method to use this one in the following way:

```
    public int calculateAge() {
        return calculateAge(LocalDate.now());
    }
```

5. In the third `calculateAge()` method, with three `int` parameters, you used a similar format to the other two, but this time you called the `LocalDate.of()` method to get the correct date from the integers specified. Again, you could use the second `calculateAge()` method to rewrite this one in a simpler and more robust way:

```
    public int calculateAge(int year, int month, int day) {
        return calculateAge(LocalDate.of(year, month, day));
    }
```

6. Offering these three `calculateAge()` methods means that other classes using the `Person` class can calculate a person's age based on the date the calculation occurs (how old is the person now?), based on a given `LocalDate` (how old was the person when they graduated high school?), and based on a given date, when the `LocalDate` class is not available to the other class or program (how old was the person on a certain year, month, and day?). This functionality may make it more reusable. By reusing one of the methods inside the others, you help improve maintainability.

INFORMATION HIDING

Information hiding, also referred to as encapsulation, is an object-oriented practice that hides the internal representation of objects. The main idea is to make member variables private, so they are not directly accessible from outside of the class. Accessor methods are created to grant access to view or modify the values of the variables. This gives the programmer control over how and when variables can be accessed.

Encapsulation offers several advantages that make it standard recommended practice for all your classes. First, as already mentioned, you can control the access to variables. For example, consider the following small program:

```java
import java.math.BigDecimal;

public class Product {
    String productName;
    String productID;
    BigDecimal productPrice;

    public Product(String name, String id, String price) {
        this.productName = name;
        this.productID = id;
        this.productPrice = new BigDecimal(price);
    }

    public String displayString() {
        return "Product " + this.productID + ": " + this.productName
                + " costs " + this.productPrice;
    }
}

public class ProductProgram {
    public static void main(String[] args) {
        Product myWidget = new Product("Widget","WID0001","11.50");
        myWidget.productPrice = new BigDecimal("-5.00");
        System.out.println(myWidget.displayString());
    }
}
```

In this example, you can create a product with a certain name, ID, and price as expected. However, after the product is created, anyone can change the price, even to a price that doesn't make any sense. It's best to restrict these changes in some way to avoid these problems, such as negative prices.

Related to this idea of limiting access, you can use the accessor methods to check for validity before changing the variable's value. If an invalid value is provided, the programmer can decide how to handle it, for example, by throwing an exception as you saw in the previous chapter. You can also add some notifications when a change occurs, so the program reacts accordingly.

On the other hand, when retrieving values from variables, you can manage this in different ways by using your accessor methods. You can provide "read-only" access to a value by providing methods to return a defensive copy but not change the value. In the Product program, lots of related classes might need to know what the price of a product is to calculate sales, tax, or profit figures, for example. However, only a few, such as a discounting application, should be able to modify it. You may also want to provide information that is collected or calculated from more than one variable. In the Product program, you might create an accessor method that adds a tax or fee to the price before returning the total price.

Finally, encapsulation can improve program maintenance by limiting the impact of changes in one class on other related classes. In the Product program, you might need to adapt the Product class later to accommodate more information about products or to change the representation in some way. However, as long your displayString() still returns a String, the other classes calling this method continue functioning as expected. If every related class printed the statements based on the instance variables directly, a change to the Product class would require adaptations to every other class to ensure the printing methods still functioned properly.

Access Modifiers

The first step to restricting access to variables or methods is to adjust the access modifiers. These were introduced in Chapter 4, where the idea of encapsulation was mentioned but not explained in full detail. There are four access modifiers that can be applied to methods and variables in Java:

➤ public: Can be accessed by any class

➤ protected: Can be accessed by subclasses or classes in the same package

➤ no modifier: Can be accessed by classes in the same package

➤ private: Can be accessed only from within the same class

You can see the access levels in Figure 7-1.

	Class	Package	Subclass	World
public	+	+	+	+
protected	+	+	+	–
no modifier	+	+	–	–
private	+	–	–	–

FIGURE 7-1

Unlike variables and methods, classes can only be given the `public` modifier or no modifier. Encapsulation calls for the member variables (class or instance) to be given only private access, meaning they are only directly accessible from within the same class. Then, the access modifiers of your accessor methods can be set according to the demands of the program. For example, you might make an employee's date of birth readable to everyone with a public accessor method, but restrict changes to the `Employee` class with a private accessor method. The `Product` program might set price changes to package protected, so subtypes of the `Product` and a `Discounter` class in the same package can adjust the price.

By now you might be wondering what these accessor methods look like. They are commonly referred to as "getter" and "setter" methods, because they are used to get and set variable values. For this reason, they are given names like `getName()` or `setPrice()`. You'll look at getters and setters in a bit more detail next.

Getters

Getters are used to access variables' values for viewing only. You should create a getter method for every private variable. Depending on the access level you want to give to the variable, you can set the access modifier of its getter method. This is demonstrated with the `Product` class. The instance variables are set to private, and public getter methods are added for each one.

```
import java.math.BigDecimal;

public class Product {
    private String productName;
    private String productID;
    private BigDecimal productPrice;

    public Product(String name, String id, String price) {
        this.productName = name;
        this.productID = id;
        this.productPrice = new BigDecimal(price);
    }

    public String getName(){
        return this.productName;
    }

    public String getID(){
        return this.productID;
    }

    public BigDecimal getPrice(){
        return this.productPrice;
    }

    public String displayString() {
        return "Product " + this.getID() + ": " + this.getName()
                + " costs " + this.getPrice();
    }
}
```

If you tried this on your own, you might notice that this causes errors in the ProductProgram class. This is because once the variables are assigned private access modifiers, the ProductProgram class can no longer access the variable productPrice directly.

Setters

Setters are the methods you use to modify the values of variables. Just like with getters, you should create setters for every variable. Setters can replace the statements you used to use in the constructor method. The Product class with the setter methods added is shown in the next example.

```java
import java.math.BigDecimal;

public class Product {
    private String productName;
    private String productID;
    private BigDecimal productPrice;

    public Product(String name, String id, String price) {
        this.setName(name);
        this.setID(id);
        this.setPrice(price);
    }

    public String getName(){
        return this.productName;
    }

    public void setName(String name){
        this.productName = name;
    }

    public String getID(){
        return this.productID;
    }

    public void setID(String id){
        this.productID = id;
    }

    public BigDecimal getPrice(){
        return this.productPrice;
    }

    public void setPrice(String price){
        this.productPrice = new BigDecimal(price);
    }

    public String displayString() {
        return "Product " + this.getID() + ": " + this.getName()
                + " costs " + this.getPrice();
    }
}
```

The setters here are very simple; they don't include any of the validity checks or access restrictions that were said to be the main advantages of information hiding. You might start by making `setID()` private. It seems logical that a `Product`'s ID number should not be changeable from outside the class. Remember, if you want to ensure that a `Product`'s ID number never changes, you can make that variable final as well. Now, to deal with the problem identified in the beginning: negative prices should not be allowed. You can add a check to see if the price is above 0, or you might store a minimum and maximum price to compare your price against. The second option is demonstrated in the next version of the `Product` class. First, two static variables have been added to indicate the absolute minimum and maximum prices any product can have. Then another method was added to compare any potential price to the minimum and maximum to see if it is a valid price. Finally, the `setPrice()` method uses the `isValidPrice()` method to check the price provided. If it is not valid, the method throws an `IllegalArgumentException`. Otherwise, the price is set to the provided price.

```java
import java.math.BigDecimal;

public class Product {
    private static BigDecimal minPrice = new BigDecimal("0.00");
    private static BigDecimal maxPrice = new BigDecimal("999.99");
    private String productName;
    private String productID;
    private BigDecimal productPrice;

    public Product(String name, String id, String price) {
        this.setName(name);
        this.setID(id);
        this.setPrice(price);
    }

    public String getName(){
        return this.productName;
    }

    public void setName(String name){
        this.productName = name;
    }

    public String getID(){
        return this.productID;
    }

    private void setID(String id){
        this.productID = id;
    }

    public BigDecimal getPrice(){
        return this.productPrice;
    }
}

    public void setPrice(String price) throws IllegalArgumentException{
        BigDecimal tempPrice = new BigDecimal(price);
        if (!isValidPrice(tempPrice)){
            throw new IllegalArgumentException(price);
```

```
        }
        this.productPrice = tempPrice;
    }

    public boolean isValidPrice(BigDecimal price){
        if (price.compareTo(minPrice)<0){
            return false;
        }
        if (price.compareTo(maxPrice)>0){
            return false;
        }
        return true;
    }

    public String displayString() {
        return "Product " + this.getID() + ": " + this.getName()
                + " costs " + this.getPrice();
    }
}
```

Now, you just need to adapt your ProductProgram class to use these new methods. You will use the setPrice() method to change the price of myWidget. Because it can throw an exception, use the try-catch blocks you learned about in the previous chapter to handle the exception appropriately. One way you could do this is shown in the next code example.

```
public class ProductProgram {
    public static void main(String[] args) {
        Product myWidget = new Product("Widget","WID0001","11.50");

        try {
            myWidget.setPrice("-5.0");
        } catch (IllegalArgumentException e){
            System.out.println(e + " is an invalid price.");
        }
        System.out.println(myWidget.displayString());
    }
}
```

Try running the program with different price values to see what happens. Or better yet, use unit testing from Chapter 6 to test all the possible cases. You might also have noticed that the ProductProgram class no longer uses the BigDecimal class because the setPrice() method takes a String as the parameter. This means that even if you decide later to use a different data type in the Product class, you would not have to change anything in the ProductProgram class.

TRY IT OUT   Information Hiding or Encapsulation

In this exercise, you start with a simple Bank Account application and adapt it to apply the principles of information hiding.

1. If you do not already have a project in Eclipse for Chapter 7, create one now.

2. Create a new class by right-clicking on the src folder in your new project. Select New ➤ and then Class. Name the new class Account. Uncheck the box to create a main method. This class should look like this:

```
public class Account {

}
```

3. Add two instance variables to the `Account` class:

```
String name;
BigDecimal amount;
```

4. Add a constructor method to set up new `Account` objects. Your constructor should accept two String parameters, one for the name and another for the starting amount of the account. Since the amount variable is a `BigDecimal` and represents currency, set the scale to two decimal points and `ROUND_HALF_UP` for the rounding mode. Your constructor should look like this:

```
public Account(String acctName, String startAmount) {
    this.name = acctName;
    this.amount = new BigDecimal(startAmount);
    this.amount.setScale(2, BigDecimal.ROUND_HALF_UP);
}
```

5. Add another new class called `AccountManager`. This time, check the box that creates the `main` method for you (you can also write the `main` method yourself after creating the class). Click Finish to create the class. Your `AccountManager` class should look something like this:

```
public class AccountManager {

    public static void main(String[] args) {
        // TODO Auto-generated method stub

    }
}
```

6. Remove the `// TODO` comment, and add a statement inside the `main` method that creates a new account with the name `FirstAccount` and amount `10.00`.

7. Add `print` statements to your `main` method so the user is given information about the account that you created. Your `main` method should look like this:

```
public static void main(String[] args) {
    Account myAccount = new Account("FirstAccount","10.00");
    System.out.println("Account Created: " + myAccount.name);
    System.out.println("Balance: " + myAccount.amount);
}
```

8. Now add another statement to change the amount in `myAccount` to `-15.00`. Print this new balance to the console. Your `main` method should look similar to this:

```
public static void main(String[] args) {
    Account myAccount = new Account("FirstAccount","10.00");
    System.out.println("Account Created: " + myAccount.name);
    System.out.println("Balance: " + myAccount.amount);
```

```
        myAccount.amount = new BigDecimal("-15.00");
        System.out.println("New Balance: " + myAccount.amount);
    }
```

9. Run the program to see the output.

```
Account Created: FirstAccount
Balance: 10.00
New Balance: -15.00
```

10. Now, make both variables in the Account class private.

11. Did you notice that this created errors in the AccountManager class? If you hover over the red x, you can see what the problem is:

```
The field Account.name is not visible.
The field Account.amount is not visible.
```

12. Because these fields are now private, they cannot be accessed from outside the Account class. Create getter methods in the Account class to allow other classes to access their values.

```
public String getName(){
    return this.name;
}

public BigDecimal getAmount(){
    return this.amount;
}
```

13. Getter methods allow you to read the values of the variables, but still you cannot modify the values. To be able to do this, you need to add setter methods to the Account class. A setter can be simple, for example:

```
public void setName(String newName){
    this.name = newName;
}
```

Or you can add conditions to control what kinds of modifications can be made. For example:

```
public void setName(String newName) {
    String pattern = "^[a-zA-Z0-9]*$";
    if (newName.matches(pattern)) {
        this.name = newName;
    }
}
```

In the second example, the matches() method checks to make sure the String contains only letters and numbers without any symbols. This, or a similar pattern, might be a requirement for an account's name. Add one of the getters for the name.

14. You need to create another setter for the amount. Remember when you directly changed the amount to -15.00 earlier in this exercise? With a bank account, you probably rarely make a direct modification like this, since all the banking transactions will need to be accounted as debits and

credits. You might find that your program is more useful with a private `setAmount()` method only for use in the constructor and other public `withdraw()` and `deposit()` methods to add or subtract funds from the amount. Inside the methods, you can check for negative balances to make sure the account is not overdrawn. Add these three methods to your `Account` class.

```
private void setAmount(String newAmount){
    this.amount = new BigDecimal(newAmount);
}

public void withdraw(String withdrawal) throws IllegalArgumentException{
    BigDecimal desiredAmount = new BigDecimal(withdrawal);

    //if desired amount is negative, throw an exception
    if (desiredAmount.compareTo(BigDecimal.ZERO) < 0){
        throw new IllegalArgumentException();
    }

    //if the amount is less than the desired amount, throw an exception
    if (amount.compareTo(desiredAmount) < 0){
        throw new IllegalArgumentException();
    }

    this.amount = this.amount.subtract(desiredAmount);
}

public void deposit(String deposit) throws IllegalArgumentException{
    BigDecimal desiredAmount = new BigDecimal(deposit);

    //if desired amount is negative, throw an exception
    if (desiredAmount.compareTo(BigDecimal.ZERO) < 0){
        throw new IllegalArgumentException();
    }

    this.amount = this.amount.add(desiredAmount);
}
```

15. Once your setters are in place, rewrite your constructor to use them.

```
public Account(String acctName, String startAmount) {
    setName(acctName);
    setAmount(startAmount);
    amount.setScale(2, BigDecimal.ROUND_HALF_UP);
}
```

16. Your complete `Account` class should look like this:

```
import java.math.BigDecimal;

public class Account {
    private String name;
    private BigDecimal amount;

    public Account(String acctName, String startAmount) {
```

```
            setName(acctName);
            setAmount(startAmount);
            amount.setScale(2, BigDecimal.ROUND_HALF_UP);
        }

        public String getName() {
            return this.name;
        }

        public BigDecimal getAmount() {
            return this.amount;
        }

        public void setName(String newName) {
            String pattern = "^[a-zA-Z0-9]*$";
            if (newName.matches(pattern)) {
                this.name = newName;
            }
        }

        private void setAmount(String newAmount){
            this.amount = new BigDecimal(newAmount);
        }

        public void withdraw(String withdrawal) throws IllegalArgumentException{
            BigDecimal desiredAmount = new BigDecimal(withdrawal);

            //if desired amount is negative, throw an exception
            if (desiredAmount.compareTo(BigDecimal.ZERO) < 0){
                throw new IllegalArgumentException();
            }

            //if the amount is less than the desired amount, throw an exception
            if (amount.compareTo(desiredAmount) < 0){
                throw new IllegalArgumentException();
            }

            this.amount = this.amount.subtract(desiredAmount);
        }

        public void deposit(String deposit) throws IllegalArgumentException{
            BigDecimal desiredAmount = new BigDecimal(deposit);

            //if desired amount is negative, throw an exception
            if (desiredAmount.compareTo(BigDecimal.ZERO) < 0){
                throw new IllegalArgumentException();
            }

            this.amount = this.amount.add(desiredAmount);
        }
    }
}
```

17. Now adapt your AccountManager class to use the getters and setters you've created. Notice how you cannot use the setAmount() method because it is also private. You need to use the withdraw() and

deposit() methods to change the amount. Since these can throw exceptions, make sure you use a try-catch block to handle invalid values. Your AccountManager class might look like this:

```
public class AccountManager {

    public static void main(String[] args) {
    Account myAccount = new Account("FirstAccount","10.00");
    System.out.println("Account Created: " + myAccount.getName());
    System.out.println("Balance: " + myAccount.getAmount());

        try {
            myAccount.withdraw("20.00");
        } catch (IllegalArgumentException e) {
            System.out.println("Invalid Withdrawal");
        } finally {
            System.out.println("New Balance: " + myAccount.getAmount());
        }
    }
}
```

How It Works

Here's how it works:

1. In the first part of the exercise, the variables in the Account class were public. This allowed you to read and change them from the AccountManager class.

2. Because the variables were public, they could be modified by any class without any checks or validations. Therefore, you were encouraged to change the variables to private, following the principle of information hiding.

3. After the variables were private, they could no longer be accessed by other classes for reading or writing. You noticed this when the errors appeared in your AccountManager class.

4. You created public getter methods for each of the variables in the Account class. This allows other classes to read their values, without being able to modify them.

5. Next, you created setter methods to modify the values of the variables in the Account class. Some were public and some were private.

6. By making private setter methods, you can still restrict the modifications to the same class. The benefit of using a setter in this case, rather than directly modifying the variable, is that you can add validations to the method to make sure the changes are allowed. For example, you might want to prevent an account's balance from being set to a negative value. Generally these conditions will be checked with if statements. If the provided parameter is not acceptable, you can handle it in several ways. You might throw an exception when an invalid value is provided. You could also simply exit the method without modifying the variable. Finally, you might modify the variable but in a valid way. For example, if a String begins with white space, and this is not allowed, you could still use the part of the String after the white space.

7. By making public (or other non-private access modifiers) setter methods, you allow them to be called from any other class. You can still control what changes are allowed with the same types of validations mentioned for private setter methods.

8. Finally, you used the newly created getter and setter methods to read and modify the variables in a safer way.

CLASS INHERITANCE

Java classes are organized in a hierarchical inheritance structure. Subclasses are derived from super-classes. The class Object is the highest-level superclass; it has no parent class above it. All other classes are either subclasses of Object or subclasses of subclasses of Object. This is illustrated in Figure 7-2.

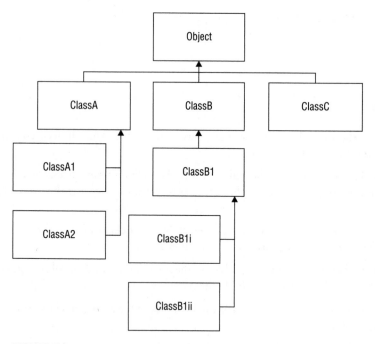

FIGURE 7-2

Inheritance represents "is a" relationship. For example, a Student is a Person, so the class Student could be a subclass of the Person class. An Employee is a Person, too, so Employee could be another subclass of Person. An undergraduate is a student and a graduate is a student, so you can create two additional subclasses of the class Student. Staff and Employee might be subclasses of the class Employee. A possible class hierarchy for this inheritance example is shown in Figure 7-3.

To indicate that a class is a subclass of another class, use the extends keyword in the class declaration, for example, public class Employee extends Person{ }. Variables and methods that are shared by all types of Persons can be placed in the Person class, and then each subclass can have specialized variables and methods that are only used by that type or its subclasses. For example,

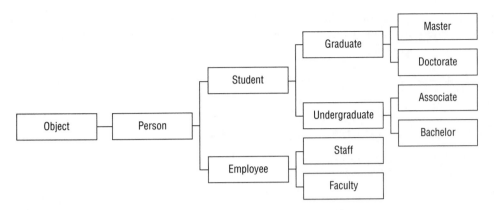

FIGURE 7-3

the `Person` class might have a `String` variable called `name`, which all `Person` objects will inherit whether they are graduate students or faculty employees. The `Student` class might have a `double` variable for their grade point average, which both graduate and undergraduate students inherit, but employees do not. A graduate student might have a `String` variable to store the title of their thesis. This would then be inherited by master and doctorate students. At the lowest level of the hierarchy, a `Doctorate` student might have a `Faculty` instance as their advisor, but with no subclasses, this will not be inherited by any other class.

The Keyword `super`

Another keyword introduced in this chapter is `super`. Super is a way of referring to the superclass. It's not so different than the `this` keyword, covered earlier in this chapter. It is used in constructors to invoke the constructor of the superclass, like the `this` keyword was used to invoke another constructor of the same class. It is also used to access the variables and methods of the superclass, like the `this` keyword was used to access the variables of the instance calling the method.

Consider a possible implementation of two of the classes from the `Person` example: `Person` and `Employee`. `Employee` is the subclass of `Person`, and `Person` is the superclass of `Employee`.

```
public class Person {
    private String name;

    public Person(String name) {
        this.setName(name);
    }

    public String getName() {
        return this.name;
    }

    public void setName(String name) {
        this.name = name;
    }
}
```

Remember, your `Employee` class should extend this `Person` class. Also, the variables `manager` and `employeeID` are added to the `Employee` class, since not all `Person` instances will have a `manager`, but all `Employee` instances will.

```
public class Employee extends Person {
    private Employee manager;
    private int id;

    public Employee(String name, Employee manager, int empID) {
        super(name);
        this.setManager(manager);
        this.setEmployeeID(empID);
    }

    public Employee getManager() {
        return manager;
    }

    public void setManager(Employee manager) {
        this.manager = manager;
    }

    public int getEmployeeID() {
        return id;
    }

    private void setEmployeeID(int employeeID) {
        this.id = employeeID;
    }

}
```

Notice how the `super` keyword is used in the first statement of the constructor. This means that the `Employee` should be constructed as a `Person` is constructed, then specialized with the `manager` and `id`.

Similar to specializing a subclass constructor by first calling the super constructor, you can also specialize methods by first calling a super method. Suppose you want to add a `displayName()` method to the `Employee` class that allows you to format their name badge.

```
public String displayName(){
    return "Employee: " + super.getName();
}
```

In the `displayName()` method, you have a specialized method for `Employee` that calls the method of the superclass to get some of the necessary information.

You can also access superclass variables using the `super` keyword. Suppose in your `Person` class you have an `int` variable called `id` that you use to uniquely identify people in your database. But you still have the `int` variable `id` in the `Employee` class that you use to store their employee ID. You might use the following method to return a `String` with both `id` numbers:

```
public String displayIdentification() {
```

```
        return "Person: " + super.id + " has EmployeeID " + this.id;
    }
```

Of course, now that you know about information hiding, it would be better still to access the ID of the superclass using a getter.

Method Overriding

It was mentioned already that subclasses inherit methods from their superclass. This means that if the Student class has a calculateGPA() method, then Graduate and Undergraduate will have this method either implicitly or explicitly as well. The subclasses can, however, override the method with a new, specialized implementation. This is called method overriding. Note, this is not related to method overloading discussed earlier in this chapter.

Consider the calculateGPA() method from the Student class. The Student class has a double[] variable called grades that lists all the students' grades. The calculateGPA() method then just calculates the average of these grades.

```
        public double calculateGPA() {
            double sum = 0;
            int count = 0;
            for (double grade : this.grades) {
                sum += grade;
                count++;
            }
            return sum/count;
        }
```

Now, suppose graduate students only get credit for grades above a certain minimum, for example only 80 percent and higher are accepted, and courses with a grade below 80 must be repeated. Then for the Graduate class, you might want to calculate the GPA based only on those higher grades. To do this, you can override the calculateGPA() method using the @Override annotation and change the implementation in the subclass.

```
        @Override
        public double calculateGPA() {
            double sum = 0;
            int count = 0;
            for (double grade : this.getGrades()) {
                if (grade > minGrade) {
                    sum += grade;
                    count++;
                }
            }
            return sum/count;
        }
```

Polymorphism

Polymorphism is a key concept in Object-Oriented Programming and is closely related to inheritance. Because inheritance models an "is a" relationship, one instance can take on the behaviors and attributes of more than one class. According to the class hierarchy of the Person example, a Master is a `Graduate`, a `Graduate` is a `Student`, and a `Student` is a `Person`, so depending on the particular functionality desired, Java might consider a particular `Master` instance as a `Master`, a `Graduate`, a `Student`, or a `Person`, because, after all, a `Master` is still a `Person`.

Static Binding

Static methods and variables have already been covered in earlier chapters. You know by now that they do not require or depend on instances of the class. Polymorphism applies to instances rather than to classes, so static methods can be bound to their implementations at compile time. This is referred to as static binding or compile-time binding. Java restricts static methods from being overridden; however, remember from earlier in this chapter that they can be overloaded. Overloaded methods differ only in the number and type of parameters, as the name is the same. To account for this possibility, the compiler will check the method signature and parameter types of static methods to find the appropriate implementation at compilation.

Dynamic Binding

Dynamic binding, also called virtual method invocation, is the binding used for instance methods to allow for polymorphism. When a method is overridden, there are multiple implementations that can be called, depending on the instance in question. Dynamic binding, as opposed to static binding, means that the binding of instance methods to the appropriate implementation is resolved at runtime, not at compile time, based on the instance and its type. During execution, the Java Virtual Machine will first check the class of the object that the reference object points to for the method implementation. If it doesn't exist, the JVM will look to the superclass. It will check the superclass above that if it still doesn't find a match, and so on throughout the class hierarchy. By searching from the bottom up, the most specific implementation, or the one from the class lowest in the hierarchy, will be the one used.

Consider again the example of the GPA calculation, which calculates the average of all grades for most `Student` instances and the average of grades above a threshold for graduate students. Suppose you create a `PersonProgram` class to run your `main` method:

```
public class PersonProgram {

    public static void main(String[] args){
        Student john = new Master("John Adams");
        john.setGrades(0.75,0.82,0.91,0.69,0.79);
        Student anne = new Associate("Anne Philips");
        anne.setGrades(0.75,0.82,0.91,0.69,0.79);

        System.out.println(john.getName() + ": " + john.calculateGPA());
        System.out.println(anne.getName() + ": " + anne.calculateGPA());
    }
}
```

You have two `Student` instances: John is a `Master` (subclass of `Graduate`) and Anne is an `Associate` (subclass of `Undergraduate`). To compare easily, assume they both have the same grades for five courses. When your `main` method reaches the print statements, it will first call the `getName()` method for each instance. For John, none of the `Master` class, the `Graduate` class, or the `Student` class contain a getName() method. Therefore, the Master instance inherits the getName() method directly from the Person class. Next, it will need to call the calculateGPA() method for John. The Master class does not contain a calculateGPA() method, but the Graduate class, the superclass of Master, does. Dynamic binding looks at the type of instance that John is: a Master and, therefore, a Graduate. Therefore, the calculateGPA() method from the Graduate class is called.

For Anne, the same decision process occurs. There is no getName() method in any of the subclasses, so the class hierarchy is considered to find that Anne is an Associate, which is an Undergraduate, which is a Student, which is a Person, and the getName() method from the Person class is called. For her GPA, neither Associate nor Undergraduate has a calculcateGPA() method, so the Student version of the method is called for Anne.

Sure enough, the console output shows two different GPAs, despite having the same grades, because dynamic method invocation allows different versions of the method to be called depending on the instance calling it.

```
John Adams: 0.865
Anne Philips: 0.792
```

The Superclass Object

As mentioned in the introduction to inheritance, all classes in Java descend from the class Object. The Object class has several methods that are, therefore, inherited by every other class. You may choose to use them directly or override them in your own classes.

➤ protected Object clone(): Creates and returns a copy of this object

➤ public boolean equals(Object obj): Indicates whether some other object is "equal to" this one

➤ protected void finalize(): Called by the garbage collector on an object when garbage collection determines that there are no more references to the object

➤ public final Class getClass(): Returns the runtime class of an object

➤ public int hashCode(): Returns a hashcode value for the object

➤ public String toString(): Returns a string representation of the object

The clone() method can be used only if the class is Cloneable. If so, the default clone() method creates a new object of the same class as the original object and with the same values for its instance variables. If your original object references another object, the clone will reference the same object. You may want to override the clone() method to create clones of both objects instead of sharing the referenced object.

The equals() method was discussed in Chapter 5. It compares two objects for equality. To compare two objects, this method uses the == operator, which gives the correct answer for primitive data types. However, for objects, it returns true if the references are equal, meaning the two variables point to exactly the same object. In most cases, you are more interested if the instance variables' values of both objects match. To accomplish this, you should override the equals() method according to the needs of your class or program. For example, you might consider two Person objects equal if their social security number is the same. Depending on the class, there might be different possible ways to check for equality, so the purposes of your program will help you determine an appropriate implementation. Two cars might be equal if they have the same vehicle identification number (the same exact car), or you might consider them equal if the make, model, and year are the same (the same kind of car).

The `finalize()` method is used as part of garbage collection. There is a brief section on this topic later in this chapter. It is worth noting that `Object`'s default `finalize()` method doesn't do anything, but it can be overridden to clean up loose ends when an object becomes garbage. Oracle notes that when and even if the `finalize()` method is called is uncertain, so it should not be relied upon to close resources.

The `getClass()` method cannot be overridden. It will always return a `Class` object that you can use to get information about the class, such as the class name, the superclass, or any interfaces it implements. The `Class` class has dozens of methods you can use to learn more about a class.

The `hashCode()` method returns a value representing the object's memory address by default. By definition, if two objects are equal, their hashcode must also be equal. Therefore, when you override the `equals()` method, you must also override the `hashCode()` method to maintain this relationship.

The `toString()` method returns a String representation of an object. The String representation depends on the object, so you should consider overriding this method in your own classes. The `toString()` method is the method called when you print an object, so if you properly override the `toString()` method, you can easily print objects in a format useful to you and your program.

Abstract Classes and Methods

Abstract classes cannot be instantiated. They are used as superclasses when you want all instances to belong to a subclass, but the subclasses share attributes or methods that are better defined in a superclass. For example, you might have an abstract class called `Shape` with several subclasses, like `Rectangle`, `Circle`, and `Triangle`. It might not make sense to be able to create a `Shape` without a more specific type, so you can make `Shape` abstract and create all shape objects as members of a subclass. The keyword `abstract` is used in the class declaration, like `public abstract class Shape { }`.

Abstract classes can also have implemented methods and abstract methods. Abstract methods are declared without an implementation. In the `Shape` example, you might declare a `calculateArea()` method in the `Shape` class, but allow each subclass to implement it in its own way, since each type of shape has a different area formula. All abstract methods must eventually be implemented in one of the subclasses. All classes that contain an abstract method must be abstract themselves. Abstract methods are declared using the `abstract` keyword, but instead of opening curly brackets, the declaration is completed with a semicolon, like `public abstract double calculateArea();`. The classes for `Shape` and `Circle` are shown as examples for the abstract class and method syntax.

```
public abstract class Shape {
    private String color;

    public Shape(String color) {
        this.setColor(color);
    }
```

```
        public String getColor() {
            return this.color;
        }

        public void setColor(String color) {
            this.color = color;
        }

        public abstract double calculateArea();
    }

    public class Circle extends Shape {
        private double radius;
        private final double PI = 3.14159;

        public Circle(String color, double radius) {
            super(color);
            this.setRadius(radius);
        }

        public double getRadius() {
            return this.radius;
        }

        private void setRadius(double radius) {
            this.radius = radius;
        }

        @Override
        public double calculateArea() {
            return PI * this.getRadius() * this.getRadius();
        }

    }
```

The following exercise will help you practice some of the main concepts associated with inheritance.

TRY IT OUT   Inheritance, Superclasses, and Subclasses

In this exercise, you continue with the Bank Account application from an earlier exercise and adapt it to apply the principles of inheritance.

1. Start from the Bank Account application from an earlier exercise. You may want to copy the files into a new package to keep both versions separate.

2. Create two new classes called SavingsAccount and CheckingAccount, which should be subclasses of the Account class.

3. Create a constructor in the SavingsAccount class that uses the superclass constructor. Assume when customers open a SavingsAccount, they receive a bonus of 10 dollars.

4. Add a private instance variable to the CheckingAccount class that indicates how many signatories are on the account. Add a getter and setter for it.

5. Create a constructor in the `CheckingAccount` class that also uses the superclass constructor and adds this instance variable initialization.

6. Make the `Account` class abstract, ensuring that all accounts are either `SavingsAccounts` or `CheckingAccounts`.

7. Override the `withdraw()` method in the `CheckingAccount` class to ensure a minimum balance is maintained in the account. Store the minimum balance required as a static variable. If the withdrawal is too large, throw an exception, otherwise use the `super.withdraw()` method.

8. Override the `toString()` method from the `Object` class to print information about `Account` instances in the `Account` class. Override the `Account` class `toString()` method to specialize it for the subclasses in `SavingsAccount` and `CheckingAccount`.

9. Adapt the `AccountManager` class to try out your new classes and methods. It should look something like this:

```
public class AccountManager {

    public static void main(String[] args) {
        Account mySavings = new SavingsAccount("Save001", "10.00");

        try {
            mySavings.withdraw("5.00");
        } catch (IllegalArgumentException e) {
            System.err.println("Invalid Withdrawal");
        }

        Account myChecking = new CheckingAccount("Check002", "10.00", 1);

        try {
            myChecking.withdraw("5.00");
        } catch (IllegalArgumentException e) {
            System.err.println("Invalid Withdrawal");
        }

        myChecking.deposit("500.00");

        try {
            myChecking.withdraw("5.00");
        } catch (IllegalArgumentException e) {
            System.err.println("Invalid Withdrawal");
        }
    }
}
```

Your `Account`, `SavingsAccount`, and `CheckingAccount` classes should resemble these:

```
import java.math.BigDecimal;

public abstract class Account {
    private String name;
    private BigDecimal amount;

    public Account(String acctName, String startAmount) {
```

```java
        this.setName(acctName);
        this.setAmount(startAmount);
        this.amount.setScale(2, BigDecimal.ROUND_HALF_UP);
        System.out.println("Account Created: " + this.getName());
    }

    public String getName() {
        return this.name;
    }

    public BigDecimal getAmount() {
        return this.amount;
    }

    public void setName(String newName) {
        String pattern = "^[a-zA-Z0-9]*$";
        if (newName.matches(pattern)) {
            this.name = newName;
        }
    }

    private void setAmount(String newAmount){
        this.amount = new BigDecimal(newAmount);
    }

    public void withdraw(String withdrawal) throws IllegalArgumentException{
        BigDecimal desiredAmount = new BigDecimal(withdrawal);

        //if desired amount is negative, throw an exception
        if (desiredAmount.compareTo(BigDecimal.ZERO) < 0){
            throw new IllegalArgumentException();
        }

        //if the amount is less than the desired amount, throw an exception
        if (this.getAmount().compareTo(desiredAmount) < 0){
            throw new IllegalArgumentException();
        }

        this.setAmount(this.getAmount().subtract(desiredAmount).toString());
        System.out.println("Withdrawal: " + this);
    }

    public void deposit(String deposit) throws IllegalArgumentException{
        BigDecimal desiredAmount = new BigDecimal(deposit);

        //if desired amount is negative, throw an exception
        if (desiredAmount.compareTo(BigDecimal.ZERO) < 0){
            throw new IllegalArgumentException();
        }

        this.setAmount(this.getAmount().add(desiredAmount).toString());
        System.out.println("Deposit: " + this);
    }

    @Override
    public String toString(){
```

```java
        return this.getName() + ": Balance = " + this.getAmount();
    }
}

import java.math.BigDecimal;

public class CheckingAccount extends Account {
    private int numberOfSigs;
    private static final BigDecimal minBalance = new BigDecimal("100.00");

    public CheckingAccount(String acctName, String startAmount, int sigs) {
        super(acctName, startAmount);
        this.setNumberOfSigs(sigs);
    }

    public int getNumberOfSigs() {
        return numberOfSigs;
    }

    public void setNumberOfSigs(int sigs) {
        this.numberOfSigs = sigs;
    }

    @Override
    public void withdraw(String withdrawal){
        BigDecimal desiredAmount = new BigDecimal(withdrawal);

        // if withdrawal would put the balance below the minimum,
        // throw an exception
        if (this.getAmount().compareTo(desiredAmount.add(minBalance)) < 0){
            throw new IllegalArgumentException();
        } else {
            super.withdraw(withdrawal);
        }
    }

    @Override
    public String toString(){
        return "Checking Account " + super.toString();
    }
}

public class SavingsAccount extends Account {

    public SavingsAccount(String acctName, String startAmount) {
        super(acctName, startAmount);
        this.deposit("10.00");
    }

    @Override
    public String toString() {
        return "Savings Account " + super.toString();
    }
}
```

How It Works

Here's how it works:

1. The Account class was made abstract because all Account instances should belong to one of the subclasses, either SavingsAccount or CheckingAccount. It was also adapted to include information hiding and accessor methods. The rest of the Account class remained unchanged. The toString() method from the Object class was overridden to allow for convenient printing of account information.

2. The SavingsAccount class is very simple; most of the methods are inherited directly from the superclass. In the SavingsAccount constructor, the super constructor is called first. The super constructor must be the first statement in a subclass constructor method. Next, an additional 10 dollars is deposited into the account as a SavingsAccount bonus. You could also save this bonus amount as a static variable. The toString() method from the Account class is overridden again to add the title "Savings Account" in front of the super toString() result.

3. The CheckingAccount class is more specialized than the SavingsAccount class. The toString() method of the Account class is similarly overridden to add the title "Checking Account." Additionally, two new variables were added: an instance variable to store the number of signatories (people who can withdraw from the account) and a static variable to store the minimum balance required in a CheckingAccount. Note that the constructor does not require a minimum balance to create the account. In order to do this, it would be better to move the minimum balance variable to the Account class and assign a different value for each subclass, so SavingsAccount minimum would be 0 and the CheckingAccount would be 100. This would allow the super constructor to check for the minimum balance while constructing an account instance. The withdraw() method is also overridden in the CheckingAccount class to check for the minimum balance. If the balance is sufficient, the super.withdraw() method is called.

4. The AccountManager class now creates two instances, one of SavingsAccount and one of CheckingAccount. The print statements are simplified since they can now use the toString() method. You can see how the withdrawal is rejected when the balance of the CheckingAccount is too low, but after a large deposit, the withdrawal becomes possible.

PACKAGES

Packages are a Java construct that function something like folders to organize your classes, but offer additional features like namespace and access control. Chapter 3 is about using Eclipse and other development environments. In that chapter, packages were discussed briefly. Indeed in your project directory, packages serve as an organizational tool to keep related classes together and less related classes separate.

You might even be organizing the exercises in this book into packages by chapter or individual exercise. If so, you may have already noticed that packages provide unique namespaces that allow several classes with the same name to exist without conflict as long as they are located in different packages. This is because the package helps to uniquely identify a specific class based on where it is located.

This same property allows you to import predefined classes and packages from other projects or even from other developers. The `import` statements you've used already in some of the exercises are an example of this. When you started using `BigDecimal`, instead of doubles, to provide more control over rounding of decimal point numbers, you used the following statement at the top of your class: `import java.math.BigDecimal;` to import the `BigDecimal` class from Java's `math` package.

In order for a program to identify a package by name, the program should be executed from the directory that contains the package, or the `CLASSPATH` must include the path to the package. The `CLASSPATH` tells the Java Virtual Machine where to find classes and packages when needed.

INTERFACES

An interface defines a protocol, or contract, of behavior. It resembles something like a template for a class, as it specifies what a class must do, but not how to do it. Instead of a `public class ClassName` heading, you should use the `public interface InterfaceName` heading. Interfaces contain headings for public methods without implementations. These are the same as abstract methods discussed earlier in the chapter, but because methods in interfaces are necessarily abstract, there is no need to use the `abstract` keyword in an interface. Comments should be provided with methods to make it clear what the method is intended for, especially since there is no implementation to read.

Interfaces must have either the `public` access modifier or no access modifier, indicating they are only accessible within the same package. An interface may have variables only if they are `final`, `static`, and initialized with a constant value.

Similar to a subclass extending a superclass, a class can implement an interface. If a class implements an interface, it must implement all methods defined in the interface. While a subclass can only extend one superclass, a single class can implement any number of interfaces. Because the methods in interfaces are unimplemented, there is no risk of ambiguity, and the class will have one single implementation for each method. Methods in an interface are implicitly assumed to be public, so the public access modifier is not necessary for interface methods.

Interfaces can extend one or more other interfaces. Any class implementing an interface must implement all methods in the interface itself, as well as any interfaces it extends.

Polymorphism applies to interfaces similar to superclasses. If the `Shape` class implements an interface `Measurable`, then you could have a variable of type `Measurable` referencing a `Rectangle` object or a variable of type `Shape` referencing a `Circle` object. Consider the following `Measurable` interface for an example of interface syntax.

```
/**
 * An interface for measuring methods.
 */
public interface Measurable{
    /** Returns the perimeter of an object */
    double calculatePerimeter();
```

```
    /** Returns the area of an object */
    double calculateArea();
}
```

Then, if Shape implements Measurable, the subclasses of Shape would also implement Measurable.

```
public abstract class Shape implements Measurable {
    private String color;

    public Shape(String color) {
        this.setColor(color);
    }

    public String getColor() {
        return this.color;
    }

    public void setColor(String color) {
        this.color = color;
    }
}

public class Circle extends Shape {
    private double radius;
    private final double pi = 3.14159;

    public Circle(String color, double radius) {
        super(color);
        this.setRadius(radius);
    }

    public double getRadius() {
        return this.radius;
    }

    private void setRadius(double radius) {
        this.radius = radius;
    }

    @Override
    public double calculateArea() {
        return pi * this.getRadius() * this.getRadius();
    }

    @Override
    public double calculatePerimeter() {
        return 2 * pi * this.getRadius();
    }

}
```

The following exercise will give you an opportunity to try out interfaces for yourself. While you work through it, keep in mind the similarities and differences between inheritance and interfaces. As you gain experience, you'll see how one or the other might be better suited to certain situations.

TRY IT OUT   Implementing Interfaces

To compare and contrast with superclasses, this exercise demonstrates the implementation of interfaces using the Bank Account examples from earlier.

1. You may want to create a new package to keep your bank account classes separated from other account classes you've been working on already.

2. Create a new interface the same way you do a class, but by selecting New ➢ Interface instead of New ➢ Class. Name it `Accountable`.

3. Add four methods to the Accountable interface:

```
boolean isValidDeposit();
void deposit();
boolean isValidWithdrawal();
void withdraw();
```

4. Write meaningful comments for the interface and each method. If you type /** and press Enter, the multiple-line comment block will be generated for you. Your `Accountable` interface may look like this:

```
/**
 * an interface to manage accounting behavior
 */
public interface Accountable {

    /**
     * Returns true if a specified String is a valid amount to deposit.
     * @param deposit: the amount to be deposited
     */
    boolean isValidDeposit(String deposit);

    /**
     * Adds the specified amount to the balance.
     * @param deposit: the amount to be deposited
     * @throws IllegalDeposit
     */
    void deposit(String deposit) throws IllegalDeposit;

    /**
     * Returns true if a specified String is a valid amount to withdraw.
     * @param withdrawal: the amount to be withdrawn
     */
    boolean isValidWithdrawal(String withdrawal);

    /**
     * Subtracts the specified amount from the balance.
     * @param withdrawal: the amount to be withdrawn
     * @throws IllegalWithdrawal
     */
    void withdraw(String withdrawal) throws IllegalWithdrawal;
}
```

5. Create a new class `SavingsAccount` that implements the `Accountable` interface. You can add interfaces in the middle of the New Java Class window, or you can type `implements Accountable` yourself after the class is created. If you add it from the window, the necessary methods will automatically be created for you to implement.

6. The `SavingsAccount` class should have two instance variables: name and amount. Follow the principle of information hiding. Use the `isValid` methods to check if a String is numeric and if it can be represented as a `BigDecimal`. Before making a deposit or withdrawal, use the `isValid` methods to check if the transaction is valid. Override the `toString()` method to print information about your accounts. Your `SavingsAccount` class may look like this:

```
import java.math.BigDecimal;

public class SavingsAccount implements Accountable {
    private String name;
    private BigDecimal amount;

    public SavingsAccount(String name, String amount) throws IllegalAccount {
        if (isValidDeposit(amount)) {
            this.setName(name);
            this.setAmount(new BigDecimal(amount));
        } else {
            throw new IllegalAccount();
        }
    }

    @Override
    public boolean isValidDeposit(String deposit) {
        BigDecimal temp;
        try {
            temp = new BigDecimal(deposit);
        } catch (Exception e) {
            return false;
        }
        return temp.compareTo(BigDecimal.ZERO) > 0;
    }

    @Override
    public void deposit(String deposit) throws IllegalDeposit {
        if (isValidDeposit(deposit)) {
            this.setAmount(this.getAmount().add(new BigDecimal(deposit)));
        } else {
            throw new IllegalDeposit();
        }
    }

    @Override
    public boolean isValidWithdrawal(String withdrawal) {
        BigDecimal temp;
        try {
            temp = new BigDecimal(withdrawal);
        } catch (Exception e) {
            return false;
```

```
        }
        if (temp.compareTo(this.getAmount()) < 0) {
            return true;
        }
        return false;
    }

    @Override
    public void withdraw(String withdrawal) throws IllegalWithdrawal {
        if (isValidWithdrawal(withdrawal)) {
            this.setAmount(this.getAmount()
                    .subtract(new BigDecimal(withdrawal)));
        } else {
            throw new IllegalWithdrawal();
        }
    }

    public String getName() {
        return name;
    }

    private void setName(String name) {
        this.name = name;
    }

    public BigDecimal getAmount() {
        return amount;
    }

    private void setAmount(BigDecimal amount) {
        this.amount = amount;
    }

    @Override
    public String toString() {
        return "SavingsAccount " + this.getName()
                + ": Balance = " + this.getAmount();
    }
}
```

7. Create another new class called `CheckingAccount`. Structure it similarly to the `SavingsAccount` class. This time add a `minBalance` static variable to maintain a minimum balance of 100 dollars in all checking accounts. Override the `toString()` method to print information about your accounts. Your `CheckingAccount` class may look like this:

```
import java.math.BigDecimal;

public class CheckingAccount implements Accountable {
    private String name;
    private BigDecimal amount = new BigDecimal("0.00");
    private static BigDecimal minBalance = new BigDecimal("100.00");

    public CheckingAccount(String name, String amount) throws IllegalAccount {
        if (isValidDeposit(amount)) {
```

```
                this.setName(name);
                this.setAmount(new BigDecimal(amount));
        } else {
            throw new IllegalAccount();
        }
    }

    @Override
    public boolean isValidDeposit(String deposit) {
        BigDecimal temp;
        try {
            temp = new BigDecimal(deposit);
        } catch (Exception e) {
            return false;
        }
        if (temp.compareTo(new BigDecimal.ZERO) > 0) {
            if (temp.add(this.getAmount()).compareTo(minBalance) > 0) {
                return true;
            }
        }
        return false;
    }

    @Override
    public void deposit(String deposit) throws IllegalDeposit {
        if (isValidDeposit(deposit)) {
            this.setAmount(this.getAmount().add(new BigDecimal(deposit)));
        } else {
            throw new IllegalDeposit();
        }
    }

    @Override
    public boolean isValidWithdrawal(String withdrawal) {
        BigDecimal temp;
        try {
            temp = new BigDecimal(withdrawal);
        } catch (Exception e) {
            return false;
        }
        if (temp.compareTo(this.getAmount().add(minBalance)) < 0) {
            return true;
        }
        return false;
    }

    @Override
    public void withdraw(String withdrawal) throws IllegalWithdrawal {
        if (isValidWithdrawal(withdrawal)) {
            this.setAmount(this.getAmount()
                    .subtract(new BigDecimal(withdrawal)));
        } else {
            throw new IllegalWithdrawal();
        }
    }
}
```

```java
    public String getName() {
        return name;
    }

    private void setName(String name) {
        this.name = name;
    }

    public BigDecimal getAmount() {
        return amount;
    }

    private void setAmount(BigDecimal amount) {
        this.amount = amount;
    }

    @Override
    public String toString() {
        return "CheckingAccount " + this.getName()
                + ": Balance = " + this.getAmount();
    }

}
```

8. Create an `AccountManager` class to test your interface-based application. You can reuse parts of the `AccountManager` class from the earlier exercise. It may look different from the one here, but should function in mostly the same way:

```java
public class AccountManager {

    public static void main(String[] args) {
        Accountable mySavings, myChecking;
        try {
            mySavings = new SavingsAccount("Save001", "10.00");
            System.out.println(mySavings);

            mySavings.withdraw("5.00");
            System.out.println(mySavings);

            myChecking = new CheckingAccount("Check002", "10.00");
            System.out.println(myChecking);

            myChecking = new CheckingAccount("Check002", "101.00");
            System.out.println(myChecking);

            myChecking.withdraw("5.00");
            System.out.println(myChecking);

            myChecking.deposit("500.00");
            System.out.println(myChecking);

            myChecking.withdraw("5.00");
            System.out.println(myChecking);
        } catch (IllegalAccount a) {
```

```
            System.out.println("Invalid Account Opening");
        } catch (IllegalDeposit d){
            System.out.println("Invalid Deposit");
        } catch (IllegalWithdrawal d){
            System.out.println("Invalid Withdrawal");
        }
    }
}
```

How It Works

Here's how it works:

1. The `Accountable` interface prescribes the types of behavior an `Accountable` class should include, namely deposit and withdraw. Some new exception types were defined to differentiate between the problems that may occur. The commenting describes the purpose of each method and any parameters or exceptions.

2. The `SavingsAccount` class implements the methods laid out in the `Accountable` interface. It also includes getters and setters for the instance variables and a `toString()` method for printing.

3. The `CheckingAccount` class is very similar to the `SavingsAccount` class, with a few small changes to account for the different rules attached to checking accounts, the minimum balance in particular. It is easy to see how these classes could easily be merged with a minimum balance of 0 for savings accounts. However, if more differences are expected or more types of accounts might be added, an interface with implementing classes may be appropriate.

4. The `AccountManager` class was organized differently than the previous exercise simply to show an alternate approach. Here the entire method is inside a `try` block, with three catch blocks to alert the user to problems with account creation, depositing, or withdrawing.

GARBAGE COLLECTION

Garbage collection is a way to reclaim memory from objects once they are no longer in use. You saw in Chapter 6 the `OutOfMemoryError` that's thrown when there is insufficient heap space for creating a new object. By removing unused objects from memory, more is available for new and existing objects. One difference between C++ and Java is that Java incorporates automatic garbage collection, so the programmer does not need to manage memory as much themselves.

An object is eligible for garbage collection when it is no longer accessible through any variable. However, if one object refers to another and that object in turn refers to the first in a cyclical dependency, they may both be eligible for garbage collection. Once an object is eligible for garbage collection, the garbage collector will eventually remove it from memory.

Recall how when a new object is created, the constructor method is called to initialize it. There is also a finalize method that's invoked just before the object is destroyed. This method is built in to the `Object` superclass, but you can override it in your classes to perform special actions before an object is destroyed.

To illustrate what is happening with garbage collection, consider the following code snippet.

```
class PersonManager {
    public static void main(String args[]) {
        Person p1 = new Person("Adam");
        Person p2 = new Person("Robert");
        p1 = p2;
        ...//Rest of program
    }
}
```

A `Person` variable `p1` is declared and initialized to a newly created `Person` object with the name `Adam`. A second `Person` variable `p2` is declared and initialized to another newly created `Person` object with the name `Robert`. See Figure 7-4.

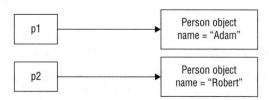

FIGURE 7-4

In the next statement, the variable `p1` is reassigned to the reference object of `p2`. See Figure 7-5.

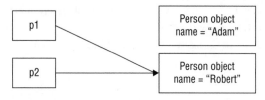

FIGURE 7-5

The `Person` object with name `Adam` no longer has any references pointing to it. So it becomes eligible for garbage collection. See Figure 7-6.

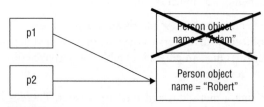

FIGURE 7-6

Handling Input and Output

WHAT YOU WILL LEARN IN THIS CHAPTER:

➤   How input and output differ

➤   How to handle interaction with users in your programs

➤   How to store and load information in files

WROX.COM CODE DOWNLOADS FOR THIS CHAPTER

The wrox.com code downloads for this chapter are found at www.wrox.com/go/ beginningjavaprogramming on the Download Code tab. The code is in the Chapter 8 download and individually named according to the names throughout the chapter.

So far, all the programs you've been writing throughout the course of this book have operated more or less on their own, without much interaction with the user at runtime, meaning that the interaction with the program happened while you were coding it, i.e. specifying all the tasks the program should perform. Once it ran, however, the program just went its course.

Interaction in programming is described as "input/output" (I/O). Of course, this communication flows in two directions, one in the form of "output," which is information the program provides to outside parties, and the other in the form of "input," which is information users provide to the program or information the program reads in from the outside world. It is easy to imagine a multitude of cases where such functionality could be useful. Imagine a program asking the user's name, for instance, or a program asking if it should terminate or ignore an error when something unexpected happens. These aspects are all covered in this chapter.

Interaction can happen not only between a program and a human end user, but can also involve other sources of information. Consider, for example, the fact that so far, whenever you closed and restarted a program, all its previous data values were lost. When writing a budget tracking application, you cannot expect your users to leave the program running indefinitely (what if the power goes out?) or expect them to re-enter all the information once they reopen the program. As such, you will also deal with ways of handling I/O between your program and data sources. This chapter covers the most basic of data sources, namely that of a file.

GENERAL INPUT AND OUTPUT

When we talk about input and output in computing, we describe all forms of communication between a program on the computer and the "outside world," which includes human end users, other programs on the same machine, or other programs running on other computers.

Input includes all the data and signals received by the running program. For instance, input can be sent to a program using input devices such as a keyboard or mouse, or can come from other computers, such as when you use your web browser to load in a specific web page. Output on the other hand includes all the signals and data sent from a program. Monitors and printers are prime examples of output devices, but again, output can involve pure data, such as when your web browser sends a request to a web server to receive a web page. The latter immediately illustrates that the same program (a web browser) can involve a series of input and output operations. The same holds for hardware devices, such as a network card or a modem.

A particular form of I/O we will be taking a closer look at in this chapter is file I/O, meaning input and output operations that read and write data to files stored on your computer. We can skip the details until we are ready to start dealing with files in Java, but two aspects are worth mentioning right now—file modes and the difference between text and binary files as they apply to programming languages other than Java.

Let's start with file modes. In many programming languages, once you specify a particular file, the language requires you to specify a particular mode (which, in many cases, is passed on to the operating system). Two general modes are fairly obvious: opening a file for reading and opening a file for writing. However, other modes can be specified as well. The following list provides an enumeration of such file modes, together with their common abbreviations used in most programming languages:

➤ r: Open a file for reading only (pointer at beginning of file).

➤ r+: Open a file for reading and writing (pointer at beginning of file).

➤ w: Open a file for writing only (pointer at beginning of file); if the file does not exist, try to create it; existing files will be truncated (made empty).

➤ w+: Open a file for reading and writing (pointer at beginning of file); if the file does not exist, try to create it; existing file will be truncated (made empty).

➤ a: Open a file for writing only (pointer at end of file, i.e. append new data at the end of the file).

➤ a+: Open a file for reading and writing (pointer at end of file, i.e. append new data at the end of the file).

➤ x: Create a file and open for writing only; fail if file already exists.

➤ x+: Create a file and open for reading and writing; fail if file already exists.

- c and c+: Open a file for writing only or for reading and writing (pointer at beginning of file); if file does not exist, try to create it; existing files will not be made empty, as opposed to w/w+, which means that writing data will overwrite existing data.

Don't panic if this list seems a bit daunting or confusing, as the most important thing for now is to remember that files can be opened for reading and writing. For writing, it is important to keep in mind that you can either empty an existing file and rewrite over it or keep the existing file in tact and append your data to the end. The reason why you don't need to remember the full list of file modes is because the Java file API makes things simple, as you'll see later.

The second general concept we highlight here is the difference between text and binary files. All the files on your computer can be categorized into these two formats. The difference lies in how the file encodes the data it contains. At the most basic level, both text and binary files store data as a series of bits (a series of zeroes and ones). However, in a text file, the bits represent characters (numbers, spaces, letters, etc.), while in a binary file, the bits represent custom data, stored and interpreted according to a particular format.

When you create a .txt file using Windows Notepad, for instance, you are creating a text file. Figure 8-1 illustrates a simple text file containing two lines of text opened in Notepad. On the right side, you can see this file in its hexadecimal representation—a compact representation of the bits stored in the file. As you can see, each byte (two hexadecimal characters) maps to exactly one character—54 maps to T and 73 maps to s.

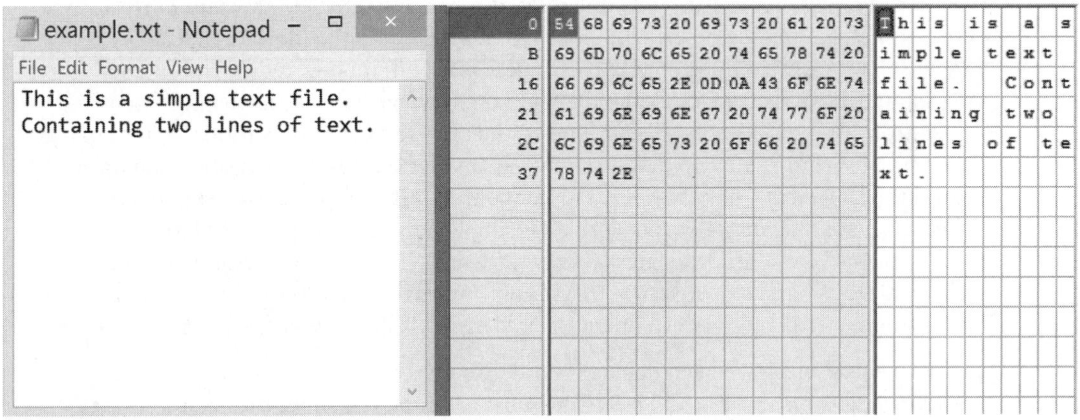

FIGURE 8-1

CHARACTER ENCODING

You might be wondering how exactly your computer knows which byte (a series of eight zeroes and ones) should be mapped to which character. The answer lies in the concept of standardization. As with every standardization process, many standards exist, all of which are compatible with one another to varying degrees (ranging from fully backward-compatible to completely incompatible). In western regions, this

continues

continued

standardization process started with standards such as EBCDIC (Extended Binary Coded Decimal Interchange Code), a character encoding scheme used by many IBM mainframes decades ago, and ASCII (American Standard Code for Information Interchange), which quickly became the standard in the early days of computing.

However, as time progressed, many vendors were confronted with the limitations of this American-centric standard, as no mapping was provided to represent accented characters (such as è, ï, and so on) used in non-English languages. As such, the International Organization for Standardization (ISO) and the International Electrotechnical Commission (IEC) proposed the ISO/IEC 8859 standard, a collection of character encodings to support European, Cyrillic, Greek, Turkish, and other languages. As ASCII used only seven out of eight bits provided in a byte (the remaining bit was sometimes used to calculate a checksum or used by vendors to map custom characters), the implementation of this standard was simple. By using the eighth bit, the range of possible characters that could be represented doubled and could thus include the accented characters. Moreover, this also ensured that all the ASCII characters could still retain their original position, which enabled backward-compatibility with existing text files.

Still, a downside of this approach was that users had to have the correct code page installed and selected on their system in order to read text files correctly. Whereas I might create a text file following the ISO/IEC 8859-1 convention (western Latin alphabet), the result will look wrong if you read the file using ISO/IEC 8859-7 (Greek). In addition, many languages were still not covered by the extending standards. Consider, for example, Asian regions, where a completely different standardization process had been followed thus far (the Chinese National Standard 11643). As such, in recent years, the ISO and IEC set out to create another standard called the Universal Character Set. This standard aims to represent all characters from the many languages of the world. The implementation comes in the form of the "Unicode" standard, the latest version of which contains a repertoire of more than 100,000 characters covering 100 scripts and various symbols. This is the standard now in use by all modern operating systems and throughout the Web.

Various encodings have been defined in order to map this wealth of characters to raw bits and bytes in a file. UTF-8 is the most common encoding format and it uses one byte for any ASCII character, all of which have the same code values in both UTF-8 and ASCII encoding (which is great news in terms of compatibility). For other characters, up to four bytes can be used. (As such, UTF-8 is called a "variable width" encoding.) Next, UCS-2 uses a two-byte code unit for each character, and thus cannot encode every character in the Unicode standard. UTF-16 extends UCS-2, using two-byte code units for the characters that were representable in UCS-2 and four-byte code units to handle each of the additional characters.

This might all seem a bit overwhelming, but the good news is that in recent years, thanks to the Unicode Consortium, things have become much simpler. The key takeaways to keep in mind are:

➤ When saving files in the old ASCII standard, you ensure compatibility but can only store a basic range of characters (fine for English).

➤ Otherwise, try to work with UTF-8. This ensures that every ASCII character is still represented by one byte, and all other characters will take up a few more bytes.

Binary files are much less structured, in the sense that they contain a sequence of bits that are structured and organized completely according to the whims of the program or programmer who created the file. This does not mean, however, that there cannot be some form of standardization behind such files. Consider, for example, image formats such as JPG or PNG, which can be opened by many image-viewing programs. Consider Figure 8-2, which shows a JPG file of a fractal opened by an image viewer capable of interpreting this format on the left side and the raw bytes on the right side.

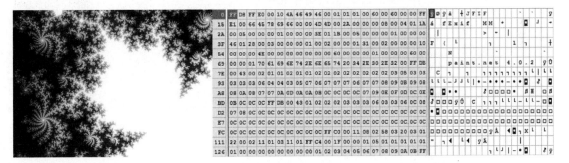

FIGURE 8-2

As you can see in Figure 8-2, the contents of this binary file cannot be represented as a series of characters in a meaningful way, although fragments and pieces of text can exist here and there, representing metadata (where the picture was taken, for instance) or strings. In many cases, many binary files will also start with a specific sequence of bytes (called a "magic number"), denoting what type of file it is. JPG files, for instance, begin with FF D8.

SPECIAL CHARACTERS

There's more to text files than character encodings alone. When dealing with text, not every character necessarily needs to represent a letter or a number. Consider for instance a special "character" representing a space or a tab, or a character representing a line break (the end of a line). Especially regarding the latter, some differences exist between operating systems. On Windows, a line break is represented by two characters (0D and 0A in hexadecimal). On most Unix-derived operating systems (such as Linux), a line break is represented by a single character (0A). The latter also holds for Mac systems, except for older Macs, where 0D is used instead. Some older operating systems also use fixed line lengths or other characters, but suffice it to say that this is something not all systems agree on. Luckily, Java helps correctly detect the end of a line in a text file, as you will see later.

INPUT AND OUTPUT IN JAVA

Dealing with input and output in Java—especially when working with files—is a topic that beginning Java programmers typically view in a begrudging manner, especially when coming in from other programming languages and looking up examples that are not yet up to par with the latest Java versions. Let's illustrate the reasons behind this with a typical example. Say you have a simple text file of a grocery list and want to go through it line by line in your program. Traditionally, examples, tutorials, and textbooks would have suggested a solution that looks like the following:

```java
import java.io.BufferedReader;
import java.io.FileReader;

public class ShowGroceries {
    public static void main(String[] args) {
        BufferedReader br = null;
        FileReader fr = null;
        try {
            fr = new FileReader("groceries.txt");
            br = new BufferedReader(fr);
            String line;
            while ((line = br.readLine()) != null) {
                System.out.println("Don't forget to pickup: " + item);
            }
        } catch (Exception x) {
            x.printStackTrace();
        } finally {
            if (fr != null) {
                try {br.close();} catch (Exception e) { e.printStackTrace(); }
                try {fr.close();} catch (Exception e) { e.printStackTrace(); }
            }
        }
    }
}
```

What is up with this large `try-catch` block? What is a `FileReader`? What is a `BufferedReader`? At first sight, dealing with file input/output in Java seems cumbersome and confusing.

A similar reasoning holds for basic user interaction. You've already seen in many examples how to show output to the user console using `System.out`:

```java
public class JavaInput {
    public static void main(String[] args) {
        System.out.println("What is your name, user?");
    }
}
```

Reading input given by the user, however, requires a more convuluted setup:

```java
import java.io.BufferedReader;
import java.io.IOException;
```

```java
import java.io.InputStreamReader;

public class JavaInput {
    public static void main(String[] args) {
        System.out.println("What is your name, user?");
        BufferedReader br = new BufferedReader(new InputStreamReader(System.in));
        String name;
        try {
            name = br.readLine();
        } catch (IOException e) {
            name = "?";
            e.printStackTrace();
        } finally {
            try { br.close(); } catch (IOException e) { e.printStackTrace(); }
        }
        System.out.println("Welcome, " + name);
    }
}
```

You might be bothered by the presence of the `try-catch` blocks and the occurrence of the `InputStreamReader`, as well as the `BufferedReader`, which makes another appearance.

Don't despair, however, as the design choices behind this, together with arcane names such as `InputStreamReader`, will all become clear in the following sections. The reason why Java's input/output model looks somewhat daunting at first is because it is based on so-called "I/O streams." A stream is simply an abstraction of a particular input source (any kind) or an output destination (also of any kind), meaning that streams can represent files, a program console, other programs, memory locations, or even hardware devices. Depending on the input source or output destination accessed, streams can support a variety of data formats, such as raw bits and bytes, but also characters, primitive data types, and even complete objects. Some streams will just pass on data, whereas others will perform some transformations. The key point, however, is that at their core, streams all represent a sequence of data. While this stream-based model can be somewhat verbose in the beginning, a great advantage is that they offer a unified model to deal with input/output, meaning that if you know how to send output to a stream with a file as its destination, you also know how to output data to the user console or to a device stream.

Even better news for beginning Java programmers is that, since Java 7, new features were added that greatly simplify the examples above. Sadly, these additions have also made the I/O landscape in Java slightly more chaotic. In Java SE 1.4, a new "Non-Blocking IO" API—oftentimes called NIO and referred to as "new I/O"—was added to the language to complement the existing I/O facilities. In Java 7, extensions were added in the form of NIO2 to offer a new, more sensible file system API. However, since backward-compatibility is a strong design goal behind Java, existing file I/O methods remained supported, so that many code samples, books, tutorials, and real-life code still apply "legacy I/O" API features. Is this a problem? Not really, except for the fact that you, the beginning Java programmer, will have to deal with both APIs, hence the illustrating examples above. The general recommendation for new projects is to use as much NIO2-based code as possible, but reverting back to the legacy API where necessary is fine. In fact, the Java language designers foresaw this issue and created a set of intercompatibility methods to quickly switch between the two, as you will see later.

> **NOTE** *As an example of how the NIO2 API improves file I/O in Java, consider the "read a grocery list" example provided earlier. Using NIO2, this code fragment can be rewritten as follows:*

```java
import java.io.IOException;
import java.nio.charset.Charset;
import java.nio.file.Files;
import java.nio.file.Paths;
import java.util.ArrayList;
import java.util.List;

public class ShowGroceries {
    public static void main(String[] args) {
        List<String> groceries = new ArrayList<>();
        try {
            groceries = Files.readAllLines(
                Paths.get("groceries.txt"),
                        Charset.defaultCharset());
        } catch (IOException | SecurityException e) {
            e.printStackTrace();
        }
        for (String item : groceries) {
            System.out.println("Don't forget to pickup: " + item);
        }
    }
}
```

> *Notice the* `readAllLines` *method, which removes the burden of having to use the* `FileReader` *and* `BufferedReader` *classes.*

You are now ready to delve into I/O with Java for real and explore the concept of streams in more detail.

STREAMS

We've mentioned before that the key abstraction behind I/O in Java is the concept of a stream. Streams represent a sequence of data as it is read from a source (an input stream) or written to a destination (an output stream). This immediately clarifies why you will not deal with file modes in Java (opening a file for reading or writing), as the type of stream (input or output) will determine whether you want to use a file as a data source or destination.

We've also stated that streams can support different kinds of data, and depending on the data type they carry, different methods are exposed. For streams carrying textual data, for instance (think back on text files), it makes sense to read in a single text line. For streams carrying byte data (raw bits and bytes), no concept of a "text line" can be defined, so this method does not make sense in this context. Apart from reading and writing data, streams can also modify or transform data as it passes through. A common example is an output stream that zips (compresses) the data while writing it to a file, in order to reduce the file size.

The following sections discuss the various types of streams in more detail.

Byte Streams

Byte streams represent sequences of data that's represented at its most basic, raw format, meaning bytes (eight bits). They form the lowest level of I/O in Java so that all other streams are built on them.

All byte streams subclass InputStream and OutputStream (inheritance, subclasses, superclasses, and interfaces were explained in the previous chapter) and always at least provide the following methods. For InputStream:

➤ int read(): Reads the next byte of data from the input stream. Returns -1 if the end of the stream is reached.

➤ int read(byte[] b): Reads some number of bytes from the input stream and stores them into the array b. Returns the total number of bytes read into the buffer or -1 if there is no more data because the end of the stream has been reached.

➤ int read(byte[] b, int off, int len): Reads up to len bytes of data from the input stream at offset off into an array b. Returns the total number of bytes read into the buffer or -1 if there is no more data because the end of the stream has been reached.

➤ long skip(long n): Skips over and discards n bytes of data from this input stream. Returns the actual number of bytes skipped.

➤ void close(): Closes this input stream and releases any system resources associated with it.

➤ int available(): Returns an estimate of the number of bytes that can be read (or skipped over) from this input stream without blocking.

➤ boolean markSupported(): Tests if this input stream supports the mark and reset methods.

➤ void mark(int readlimit): Marks the current position in this input stream.

➤ void reset(): Repositions this stream to the position at the time the mark method was last called on this input stream.

INTEGERS AS BYTES

You might be surprised by the fact that the read methods in the previous list return ints and not bytes, which is also a primitive data type and would be a logical sounding choice for a stream-reading and -writing byte. The reason for this is twofold. First, the byte type in Java is signed, meaning that after conversion to a number, it represents the range of -128 to 127, which makes calculation more cumbersome when an unsigned number ranging between 0 and 255 is expected. Furthermore, note that the read methods return -1 when the end of a stream is reached, which would then not be able to fall inside the range of an 8-bit range (0 to 255).

continues

continued

Very astute readers will note that the short primitive data type would also be fine to represent a byte, as it ranges from -32,768 to 32,767 and thus has plenty of space to represent both -1 and 0 to 255. The reason for this is simply because working with `int`s is faster than shorts in the JVM (as this 32-bit type maps more closely to underlying modern hardware), and that `int` has become sort of a standard means to hold a byte of data. Secondly, you might also wonder why `read` returns -1 instead of throwing an exception when the end of a stream is reached. Again a good point, and this is due to historic reasons and standardized practices (coming mainly from the world of the C programming language).

For `OutputStream`, we get:

➤ `void write(int b):` Writes the specified byte (represented using an `int` variable) to this output stream.

➤ `void write(byte[] b):` Writes the specified byte array `b` to this output stream.

➤ `void write(byte[] b, int off, int len):` Writes `len` bytes from the `b` starting at offset `off` to this output stream.

➤ `void close():` Closes this output stream and releases any system resources associated with this stream.

➤ `void flush():` "Flushes" this output stream, i.e. forces any buffered output bytes to be written out.

It's worth underlining the fact that the `close` method appears in both the `InputStream` and `OutputStream` classes. It is extremely important to always close streams when you no longer need them. In fact, this is so important that, even when an error occurs, you should still attempt to close streams. Keeping streams open can lead to resource leaks, i.e. files remain opened by the JVM and take up memory in your program. When the data source or destination is something other than a file, the `close` method of the byte stream class might also be responsible for ensuring that everything is tidied up correcly.

To get you started with byte streams, the following Try It Out shows you how to copy a file using `FileInputStream` and `FileOutputStream`, two basic byte stream classes aimed at working with files.

TRY IT OUT   Copying Files with Byte Streams

In this Try It Out, you will copy a grocery list using byte streams.

1. Create a new project in Eclipse if you haven't done so already.

2. In the Eclipse Package Explorer, create a new file called `groceries.txt` within the project root (not in the `src` folder). See Figure 8-3.

3. Enter a grocery list in this TXT file and save it (one item per line). This example uses the following shopping list:

```
apples
bananas
water
orange juice
milk
bread
```

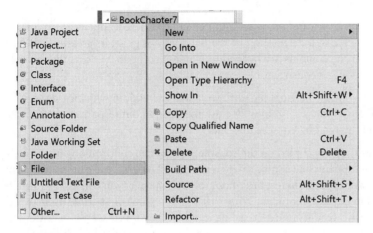

FIGURE 8-3

4. Create a `FileCopier` class with the following contents:

```java
import java.io.FileInputStream;
import java.io.FileOutputStream;
import java.io.IOException;

public class FileCopier {
    public static void main(String[] args) {
        FileInputStream in = null;
        FileOutputStream out = null;
        try {
            in = new FileInputStream("groceries.txt");
            out = new FileOutputStream("groceries (copy).txt");
            int c;
            while ((c = in.read()) != -1) {
                out.write(c);
                System.out.print((char) c);
            }
        } catch (IOException e) {
            e.printStackTrace();
        } finally {
            if (in != null) try { in.close(); } catch (IOException e)
                { e.printStackTrace(); }
            if (out != null) try { out.close(); } catch (IOException e)
                { e.printStackTrace(); }
        }
    }
}
```

5. Execute the program. If you refresh your project (right-click and select Refresh or press F5), you will see that a file called `groceries (copy).txt` has appeared. In addition, the copied bytes are shown on Eclipse's console.

How It Works

Here's how it works:

1. We're using both a `FileInputStream` and `FileOutputStream` class here to open the original file as a data source and a new file as a destination. If the file does not exist, its creation will be attempted. If the file does exist, its contents are overridden, unless you pass `true` as the second argument of the `FileOutputStream` constructor.

2. Next, we keep reading bytes from the original file until we reach the end, in which case the `read` method will return -1. Inside the `while` loop, we use the `write` counterpart method of the `FileOutputStream` to write the read byte to the new file.

3. We also show the contents as they are copied on the console, so you can follow along as the file is being copied (the `System.out.print` line can be safely removed). To do so, we cannot just print the `int c` variable, as doing so would result in a series of numbers as output (you can try this yourself). Therefore, we first cast the integer to a character. Note that this is a somewhat crude approach that assumes that we are dealing with readable, text-based data (which is not necessarily the case when working with byte streams) and that the original data is stored using a standard ASCII-based encoding. For the sake of this example, these assumptions are not problematic, though.

4. An `IOException` is caught in case some error occurs (for instance, when the original file does not exist). A `finally` block closes the streams. Note that closing streams can also throw exceptions, but we just give up in that case and ignore those.

5. Note that streams provide an excellent opportunity to make use of a Java 7–specific feature called ARM (Automatic Resource Management), also known under the name *try-with-resources*. As you saw in Chapter 6, a try-with-resources block is a `try` statement that declares one or more resources. These resources will be closed at the end of the code included in the `try` block. Any objects that implement the `AutoCloseable` interface (which includes streams) can be used in such a try-with-resources block. As such, the previous code can be rewritten as follows:

```
import java.io.FileInputStream;
import java.io.FileOutputStream;
import java.io.IOException;

public class FileCopier {
    public static void main(String[] args) {
        try (
            FileInputStream in = new FileInputStream("groceries.txt");
            FileOutputStream out = new FileOutputStream("groceries (copy).txt");
        ) {
            int c;
            while ((c = in.read()) != -1) {
                out.write(c);
                System.out.print((char) c);
            }
        } catch (IOException e) {
```

```
            e.printStackTrace();
        }
    }
}
```

The `PrintStream` class is another interesting example that implements extra methods to allow for easy output formatting on top of a normal byte output stream:

➤ `void print(String s)`: Writes the specified string to this print stream. Note that this method is overridden to also accept other primitive types (char, double, etc.).

➤ `void println(String s)`: Writes the specified string to this print stream, but also terminates the line (i.e. starts a new line). Note that this method is overridden to also accept other primitive types (char, double, etc.).

➤ `void format(String format, Object... args)`: This function takes a "format string" as its first argument and the variables you want to format as the following arguments. The format string contains a number of percentage (%) fields representing where, which, and how variables should be formatted. The most basic conversions are:

   ➤ %d: to format an integer value as a decimal value

   ➤ %f: to format a floating-point value as a decimal value

   ➤ %n: to output a line terminator

   ➤ %x: to format an integer value as a hexadecimal value (less useful)

   ➤ %s: to format any value as a string (effectively calling the `toString` method)

   ➤ %%: to output a percentage sign

Note that the `System.out` object we've been using to send output to the console is in fact an example of a `PrintStream`. It is opened at the start of your program and closed automatically at the end, so you can use it directly without further management. The following Try It Out shows some examples of `PrintStream`'s methods.

TRY IT OUT Formatting Output with PrintStream

This Try It Out shows some examples of formatting output with a `PrintStream` byte stream.

1. Create a new project in Eclipse if you haven't done so already.

2. Create the following class and execute it to see the examples in action:

```java
public class FormattingOutput {
    public static void main(String[] args) {
        /* System.out is a PrintStream, but a PrintStream class
        is a specialization of an OutputStream. The write() method
        is thus available: */
        System.out.write(50); // 50 corresponds to '2'
        System.out.write((int)'\n'); // newline
```

```
            // However, it is much easier to use print and println:
            System.out.print("Text without newline");

            System.out.print("\r\nYou can enter a newline\r\n"
                    + "manually, as well as tabs using \t tab \t tab \t ...\r\n"
                    + "Backslashes themselves are entered with \\...\r\n");

            System.out.println("println is easier to show a "
                    + "string with a newline");

            // The format method can be used to format arguments in a string
            int number = 10;
            double othernumber = 1.134;
            System.out.println("Using + is okay in most cases: " + number
                    + ", " + othernumber);
            System.out.format("But format allows for more flexibility: %d, %3.2f %n",
                    number, othernumber);
            System.out.format("Another %3$s: %2$+020.10f, %1$d%n",
                    number, othernumber, "example");
        }
    }
```

3. Executing this program shows the following output in the console. Try experimenting with the print, println, and format methods at your own leisure.

```
2
Text without newline
You can enter a newline
manually, as well as tabs using        tab         tab          ...
Backslashes themselves are entered with \...
println is easier to show a string with a newline
Using + is okay in most cases: 10, 1.134
But format allows for more flexibility: 10, 1.13
Another example: +00000001.1340000000, 10
```

How It Works

Here's how it works:

1. We're using the standard System.out PrintStream to illustrate the workings of this class.

2. Since a PrintStream extends an OutputStream, you can still call the write method on System.out as well. The code sample does so by first sending the byte 50 (represented using an int variable and corresponding to the character 2) and a newline character (by casting it to an int) to System.out.

3. The workings of the print and println methods should be familiar by now. Note, however, the use of \n, \r, \t, and \\ within the strings to insert special characters. These special backslash combinations are called "escape sequences."

4. The format method on the other hand is new. As explained above, this function takes a "format string" as its first argument and the variables you want to format as the following arguments.

5. Using this method, numbers can be formatted with advanced formatting parameters. For example, %3.2f in our code shows "1.134" as "1.13". The full set of formatting parameters are given by the example %2$+020.10f, with:

➤ 2$ denotes the argument index (2). Use this if the variables to be formatted do not follow the same order as provided in the format string or if you want to output the same variable more than once.

➤ +0 for flags. This is a series of characters including + to specify that a number should be formatted with a sign, 0 to specify that 0 is the padding character (if not provided, a space is used instead), - to specify that padding should be added on the right (the number will be left aligned), and , to specify that a locale-specific thousands separator should be used.

➤ 20 is the minimum width of the formatted value. The value will be padded if necessary to obtain this width.

➤ .10 is the precision (10). For decimals, this is the mathematical precision of the formatted value. For %s and other conversions, this is the maximum width of the formatted value, truncated if necessary.

➤ f is the actual conversion.

Returning to the file copy program we introduced before, recall that we're copying the file in a raw, byte-by-byte manner. While this is fine, byte streams actually represent low-level input/output. Since the grocery list is a text file containing character data, it might be better to use a higher-level stream type geared more toward this purpose, namely character streams.

Character Streams

Character streams translate Unicode characters (used internally within Java) to and from the character locale specified. This stream is equal to a byte stream but adapts to the local character set and is thus ready for internationalization.

All character streams subclass Reader and Writer, e.g., FileReader and FileWriter. These classes are *not* subclasses of the byte stream InputStream and OutputStream classes, but offer a similar set of methods, e.g., read and write. The next Try It Out reworks the file copier example to use character streams instead of byte streams.

TRY IT OUT Copying Files with Character Streams

In this Try It Out, you will copy a grocery list using character streams.

1. We will modify the FileCopier class we created earlier. Refer to the earlier Try It Out if you have not done so already. Make sure the groceries.txt file is still present.

2. Edit the FileCopier class to look as follows:

```
import java.io.FileReader;
import java.io.FileWriter;
import java.io.IOException;

public class FileCopier {
    public static void main(String[] args) {
        try {
            Reader in = new FileReader("groceries.txt");
```

```
            Writer out = new FileWriter("groceries (copy).txt");
        ) {
            int c;
            while ((c = in.read()) != -1) {
                out.write(c);
                System.out.print((char) c);
            }
        } catch (IOException e) {
            e.printStackTrace();
        }
    }
}
```

3.   Execute the program. You'll see that it behaves similarly as before.

How It Works

Here's how it works:

1.   We're now using the FileReader and FileWriter classes here to open the original file as a data source and a new file as a destination. If the file does not exist, the program will attempt to create it. If the file does exist, its contents are overridden, unless you pass true as the second argument of the FileWriter constructor.

2.   The rest of the program is performed very similarly to using byte streams. Note that we're using a try-with-resources block to handle the closing of the Reader and the Writer automatically. If you use a traditional try-catch block, do not forget to add a finally clause when you close the Reader and Writer.

3.   With our Reader and Writer acting so similarly to our InputStream and OutputStream, you might be wondering why it makes sense to use character streams in the first place. The first difference lies in the fact that Readers and Writers store characters in the last 16 bits of an int, and thus support a wider range of characters. Byte streams read and write bytes, that is, they store a byte in the last eight bits of an int. For this simple English grocery list, the difference is not noticeable, but once you start adding a wider range of characters, you'll see that character streams are the right route to follow. Second, when dealing with text files, you might often be interested in working with bigger units than just a single byte (or character), for example to read and show lines. With Readers and Writers, you can do so, although you first need to add another stream type to the mix, as you'll see in the following section on buffered streams.

Next, note the existance of InputStreamReader and OutputStreamReader to create byte-to-character bridges when no native character stream class exists to meet your data source/destination (you will see a situation later on where this becomes useful). The PrintWriter class, finally, is the character stream counterpart of the PrintStream class.

Buffered Streams

Most streams in Java are unbuffered, meaning that each write and read request is handled directly by the operating system. This makes programs less efficient, as every write request to a file, for instance, will trigger disk access or some other time-consuming operation. Therefore, buffered streams can be used to wrap around other streams. They provide a dedicated space in memory (a buffer) to store data in an efficient manner, and will request time-expensive operations only if necessary (such as when the buffer is full and ready to be written to disk).

Four buffer classes exist which can be wrapped around a byte or character input/output stream: `BufferedInputStream`, `BufferedOutputStream`, `BufferedReader`, and `BufferedWriter`. The latter two classes are especially helpful when dealing with text files, as they allow you to work with data in a line-oriented manner. The following Try It Out once again shows the file copier example rewritten.

TRY IT OUT   Copying and Showing Files Line by Line with Buffered Streams

In this Try It Out, you will copy a grocery list using buffered character streams.

1.   You will modify the `FileCopier` class created earlier. Refer to the earlier Try It Out if you have not done so already. Make sure the `groceries.txt` file is still present.

2.   Edit the `FileCopier` class to look as follows:

```java
import java.io.BufferedReader;
import java.io.BufferedWriter;
import java.io.FileReader;
import java.io.FileWriter;
import java.io.IOException;

public class FileCopier {
    public static void main(String[] args) {
        try (
            Reader in = new BufferedReader(
                    new FileReader("groceries.txt"));
            Writer out = new BufferedWriter(
                    new FileWriter("groceries (copy).txt"));
        ) {
            String line;
            while ((line = in.readLine()) != null) {
                out.write(line + System.lineSeparator());
                System.out.println(line);
            }
        } catch (IOException e) {
            e.printStackTrace();
        }
    }
}
```

3.   Execute the program. You'll see that it behaves similarly as before.

How It Works

Here's how it works:

1.   We're now using `BufferedReader` and `BufferedWriter` classes here to open the original file as a data source and a new file as a destination. Note that these classes wrap around normal `Reader` and `Writer` classes (just as `BufferedInputStream` and `BufferedOutputStream` wrap around `InputStream` and `OutputStream` classes).

2. Note earlier that we mentioned that you can use `InputStreamReader` and `OutputStreamReader` to create byte-to-character bridges. It is therefore, in theory, possible to write the following:

```
BufferedReader in = new BufferedReader(
    new InputStreamReader(
        new FileInputStream("groceries.txt")));
```

But it goes without saying that this is not an efficient nor clear manner to achieve the desired effect. Therefore, only use `InputStreamReader` and `OutputStreamReader` when no other option is available.

3. The rest of the program works similarly, but now reads data line by line. Note that the newline terminator will be stripped from the read line, so we use `System.lineSeparator()` to add a platform-dependent line ending (\r or \n or \r\n) when writing the line to the output file. Note that the system line separator might be different than the one used in the original file, so this implementation of our file copier might not make exact copies in this case (if you do want to create an exact copy, you can use the `read()` method, but this will result in the code working more slowly, as now every character is read, returned, and copied one by one). Note also that the `readLine` method returns null when the end of a stream is reached.

> **NOTE** *When not using try-with-resources blocks and closing your streams manually, you might wonder which streams you need to close when wrapping streams (such as is the case with buffered streams) and in which order. The answer is simple: just close the topmost stream. The underlying ones will be closed and tidied up as well.*

Data and Object Streams

Data streams support binary input and output of primitive data type values (boolean, char, byte, short, int, long, float, and double) as well as String values. They thus offer a simple generic means to load and store primitive data values. All data streams implement either the `DataInput` interface or the `DataOutput` interface, i.e. `DataInputStream` and `DataOutputStream`. Note that these streams subclass `InputStream` and `OutputStream` and are thus a specialization of byte streams.

Object streams are similar to data streams, but allow the serialization of all objects that implement the `Serializable` marker interface. The object streams implement either the `ObjectInput` or `ObjectOutput` interfaces (which themselves are subinterfaces of `DataInput` and `DataOutput`), i.e. `ObjectInputStream` and `ObjectOutputStream`. Note that these streams subclass `InputStream` and `OutputStream` and are thus a specialization of byte streams.

The following Try It Out shows you how to work with data and object streams.

TRY IT OUT   Working with Data and Object Streams

In this Try It Out, you create a small class to illustrate the workings of an `ObjectOutputStream`. Note that an `ObjectOutputStream` can write primitive data types as well (as a `DataOutputStream` using the same method names), but can also serialize objects.

1. Create a class called `ObjectOutputStreamTest` with the following contents:

```java
import java.io.FileOutputStream;
import java.io.IOException;
import java.io.ObjectOutputStream;
import java.util.ArrayList;
import java.util.List;

public class ObjectOutputStreamTest {
    public static void main(String[] args) {
        int number1 = 5;
        double number2 = 10.3;
        String string = "a string";
        List<String> list = new ArrayList<>();
        list.add("a");
        list.add("b");

        try (
            ObjectOutputStream out = new ObjectOutputStream(
                    new FileOutputStream("saved.txt"));
        ) {
            out.writeInt(number1);
            out.writeDouble(number2);
            out.writeBytes(string);
            out.writeObject(list);
        } catch (IOException e) {
            e.printStackTrace();
        }
    }
}
```

2. Execute the program and refresh your Eclipse project. A file called `saved.txt` should appear with contents similar to these:

```
    @$™™™™™™ša string¬í sr FileCopier$1ÍÉJ;¹-
\-------------------------------------------------------------------------
xr java.util.ArrayListxÒ&traed;Ça•---------------------------------
I -------------------------------------------------------------------------
sizexpw---------------------------------------------------------------------
t at bx¬í w    @$™™™™™™ša stringsr FileCopier$1ÍÉJ;¹
\-------------------------------------------------------------------------
xr java.util.ArrayListxÒ™Ça------------------------------------- I
-------------------------------------------------------------------------
sizexpw---------------------------------------------------------------------
t at bx
```

How It Works

Here's how it works:

1. The `ObjectOutputStream` class is created as a wrapper around a normal `FileOutputStream`.

2. Next, `ObjectOutputStream` exposes a number of methods, i.e. `writeInt`, `writeDouble`, and so on, to write data to the stream.

3. Although you save the data to a file named `saved.txt`, the reality is that you are creating a binary file and not a text file, which explains why the text looks all garbled when you try to open it with a text editor. You are looking at raw binary data representing primitive values and objects, stored according to a format defined by the JVM.

4. Things to try: change `ObjectOutputStream` to `DataOutputStream`. Which variables can be written? Which cannot? Try expanding this class to use `ObjectInputStream` to read the saved data back in again. Take care to read the data in the correct order as saved in the file.

A common use case for using data and object streams is to implement input and output (communication) between different running programs, for example to send objects or data from one process to another. This concept is called inter-process communication (IPC). While discussing the details of IPC is too advanced for a beginner's book on programming, it is worth knowing that this exists and can in fact be implemented in various ways:

➤ **Using a file:** One program writes information to a file, which is then read out by another program. This method is crude, but works and is relatively simple to implement. After reading through this chapter, you'll know how to read and write from files, and the Data and Object streams mentioned above can be utilized here to read from and write to these files.

➤ **Sending a signal:** This works only if signaling capabilities are provided by the underlying operating system. Oftentimes it's used to send commands instead of larger data.

➤ **A network socket:** A data stream sent over a network interface. Note that this allows the communicating programs to also reside on different machines. Chapter 10 provides a basic introduction regarding building web services using Java, which can also be used to enable IPC.

➤ **A pipe:** This is a data stream that allows two-way character-by-character communication, supported and provided by most operating systems.

➤ **A message queue:** Also provided by the operating system. Similar to a pipe, but messages are sent in packets rather than streamed character by character.

➤ **Shared memory:** Two programs are given access to the same part of memory.

A WORD ABOUT SERIALIZATION

We have stated that objects can be saved and read using `ObjectOutputStream` and `ObjectInputStream` as long as they implement the `Serializable` marker interface. We call this a "marker" interface, as the interface does not actually specify any methods that must be implemented by the class that is to be serialized. Any object can be serialized, as long as it implements this marker interface and all its fields can be serialized, meaning that the fields that should be primitive types are other objects that can be serialized (implementing the `Serializable` interface).

Note that it is possible to specifiy fields that should not be serialized using the `transient` keyword, for instance:

> ```
> private transitent String secretCreditCardNumber;
> ```
>
> The reason why you might want to make fields transient is because they are stored
> in an unencrypted format when they're serialized.
>
> Finally, note that you can override two hidden methods: `private void readObject`
> `(ObjectInputStream s)` and `private void writeObject(ObjectOutputStream`
> `s)` in order to define a custom (de)serialization scheme. In most cases, the default
> serialization scheme works just fine, though.

Other Streams

Finally, a multitude of various other streams exist. Consider for instance `AudioInputStream`, which
reads in audio-based data (sample frames). Or `ZipOutputStream`, which implements an output
stream for writing ZIP (compressed) files. The latter is a subclass of the `FilterOutputStream`,
which acts as a superclass of other transforming output stream classes as well.

Most of these other streams subclass `InputStream` and `OutputStream`, i.e. byte streams, which you
have seen before. Browse through the Java API docs in order to get an overview of all the stream
types included in the standard Java API.

SCANNERS

Earlier, you saw how you can perform advanced output formatting using the format method of the
`PrintWriter` and `PrintStream` stream classes. This might have left you wondering: what about
input? If a text file is formatted in a known manner, how can you easily read out all the data?

In fact, you've already seen a few ways to tackle this problem. If you don't mind your input data
being binary, you can use data or object streams to read in the various data types correctly. If your
data is given as text, you have seen how the `BufferedReader` class can help read the data line by
line. But what if a line of text contains different fragments you want to parse out?

Luckily, Java provides a simple means to break down input into various fragments—or *tokens*, as
they are called—and translate them according to their data type. The class that helps you do this is
the `Scanner`, found under `java.util.Scanner`. The following Try It Out shows how it works.

TRY IT OUT   Scanning a Grocery List with Prices

In this Try It Out, you use the `Scanner` class to read in text fragments and translate them according to
their data type.

1. You will continue working in the same project as before. Create a new text file next to `groceries.`
    `txt` called `grocerieswithprices.txt` with the following content:

    ```
    apples, 5.33

    bananas, 4.61
    ```

```
water, 1.00

orange juice, 2.50

milk, 3.20

bread, 1.11
```

2. Create a new class called `ShowGroceries`. First of all, you will take a look at how you would read out the grocery list and show it without using a `Scanner`:

```java
import java.io.BufferedReader;
import java.io.FileReader;
import java.io.IOException;

public class ShowGroceries {
    public static void main(String[] args) {
        try (
            BufferedReader in = new BufferedReader(new FileReader(
                "grocerieswithprices.txt"));
        ) {
            String line;
            while ((line = in.readLine()) != null) {
                String[] splittedLine = line.split(", ");
                String item = splittedLine[0].trim();
                double price = Double.parseDouble(splittedLine[1].trim());
                System.out.format("Price of %s is: %.2f%n", item, price);
            }
        } catch (IOException e) {
            e.printStackTrace();
        }

    }
}
```

3. This approach works fine for simple cases, but depending on the nature and structure of your input text, you might want to resort to a `Scanner` instead, as follows:

```java
import java.io.BufferedReader;
import java.io.FileReader;
import java.io.IOException;
import java.util.Locale;
import java.util.Scanner;
import java.util.regex.Pattern;

public class ShowGroceries {
    public static void main(String[] args) {
        try (
            Scanner sc = new Scanner(
                    new FileReader("grocerieswithprices.txt"));
        ) {
            sc.useDelimiter(Pattern.compile("(, )|(\r\n)"));
            sc.useLocale(Locale.ENGLISH);
            while (sc.hasNext()) {
                String item = sc.next();
```

```
                    double price = sc.nextDouble();
                    System.out.format("Price of %s is: %.2f%n", item, price);
            }
        } catch (IOException e) {
            e.printStackTrace();
        }

    }
}
```

How It Works

Here's how it works:

1. The `Scanner` class wraps around a `BufferedReader` in this example, but can also be directly applied to a string if so desired.

2. Next, we set the delimiter pattern of the `Scanner`. A delimiter is a piece of string by which we want to split up text fragments. By default, the delimiter of a `Scanner` equals all white-space characters (newline, a space, a tab), but in our case, we change it to match either a comma followed by a space (", ") or a newline (\r\n).

3. We also set the `Locale` of the `Scanner` to English to make sure the decimal prices are read in and interpreted correctly. `Locale` is a Java provided class to represent geographical regions. Instead of instantiating a new object, the class provides a series of static members (themselves `Locale` objects) that can be accessed and used directly, such as `Locale.ENGLISH` or `Locale.KOREA`. Your computer might already use English as a default locale, in which case this line can also be removed.

4. Next, a `while` loop is iterated over so long as the `Scanner` is able to feed text fragments. If this is the case, we know we can immediately read in two pieces of fragments at once—the item and the price—using the `nextDouble` method.

5. Note that we use the `Pattern` class here to supply a regular expression, a relatively advanced format that specifies text patterns. Normally, you could also supply the delimiter as a single string, in which case you might be tempted to try ", ", but this will not work, as the `Scanner` will then continue to read text even after the end of a line is encountered, which we do not want in this case. Therefore, as a general recommendation, it is best to either stick to newline delimiters only, or use a delimiter that can be easily expressed as a single string, for instance ", " and put all the data on the same line.

INPUT AND OUTPUT FROM THE COMMAND-LINE

You've seen how to use streams to perform input and output operations, e.g., to read and write data to files. In the following section, we'll explore file I/O a bit deeper, but we first take a slight detour in order to show off input and output with the command-line.

Although most programs you run on your computer nowadays offer some sort of Graphical User Interface (GUI), this has not always been the case. In the old days of computing, programs oftentimes only offered text-like communication possibilities, showing their output and taking input from a so-called "console," or command-line. Even in modern operating systems, this command-line interface is still present under the hood. In Windows, for instance, you can try firing up the `cmd.exe` program to get the command prompt shown in Figure 8-4.

FIGURE 8-4

When you execute Java programs in Eclipse, they will also show their output and take their input from a command-line interface, unless you program in some kind of GUI features. We refer here to the Eclipse console. Refer back to Chapter 3 if you want to know how you can run Java programs from the common Windows command-line.

In every console application, three mechanisms exist to communicate with the user. In Java, these are implemented as the "standard streams," corresponding to the following:

➤ `System.in`: A byte `InputStream` to take user input (you might have expected this to be a character stream, but for historical reasons, this is not the case)

➤ `System.err`: A `PrintStream` to output error messages

➤ `System.out`: A `PrintStream` to output normal messages

You can use these streams just as you would use normal Java streams, with the difference, however, that you don't need to open or close them. The following Try It Out shows how it works.

TRY IT OUT   Input and Output from the Command-Line

This Try It Out illustrates the basic use of `System.in`, `System.err`, and `System.out` by means of a simple greeter application.

1.   Create a single class named `ReadName` with the following content:

```java
import java.io.BufferedReader;
import java.io.IOException;
import java.io.InputStreamReader;

public class ReadName {
    public static void main(String[] args) {
        try(
            BufferedReader reader = new BufferedReader(
                    new InputStreamReader(System.in));
        ) {
            System.out.println("What is your name, user?");
            String name = reader.readLine();
```

```
            if (name.trim().equals(""))
                throw new IllegalArgumentException();
            System.out.println("Welcome, " + name);
        } catch (IllegalArgumentException e) {
            System.err.println("Error: name cannot be blank!");
        } catch (IOException e) {
            e.printStackTrace();
        }

    }
}
```

2. Execute the class and watch what happens in Eclipse's console. Try to enter your name. What happens when you enter a blank name?

How It Works

Here's how it works:

1. `System.in`, `System.out`, and `System.err` all act as normal streams as you've seen before. Note, however, the use of the `InputStreamReader` class to make a bridge from `System.in` (a byte stream) to a `BufferedReader`, which expects a character stream. Why do we use `BufferedReader` instead of `BufferedInputStream` here? Because we want to use the `readLine` method to read in a complete line of user input. This is one of the valid use cases for `InputStreamReader`. As an alternative, it is also possible to make use of a `Scanner` as seen above, in which case the class would look like follows:

```
import java.util.Scanner;

public class ReadName {
    public static void main(String[] args) {
        try(
            Scanner sc = new Scanner(System.in);
        ) {
            System.out.println("What is your name, user?");
            String name = sc.nextLine();
            if (name.trim().equals(""))
                throw new IllegalArgumentException();
            System.out.println("Welcome, " + name);
        } catch (IllegalArgumentException e) {
            System.err.println("Error: name cannot be blank!");
        }

    }
}
```

2. Note also that we define two `catch` blocks: one to catch I/O errors as we've done before, and one to catch our own thrown exception in case the user enters a blank name.

The reason why both normal output and error streams are provided is not native to Java, but is due to historical reasons and standardization of command-line I/O in modern operating systems. Both normal output and error streams are provided to allow users to redirect output to a file, while still showing error messages on the command line. This concept is not native to Java, but is included for historical reasons due to the standardization of command-line I/O in modern operating systems.

An example can help to clarify this. Let's assume that you want to make a class that accepts lines from System.in and then shows the reversed line on System.out. When a palindrome is given, however (a line that reads the same forward or reversed), we'll also show a toy "warning" on System.err. When a blank line is given, execution is stopped. The final class looks like this:

```java
import java.io.BufferedReader;
import java.io.IOException;
import java.io.InputStreamReader;


public class LineReverser {
    public static void main(String[] args) {
        try(
            BufferedReader reader = new BufferedReader(
                    new InputStreamReader(System.in));
        ) {
            String line = null;
            while (true) {
                line = reader.readLine();
                if (line == null || "".equals(line))
                    break;
                String reverse = new StringBuilder(line).reverse().toString();
                System.out.println(reverse);
                if (line.equals(reverse))
                    System.err.format("The string '%s' is a palindrome!%n", line);
            }
        } catch (IOException e) {
            e.printStackTrace();
        }

    }
}
```

Take some time to execute this class and familiarize yourself with the code. Try to enter a palindrome such as "amoreroma" and see what happens.

Now, we will take this a step further. Right-click on the LineReverser class in Eclipse and choose Export. Next, select Runnable JAR File. See Figure 8-5.

In the next screen, select LineReverser as the "launch configuration" (this requires that you ran the class in Eclipse at least once). Set the Export Destination to linereverser.jar on your desktop.

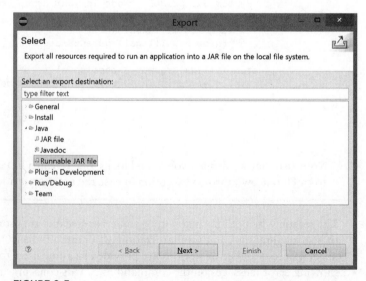

FIGURE 8-5

Once this is done, open a command-line window (start `cmd.exe` on Windows) and navigate to your Desktop folder. Usually, typing `cd %HOMEPATH%\Desktop` does the trick, but if not, navigate to your Desktop folder by using a combination of `cd ..` and `cd foldername` commands, as shown in Figure 8-6.

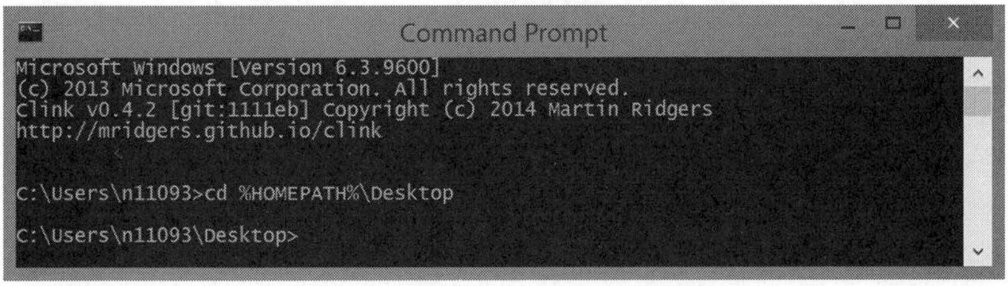

FIGURE 8-6

Next, on the command-line, start your Java program using the command `java -jar linereverser.jar`. The program will start and you will be able to interact with it just as you did from Eclipse's console. See Figure 8-7.

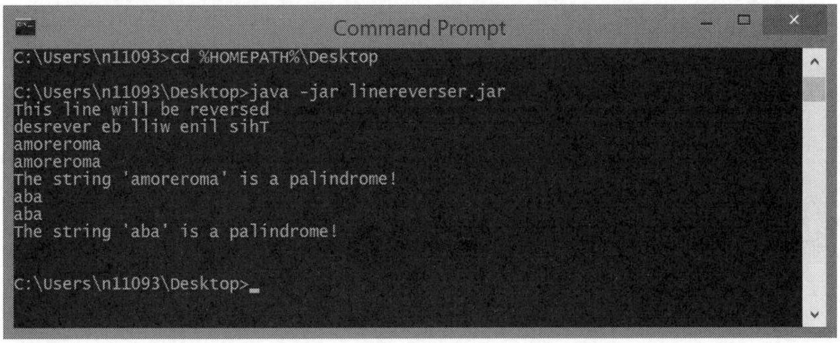

FIGURE 8-7

Note how both the standard output and standard error streams are shown on the command-line by default. However, we can perform a neat little trick now by what is called "stream redirection." Let's say we want to save our reversed lines to a text file, but we do not want to save the error messages. In this case, we can execute the following command: `java -jar linereverser.jar > output.txt`. See Figure 8-8.

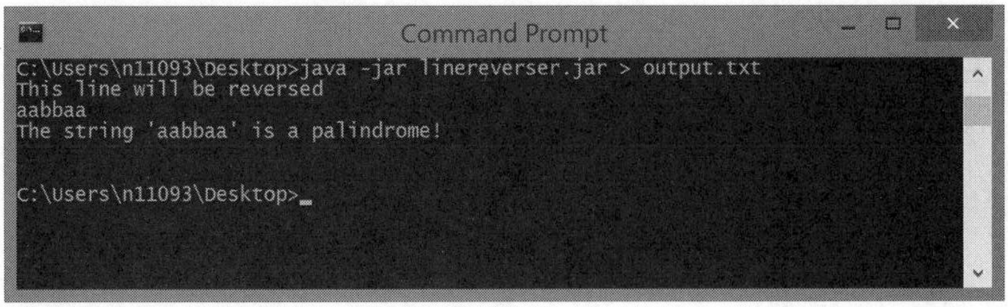

FIGURE 8-8

Note how the error messages are still shown on the console, whereas standard output is now saved in the `output.txt` text file (verify this by opening the file). Is there a way to redirect error messages as well? Indeed there is, by using `2>`: `java -jar linereverser.jar > output.txt 2> error.txt`. Note that `>` (standard output redirection) can then also be written as `1>`. If you want to append to the end of a file instead of creating a new one, you can use `>>` (two arrows) instead of `>`. Try this out if you like.

Let us now take this a step further. Create a text file called `input.txt` on your Desktop containing the following:

`apple`

`amoreroma`

`test`

`aabbaa`

No doubt you can see where this is going; we would like to use the contents of this file as input instead of typing the lines ourselves. Again, this is easy, using the `<` redirection operator, like so: `java -jar linereverser.jar < input.txt`. See Figure 8-9.

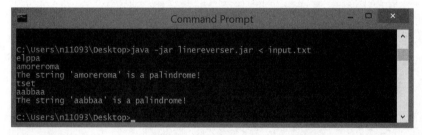

FIGURE 8-9

Indeed, you can also combine these operators to construct something like this: `java -jar linereverser.jar < input.txt > output.txt 2> errors.txt`.

So far, you've been taking input and sending output from and to files, but it is also possible to redirect the standard streams from one program to another program. To illustrate this, we will use a standard Windows command-line program called `type`. This program just shows the contents of a file on the standard output. Try it out by typing `type input.txt`. See Figure 8-10.

```
Command Prompt                                           _ □ ×
C:\Users\n11093\Desktop>type input.txt
apple
amoreroma
test
aabbaa

C:\Users\n11093\Desktop>
```

FIGURE 8-10

Now, how can you send the standard output of the type program to the program? Using > will not work here, as you're not sending the output to a file. Instead, you can use the | operator, called the *pipe*, as it pipes the output from one program to another, i.e.: type input.txt | java -jar linereverser.jar. See Figure 8-11.

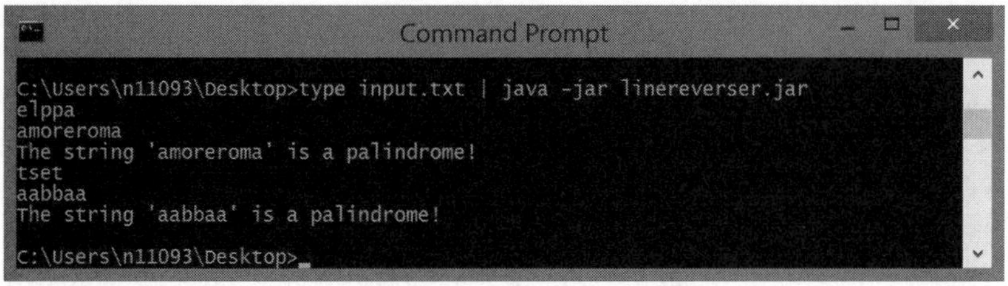

FIGURE 8-11

Piping and output redirection are two very powerful features of command-line programs. They allow for writing simple, one-task-only programs that can then be combined and chained together in a manner that's more flexible than what most GUI applications can offer. This aspect forms one of the key reasons why command-line programs remain useful and used in server environments.

Before we end this section, let us return to Eclipse and Java to highlight a more advanced alternative of the standard streams, named the Console. This is a class that lives under java.io.Console and can be accessed through System.console(). This object provides all features the standard streams have, as well as some other features, such as secure input mechanisms (such as for password entry). The Console also provides input and output streams that are character streams. A downside of this technique however is that the Console is not available in all operating systems or environments, so the recommended approach remains to use the standard streams, unless you really need a feature Console provides. The following Try It Out shows how to read passwords in a secure manner using the Console.

TRY IT OUT Advanced Command-Line Interaction Using the Console

In this Try It Out, we will use System.console() to read in a password in a secure manner.

1. You will create a single class named GetPassword with the following content:

```java
import java.io.Console;
import java.io.IOException;

public class GetPassword {
    public static void main (String args[]) throws IOException {
        Console c = System.console();
        if (c == null) {
            System.err.println("Console object is not available");
            System.exit(1);
        }

        String username = c.readLine("Enter your username: ");
        char[] password = c.readPassword("Enter your password: ");
```

```
            if (username.equals("admin") && new String(password).equals("swordfish")) {
                c.writer().println("Access granted");
            } else {
                c.writer().println("Oops, didn't recognize you there");
            }
        }

    }
```

2. Executing this program in Eclipse's console will not work, as Eclipse does not provide a so-called "interactive command-line." You will need to export the class as a Runnable JAR file like you did before. Make sure to select GetPassword as the launch configuration (execute the program in Eclipse if this does not appear in the list).

3. Once you have exported the program, you can test it using a Windows command-line. Note that the characters you type for the password will not appear on the screen. See Figure 8-12.

FIGURE 8-12

How It Works

This class is fairly straightforward, as most methods of System.console() are self-explanatory. The only thing you need to keep in mind is to first test whether you can access the console in your environment by performing a null check. Next, you use the readLine and readPassword methods to get user input. Note that the latter does not return a string but an array of characters, which you thus convert to a string to perform the username/password check.

We now turn our attention back to files and continue our discussion on working with file I/O in Java in the following section.

INPUT AND OUTPUT FROM FILES

You've already seen some example programs that dealt with files in Java. The file copying programs, for instance, illustrated how you can use byte, character, and buffered streams to get input from and send output to files.

However, there's more to file I/O than just taking and dropping contents from and into files. Files can be checked for existence, deleted, moved, copied, created, can contain metadata of various sorts, and can be organized into directories, which are also traversable in Java. The following sections teach you how to handle all of these things.

Java NIO2 File Input and Output

Recall from the introduction that Java 7 introduced the "NIO2" API to offer a new file system API. Existing legacy file I/O methods remain supported, so that many code samples, books, tutorials, and real-life code still apply "legacy I/O" API features.

Since newer means better in this case, we will start by applying the NIO2 API toward working with files. The central player in NIO2 is the `Path` type and its little helper class `Paths`.

The Path Interface

On your computer, files are stored in a way so that they can be easily retrieved and accessed later. On most file systems, files are stored in a hierarchical structure, meaning as a tree. The top of a tree is called a root node (e.g., `C:\`) under which a hierarchy of folders can be found. Each folder can contain other folders or files.

This implies that all files on your computer can be identified by a unique path of traversal through the tree. For example, on Windows, the `"C:\projects\java book\structure outline.txt"` path refers to a text file that lives in the folder named `java book`, which in turn lives in the folder `projects`.

> **NOTE** On Linux, Unix, and BSD, paths use a different separator character, namely / instead of \. When programming in Java on Windows, you can also use / instead of \. If you want to retrieve the separator in a programmatic manner, you can call the following method, which returns a string:
>
> ```
> FileSystems.getDefault().getSeparator();
> ```

The example we provided illustrated a so-called "absolute" path, meaning that the path started from the root element in the file system hierarchy (`C:\`) and worked its way down from there. A path can also be "relative." Relative paths need to be combined with other paths to access a file. For example, when the current path is `"C:\projects\"`, the relative path `"java book\structure outline.txt"` would lead you to the file you had before. The relative path `overview.txt` would resolve to `"C:\projects\overview.txt"` and the relative path `"..\movies\vacation.avi"` would resolve to `"C:\movies\vacation.avi"`. Note the use of `".."`, which traverses one level up the directory tree. A single dot (`.`) in a path refers to the current directory.

Finally, on some systems, file systems can also support links, apart from files and folders. A link is a special file that serves as a reference to another file. Operations on these links are automatically redirected to the target location of the link. You don't need to concern yourself further regarding this aspect, as they are very uncommon on Windows systems and you won't use them for most purposes.

In Java, the `Path` type, found under the `java.nio.file` package, represents a path in the file system. `Path` objects contain the filename and directory list used to build the path, and can be used to examine and work with files. Creating a path is done by using the `get` method on the `Paths` class, also under `java.nio.file`, like so:

```
Path myPath = Paths.get("C:\\projects\\outline.txt");
```

> **NOTE** *An important thing to note here is that* `Path` *is an interface type, whereas* `Paths` *is a normal class (albeit a very simple one, without a public constructor). In case you're wondering why the former is an interface, the reason for this is to allow developers of custom file systems to be able to implement (or extend) it.*
>
> *The usage of the* `s` *suffix of* `Path` *versus* `Paths` *is also in line with other concepts in NIO2, for instance Files (which you'll encounter later on) and* `FileSystem` *versus* `FileSystems`. *In fact, calling the* `get` *method of* `Paths` *is a shorthand for:*
>
> ```
> FileSystems // A static utility class containing methods to create
>     FileSystem objects
>     .getDefault() // Get the default file system FileSystem
>         .getPath("C:\\projects\\outline.txt") // Return a Path
> ```

Once you have created a `Path` object, there are a number of methods you can execute on them to retrieve information about the path. These methods do not require that the file corresponding to the path actually exist:

➤   `String myPath.toString()`: Returns the string representation of the `Path` object. Note that this method will attempt to perform syntactic cleanup.

➤   `Path myPath.getFileName()`: Returns the filename or the last element in the `Path` object.

➤   `Path myPath.getName(int i)`: Returns the `Path` element corresponding to the specified index. Note that `index 0` does not represent the root, but the element closest to the root.

➤   `int myPath.getNameCount()`: Returns the number of elements in the path.

➤   `Path myPath.subpath(int i, int j)`: Returns the subsequence of the `Path` (not including a root element) as specified by beginning and ending indices.

➤   `Path myPath.getParent()`: Returns the `Path` of the parent directory of this path.

➤   `Path myPath.getRoot()`: Returns the root of the path.

➤   `Path myPath.normalize()`: Cleans up redundancies from a path and returns the cleaned-up result. For example, "`C:\.\projects\..\movies\vacation.avi`" is converted to "`C:\movies\vacation.avi`".

➤   `Path myPath.resolve(String partialPath)`: The partial path (not including a root element) is added to the original path and the new path is returned. If you pass in an absolute path, the absolute `Path` itself will be returned.

➤   `Path myPath.relativize(Path otherPath)`: Constructs a new `Path` object originating from the original path and ending at the location specified by `otherPath`. This returns a relative `Path`.

In addition, methods exist to convert a path:

➤   `URI myPath.toUri()`: Converts the path to a string that can be opened by web browsers.

➤ `Path myPath.toAbsolutePath()`: Converts a relative path to an absolute one.

➤ `Path myPath.toRealPath(LinkOption... options)`: Returns the real path of an existing file. If `true` is passed in the `options` parameters, links will be resolved to their real paths (if the file system supports links). In addition, relative paths will be converted to absolute ones and redundant elements will be removed.

The Files Class

Apart from the `Path` interface, the `Files` class is the other most important class contained in the `java.nio.file` package. This utility class offers a set of static methods for reading, writing, and manipulating files and folders (do not be thrown off by the fact that the class itself is named `Files` and not `FilesAndFolders`).

> **NOTE** Similarly to `Path` with its `Paths` helper and `FileSystem` with its `FileSystems` counterpart, you might expect `Files` to contain methods that return `File` objects. However, the `File` class already existed before the advent of NIO2 (you'll meet it in the legacy file section ahead), so that all methods in the `Files` class that do return an object representing an entity in a file system will return it as a `Path` object, not `File`.

Checking Existence

The first and most basic operation you can execute using the `Files` class is performing checks on files and folders. Let's say you have created a `Path` object representing a file or folder. How do you check whether this path actually exists? Two methods exist (no pun intended) to do so:

➤ `boolean Files.exists(Path pathToCheck, LinkOption... options)`

➤ `boolean Files.notExists(Path pathToCheck, LinkOption... options)`

Ignore the options parameter for now. As we've said, this parameter is there to specify how links should be dealt with. A more interesting question is why two methods are provided. Couldn't you just use `!Files.exists(path)` instead of `Files.notExists(path)`? The reason for this is because—when checking the existence of a path—three results can occur: the file exists, the file does not exist, or your program cannot determine the existence, for instance, when access rules block your program from reaching the path. If both `exists` and `notExists` return `false`, this means the existence of the path cannot be verified. If exists returns `true`, this means you can safely continue working with this file, as it exists and can be accessed from your program.

There are also a number of other methods to check a file's status:

➤ `boolean Files.isReadable(Path pathToCheck)`: Tests whether a path is readable.

➤ `boolean Files.isWritable(Path pathToCheck)`: Tests whether a path is writable.

➤ `boolean Files.isExecutable(Path pathToCheck)`: Tests whether a path is executable.

➤ `boolean Files.isDirectory(Path pathToCheck)`: Tests whether the path represents a directory.

➤ `boolean Files.isSameFile(Path firstPath, Path secondPath)`: Tests whether two paths resolve to the same location, taking into account redundant syntax and links.

> **NOTE** Note that the result of performing a check on a `Path` is atomic and might be violated almost immediately after you continue in your code. Meaning that a file might be deleted, for instance, after you perform an existence check and move on with the rest of your code. This aspect can lead to a particular kind of software bug called TOCTTOU (time of check to time of use) and can also lead to security problems in serious cases. Therefore, never assume too strongly that the result of your check will remain absolutely true throughout the execution of your program, and always be ready to handle exceptions thrown by the `Files` methods in a graceful manner.

Deleting Files and Folders

The next operation you can perform using the `Files` class is a bit more volatile, i.e. deletion. It is possible to delete both files and folders, but for folders, the folder needs to be empty before it can be deleted, otherwise an exception will be thrown. The following code snippet shows how the `delete` method works:

```
try {
    Files.delete(path);
} catch (NoSuchFileException x) {
    // File does not exist
} catch (DirectoryNotEmptyException x) {
    // The directory is not empty
} catch (IOException x) {
    // File permission problem, no access
}
```

Note that there is also a `Files.deleteIfExists(Path pathToDelete)` method. This method works in a similar manner, but will not throw an exception when the file does not exist. It just does nothing in that case.

Copying and Moving Files and Folders

Next up, you look at two methods for copying and moving files:

➤ `Path copy(Path source, Path target, CopyOptions... options)`: Copies a source file to a target file. The `options` specify how the copy is performed. By default, the copy operation will fail if the target file already exists (except when both are the same file), unless you pass `REPLACE_EXISTING` as an option. If the file to copy is a directory, an empty directory is created in the target location, but the entries in the directory are not copied. You will see later how to easily copy over a complete directory using this method.

➤ `Path move(Path source, Path target, CopyOptions... options)`: Moves a source file to a target file. The `options` specify how the move is performed. By default, the move operation will fail if the target file already exists (except when both are the same file), unless you pass `REPLACE_EXISTING` as an option. If the file to copy is a directory, the move will be successful if the directory is empty. Otherwise, the result of the move depends on the underlying file system and can throw an `IOException` in some cases. In that case, a copy should be performed first followed by a manual cleanup of the original source directory.

> **NOTE** *Note that these methods provide a more straightforward means to copy and move files than the stream-based file copy programs you've seen before. Again, one of the nice improvements of the NIO2 API.*

Reading, Writing, and Creating Files

Next, let's take a look at how to read, write, and create files using the NIO2 API. In this chapter, you've already seen how to use stream-based methods to do this, and the NIO2 API will build on the concept of streams, while also making our lives easier with some helpful methods.

First of all, when you just want to get all bytes or lines from a file, you can use the following methods:

➤ `byte[] Files.readAllBytes(Path path)`: Reads all the bytes from a file to a byte array. This method takes care of opening and closing the file for you.

➤ `List<String> readAllLines(Path path, Charset cs)`: Reads all lines from a file to a list of strings. This method takes care of opening and closing the file for you. The `Charset` parameter specifies which character set should be used for decoding the file. Using `Charset.defaultCharset()` or `Charset.forName("UTF-8")` works best in most cases.

Note, however, that these methods will read the complete contents of a file at once, and thus will fail to work when you are dealing with large files. For small files, however, this approach is straightforward and works just fine. As an example, recall the grocery-reading application we showed off in the introduction. Note that you can completely avoid dealing with streams thanks to the `Files` class:

```
import java.io.IOException;
import java.nio.charset.Charset;
import java.nio.file.Files;
import java.nio.file.Paths;
import java.util.ArrayList;
import java.util.List;

public class ShowGroceries {
    public static void main(String[] args) {
        List<String> groceries = new ArrayList<>();
```

```
            try {
                groceries = Files.readAllLines(
                        Paths.get("groceries.txt"),
                                Charset.defaultCharset());
            } catch (IOException e) {
                e.printStackTrace();
            }
            for (String item : groceries) {
                System.out.println("Don't forget to pickup: " + item);
            }
        }
    }
```

Similarly, two methods exist to write all bytes or lines to a file:

➤ `Path write(Path path, byte[] bytes, OpenOption... options)`: Writes bytes to a file. By default, this method creates a new file or overwrites an existing file.

➤ `Path write(Path path, Iterable<? extends CharSequence> lines, Charset cs, OpenOption... options)`: Writes lines of text to a file. By default, this method creates a new file or overwrites an existing file. Don't be confused by the signature of the `lines` argument. In practical cases, this will work with a `List<String>`, for instance. The `Charset` parameter specifies which character set should be used for encoding the file. Using `Charset.defaultCharset()` or `Charset.forName("UTF-8")` works best in most cases.

You might be wondering what the `OpenOptions` parameters are for in these methods. These options are used in various methods and will tell the NIO2 API how you want to open the file. You can pass in the following `StandardOpenOptions` values:

➤ `WRITE`: Opens a file for write access.

➤ `APPEND`: Appends new data to the end of the file (use together with `WRITE` or `CREATE`).

➤ `TRUNCATE_EXISTING`: Empties the file before writing (use with `WRITE`).

➤ `CREATE_NEW`: Creates a new file or throws an exception if the file exists.

➤ `CREATE`: Opens the file or creates it if it does not exist.

➤ `DELETE_ON_CLOSE`: Deletes the file when the handling stream is closed.

➤ `SPARSE, SYNC, DSYNC`: A set of advanced options that we do not describe in detail here.

If you've been paying attention, you'll notice that these options strongly resemble the file operation modes introduced in the beginning of this chapter. In most cases, there's no need to provide any options at all, however, as the API will assume sensible defaults when you leave them out (`CREATE`, `TRUNCATE_EXISTING`, and `WRITE` for the `write` methods, for instance). When you do supply your own options, take care not to supply an infeasible combination or a combination that does not match the operation you're trying to perform with the method you're calling.

The methods mentioned so far are fine when you're dealing with small files, but when you need to work with large files, you cannot store the contents of the file in memory all at the same time. We already know how we would approach this problem using buffered character streams:

```
Reader fr = new FileReader("groceries.txt");
BufferedReader br = new BufferedReader(fr);
```

However, the NIO2 API provides a cleaner way to read and write files (note for instance that we hardcoded the filename in the code snippet) using the following two methods:

➤   `BufferedReader Files.newBufferedReader(Path path, Charset cs)`: Returns a buffered character stream to read a text file in an efficient manner using the given character set to decode.

➤   `BufferedReader Files.newBufferedReader(Path path)`: Same as above, but using UTF-8 as the character set.

➤   `BufferedWriter Files.newBufferedWriter(Path path, Charset cs, OpenOption...` `options)`: Returns a buffered character stream to write a text file in an efficient manner using the given character set to encode. If no options are provided, CREATE, TRUNCATE_ EXISTING and WRITE are used.

➤   `BufferedWriter Files.newBufferedWriter(Path path, OpenOption... options)`: Same as above, but using UTF-8 as the character set.

Note how these neatly work together with the `Files` and `Path` types. Once called, you can just use the `BufferedReader` and `BufferedWriter` streams as you've seen before. The following code fragment shows an example using a try-with-resources block, which remains the recommended approach:

```
Path file = Paths.get("groceries.txt");
try (BufferedReader reader = Files.newBufferedReader(file)) {
    String line = null;
    while ((line = reader.readLine()) != null) {
        System.out.println(line);
    }
} catch (IOException x) {
    System.err.println("Something went wrong");
}
```

Next, if you do not want to use buffered character streams but want to use byte streams instead, you'll need to use the `newInputStream` and `newOutputStream` methods. They work similarly to the previous methods, but return `InputStream` and `OutputStream` object respectively, which you can then wrap in `BufferedInputStream` and `BufferedOutputStream` objects if you want to obtain a buffered byte stream.

> **NOTE** *You might be wondering why the character stream variant of these methods return a buffered stream, whereas the byte stream ones return a non-buffered one. This is mainly due to convention: in cases where you will use a character stream, using a buffered approach almost always make sense. You can still obtain an unbuffered character stream if you really need it by using the* `InputStreamReader` *and* `OutputStreamWriter` *classes and wrapping them around the* `InputStream` *and* `OutputStream` *objects you get with the* `newIn-putStream` *and* `newOutputStream` *methods.*

Note that the Java NIO2 API also provides a different method to read and write files, named *channel I/O*, as an alternative to stream-based I/O. Whereas streams read one character or byte at a time, channels can read or write buffers at a time (and thus avoid the use of a separate buffering mechanism). In addition, channels exist that allow for more fine-grained seeking within a file through a concept called Random Access Files, which permit non-sequential access to files and which allow you to map the contents of a file directly to computer memory. We mention it here for the sake of completeness, but in most "normal" file I/O environments, stream-based I/O works just fine.

Lastly, we can take a look at the methods to create files. While you might just use one of the earlier writing functions to open a new file and immediately close it, it is much cleaner to use the `Files.createFile(Path path)` method to create an empty file. Note that this method will—by default—throw a permission if a path exists, contrary to the writing methods shown previously, which will overwrite a file if it exists. It is thus a good idea to use this method as an extra fail-safe in cases where this matters. You can also use another method—`Files.createTempFile(Path folder, String prefix, String suffix`—to create temporary files in the specified folder, using a given prefix, suffix, and a randomized body as a name. Note that you can leave the `folder` argument out, in which case the standard temporary-file directory provided by your operating system will be used. These methods are helpful to create quick "throwaway" files.

Reading and Creating Folders

Some path operation methods, such as deletion or copying, can work on files and folders. But directories also require an additional set of methods. For example, how would you list all the contents of a folder?

First of all, though, let's quickly take a look at creating folders. This can be done using the `Files.createDirectory(Path path)` method or the `createTempDirectory(Path folder, String prefix)` method in case you want to create a temporary `folder` (again, the `folder` argument can be left out).

You list all the contents of a folder using the `Files.newDirectoryStream(Path folder)` method. Note that this method returns an object that implements the `DirectoryStream` and `Iterable` interfaces, so you can loop over this object to read all of the entries. However, since this object is a stream, don't forget to close it in your `finally` block (or use a try-with-resources block as we've been recommending so far). The following example class shows how to list the contents of a directory:

```
import java.io.IOException;
import java.nio.file.DirectoryIteratorException;
import java.nio.file.DirectoryStream;
import java.nio.file.Files;
import java.nio.file.Path;
import java.nio.file.Paths;

public class ShowDirectory {
    public static void main(String[] args) {
        Path folder = Paths.get("C:\\");
        try (DirectoryStream<Path> stream = Files.newDirectoryStream(folder)) {
```

```
                    for (Path entry: stream) {
                        System.out.println(entry.getFileName());
                    }
                } catch (IOException | DirectoryIteratorException x) {
                    System.err.println("An error occurred");
                }
            }
        }
    }
```

Example output:

```
$Recycle.Bin
BOOTNXT
Documents and Settings
eclipse
hiberfil.sys
MSOCache
pagefile.sys
PerfLogs
Program Files
Program Files (x86)
ProgramData
swapfile.sys
System Volume Information
temp
Users
Windows
```

Note that this approach returns all the contents of a directory: files, subdirectories, hidden files, and links. If you only need a subset, you can just add checks to the `for` loop using methods you've seen before. Another way to filter a directory listing is by using a concept called *globbing*, using the `Files.newDirectoryStream(Path folder, String glob)` method. A glob is a special kind of syntax to specify pattern-matching behavior. An asterisk (`*`), for instance, matches any number of characters; a question mark (`?`) matches exactly one character. Braces (`{one,two}`) specify a collection of subpatterns, whereas square patterns (`[qwerty]`) convey a set or range (`[0-9]`) of characters. The following method call, for example, only returns DOC, PDF, and TXT files:

```
Files.newDirectoryStream(dir, "*.{txt,doc,pdf}"));
```

If you only want to retrieve directories, you'll need to write your own filter. To do so, you can create a class implementing the `DirectoryStream.Filter<T>` interface (and implementing the `accept` method) and use this to invoke the `Files.newDirectoryStream(Path folder, DirectoryStream.Filter filter)` method. Just using an `if (Files.isDirectory(entry))` `continue;` line might be easier in this case, however.

Recursing Folders

The last operation we'll take a closer look at involves recursing over the folder tree. When discussing how to copy, move, or delete paths, we've stated that copying folders just creates an empty folder, moving folders can fail in some cases, and deleting folders only works when the folder is empty. In addition, you might be interested in writing a method that looks for a file or directory in a directory as well as subdirectories.

For all these tasks, interfaces have been defined by the NIO2 API to do this. The reality, however, is that implementing all interfaces and setting up everything can be a bit daunting for newcomers. For instance, to walk over a directory tree, you'll need to implement `FileVisitor<Path>` with the `pre-VisitDirectory`, `visitFile`, `postVisitDirectory`, and `visitFileFailed` methods. Look up the Java API docs if you're interested to learn more.

Instead, the following Try It Out will present a set of alternative recursive methods you can use to copy, move, delete, and search through directories, which you can use as a starting point in your own code as well.

TRY IT OUT   Using Recursive Operations

In this Try It Out, you implement a set of methods to search, delete, copy, and move complete directories at once.

1.   In Eclipse, create a class called `RecursiveOperations`.

2.   First, add a method to delete files:

```
public static void delete(Path source) throws IOException {
    if (Files.isDirectory(source)) {
        for (Path file : getFiles(source))
            delete(file);
    }
    Files.delete(source);
    System.out.println("DELETED "+source.toString());
}
```

3.   Next, you need to provide the `getFiles` method. This helper method returns all files and subdirectories in a given folder. However, since deletion will only work on empty folders, you want this method to first return all directories, followed by all files to ensure that the `delete` method first goes through all directories as far as possible:

```
public static List<Path> getFiles(Path dir) {
    // Gets all files, but puts directories first
    List<Path> files = new ArrayList<>();
    if (!Files.isDirectory(dir))
        return files;
    try (DirectoryStream<Path> stream = Files.newDirectoryStream(dir)) {
        for (Path entry : stream)
            if (Files.isDirectory(entry))
                files.add(entry);
    } catch (IOException | DirectoryIteratorException x) {
    }
    try (DirectoryStream<Path> stream = Files.newDirectoryStream(dir)) {
        for (Path entry : stream)
            if (!Files.isDirectory(entry))
```

```
                    files.add(entry);
            } catch (IOException | DirectoryIteratorException x) {
            }
            return files;
        }
```

4. Next up, you can define a `copy` method in a similar fashion:

```java
public static void copy(Path source, Path target) throws IOException {
    if (Files.exists(target) && Files.isSameFile(source, target))
        return;
    if (Files.isDirectory(source)) {
        Files.createDirectory(target);
        System.out.println("CREATED "+target.toString());
        for (Path file : getFiles(source))
            copy(file, target.resolve(file.getFileName()));
    } else {
        Files.copy(source, target);
        System.out.println(
            "COPIED "+source.toString()+" -> "+target.toString());
    }
}
```

5. The `move` method just reuses the `copy` and `delete` methods:

```java
public static void move(Path source, Path target) throws IOException {
    if (Files.exists(target) && Files.isSameFile(source, target))
        return;
    copy(source, target);
    delete(source);
}
```

6. The `search` method is added as follows, and uses a `PathMatcher` object to match a filename to a provided glob:

```java
public static Set<Path> search(Path start, String glob,
        boolean includeDirectories, boolean includeFiles) {

    PathMatcher matcher = FileSystems.getDefault().getPathMatcher
        ("glob:" + glob);
    Set<Path> results = new HashSet<>();
    search(start, matcher, includeDirectories, includeFiles, results);
    return results;
}

private static void search(Path path, PathMatcher matcher,
        boolean includeDirectories, boolean includeFiles, Set<Path> results) {

    if (matcher.matches(path.getFileName())
            && ((includeDirectories && Files.isDirectory(path))
                || (includeFiles && !Files.isDirectory(path)))) {
        results.add(path);
```

```
        }

        for (Path next : getFiles(path))
            search(next, matcher, includeDirectories, includeFiles, results);
    }
```

7. Finally, you can add a `main` class to test these methods:

```
public static void main(String args[]) throws IOException {
    // WARNING: TAKE CARE WHEN TESTING THESE FUNCTIONS ON
    // EXISTING FOLDERS ON YOUR SYSTEM

    // Set up test directory
    try {
        delete(Paths.get("C:\\javatest\\"));
        delete(Paths.get("C:\\javatest2\\"));
    } catch(NoSuchFileException e) {}
    Files.createDirectory(Paths.get("C:\\javatest\\"));
    Files.createDirectory(Paths.get("C:\\javatest\\subdir\\"));
    Files.createFile(Paths.get("C:\\javatest\\text1.txt"));
    Files.createFile(Paths.get("C:\\javatest\\text2.txt"));
    Files.createFile(Paths.get("C:\\javatest\\other.txt"));
    Files.createFile(Paths.get("C:\\javatest\\subdir\\text3.txt"));
    Files.createFile(Paths.get("C:\\javatest\\subdir\\other.txt"));

    // Test our methods
    copy(Paths.get("C:\\javatest\\subdir\\"),
        Paths.get("C:\\javatest\\subdircopy\\"));
    System.out.println(search(Paths.get("C:\\javatest"),
        "text*.txt", true, true));
    move(Paths.get("C:\\javatest\\subdircopy\\"),
        Paths.get("C:\\javatest\\subdircopy2\\"));
    System.out.println(search(Paths.get("C:\\javatest\\"),
        "text*.txt", true, true));
    copy(Paths.get("C:\\javatest\\"), Paths.get("C:\\javatest2\\"));

}
```

8. Executing this code yields the following output:

```
CREATED C:\javatest\subdircopy
COPIED C:\javatest\subdir\other.txt -> C:\javatest\subdircopy\other.txt
COPIED C:\javatest\subdir\text3.txt -> C:\javatest\subdircopy\text3.txt
[C:\javatest\subdir\text3.txt, C:\javatest\text2.txt,
    C:\javatest\subdircopy\text3.txt, C:\javatest\text1.txt]
CREATED C:\javatest\subdircopy2
COPIED C:\javatest\subdircopy\other.txt -> C:\javatest\subdircopy2\other.txt
COPIED C:\javatest\subdircopy\text3.txt -> C:\javatest\subdircopy2\text3.txt
DELETED C:\javatest\subdircopy\other.txt
DELETED C:\javatest\subdircopy\text3.txt
DELETED C:\javatest\subdircopy
[C:\javatest\subdir\text3.txt, C:\javatest\subdircopy2\text3.txt,
    C:\javatest\text2.txt, C:\javatest\text1.txt]
```

```
CREATED C:\javatest2
CREATED C:\javatest2\subdir
COPIED C:\javatest\subdir\other.txt -> C:\javatest2\subdir\other.txt
COPIED C:\javatest\subdir\text3.txt -> C:\javatest2\subdir\text3.txt
CREATED C:\javatest2\subdircopy2
COPIED C:\javatest\subdircopy2\other.txt -> C:\javatest2\subdircopy2\other.txt
COPIED C:\javatest\subdircopy2\text3.txt -> C:\javatest2\subdircopy2\text3.txt
COPIED C:\javatest\other.txt -> C:\javatest2\other.txt
COPIED C:\javatest\text1.txt -> C:\javatest2\text1.txt
COPIED C:\javatest\text2.txt -> C:\javatest2\text2.txt
```

How It Works

Here's how it works:

1. Although the class is relatively large, most of the operations we've included follow the same general reasoning: loop over subdirectories until you cannot go any further, then perform operations on the included files.

2. Two important notes to keep in mind are that the getFiles method first returns a list of directories, followed by normal files, so that deletion can first clean up the deepest directory before working its way up. Another interesting aspect is how we use the PathMatcher class to match a filename to a glob. The following code snippet can come in handy in other scenarios as well:

```
Path path = ...;
PathMatcher matcher = FileSystems.getDefault().getPathMatcher("glob:" + glob);
if (matcher.matches(path.getFileName())
    // do something
```

3. The "glob:" prefix in the getPathMatcher method should be provided by convention to indicate your pattern is a glob type.

4. We've added a check to prevent copying and moving a source to the same target. What would happen if you tried to move a directory under one of its subdirectories? Can you imagine ways to prevent this (or deal with this case)?

5. If you're interested in knowing how to copy directories using the visitor pattern offered by the NIO2 API, you can take a look at this example online: http://docs.oracle.com/javase/tutorial/essential/io/examples/Copy.java.

Other Methods

Finally, there are a number of additional methods in the Files class that can come in handy. First, metadata methods such as Files.size(Path p) (returns the size of the file in bytes), Files.getOwner(Path p, LinkOption... options), and Files.getLastModifiedTime(Path p, LinkOption... options) can be used to retrieve (and set) metadata. Secondly, functionality exists to watch a file for changes. Look up NIO's WatchService if you ever need this feature. Lastly, we briefly touched on the concept of link. The NIO2 API also provides functionality to create and modify such links in the file system, but we skipped an in-depth discussion and refer interested intermediate readers to other sources, such as the Java API docs.

Legacy File Input and Output

Prior to the Java 7 release, the `java.io.File` class was the default mechanism used for file I/O. This class is still present for reasons of backward-compatibility, but has several drawbacks:

➤ Some methods don't throw exceptions when an error occurs, or do not provide enough information to know the root cause behind a failure.

➤ Well-defined support for links is lacking.

➤ Accessing file metadata can be difficult and slow.

➤ Fetching information over a network introduces scalability issues.

➤ Some methods do not work consistently on various operating systems and platforms.

That being said, a great deal of real-life code still uses the legacy file input and output, so we discuss it here in brief. Creating a file object is simple:

```
File myFile = new File("groceries.txt");
```

Whenever you can, a good way to deal with methods returning legacy `File` objects is to immediately convert them to a `Path` using the `myFile.toPath()` method. Similarly, the `Path` interface defines a `toFile()` method you can use to get a legacy `File` object from a `Path` object.

Operations you wish to execute on a `File` object (such as checking for existence) are not done through a helper class like `Files` did on `Path` objects, but directly on the `File` object itself, for example by calling one of its methods. The following list shows the corresponding `File` methods for most of the `Files` equivalents we've discussed:

➤ `Path.getFileName(...)` was `File.getName()`

➤ `Files.isDirectory(...)` was `File.isDirectory(...)`

➤ `Files.isRegularFile(...)` was `File.isFile(...)`

➤ `Files.size(...)` was `File.length(...)`

➤ `Files.move(...)` was `File.renameTo(...)`

➤ `Files.delete(...)` was `File.delete(...)`

➤ `Files.createFile(...)` was `File.createNewFile(...)`

➤ `Files.createTempFile(...)` was `File.createTempFile(...)`

➤ `File.deleteOnExit(...)` is now handled by passing `DELETE_ON_CLOSE` as an option to `Files.createFile(...)`

➤ `Files.exists(...)` and `Files.notExists(...)` was `File.exists(...)`

➤ `Path.newDirectoryStream(...)` was `File.list(...)` and `File.listFiles(...)`

➤ `Path.createDirectory(...)` was `File.mkdir(...)`

As an example, the following code fragment shows how to loop over the contents of a directory using the legacy API:

```java
import java.io.File;


public class ShowDirectory {
    public static void main(String[] args) {
        File folder = new File("C:\\");
        for (File entry : folder.listFiles()) {
            System.out.println(entry.getName());
        }
    }
}
```

This particular example might appear simple compared to the corresponding NIO2 implementation (fewer imports are used), but keep in mind the other advantages of NIO2 (reading and writing, for instance). The NIO2 approach remains the recommended one.

A Word on FileUtils

Java's file input/output classes—and the legacy ones in particular—miss some widely used features that are both somewhat annoying and time consuming to implement yourself, or require a great amount of exception juggling to implement gracefully. You've already seen an example of this in the form of the implementation of copy, move, and delete operations for whole directories.

When you're looking for an implementation to properly copy, clean, and move directories or perform many other common file operations, the `FileUtils` utility class by the Apache Commons project is worth looking at. In fact, many programmers consider this class so helpful and so essential that they will include it as a library in any new Java project they set up. Take a look at the following website if you're interested in knowing more or want to download and use the library (add it to Eclipse's build path in order to use it): `http://commons.apache.org/proper/commons-io/`.

One downside of the `FileUtils` library, however, is that it is built with Java 6 compatibility in mind, meaning that the legacy `File` class is used in its method arguments, without `Path` and `Files` being present. If you use the `FileUtils` library, consider using the previously discussed `Path.toFile()` method to keep the rest of your code base NIO-ready.

CONCLUSION

This concludes this chapter on basic input/output with Java and file input/output. You've seen what is meant by stream-based input/output, learned how to interact with users over the command-line, and learned how to write and read content to and from files, using both the NIO2 and legacy API. As always, don't be afraid to peruse the Java docs or explore the methods offered by `Path` and `Files` and other classes using Eclipse's autosuggest functionality. It is a great way to experiment and learn.

This chapter was largely about saving and reading data to and from files. The next chapter introduces databases, a more advanced and powerful method to store and retrieve information.

Working with Databases in Java

WHAT YOU WILL LEARN IN THIS CHAPTER:

➤ Basic concepts of relational databases

➤ Key problems when working with relational databases in Java

➤ How to use JDBC and SQLJ

➤ How to use an object relational mapper like Hibernate

➤ How to use object-oriented databases

➤ Key advantages and disadvantages of different approaches

WROX.COM CODE DOWNLOADS FOR THIS CHAPTER

The wrox.com code downloads for this chapter are found at www.wrox.com/go/
beginningjavaprogramming on the Download Code tab. The code is in the Chapter 9
download and individually named according to the names throughout the chapter.

Many Java applications need to either retrieve, update, delete, or store data. In Chapter 8, you
discovered how files can be used for this purpose. For small applications, it is definitely possible to use files for data storage. However, for larger-scale applications, the file-based approach
to data storage and management creates several problems. First, since every Java program
needs to explicitly define the structure of the file, a strong dependency is created between files
and Java programs. In other words, the Java program is strongly tied to the physical representation of the file. This creates substantial maintenance issues when the files are being accessed
by multiple Java programs simultaneously. For example, when the physical storage structure of
a file is changed, such as distributing its content over a network, all Java classes working with
the file would need to be updated. Likewise, when changing its internal content and/or representation, such as by adding, deleting, or changing data elements, changes need to be made to
all the Java programs that access it. Moreover, in a multi-application distributed environment,
many files will contain duplicate data, which obviously not only implies a waste of storage

space, but also increases the risk of inconsistent data manipulation, in case the data is updated in one file but not in other files. Finally, from an application integration perspective, the file-based approach to data management comes with high difficulty and thus substantial cost.

To store and manage data in a more structured way, databases have been introduced. A database represents a subset of a particular real-world problem and has an intrinsic meaning to a specific group of users. It is being managed by a database management system (DBMS). This is a collection of programs that facilitates the process of defining, constructing, and manipulating databases for various applications. Throughout the past decades, many different types of DBMSs have been introduced in the industry: hierarchical DBMSs, Codasyl DBMSs, relational DBMSs, object-oriented DBMSs, object relational DBMSs, and so on. Undoubtedly, the most popular DBMS technology in use nowadays is the relational DBMS (RDBMS). Various software implementations of RDBMSs have been provided by leading firms such as Microsoft, Oracle, and IBM. A key characteristic of an RDBMS is that it stores both data and data definitions in a comprehensive and transparent way. This is illustrated in Figure 9-1.

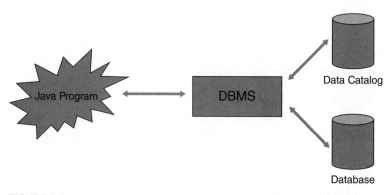

FIGURE 9-1

In this chapter, you learn how to access RDBMSs from within Java. First, there is an introduction or refresher covering the basic concepts of relational database technology. Next, Java Database Connectivity (JDBC) as a popular application programming interface (API) for accessing tabular data is discussed. Following that, SQLJ, structured query language combined with Java, and Hibernate, a popular object relational mapping framework capable of mapping Java objects to relational databases in a transparent way, are both introduced. Java-friendly object-oriented database management systems (OODBMS) are presented as an alternative to relational databases. Then you will find a brief comparison of these technologies and their place in the business world.

COVERING THE BASICS OF RELATIONAL DATABASES

A fundamental building block of a relational database is a relational scheme that's a gathering of various database tables and related constructs (queries, views, and indexes) describing real-life concepts. It is typically developed during database design and is not expected to change too frequently. Every relational scheme has one or more relational tables that store information about a particular item of interest. Table 9-1 shows an example relational table that stores information about employees.

TABLE 9-1: Employee Relational Table

EMPLOYEEID	NAME	GENDER	DNR
1	Bart Baesens	Male	1
2	Aimée Backiel	Female	1
3	Seppe vanden Broucke	Male	1
4	Michael Jackson	Male	2
5	Sarah Adams	Female	3

The table has four columns, also called attribute types, which specify the employee characteristics that should be stored. The first attribute type, EmployeeID, is called the primary key and is unique for each employee. The table has five rows, which are also called tuples. Conceptually, a relational database table corresponds to a mathematical set, which implies that every row is unique and there are no duplicate rows. Every row consists of a series of values, whereby every value comes from a specific type (integer, text, date, and so on) or can also be NULL, which means that the value is unknown or not applicable. The last column, DNR, is a foreign key that refers to the department number in the table Department, which is defined as shown in Table 9-2.

TABLE 9-2: Department Relational Table

DNR	DNAME	DADDRESS
1	ICT	Brussels
2	Marketing	New York
3	Finance	Singapore
4	Accounting	Sydney

Note that by using foreign keys, relationships can be established between various tables. As such, it can be easily seen that in the example, employees Bart Baesens, Aimée Backiel, and Seppe vanden Broucke work in ICT, whereas Michael Jackson works in Marketing and Sarah Adams in Finance.

RDBMSs use structured query language (SQL) as the underlying language to both define and manipulate the database concepts. In fact, SQL has a subset of instructions to define data structures, called data definition language (DDL), as well as to manipulate data, called data manipulation language (DML). SQL is a declarative language. Hence, as discussed in Chapter 1, you need only to specify which data to retrieve, in contrast to procedural languages, where you have to explicitly declare how to retrieve the data.

The SQL DDL needed to define Tables 9-1 and 9-2 is illustrated in the following code:

```
CREATE TABLE 'EmployeeSchema'.'Employee' (
    'EmployeeID' INT NOT NULL,
    'Name' VARCHAR(45) NULL,
    'Gender' VARCHAR(45) NULL,
    'DNR' INT NULL,
    PRIMARY KEY ('EmployeeID'),
    INDEX 'DNRForeign_idx' ('DNR' ASC),
    CONSTRAINT 'DNRForeign'
    FOREIGN KEY ('DNR')
    REFERENCES 'EmployeeSchema'.'Department' ('DNR')
    ON DELETE NO ACTION
    ON UPDATE NO ACTION)

CREATE TABLE 'EmployeeSchema'.'Department' (
    'DNR' INT NOT NULL,
    'DName' VARCHAR(45) NULL,
    'DAddress' VARCHAR(45) NULL,
    PRIMARY KEY ('DNR'))
```

The SQL DML instructions allow you to query, insert, update, and delete the data. Some examples are presented in Table 9-3.

TABLE 9-3: Examples of SQL Queries

SQL QUERY	MEANING
Select * From Employeeschema.Employee;	Select all information from the Employee table.
Select Name From Employeeschema.Employee Where DNR=1;	Select the name of all employees working in department number 1.
Select count(*) From Employeeschema. Department;	Select the number of departments from the Department table.
Select E.Name, D.Dname From Employeeschema.Employee E, Employeeschema. Department D Where E.DNR=D.DNR;	Select the names of all employees together with the names of the departments they work in.
Insert Into Employeeschema.Employee Values (6, "David Peeters", "Male",2);	Add a new employee to the Employee table.
Update Employeeschema.Employee Set DNR=3 Where Name="David Peeters";	Change the department of an employee.
Delete From Employeeschema.Employee Where Name="David Peeters";	Delete an employee from the Employee table.

In the remainder of this chapter, MySQL is used to demonstrate relational database access from within Java. MySQL is a popular open-source RDBMS currently maintained by Oracle (www.mysql.com). It has been very popular in web applications and is also part of the LAMP (Linux, Apache, MySQL, and Perl/PHP/Python) open-source software stack.

TRY IT OUT Creating a Relational Database in MySQL

This exercise shows you how to create a simple relational database using MySQL.

1. Download and install the MySQL Community Edition (GPL) from `http://www.mysql.com/downloads/`.

2. Open the MySQL workbench application. See Figure 9-2.

3. Create a new MyConnection connection by clicking the + button next to MySQL Connections, as shown in Figure 9-3.

FIGURE 9-2

4. Open MyConnection and create a schema called `Employeeschema`. Your screen now looks as shown in Figure 9-4.

5. Create two tables—Employee and Department—as shown in Figures 9-5 and 9-6.

6. Make sure to also create a foreign key relationship between DNR in Employee and DNR in Department. The SQL DDL corresponding to both these tables is:

```
CREATE TABLE IF NOT EXISTS 'EmployeeSchema'.'Employee' (
    'EmployeeID' INT NOT NULL,
    'Name' VARCHAR(45) NULL,
    'Gender' VARCHAR(45) NULL,
    'DNR' INT NULL,
    PRIMARY KEY ('EmployeeID'),
    INDEX 'DNRForeign_idx' ('DNR' ASC),
    CONSTRAINT 'DNRForeign'
      FOREIGN KEY ('DNR')
```

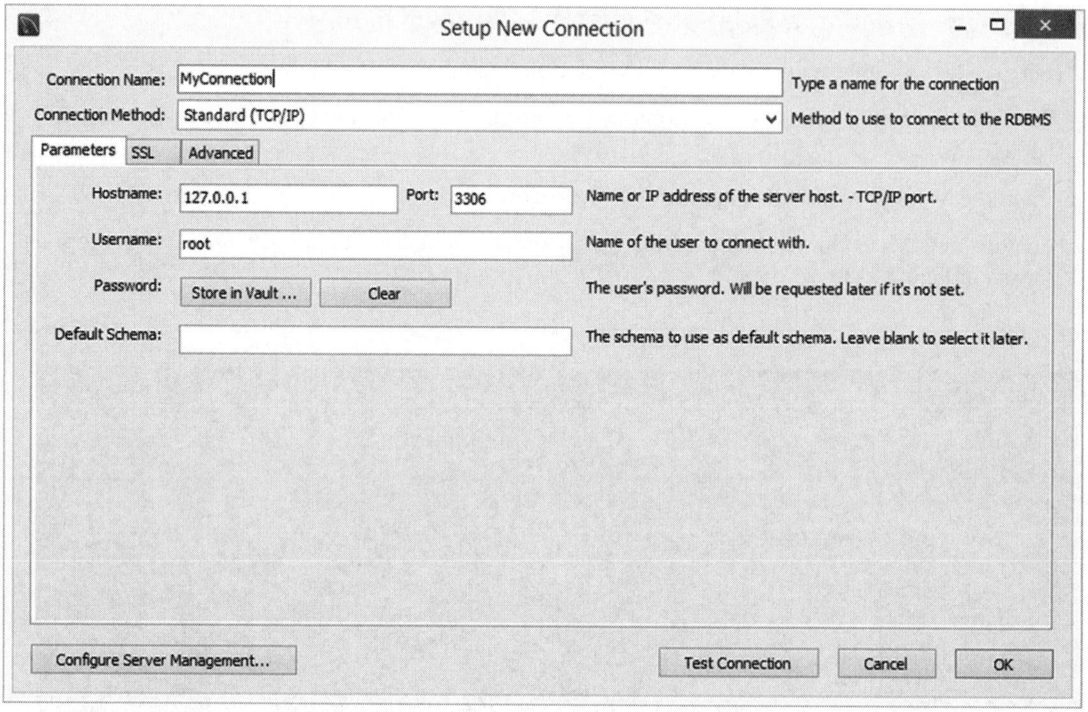

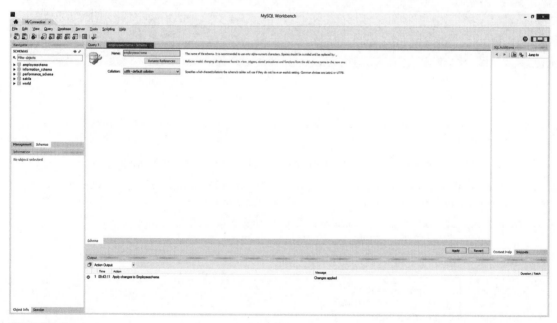

FIGURE 9-3

FIGURE 9-4

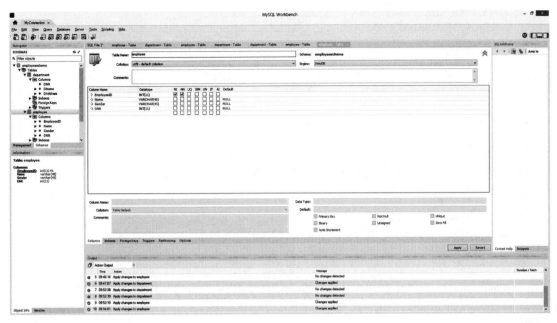

FIGURE 9-5

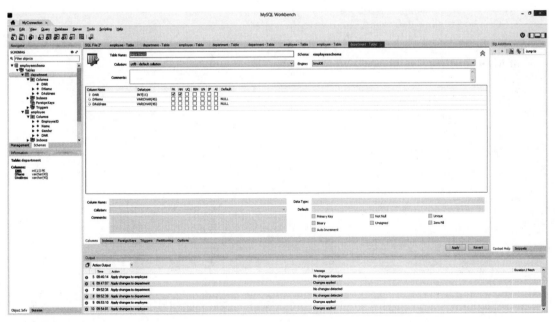

FIGURE 9-6

```
            REFERENCES 'EmployeeSchema'.'Department' ('DNR')
                 ON DELETE NO ACTION
                 ON UPDATE NO ACTION)
ENGINE = InnoDB

CREATE TABLE IF NOT EXISTS 'EmployeeSchema'.'Department' (
     'DNR' INT NOT NULL,
     'DName' VARCHAR(45) NULL,
     'DAddress' VARCHAR(45) NULL,
     PRIMARY KEY ('DNR'))
ENGINE = InnoDB
```

7. Use an SQL `insert` statement to add the following tuples to the Department table:

```
insert into employeeschema.department
values
    (1,     'ICT',       'Brussels'),
    (2,     'Marketing',     'New York'),
    (3,     'Finance',     'Singapore'),
    (4,     'Accounting',     'Sydney');
```

8. Use an SQL `insert` statement to add the following tuples to the Employee table:

```
insert into employeeschema.employee
values
    (1,     'Bart Baesens',      'Male',     1),
    (2,     'Aimée Backiel',      'Female',     1),
    (3,     'Seppe vanden Broucke',      'Male',     1),
    (4,     'Michael Jackson',      'Male',     2),
    (5,     'Sarah Adams',      'Female',     3);
```

9. Your MySQL screen should now look like Figure 9-7.

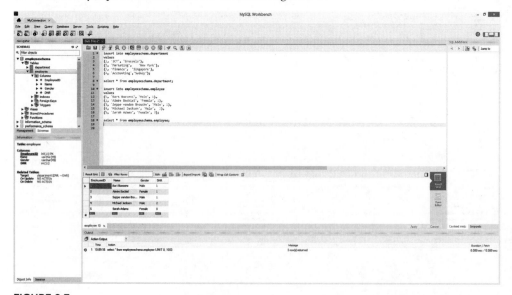

FIGURE 9-7

ACCESSING RELATIONAL DATABASES FROM JAVA

Accessing relational databases from Java is not a straightforward exercise. Various issues arise due to the intrinsic conceptual differences between Java as an object-oriented programming environment and the database, which is typically based on relational concepts and SQL. The discrepancy between both environments is often referred to as the *impedance mismatch problem.*

The first problem concerns the incompatibility between the data types implemented in Java and the types available in SQL. Some SQL data types are directly equivalent to a Java type. An example of this is the SQL INTEGER data type, which is identical to the Java int data type. Other SQL data types need to be converted. Examples are the SQL CHAR, VARCHAR, and LONGVARCHAR data types, which can be easily converted to the Java equivalent String data type. For the SQL DATE data type, a special Java data type, Java.Date, was created.

Another complication is that SQL relations are sets of records with no prior limitation on the number. Hence, Java needs to foresee a mechanism to appropriately import and handle the results of SQL queries. One popular approach here is a cursor mechanism that will allow you to iteratively loop through a set of records and process them one at a time in Java.

A discussion on the various ways of accessing databases from Java, each with their own approach to dealing with both of these problems, follows. It begins with an introduction to JDBC, which is a standard database application programming interface (API) available in Java. This is followed by a discussion of SQLJ, which allows SQL statements to be directly embedded into Java programs.

Java Database Connectivity (JDBC)

Every database vendor provides its own application programming interface (API). Hence, when connecting to a particular database, you need to be aware of the proprietary routines that make up the particular API. This makes it tedious and difficult to use different databases in an application. Java database connectivity (JDBC) is a popular standardized application programming interface (API) that gives database-independent access to tabular data typically stored in relational databases or Microsoft Excel. It allows you to set up a connection with the database (or tabular data source), exchange SQL statements (such as CREATE, SELECT, INSERT, UPDATE, and DELETE), and process the results. A key advantage of JDBC is that it provides an easy access mechanism to various existing data sources. Moreover, since it is based on Java technology, it is easy to learn and use in your Java programs. Given its popularity, many database vendors provide support for it, such as Oracle, IBM, Microsoft, and more. The most recent version is JDBC 4.2 and is included in Java SE 8. The JDBC classes are implemented using the packages java.sql and javax.sql. There are four types of JDBC drivers to access the data, as shown in Table 9-4.

TABLE 9-4: JDBC Driver Types

DRIVER TYPE	DESCRIPTION
JDBC type 1 driver	JDBC/ODBC bridge. Open Database Connectivity (ODBC) is another standard API for accessing databases developed by Microsoft. This driver will convert JDBC calls to client-side ODBC calls, which then communicate with the network database.

continues

TABLE 9-4: *(continued)*

DRIVER TYPE	DESCRIPTION
JDBC type 2 driver	This driver converts JDBC calls into client-side API calls, which will then further communicate to the network database.
JDBC type 3 driver	This is a 100% Java driver whereby JDBC calls are translated to the protocol adopted by a separate middleware application server, which then further communicates to the database.
JDBC type 4 driver	This is a 100% Java driver whereby JDBC calls are directly translated into the network protocol used by the database.

From Table 9-4, it is clear that the JDBC type 4 driver is the most powerful. Its workings are further clarified in Figure 9-8.

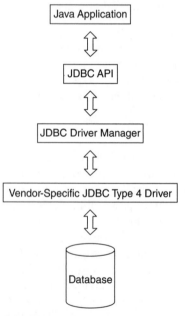

FIGURE 9-8

Table 9-5 describes the core JDBC classes and methods.

TABLE 9-5: JDBC Classes and Purpose

JDBC CLASS	PURPOSE
DriverManager	Locate the JDBC driver.
Connection	Set up a database connection.
Statement	Define a static SQL statement.

`PreparedStatement`	Define a dynamic SQL statement.
`CallableStatement`	Execute stored procedures in the database.
`ResultSet`	Provide a JDBC cursor mechanism.

In the next exercise, you see how these classes can be used to access data from a MySQL database.

TRY IT OUT   Accessing a Relational Database Using JDBC

1. Download and install the JDBC driver for MySQL. In my case (working on a Windows 8 computer), I downloaded MySQL Connector/J from `http://dev.mysql.com/downloads/connector/j/5.0.html`, which is the official JDBC type 4 driver for MySQL. The file called `mysql-connector-java-5.1.30-bin.jar` was then installed in my directory `C:\Program Files (x86)\MySQL\Connector J 5.1.30`. Make sure to add the directory `C:\Program Files (x86)\MySQL\Connector J 5.1.30` to the `CLASSPATH` environment variable. As an alternative, you could also right-click the project in Eclipse, choose Build Path ➢ Configure Build Path ➢ Add External JARs, and then explicitly add the file `mysql-connector-java-5.1.30-bin.jar`.

2. Create a new project in Eclipse. Perhaps call it `Chapter9` to keep the exercises organized according to the chapters in this book.

3. Create a new class by right-clicking on the `src` folder in your new project. Select New ➢ Class.

4. In the Name field, enter the name of your class, `JDBCExample1`. In the bottom portion of the New Java Class window, there is a section that reads, "Which method stubs would you like to create?" You may choose to check the box next to "public static void main(String[] args)" to automatically create a `main` method.

5. You should automatically have the basis for the class body shown here:

```
public class JDBCExample1 {

    public static void main(String[] args) {
        // TODO Auto-generated method stub
    }
}
```

6. Adapt this class definition as follows:

```
import java.sql.*;

public class JDBCExample1 {

public static void main(String[] args) {
        try {
            System.out.println("Loading JDBC driver...");
            Class.forName("com.mysql.jdbc.Driver");
            System.out.println("JDBC driver successfully loaded!");
        } catch (ClassNotFoundException e) {
            throw new RuntimeException(e);
        }
```

```java
String url = "jdbc:mysql://localhost:3306/employeeschema";
String username = "root";
String password = "mypassword123";
String query = "select E.Name, D.DName" +
    "from employee E, department D" +
    "where E.DNR=D.DNR;";
Connection connection = null;
Statement stmt=null;

try {
    System.out.println("Connecting to the MySQL database...");
    connection = DriverManager.getConnection(url, username, password);
    System.out.println("MySQL Database connected!");
    stmt = connection.createStatement();
    ResultSet rs = stmt.executeQuery(query);
    while (rs.next()) {
        System.out.print(rs.getString(1));
        System.out.print("  ");
        System.out.println(rs.getString(2));
    }
    stmt.close();
} catch (SQLException e) {
    System.out.println(e.toString());
} finally {
    System.out.println("Closing the connection.");
    if (connection != null) {
        try {
            connection.close();
        } catch (SQLException ignore) {
        }
    }
}
```

7. Save the class by clicking the disk icon or selecting File ➤ Save.

8. Run the application by clicking the green play icon or selecting Run ➤ Run.

9. You should receive the following output:

```
Loading JDBC driver...
JDBC driver successfully loaded!
Connecting to the MySQL database...
MySQL Database connected!
Bart Baesens  ICT
Aimée Backiel  ICT
Seppe vanden Broucke  ICT
Michael Jackson  Marketing
Sarah Adams  Finance
Closing the connection.
```

How It Works

The program starts by importing the JDBC package by using the statement `import java.sql.*;`. The first part of the code then sets up the connection with the database. The statement

`Class.forName("com.mysql.jdbc.Driver")` dynamically loads the MySQL database driver. It is embedded in a `try catch` block in case exceptions occur. The URL variable contains the location of the database schema, and the username and password variables store the logon credentials. The query variable is a string containing the SQL query you want to execute. Note that it is a join query, whereby the Employee and Department tables are joined. The statement `connection = DriverManager.getConnection(url, username, password)` establishes a connection to the MySQL database by creating a connection object using the logon information. In JDBC, all SQL statements are executed within the context of a connection object. A Java program can have multiple connections to different databases. The statement `stmt = connection.createStatement()` creates a statement object for sending SQL statements to the MySQL database. The statement `ResultSet rs = stmt.executeQuery(query);` executes the query and stores the result thereof into the `rs` object. It's important to note that in JDBC, all SQL queries are compiled and processed at runtime. The `rs` resultset object contains a cursor pointing to a particular row of data in the result. Initially, it is put before the first row and can be moved using the method `next`. The latter returns `false` when there are no more rows in the resultset. The `while` loop, which follows, now navigates through the results of the resultset. The statement `System.out.print(rs.getString(1));` then retrieves the first element (`E.Name`) of the row where the cursor is positioned. The statement `System.out.print(" ");` then adds some extra space and is followed by the statement `System.out.println(rs.getString(2));` which retrieves the second element (i.e. `D.DName`) of the row where the cursor is positioned and adds a line break. To conclude the program, the statement and connection objects are properly closed.

In the following example, you will use JDBC to access a MySQL database in combination with user-provided input.

TRY IT OUT Accessing a Relational Database Using JDBC and User Input

In this example, you will allow the user to provide input for the query in the JDBC program.

1. Create a new class by right-clicking on the `src` folder in your `Chapter9` project. Select New ➤ Class.

2. In the Name field, enter the name of your class, `JDBCExample2`. In the bottom portion of the New Java Class window, there is a section that reads, "Which method stubs would you like to create?" You may choose to check the box next to "`public static void main(String[] args)`" to automatically create a `main` method.

3. You should automatically have the basis for the class body shown here:

```
public class JDBCExample2 {

    public static void main(String[] args) {
        // TODO Auto-generated method stub
    }
}
```

4. Adapt this class definition as follows:

```
import java.sql.*;
import java.util.*;

public class JDBCExample2 {
```

```java
public static void main(String[] args) {
    int DeptNr=0;
    try {
        System.out.println("Loading JDBC driver...");
        Class.forName("com.mysql.jdbc.Driver");
        System.out.println("JDBC driver successfully loaded!");
    } catch (ClassNotFoundException e) {
        throw new RuntimeException(e);
    }

    Scanner keyboard = new Scanner(System.in);
    try {
        System.out.println("Please enter the department number: ");
        DeptNr=keyboard.nextInt();
    } catch(InputMismatchException err) {
        System.out.println("Incorrect input");
    }
    String url = "jdbc:mysql://localhost:3306/employeeschema";
    String username = "root";
    String password = "mypassword123";
    String query="select Name, Gender, DNR" +
        " from employee where DNR=?";
    Connection connection = null;
    Statement stmt = null;
    try {
        System.out.println("Connecting to the MySQL database...");
        connection = DriverManager.getConnection(url, username, password);
        System.out.println("MySQL Database connected!");
        PreparedStatement preparedStatement =
            connection.prepareStatement(query);
        preparedStatement.setInt(1, DeptNr);
        ResultSet rs = preparedStatement.executeQuery();
        while (rs.next()) {
            System.out.print(rs.getString(1));
            System.out.print((" "));
            System.out.print(rs.getString(2));
            System.out.print((" "));
            System.out.println(rs.getInt(3));
        }
        preparedStatement.close();
    } catch (SQLException e) {
        System.out.println(e.toString());
    } finally {
        System.out.println("Closing the connection.");
        if (connection != null) {
            try {
                connection.close();
            } catch (SQLException ignore) {
            }
        }
    }
}
```

5.   Save the class by clicking the disk icon or selecting File ➤ Save.

6. Run the application by clicking the green play icon or selecting Run ➤ Run. Enter 1 for the department number.

7. You will now get the output shown in Figure 9-9.

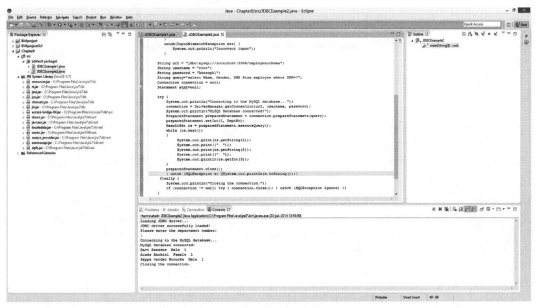

FIGURE 9-9

How It Works

The first part of the code is similar to the previous example. The only thing that is different is that a Scanner object is created (using the `java.util.*` package) to provide input using the keyboard. The `DeptNr` variable stores the number of the department for which you want to list the employees. This is accomplished using a `PreparedStatement` object. This object can take parameters that are being input using the keyboard or from a GUI application. In this example, the statement `PreparedStatement`
`preparedStatement = connection.prepareStatement(query);` creates a `preparedStatement` object based upon the query string variable, which is defined as follows: `String query="select Name, Gender, DNR from employee where DNR=?";`. The question mark in the query variable refers to a value that needs to be specified before the query can be executed. In this example, this variable will be set to `DeptNr` (which was obtained via the keyboard) using the following statement: `preparedStatement.setInt(1, DeptNr);`. The prepared statement object can then be executed and the results stored in a resultset object using the following statement: `ResultSet rs = preparedStatement.executeQuery();`. A `while` loop can then be used to navigate through the results of this resultset object as in the previous example.

SQLJ

SQLJ is built on top of JDBC and allows you to embed SQL statements directly into Java programs. A preprocessor will then translate the SQL statements into Java/JDBC statements, which are then further compiled by the Java compiler to bytecode. This is illustrated in Figure 9-10.

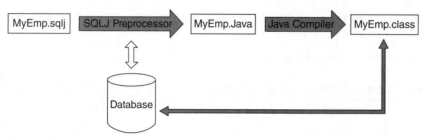

FIGURE 9-10

The preprocessor can perform syntax checks, Java/SQL type matching, and verify the query against the database schema at design time. This will not only result in fewer errors at runtime, but will also improve the performance of the query. Another key difference with JDBC is that SQL statements are compiled at runtime.

Note that as illustrated in Figure 9-10, a Java program with embedded SQLJ statements should have an `*.sqlj` filename extension. Both SQLJ and JDBC statements can be used in the same program. This allows you to combine the benefits of static, pre-compiled SQL offered by SQLJ with the runtime flexibility offered by JDBC.

The `sqlj.runtime` and `sqlj.runtime.ref` packages contain the Java runtime classes and interfaces used by SQLJ and should be imported at the start of the program. The JDBC `java.sql` package will also be imported to set up the JDBC connection and perform error handling:

```
import sqlj.runtime.*;
import sqlj.runtime.ref.*;
import java.sql.*;
```

A SQLJ program starts by loading a JDBC driver and creating a connection context (similar to a JDBC connection object) as follows:

```
try {
    System.out.println("Loading JDBC driver...");
    Class.forName("com.mysql.jdbc.Driver");
    DefaultContext.setDefaultContext(new DefaultContext(
        "jdbc:mysql://localhost:3306/employeeschema","root","mypassword123"));
} catch (Exception e) {
    //do something
}
```

By default, all SQLJ statements will then be executed within the defined default connection context.

SQLJ statements start with an `#sql` delimiter and are terminated with a semicolon as follows:

```
#sql {<sql-statement>};
```

This allows the SQLJ preprocessor to easily recognize the SQL instructions. The SQLJ statement itself can span multiple lines and may also include host variables and/or expressions. Host variables are variables defined within the Java program and can be included in a SQLJ statement preceded by a colon, such as the following:

```
#sql {select EmployeeID, Name
    into :empID,:ename
    from EmployeeSchema.Employee
    where DNR = :dnr };
```

SQLJ has two types of cursors: iterators and positional iterators. They are always defined at the start of the Java class file and not within a class. Remember the Employee table defined earlier:

```
CREATE TABLE 'EmployeeSchema'.'Employee' (
    'EmployeeID' INT NOT NULL,
    'Name' VARCHAR(45) NULL,
    'Gender' VARCHAR(45) NULL,
    'DNR' INT NULL,
    PRIMARY KEY ('EmployeeID'),
    INDEX 'DNRForeign_idx' ('DNR' ASC),
    CONSTRAINT 'DNRForeign'
        FOREIGN KEY ('DNR')
        REFERENCES 'EmployeeSchema'.'Department' ('DNR')
        ON DELETE NO ACTION
        ON UPDATE NO ACTION)
```

Let's now define a named iterator as follows:

```
#sql iterator EmpNameIter (int EmployeeID, String Name, int DNR);
class SQLJEx1 {
    void AccessEmpData() throws SQLException {

        EmpNameIter MyNamedIter;
        #sql MyNamedItter =
            {SELECT Name, EmployeeID, DNR FROM EmployeeSchema.Employee };
    }
}
```

Note that the iterator column names match the table column names. Also observe that the order of the columns in the SQL statement should not match the order in the iterator statement or table since data is matched by name and not by position, which is very convenient. You can then access the columns by their name, as follows:

```
while (MyNamedItter.next()) {
    System.out.println(MyNamedItter.EmployeeID +
        " " + MyNamedItter.Name + " " + MyNamedItter.DNR));
}
```

The method next retrieves the next row of the iterator and then returns true unless there are no more rows to be retrieved, in which case it returns false.

A positional iterator defines only the data type of each column and not its name. An example is as follows:

```
#sql iterator EmpPosIter (int, String, in);

class SQLJEx2 {
    void AccessEmpData () throws SQLException {
        EmpPosIter MyPosIter;
        #sql MyPosItter =
```

```
                    { SELECT EmployeeID, Name, DNR FROM EmployeeSchema.Employee };
        }
    }
```

Observe that the order is the same for the table, iterator, and SQL statement. To retrieve data from a positional iterator, you must use the FETCH INTO statement and the endfetch() method to verify if the end of the data has been reached as follows:

```
while (true) {
    #sql {FETCH : MyPosIter INTO :EmployeeID, :Name, :DNR} ;
    if (MyPosIter.endFetch()) {
        break;
    }
}
```

As with other database objects, it is important to close every iterator using the close() method to free the occupied resources.

When compared to JDBC, SQLJ programs are usually more concise and thus easier to debug. As discussed, SQLJ also allows you to do syntactic and semantic query checking at design time, in contrast to JDBC where queries are verified at runtime. Despite its advantages, the SQLJ standard has been less popular than JDBC in the industry.

PUSHING COMPLEX DATA PROCESSING TO THE DATABASE

SQL is a very powerful database manipulation language that allows complex data-processing operations in the RDBMS itself. When using JDBC or SQLJ, it is highly recommended to push as many complex data operations as possible to the database instead of programming them in Java. Every RDBMS has built-in sophisticated facilities for indexing and caching, which have a huge impact on query performance.

In the first JDBC example in this chapter, the SQL query performs a join between two tables. Alternatively, you could opt to retrieve the data from both tables into the Java program and program the join in Java. However, from a performance viewpoint, this is highly discouraged as it would create more network traffic and processing time. Hence, it is of key importance that a Java developer accessing a RDBMS through JDBC or SQLJ possess a deep understanding of SQL in order to write high-performing Java database applications!

ENSURING OBJECT PERSISTENCE

During Java program execution, a distinction can be made between transient objects, which only exist during program execution, and persistent objects, which need to be permanently stored in a database. Earlier in this chapter, you learned about the impedance mismatch problem, which refers to the intrinsic incompatibility between Java objects and relational SQL tables. To bridge this incompatibility problem, two solutions can be pursued. A first solution is to use an object relational mapping (ORM) framework, which tackles the impedance problem by directly mapping Java objects to relational concepts and vice versa. Every plain old Java object (POJO) or JavaBean that needs to be made persistent can be directly mapped by the ORM to one or more tuples in a relational database without having to implement (vendor-) specific interfaces or classes. The ORM provides full support of all CRUD (CREATE, READ, UPDATE, and DELETE) database operations. A key advantage of using an object relational mapper is that it waives the Java developer from fully understanding and mastering all details of relational database design and advanced SQL query tuning, since all database interactions are directly handled and optimized by the ORM. This will result in more compact Java code, a potential decrease in database calls, more efficient queries, and higher portability across database platforms.

A second solution is to abandon the idea of using a relational database and use an object-oriented DBMS (OODBMS) instead. OODBMSs support the storage of objects rather than relational tuples. This will allow the storage of all POJOs directly and transparently as objects in an OODBMS without having to perform any translation. Obviously, avoiding all the mapping operations will greatly benefit the performance of the Java application.

The Java community has introduced various standards for object persistence. The most popular are the Java Persistence API (JPA) and Java Data Objects (JDO). Both provide a set of rules and guidelines to make POJOs persistent for both Java SE and Java EE environments using either an ORM, OODBMS, or another storage format (such as XML). JPA was mainly designed for relational databases, whereas JDO was more targeted toward OODBMSs, which are less popular in the industry. Hence, given the widespread availability of relational databases, this discussion will continue with JPA. For more details about JDO, refer to `http://www.oracle.com/technetwork/java/index-jsp-135919.html`.

JPA was first developed in 2006. The most recent version, JPA 2.1, was released in 2013. The JPA API is specified in the `javax.persistence` package. To facilitate the mapping between the Java application and the database (either relational or OO), annotations are used. JPA also includes the Java Persistence Query Language (JPQL) as an SQL-like standard to define object-oriented queries on objects. JPQL queries are also formulated as `Select... From...` queries but can now return objects rather than field values, as is the case in SQL. When using an ORM, the JPQL queries will be translated to relational SQL queries, whereas when using an OODBMS, the JPQL queries can be directly executed on the database, thereby increasing the performance of the query. JPQL provides full support of all OO concepts such as (multiple) inheritance, dynamic binding, polymorphism, and so on. Example implementations of the JPA standard are:

➤ ORM: Hibernate, EclipseLink (formerly Oracle TopLink), and OpenJPA

➤ OODBMS: ObjectDB

It is important to keep in mind that JPA was developed after many of the ORMs (such as Hibernate and TopLink) were already available. The result is one overall, uniform interface that facilitates switching between different persistence providers.

Two examples to illustrate the use of JPA follow. Hibernate is an example of an ORM implementation of JPA, and ObjectDB is an example of an OODBMS implementation of JPA.

Hibernate

We will start by discussing Hibernate, one of the most commonly used ORMs in the industry. It is an open-source ORM currently maintained by Red Hat at `http://hibernate.org/`. It provides support for most commercial database platforms such as MySQL, Oracle, Sybase, and so on. Just like SQLJ, it uses JDBC to communicate to the database. It also includes facilities for transaction management, concurrency control, caching, and connection pooling. Figure 9-11 gives a high-level outline of the Hibernate architecture.

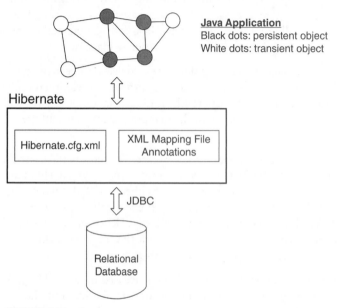

FIGURE 9-11

A first important building block when creating a Hibernate application is the `hibernate.cfg.xml` configuration file. This is one application-specific XML file containing the essential information to set up the database connection by specifying the JDBC driver, connection URL, the database username and password, and the Java classes that need to be mapped. The object relational mapping itself can then be specified using either an XML file or annotations. By convention, the XML file has the same name as the class that's to be mapped and is in the same directory. An example `employee.hbm.xml` file providing a mapping of the Java class `Employee` to the MySQL relational Employee table could be a follows:

```
<?xml version="1.0" encoding="utf-8"?>
<!DOCTYPE hibernate-mapping PUBLIC
    "-//Hibernate/Hibernate Mapping DTD//EN"
    "http://www.hibernate.org/dtd/hibernate-mapping-3.0.dtd">

<hibernate-mapping>
    <class name="Employee" table="EMPLOYEE">
        <meta attribute="class-description">
            This class contains the employee detail.
        </meta>
        <id name="id" type="int" column="id">
            <generator class="native"/>
        </id>
```

```
            <property name="JEmpID" column="EmployeeID" type="int"/>
            <property name="JName" column="Name" type="string"/>
            <property name="JGender" column="Gender" type="string"/>
            <property name="JDNR" column="DNR" type="int"/>
    </class>
</hibernate-mapping>
```

This example clearly illustrates how the various class properties are mapped to relational database columns.

When using annotations, the mapping is directly specified in the POJO class definition itself. Table 9-6 provides an overview of commonly used annotations available in Hibernate. See `http://hibernate.org/` for a comprehensive overview.

TABLE 9-6: Common Hibernate Annotations

ANNOTATION	DESCRIPTION
@Entity	Declares a persistent POJO class.
@Table	Allows you to explicitly specify the name of the relational table to map the persistent POJO class to, in case both names are different.
@Column	Allows you to explicitly specify the name of the relational table column in case it is different from the persistent POJO class field.
@ID	Maps a persistent POJO class field to a primary key of a relational table.
@Transient	Allows you to define POJO class fields that are transient and thus should not be made persistent.

As opposed to XML, annotations are directly compiled to bytecode and thus provide better performance. This is a key reason why most developers nowadays use annotations to perform the mapping. A disadvantage of both XML and annotations is that the persistence details are spread across different classes or XML files instead of being centralized, which may hamper the maintenance.

Although Hibernate allows you to directly embed SQL queries in Java, it also comes with a new full-fledged, database agnostic query language called Hibernate Query Language (HQL). HQL is object-oriented and works with classes and properties instead of tables and columns. It is less verbose than SQL and includes support for inner/outer joins, polymorphism, subqueries, aggregation, grouping, and ordering. Queries can be formulated by navigating object relations rather than relational tables. All HQL queries are translated to relational SQL queries at runtime. JPQL is based on HQL, since JPA was introduced after Hibernate was created.

In the "Try It Out" that follows, you develop your first Hibernate application.

TRY IT OUT   Accessing a Relational MySQL Database Using Hibernate

In this example, you will be able to access a relational MySQL database using Hibernate.

1. First, install Hibernate from `http://hibernate.org/orm/downloads/`. In this example, hibernate release `4.3.5.final` is installed in the directory `C:\hibernate-release-4.3.5.Final`.

2. Now add the Hibernate JARs to the build path of the project. Right-click the project, choose Properties ➤ Java Build Path ➤ Add Library. Define a User Library called `MyHibernateLibrary` and add the files from `C:\hibernate-release-4.3.5.Final\lib\required`, as shown in Figure 9-12.

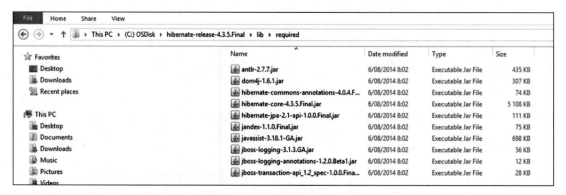

FIGURE 9-12

3. Make sure to also add the `mysql-connector-java-5.1.30-bin.jar` to the Build Path. Your Eclipse project now looks like Figure 9-13.

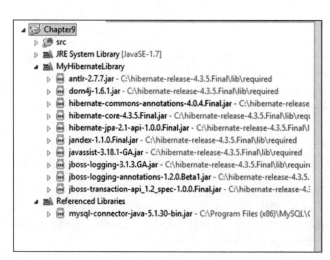

FIGURE 9-13

4. Create a file called `hibernate.cfg.xml` with the following content:

```xml
<?xml version='1.0' encoding='utf-8'?>
<!DOCTYPE hibernate-configuration PUBLIC
"-//Hibernate/Hibernate Configuration DTD//EN"
"http://www.hibernate.org/dtd/hibernate-configuration-3.0.dtd">
<hibernate-configuration>
    <session-factory>
        <property name="hibernate.connection.driver_class">
            com.mysql.jdbc.Driver</property>
        <property name="hibernate.connection.url">
            jdbc:mysql://localhost:3306/employeeschema</property>
        <property name="hibernate.connection.username">
            root</property>
        <property name="hibernate.connection.password">
            mypassword123</property>
        <property name="hibernate.connection.pool_size">
            10</property>
        <property name="show_sql">true</property>
        <property name="dialect">
            org.hibernate.dialect.MySQLDialect</property>
        <property name="hibernate.current_session_context_class">
            thread</property>
        <mapping class="Employee" />
    </session-factory>
</hibernate-configuration>
```

5. Add the file to the `src` directory of your project. Your Eclipse environment now looks like Figure 9-14.

FIGURE 9-14

6. Create a new class called `Employee.java`, as follows:

```java
import javax.persistence.Entity;
import javax.persistence.Id;

@Entity
public class Employee {
    private int EmployeeID;
    private String Name;
    private String Gender;
    private int DNR;

    @Id
    public int getEmployeeID() {
        return EmployeeID;
    }

    public void setEmployeeID( int id ) {
        this.EmployeeID = id;
    }

    public String getName() {
        return Name;
    }

    public void setName( String name ) {
        this.Name = name;
    }

    public String getGender() {
        return Gender;
    }

    public void setGender( String gender ) {
        this.Gender = gender;
    }

    public int getDNR() {
        return DNR;
    }

    public void setDNR( int dnr) {
        this.DNR = dnr;
    }

}
```

7. Create a class called `myDBApp.java`, as follows:

```java
import org.hibernate.SessionFactory;
import org.hibernate.Session;
import org.hibernate.cfg.Configuration;
import org.hibernate.Query;

import java.util.List;
```

```
public class myDBApp {
    public static void main(String[] args) {
        // Create new employee and store in MySQL
        Employee Myemp=new Employee();
        Myemp.setName("Hibernate dude");
        Myemp.setGender("Male");
        Myemp.setEmployeeID(6);
        Myemp.setDNR(2);

        SessionFactory sessionFactory =
            new Configuration().configure().buildSessionFactory();
        Session session=sessionFactory.openSession();
        session.beginTransaction();
        session.save(Myemp);
        session.getTransaction().commit();
        // Retrieve employee data from MySQL
        Query query = session.createQuery("from Employee where EmployeeID = 6");
        List<?> list = query.list();
        Employee emp = (Employee)list.get(0);
        System.out.println(emp.getName());
        System.out.println(emp.getGender());
        System.out.println(emp.getDNR());
        session.close();
        sessionFactory.close();
    }
}
```

8. Run the class and inspect its output. It should now look like Figure 9-15.

FIGURE 9-15

9. Also inspect the Employee table in MySQL to verify if the new employee has been successfully added, as shown in Figure 9-16.

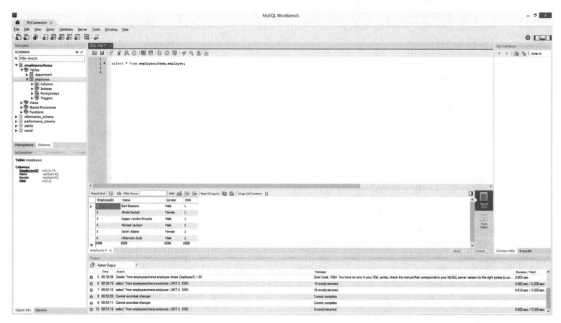

FIGURE 9-16

How It Works

1. It begins with installing all the necessary JARs to use both Hibernate and MySQL. The hibernate.cfg.xml file contains all the Hibernate configuration details that will be used by the sessionFactory object to set up a database connection. Note that Hibernate will communicate with the MySQL database using JDBC. The following properties were set:

```
hibernate.connection.driver_class: JDBC driver class
hibernate.connection.url: JDBC URL
hibernate.connection.username: database user
hibernate.connection.password: database user password
hibernate.connection.pool_size: maximum number of pooled JDBC connections
```

2. By setting the show_SQL property to true, the SQL commands generated by Hibernate are displayed in the console. This is very handy for debugging. The dialect property allows you to specify which SQL language should be used to communicate with the relational database, for example, Oracle9Dialect, PostgreSQLDialect, SybaseDialect, and so on. Since you are working with a MySQL database, it was set to MySQLDialect. By setting the hibernate.current_session_context_class property to thread, the Hibernate session is executed in the thread in which it was created. The <mapping class="Employee" /> statement then defined the class for which you want to create the mapping to the MySQL database.

3. Then the `Employee` class was created. It contains the same four attributes as in the MySQL database: `EmployeeID`, `Name`, `Gender`, and `DNR`. The mapping to the Employee MySQL table is performed using the `@Entity` and `@Id` annotations. The `@Entity` annotation is included before the class definition and maps the class to the relational MySQL Employee table. The `@Id` annotation then defines the identifier of the class that will be mapped to the primary key of the MySQL Employee table. Note that the Java class may have a different name than the MySQL table. In this case, the `@Table` annotation can be used to define the mapping. If no `@Table` annotation is used, the name of the class is used, which is fine in this case since it is identical to the name of the MySQL table. Likewise, the `@Column` annotation can be used to map Java properties to MySQL columns. Refer to `http://hibernate.org/` for other examples of annotations.

4. In Step 7 of the Try It Out, the `myDBApp` class was created to perform some basic database operations. It starts with creating a new employee object `Myemp` and setting its characteristics. Then a `sessionFactory` object was created, which will in turn allow the creation of a `session` object. The latter represents a single-threaded wrapped JDBC connection with the database. Note that Hibernate often introduces new classes and methods to create both `sessionFactory` and `session` objects, and it is thus recommended to check `http://hibernate.org/` regularly for updates.

5. The `session` object serves as a factory for creating database transactions. The statement `session.beginTransaction();` initiates a database transaction that represents an atomic unit of database operations. If needed, multiple transactions per session can be created. The `Myemp` employee object will then be made persistent in the MySQL database using the method `session.save(Myemp)` followed by `session.getTransaction().commit()`. Then the insert is verified by issuing the HQL query: `Query query = session.createQuery("from Employee where EmployeeID = 6")`. The results of the query are stored in a list object `List<?> list = query.list()`. The query will return one result, which will be stored in the object emp as follows: `Employee emp = (Employee)list.get(0)`. This is followed by retrieving the various attributes and displaying them on the console. The program finishes by closing the `session` and `sessionFactory` objects.

6. Since the `show_SQL` property was set to `true` in the configuration file, you can see the SQL statements that are being generated by Hibernate as follows:

```
Hibernate: insert into Employee (DNR, gender, name, employeeID) values (?, ?, ?, ?)
Hibernate: select employee0_.employeeID as employee1_0_, employee0_.DNR as DNR2_0_,
    employee0_.gender as gender3_0_, employee0_.name as name4_0_
    from Employee employee0_
    where EmployeeID=6
```

The result of the query is then:

```
Hibernate dude
Male
2
```

This is also confirmed by inspecting the table directly in MySQL.

In most applications, Java objects and their corresponding relational tables will be associated using relationships. Hibernate also has facilities for managing the object relational mapping of these associations. Obviously, the mapping depends on the type and the multiplicity of the association.

Associations can be implemented as unidirectional or bidirectional depending upon how they are being used and navigated. A unidirectional association always navigates from a parent object (owning side) to a child object (inverse side), whereas in a bidirectional association, both directions of navigation are supported. Depending upon the multiplicity, the association can then be qualified using the following annotations: `@OnetoMany`, `@ManytoOne`, or `@ManytoMany`. An example of mapping a unidirectional many-to-many relationship in Hibernate follows.

TRY IT OUT Many-to-Many Relationship Mapping Using Hibernate

In this example, you perform a many-to-many mapping using annotations in Hibernate.

1. Start by creating a new table called `project` in MySQL. The table has two attributes—`ProjectID` is the primary key and `PName` contains the name of the project. The SQL DDL for the project table is as follows:

```
CREATE TABLE 'project' (
    'ProjectID' int(11) NOT NULL,
    'PName' varchar(45) DEFAULT NULL,
    PRIMARY KEY ('ProjectID')
) ENGINE=InnoDB DEFAULT CHARSET = utf8;
```

2. Now assume that there is a many-to-many relationship between the tables `employee` and `project`. In other words, an employee can work on at least 0 and at most m projects, whereas a project is assigned to at least 0 and at most n employees. This can be visualized in an Entity Relationship (ER) diagram, as shown in Figure 9-17.

FIGURE 9-17

3. In order to implement this many-to-many relationship in MySQL, create a new table called `works_on` as follows:

```
CREATE TABLE 'works_on' (
    'EmployeeID' int(11) NOT NULL,
    'ProjectID' int(11) NOT NULL,
    PRIMARY KEY ('EmployeeID','ProjectID'),
    KEY 'works_onProj_idx' ('ProjectID'),
    CONSTRAINT 'works_onEmp' FOREIGN KEY ('EmployeeID')
        REFERENCES 'employee' ('EmployeeID')
        ON DELETE NO ACTION
        ON UPDATE NO ACTION,
    CONSTRAINT 'works_onProj' FOREIGN KEY ('ProjectID')
        REFERENCES 'project' ('ProjectID')
        ON DELETE NO ACTION
        ON UPDATE NO ACTION
) ENGINE = InnoDB DEFAULT CHARSET = utf8;
```

The `works_on` table has two attributes—`EmployeeID` and `ProjectID`—which make up the primary key and are at the same time foreign keys referring to the primary keys of the Employee and Project tables, respectively.

4. Now write a Java application that will create POJO objects that will be made persistent in both the `project` and `works_on` tables using Hibernate. Start by creating a new class called `Project.java`, as follows:

```java
import javax.persistence.Entity;
import javax.persistence.Id;

@Entity
public class Project {
    private int ProjectID;
    private String PName;

    public Project(int ProjectID, String PName) {
        super();
        this.ProjectID = ProjectID;
        this.PName = PName;
    }

    @Id
    public int getProjectID() {
        return ProjectID;
    }

    public void setProjectID(int projectID) {
        ProjectID = projectID;
    }

    public String getPName() {
        return PName;
    }

    public void setPName(String pName) {
        PName = pName;
    }
}
```

5. Adjust the `Employee` class as follows:

```java
import java.util.HashSet;
import java.util.Set;

import javax.persistence.Entity;
import javax.persistence.CascadeType;
import javax.persistence.ManyToMany;
import javax.persistence.JoinTable;
import javax.persistence.JoinColumn;
import javax.persistence.Id;

@Entity
public class Employee {
        private int EmployeeID;
        private String Name;
        private String Gender;
        private int DNR;
        private Set<Project> projects=new HashSet<Project>(0);
```

```java
public Employee(int EmployeeID, String Name, String Gender,
    int DNR, Set<Project> projects) {
        super();
        this.EmployeeID = EmployeeID;
        this.Name = Name;
        this.Gender = Gender;
        this.DNR = DNR;
        this.projects = projects;
    }

@Id
public int getEmployeeID() {
    return EmployeeID;
}

public void setEmployeeID( int id ) {
    this.EmployeeID = id;
}

public String getName() {
    return Name;
}

public void setName( String name ) {
    this.Name = name;
}

public String getGender() {
    return Gender;
}

public void setGender( String gender ) {
    this.Gender = gender;
}

public int getDNR() {
    return DNR;
}

public void setDNR( int dnr) {
    this.DNR = dnr;
}

@ManyToMany (cascade = CascadeType.ALL)
@JoinTable(name = "works_on", joinColumns =
    { @JoinColumn(name = "EmployeeID") },
    inverseJoinColumns = { @JoinColumn(name = "ProjectID") })

public Set<Project> getProjects(){
    return this.projects;
}

public void setProjects (Set<Project> projects) {
    this.projects = projects;
}
}
```

6. Make sure to include the `Project` class in the `hibernate.cfg.xml` file, as follows:

```xml
<?xml version='1.0' encoding='utf-8'?>
<!DOCTYPE hibernate-configuration PUBLIC
    "-//Hibernate/Hibernate Configuration DTD//EN"
    "http://www.hibernate.org/dtd/hibernate-configuration-3.0.dtd">
<hibernate-configuration>
    <session-factory>
        <property name="hibernate.connection.driver_class">
            com.mysql.jdbc.Driver</property>
        <property name="hibernate.connection.url">
            jdbc:mysql://localhost:3306/employeeschema</property>
        <property name="hibernate.connection.username">
            root</property>
        <property name="hibernate.connection.password">
            mypassword123</property>
        <property name="hibernate.connection.pool_size">
            10</property>
        <property name="show_sql">true</property>
        <property name="dialect">
            org.hibernate.dialect.MySQLDialect</property>
        <property name="hibernate.current_session_context_class">
            thread</property>
        <mapping  class="Employee" />
        <mapping  class="Project" />
    </session-factory>
</hibernate-configuration>
```

7. Create a new class called `myDBApp2` as follows:

```java
import org.hibernate.Session;
import org.hibernate.SessionFactory;
import org.hibernate.cfg.Configuration;

import java.util.HashSet;
import java.util.Set;

public class myDBApp2 {
    public static void main(String[] args) {
        Set<Project> projects=new HashSet<Project>();
        projects.add(new Project(1,"Hibernate Basic Project"));
        projects.add(new Project(2, "Hibernate Many to Many Project"));

        Employee Myemp=new Employee(7,"Hibernate freak", "Male", 1, projects );

        SessionFactory sessionFactory =
            new Configuration().configure().buildSessionFactory();
        Session session=sessionFactory.openSession();
        session.beginTransaction();
        session.save(Myemp);
        session.getTransaction().commit();

        session.close();
        sessionFactory.close();
    }
}
```

8. Run the myDBApp2 class and inspect its output. It should look like Figure 9-18 now.

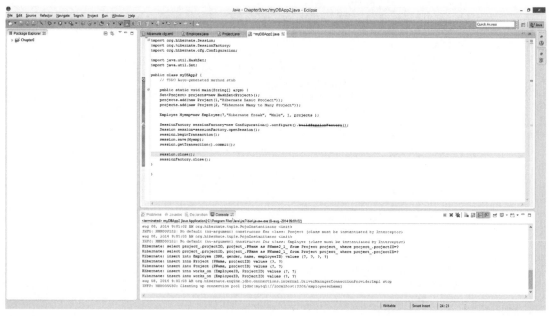

FIGURE 9-18

9. Also inspect the relational tables called employee, project, and works_on in MySQL. You will see that they look as shown in Figure 9-19, 9-20, and 9-21.

```
1 •   SELECT * FROM employeeschema.employee;
```

	EmployeeID	Name	Gender	DNR
▶	1	Bart Baesens	Male	1
	2	Aimée Backiel	Female	1
	3	Seppe vanden Broucke	Male	1
	4	Michael Jackson	Male	2
	5	Sarah Adams	Female	3
	6	Hibernate dude	Male	2
	7	Hibernate freak	Male	1
*	NULL	NULL	NULL	NULL

FIGURE 9-19

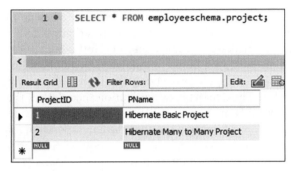

FIGURE 9-20

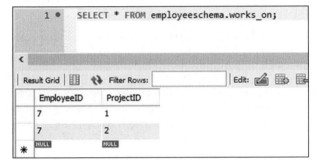

FIGURE 9-21

10. In these tables, you can see the new employee who is added to the employee table, both new projects in the project table, and the rows that have been added to the works_on table connecting the new employee to both new projects.

How It Works

1. The first three steps created the tables project and works_on in MySQL. Note that both tables are empty and will be populated from Java using Hibernate.

2. Next, the Project Java class was defined. Again, note that the @Entity annotation was included before the class definition to specify the mapping to the project MySQL table. The Project class also has a constructor method with two input arguments—ProjectID and PName. Finally, the @Id annotation maps the ProjectID property to the primary key of the Project MySQL table.

3. The Employee class was defined next. It starts with the annotation @Entity and includes a constructor method. Note that besides EmployeeID, Name, Gender, and DNR, this method also takes a set of project objects as input, which are to be assigned to the employee object upon creation. In other words, during object creation and manipulation, you navigate unidirectionally from the employee object (owning object) to the project objects (non-owning objects). You could also define this in the opposite direction from a project object (owning object) to the employee objects (non-owning objects) or implement it bidirectionally. In this last case, both objects would be considered owning objects. Again, the @Id annotation is used to map the EmployeeID property to the corresponding primary key in the relational Employee MySQL table.

4. The many-to-many mapping between `Employee` and `Project` is then implemented using the `@ManyToMany` annotation. The option `cascade=CascadeType.ALL` indicates that all data manipulations of `employee` objects will be immediately propagated to both the `employee` and `works_on` MySQL tables. For example, if an `employee` object is removed, then Hibernate will not only remove the corresponding tuple from the `employee` MySQL table, but also all referring tuples from the `works_on` MySQL table. The `@JoinTable` annotation then defines the connection to the join table. It is always specified in the class representing the owning side, which in this case is the `Employee` class. The `name` property specifies the corresponding join `works_on` MySQL table. The `joinColumns` property connects to the relevant MySQL attribute of the owning side (`Employee`) using the `@JoinColumn` annotation. The `inverseJoinColumns` property connects to the relevant MySQL attribute of the non-owning side (`Project`), again by using the `@JoinColumn` annotation. This is then followed by the setter and getter methods for the project's attribute.

5. In Step 6 of the Try It Out, you made sure that the `Project` class was now also included in the `hibernate.cfg.xml` mapping file.

6. In the next step, the class `myDBApp2` was created. First, a set object `projects` was defined and two new `project` objects were added to it. Then a new `Employee` object called `Myemp` was created and the `projects` set object was added to it. As in the previous example, a `sessionFactory` object was created, which then opened a `session` object, which in turn started a transaction. The `Myemp` object was then saved, the transaction was committed, and the `session` and `sessionFactory` objects were closed.

7. As in the previous example, since the `show_SQL` property was set to `true` in the configuration file, you can see the SQL statements that are being generated by Hibernate as follows:

```
Hibernate: select project_.projectID, project_.PName as PName2_1_
    from Project project_ where project_.projectID=?
Hibernate: select project_.projectID, project_.PName as PName2_1_
    from Project project_ where project_.projectID=?
Hibernate: insert into Employee (DNR, gender, name, employeeID) values (?, ?, ?, ?)
Hibernate: insert into Project (PName, projectID) values (?, ?)
Hibernate: insert into Project (PName, projectID) values (?, ?)
Hibernate: insert into works_on (EmployeeID, ProjectID) values (?, ?)
Hibernate: insert into works_on (EmployeeID, ProjectID) values (?, ?)
```

8. The results can then also be confirmed by inspecting the `employee`, `project`, and `works_on` tables in MySQL.

NOTE *For small-scale, single-user applications, you could also opt to adopt SQLite (or its Java implementation SQLJet) instead of MySQL. This is an in-process library implementing a lightweight, self-contained, server-less, zero-configuration SQL-based RDBMS. No external client-server based communication (using something like sockets or ports) is needed since all database communication is handled directly in the process in which the application runs. The database itself is then stored in a simple file that can be easily accessed and moved.*

Object-Oriented Database Access from Java

As mentioned, OODBMs store objects rather than relational tuples. Hence, no mapping is needed to store Java objects into an OODBMS. Although this may seem conceptually appealing at first sight, the success of OODBMSs in the industry has been limited to niche sectors, such as spatial and scientific applications. One of the reasons often mentioned for this is their intrinsic complexity when compared to RDBMSs.

In the next exercise, you see how Java can work with ObjectDB, a popular OODBMS, providing support for all the common database operations (such as transaction management, query processing, indexing, and so on). This is an example using the JPA and JDO APIs you saw earlier in the chapter. It is implemented as a single JAR and the database is stored as a single file.

TRY IT OUT Working with ObjectDB from Java

In this example, you will use ObjectDB to see how OODBMSs interact with Java directly.

1. Start by installing ObjectDB from `http://www.objectdb.com/object/db/database/download`. In this example, ObjectDB version 2.5.6_04 was installed in the directory `C:\objectdb-2.5.6_04`.

2. Continue from your previous Java project, `Chapter9`, and add the file `C:\objectdb-2.5.6_04\objectdb-2.5.6_04\bin\objectdb.jar` to the build path of the project. Remember, you can do this by right-clicking the project and choosing Build Path ≻ Add External Archives.

3. Make sure the classes `Employee.java` and `Project.java`, as defined in the previous activity, are still available in the current project.

4. Create a new class called `myDBApp3` as follows:

```java
import javax.persistence.*;
import java.util.*;
public class myDBApp3 {
    public static void main(String[] args) {
        EntityManagerFactory emf =
            Persistence.createEntityManagerFactory(
            "C:/objectdb-2.5.6_04/db/employeeadm.odb");
        EntityManager em = emf.createEntityManager();
        em.getTransaction().begin();
        Set<Project> projects=new HashSet<Project>();
        projects.add(new Project(1,"Basic ObjectDB Project"));
        projects.add(new Project(2, "Advanced ObjectDB Project"));
        Employee Myemp=new Employee(1,"Object DB freak", "Male", 1, projects );
        em.persist(Myemp);
        em.getTransaction().commit();
        Query q1 = em.createQuery("SELECT COUNT(emp) FROM Employee emp");
        System.out.println("Total Employees: " + q1.getSingleResult());
        TypedQuery<Project> query =
                em.createQuery("SELECT proj FROM Project proj", Project.class);
        List<Project> results = query.getResultList();
        for (Project proj : results) {
            System.out.print(proj.getProjectID());
            System.out.print(" ");;
```

```
                    System.out.println(proj.getPName());
            }
        em.close();
        emf.close();
    }
}
```

5. Run the `myDBApp3` class and inspect its output on the console. It should look like Figure 9-22.

FIGURE 9-22

6. Now open the ObjectDB explorer by double-clicking the file: `C:\objectdb-2.5.6_04\objectdb-2.5.6_04\bin\explorer.exe`.

7. Right-click the Employee Entity Class and choose Open Tree Window. Double-click the `Employee` object and the project's `HashSet` object. You will now get the results shown in Figure 9-23.

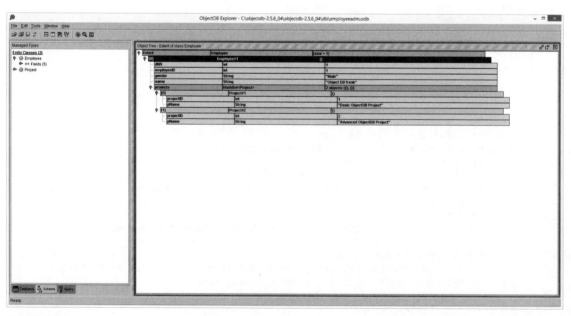

FIGURE 9-23

How It Works

1. The class `MyDBApp3` starts by importing the JPA `javax.persistence.*` package.

2. An `EntityManagerFactory` object `emf` is defined for the database in `C:\objectdb-2.5.6_04\` `objectdb-2.5.6_04\db\employeeadm.odb` using a static factory method of the JPA bootstrap class `Persistence`. If the database does not exist, which is the case in this example, then a new one will be created. Note that an URL combined with a username and a password can also be used when creating the `EntityManagerFactory` object. The connection to the database is then represented by the `EntityManager` object `em`, which is created by the `emf` object. The `emf` object may create multiple `EntityManager` objects in case multiple database connections are needed, which can then be efficiently pooled by the `emf` object. The method `em.getTransaction().begin();` then initiates a database transaction. The next lines of Java code then create two new `Project` objects and a new `Employee` object to which the `Project` objects are assigned using a `HashSet` object called `projects`. The `Employee` object is then stored in ObjectDB using the method `em.persist(Myemp);` and the transaction is committed by `em.getTransaction().commit();`. The `Employee` object has now been made persistent and can now be queried. Note how easy this is here, compared to the Hibernate approach where a configuration file had to be defined to specify the mapping details.

3. In JPA, queries can be implemented using the (old) `Query` or (new) `TypedQuery` interface. The `Query` interface can be used when the result type of the query is unknown, whereas the `TypedQuery` interface is used when a known result type is expected. Note that queries are always formulated in JPQL.

4. The statement `Query q1 = em.createQuery("SELECT COUNT(emp) FROM Employee emp");` creates a JPQL query object called `q1`, which counts the number of employees in the Employee Entity Class in ObjectDB. The result of the query is a single value and is written to the console using the method `System.out.println("Total Employees: " + q1.getSingleResult());`.

5. A JPQL query will now retrieve all `Project` objects and list them on the console. The statement `TypedQuery<Project> query = em.createQuery("SELECT proj FROM Project proj",` `Project.class);` creates a `TypedQuery` object whereby the return type of the query, i.e. `Project`, is now explicitly specified. The statement `List<Project> results = query.getResultList();` then executes the query and stores the results in a list of `Project` objects. A `for` loop is then used to iterate through this list and display the relevant information to the console. Finally, the `em` and `emf` objects are closed using the methods `em.close();` and `emf.close();`.

6. Finally, the object tree for the `Employee` and `Project` objects is displayed.

COMPARING JAVA DATABASE ACCESS TECHNOLOGIES

In this chapter, you have seen several ways to access databases from Java: JDBC, SQLJ, Hibernate as an ORM framework example, and OpenDB as an OODBMS example. In the industry, the most popular approaches currently adopted are JDBC and Hibernate. Despite their intrinsic advantages, SQLJ and OODBMSs are only seldom used because both are often perceived (rightfully or not) as complex to work with.

For simple applications working with only one database and less than 10 relational tables, it is advised to use JDBC. It's quite easy to install and use when compared to Hibernate, which has a rather steep learning curve and bigger footprint.

Hibernate is typically recommended when working with complex database models consisting of hundreds of relational tables with complex relationships between them. One of the key benefits of Hibernate is that it allows the complex underlying database design to be completely abstracted. Managing all these tables and relationships in JDBC would be a very cumbersome exercise. Since many professional software development methodologies are object-oriented, another key advantage of Hibernate is that it provides a straightforward mapping from a conceptual OO model to a Java application without having to bother with database design issues. Furthermore, Hibernate is a very portable solution, making it easy to switch to another ORM if desired. However, a key concern that is often heard by many Java developers working with ORM frameworks in general is that many ORMs could benefit from further query optimization and tuning, for example, improved indices and caching. Because of this performance issue, some developers use a mixed approach, using native SQL for read operations (which typically make up the majority of an application anyway) and Hibernate for the remaining create, update, and delete operations.

WHAT'S AHEAD

Nowadays, databases are expanding massively in size. IBM estimates that every day 2.5 quintillion bytes of data are generated. In relative terms, this means that 90% of the data in the world has been created in the last two years. New database technologies have been introduced to efficiently cope with this big data storm. NoSQL (Not only SQL) is one of these newer technologies. NoSQL databases abandon the well-known and popular relational database scheme in favor of a more flexible, schema-less database structure that more closely aligns with the needs of a big data-generating business process. One of its key advantages is that it more easily scales horizontally in terms of storage. Four popular types of NoSQL database technologies are key-value-based databases, document-based databases, column-based databases, and graph-based databases. This chapter concludes with a brief discussion of these technologies.

Key-value-based databases access data by means of keys. In other words, data is stored as a table with only two columns: a (primary) key and a corresponding value, similar to a dictionary. The value itself is stored as a meaningless binary large object (blob), and it is the responsibility of the application to understand its content. An example of a key-value-based database is Amazon's Dynamo.

Document-based databases are very similar to key-value-based databases except that the value is now a document. Various document formats can be supported, such as XML, JSON, BSON, PDF, Microsoft Word, and others. Unlike in key-value-based databases where the values are unstructured, a document consists of semi-structured elements specified using a predefined set of tags. A very popular example of a document-based database is MongoDB.

Contrary to classical relational databases where the data is stored row by row, column-based databases store data in a column-by-column format. Every column then contains a name, a value, and a timestamp (which can be used to verify how recent the data is). A column family then groups various columns together, much like a table in a relational database environment. Two popular examples of column-based databases are Google's BigTable and Facebook's Casandra.

Graph databases store database objects using a graph-based format consisting of nodes, properties, and edges. A node can have 0 or more properties. Nodes are linked by means of edges. Just like nodes, edges can also have properties. Graph databases can be easily navigated through by hopping from one node to another along the existing edges. Hence, they provide a transparent storage format for Java objects, which are typically also highly interlinked. Every node in the graph then corresponds to a Java object—the node properties to the fields of the Java object and the edges to the associations between the Java objects. A key advantage of graph databases compared to relational databases is that they are schema-less, meaning that node properties and edges can be dynamically added. Furthermore, they are more efficient at querying highly interlinked data structures, which can now be tackled using path traversal through the graph, instead of resource-expensive SQL join operations as would be the case with an RDBMS. Popular examples of graph databases are Oracle NoSQL, HyperGraphDB, and Neo4j.

Although the JDBC and JPA specifications were originally developed for relational database access, some vendors have provided JDBC/JPA access to NoSQL databases. Hibernate has introduced the Object/Grid Mapper (OGM), which uses its ORM engine to provide Java persistence (JPA) support for NoSQL databases. It currently supports key-value, document, and graph databases. EclipseLink also provides JPA support for NoSQL databases.

To summarize, as also illustrated by a recent KDnuggets poll (see `http://goo.gl/KCTCoA`), SQL is far from dead, and given its widespread adoption will still remain an important data-manipulation language for years to come. In fact, despite the name NoSQL, many of the database systems discussed in this chapter still provide active support for SQL to manipulate the data. Moreover, in response to the NoSQL stream, some vendors came up with NewSQL database products by equipping traditional RDBMs with facilities to provide the same scalability as their NoSQL counterparts. A popular example here is Google's Spanner. Hence from a Java programmer's perspective, it will remain important to know the basic concepts of SQL in order to develop high-performing Java database applications.

10

Accessing Web Sources

WHAT YOU WILL LEARN IN THIS CHAPTER:

➤ How computers communicate with each other over networks and the Internet

➤ What web services are and what the common web service standards are

➤ How to access web services and information on the Internet with Java

➤ How to set up your own web services with Java

WROX.COM CODE DOWNLOADS FOR THIS CHAPTER

The wrox.com code downloads for this chapter are found at www.wrox.com/go/ beginningjavaprogramming on the Download Code tab. The code is in the Chapter 10 download and individually named according to the names throughout the chapter.

Since its inception, Java has always been merited for its strong networking support, enabling computers to communicate with each other and transmit information between Java programs over networks and the Internet. To say it in the words of John Cage—the 21st employee of Sun Microsystems (where Java originated)—"the network is the computer." This phrase was reflected in Sun's philosophy and can be observed in Java as well.

In this day and age, programs rarely behave as an "island," but communicate instead with a vast array of other platforms. In fact, you have seen one example of this in the previous chapter on how to communicate with database management systems in Java. This chapter takes you a step further and shows you how to interact with websites and web services, and how to create your own web services in Java to provide information to other parties.

Web applications are an incredibly important application area for Java, so much so that entire books have been devoted to the topic. Thus, this chapter will not be able to cover each and every detail regarding networking, web applications, and web services, but it will provide you with enough information to get started in terms of being able to retrieve information from the web, and even in making your own programs accessible from the outside world.

This chapter is organized as follows: as each web application builds on top of a networking infrastructure, the first section provides a brief, general introduction to computer networks. The goal here is just to provide you with enough information to bring you up to speed, but it will not cover how to program so-called low-level networking applications in Java. That's an advanced area of programming entailing a great deal of complexity. Instead, you can use the higher-level classes and techniques to abstract away some of this complexity by using Java's strong support for interacting with so-called web services.

A large number of web service technologies exist—each of which differs in terms of complexity, flexibility, and ease of use. This chapter discusses Remote Procedure Calls (RPC), Remote Method Invocation (RMI), Simple Object Access Protocol (SOAP), and Representational State Transfer (REST). After explaining these techniques, you will see how to access such services with Java. Note, however, that not all information you want to access online will be provided to you in the form of a neatly packaged web service, so you will also learn how to make Java act as a web browser and retrieve information from web sources in that way.

Finally, the last section in this chapter shows you how to create your own web services with Java and make your programs accessible to the outside world. Note that this chapter is one of the harder ones in this book. As such, don't be afraid to take your time to explore the different code examples or skip parts you don't feel comfortable with yet. Especially if you've never worked with web technologies before, some of the concepts discussed in this chapter can seem a bit daunting at first. Additionally, note that this chapter follows a more hands-on approach than other chapters. As such, each section immediately guides you through an example program to illustrate the different topics.

A BRIEF INTRODUCTION TO NETWORKING

Nowadays, computer networks have become so integrated into our day-to-day computing activities that you rarely think about their complexity. Whenever you surf the web, access social networks, use e-mail clients, use smartphone apps, or upload files on a company's intranet site, information is being passed over some sort of computer network. Put simply, a computer network is no more than a series of connected machines that allow devices to exchange data with one another, be it PCs, phones, or servers.

Although this description looks simple enough, computer networks are composed of so many different protocols (a protocol is a standard "agreement" on how to communicate) and services, that it is just short of amazing that they work and work fast. As an example, consider what happens when you try to access a website, say, www.wrox.com for example:

1.   You enter www.wrox.com into your web browser, so the browser needs to figure out the IP address for this site. IP stands for "Internet Protocol." It's the core protocol of the Internet, as it enables networks to route and redirect communication packets between connected computers, which are all given a so-called IP address. To communicate with the Wrox web server, you need to know its IP address. Since the IP address is basically a number, users cannot be expected to remember all addresses for all websites they want to visit (this would be the same as remembering a telephone book!). Therefore, your browser sets off to figure out the correct address for you.

2. In order to retrieve the IP address for a website, web browsers use another protocol, called DNS (Domain Name System). First, the web browser will inspect its own cache (its "short-term memory," if you will) to see whether you've visited this website in the past. If you have, the browser can reuse the stored address. If not, the browser will ask the underlying operating system (Windows, for instance) to see whether it knows the address for `www.wrox.com`. In case you already know the IP address up front (not likely) and type it in your browser's URL bar directly, this address lookup step can, of course, be skipped.

3. If the operating system is also unaware of this domain, the browser will send a DNS request to your router, which is the machine that connects you to the Internet and typically keeps its own DNS cache.

4. If your router is also unaware of the correct address, your browser will start sending a number of data packets to known DNS servers, for example, to those maintained by your Internet service providers. To send these requests, a number of protocols are used on top of each other. First, IEEE 802.3 (Ethernet) communicates with machines on the same network; IP correctly routes the request to the IP address of the DNS server; UDP (a "transport protocol") builds on top of IP to provide a standardized simple messaging facility; and finally, DNS governs how the actual DNS request message should look. A simple "tell me the address for www.wrox.com" message looks like Figure 10-1 if you capture it from the network.

```
⊞ Frame 186: 72 bytes on wire (576 bits), 72 bytes captured (576 bits)
⊞ Ethernet II, Src: Dell_7f:6c:8f (5c:26:0a:7f:6c:8f), Dst: Cisco_93:9a:7f (d0:d0:fd:93:9a:7f)
⊟ Internet Protocol Version 4, Src: 10.33.200.175 (10.33.200.175), Dst: 8.8.8.8 (8.8.8.8)
    Version: 4
    Header length: 20 bytes
  ⊞ Differentiated Services Field: 0x00 (DSCP 0x00: Default; ECN: 0x00: Not-ECT (Not ECN-Capable Transport))
    Total Length: 58
    Identification: 0x677c (26492)
  ⊞ Flags: 0x00
    Fragment offset: 0
    Time to live: 128
    Protocol: UDP (17)
  ⊞ Header checksum: 0xf056 [correct]
    Source: 10.33.200.175 (10.33.200.175)
    Destination: 8.8.8.8 (8.8.8.8)
⊟ User Datagram Protocol, Src Port: 61796 (61796), Dst Port: domain (53)
    Source port: 61796 (61796)
    Destination port: domain (53)
    Length: 38
  ⊟ Checksum: 0xefd4 [validation disabled]
    [Good Checksum: False]
    [Bad Checksum: False]
⊟ Domain Name System (query)
    [Response In: 187]
    Transaction ID: 0x0008
  ⊞ Flags: 0x0100 (Standard query)
    Questions: 1
    Answer RRs: 0
    Authority RRs: 0
    Additional RRs: 0
  ⊟ Queries
    ⊟ www.wrox.com: type A, class IN
        Name: www.wrox.com
        Type: A (Host address)
        Class: IN (0x0001)
```

FIGURE 10-1

> **NOTE** *The excellent free and open source Wireshark tool is used to capture and show network packets here.*

Figure 10-1 shows the "stack" of protocols discussed previously. At the top, you can see a "frame" message, which describes your message in its most basic "physical" terms—a series of bytes, 0 and 1 pulses on a wire. Below this, you find "Ethernet," which in this case shows that communication is going on between a Dell laptop and a Cisco router (the manufacturer information can be derived from a unique identifier which is associated with every Ethernet device). Under this, you have the Internet Protocol, which shows that a message is sent from the address 10.33.200.175 (the laptop) to 8.8.8.8 (Google's DNS server). The IP protocol includes some basic checksums to make sure the receiver can check the integrity of the package (errors occur when the transmission is sent over wires). Next, you see the "User Datagram Protocol" (UDP), which shows that a message is being sent to port 53, the standard port DNS servers are listening on. Assigning messages a destination port number provides a simple way for the receiving party to know for which application the message is intended. The computer also specifies a temporary source port (61796) to indicate that a reply is expected to be sent to this port. Finally, at the bottom, you find the "Domain Name System" (DNS) message, which tells you that this message contains a query for www.wrox.com.

5. You're not out of the woods yet, as the DNS server still has to send back a reply. Again, a complex message is constructed and sent back, as shown in Figure 10-2.

```
⊞ Frame 187: 102 bytes on wire (816 bits), 102 bytes captured (816 bits)
⊞ Ethernet II, Src: Cisco_93:9a:7f (d0:d0:fd:93:9a:7f), Dst: Dell_7f:6c:8f (5c:26:0a:7f:6c:8f)
⊞ Internet Protocol Version 4, Src: 8.8.8.8 (8.8.8.8), Dst: 10.33.200.175 (10.33.200.175)
⊞ User Datagram Protocol, Src Port: domain (53), Dst Port: 61796 (61796)
⊟ Domain Name System (response)
     [Request In: 186]
     [Time: 0.015278000 seconds]
     Transaction ID: 0x0008
   ⊞ Flags: 0x8180 (Standard query response, No error)
     Questions: 1
     Answer RRs: 2
     Authority RRs: 0
     Additional RRs: 0
   ⊞ Queries
   ⊟ Answers
      ⊟ www.wrox.com: type CNAME, class IN, cname wrox.com
          Name: www.wrox.com
          Type: CNAME (Canonical name for an alias)
          Class: IN (0x0001)
          Time to live: 9 minutes, 16 seconds
          Data length: 2
          Primaryname: wrox.com
      ⊟ wrox.com: type A, class IN, addr 208.215.179.178
          Name: wrox.com
          Type: A (Host address)
          Class: IN (0x0001)
          Time to live: 9 minutes, 16 seconds
          Data length: 4
          Addr: 208.215.179.178 (208.215.179.178)
```

FIGURE 10-2

The Ethernet protocol informs you that a message is coming in from the Cisco router back to the laptop. The IP protocol specifies that the message is coming from address 8.8.8.8 and back to your address 10.33.200.175. The UDP protocol tells you that the message originates from port 53 and is destined for port 61796—the one you're listening on to receive a reply. The DNS message contains a structured answer, telling you that www.wrox.com is the same as wrox.com, and that wrox.com has the IP address 208.215.179.178.

6. All of this was done just to figure out the IP address of www.wrox.com. Your browser can now establish a connection to 208.215.179.178. Again, a number of protocols are combined to construct a complex message. You have already seen IEEE 802.3 (Ethernet) and IP. Instead of UDP, another transport protocol is used on top of this, called TCP (Transmission Control Protocol). TCP provides a more reliable means of delivering network messages, as it includes functionality for error-checking, makes sure that packets are delivered in the right order, and takes care of resending packets when they are lost in transmission. Finally, HTTP (HyperText Transfer Protocol) is used to request and receive the web page. Figure 10-3 shows the complete package the browser sends to request a web page from www.wrox.com (208.215.179.178).

```
⊟ Frame 151: 404 bytes on wire (3232 bits), 404 bytes captured (3232 bits)
⊞ Ethernet II, Src: Dell_7f:6c:8f (5c:26:0a:7f:6c:8f), Dst: Cisco_93:9a:7f (d0:d0:fd:93:9a:7f)
⊞ Internet Protocol Version 4, Src: 10.33.200.175 (10.33.200.175), Dst: 208.215.179.178 (208.215.179.178)
⊟ Transmission Control Protocol, Src Port: 49421 (49421), Dst Port: http (80), Seq: 1, Ack: 1, Len: 350
    Source port: 49421 (49421)
    Destination port: http (80)
    [Stream index: 13]
    Sequence number: 1      (relative sequence number)
    [Next sequence number: 351      (relative sequence number)]
    Acknowledgement number: 1      (relative ack number)
    Header length: 20 bytes
  ⊞ Flags: 0x018 (PSH, ACK)
    Window size value: 64240
    [Calculated window size: 64240]
    [Window size scaling factor: -2 (no window scaling used)]
  ⊞ Checksum: 0xb571 [validation disabled]
  ⊞ [SEQ/ACK analysis]
⊟ Hypertext Transfer Protocol
  ⊞ GET / HTTP/1.1\r\n
    Host: www.wrox.com\r\n
    Connection: keep-alive\r\n
    Accept: text/html,application/xhtml+xml,application/xml;q=0.9,image/webp,*/*;q=0.8\r\n
    User-Agent: Mozilla/5.0 (Windows NT 6.1; WOW64) AppleWebKit/537.36 (KHTML, like Gecko) Chrome/33.0.1750.154
    Accept-Encoding: gzip,deflate,sdch\r\n
    Accept-Language: en-US,en-GB;q=0.8,nl;q=0.6\r\n
    \r\n
    [Full request URI: http://www.wrox.com/]
```

FIGURE 10-3

Figure 10-3 shows the whole stack of protocols at work here. Note the sequence number, the acknowledgement number, and the checksum in the TCP message, which make sure messages are delivered correctly and in the right order. Note also that, just as with UDP, TCP uses the ports mechanism to organize messages. The HTTP message looks like the following:

```
GET / HTTP/1.1
Host: www.wrox.com
Connection: keep-alive
Accept: text/html,application/xhtml+xml,application/xml;q=0.9,image/webp,*/*;
```

```
       q=0.8
User-Agent: Mozilla/5.0 (Windows NT 6.1; WOW64) AppleWebKit/537.36
    (KHTML, like Gecko) Chrome/33.0.1750.154 Safari/537.36
Accept-Encoding: gzip,deflate,sdch
Accept-Language: en-US,en-GB;q=0.8,nl;q=0.6
```

The HTTP request is composed of an HTTP verb (GET) to a location (/) and version specification (HTTP/1.1) (the first line), followed by the number of headers, followed by a blank line to close the request. Browsers are free to include as many headers as they want to request information from and send instructions to the web server. Since HTTP will be used throughout the remainder of this chapter, this simple request message is explained line by line here:

➤ GET / HTTP/1.1 denotes that you are performing a GET request for the URL / on this web server. HTTP/1.1 denotes that you are compatible with version 1.1 of the HTTP protocol.

➤ Since the same web server can host multiple websites, the "Host" header specifies that you are requesting a web page from www.wrox.com, so the web server knows from which site it should return a page.

➤ The "Connection" header instructs the server to keep the connection open, if possible. This allows the following HTTP requests to speed up. If this header is not provided (or the server is not willing to accept keep-alive connections), a new complete HTTP transaction will be set up for each request.

➤ The "Accept" header informs the web server that the web browser is capable of receiving the following formats. Web servers can use this information to adapt their response accordingly.

➤ The "User-Agent" header provides information about the browser and operating system the user is using to visit the websites. This is one of the easiest ways for sites to detect which browser you are using.

➤ The "Accept-Encoding" and "Accept-Language" headers also inform the web server about formats and languages the browser accepts. This can be used by the web server to compress the reply before sending it (as the browser accepts GZIP), for instance, or to send a translated version of the requested page if the user desires.

NOTE *If TCP is so much more reliable than UDP, you might be wondering why it's not used by default. For most applications, TCP is the transport protocol of choice to be used in combination with IP. So commonly, in fact, that the whole stack of protocols (Ethernet, IP, and TCP) is oftentimes just denoted as TCP/IP. Then why use UDP? Well, sometimes network applications need to be fast above all else, so programmers might prefer to use the bare-bones offerings of UDP above TCP and are willing to sacrifice reliability aspects. Games, for example, typically apply UDP instead of TCP in order to minimize latency. Lost packets can then just be dealt with by the application and re-sent if necessary.*

7. Next, you receive the following HTTP reply from the web server. The complete protocol stack is not shown this time (Ethernet, IP, TCP, and HTTP); it just shows the HTTP message contained within:

```
HTTP/1.0 302 Found
Date: Fri, 11 Apr 2014 09:45:49 GMT
Server: Apache
Location: http://www.wrox.com/WileyCDA/
Vary: Accept-Encoding
Content-Encoding: gzip
Content-Length: 190
Connection: close
Content-Type: text/html; charset=iso-8859-1

<!DOCTYPE HTML PUBLIC "-//IETF//DTD HTML 2.0//EN">
<html><head>
<title>302 Found</title>
</head><body>
<h1>Found</h1>
<p>The document has moved <a href="http://www.wrox.com/WileyCDA/">here</a>.</p>
</body></html>
```

HTTP replies are structured mostly in the same manner as an HTTP request. The first line indicates the HTTP protocol version the server adheres to (HTTP/1.0), together with a status message (302) and a textual description of the status (Found). Next, the server sends a number of headers followed by a newline, followed by the actual contents of the page, which is the message body. In this case, the server is telling you that your requested resource (/) was found, but should be retrieved at another location: www .wrox.com/WileyCDA/. The server was able to adhere to the request to compress the contents (GZIP), but is unwilling to keep the connection open ("Connection: close"). Note that the actual contents have been uncompressed to show you what is returned to the browser.

8. If you were using an archaic or broken web browser, the browser would display the received body to the user. The actual body is formatted in HTML (HyperText Markup Language), which is the standard language used to create web pages. Luckily, your browser is smart enough to understand the 302 status code, so it fires off another request to the given location: http://www.wrox.com/WileyCDA/.

9. Luckily, this time the browser remembers the IP address for www.wrox.com, so it can immediately send a new HTTP request:

```
GET /WileyCDA/ HTTP/1.1
Host: www.wrox.com
Connection: keep-alive
Accept: text/html,application/xhtml+xml,application/xml;q=0.9,image/webp,*/*;
    q=0.8
User-Agent: Mozilla/5.0 (Windows NT 6.1; WOW64) AppleWebKit/537.36
    (KHTML, like Gecko) Chrome/33.0.1750.154 Safari/537.36
Accept-Encoding: gzip,deflate,sdch
Accept-Language: en-US,en-GB;q=0.8,nl;q=0.6
```

This request looks similar to the previous one, except that now, the location `/WileyCDA/` is accessed. The server now happily replies:

```
HTTP/1.0 200 OK
Date: Fri, 11 Apr 2014 09:45:50 GMT
Server: Apache
X-Powered-By: SPA
Set-Cookie: JSESSIONID=495BF51CF5892A07BBF54D9F6CA32D48; Path=/
Instance: p4
Vary: Accept-Encoding
Content-Encoding: gzip
Connection: close
Content-Type: text/html;charset=ISO-8859-1

<!DOCTYPE HTML PUBLIC "-//W3C//DTD HTML 4.01 Transitional//EN">
<!-- Build: R16B063 -->
<!-- Strand Id: 0229556601 -->

<!-- layout( Wrox Homepage ) -->
 <html>
  <head>
  <link rel="canonical" href="http://www.wrox.com" />
  <link href="http://media.wiley.com/spa_assets/R16B063/site/wrox/include/
    style.css" type="text/css" rel="stylesheet" />
   <title>Programming Books, Free Code Downloads, Ebooks, Blogs, Articles,
     Forums - Wrox</title>
                    ... LOTS OF HTML CODE ...
</html>
<!-- / layout( Wrox Homepage ) -->
```

Most of the HTML reply is omitted here, as printing the whole thing would take multiple pages. Just note that the server now replies a `200` status message, indicating the request could be handled successfully.

> **NOTE** Many other HTTP status codes exist. Most of us are familiar with the `404` ("Not Found") status code. One other peculiar "error" status code is `418` ("I'm a teapot"), which was added to the standard as a 1998 April Fools' joke, but is not expected to be implemented by actual HTTP servers.

10. The web browser starts interpreting the HTML code and displays the page to the user. The web browser sees, however, that the page also includes a number of images. For each image, the browser will have to fire off a new HTTP request. As such, rendering just one web page might involve a large number of HTTP requests. Modern browsers, such as Firefox and Chrome, allow you to show a timeline of all requests being made, such as the one shown in Figure 10-4 for rendering `www.wrox.com`.

Luckily, browsers are smart and will start rendering the page as soon as information is coming in, showing images and other visuals as they are retrieved. In addition, as can be observed from the timeline shown in Figure 10-4, browsers will send a number of HTTP requests in parallel to speed up the loading process.

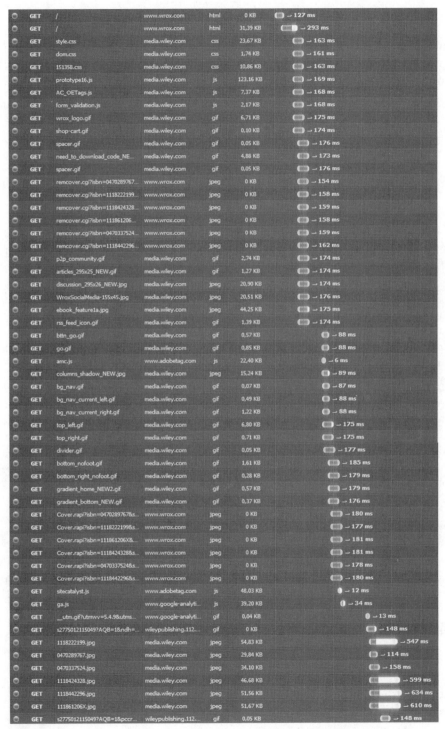

	GET	/	www.wrox.com	html	0 KB	→ 127 ms
	GET	/	www.wrox.com	html	31,39 KB	→ 293 ms
	GET	style.css	media.wiley.com	css	23,67 KB	→ 163 ms
	GET	dom.css	media.wiley.com	css	1,74 KB	→ 161 ms
	GET	151358.css	media.wiley.com	css	10,86 KB	→ 163 ms
	GET	prototype16.js	media.wiley.com	js	123,16 KB	→ 169 ms
	GET	AC_OETags.js	media.wiley.com	js	7,37 KB	→ 168 ms
	GET	form_validation.js	media.wiley.com	js	2,17 KB	→ 168 ms
	GET	wrox_logo.gif	media.wiley.com	gif	6,71 KB	→ 175 ms
	GET	shop-cart.gif	media.wiley.com	gif	0,10 KB	→ 174 ms
	GET	spacer.gif	media.wiley.com	gif	0,05 KB	→ 176 ms
	GET	need_to_download_code_NE...	media.wiley.com	gif	4,88 KB	→ 173 ms
	GET	spacer.gif	media.wiley.com	gif	0,05 KB	→ 176 ms
	GET	remcover.cgi?isbn=0470289767...	www.wrox.com	jpeg	0 KB	→ 154 ms
	GET	remcover.cgi?isbn=1118222199...	www.wrox.com	jpeg	0 KB	→ 158 ms
	GET	remcover.cgi?isbn=1118424328...	www.wrox.com	jpeg	0 KB	→ 159 ms
	GET	remcover.cgi?isbn=111861206...	www.wrox.com	jpeg	0 KB	→ 158 ms
	GET	remcover.cgi?isbn=0470337524...	www.wrox.com	jpeg	0 KB	→ 159 ms
	GET	remcover.cgi?isbn=1118442296...	www.wrox.com	jpeg	0 KB	→ 162 ms
	GET	p2p_community.gif	media.wiley.com	gif	2,74 KB	→ 174 ms
	GET	articles_295x25_NEW.gif	media.wiley.com	gif	1,27 KB	→ 174 ms
	GET	discussion_295x26_NEW.jpg	media.wiley.com	jpeg	20,90 KB	→ 174 ms
	GET	WroxSocialMedia-155x45.jpg	media.wiley.com	jpeg	20,51 KB	→ 176 ms
	GET	ebook_feature1a.jpg	media.wiley.com	jpeg	44,25 KB	→ 175 ms
	GET	rss_feed_icon.gif	media.wiley.com	gif	1,39 KB	→ 174 ms
	GET	bttn_go.gif	media.wiley.com	gif	0,57 KB	→ 88 ms
	GET	go.gif	media.wiley.com	gif	0,85 KB	→ 88 ms
	GET	amc.js	www.adobetag.com	js	22,40 KB	→ 6 ms
	GET	columns_shadow_NEW.jpg	media.wiley.com	jpeg	15,24 KB	→ 89 ms
	GET	bg_nav.gif	media.wiley.com	gif	0,07 KB	→ 87 ms
	GET	bg_nav_current_left.gif	media.wiley.com	gif	0,49 KB	→ 88 ms
	GET	bg_nav_current_right.gif	media.wiley.com	gif	1,22 KB	→ 88 ms
	GET	top_left.gif	media.wiley.com	gif	6,80 KB	→ 175 ms
	GET	top_right.gif	media.wiley.com	gif	0,71 KB	→ 175 ms
	GET	divider.gif	media.wiley.com	gif	0,05 KB	→ 177 ms
	GET	bottom_nofoot.gif	media.wiley.com	gif	1,61 KB	→ 185 ms
	GET	bottom_right_nofoot.gif	media.wiley.com	gif	0,28 KB	→ 179 ms
	GET	gradient_home_NEW2.gif	media.wiley.com	gif	0,57 KB	→ 179 ms
	GET	gradient_bottom_NEW.gif	media.wiley.com	gif	0,37 KB	→ 176 ms
	GET	Cover.rapi?isbn=0470289767&s...	www.wrox.com	jpeg	0 KB	→ 180 ms
	GET	Cover.rapi?isbn=1118222199&s...	www.wrox.com	jpeg	0 KB	→ 177 ms
	GET	Cover.rapi?isbn=111861206X&...	www.wrox.com	jpeg	0 KB	→ 181 ms
	GET	Cover.rapi?isbn=1118424328&s...	www.wrox.com	jpeg	0 KB	→ 181 ms
	GET	Cover.rapi?isbn=0470337524&s...	www.wrox.com	jpeg	0 KB	→ 178 ms
	GET	Cover.rapi?isbn=1118442296&s...	www.wrox.com	jpeg	0 KB	→ 180 ms
	GET	sitecatalyst.js	www.adobetag.com	js	48,03 KB	→ 12 ms
	GET	ga.js	www.google-analyti...	js	39,20 KB	→ 34 ms
	GET	_utm.gif?utmwv=5.4.9&utms...	www.google-analyti...	gif	0,04 KB	→ 13 ms
	GET	s2775012115049?AQB=1&ndh=...	wileypublishing.112...	0 KB	→ 148 ms
	GET	1118222199.jpg	media.wiley.com	jpeg	54,83 KB	→ 547 ms
	GET	0470289767.jpg	media.wiley.com	jpeg	29,84 KB	→ 114 ms
	GET	0470337524.jpg	media.wiley.com	jpeg	34,10 KB	→ 158 ms
	GET	1118424328.jpg	media.wiley.com	jpeg	46,68 KB	→ 599 ms
	GET	1118442296.jpg	media.wiley.com	jpeg	51,56 KB	→ 634 ms
	GET	111861206X.jpg	media.wiley.com	jpeg	51,67 KB	→ 610 ms
	GET	s2775012115049?AQB=1&pccr...	wileypublishing.112...	gif	0,05 KB	→ 148 ms

FIGURE 10-4

With so many protocols, requests, and back-and-forth communication going on, it is nothing short of amazing that you are able to view a simple web page in less than one second. To standardize this wealth of protocols, the International Organization of Standardization (ISO) maintains the so-called Open Systems Interconnection (OSI) model, which defines aspects of communication into seven layers, from bottom to top:

➤ Layer 1: Physical layer: Includes the Ethernet protocol, but also USB, Bluetooth, and other radio protocols

➤ Layer 2: Data link layer: Includes the Ethernet protocol

➤ Layer 3: Network layer: Includes IP (Internet Protocol)

➤ Layer 4: Transport layer: TCP and UDP

➤ Layer 5: Session layer: Includes protocols for opening/closing and managing sessions. TCP's session management is found on this layer.

➤ Layer 6: Presentation layer: Includes protocols to format and translate data. This layer also includes encryption protocols.

➤ Layer 7: Application layer: HTTP and DNS, for instance

Not all network communications need to use protocols from all these layers. To request a web page for instance, layers 1 (physical), 2 (Ethernet), 3 (IP), 4 (TCP), and 7 (HTTP) are involved, but the layers are constructed so that each protocol found at a higher level can be contained inside the message of a lower-layer protocol. When you request a secure web page, for instance, the HTTP message (layer 7) will be encoded in an encrypted SSL or TLS message (layer 6).

The lower the layer you aim for when programming networked applications, the more functionality and complexity you need to deal with. In Java, for example, it is possible to set up so-called server and client "sockets," which are networking endpoints that define a TCP/IP, UDP/IP, or raw IP connection. Once this connection is established, it is up to you, the programmer, to define how the actual messages you transmit should look, so that you are then effectively creating a higher-layered protocol on top of this.

TRY IT OUT Creating a Simple Networked Application in Java

Now that you have the basics of networking under your belt, take a quick look at how you would implement the most basic client-server networking application in Java using a simple example. Similarly to how HTTP works, you will create a simple request-reply program using TCP/IP sockets in Java.

Note that this is the only time when you will be applying Java sockets directly. Earlier in this chapter, you read that programming this close to the "networking metal" is a complex and challenging task, and in this Try It Out, you'll see the reasons why.

1. Create two classes in Eclipse: TCPServer and TCPClient. Put them in a package called socketexample.

2. Write the following source code for the TCPServer class:

```
package socketexample;

import java.io.*;
import java.net.*;

public class TCPServer {
    public static void main(String args[]) {
        // Listen to incoming connections at port 9000
        try (ServerSocket serverSocket = new ServerSocket(9000)) {
            String message = null;
            while (!"STOP".equals(message)) {
                // Accept incoming client
                System.out.println("Waiting for connection...");
                try (    // Set up socket for connection with client
                        Socket connectionSocket = serverSocket.accept();
                        // Set up input stream reader (from client)
                        DataInputStream incoming =
                        new DataInputStream(connectionSocket.getInputStream());
                        // Set up output stream writer (to client)
                        DataOutputStream outgoing =
                        new DataOutputStream(connectionSocket.getOutputStream());
                ) {
                    // Get the message the client sent
                    System.out.println("Waiting for message...");
                    message = incoming.readUTF().trim();
                    System.out.println("CLIENT SAID: " + message);
                    // Send message back
                    outgoing.writeUTF("MESSAGE RECEIVED\n");
                    if ("STOP".equals(message))
                        // Send additional line
                        outgoing.writeUTF("SERVER CLOSING DOWN\n");
                    // Close output stream to indicate that no more data is to be
                        sent
                    outgoing.close();
                } catch (IOException e) {
                    e.printStackTrace();
                }
            }
        } catch (IOException e) {
            e.printStackTrace();
        }
    }
}
```

3. For the TCPClient class, the code reads as follows:

```
package socketexample;

import java.io.*;
import java.net.*;

public class TCPClient {
    public static void main(String args[]) {
```

```
            try (    // Create a socket connecting to server
                    Socket clientSocket = new Socket("localhost", 9000);
                    // Set up input stream reader to read keyboard input
                    BufferedReader keyboardReader =
                      new BufferedReader(new InputStreamReader(System.in, "UTF-8"));
                    // Set up input stream reader (from server)
                    DataInputStream incoming =
                      new DataInputStream(clientSocket.getInputStream());
                    // Set up output stream writer (to server)
                    DataOutputStream outgoing = new
                      DataOutputStream(clientSocket.getOutputStream());
            ) {
                // Read message from user
                System.out.println("Enter message to send to server: ");
                String message = keyboardReader.readLine();
                // Send message to server
                outgoing.writeUTF(message + '\n');
                // Read the reply from server
                System.out.println("Server replied: ");
                try {
                    String reply = incoming.readUTF();
                    System.out.print(reply);
                } catch (EOFException eof) {
                    // Do nothing... server has closed the connection
                }
                // Close the connection
                clientSocket.close();
                System.out.println("Connection closed gracefully");
            } catch (IOException e) {
                e.printStackTrace();
            }
        }
    }
```

4. To try out this code, start `TCPServer` first, followed by `TCPClient`. Note that you might get a warning from your firewall telling you that network activity is being requested by Java. Naturally, to make the code work, you should allow this. You should be able to type a message in the `TCPClient` console window and receive a reply. The output for `TCPServer` will then read like so:

```
Waiting for connection...
Waiting for message...
CLIENT SAID: Hello there server!
Waiting for connection...
```

Whereas for the client, you will see:

```
Enter message to send to server:
Hello there server!
Server replied:
MESSAGE RECEIVED
Connection closed gracefully
```

How It Works

Now take a look at the way this code works.

1. On the server's side, a `ServerSocket` is created that will listen for incoming connections on the local computer (the default) on port `9000`, using TCP/IP. (UDP/IP server-client programs, on the other hand, are created through another class, `DatagramSocket`.)

2. Next, the server performs a loop that accepts a client connection (using a second socket), reads a message from the client, sends back an acknowledgement, and closes the output stream. If a client sends a `STOP` message, the server will stop accepting new connections and will close itself down. Note that the stream types are matching on both sides of the connection (data input and output streams). Also note the use of `writeUTF` and `readUTF` to make sure the client and server can communicate by using the full Unicode spectrum (e.g., also in Mandarin).

3. On the client's side, a normal socket is created to connect to `localhost` (the hostname denoting the local computer; you can also use the special IP address `127.0.0.1`, which also refers to the local computer). The user is then asked to enter a message, which is sent to the server. Next, as long as the server is sending back data, the reply to the user is printed out before closing the connection.

4. If you get a `"java.net.BindException: Address already in use: JVM_Bind"` exception on the server's side, this means that a TCP/IP socket is already listening on port `9000`. Make sure you haven't started `TCPServer` multiple times, or try to change the port number in `TCPServer` and `TCPClient` to something else—perhaps there is another program on your computer listening to this port number.

5. Take some time if you want to experiment with the program and try out some simple modifications. For instance, try changing the client and server classes to allow the client to send multiple lines before receiving a reply from the server. To indicate when the client has finished sending its message, you can use another terminator string (such as a blank newline, like the one used in the HTTP protocol).

The setup of this example might not seem too difficult to understand, but this example has been kept deliberately simple. Once more functionality is required, things start getting more complex rather quickly. For example, you have created a simple request-reply "protocol" here, which is much simpler to implement than a program where both the client and the server transmit a number of messages to each other. In addition, try launching multiple client programs at once. You'll note how the server is able to deal with only one client at once, forcing the other one to wait to establish its connection. This means that, if you run this program in a real-life setting, one single client can block access to the service by just waiting indefinitely to send its message. To overcome this problem, you need to use a multithreaded setup where multiple connections can be active at once (and dealt with separately in parallel running threads). Finally, this program is also "blocking," meaning that when you write something like `reply = incoming.readUTF()`, the execution of the program will stop until actual data is received (this is why you close the outgoing stream explicitly on the server's side). So-called "asynchronous" (non-blocking) communication is also possible in Java, but is harder to implement correctly.

Luckily, Java comes with a number of libraries and frameworks that help to abstract away a lot of this complexity, so that you can focus on the task at hand—accessing actual information over the networks and the Internet.

This concludes the brief introduction to basic networking. From now on, a variety of built-in Java classes and libraries will be used to help you access and retrieve information stored on computer networks—such as the Internet—which is made accessible in a standardized, structured way.

WEB SERVICES

This section first provides a short introduction on web services and how they help to make information accessible over the network.

On a conceptual level, web service standards are frequently separated into two large categories. The first category can be denoted as "heavyweight" web services, which typically use XML-based formats to exchange messages, involving a variety of protocols and standards to pass information, as well as define which kinds of information can be accessed and how. For example, a complex web service may involve the HTTP protocol (which is now used as a transport protocol to pass the actual message); SOAP, the messaging protocol that encodes messages in XML; WSDL (Web Services Description Language), a protocol used to describe the functionalities offered by the web service, and UDDI (Universal Description Discovery and Integration), which can be used to make web services discoverable by registering them in a central location.

Due to the complexity of heavyweight web services, a new web service standard, called REST (Representational State Transfer), has been gaining traction in recent years. REST is built directly on top of HTTP and is completely stateless and light in terms of bandwidth consumption. It has been adopted by most websites offering some kind of API. For example, most social networks use a REST-based API to handle the communication between the service and mobile apps.

RPC and RMI

RPC stands for "Remote Procedure Call," and it's used as a general term to denote any form of communication between computer programs where one program accesses a routine or procedure in another program, often over the network. In Object-Oriented Programming, the term RMI is used, which stands for "Remote Method Invocation."

RPC messages are initiated by the client, which sends a message to request the execution of a certain method to a server, together with the parameters to send to this method. The remote server sends a response back to the client, which can then be processed. As explained in the Try It Out, "A Simple Networked Application in Java," earlier in "A Brief Introduction to Networking" section, RPC calls can come in two varieties: synchronous (where the client blocks and waits until it receives a reply) and asynchronous (where the client can continue to execute some tasks while waiting for the reply). Of course, since communication is performed over a network, you must take special care when handling failures such as the network going down, without the client knowing if part of the RPC call was actually executed. If the called method performs data changes on the server's side, rollback mechanisms must be provided to undo these changes in the event of a failure.

RPC and RMI have a long history. RPC was originally invented by Sun Microsystems (the same company from which Java originated) and was ultimately standardized and implemented as the Open Network Computing Remote Procedure Call. Java also provides built-in mechanisms to perform RMI, called Java RMI. This book will not go into much detail on how Java RMI works, but the following Try It Out briefly shows how it works.

TRY IT OUT RMI in Java

This exercise will help you see how Java RMI works. You will create a simple server for two basic number manipulations: addition and subtraction.

1. Create two classes and an interface: `RMIClient`, `RMIServer`, and `RMIInterface`. Create a package called `rmiexample` to hold them.

2. Start with `RMIInterface`. This interface defines the methods the server will expose to the client without specifying the actual code to be executed, just as a normal interface would. The code for `RMIInterface` looks like this:

```java
package rmiexample;

import java.rmi.Remote;
import java.rmi.RemoteException;

public interface RMIInterface extends Remote {
    public int addTwoNumbers(int a, int b) throws RemoteException;
    public int substractTwoNumbers(int a, int b) throws RemoteException;
}
```

3. The `RMIServer` class implements this interface and thus specifies the method body for `addTwoNumbers` and `substractTwoNumbers`. A `main` method is also included in this class and it instantiates an `RMIServer` object:

```java
package rmiexample;

import java.rmi.Naming;
import java.rmi.RemoteException;
import java.rmi.server.UnicastRemoteObject;
import java.rmi.registry.*;

public class RMIServer
    extends UnicastRemoteObject implements RMIInterface {

    public RMIServer() throws RemoteException {
        super();
    }

    public int addTwoNumbers(int a, int b) throws RemoteException {
        System.out.println("addTwoNumbers was called");
        return a + b;
    }

    public int substractTwoNumbers(int a, int b) throws RemoteException {
        System.out.println("substractTwoNumbers was called");
        return a - b;
    }

    public static void main(String args[]) throws Exception {
        System.out.println("Starting server...");
```

```
        try {
            // Create registry on local machine running on port 1099
            LocateRegistry.createRegistry(1099);
            System.out.println("RMI registry was created");
        } catch (RemoteException e) {
            System.out.println("RemoteException occurred: ");
            e.printStackTrace();

        }

        RMIServer theServer = new RMIServer();

        // Bind the server instance to the name "RMIServer"
        Naming.rebind("//localhost/RMIServer", theServer);
        System.out.println("RMIServer bound in registry");
    }
}
```

4. `RMIClient` just contains a `main` method to try out the RMI server:

```
package rmiexample;

import java.rmi.registry.LocateRegistry;
import java.rmi.registry.Registry;

public class RMIClient {
    public static void main(String args[]) throws Exception {
        // Get RMI registry running at the local computer
        Registry registry = LocateRegistry.getRegistry("localhost");
        // Request interface bound on name "RMIServer"
        RMIInterface serverInterface = (RMIInterface) registry.lookup("RMIServer");

        // Execute methods over RMI
        System.out.println(serverInterface.addTwoNumbers(3, 4));
        System.out.println(serverInterface.substractTwoNumbers(10, 3));
    }
}
```

5. To try out this code, start the `main` class of `RMIServer` first, followed by `RMIClient`. If everything goes right, you should see this on the server's console:

```
Starting server...
RMI registry was created
RMIServer bound in registry
addTwoNumbers was called
substractTwoNumbers was called
```

With the results of the two method calls on the client's console:

```
7
7
```

How It Works

Here's how it works:

1. RMIInterface defines the methods the server will expose to the client without actually specifying the code to be executed, just as a normal interface would. However, unlike normal interfaces, note that RMI interfaces need to extend the remote interface in order to be used as an RMI service. In addition, each method you define in the interface needs to throw a RemoteException exception.

2. Concerning RMIServer, most of the code should be self-explanatory, especially the implementation of the two provided methods. Two important aspects should be noted: first, the class should implement the interface you've defined earlier. Second, you are extending another class—UnicastRemoteObject—which is a built-in class that allows you to automatically export a so-called "stub" for RMIServer. A stub is basically a bare-bones version of the RMIServer class that includes functionality for parameter conversion. Since the server and client code of an RMI program can run on different machines with different architectures, they might not agree on the data representation of different parameters. Consider, for example, 32- and 64-bit machines using different sizes to represent number types. A stub handles the conversion of passed method arguments and deconversion of returned results automatically. There are two ways to generate stubs: manually, using the rmic program included in the Java JDK (this would create an RMIServer_Stub.class file), or automatically, like you've done here by extending UnicastRemoteObject.

3. Next, take a look at the main method of RMIServer. First, this method uses the LocateRegistry built-in class to create an RMI registry running on port 1099. An RMI registry keeps track of the services provided by an RMI server by binding objects providing methods over RMI to specific names. Again, it is possible to start this registry from the operating system (using the rmiregistry program included in the Java JDK), but you're taking the programmatic route here. Next, the main class instantiates an RMIServer object and binds it to the name RMIServer on the local machine, localhost.

4. The client (RMIClient) uses the LocateRegistry class to retrieve the registry running on localhost, and then an interface object is created by looking up the bound object to the name RMIServer in the registry. Finally, everything is set for methods to be executed on this object, just as you would with a normal object. The difference, however, is that the method arguments will now be sent over the network.

Apart from Java RMI, a large number of additional RPC-based standards and protocols have been defined throughout the past years, not all of them being specific to Java, of course. For example, the Common Object Request Broker Architecture (CORBA) is a standard that was defined by the OMG (Object Management Group) and enables communication between systems. The reason I mention it is because it is the only OMG standard that's been incorporated in Java SE as a built-in library, with classes being located in the org.omg.CORBA package. Conceptually speaking, CORBA enables the same functionality as Java RMI, with the difference that CORBA allows communication between very diverse systems (i.e., not only between Java programs) running on different architectures, different operating systems, and written using different programming languages. However, CORBA has been subject to quite a bit of criticism—some of it relating to technical aspects, some of it to design choices—and the complexity of the standard means that it is not very widely adapted. As such, I will not discuss it in more detail here, but if you ever hear the name again, you know what it relates to.

SOAP

Another RPC-based protocol that enables accessing objects over a network is called SOAP, and it was designed as the successor of XML-RPC (XML-based RPC). SOAP is quite popular in "enterprise" environments as a method to access and provide web services.

SOAP stands for "Simple Object Access Protocol," although the W3 standards body has dropped the use of the name as an acronym in a recent revision of the standard in favor of just using "SOAP" as is. While this protocol is easier to use than CORBA, it can be argued that it is still not really. . . simple. Recall that the introduction stated that web service technologies are typically separated into "heavyweight" and "lightweight" categories, and SOAP—like other RPC-based technologies—is one of the former. The basic idea behind SOAP is to provide an XML-based messaging framework that's extensible (new features can be easily added), neutral (SOAP messages can travel on top of HTTP and a variety of other protocols), and independent (can be used independently of the programming language and architecture used). These aspects make SOAP very versatile, but the standard is also slower and more verbose than other RPC standards, as XML messages can grow large quickly. For example, the following code snippet shows a SOAP request to call a method `AddTwoNumbers`, which is embedded inside an HTTP request:

```
POST /mathematicsService HTTP/1.1
Host: www.example.org
Content-Type: application/soap+xml; charset=utf-8
Content-Length: *LENGTH*

<?xml version="1.0"?>
<soap:Envelope
    xmlns:soap="http://www.w3.org/2001/12/soap-envelope"
    soap:encodingStyle="http://www.w3.org/2001/12/soap-encoding">

<soap:Body xmlns:m="http://www.example.org/mathematics">
    <m:AddTwoNumbers>
        <m:FirstNumber>3</m:FirstNumber >
        <m:SecondNumber>6</m:SecondNumber>
    </m:AddTwoNumbers>
</soap:Body>

</soap:Envelope>
```

And the server answers with the following reply:

```
HTTP/1.1 200 OK
Content-Type: application/soap+xml; charset=utf-8
Content-Length: *LENGTH*

<?xml version="1.0"?>
<soap:Envelope
    xmlns:soap="http://www.w3.org/2001/12/soap-envelope"
```

```
        soap:encodingStyle="http://www.w3.org/2001/12/soap-encoding">

<soap:Body xmlns:m="http://www.example.org/mathematics">
    <m:AddTwoNumbersResult>
        <m:Result>9</m:Result>
    </m:AddTwoNumbersResult>
</soap:Body>

</soap:Envelope>
```

As you can see from this example, XML—just like HTML—is another markup language that's used to encode documents in a format that is both human- and machine-readable. It is similar to HTML in the sense that documents are formatted as a tree of tags. For example, the following XML document describes a simple book listing:

```
<?xml version="1.0"?>
<books>
    <book>
        <title>My First Book</title>
            <authors>
                <author>
                    <firstname>Anton</firstname>
                    <lastname>Anonymous</lastname>
                </author>
            </authors>
    </book>
    <book>
        <title>Another Book</title>
            <authors>
                <author>
                    <firstname>Anton</firstname>
                    <lastname>Anonymous</lastname>
                </author>
                <author>
                    <firstname>Bruce</firstname>
                    <lastname>McAuthor</lastname>
                </author>
            </authors>
    </book>
</books>
```

SOAP is often combined with another standard, called WSDL (Web Services Description Language). WSDL is used to describe the functionalities offered by the web service. You will see more about WSDL later, when you learn how to access SOAP services with Java.

Java provides excellent functionalities to communicate with SOAP services, as you will see later. However, the verbosity and "heaviness" of this technique have caused a shift toward simpler protocols in recent years. Traditionally, the Java ecosystem has always been very "XML friendly," with many messaging formats and configuration files being defined and stored as XML. In recent years, especially with the rise of "modern" web frameworks such as Ruby on Rails, a shift has been occurring toward simpler architectures, which prefer to use simpler data description languages such as JSON or YAML. For example, here is how the "books" data structure as provided in the previous

XML could be represented as a YAML document, which is arguably more readable and definitely more concise:

```
---
books:
    - title: My First Book
      authors:
          - {Anton, Anonymous}

    - title: Another Book
      authors:
          - {Anton, Anonymous}
          - {Bruce, McAuthor}
```

However, every technology comes with advantages and disadvantages, and SOAP remains in wide use, especially in enterprise environments that have a strong need for its versatility.

REST

This section looks at how REST—Representational State Transfer—works. REST is extremely well suited for basic, ad hoc web services. In addition, as the standard is very tightly coupled with HTTP, it has become the architecture of choice by "modern" web companies (think of social networks, for example) to provide APIs with which third-party developers can develop applications. In fact, a shift is going on where developers can be seen first constructing a REST API (API-first development) and then building their own applications and websites around this API.

One of the biggest differences between REST and SOAP is that SOAP is communication agnostic (remember that SOAP messages can be transferred on top of HTTP or any other network protocol), whereas REST is tightly integrated with HTTP and "embraces" the protocol. In fact, a REST request looks completely similar to a normal HTTP request:

```
GET /books/B101 HTTP/1.1
Host: www.example.com
```

This is a normal HTTP GET request for the URI /books/B101 sent to the host www.example.com. The server can then respond with a formatted representation of the book with ID B101. Other HTTP request types—apart from GET—exist. In the previous discussion on SOAP, for example, the SOAP request message was sent using a POST request type. GET and POST are the most commonly used HTTP methods. In fact, your browser will typically execute GET requests to request an URL and will perform POST requests to send web forms to the server. In the context of "RESTful" web services, however, the following HTTP methods are used, which are typically requested on collection resources (with an URI such as http://www.example.com/books) or specific resource elements (such as http://www.example.com/books/B101 as shown previously):

➤ GET: Retrieve a list of resources belonging to a collection, or a formatted representation of information on a resource element.

➤ PUT: Replace the entire collection with a new one, replace the resource element with a new one, or create a resource element if its identifier does not exist.

➤ POST: Create a new entry in a collection, or create a new entry in a resource element (less commonly used).

➤ DELETE: Delete an entire collection or a resource element.

Unlike SOAP, REST does not have an official standard, so different APIs may apply different conventions in terms of how they deal with the HTTP methods listed previously. Additionally, REST does not specify a formatting language or standard for the actual request and response messages to represent data, which means that the server may answer the GET /books/B101 query shown previously with a JSON, YAML, XML or even plain English description of the book. Some developers choose to support multiple formats, either by using and adhering to the "Accept" header in the HTTP request, or by adding an extension prefix to the requested URI, for example, GET /books/B101.xml.

Nowadays, companies such as Twitter, Facebook, and PayPal are all providing a REST interface to access their services, information, and functionalities (Facebook calls this their "Graph API," but it works the same way). Due to the fact that there is no real REST standard, conventions might differ among implementations—so you will need to browse through the API documentation of each service you want to access—but they all agree on using simple HTTP-based request-response communication.

TRY IT OUT   Accessing Facebook's REST Interface

This small exercise illustrates how RESTful web services are defined on top of simple HTTP requests.

1. Navigate to http://graph.facebook.com/me with your web browser.

2. You should receive the following reply:

```
{
    "error": {
        "message": "An active access token must be used to query information
            about the current user.",
        "type": "OAuthException",
        "code": 2500
    }
}
```

How It Works

Here's how it works:

1. Navigating to http://graph.facebook.com/me with a web browser will result in the browser executing an HTTP GET request for the /me endpoint.

2. Facebook uses JSON to format its REST replies.

3. As can be read from the reply, the server refuses to provide you with any information, as you have not authenticated yourself first. Most RESTful web services nowadays use the so-called "OAuth" validation technology to perform the authentication step.

4. Luckily, Facebook also provides a "sandbox" where you can play around with their REST API at `https://developers.facebook.com/tools/explorer`, which will automatically handle the authentication for you. Now, execute a GET request on `/me?fields=id,name,birthday`. The server responds with something similar to:

```
{
  "id": "507162275",
  "name": "Seppe Vanden Broucke",
  "birthday": "11/09/1986"
}
```

5. Note how you have supplied arguments with your request this time. You provided one `fields` argument with content `id,name,birthday` to specify which fields you want to get back. This way of passing arguments to REST requests is comparable to method-argument passing in SOAP or RMI.

ACCESSING WEB SERVICES AND SOURCES WITH JAVA

Now that you know what web services are and how they work, it's high time you get to see how you can access them using Java. This section discusses how to access three kinds of web services: services offered over SOAP, RESTful web services, and web services that are, in fact, not offered as a web service at all, using a technique called "screen scraping," for when you really, absolutely want to get some information out of a website.

Accessing SOAP Services

The first of the three kinds of web services discussed in this section is SOAP. This protocol was introduced earlier in this chapter. Here you learn how to use it.

Installing JAX-WS

JAX-WS Java library will be used to access SOAP services. If you're using Eclipse with the Java JRE (that is, you don't have the JDK installed), you'll need to perform the following steps to get JAX-WS running. If you're using the JDK, you're already up and running and can skip the installation steps below.

1. Browse to `https://jax-ws.java.net` and download the ZIP file offered there (this book uses `jaxws-ri-2.2.8.zip` at the time of writing).

2. This ZIP file contains a `docs` folder with documentation, a `bin` folder with some executables, a `samples` folder containing code samples, and a `lib` folder with the actual library and support classes, stored in compressed Java Archives (or JAR) files. Extract the `lib` folder somewhere you can easily find it (e.g., on your desktop).

3. Open Eclipse and create a new Java project, e.g., `SOAPWithJava`.

4. Drag the extracted `lib` folder to your Eclipse project, i.e., to the `SOAPWithJava` entry in the package explorer.

5. Eclipse will ask you how it should import your files. You should copy them in the Eclipse project to keep things neatly in one place, as shown in Figure 10-5.

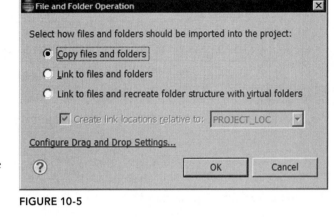

FIGURE 10-5

6. The package explorer should now list a `lib` folder under the `SOAPWithJava` project. It's best to rename this folder `jaxws` (right-click, select Refactor and then Rename). Do this before you move on to the next step.

7. You now need to add all the JAR files in the `jaxws` folder to the build path, so Eclipse and Java know that you want to use the classes contained in these files in your project. You do so by selecting all JAR files in `jaxws` and in the `plugins` subdirectory, right-clicking, and then selecting Add to Build Path under Build Path, as shown in Figure 10-6.

8. The JAR files will now show up under "Referenced Libraries" in the package explorer.

9. Finally, keep the extracted ZIP file around, as you'll need to use the executables provided in the `bin` folder.

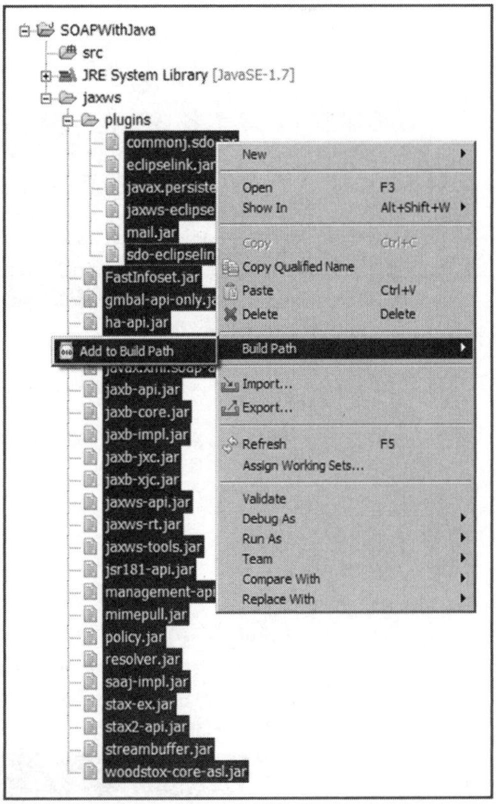

You're now ready to move on with the implementation of the actual client.

Accessing SOAP Services with JAX-WS Without WSDL

FIGURE 10-6

In this section, you first take a look at how to access web services without using the WSDL descriptor file.

To test the examples in this chapter, you'll need a server that can respond to SOAP queries. To this end, you'll be using the services offered by the following website: http://www.webservicex.net. This website hosts a number of small, working, example web services, and serves over six million requests a day. The following Try It Out will help you explore the website.

Exploring SOAP Services

This exercise will let you explore the webservicex.net website and its services to get a feel for how they work.

1. Navigate to http://www.webservicex.net in your web browser. You'll see a page appearing with a list of web services you can choose from.

2. In this example, use the "Stock Quote" web service, retrievable at http://www.webservicex .net/ws/WSDetails.aspx?CATID=2&WSID=9.

3. The page shown in Figure 10-7 should appear for the "Stock Quote" web service.

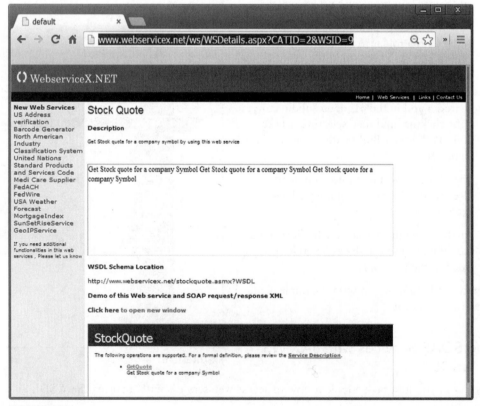

FIGURE 10-7

4. In the lower pane, you'll see a list of operations—methods—this web service supports. For the "Stock Quote" service, only one operation is available: GetQuote. Click this operation to get some more information about it, as shown in Figure 10-8.

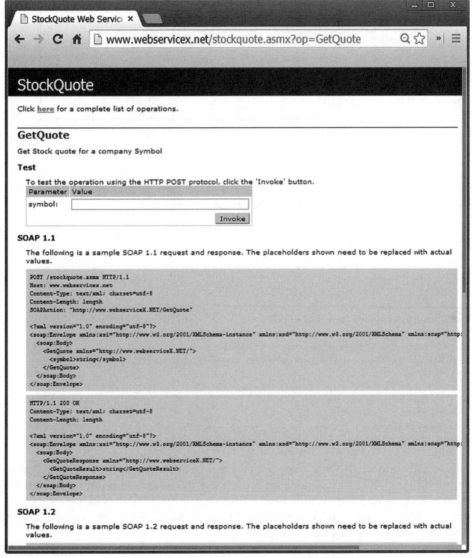

FIGURE 10-8

5. The web service tells you that one parameter, "symbol," is required to pass to this operation. You can test the web service using your browser. For example, try typing in IBM and pressing Invoke. The web service should show the result demonstrated in Figure 10-9.

FIGURE 10-9

6. Finally, the web service also provides an example of a SOAP request-reply interchange to access this web service. Let's take a look at the example request:

```
POST /stockquote.asmx HTTP/1.1
Host: www.webservicex.net
Content-Type: text/xml; charset=utf-8
Content-Length: length
SOAPAction: "http://www.webserviceX.NET/GetQuote"

<?xml version="1.0" encoding="utf-8"?>
<soap:Envelope xmlns:xsi="http://www.w3.org/2001/XMLSchema-instance"
       xmlns:xsd="http://www.w3.org/2001/XMLSchema"
       xmlns:soap="http://schemas.xmlsoap.org/soap/envelope/">
    <soap:Body>
        <GetQuote xmlns="http://www.webserviceX.NET/">
            <symbol>string</symbol>
        </GetQuote>
    </soap:Body>
</soap:Envelope>
```

This request message tells you a few things. First, you now know that you should make a request to the URL /stockquote.asmx at the host www.webservicex.net. Next, you should also provide a SOAPAction header with the content http://www.webserviceX.NET/GetQuote. Finally, the XML encoded SOAP message itself contains the GetQuote operation call with a symbol tag to pass the argument.

If all goes well, the server replies with the following:

```
HTTP/1.1 200 OK
Content-Type: text/xml; charset=utf-8
Content-Length: length

<?xml version="1.0" encoding="utf-8"?>
```

```
<soap:Envelope xmlns:xsi="http://www.w3.org/2001/XMLSchema-instance"
    xmlns:xsd="http://www.w3.org/2001/XMLSchema"
    xmlns:soap="http://schemas.xmlsoap.org/soap/envelope/">
  <soap:Body>
    <GetQuoteResponse xmlns="http://www.webserviceX.NET/">
      <GetQuoteResult>string</GetQuoteResult>
    </GetQuoteResponse>
  </soap:Body>
</soap:Envelope>
```

So now you know you can expect a SOAP reply message with a `GetQuoteResponse` tag containing one internal tag—`GetQuoteResult`–which you can parse in your program.

7. Finally, note that the web service also provides a WSDL file, which you will see later on in a bit more depth.

How It Works

Here's how it works:

1. The `http://www.webservicex.net` website hosts a number of useful SOAP services, one of which is the stock quote provider.

2. Each SOAP service provides a number of "operations." Think of these as "methods" you can call on the service. In the case of the stock quote provider, only one operation is provided: `GetQuote`.

3. SOAP requests can be sent to invoke a service operation. To do so, a request message needs to be constructed that will be sent to the service URI (the endpoint). That method must contain a `SOAPAction` header with the operation you want to call and a message body containing the parameters you want to send to the operation handler. The `WebserviceX.NET` websites provides example messages for each of its operations.

4. If the request succeeds, you know you will receive a reply formatted to the specifications as shown on the example page. You know you can expect a SOAP reply message with a `GetQuoteResponse` tag containing one internal tag: `GetQuoteResult`. This tag contains a "string"—you can't be sure yet how this string is formatted or what information it contains, so you'll need to take a closer look at it once you receive SOAP replies in your program.

It's time to get started and see how you can access this service in Java. Create a class called `ClientWithoutWSDL` to do so. From the example in the Try It Out, you know that you will need the following to access the web service:

➤ The hostname of the service. In this case, this is `www.webservicex.net`.

➤ The "endpoint" to which you should send the request using HTTP. For the "Stock Quote" web service, this is `/stockquote.asmx`. Together with the hostname, this forms the full endpoint URI: `http://www.webservicex.net/stockquote.asmx`.

➤ The name of the operation you want to invoke. In this case, this is `GetQuote`. The name of the operation is also used to construct the `SOAPAction` header: `http://www.webserviceX.NET/GetQuote`.

To keep things orderly, you can set up a number of static variables to hold this information, so the first iteration of the `ClientWithoutWSDL` class should look like this:

```
public class ClientWithoutWSDL {

    private final static String SERVICE_HOST = "http://www.webserviceX.NET/";
    private final static String SERVICE_METHOD = "GetQuote";
    private final static String SERVICE_ENDPOINT = "stockquote.asmx";

    public static void main(String args[]) {

    }

}
```

Take special care to enter these constants exactly as listed in the code snippet. Note that you should be using `http://www.webserviceX.NET/` and not `http://www.webservicex.net/` or `www.webservicex.net`. These addresses are case sensitive. The reasons for this will become apparent later on.

> **NOTE** *The Internet is a rapidly changing place, and with a chapter on web services, we risk the possibility that websites might no longer work (or have been changed) by the time you read this chapter. That said, all web resources used here have been chosen based on the amount of time they have been around and their maturity (e.g., WebServiceX responds to millions of queries a day). Keep an eye on the online resources for this book at www.wrox.com to get notified in case things break.*

Next, you will start creating the actual SOAP request message. To do so, you will use a number of classes made available under `javax.xml.soap`:

```
import javax.xml.soap.SOAPConnection;
import javax.xml.soap.SOAPConnectionFactory;
import javax.xml.soap.SOAPMessage;

public class ClientWithoutWSDL {

    private final static String SERVICE_HOST = "http://www.webserviceX.NET/";
    private final static String SERVICE_METHOD = "GetQuote";
    private final static String SERVICE_ENDPOINT = "stockquote.asmx";

    private final static String STOCK_SYMBOL = "IBM";

    public static void main(String args[]) {
      try {
        // Create a new SOAP connection
        SOAPConnectionFactory soapConnectionFactory =
        SOAPConnectionFactory.newInstance();
        SOAPConnection soapConnection = soapConnectionFactory.createConnection();
```

```
            // Send a SOAP Message to SOAP server
            // Send this message to http://www.webserviceX.NET/stockquote.asmx
            SOAPMessage soapResponse = soapConnection.call(
                createSOAPRequest(STOCK_SYMBOL),
                SERVICE_HOST + SERVICE_ENDPOINT);

            // Close the connection
            soapConnection.close();
        } catch (Exception e) {
            System.err.println("Fatal error occurred");
            e.printStackTrace();
        }
    }

    private static SOAPMessage createSOAPRequest(String stockSymbol) {
        // Construct a new SOAP request message
        return null;
    }

}
```

Now take a look at the changes you've made. First, you created a global exception catcher in the main class to print out any errors that might occur. Using a global exception catcher is not good practice in general, but it's fine to create the prototype. Next, you use a class called SOAPConnectionFactory to instantiate a SOAPConnection object.

There are a number of programming patterns at work here. First, note that you do not call the constructor for SOAPConnection directly (using the new keyword), but instead ask the factory class to instantiate this object for you. "Factories" are a common Object-Oriented Programming pattern and are used for a couple of reasons. First, it allows the factory object to keep track of all objects it has instantiated, providing a centralized means to itemize them and access them later. Second, since factories take care of the actual instantiation of an object, the factory can decide which subclass is best suited whenever multiple subclasses are available. Indeed, SOAPConnection is an abstract class, which is why you cannot instantiate it directly (even if you wanted to do so), so the factory can decide which actual subclass of SOAPConnection is best suited for your needs.

You can see a similar pattern occurring for the instantiation of the SOAPConnectionFactory object. Again, you are not constructing this object directly using the new keyword, but instead calling the static newInstance method to instantiate a factory object. The reasoning behind this is also similar: it allows the internals of the library to keep track of all the factories that have been created and to select the proper factory subclass to use. In some cases, you'll also see the so-called "Singleton" pattern at work here, where the newInstance method—or getOrCreateInstance, which would be a better name in this case—will create a new factory if no factory exists and return the existing factory if it does exist, effectively only allowing one single instantiation of this class (one single factory). Both the Factory and Singleton patterns are heavily used design patterns in Object-Oriented Programming. Chapter 12 provides more insights on object-oriented patterns, but it's good to briefly mention them here.

Further on in the code, the call method is called on your SOAPConnection object to send a SOAP request to http://www.webserviceX.NET/stockquote.asmx, the full endpoint URI. You also need to pass a SOAPMessage object to send, which you create using another—currently empty—method you've added: createSOAPRequest. The stock symbol is passed to this method as an argument, and a constant is added to set the symbol "IBM."

Let's now start to fill in the `createSOAPRequest` method. You can start by creating an empty SOAP message, so that your code now looks like the following:

```java
import javax.xml.namespace.QName;
import javax.xml.soap.MessageFactory;
import javax.xml.soap.MimeHeaders;
import javax.xml.soap.SOAPBody;
import javax.xml.soap.SOAPBodyElement;
import javax.xml.soap.SOAPConnection;
import javax.xml.soap.SOAPConnectionFactory;
import javax.xml.soap.SOAPElement;
import javax.xml.soap.SOAPMessage;

public class ClientWithoutWSDL {

    private final static String SERVICE_HOST = "http://www.webserviceX.NET/";
    private final static String SERVICE_METHOD = "GetQuote";
    private final static String SERVICE_ENDPOINT = "stockquote.asmx";
    private final static String STOCK_SYMBOL = "IBM";

    public static void main(String args[]) {
      try {
        // Create a new SOAP connection
        SOAPConnectionFactory soapConnectionFactory =
        SOAPConnectionFactory.newInstance();
        SOAPConnection soapConnection = soapConnectionFactory.createConnection();

        // Send a SOAP Message to SOAP server
        // Send this message to http://www.webserviceX.NET/stockquote.asmx
        SOAPMessage soapResponse = soapConnection.call(
            createSOAPRequest(STOCK_SYMBOL),
            SERVICE_HOST + SERVICE_ENDPOINT);

        // Close the connection
        soapConnection.close();
      } catch (Exception e) {
        System.err.println("Fatal error occurred");
        e.printStackTrace();
      }
    }

    private static SOAPMessage createSOAPRequest(String stockSymbol)
        throws Exception {
        // Construct a new SOAP request message
        MessageFactory messageFactory = MessageFactory.newInstance();
        SOAPMessage soapMessage = messageFactory.createMessage();

        // Construct the SOAP "body" with the method arguments
        soapMessage.saveChanges();

        // Print out the request message:
        System.out.println("Sending SOAP request:");
        soapMessage.writeTo(System.out);
        System.out.printf("%n");
```

```
        return soapMessage;
    }
}
```

Again, the same Factory patterns are being applied here to construct the SOAPMessage object. You will need to modify this actual message—which you will do in the next step—but you should call the saveChanges method after you're done constructing your SOAP request. This seems a bit ad hoc. Normally, most objects you have worked with so far immediately perform any changes you apply and do not need to have a special save method called. In some cases, however, complex methods might need to perform a series of CPU or disk-intensive operations when performing changes, so that programmers will wait to execute these steps until the programmer explicitly indicates that they are finished modifying the object and all intensive steps can be performed. The SOAPMessage object works exactly like this.

> **NOTE** You might be wondering how you can possibly know when programmers decide that a special saveChanges method needs to be called on the objects they provide in their libraries. The answer is that you can't, really. The context sensitive pop-ups in Eclipse can provide an indication (if you see a saveChanges method appearing, it might be a strong indication that you'll need to call it at some point), but it's easy to miss this. Another way to find this out is by reading the documentation and API reference for the libraries you use. Finally—and what will happen in most real-life situations—it's also possible to discover this just by doing. If you forget to call this method, things might not work as expected, but reported error messages will lead you in the right direction. As always, don't be afraid to search around on the Internet to find an answer for your problem.

You also add a number of statements to print out the constructed SOAP message for inspection by asking the object to print out its string representation to the output stream System.out, using the writeTo method.

Finally, note that you have added a throws Exception declaration to your method definition to "bubble up" any errors to the try-catch block in your main method. At this point, your code is runnable, so why not test it? If you run the main method, you'll see something like this appear:

```
Sending SOAP request:
<SOAP-ENV:Envelope xmlns:SOAP-ENV="http://schemas.xmlsoap.org/soap/envelope/">
<SOAP-ENV:Header/><SOAP-ENV:Body/></SOAP-ENV:Envelope>
```

Does this mean your code is working? The SOAP message does not seem to contain much. To figure out what's going on, take a closer look at the soapResponse object you get back, which is also a SOAPMessage object, by simply printing out its contents:

```
import javax.xml.namespace.QName;
import javax.xml.soap.MessageFactory;
import javax.xml.soap.MimeHeaders;
import javax.xml.soap.SOAPBody;
import javax.xml.soap.SOAPBodyElement;
```

```java
import javax.xml.soap.SOAPConnection;
import javax.xml.soap.SOAPConnectionFactory;
import javax.xml.soap.SOAPElement;
import javax.xml.soap.SOAPMessage;

public class ClientWithoutWSDL {

    private final static String SERVICE_HOST = "http://www.webserviceX.NET/";
    private final static String SERVICE_METHOD = "GetQuote";
    private final static String SERVICE_ENDPOINT = "stockquote.asmx";

    private final static String STOCK_SYMBOL = "IBM";

    public static void main(String args[]) {
      try {
          // Create a new SOAP connection
          SOAPConnectionFactory soapConnectionFactory =
          SOAPConnectionFactory.newInstance();
          SOAPConnection soapConnection = soapConnectionFactory.createConnection();

          // Send a SOAP Message to SOAP server
          // Send this message to http://www.webserviceX.NET/stockquote.asmx
          SOAPMessage soapResponse = soapConnection.call(
              createSOAPRequest(STOCK_SYMBOL),
              SERVICE_HOST + SERVICE_ENDPOINT);

          System.out.println("Received SOAP reply:");
          soapResponse.writeTo(System.out);
          System.out.println("\r\n");

          // Close the connection
          soapConnection.close();
      } catch (Exception e) {
          System.err.println("Fatal error occurred");
          e.printStackTrace();
      }
    }

    private static SOAPMessage createSOAPRequest(String stockSymbol)
        throws Exception {
        // *UNCHANGED*
    }

}
```

If you run the code again, you'll see:

```
Sending SOAP request:
<SOAP-ENV:Envelope xmlns:SOAP-ENV="http://schemas.xmlsoap.org/soap/envelope/">
<SOAP-ENV:Header/><SOAP-ENV:Body/></SOAP-ENV:Envelope>

Received SOAP reply:
<?xml version="1.0" encoding="utf-8"?><soap:Envelope
xmlns:soap="http://schemas.xmlsoap.org/soap/envelope/"
xmlns:xsi="http://www.w3.org/2001/XMLSchema-instance"
xmlns:xsd="http://www.w3.org/2001/XMLSchema"><soap:Body>
```

```
<soap:Fault><faultcode>soap:Client</faultcode><faultstring>
System.Web.Services.Protocols.SoapException:
Server did not recognize the value of HTTP Header SOAPAction: .
    at System.Web.Services.Protocols.Soap11ServerProtocolHelper.RouteRequest()
    at System.Web.Services.Protocols.SoapServerProtocol.RouteRequest
        (SoapServerMessage message)
    at System.Web.Services.Protocols.SoapServerProtocol.Initialize()
    at System.Web.Services.Protocols.ServerProtocolFactory.Create(Type type,
        HttpContext context, HttpRequest request, HttpResponse response,
        Boolean&amp; abortProcessing)</faultstring><detail
        /></soap:Fault></soap:Body></soap:Envelope>
```

Apparently, the server is not too happy with the message you've sent and complains that it needs a value for the `SOAPAction` header. Add one to your request message by changing your `createSOAPRequest` method to look like this:

```java
private static SOAPMessage createSOAPRequest(String stockSymbol)
    throws Exception {
    // Construct a new SOAP request message
    MessageFactory messageFactory = MessageFactory.newInstance();
    SOAPMessage soapMessage = messageFactory.createMessage();

    // Construct the SOAP "body" with the method arguments

    // Add a SOAP action header to the request
    // Action: http://www.webserviceX.NET/GetQuote
    MimeHeaders headers = soapMessage.getMimeHeaders();
    headers.addHeader("SOAPAction", SERVICE_HOST + SERVICE_METHOD);

    // Save our changes
    soapMessage.saveChanges();

    // Print out the request message:
    System.out.println("Sending SOAP request:");
    soapMessage.writeTo(System.out);
    System.out.println("\r\n");

    return soapMessage;
}
```

This piece of code will add the following HTTP header to your request:

```
SOAPAction: "http://www.webserviceX.NET/GetQuote"
```

If you followed along with the "Exploring SOAP Services" Try It Out, you already saw this `SOAPAction` header in the example provided by `WebserviceX.NET`. In most cases, the `SOAPAction` header combines the hostname with the SOAP operation (`GetQuote`). Later on in this chapter, you'll see how you can use WSDL to provide this information.

If you execute this code once more, you now get a different reply from the server.

Sending SOAP request:

```
<SOAP-ENV:Envelope xmlns:SOAP-ENV="http://schemas.xmlsoap.org/soap/envelope/">
```

```
<SOAP-ENV:Header/><SOAP-ENV:Body/></SOAP-ENV:Envelope>

Received SOAP reply:
<?xml version="1.0" encoding="utf-8"?><soap:Envelope
xmlns:soap="http://schemas.xmlsoap.org/soap/envelope/"
xmlns:xsi="http://www.w3.org/2001/XMLSchema-instance"
xmlns:xsd="http://www.w3.org/2001/XMLSchema">
<soap:Body><GetQuoteResponse xmlns="http://www.webserviceX.NET/">
<GetQuoteResult>exception</GetQuoteResult></GetQuoteResponse>
</soap:Body></soap:Envelope>
```

You're making progress, but this is still not the expected reply. The "exception" result seems to indicate that something went wrong, although the server is not too helpful in detailing exactly what. Debugging sessions with limited information can get very frustrating quickly, but in this case, you have a good idea of what's wrong: your actual SOAP message does not contain any content and is empty. Let's start filling it up.

> **NOTE** *Remember how you've read before that it's important to use* `http://www.webserviceX.NET/` *for the* `SERVICE_HOST` *variable. Servers can be very picky about how they parse the* `SOAPAction` *header. In this case, using another capitalization of* `http://www.webservicex.NET/` *will cause the server to continue complaining about the* `SOAPAction` *header.*

Modify your `createSOAPRequest` method once again to look like this:

```java
private static SOAPMessage createSOAPRequest(String stockSymbol) throws Exception {
    // Construct a new SOAP request message
    MessageFactory messageFactory = MessageFactory.newInstance();
    SOAPMessage soapMessage = messageFactory.createMessage();

    // Construct the SOAP "body" with the method arguments
    SOAPBody soapBody = soapMessage.getSOAPBody();
    QName bodyName = new QName(SERVICE_HOST, SERVICE_METHOD);
    SOAPBodyElement bodyElement = soapBody.addBodyElement(bodyName);

    SOAPElement soapBodyArgument1 = bodyElement.addChildElement("symbol");
    soapBodyArgument1.addTextNode(stockSymbol);

    // Add a SOAP action header to the request
    // Action: http://www.webserviceX.NET/GetQuote
    MimeHeaders headers = soapMessage.getMimeHeaders();
    headers.addHeader("SOAPAction", SERVICE_HOST + SERVICE_METHOD);

    soapMessage.saveChanges();

    // Print out the request message:
    System.out.println("Sending SOAP request:");
    soapMessage.writeTo(System.out);
```

```
    System.out.printf("%n");

    return soapMessage;
}
```

This piece of code will add a body to your SOAP message containing a GetQuote element (SERVICE_METHOD). Within this XML tag, you add another element—symbol—with your provided stock quote as the content.

The use of the QName object to add an XML element is a bit peculiar. The reason for this is that the web service specifies that you need to add a GetQuote element, which looks like this:

```
<GetQuote xmlns="http://www.webserviceX.NET/">...</GetQuote>
```

And not just:

```
<GetQuote>...</GetQuote>
```

If you use the following piece of code to construct your message:

```
// Construct the SOAP "body" with the method arguments
SOAPBody soapBody = soapMessage.getSOAPBody();
SOAPElement bodyElement = soapBody.addChildElement(SERVICE_METHOD);
SOAPElement soapBodyArgument1 = bodyElement.addChildElement("symbol");
soapBodyArgument1.addTextNode(stockSymbol);
```

You get the following request message—which looks okay:

```
<SOAP-ENV:Envelope xmlns:SOAP-ENV="http://schemas.xmlsoap.org/soap/envelope/">
  <SOAP-ENV:Header/>
  <SOAP-ENV:Body>
    <GetQuote><symbol>IBM</symbol></GetQuote>
  </SOAP-ENV:Body>
</SOAP-ENV:Envelope>
```

But the server still responds with an "exception" reply. Again, servers can be very picky about how they parse request messages, so take care to construct messages exactly as indicated by the service provider.

With your code, however, you now see the following interchange happening:

```
Sending SOAP request:
<SOAP-ENV:Envelope xmlns:SOAP-ENV="http://schemas.xmlsoap.org/soap/envelope/">
    <SOAP-ENV:Header/>
    <SOAP-ENV:Body>
        <GetQuote xmlns="http://www.webserviceX.NET/">
        <symbol>IBM</symbol>
        </GetQuote>
    </SOAP-ENV:Body>
</SOAP-ENV:Envelope>
```

```
Received SOAP reply:
<?xml version="1.0" encoding="utf-8"?>
<soap:Envelope xmlns:soap="http://schemas.xmlsoap.org/soap/envelope/"
    xmlns:xsi="http://www.w3.org/2001/XMLSchema-instance"
    xmlns:xsd="http://www.w3.org/2001/XMLSchema">
    <soap:Body>
        <GetQuoteResponse xmlns="http://www.webserviceX.NET/">
            <GetQuoteResult>
            &lt;StockQuotes&gt;&lt;Stock&gt;&lt;Symbol&gt;IBM&lt;
            /Symbol&gt;&lt;Last&gt;196.40&lt;/Last&gt;&lt;Date&gt;
            4/16/2014&lt;/Date&gt;&lt;Time&gt;4:01pm&lt;/Time&gt;
            &lt;Change&gt;-
            0.62&lt;/Change&gt;&lt;Open&gt;197.77&lt;/Open&gt;&lt;
            High&gt;198.71&lt;/High&gt;&lt;Low&gt;195.00&lt;/Low&gt;
            &lt;Volume&gt;8527415&lt;/Volume&gt;&lt;MktCap&gt;204.5B&lt;
            /MktCap&gt;&lt;PreviousClose&gt;197.02&lt;/PreviousClose&gt;
            &lt;PercentageChange&gt;-0.31%&lt;/PercentageChange&gt;&lt;
            &gt;172.19 - 11.98&lt;/AnnRange&gt;&lt;Earns&gt;
            14.942&lt;/Earns&gt;&lt;P-E&gt;13.19&lt;/P-E&gt;&lt;Name&gt;
            International Bus&lt;/Name&gt;&lt;/Stock&gt;&lt;/StockQuotes&gt;
            </GetQuoteResult>
        </GetQuoteResponse>
    </soap:Body>
</soap:Envelope>
```

Great! You seem to be getting something back now. However, as you can observe, this particular service has chosen to encode its result as one big mess within the GetQuoteResult tag. In fact, the text included herein is a so-called "escaped" XML string. Note how all the < and > characters have been replaced with < and >. Why this particular server is behaving like this instead of including the XML as is—which would be easier to parse—remains a mystery, but to parse your result, you'll need to get out the escaped XML string and then interpret it again as XML.

> **NOTE** If you're paying very close attention, you might note that this SOAP message still looks somewhat different from the example provided at the WebserviceX.NET website. Most notable is that all your tags start with SOAP-ENV, whereas the example uses soap. Funnily enough, the server is not picky regarding this aspect. The reason for this is that a so-called "namespace" definition is explicitly provided in the message. In the example provided, this is done by xmlns:soap="http://schemas.xmlsoap.org/soap/envelope/". In your message, the same namespace is provided, but with the name SOAP-ENV. A namespace is basically a way to indicate the following: "Let's agree to use a set of tags we both know about. You can find their definition and description on this URL, and I'm going to prepend the tag names with SOAP-ENV." As long as the server knows about the namespace being used, it does not matter what shorthand name you use to prepend the tags.

To parse the information contained in the reply, you can add a new method, showSOAPResponse. You can also remove all the System.out.println statements as you do not need them anymore—you know your messages are working:

```java
import javax.xml.namespace.QName;
import javax.xml.soap.MessageFactory;
import javax.xml.soap.MimeHeaders;
import javax.xml.soap.SOAPBody;
import javax.xml.soap.SOAPBodyElement;
import javax.xml.soap.SOAPConnection;
import javax.xml.soap.SOAPConnectionFactory;
import javax.xml.soap.SOAPElement;
import javax.xml.soap.SOAPMessage;

public class ClientWithoutWSDL {

    private final static String SERVICE_HOST = "http://www.webserviceX.NET/";
    private final static String SERVICE_METHOD = "GetQuote";
    private final static String SERVICE_ENDPOINT = "stockquote.asmx";

    private final static String STOCK_SYMBOL = "IBM";

    public static void main(String args[]) {
        try {
            // Create a new SOAP connection
            SOAPConnectionFactory soapConnectionFactory = SOAPConnectionFactory
                .newInstance();
            SOAPConnection soapConnection = soapConnectionFactory
                .createConnection();

            // Send a SOAP Message to SOAP server
            // Send this message to http://www.webserviceX.NET/stockquote.asmx
            SOAPMessage soapResponse = soapConnection.call(
                createSOAPRequest(STOCK_SYMBOL), SERVICE_HOST
                    + SERVICE_ENDPOINT);

            showSOAPResponse(soapResponse);

            // Close the connection
            soapConnection.close();
        } catch (Exception e) {
            System.err.println("Fatal error occurred");
            e.printStackTrace();
        }
    }

    private static SOAPMessage createSOAPRequest(String stockSymbol)
            throws Exception {
        // Construct a new SOAP request message
        MessageFactory messageFactory = MessageFactory.newInstance();
        SOAPMessage soapMessage = messageFactory.createMessage();

        // Construct the SOAP "body" with the method arguments
        SOAPBody soapBody = soapMessage.getSOAPBody();
```

```
        QName bodyName = new QName(SERVICE_HOST, SERVICE_METHOD);
        SOAPBodyElement bodyElement = soapBody.addBodyElement(bodyName);
        SOAPElement soapBodyArgument1 = bodyElement.addChildElement("symbol");
        soapBodyArgument1.addTextNode(stockSymbol);

        // Add a SOAP action header to the request
        // Action: http://www.webserviceX.NET/GetQuote
        MimeHeaders headers = soapMessage.getMimeHeaders();
        headers.addHeader("SOAPAction", SERVICE_HOST + SERVICE_METHOD);

        soapMessage.saveChanges();

        return soapMessage;
    }

    private static void showSOAPResponse(SOAPMessage soapResponse)
        throws Exception {

    }

}
```

Let's start filling in this method. First, add the following two lines:

```
Node responseNode = soapResponse.getSOAPBody().getFirstChild();
System.out.println(responseNode.getTextContent());
```

This will take the SOAP body part from the response message (which is an XML document), and then take the first child node in this body. Then you print the text content of this node, i.e., the text between the tags in the XML message, which gives you the following:

```
<StockQuotes><Stock><Symbol>IBM</Symbol><Last>196.40</Last>
<Date>4/16/2014</Date><Time>4:01pm</Time><Change>-
0.62</Change><Open>197.77</Open><High>198.71</High><Low>195.00
</Low><Volume>8527415</Volume><MktCap>204.5B</MktCap>
<PreviousClose>197.02</PreviousClose><PercentageChange>-
0.31%</PercentageChange><AnnRange>172.19 - 211.98</AnnRange>
<Earns>14.942</Earns><P-E>13.19</P-E><Name>International
Bus</Name></Stock></StockQuotes>
```

You can see that Java has already "un-escaped" the XML for you, but it is still regarded as one big string. To parse this information, you need to construct a new object representing an XML document out of this string, so you change the method to look like so:

```
private static void showSOAPResponse(SOAPMessage soapResponse) throws Exception {
    Node responseNode = soapResponse.getSOAPBody().getFirstChild();
    String xmlText = responseNode.getTextContent();
    DocumentBuilderFactory factory = DocumentBuilderFactory.newInstance();
    DocumentBuilder builder = factory.newDocumentBuilder();
    Document document = builder.parse(new InputSource(
        new StringReader(xmlText)));
}
```

This code will create an `org.w3c.dom.Document` object representing an XML tree. You can now traverse this tree to get out your information. Looking at the result, you can see that stock information is provided in "Stock" tags, with each piece of information being stored in a separate subtag. So modify your method once again, so that the complete class will look like this:

```java
import java.io.StringReader;

import javax.xml.namespace.QName;
import javax.xml.parsers.DocumentBuilder;
import javax.xml.parsers.DocumentBuilderFactory;
import javax.xml.soap.MessageFactory;
import javax.xml.soap.MimeHeaders;
import javax.xml.soap.SOAPBody;
import javax.xml.soap.SOAPBodyElement;
import javax.xml.soap.SOAPConnection;
import javax.xml.soap.SOAPConnectionFactory;
import javax.xml.soap.SOAPElement;
import javax.xml.soap.SOAPMessage;

import org.w3c.dom.Document;
import org.w3c.dom.Node;
import org.w3c.dom.NodeList;
import org.xml.sax.InputSource;

public class ClientWithoutWSDL {

    private final static String SERVICE_HOST = "http://www.webserviceX.NET/";
    private final static String SERVICE_METHOD = "GetQuote";
    private final static String SERVICE_ENDPOINT = "stockquote.asmx";

    private final static String STOCK_SYMBOL = "IBM";

    public static void main(String args[]) {
        try {
            // Create a new SOAP connection
            SOAPConnectionFactory soapConnectionFactory = SOAPConnectionFactory
                .newInstance();
            SOAPConnection soapConnection = soapConnectionFactory
                .createConnection();

            // Send a SOAP Message to SOAP server
            // Send this message to http://www.webserviceX.NET/stockquote.asmx
            SOAPMessage soapResponse = soapConnection.call(
                createSOAPRequest(STOCK_SYMBOL), SERVICE_HOST
                    + SERVICE_ENDPOINT);

            showSOAPResponse(soapResponse);

            // Close the connection
            soapConnection.close();
        } catch (Exception e) {
            System.err.println("Fatal error occurred");
            e.printStackTrace();
        }
```

```
        }

        private static SOAPMessage createSOAPRequest(String stockSymbol)
                throws Exception {
            // Construct a new SOAP request message
            MessageFactory messageFactory = MessageFactory.newInstance();
            SOAPMessage soapMessage = messageFactory.createMessage();

            // Construct the SOAP "body" with the method arguments
            SOAPBody soapBody = soapMessage.getSOAPBody();
            QName bodyName = new QName(SERVICE_HOST, SERVICE_METHOD);
            SOAPBodyElement bodyElement = soapBody.addBodyElement(bodyName);
            SOAPElement soapBodyArgument1 = bodyElement.addChildElement("symbol");
            soapBodyArgument1.addTextNode(stockSymbol);

            // Add a SOAP action header to the request
            // Action: http://www.webserviceX.NET/GetQuote
            MimeHeaders headers = soapMessage.getMimeHeaders();
            headers.addHeader("SOAPAction", SERVICE_HOST + SERVICE_METHOD);

            soapMessage.saveChanges();

            return soapMessage;
        }

        private static void showSOAPResponse(SOAPMessage soapResponse)
          throws Exception {
            Node responseNode = soapResponse.getSOAPBody().getFirstChild();
            String xmlText = responseNode.getTextContent();
            DocumentBuilderFactory factory = DocumentBuilderFactory.newInstance();
            DocumentBuilder builder = factory.newDocumentBuilder();
            Document document = builder.parse(new InputSource(
                new StringReader(xmlText)));

            NodeList stockElements = document.getElementsByTagName("Stock");
            for (int i = 0; i < stockElements.getLength(); i++) {
                System.out.println("----- Stock nr. " + i + " ------");
                NodeList infoElements = stockElements.item(i).getChildNodes();
                for (int j = 0; j < infoElements.getLength(); j++) {
                    System.out.println(infoElements.item(j).getNodeName() +
                        "\t --> " +
                            infoElements.item(j).getTextContent());
                }
            }
        }

    }
}
```

If you execute this code, the program will show the following result:

```
----- Stock nr. 0 -----
Symbol  --> IBM
Last    --> 196.40
```

```
Date      --> 4/16/2014
Time      --> 4:01pm
Change    --> -0.62
Open      --> 197.77
High      --> 198.71
Low       --> 195.00
Volume    --> 8527415
MktCap    --> 204.5B
PreviousClose  --> 197.02
PercentageChange  --> -0.31%
AnnRange  --> 172.19 - 211.98
Earns     --> 14.942
P-E       --> 13.19
Name      --> International Bus
```

Take some time to explore the code you've written at your own leisure. Try experimenting with different stock symbols, or if you feel up to it, try selecting one of the other provided web services at WebserviceX.NET and see whether you can get it to work (the "Global Weather" service—http://www.webservicex.net/ws/WSDetails.aspx?CATID=12&WSID=56—works nicely).

In this section, you've been accessing SOAP services in a very ad hoc manner, constructing SOAP messages by hand and parsing the responses manually. You had to look up the correct endpoint URI and hostname to use, and had to deal with picky server error messages. Luckily, many SOAP web services also provide a so-called WSDL file that describes the operations the service offers, together with the ways they can be accessed. JAX-WS contains a handy feature to automatically construct a set of service-interacting classes from this WSDL file, as you'll see in the following section.

First, however, this section ends with a hands-on Try It Out. It shows you how to clean up the code you've written some more, if you're up for it.

TRY IT OUT   A True Object-Oriented SOAP Client

The code you wrote to access a SOAP client does not really look like clean, object-oriented Java code. In fact, the code has more similarities to a procedural scripting language, with one big `main` method delegating some tasks to other static methods.

For building a quick prototype—e.g., when you're just starting out and trying to see if you can get your SOAP client to work—this is fine, but in real-life applications, you'll want to clean up your code to be more in line with the object-oriented paradigm.

Let's see how you can do this for the stock quote client. The goal is to abstract away the complexity of SOAP interaction and to provide an object structure for your applications to work with.

1. Create a new package called `withoutwsdlobjectoriented` to hold your classes (feel free to pick a more suitable or creative name, but this one will match the code provided with this book). As you know by now, when you think about objects and classes, you want your classes to represent your domain concepts. What is your most primary concept in a stock quote application? Naturally, a class representing a stock symbol and its information. As such, create a `Stock` class as follows:

```
package withoutwsdlobjectoriented;

import java.util.Date;
```

```java
public class Stock {
    private String symbol, name;
    private double last, open, high, low;
    private long volume;
    private Date timestamp;
    private double marketCap;
    private double previousClose;
    private double change, percentageChange;
    private double annRangeLow, annRangeHigh;
    private double earns;
    private double pe;

    public Stock(String symbol, String name, double last, double open, double high,
        double low, long volume, Date timestamp, double marketCap,
        double previousClose, double change, double percentageChange,
        double annRangeLow, double annRangeHigh, double earns, double pe) {
        this.symbol = symbol;
        this.name = name;
        this.last = last;
        this.open = open;
        this.high = high;
        this.low = low;
        this.volume = volume;
        this.timestamp = timestamp;
        this.marketCap = marketCap;
        this.previousClose = previousClose;
        this.change = change;
        this.percentageChange = percentageChange;
        this.annRangeLow = annRangeLow;
        this.annRangeHigh = annRangeHigh;
        this.earns = earns;
        this.pe = pe;
    }

    public String getSymbol() {
        return symbol;
    }

    public String getName() {
        return name;
    }

    public double getLast() {
        return last;
    }

    public double getChange() {
        return change;
    }

    public double getOpen() {
        return open;
    }

    public double getHigh() {
        return high;
    }
```

```java
    public double getLow() {
        return low;
    }

    public long getVolume() {
        return volume;
    }

    public Date getTimestamp() {
        return timestamp;
    }

    public double getMarketCap() {
        return marketCap;
    }

    public double getPreviousClose() {
        return previousClose;
    }

    public double getPercentageChange() {
        return percentageChange;
    }

    public double getAnnRangeLow() {
        return annRangeLow;
    }

    public double getAnnRangeHigh() {
        return annRangeHigh;
    }

    public double getEarns() {
        return earns;
    }

    public double getPe() {
        return pe;
    }

    public String toString() {
        String r = "";
        r += "STOCK " + symbol + ": " + name + "\r\n";
        int l = r.length() - 2;
        for (int i = 0; i < l; i++)
            r += "=";
        r += "\r\n";
        r += "* Retrieved at: " + timestamp + "\r\n";
        r += "* Last / High / Low / Open: " +
                last + " / " + high + " / " + low + " / " + open + "\r\n";
        r += "* Previous close: " + previousClose + "\r\n";
        r += "* Volume: " + volume + "\r\n";
        r += "* Market Cap: " + marketCap + "B" + "\r\n";
        r += "* Change (%): " + change + " (" + percentageChange + "%)" + "\r\n";
        r += "* Annual range High / Low: " +
                annRangeHigh + " / " + annRangeLow + "\r\n";
        r += "* Earns: " + earns + "\r\n";
```

```
                r += "* P/E: " + pe + "\r\n";
                return r;
        }
    }
```

2. You need a way to instantiate a `Stock` object based on the response you receive from the web service. There are multiple ways to approach this. You can create an additional constructor, add a static method (e.g., `createStockFromXML`) to the `Stock` class, or abstract out this functionality using a separate class. In this exercise the last method is used, to keep your Stock class as clean as possible and to add a layer of abstraction between domain logic and web-service-oriented logic. As such, create a `StockFactory` class that will just contain some static methods to help instantiate a `Stock` object using a received SOAP reply:

```java
package withoutwsdlobjectoriented;

import java.io.IOException;
import java.io.StringReader;
import java.text.ParseException;
import java.text.SimpleDateFormat;
import java.util.Date;
import java.util.Locale;
import java.util.Set;
import java.util.HashSet;

import javax.xml.parsers.DocumentBuilder;
import javax.xml.parsers.DocumentBuilderFactory;
import javax.xml.parsers.ParserConfigurationException;
import javax.xml.soap.SOAPException;
import javax.xml.soap.SOAPMessage;

import org.w3c.dom.Document;
import org.w3c.dom.Element;
import org.w3c.dom.Node;
import org.w3c.dom.NodeList;
import org.xml.sax.InputSource;
import org.xml.sax.SAXException;

public class StockFactory {
    public static Set<Stock> newStocksFromSOAPReplyMessage(SOAPMessage soapResponse) {
        try {
            Node responseNode = soapResponse.getSOAPBody().getFirstChild();
            String xmlText = responseNode.getTextContent();
            return newStocksFromXMLString(xmlText);
        } catch (SOAPException e) {
            e.printStackTrace();
        }
        // If we end up here, something went wrong:
        return null;
    }

    public static Set<Stock> newStocksFromXMLString(String xmlText) {
        try {
            DocumentBuilderFactory factory = DocumentBuilderFactory.newInstance();
```

```java
        DocumentBuilder builder = factory.newDocumentBuilder();
        Document document =
            builder.parse(new InputSource(new StringReader(xmlText)));
        return newStocksFromXMLDocument(document);
    } catch (ParserConfigurationException e) {
        e.printStackTrace();
    } catch (SAXException e) {
        e.printStackTrace();
    } catch (IOException e) {
        e.printStackTrace();
    }
    // If we end up here, something went wrong:
    return null;
}

public static Set<Stock> newStocksFromXMLDocument(Document document) {
    Set<Stock> stocksSet = new HashSet<Stock>();
    NodeList stockElements = document.getElementsByTagName("Stock");
    for (int i = 0; i < stockElements.getLength(); i++) {
        Stock stock = newStockFromXMLElement(
            (Element) stockElements.item(i));
        stocksSet.add(stock);
    }
    return stocksSet;
}

public static Stock newStockFromXMLElement(Element node) {
    String symbol, name;
    double last, open, high, low, marketCap,
        previousClose, change, percentageChange, annRangeLow,
        annRangeHigh, earns, pe;
    long volume;
    Date timestamp;

    symbol = getEl(node, "Symbol");
    name = getEl(node, "Name");
    last = Double.parseDouble(getEl(node, "Last"));
    open = Double.parseDouble(getEl(node, "Open"));
    high = Double.parseDouble(getEl(node, "High"));
    low = Double.parseDouble(getEl(node, "Low"));
    volume = Long.parseLong(getEl(node, "Volume"));
    marketCap = Double.parseDouble(getEl(node, "MktCap").replace("B", ""));
    previousClose = Double.parseDouble(getEl(node, "PreviousClose"));
    percentageChange = Double.parseDouble(getEl(node, "PercentageChange")
            .replace("%", "")
            .replace("+", "")
            .replace("-", ""));
    change = Double.parseDouble(getEl(node, "Change")
            .replace("+", "")
            .replace("-", ""));
    String[] annRange = getEl(node, "AnnRange").split(" - ");
    annRangeLow = Double.parseDouble(annRange[0]);
    annRangeHigh = Double.parseDouble(annRange[1]);
    earns = Double.parseDouble(getEl(node, "Earns"));
    pe = Double.parseDouble(getEl(node, "P-E"));
```

```
            try {
                String fullDate = getEl(node, "Date")+" "+getEl(node, "Time");
                fullDate = fullDate.replace("pm", " pm").replace("am", " am");
                timestamp = new SimpleDateFormat("M/d/y K:m a",
                    Locale.ENGLISH).parse(fullDate);
            } catch (ParseException e) {
                e.printStackTrace();
                timestamp = new Date();
            }

            return new Stock(symbol, name,
                    last, open, high, low,
                    volume, timestamp, marketCap,
                    previousClose, change,
                    percentageChange, annRangeLow,
                    annRangeHigh, earns, pe);
        }

        private static String getEl(Element node, String n) {
            return node.getElementsByTagName(n).item(0).getTextContent();
        }

    }
```

3. Also define another helper class, called `StockServiceClient`, which will communicate with the SOAP service, like so:

```
package withoutwsdlobjectoriented;

import javax.xml.namespace.QName;
import javax.xml.soap.MessageFactory;
import javax.xml.soap.MimeHeaders;
import javax.xml.soap.SOAPBody;
import javax.xml.soap.SOAPBodyElement;
import javax.xml.soap.SOAPConnection;
import javax.xml.soap.SOAPConnectionFactory;
import javax.xml.soap.SOAPElement;
import javax.xml.soap.SOAPException;
import javax.xml.soap.SOAPMessage;

public class StockServiceClient {
    private final static String SERVICE_HOST = "http://www.webserviceX.NET/";
    private final static String SERVICE_METHOD = "GetQuote";
    private final static String SERVICE_ENDPOINT = "stockquote.asmx";

    public static SOAPMessage getStockQuote(String stockSymbol) {
        SOAPConnection soapConnection = null;
        try {
            SOAPConnectionFactory soapConnectionFactory =
                    SOAPConnectionFactory.newInstance();
            soapConnection =
                    soapConnectionFactory.createConnection();

            SOAPMessage soapResponse = soapConnection.call(
```

```
                        createSOAPRequest(stockSymbol),
                        SERVICE_HOST + SERVICE_ENDPOINT);

                soapConnection.close();

                return soapResponse;
            } catch (UnsupportedOperationException | SOAPException e) {
                e.printStackTrace();
            } finally {
                if (soapConnection != null)
                    try { soapConnection.close(); } catch (SOAPException i) {}
            }

            return null;
        }

        private static SOAPMessage createSOAPRequest(String stockSymbol) {
            try {
                MessageFactory messageFactory = MessageFactory.newInstance();
                SOAPMessage soapMessage = messageFactory.createMessage();

                SOAPBody soapBody = soapMessage.getSOAPBody();
                QName bodyName = new QName(SERVICE_HOST, SERVICE_METHOD);
                SOAPBodyElement bodyElement = soapBody.addBodyElement(bodyName);
                SOAPElement soapBodyArgument1 = bodyElement.addChildElement("symbol");
                soapBodyArgument1.addTextNode(stockSymbol);

                MimeHeaders headers = soapMessage.getMimeHeaders();
                headers.addHeader("SOAPAction", SERVICE_HOST + SERVICE_METHOD);

                soapMessage.saveChanges();

                return soapMessage;
            } catch (SOAPException e) {
                e.printStackTrace();
            }

            return null;
        }
    }
```

4. Finally, you can create a test class containing a main method, called StockQuoteProgram:

```
package withoutwsdlobjectoriented;

import java.util.Set;
import javax.xml.soap.SOAPMessage;

public class StockQuoteProgram {
    public static void main(String[] args) {
        SOAPMessage soapReply = StockServiceClient.getStockQuote("IBM");

        Set<Stock> stocks =
            StockFactory.newStocksFromSOAPReplyMessage(soapReply);
```

```
            for (Stock stock : stocks) {
                System.out.println(stock.toString());
            }
        }
    }
```

5. Run the program. If all goes well—the website or your Internet connection might be down—you should see the following:

```
STOCK IBM: International Bus
=============================
* Retrieved at: Thu Apr 17 16:02:00 CEST 2014
* Last / High / Low / Open: 190.01 / 190.7 / 187.01 / 187.29
* Previous close: 196.4
* Volume: 11255493
* Market Cap: 197.9B
* Change (%): 6.39 (3.25%)
* Annual range High / Low: 211.98 / 172.19
* Earns: 14.942
* P/E: 13.14
```

How It Works

Here's how it works:

1. In the `Stock` class, you created instance variables to hold all the information the web service will provide, together with a constructor to initialize `Stock` objects. You used private variables with generated getters and setters to do so. While it is generally a good idea to access data in objects from the outside world by using methods provided by the object (instead of using public fields), for "data-heavy" classes such as the `Stock` class, feel free to resort to public final fields if you don't want to make your code too verbose. Especially when none of the getters and the setters have side effects (meaning that they just return or change one field), this is an okay approach.

2. At this point, it might also be prudent to note that—generally speaking—it is not a good idea to store monetary values and amounts as doubles or floats, not only in Java, but in most programming languages. The reason for this is that the internal representation of a floating point number cannot accurately represent fractions, which will introduce subtle rounding errors over time once you start performing addition, multiplication, subtraction, and division on them, as monetary software tends to do. There are ways to work around this, for example, by using the built-in `BigDecimal` class in Java. For these exercises, it's simpler to work with doubles, but keep this remark in mind when working with monetary values in a real-life setting.

3. The `StockFactory` class includes a number of methods to construct a set of `Stock` objects from a received SOAP message. The `newStocksFromSOAPReplyMessage` method extracts the reply string from the message, which is then passed to a separate method, `newStocksFromXMLString`. This method converts the string to an XML document, which is then passed to another method, `newStocksFromXMLDocument`, which iterates over all the "Stock" tags and parses them using `newStockFromXMLElement`. `getEl` is a helper method defined to get the text content from the

first XML tag within a node given a specific tag name. Note that you need to parse some of the information you receive from the server. For example, since the server returns the string `"172.19 - 211.98"` to specify the annual range, you need to split up this string and parse it using `Double.parseDouble()` to store it in your variables. Note also the use of the `SimpleDateFormat` class to parse a string to a `Date` object.

4. `StockServiceClient` contains most of the same logic you've seen before to communicate with the SOAP service.

5. Finally, your now nimble `main` method just invokes the `StockServiceClient` and `StockFactory` classes to do the heavy lifting. You have neatly separated all aspects of this program—the domain logic (`Stock`), the service interaction logic (`StockServiceClient`), and the parsing logic (`StockFactory`). If you want, you can continue to expand on this program some more. For example, try expanding the `main` method to take a list of stock symbols, retrieve their information, and show a ranking based on price/earnings ratio.

Accessing SOAP Services with JAX-WS with WSDL

You have seen how to access a web service by constructing SOAP request messages manually. However, this method assumes that you are aware of the endpoints the service provides, the operations, and the parameters to be passed.

To overcome this issue, most SOAP-based web services provide a so-called WSDL file. WSDL, or "Web Services Description Language," is an XML format for describing network services and their endpoints, together with the operation they support and the arguments they expect. You can use the information stored in such files to allow JAX-WS to do a lot of the work for you.

Let's take another look at the Stock Quote service page at `WebserviceX.NET`: `http://www.webservicex.net/WS/WSDetails.aspx?CATID=2&WSID=9`. The description mentions that a WSDL file is provided at `http://www.webservicex.net/stockquote.asmx?WSDL`, which you can request with your web browser, and indeed looks like an XML document containing the following:

```
<wsdl:definitions xmlns:tm="http://microsoft.com/wsdl/mime/textMatching/"
xmlns:soapenc="http://schemas.xmlsoap.org/soap/encoding/"
xmlns:mime="http://schemas.xmlsoap.org/wsdl/mime/"
xmlns:tns="http://www.webserviceX.NET/"
xmlns:soap="http://schemas.xmlsoap.org/wsdl/soap/"
xmlns:s="http://www.w3.org/2001/XMLSchema"
xmlns:soap12="http://schemas.xmlsoap.org/wsdl/soap12/"
xmlns:http="http://schemas.xmlsoap.org/wsdl/http/"
xmlns:wsdl="http://schemas.xmlsoap.org/wsdl/"
targetNamespace="http://www.webserviceX.NET/">
  <wsdl:types>
    <s:schema elementFormDefault="qualified"
        targetNamespace="http://www.webserviceX.NET/">
    <s:element name="GetQuote">
    <s:complexType>
```

```
      <s:sequence>
      <s:element minOccurs="0" maxOccurs="1" name="symbol" type="s:string"/>
      </s:sequence>
      </s:complexType>
      </s:element>
      <s:element name="GetQuoteResponse">
      <s:complexType>
      <s:sequence>
      <s:element minOccurs="0" maxOccurs="1" name="GetQuoteResult" type="s:string"/>
      </s:sequence>
      </s:complexType>
      </s:element>
      <s:element name="string" nillable="true" type="s:string"/>
      </s:schema>
  </wsdl:types>

    <wsdl:message name="GetQuoteSoapIn">
        <wsdl:part name="parameters" element="tns:GetQuote"/>
    </wsdl:message>

    <wsdl:message name="GetQuoteSoapOut">
        <wsdl:part name="parameters" element="tns:GetQuoteResponse"/>
    </wsdl:message>

    <wsdl:message name="GetQuoteHttpGetIn">
        <wsdl:part name="symbol" type="s:string"/>
    </wsdl:message>

    <wsdl:message name="GetQuoteHttpGetOut">
        <wsdl:part name="Body" element="tns:string"/>
    </wsdl:message>

    <wsdl:message name="GetQuoteHttpPostIn">
        <wsdl:part name="symbol" type="s:string"/>
    </wsdl:message>

    <wsdl:message name="GetQuoteHttpPostOut">
        <wsdl:part name="Body" element="tns:string"/>
    </wsdl:message>

    <wsdl:portType name="StockQuoteSoap">
        <wsdl:operation name="GetQuote">
        <wsdl:documentation xmlns:wsdl="http://schemas.xmlsoap.org/wsdl/">
          Get Stock quote for a company Symbol</wsdl:documentation>
        <wsdl:input message="tns:GetQuoteSoapIn"/>
        <wsdl:output message="tns:GetQuoteSoapOut"/>
        </wsdl:operation>
    </wsdl:portType>

    <wsdl:portType name="StockQuoteHttpGet">
        <wsdl:operation name="GetQuote">
        <wsdl:documentation xmlns:wsdl="http://schemas.xmlsoap.org/wsdl/">
          Get Stock quote for a company Symbol</wsdl:documentation>
        <wsdl:input message="tns:GetQuoteHttpGetIn"/>
```

```
        <wsdl:output message="tns:GetQuoteHttpGetOut"/>
        </wsdl:operation>
</wsdl:portType>

<wsdl:portType name="StockQuoteHttpPost">
        <wsdl:operation name="GetQuote">
        <wsdl:documentation xmlns:wsdl="http://schemas.xmlsoap.org/wsdl/">
           Get Stock quote for a company Symbol</wsdl:documentation>
        <wsdl:input message="tns:GetQuoteHttpPostIn"/>
        <wsdl:output message="tns:GetQuoteHttpPostOut"/>
        </wsdl:operation>
</wsdl:portType>

<wsdl:binding name="StockQuoteSoap" type="tns:StockQuoteSoap">
        <soap:binding transport="http://schemas.xmlsoap.org/soap/http"/>
        <wsdl:operation name="GetQuote">
        <soap:operation soapAction="http://www.webserviceX.NET/GetQuote"
            style="document"/>
        <wsdl:input>
        <soap:body use="literal"/>
        </wsdl:input>
        <wsdl:output>
        <soap:body use="literal"/>
        </wsdl:output>
        </wsdl:operation>
</wsdl:binding>

<wsdl:binding name="StockQuoteSoap12" type="tns:StockQuoteSoap">
        <soap12:binding transport="http://schemas.xmlsoap.org/soap/http"/>
        <wsdl:operation name="GetQuote">
        <soap12:operation soapAction="http://www.webserviceX.NET/GetQuote"
            style="document"/>
        <wsdl:input>
        <soap12:body use="literal"/>
        </wsdl:input>
        <wsdl:output>
        <soap12:body use="literal"/>
        </wsdl:output>
        </wsdl:operation>
</wsdl:binding>

<wsdl:binding name="StockQuoteHttpGet" type="tns:StockQuoteHttpGet">
        <http:binding verb="GET"/>
        <wsdl:operation name="GetQuote">
        <http:operation location="/GetQuote"/>
        <wsdl:input>
        <http:urlEncoded/>
        </wsdl:input>
        <wsdl:output>
        <mime:mimeXml part="Body"/>
        </wsdl:output>
        </wsdl:operation>
</wsdl:binding>
```

```
        <wsdl:binding name="StockQuoteHttpPost" type="tns:StockQuoteHttpPost">
            <http:binding verb="POST"/>
            <wsdl:operation name="GetQuote">
            <http:operation location="/GetQuote"/>
            <wsdl:input>
            <mime:content type="application/x-www-form-urlencoded"/>
            </wsdl:input>
            <wsdl:output>
            <mime:mimeXml part="Body"/>
            </wsdl:output>
            </wsdl:operation>
        </wsdl:binding>

        <wsdl:service name="StockQuote">
            <wsdl:port name="StockQuoteSoap" binding="tns:StockQuoteSoap">
            <soap:address location="http://www.webservicex.net/stockquote.asmx"/>
            </wsdl:port>
            <wsdl:port name="StockQuoteSoap12" binding="tns:StockQuoteSoap12">
            <soap12:address location="http://www.webservicex.net/stockquote.asmx"/>
            </wsdl:port>
            <wsdl:port name="StockQuoteHttpGet" binding="tns:StockQuoteHttpGet">
            <http:address location="http://www.webservicex.net/stockquote.asmx"/>
            </wsdl:port>
            <wsdl:port name="StockQuoteHttpPost" binding="tns:StockQuoteHttpPost">
            <http:address location="http://www.webservicex.net/stockquote.asmx"/>
            </wsdl:port>
        </wsdl:service>
    </wsdl:definitions>
```

Certainly, this is a pretty hefty WSDL descriptor, but it does provide a good general overview on how they are defined. First, the WSDL document lists a number of types that are used throughout the service. Note the `symbol` and `GetQuoteResult` types. By looking at `GetQuoteResult`, there's no doubt that this type provides a single string that you will need to parse. Next, the WSDL document lists a number of messages to define the various messages that will be interchanged. These are used in the definition of WSDL "ports." For example, `StockQuoteHttpPost` indicates that it's possible to interchange messages by an HTTP POST request to perform the `GetQuote` operation, and it will use the `GetQuoteHttpPostIn` and `GetQuoteHttpPostOut` messages to do so (which is exactly what you're doing when trying out the service using your browser, as seen earlier). Finally, to make ports available for public access, they need to be "bound" to endpoints. You can see, for example, that a binding named `StockQuoteSoap` has been defined for the `GetQuote` operation, which is bound to the endpoint `http://www.webserviceX.NET/GetQuote`.

While WSDL files are certainly not meant for human reading, they do provide a means to easily construct clients to consume the web services defined therein.

Here you will see how to use the `wsimport` tool provided by JAX-WS. Contrary to what we've seen thus far, you'll now need to have the Java Development Kit (JDK) installed. The tool itself is located in the `bin` folder of your JDK installation.

Next, open a command prompt and navigate to the location of the `wsimport` executable (using the `cd` command, as shown in Figure 10-10). Most likely, you will get the error message shown in Figure 10-10.

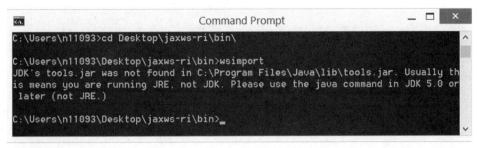

FIGURE 10-10

To fix this, you'll need to explicitly provide the location of the JDK. Depending on the version you installed and the architecture you're using, this might either be located in `C:\Program Files\Java\jdk*VERSION*` or `C:\Program Files (x86)\Java\jdk*VERSION*`. Make sure to check the exact location. In this case, it's `C:\Program Files\Java\jdk1.8.0_05`. Execute the following command to point `wsimport` in the right direction:

```
set JAVA_HOME=C:\Program Files\Java\jdk1.8.0_05
```

Run `wsimport` again; you should now get back some helpful information, as shown in Figure 10-11.

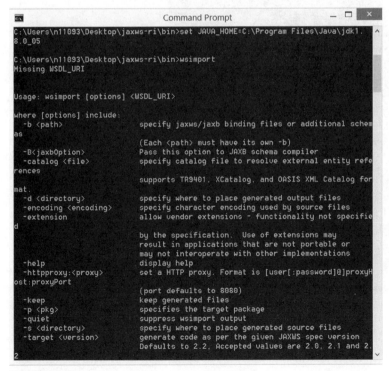

FIGURE 10-11

> **NOTE** *You'll need to execute the* `set JAVA_HOME` *command every time you want to run* `wsimport` *and open a command prompt. If you want to avoid this, you can also edit the* `wsimport.bat` *file in a text editor and add the command after the* `:LAUNCH` *line, so it looks like this:*
>
> ```
> :LAUNCH
> set JAVA_HOME=C:\Program Files\Java\jdk1.8.0_05
> %JAVA% %WSIMPORT_OPTS% -jar "%JAXWS_HOME%\lib\jaxws-tools.jar" %*
> ```

Try to execute `wsimport` using the WSDL URL:

```
wsimport http://www.webservicex.net/stockquote.asmx?WSDL
```

However, you'll get an error message telling you that a schema document could not be read because file access is not allowed, as shown in Figure 10-12.

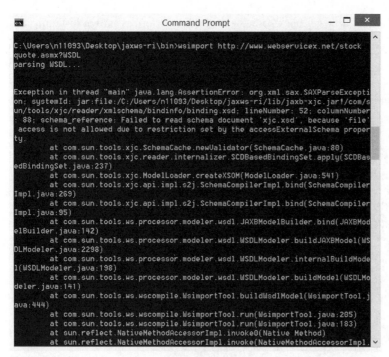

FIGURE 10-12

To work around this, you need to set another variable, called `WSIMPORT_OPTS`, with the following command:

```
set WSIMPORT_OPTS=-Djavax.xml.accessExternalSchema=all
```

Pay close attention when entering this command (there is only one space and note the capitalization). Once you've executed this command, you can run `wsimport` again. You should now get the results shown in Figure 10-13.

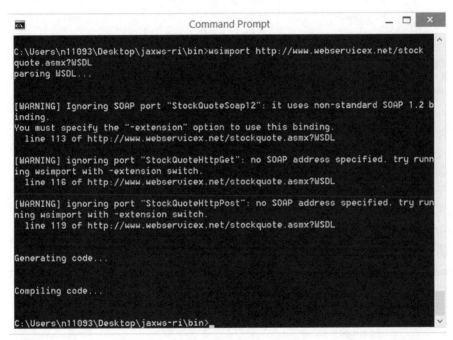

FIGURE 10-13

`wsimport` is warning you that it found some ports that are not SOAP-specific or using a non-standard binding. You can safely ignore this warning, as you're interested in the SOAP 1.1 endpoint only.

What has happened here? `wsimport` downloaded the WSDL file, parsed its contents, constructed some classes, and compiled them, placing them in the location where you executed the tool (the `bin` folder in this case). If you take a look with the file explorer, you'll see that a new folder called `net` has been added, as shown in Figure 10-14.

When exploring this folder deeper, you'll see a listing of class files, as shown in Figure 10-15.

These generated class files can immediately be used in your project to interact with the web service. However, since you would like to take a look at the generated source code, run the `wsimport` tool again, but this time with the `-keep` option set, like so:

```
wsimport -keep http://www.webservicex.net/stockquote.asmx?WSDL
```

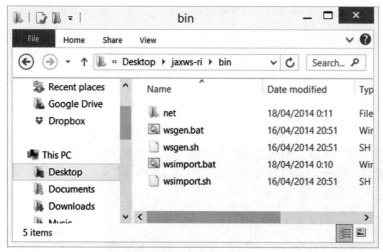

FIGURE 10-14

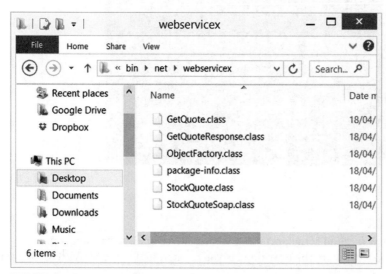

FIGURE 10-15

The generated files will now also include Java source files. Now, take a look at them in Eclipse. You can continue to use the SOAPWithJava project, as this contains the references to JAX-WS, but you can also set up a new project if you want. Create a new package in Eclipse called net .webservicex, and drag all the .java files (you should have six of them) located in the net\ webservicex folder to this package in the Eclipse package explorer.

Take a look at the classes wsimport has generated:

➤   package-info is a meta file containing no real information.

➤   ObjectFactory is a Factory class containing methods to create GetQuote and GetQuoteResponse objects.

> ➤ StockQuote is a class to wrap access to the service, with methods returning StockQuoteSoap objects to access one of the service endpoints.

> ➤ StockQuoteSoap is a class to wrap access to an endpoint provided by the service, in this case a SOAP endpoint. It contains a single method, called getQuote, to perform the GetQuote operation.

> ➤ GetQuote and GetQuoteResponse wrap the XML messages themselves.

Based on the classes wsimport has created for you from the WSDL file, it becomes very easy to access SOAP services. You no longer have to be concerned with manually constructing the SOAP request message with the proper parameters and knowing the endpoints you need to access. Try this out by creating a new class called ClientWithWSDL:

```java
package withwsdl;

import net.webservicex.StockQuote;
import net.webservicex.StockQuoteSoap;

public class ClientWithWSDL {
    public static void main(String[] args) {
        StockQuote service = new StockQuote();
        StockQuoteSoap soapService = service.getStockQuoteSoap();

        String stock = soapService.getQuote("IBM");

        System.out.println(stock);
    }
}
```

Just as before, this should give you the following output (note that executing this code might take some time):

```
<StockQuotes><Stock><Symbol>IBM</Symbol><Last>190.01</Last><Date>4/17/2014</Date>
<Time>4:02pm</Time><Change>-
6.39</Change><Open>187.29</Open><High>190.70</High><Low>187.01</Low>
<Volume>11255493</Volume><MktCap>197.9B</MktCap><PreviousClose>196.40
</PreviousClose><PercentageChange>-3.25%</PercentageChange><AnnRange>
172.19 - 211.98</AnnRange><Earns>14.942</Earns><P-E>13.14</P-E>
<Name>International Bus</Name></Stock></StockQuotes>
```

You only need to use the service-providing classes. All the rest is dealt with automatically. The ObjectFactory class is used by the service classes to construct the GetQuote and GetQuoteResponse objects—you do not need to construct them manually, but can instead call your desired method directly with the stock symbol ("IBM") as the method argument.

Naturally, since this SOAP service is still returning a single string, you still need to perform the parsing of this string manually, just like earlier:

```java
package withwsdl;

import java.io.IOException;
import java.io.StringReader;

import javax.xml.parsers.DocumentBuilder;
import javax.xml.parsers.DocumentBuilderFactory;
```

```
import javax.xml.parsers.ParserConfigurationException;
import org.w3c.dom.Document;
import org.w3c.dom.NodeList;
import org.xml.sax.InputSource;
import org.xml.sax.SAXException;

import net.webservicex.StockQuote;
import net.webservicex.StockQuoteSoap;

public class ClientWithWSDL {
    public static void main(String[] args) {
        StockQuote service = new StockQuote();
        StockQuoteSoap soapService = service.getStockQuoteSoap();
        String stock = soapService.getQuote("IBM");

        showSOAPResponse(stock);
    }

    private static void showSOAPResponse(String responseString) {
        Document document = null;

        try {
            DocumentBuilderFactory factory = DocumentBuilderFactory.newInstance();
            DocumentBuilder builder = factory.newDocumentBuilder();
            document = builder.parse(new InputSource(
                    new StringReader(responseString)));
        } catch (SAXException | IOException | ParserConfigurationException e) {
            e.printStackTrace();
            return;
        }

        NodeList stockElements = document.getElementsByTagName("Stock");
        for (int i = 0; i < stockElements.getLength(); i++) {
            System.out.println("----- Stock nr. " + i + " ------");
            NodeList infoElements = stockElements.item(i).getChildNodes();
            for (int j = 0; j < infoElements.getLength(); j++) {
                System.out.println(infoElements.item(j).getNodeName() +
                        "\t --> " +
                        infoElements.item(j).getTextContent());
            }
        }
    }
}
```

In most cases, it's best to access SOAP services in this manner, i.e., by using wsimport to generate service-wrapping classes and use those in your projects. One final remark concerns the fact that the WSDL file will continue to be accessed by the generated classes every time you use them. To see how, take a look at the generated StockQuote class and note the following lines:

```
static {
    URL url = null;
    WebServiceException e = null;
    try {
```

```
        url = new URL("http://www.webservicex.net/stockquote.asmx?WSDL");
    } catch (MalformedURLException ex) {
        e = new WebServiceException(ex);
    }
    STOCKQUOTE_WSDL_LOCATION = url;
    STOCKQUOTE_EXCEPTION = e;
}
```

> **NOTE** The code snippet that shows the generated `StockQuote` class
> shows a so-called "static block," which you have not worked with explic-
> itly before. Static code blocks are helpful when you want to instantiate
> some static variables, but need to catch some error conditions with a
> `try-catch` block as well, as can be observed here. Just typing the follow-
> ing would not work, as Java expects you to catch a possible exception—a
> `MalformedURLException`—which can occur during the instantiation of an URL
> object:
>
> ```
>     private final static URL STOCKQUOTE_WSDL_LOCATION = new
>         URL("http://www.webservicex.net/stockquote.asmx?WSDL");
> ```

To speed up the code somewhat, and to prevent the code from breaking down when the WSDL file is unavailable (but the SOAP service itself still works), it's also possible to store this file on your local machine.

To do so, navigate to `http://www.webservicex.net/stockquote.asmx?WSDL` in your web browser and save this file somewhere, for instance on your desktop, as `stockquote.wsdl`. Next, in Eclipse, right-click the `SOAPWithJava` project in the package explorer (or on your project name if you're using a different one) and create a new "Folder" (not a "Source Folder"). Call it `wsdl`. See Figure 10-16.

Next, drag your saved `stockquote.wsdl` file over to the `wsdl` folder in the package explorer and create a copy (you may now remove your originally saved file). Next, edit the code in `StockQuote` to look like the following:

```
static {
    ClassLoader classloader = Thread.currentThread().getContextClassLoader();
        WebServiceException e = null;
        URL url = classloader.getResource("wsdl/stockquote.wsdl");
        STOCKQUOTE_WSDL_LOCATION = url;
        STOCKQUOTE_EXCEPTION = e;
}
```

The generated class will now use the locally stored WSDL file instead of retrieving it online.

You have now seen how to access SOAP web services, both by constructing SOAP messages manually and by using the `wsimport` tool to automatically generate classes. Obviously, in most cases, the functionality offered by `wsimport` is the recommended way to write clients using SOAP

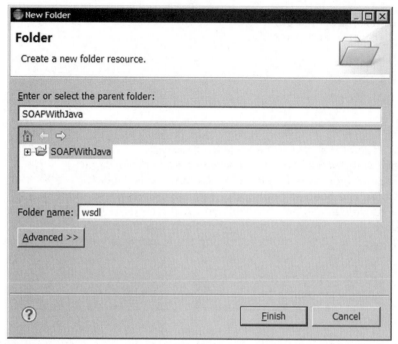

FIGURE 10-16

services. Again, take some time to go over all the code you've seen to make sure you understand everything. If you're up for it, you can try some of the other web services offered at WebserviceX. NET and see if you can get them to work with wsimport.

One aspect of SOAP you'll probably agree on is the fact that its services are not really "simple" at all. They involve a wealth of protocols and message formats, involving terminology such as ports, bindings, and endpoints. In enterprise environments, however, SOAP services remain very popular, so it is helpful to know how to access them in the programs you write. In the next section, you'll take a look at a simpler web service "standard," which is not really a standard, but more like an agreed-upon method to access web sources using the infrastructure that's already in place to serve websites to end users: HTTP.

Accessing REST Services

REST stands for "Representational State Transfer" and describes a simple, common methodology for accessing ad hoc web services. In recent years, it has become the methodology of choice by "modern" web companies to provide APIs to access their information.

Recall from the introduction that one of the biggest differences between REST and SOAP is that REST is stateless and SOAP is stateful. However, as you've seen in the preceding section, since many SOAP services do not track state (in fact, only complex SOAP services do), this is not really an issue for most applications.

Recall also that REST builds heavily on the existing HTTP protocol. If you're very observant, you might recall that SOAP can wrap its messages inside the HTTP protocol. Take, for instance, the example provided by `WebserviceX.NET` to access the stock quote service:

```
POST /stockquote.asmx HTTP/1.1
Host: www.webservicex.net
Content-Type: text/xml; charset=utf-8
Content-Length: length
SOAPAction: "http://www.webserviceX.NET/GetQuote"

<?xml version="1.0" encoding="utf-8"?>
<soap:Envelope xmlns:xsi="http://www.w3.org/2001/XMLSchema-instance"
    xmlns:xsd="http://www.w3.org/2001/XMLSchema"
    xmlns:soap="http://schemas.xmlsoap.org/soap/envelope/">
        <soap:Body>
            <GetQuote xmlns="http://www.webserviceX.NET/">
                <symbol>string</symbol>
            </GetQuote>
        </soap:Body>
</soap:Envelope>
```

So what is the difference here? In SOAP, the HTTP protocol is just one way to "encapsulate" a SOAP message. Other methods exist. For example, it is possible to send SOAP messages over the so-called SMTP protocol, the Simple Mail Transfer Protocol that is used to send e-mails. When you are coding SOAP clients, however, JAX-WS assumes by default that you're going to send SOAP messages over HTTP, and the main concern then is to construct the actual XML SOAP message.

In REST, the HTTP protocol *is* the complete exchange protocol, meaning that REST basically instructs programmers to use the same protocol as your web browser uses to access websites, with the difference being that web servers will not return HTML data to be rendered by a web browser, but structured data that can be parsed by a computer. This can be in XML as well, but with the difference that this XML will not contain any of the SOAP-defined tags. For example, you could send the following HTTP GET request to a RESTful web service:

```
GET /stockquote/IBM HTTP/1.1
Host: www.example.com
Connection: keep-alive
Accept: application/xml
```

And simply get back the following reply:

```
HTTP/1.0 200 OK
Content-Type: application/xml

<StockQuotes>
    <Stock>
        <Symbol>IBM</Symbol>
        <Last>190.01</Last>
        <Date>4/17/2014</Date>
```

```
            <Time>4:02pm</Time>
            <Change>-6.39</Change>
            <Open>187.29</Open>
            <High>190.70</High>
            <Low>187.01</Low>
            <Volume>11255493</Volume>
            <MktCap>197.9B</MktCap>
            <PreviousClose>196.40</PreviousClose>
            <PercentageChange>-3.25%</PercentageChange>
            <AnnRange>172.19 - 211.98</AnnRange>
            <Earns>14.942</Earns>
            <P-E>13.14</P-E>
            <Name>International Bus</Name>
        </Stock>
    </StockQuotes>
```

The idea behind REST stems from the realization that most web services just provide simple request-reply functionality, for which HTTP is already perfectly suited, and thus extra standards, such as SOAP, which add extra overhead and complexity, are not needed. REST just uses HTTP as-is, with some extra conventions added to it—one of them being that messages should be structured to be parsed and understood by machines, and the other one being that HTTP methods other than GET and POST (used by your browser) should be used on a structured set of URLs, either on an URL representing a collection (http://www.example.com/books) or specific resource elements (http://www.example.com/books/B101). To repeat, the four common HTTP methods being used are:

➤ GET: Retrieves a list of resources belonging to a collection or a formatted representation of information on a resource element.

➤ PUT: Replaces the entire collection with a new one, or replaces the resource element with a new one, or creates a resource element if its identifier does not exist.

➤ POST: Creates a new entry in a collection or creates a new entry in a resource element (less commonly used).

➤ DELETE: Deletes an entire collection or a resource element.

Do keep in mind, however, that unlike SOAP, REST does not have an official standard, so different APIs may apply different conventions in terms of how they deal with these HTTP methods. Some providers choose to use GET and POST only, or to define different URLs to deal with different actions (/book/retrieve/B101, /book/insert/B101, and so on). However, since RESTful web services are easy to understand—as they're built straight on top of HTTP—perusing the documentation given by the service provider is in most cases enough to get going.

Accessing REST Services Without Authentication

To get started, you will see how you can access a REST service without authentication. As before, the examples use publicly offered services, the first of which is a simple service located at http://www.thomas-bayer.com/sqlrest/.

Try opening this URL in your web browser. You'll see the results shown in Figure 10-17.

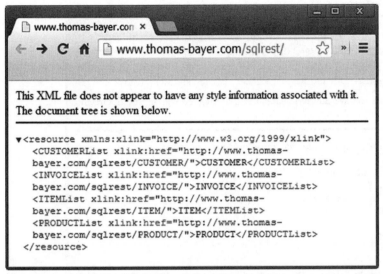

FIGURE 10-17

Now try following the link `http://www.thomas-bayer.com/sqlrest/CUSTOMER/`, which is a collection URL and thus provides a list of customers. See Figure 10-18.

Now try accessing a specific customer, e.g., `http://www.thomas-bayer.com/sqlrest/CUSTOMER/8/`, which is a resource element. See Figure 10-19.

FIGURE 10-18

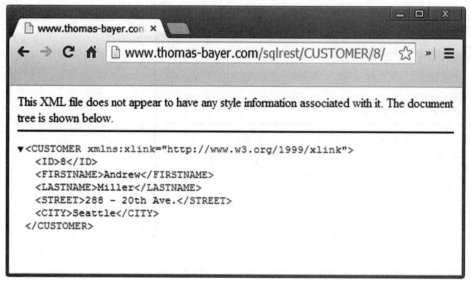

FIGURE 10-19

As you can observe, your browser is making simple HTTP GET requests to specified, agreed-upon URLs and getting back structured information, in this case formatted as XML.

To access REST web services using Java, you'll need a way to work with the HTTP protocol directly. Many good libraries exist to do so, but for now, take a look at Java's built-in HTTP connection class: `java.net.HttpURLConnection`. Create a new project in Eclipse—RESTWithJava—and use it throughout this section.

Instead of writing Java code like a script (as you've done before to show off SOAP services), make sure the resources you request from the web service are immediately converted to objects, which is the proper object-oriented way to go. If you take a look at the web service, you'll see that it defines four kinds of resources:

➤ A customer: With an ID, first name, last name, street, and city

➤ An invoice: With an ID, which is the customer ID the invoice relates to and a total sum

➤ A product: With an ID, name, and price

➤ An item line: Relates to an invoice, a product, quantity, and total cost

You can verify this by exploring the other URLs in your browser. You should create classes to represent each of these and place them in the `com.thomasbayer.sqlrest` package, starting with a customer:

```
package com.thomasbayer.sqlrest;

public class Customer {
    private int id;
    private String firstName, lastName;
```

```java
private String street, city;

public Customer(int id) {
    this.id = id;
}

public Customer(int id,
        String firstName, String lastName,
        String street, String city) {
    this(id);
    this.firstName = firstName;
    this.lastName = lastName;
    this.street = street;
    this.city = city;
}

public int getId() {
    return id;
}

public String getFirstName() {
    return firstName;
}

public void setFirstName(String firstName) {
    this.firstName = firstName;
}

public String getLastName() {
    return lastName;
}

public void setLastName(String lastName) {
    this.lastName = lastName;
}

public String getStreet() {
    return street;
}

public void setStreet(String street) {
    this.street = street;
}

public String getCity() {
    return city;
}

public void setCity(String city) {
    this.city = city;
}

public String toString() {
    return String.format(
        "Customer[#%s: %s, %s -- %s, %s]",
```

```
                  id, lastName, firstName,
                  street, city);
     }
  }
```

Recall that you can use the "Generate Getters and Setters. . ." function under "Source" when right-clicking in Eclipse's code window to generate getter and setter methods. Note also that here the `String.format` method is used to format the string representation in the `toString` method. This is a more readable alternative than having to work with long, concatenated strings.

Next up, create a class to represent a product:

```java
package com.thomasbayer.sqlrest;

public class Product {
    private int id;
    private String name;
    private double price;

    public Product(int id) {
        this.id = id;
    }

    public Product(int id, String name, double price) {
        this(id);
        this.name = name;
        this.price = price;
    }

    public int getId() {
        return id;
    }

    public String getName() {
        return name;
    }

    public void setName(String name) {
        this.name = name;
    }

    public double getPrice() {
        return price;
    }

    public void setPrice(double price) {
        this.price = price;
    }

    public String toString() {
        return String.format(
            "Product #%s: %s: priced at %s",
            id, name, price);
    }
```

```
    }
```

Followed by an invoice:

```
package com.thomasbayer.sqlrest;

import java.util.ArrayList;
import java.util.List;

public class Invoice {
    private int id;
    private Customer customer;
    private double totalSum;
    private final List<Item> items;

    public Invoice(int id) {
        this.id = id;
        this.items = new ArrayList<Item>();
    }

    public Invoice(int id, Customer customer, double totalSum, List<Item> items) {
        this(id);
        this.customer = customer;
        this.totalSum = totalSum;
        this.items.addAll(items);
    }

    public Customer getCustomer() {
        return customer;
    }

    public void setCustomer(Customer customer) {
        this.customer = customer;
    }

    public double getTotalSum() {
        return totalSum;
    }

    public void setTotalSum(double totalSum) {
        this.totalSum = totalSum;
    }

    public int getId() {
        return id;
    }

    public void addItem(Item item) {
        items.add(item);
    }

    public void removeItem(Item item) {
        items.remove(item);
    }
```

```java
    public List<Item> getItems() {
        return new ArrayList<Item>(items);
    }

    public void setItems(List<Item> items) {
        this.items.clear();
        this.items.addAll(items);
    }

    public String toString() {
        return String.format(
            "Invoice #%s: total sum %s" +
            "%n%s",
            id, totalSum,
            customer );
    }
}
```

And finally, an item:

```java
package com.thomasbayer.sqlrest;

public class Item {
    private Invoice invoice;
    private Product product;
    private int quantity;
    private double cost;

    public Item(Invoice invoice, Product product) {
        this.invoice = invoice;
        this.product = product;
    }

    public Item(Invoice invoice, Product product, int quantity, double cost) {
        this(invoice, product);
        this.quantity = quantity;
        this.cost = cost;
    }

    public Invoice getInvoice() {
        return invoice;
    }

    public Product getProduct() {
        return product;
    }

    public int getQuantity() {
        return quantity;
    }

    public void setQuantity(int quantity) {
        this.quantity = quantity;
    }
```

```java
    public double getCost() {
        return cost;
    }

    public void setCost(double cost) {
        this.cost = cost;
    }

    public String toString() {
        return String.format(
            "Item: quantity: %s, cost: %s" +
            "%n%s" +
            "%n%s",
            quantity, cost,
            invoice,
            product);
    }
}
```

Next, create a `RestServiceClient` class to communicate with the web service:

```java
package com.thomasbayer.sqlrest;

import java.io.BufferedReader;
import java.io.IOException;
import java.io.InputStreamReader;
import java.io.StringReader;
import java.io.StringWriter;
import java.net.HttpURLConnection;
import java.net.URL;

import javax.xml.parsers.DocumentBuilder;
import javax.xml.parsers.DocumentBuilderFactory;
import javax.xml.parsers.ParserConfigurationException;
import javax.xml.transform.Transformer;
import javax.xml.transform.TransformerException;
import javax.xml.transform.TransformerFactory;
import javax.xml.transform.dom.DOMSource;
import javax.xml.transform.stream.StreamResult;

import org.w3c.dom.Document;
import org.xml.sax.InputSource;
import org.xml.sax.SAXException;

public class RestServiceClient {
    private final static String URL_API_ROOT =
      "http://www.thomas-bayer.com/sqlrest/";

    public enum Resource {
        CUSTOMER, PRODUCT, INVOICE, ITEM
    };

    public Document getResourceCollection(Resource resource) {
```

```java
        return stringToXMLDocument(getHttpUrl(URL_API_ROOT + resource.name()));
    }

    public Document getResourceItem(Resource resource, int itemId) {
        return stringToXMLDocument(
          getHttpUrl(URL_API_ROOT + resource.name() + "/" + itemId));
    }

    public String getHttpUrl(String url) {
        HttpURLConnection connection = null;
        try {
            URL u = new URL(url);
            connection = (HttpURLConnection) u.openConnection();
            // We will be making GET requests only to this service
            connection.setRequestMethod("GET");
            connection.connect();
            int responseCode = connection.getResponseCode();
            if (responseCode != HttpURLConnection.HTTP_OK) {
                // We got a non 200 (OK) status code: error or server is down
                System.err.println("Server returned status code: " + responseCode);
                return null;
            }
            // Fetch the response from the server
            StringBuilder stringBuilder = new StringBuilder();
            // getInputStream is data coming back from the server
            // getOutputStream is meant for sending data to the server
            try (BufferedReader reader = new BufferedReader(
                    new InputStreamReader(connection.getInputStream(), "UTF-8"))) {
                String s;
                while ((s = reader.readLine()) != null) {
                    stringBuilder.append(s + "\n");
                }
            } catch (IOException e) {
                e.printStackTrace();
            }
            connection.disconnect();
            return stringBuilder.toString();
        } catch (IOException e) {
            e.printStackTrace();
        } finally {
            if (connection != null)
                connection.disconnect();
        }
        return null;
    }

    static public Document stringToXMLDocument(String xmlText) {
        try {
            DocumentBuilderFactory factory = DocumentBuilderFactory.newInstance();
            DocumentBuilder builder = factory.newDocumentBuilder();
            Document document = builder.parse(new InputSource(
                    new StringReader(xmlText)));
            return document;
        } catch (ParserConfigurationException | SAXException | IOException e) {
            e.printStackTrace();
```

```
        }
        return null;
    }

    public static void main(String args[]) throws TransformerException {
        // Testing our RestServiceClient
        RestServiceClient client = new RestServiceClient();

        // Set up a transformer to properly convert an XML document to a string
        Document d;
        TransformerFactory tf = TransformerFactory.newInstance();
        Transformer transformer = tf.newTransformer();

        // Test collection URL
        StringWriter writer = new StringWriter();
        d = client.getResourceCollection(Resource.CUSTOMER);
        transformer.transform(new DOMSource(d), new StreamResult(writer));
        System.out.println(writer);

        // Test item URL
        writer = new StringWriter();
        d = client.getResourceItem(Resource.PRODUCT, 3);
        transformer.transform(new DOMSource(d), new StreamResult(writer));
        System.out.println(writer);
    }
}
```

Pay particular attention to the `HttpUrlConnection` class used here to establish an HTTP connection and get a response from the server. This object exposes two streams using the `getInputStream` and `getOutputStream` methods. The first enables you to get information from the server (the input), whereas the second allows you to send information to the server (the output), which you do not have to use here as the URL on its own is enough for the server to know which information you want to retrieve. A short `main` method is added here to test the functionality of this class, using a Transformer to convert an XML document back to a string (just using `toString()` will not work for document objects). Finally, note that a `BufferedReader` is used together with a `StringBuilder` object to quickly construct a string of the HTTP response received.

Next up, create an `ObjectFactory` to convert received XML replies to your Java objects:

```
package com.thomasbayer.sqlrest;

import java.util.ArrayList;
import java.util.List;

import org.w3c.dom.Document;
import org.w3c.dom.Element;
import org.w3c.dom.Node;
import org.w3c.dom.NodeList;

import com.thomasbayer.sqlrest.RestServiceClient.Resource;

public class ObjectFactory {
    private final static RestServiceClient client = new RestServiceClient();
```

```java
public static int[] getCustomerIds() {
    return getCollectionIds(Resource.CUSTOMER);
}

public static int[] getProductIds() {
    return getCollectionIds(Resource.PRODUCT);
}

public static int[] getItemIds() {
    return getCollectionIds(Resource.ITEM);
}

public static int[] getInvoiceIds() {
    return getCollectionIds(Resource.INVOICE);
}

public static Customer createCustomer(int id) {
    Document document = client.getResourceItem(Resource.CUSTOMER, id);
    Customer customer = new Customer(id);
    customer.setFirstName(getEl(document, "FIRSTNAME"));
    customer.setLastName(getEl(document, "LASTNAME"));
    customer.setStreet(getEl(document, "STREET"));
    customer.setCity(getEl(document, "CITY"));
    return customer;
}

public static Product createProduct(int id) {
    Document document = client.getResourceItem(Resource.PRODUCT, id);
    Product product = new Product(id);
    product.setName(getEl(document, "NAME"));
    product.setPrice(Double.parseDouble(getEl(document, "PRICE")));
    return product;
}

public static Invoice createInvoice(int id) {
    Document document = client.getResourceItem(Resource.INVOICE, id);
    Invoice invoice = new Invoice(id);
    invoice.setCustomer(
            createCustomer(Integer.parseInt(getEl(document, "CUSTOMERID"))));
    invoice.setTotalSum(Double.parseDouble(getEl(document, "TOTAL")));
    invoice.setItems(createItems(id, invoice));
    return invoice;
}

public static List<Item> createItems(int id, Invoice invoice) {
    Item item;
    Product product = null;
    int quantity = 0;
    double cost = 0D;
    Document document = client.getResourceItem(Resource.ITEM, id);
    List<Item> items = new ArrayList<Item>();
    if (document.getChildNodes().getLength() == 0)
        return items;
    NodeList children = document.getChildNodes().item(0).getChildNodes();
    // Loop over the XML document
```

```
        for (int i = 0; i < children.getLength(); i++) {
            Node node = children.item(i);
            switch (node.getNodeName()) {
            case "PRODUCTID":
                product = createProduct(Integer.parseInt(node.getTextContent()));
                break;
            case "QUANTITY":
                quantity = Integer.parseInt(node.getTextContent());
                break;
            case "COST":
                cost = Double.parseDouble(node.getTextContent());
                // This is the last line, commit our item to the list
                item = new Item(invoice, product, quantity, cost);
                items.add(item);
                break;
            default:
                break;
            }
        }


        return items;
    }
    private static int[] getCollectionIds(Resource resource) {
        Document document = client.getResourceCollection(resource);
        NodeList elements = document.getElementsByTagName(resource.name());
        int[] ids = new int[elements.getLength()];
        for (int i = 0; i < ids.length; i++) {
          ids[i] = Integer.parseInt(((Element) elements.item(i)).getTextContent());
        }
        return ids;
    }

    private static String getEl(Document document, String n) {
        return document.getElementsByTagName(n).item(0).getTextContent();
    }

}
```

Finally, you can create a `RestClientProgram` class to test what you've built:

```
package com.thomasbayer.sqlrest;

public class RestClientProgram {
    public static void main(String[] args) {
        int[] customerIds = ObjectFactory.getCustomerIds();

        System.out.println("----------- Collection test -----------");
        System.out.println("First three customer ids: " +
                customerIds[0] + ", " +
                customerIds[1] + ", " +
                customerIds[2]);
```

```
        System.out.println("---------- Customer test ----------");
        Customer customer = ObjectFactory.createCustomer(customerIds[1]);
        System.out.println(customer);

        System.out.println("---------- Product test ----------");
        Product product = ObjectFactory.createProduct(0);
        System.out.println(product);

        System.out.println("---------- Invoice test ----------");
        Invoice invoice = ObjectFactory.createInvoice(0);
        System.out.println(invoice);

        System.out.println("---------- Invoice items test ----------");
        System.out.println(invoice.getItems());
    }
}
```

If you run this class, you should get something like the following:

```
---------- Collection test ----------
First three customer ids: 0, 1, 2
---------- Customer test ----------
Customer #1: King, Susanne – 366 - 20th Ave., Olten
---------- Product test ----------
Product #0: Iron Iron: priced at 5.4
---------- Invoice test ----------
Invoice #0: total sum 2607.6
Customer #0: Steel, Laura – 429 Seventh Av., Dallas
---------- Invoice items test ----------
[Item: quantity: 12, cost: 12.6
Invoice #0: total sum 2607.6
Customer #0: Steel, Laura -- 429 Seventh Av., Dallas
Product #7: Telephone Shoe: priced at 8.4, Item: quantity: 19, cost: 18.6
Invoice #0: total sum 2607.6
Customer #0: Steel, Laura -- 429 Seventh Av., Dallas
Product #14: Telephone Iron: priced at 12.4, Item: quantity: 3, cost: 26.7
```

That's all there is to the basics of accessing RESTful web services. Note that the essential code is found in the `RestServiceClient` class, where the `HttpUrlConnection` class is used to establish the connection. All the other classes deal with parsing the responses received from the server and establishing an object representation for them.

> **NOTE** If you've already worked through the previous chapter on databases, you might recognize that what is built here is quite similar to Object Relational Mapping (ORM), where the relational structure of a database is mapped to objects in Java, abstracting the aspect of having to deal with SQL manually by or and just working with plain objects and their methods. What you're doing here is similar: abstracting communication with the REST service in a separate class.

Again, take some time to explore this code at your own leisure. One "issue" that's still present is that you are creating objects in an ad hoc manner, even if an object might already exist. For instance, if you create two `Invoice` objects belonging to the same customer, the customer information is requested twice, and two separate `Customer` objects are created containing the same information. You might try to modify the code to work around this. To do so, you need a global set of object "managing" classes, which keep track of a set of objects (customers, for instance). This class can then provide a method—e.g., `createOrGetCustomer`—that returns a `Customer` object for a given ID if it has been created earlier (stored in a map, for example) or fetches and creates a new `Customer` object and returns that one (after adding it to its map for quick retrieval later). You can also try to add constructors to the resource objects to create a resource by fetching information from a web service (using the `ObjectFactory`), instead of directly accessing the methods of `ObjectFactory`. You will often have to think about these kinds of architectural decisions when writing more complex programs. Different solutions to solve the same problem exist, and depending on your needs, you might need to add more abstraction or managing classes. As you get more experienced in programming in Java, the right "patterns" to use for a given circumstance will present themselves more quickly and easily, but don't be afraid to iterate over your code and refactor when necessary.

> **NOTE** *Another interesting aspect is the way to fetch "related" objects. For example, when an* `Invoice` *object is created, the information for* `Customer` *is requested immediately to construct a* `Customer` *object and store this in the* `Invoice` *object. This technique is called "eager" loading, where you immediately request all information you need, potentially leading to slower code. For instance, consider an object with a very large related object. If you only need basic information, eagerly loading the related object leads to bandwidth and time overhead.*
>
> *As such, it would be possible to adapt your classes to only store the customer ID for an invoice, for instance, and keep the* `Customer` *field set to null. Once the programmer requests the full customer information (using the* `getCustomer` *method), an additional request to the server to instantiate and set the customer field can be fired. If you feel up for it, you can try modifying the code to allow for "lazy" loading.*
>
> *Note that the same terminology pops up when working with Object Relational Mappers to interact with databases, for instance, to indicate whether you want to immediately fetch all relations in a one-to-many connection or wait until the programmer explicitly requests to do so.*

In any case, now you know how to access a simple RESTful service using Java. Now, take a look at a more complex RESTful service, which involves authentication and requests other than GET, in order to send information to the service.

Accessing REST Services with Authentication

Not all RESTful services are as simple as the one used in the previous section. In fact, many RESTful services involve authentication of some kind.

Depending on the REST service you're using, different authentication schemes can be used:

➤ Sending a username and password with every request as an URL parameter. You then send requests to the following URL, for instance: `http://www.example.com/books/B101?usern ame=me&password=secret`.

➤ Sending a so-called "key" with every request as an URL parameter. This is a secret "password" given to you by the service provider. You then send requests to the following URL, for instance: `http://www.example.com/books/B101?api_key=1234567890/`.

➤ Username/password or key-based authentication schemes where the key is sent in an HTTP header.

➤ Username/password or key-based authentication schemes using HTTP cookies. Users then first authenticate once and send the given cookie in each of the subsequent requests.

➤ RESTful services using middleware—such as OAuth—to handle authentication; this is especially helpful when you need more fine-grained authentication (instead of just allowing or disallowing requests).

URL parameter and cookie-based authentication is becoming quite rare in modern REST services. The reason for this is that keys and passwords can be stolen by intercepting network traffic, especially when services are exposed over non-secured HTTP connections.

For all of the authentication schemes mentioned previously, Java's built-in `HttpUrlConnection` class will work fine (just add the URL parameters in the URL you request). When you need to work with cookies, you can use the `java.net.CookieManager` class to help out—in the "Screen Scraping" section that follows, there is an example on how to use this class. However, for REST services using OAuth, you might want to resort to another library to handle the authentication aspect for you, as doing this step manually is somewhat complex.

To this end, these examples will use Google's Java OAuth Client Library. This library is built on top of Google's HTTP Library for Java, which in turn can wrap using `HttpUrlConnection` or the Apache HTTP Client Library for Java, an alternative third-party class to communicate with HTTP servers. To set up this library, navigate to `https://code.google.com/p/google-oauth-java-client/` and download the latest version of the library (`google-oauth-java-client-1.17.0-rc.zip` is used here). Extract this ZIP file somewhere. Next, create a new folder in your Eclipse project (this book continues to use `RESTWithJava`, but you can create a new one) named `google-http`. Next, drag and copy the contents of the `libs` folder in the extracted ZIP to this folder. Finally, add all the JAR files in the `google-http` folder to the build path in Eclipse.

Twitter's REST service is used here to build a sample client. Twitter is a social networking service that enables users to send and read short messages, called "tweets." Take a look at Twitter's documentation concerning its REST service at `https://dev.twitter.com/docs/api/1.1`. The documentation lists a number of resources that can be accessed using only GET and POST HTTP requests. For example, the page on "statuses/home_timeline"—see `https://dev.twitter.com/docs/api/1.1/get/statuses/home_timeline`—mentions that this resource can be used to return a collection of tweets posted by the authenticated user and the users they follow. The page mentions that accessing this resource requires a "user context." The page also lists parameters that can be submitted with the request and an example request message. Try to open the URL `https://api.twitter.com/1.1/statuses/home_timeline.json` in your browser, and you'll get the following response:

```
{"errors":[{"message":"Bad Authentication data","code":215}]}
```

Clearly, Twitter requires you to perform some additional steps before you can access its REST service. However, you can see already that Twitter does not return XML-formatted responses, but instead uses JSON, another notation to structure documents. You will see how to deal with parsing JSON soon.

Now take a look at setting up OAuth authentication to access the Twitter service. Even without knowing it, you might be familiar with OAuth if you've accessed Twitter—or services such as Facebook—before. Whenever you see a pop-up in your browser asking you if you want to grant a third-party application access to your Twitter information, OAuth is under the hood. Every OAuth authentication basically involves these three steps:

1. Get a "request token," which is a temporary identifier shared between your application and the service that will be used to authorize an access token.

2. Ask the user to identify and allow access, basically indicates that this "request token" has been granted access.

3. If the user authorizes access, an "access token" can be given to the requesting application, which is requested using the request token. Once this is done, the request token is discarded and the access token is used for following requests.

    The documentation of Twitter's REST service also provides excellent documentation regarding OAuth. Take a look at `https://dev.twitter.com/docs/auth/3-legged-authorization` and `https://dev.twitter.com/docs/auth/authorizing-request`. The latter mentions that normally, you would be able to send a REST HTTP POST request like this to post a tweet:

```
POST /1/statuses/update.json?include_entities=true HTTP/1.1
Accept: */*
Connection: close
User-Agent: OAuth gem v0.4.4
Content-Type: application/x-www-form-urlencoded
Content-Length: 76
Host: api.twitter.com

status=Hello%20Ladies%20%2b%20Gentlemen%2c%20a%20signed%20OAuth%20request%21
```

However, this request would be considered invalid, since Twitter would not know which application makes the request, for which user the request is being posed, if the user is allowed to post this tweet, and whether the request has been tampered with. A valid request thus needs to look like this:

```
POST /1/statuses/update.json?include_entities=true HTTP/1.1
Accept: */*
Connection: close
User-Agent: OAuth gem v0.4.4
```

```
Content-Type: application/x-www-form-urlencoded
Authorization:
    OAuth oauth_consumer_key="xvz1evFS4wEEPTGEFPHBog",
        oauth_nonce="kYjzVBB8Y0ZFabxSWbWovY3uYSQ2pTgmZeNu2VS4cg",
        oauth_signature="tnnArxj06cWHq44gCs1OSKk%2FjLY%3D",
        oauth_signature_method="HMAC-SHA1",
        oauth_timestamp="1318622958",
        oauth_token="370773112-GmHxMAgYyLbNEtIKZeRNFsMKPR9EyMZeS9weJAEb",
        oauth_version="1.0"
Content-Length: 76
Host: api.twitter.com

status=Hello%20Ladies%20%2b%20Gentlemen%2c%20a%20signed%20OAuth%20request%21
```

This request is similar, except that it now contains a special "Authorization" OAuth header. This header contains the following information:

➤ `oauth_consumer_key`: Identifies the application making the REST request.

➤ `oauth_nonce`: A unique token generated for each request. This is to prevent the same request being sent multiple times.

➤ `oauth_signature`: A hash of the request and some secret values that can be used to check the request on the server's side to make sure it has not been tampered with.

➤ `oauth_signature_method`: The method that was used to construct the signature.

➤ `oauth_timestamp`: Indicates when the request was created. OAuth services will reject requests that were created too far in the past.

➤ `oauth_token`: The access token representing the permission by the user to share access to your application.

➤ `oauth_version`: The version of the OAuth protocol being used.

It is possible to construct this header manually and send it along every request, e.g., using `HttpUrlConnection`. Since this is a complex process involving a great deal of steps, you can use Google's Java OAuth Client Library instead.

The first thing you'll need to do is create a Twitter API key to identify your application. This is the `oath_consumer_key` mentioned previously. To create it, navigate to `https://apps.twitter.com/`, log in with your Twitter account (it's easy to create one if you haven't already), and select Create New App. You will need to fill in some details:

➤ Name: The name given to your application. For this example, the name `NAMEJavaTestClient` is used. Fill in your name instead of "NAME" (application names need to be unique).

➤ Description: "Testing Twitter's REST Service in Java."

➤ Website: You can just put a placeholder here, e.g., `http://www.example.com`.

➤ Callback URL: Fill in nothing.

Accept the agreements and press Create Your Twitter Application. If all goes well, you'll be brought to a page with details for your app. See Figure 10-20.

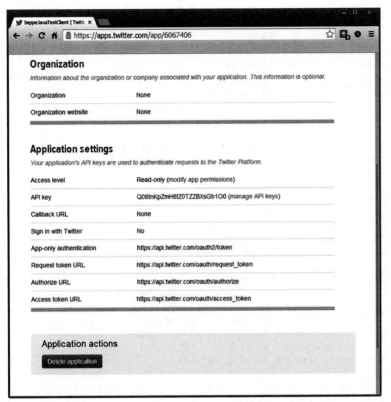

FIGURE 10-20

Note your API key and take note of the request token, authorize, and access token URLs. They'll reappear in your code soon. You'll also need to modify your app permissions (click the link) and allow for Read and Write access. Update your settings and go back to the Details tab. There, next to the API key, click Manage API Keys and note your API Secret as well. Also note that the access level has been set to Read and Write. As the Twitter page mentions, never give out your secret key to anyone, as this will allow others to pose as your application. In real-life applications, you'll want to store this key in an encrypted form, but for these purposes, you can just use it in plain form in the code.

Next, create a `TwitterTest` class in a new `com.twitter.api` package to build a prototype working with OAuth. The code should like the following:

```
package com.twitter.api;

import java.io.BufferedReader;
import java.io.InputStreamReader;

import com.google.api.client.auth.oauth.OAuthAuthorizeTemporaryTokenUrl;
import com.google.api.client.auth.oauth.OAuthCredentialsResponse;
import com.google.api.client.auth.oauth.OAuthGetAccessToken;
import com.google.api.client.auth.oauth.OAuthGetTemporaryToken;
import com.google.api.client.auth.oauth.OAuthHmacSigner;
```

```java
import com.google.api.client.auth.oauth.OAuthParameters;
import com.google.api.client.http.GenericUrl;
import com.google.api.client.http.HttpRequest;
import com.google.api.client.http.HttpRequestFactory;
import com.google.api.client.http.HttpResponse;
import com.google.api.client.http.HttpTransport;
import com.google.api.client.http.javanet.NetHttpTransport;

public class TwitterTest {

    private static final String CONSUMER_KEY = "FILL IN YOUR API KEY";
    private static final String CONSUMER_SECRET = "FILL IN YOUR SECRET KEY";

    private static final String REQUEST_TOKEN_URL =
       "https://api.twitter.com/oauth/request_token";
    private static final String AUTHORIZE_URL =
       "https://api.twitter.com/oauth/authenticate";
    private static final String ACCESS_TOKEN_URL =
       "https://api.twitter.com/oauth/access_token";

    private static final String API_ENDPOINT_URL =
       "https://api.twitter.com/1.1/statuses/home_timeline.json";

    public static void main(String[] args) throws Exception {
        // HttpTransport will be used to handle the HTTP requests
        // This is part of the google-http library
        HttpTransport transport = new NetHttpTransport();

        // The OAuthHmacSigner will be used to create the oauth_signature
        // Using HMAC-SHA1 as the oauth_signature_method
        // The signer needs the secret key to sign requests
        OAuthHmacSigner signer = new OAuthHmacSigner();
        signer.clientSharedSecret = CONSUMER_SECRET;

        // Step 1: Get a request token
        // ---------------------------

        // We need to provide our application key
        // We also need to provide an HTTP transport object
        // And the signer which will sign the request
        OAuthGetTemporaryToken requestToken =
            new OAuthGetTemporaryToken(REQUEST_TOKEN_URL);
        requestToken.consumerKey = CONSUMER_KEY;
        requestToken.transport = transport;
        requestToken.signer = signer;

        // Get back our request token
        OAuthCredentialsResponse requestTokenResponse = requestToken.execute();

        System.out.println("Request Token:");
        System.out.println("- oauth_token        = " + requestTokenResponse.token);
        System.out.println("- oauth_token_secret = " +
            requestTokenResponse.tokenSecret);

        // Update the signer to also include the request token
        signer.tokenSharedSecret = requestTokenResponse.tokenSecret;
```

```java
// Step 2: User grants access
// --------------------------

// Construct an authorization URL using the temporary request token
OAuthAuthorizeTemporaryTokenUrl authorizeUrl =
        new OAuthAuthorizeTemporaryTokenUrl(AUTHORIZE_URL);
authorizeUrl.temporaryToken = requestTokenResponse.token;

// We ask the user to open this URL and grant access
// Twitter includes an extra safety measure, asks the user to provide PIN
String pin = null;
System.out.println("Go to the following link:\n" + authorizeUrl.build());
InputStreamReader converter = new InputStreamReader(System.in, "UTF-8");
BufferedReader in = new BufferedReader(converter);
while (pin == null) {
    System.out.println("Enter the verification PIN provided by Twitter:");
    pin = in.readLine();
}

// Step 3: Request the access token the user has approved
// -------------------------------------------------------

// Get the access token
// We need to provide our application key
// The signer, the transport objects
// The temporary request token
// And a verifier string (the PIN number provided by Twitter)
OAuthGetAccessToken accessToken = new OAuthGetAccessToken(ACCESS_TOKEN_URL);
accessToken.consumerKey = CONSUMER_KEY;
accessToken.signer = signer;
accessToken.transport = transport;
accessToken.temporaryToken = requestTokenResponse.token;
accessToken.verifier = pin;

// Get back our access token
OAuthCredentialsResponse accessTokenResponse = accessToken.execute();

System.out.println("Access Token:");
System.out.println("- oauth_token        = " + accessTokenResponse.token);
System.out.println("- oauth_token_secret = " +
    accessTokenResponse.tokenSecret);

// Update the signer again
// We now replace the temporary request token with the final access token
signer.tokenSharedSecret = accessTokenResponse.tokenSecret;

// Set up OAuth parameters which can now be used in authenticated requests
OAuthParameters parameters = new OAuthParameters();
parameters.consumerKey = CONSUMER_KEY;
parameters.token = accessTokenResponse.token;
parameters.signer = signer;

// OAuth steps finished, we can now start accessing the service
// ------------------------------------------------------------

HttpRequestFactory factory = transport.createRequestFactory(parameters);
```

```
        GenericUrl url = new GenericUrl(API_ENDPOINT_URL);
        HttpRequest req = factory.buildGetRequest(url);
        HttpResponse resp = req.execute();

        System.out.println(resp.getStatusCode());
        System.out.println(resp.parseAsString());

    }

}
```

Take some time to read through the code and the comments. Don't forget to fill in the keys you received from Twitter in the CONSUMER_KEY and CONSUMER_SECRET variables. Note also the REQUEST_TOKEN_URL, AUTHORIZE_URL, and ACCESS_TOKEN_URL variables, containing the OAuth URLs provided to you earlier by Twitter.

Execute this code in Eclipse; you'll see the following output:

```
Request Token:
- oauth_token        = QEaZwniqkgRcB25gAuGGQg7rHz48OR5a8uoZ3AJs
- oauth_token_secret = scnIHqN59V0WAe2nyEoxiOWRejcBA7WPmQv5Ah5Q
Go to the following link:
https://api.twitter.com/oauth/authenticate?oauth_token=
    QEaZwniqkgRcB25gAuGGQg7rHz48OR5a8uoZ3AJs
Enter the verification PIN provided by Twitter:
```

(Your tokens will differ.) Open the given link in your web browser. A Twitter page will appear asking you if you want to allow access to an external application. See Figure 10-21.

Press Authorize App. Next, Twitter will provide you with a PIN that you'll need to provide to the application. See Figure 10-22.

Go back to the running Eclipse console, enter the PIN, and press Enter. The program will resume and execute the REST call:

```
Enter the verification PIN provided by Twitter:
2162766
Access Token:
- oauth_token        = 9807092-pEFWjo4juyL3MhZ1IruqvUeq1bvbpb83ZcDGCBtVEB
- oauth_token_secret = QlG4enz5Zo4YKMXq6Pv4kgoLFH5x7cLBZpHsYshhNynwz
200
[*REALLY LONG JSON RESPONSE*]
```

> **NOTE** *If you had set a callback URL, Twitter would not provide a PIN but would refer the user back to an URL you specify with the access token provided as an URL parameter, which your application can then intercept automatically. Since setting up web servers with Java hasn't been covered yet, here you can use the PIN-based approach.*

FIGURE 10-21

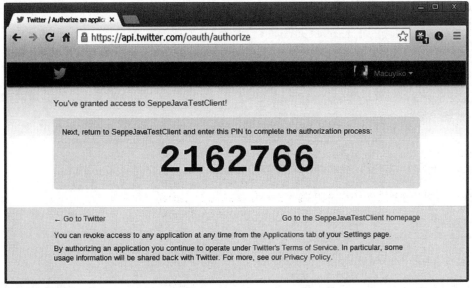

FIGURE 10-22

Great, everything works. However, the code is contained in one huge `main` method and thus could use some cleaning up. You'll also need to find a way to parse the received JSON, and it would be better to avoid users having to grant permission to your application each time it is run, as you can just as well reuse the same access token for future requests.

Start by creating an `OAuthParametersProvider` class, which you can use to perform a three-step OAuth authentication, and will be able to store access tokens for later use. First, create a new folder (not a source folder) in your `RESTWithJava` project called `tokens`. Next, enter the following code:

```java
package com.twitter.api;

import java.awt.Desktop;
import java.io.BufferedReader;
import java.io.FileNotFoundException;
import java.io.IOException;
import java.io.InputStreamReader;
import java.io.PrintWriter;
import java.io.UnsupportedEncodingException;
import java.net.URI;
import java.net.URISyntaxException;
import java.nio.charset.StandardCharsets;
import java.nio.file.Files;
import java.nio.file.Paths;
import java.util.List;

import com.google.api.client.auth.oauth.OAuthAuthorizeTemporaryTokenUrl;
import com.google.api.client.auth.oauth.OAuthCredentialsResponse;
import com.google.api.client.auth.oauth.OAuthGetAccessToken;
import com.google.api.client.auth.oauth.OAuthGetTemporaryToken;
import com.google.api.client.auth.oauth.OAuthHmacSigner;
import com.google.api.client.auth.oauth.OAuthParameters;
import com.google.api.client.http.HttpTransport;
import com.google.api.client.http.javanet.NetHttpTransport;

public class OAuthParametersProvider {
    protected final String configurationName;

    protected final String consumerKey;
    protected final String consumerSecret;

    protected final String requestTokenUrl;
    protected final String authorizeUrl;
    protected final String accessTokenUrl;

    protected final boolean requiresVerification;

    protected final HttpTransport transport;
    protected final OAuthHmacSigner signer;

    public OAuthParametersProvider(String configurationName,
            String consumerKey, String consumerSecret,
            String requestTokenUrl, String authorizeUrl, String accessTokenUrl,
```

```java
        boolean requiresVerification) {
    this.configurationName = configurationName;
    this.consumerKey = consumerKey;
    this.consumerSecret = consumerSecret;
    this.requestTokenUrl = requestTokenUrl;
    this.authorizeUrl = authorizeUrl;
    this.accessTokenUrl = accessTokenUrl;
    this.requiresVerification = requiresVerification;

    this.transport = new NetHttpTransport();
    this.signer = new OAuthHmacSigner();
    this.signer.clientSharedSecret = consumerSecret;
}

public OAuthParameters getOAuthParameters() {
    OAuthParameters parameters = new OAuthParameters();
    parameters.consumerKey = consumerKey;
    OAuthCredentialsResponse accessToken = getAccessToken();
    parameters.token = accessToken.token;

    // Construct a new signer
    OAuthHmacSigner requestSigner = new OAuthHmacSigner();
    requestSigner.clientSharedSecret = consumerSecret;
    requestSigner.tokenSharedSecret = accessToken.tokenSecret;

    parameters.signer = requestSigner;

    return parameters;
}

public OAuthCredentialsResponse getAccessToken() {
    return getAccessToken(false);
}

public OAuthCredentialsResponse getAccessToken(boolean forceNewToken) {
    OAuthCredentialsResponse token = getStoredAccessToken();
    if (!forceNewToken && token != null)
        return token;

    OAuthCredentialsResponse requestToken = getRequestToken();
    OAuthCredentialsResponse accessToken = getAccessToken(requestToken);

    return accessToken;
}

protected OAuthCredentialsResponse getStoredAccessToken() {
    String path = "tokens/"+configurationName+".txt";
    if (Files.notExists(Paths.get(path)))
        return null;
    try {
        List<String> lines = Files.readAllLines(Paths.get(path),
            StandardCharsets.UTF_8);
        OAuthCredentialsResponse accessToken = new OAuthCredentialsResponse();
        accessToken.token = lines.get(0);
```

```java
            accessToken.tokenSecret = lines.get(1);
            return accessToken;
        } catch (IOException e) {
            e.printStackTrace();
        }
        return null;
    }

    protected String getStoredVerifier() {
        String path = "tokens/"+configurationName+".txt";
        if (!Files.exists(Paths.get(path)))
            return null;
        try {
            List<String> lines = Files.readAllLines(Paths.get(path),
                StandardCharsets.UTF_8);
            return lines.get(2);
        } catch (IOException e) {
            e.printStackTrace();
        }
        return null;
    }

    protected void storeAccessTokenAndVerifier(OAuthCredentialsResponse accessToken,
            String verifier) {
        String path = "tokens/"+configurationName+".txt";
                try (PrintWriter writer = new PrintWriter(path, "UTF-8")) {
            writer.println(accessToken.token);
            writer.println(accessToken.tokenSecret);
            writer.println(verifier);            }
            catch (FileNotFoundException | UnsupportedEncodingException e) {
            e.printStackTrace();
        }
    }

    protected OAuthCredentialsResponse getRequestToken() {
        signer.tokenSharedSecret = null;

        OAuthGetTemporaryToken requestToken =
            new OAuthGetTemporaryToken(requestTokenUrl);
        requestToken.consumerKey = consumerKey;
        requestToken.transport = transport;
        requestToken.signer = signer;

        try {
            OAuthCredentialsResponse requestTokenResponse = requestToken.execute();
            return requestTokenResponse;
        } catch (IOException e) {
            e.printStackTrace();
        }

        return null;
    }

    protected OAuthCredentialsResponse getAccessToken(
            OAuthCredentialsResponse requestToken) {
```

```java
        signer.tokenSharedSecret = requestToken.tokenSecret;
        OAuthAuthorizeTemporaryTokenUrl oAuthAuthorizeUrl =
                new OAuthAuthorizeTemporaryTokenUrl(authorizeUrl);
        oAuthAuthorizeUrl.temporaryToken = requestToken.token;
        System.out.println("Go to the following link in your browser:\n"
                + oAuthAuthorizeUrl.build());
        try {
            // Try to open browser automatically
            Desktop.getDesktop().browse(new URI(oAuthAuthorizeUrl.build()));
        } catch (IOException | URISyntaxException e1) {
            e1.printStackTrace();
        }
        String verifier = null;
        if (requiresVerification)
            verifier = getVerificationCode();

        OAuthGetAccessToken accessToken = new OAuthGetAccessToken(accessTokenUrl);
        accessToken.consumerKey = consumerKey;
        accessToken.signer = signer;
        accessToken.transport = transport;
        accessToken.temporaryToken = requestToken.token;
        if (requiresVerification)
            accessToken.verifier = verifier;

        OAuthCredentialsResponse accessTokenResponse;
        try {
            accessTokenResponse = accessToken.execute();
            storeAccessTokenAndVerifier(accessTokenResponse, verifier);
            return accessTokenResponse;
        } catch (IOException e) {
            e.printStackTrace();
        }

        return null;
    }

    protected String getVerificationCode() {
        String verifier = null;
        InputStreamReader converter = new InputStreamReader(System.in, "UTF-8");
        BufferedReader in = new BufferedReader(converter);
        while (verifier == null) {
            System.out.println(
                "Enter the verification code provided by the service:");
            try {
                verifier = in.readLine();
            } catch (IOException e) {}
        }
        return verifier;
    }
}
```

This code contains much of the same logic you've seen earlier, but now neatly separated into different methods. There is also the added functionality to store access tokens in text files and retrieve them later. A few lines of code were added to automatically open a browser window:

```
            try {
                // Try to open browser automatically
                Desktop.getDesktop().browse(new URI(oAuthAuthorizeUrl.build()));
            } catch (IOException | URISyntaxException e1) {}
```

Note also that `protected` fields and methods are used in this class, in order to extend it later (the reason will be made clear soon).

Next, create a `TwitterRESTClient` class:

```
package com.twitter.api;

import java.io.IOException;
import java.util.Map;
import java.util.Map.Entry;

import com.google.api.client.http.GenericUrl;
import com.google.api.client.http.HttpRequest;
import com.google.api.client.http.HttpRequestFactory;
import com.google.api.client.http.HttpResponse;
import com.google.api.client.http.HttpTransport;
import com.google.api.client.http.UrlEncodedContent;
import com.google.api.client.http.javanet.NetHttpTransport;

public class TwitterRESTClient {
    private static final String API_ENDPOINT_URL = "https://api.twitter.com/1.1/";

    private final HttpTransport transport;
    private final OAuthPostSignatureParametersProvider parametersProvider;

    public TwitterRESTClient(
            OAuthPostSignatureParametersProvider parametersProvider) {
        this.transport = new NetHttpTransport();
        this.parametersProvider = parametersProvider;
    }

    public String makeRequest(String operation) {
        return makeRequest(operation, "GET");
    }

    public String makeRequest(String operation, String method) {
        return makeRequest(operation, method, true, null);
    }

    public String makeRequest(String operation, Map<String, String> parameters) {
        return makeRequest(operation, "GET", true, parameters);
    }

    public String makeRequest(String operation, String method,
        Map<String, String> parameters) {
        return makeRequest(operation, method, true, parameters);
    }

    public String makeRequest(String operation, String method, boolean useOAuth,
            Map<String, String> parameters) {
```

```
        HttpRequestFactory factory;
        if (useOAuth)
            factory = transport.createRequestFactory(
                parametersProvider. getOAuthPostSignatureParameters());
        else
            factory = transport.createRequestFactory();

        String url = API_ENDPOINT_URL + operation;
        GenericUrl reqUrl = new GenericUrl(url);
        UrlEncodedContent content = null;
        if (parameters != null && method.equals("POST"))
            content = new UrlEncodedContent(parameters);
        if (parameters != null && method.equals("GET"))
            for (Entry<String, String> parameter : parameters.entrySet())
                reqUrl.put(parameter.getKey(), parameter.getValue());

        HttpRequest req = null;
        try {
            req = factory.buildRequest(method, reqUrl, content);
            HttpResponse resp = req.execute();
            if (resp.isSuccessStatusCode()) {
                return resp.parseAsString();
            } else {
                System.err.println("Request failed with status code: " +
                    resp.getStatusCode());
            }
        } catch (IOException e) {
            e.printStackTrace();
        }

        return null;
    }

}
```

Again, much of the same logic is at work here. The makeRequest method allows you to send an OAuth authenticated request to the Twitter REST service and takes parameters (and adds them to the URL in the case of a GET request or to the HTTP request body in case of a POST request) before firing off the request.

Note that OAuthParametersProvider is not used here. Instead, the code uses OAuthPostSignatureParametersProvider, which is a class that still needs to be made:

```
package com.twitter.api;

import com.google.api.client.auth.oauth.OAuthCredentialsResponse;
import com.google.api.client.auth.oauth.OAuthHmacSigner;

public class OAuthPostSignatureParametersProvider extends OAuthParametersProvider {

    public OAuthPostSignatureParametersProvider(String configurationName,
            String consumerKey, String consumerSecret, String requestTokenUrl,
            String authorizeUrl, String accessTokenUrl,
            boolean requiresVerification) {
        super(configurationName, consumerKey, consumerSecret, requestTokenUrl,
```

```
                       authorizeUrl, accessTokenUrl, requiresVerification);
        }

        public OAuthPostSignatureParameters getOAuthPostSignatureParameters() {
            OAuthPostSignatureParameters parameters = new OAuthPostSignatureParameters();
            parameters.consumerKey = consumerKey;
            OAuthCredentialsResponse accessToken = getAccessToken();
            parameters.token = accessToken.token;

            // Twitter is sometimes picky on requiring a callback in every request
            // As well as the original verifier
            parameters.callback = "http://127.0.0.1/";
            if (requiresVerification)
                parameters.verifier = getStoredVerifier();

            // Construct a new signer
            OAuthHmacSigner requestSigner = new OAuthHmacSigner();
            requestSigner.clientSharedSecret = consumerSecret;
            requestSigner.tokenSharedSecret = accessToken.tokenSecret;

            parameters.signer = requestSigner;

            return parameters;
        }

    }
```

This class simply extends `OAuthParametersProvider` and adds an extra method, which does not return a set of `OAuthParameters`, but `OAuthPostSignatureParameters` instead. The reason for this is that Google's OAuth Client Library for Java does not allow you to include POST parameters in the signature, something that Twitter requires (see `https://dev.twitter.com/docs/auth/creating-signature`). Thus, you need to roll your own `OAuthPostSignatureParameters`, which is very similar to Google's `OAuthParameters`:

```
package com.twitter.api;

import com.google.api.client.auth.oauth.OAuthSigner;
import com.google.api.client.http.GenericUrl;
import com.google.api.client.http.HttpContent;
import com.google.api.client.http.HttpExecuteInterceptor;
import com.google.api.client.http.HttpRequest;
import com.google.api.client.http.HttpRequestInitializer;
import com.google.api.client.http.UrlEncodedContent;
import com.google.api.client.util.escape.PercentEscaper;

import java.io.IOException;
import java.security.GeneralSecurityException;
import java.security.SecureRandom;
import java.util.Collection;
import java.util.Map;
import java.util.TreeMap;

public final class OAuthPostSignatureParameters
```

```java
implements HttpExecuteInterceptor, HttpRequestInitializer {

/*
 * Due to a limitation in OAuthParameters, form parameters (as those
 * used by POST requests) are not included in the construction of the
 * OAuth signature. As such, we build a new class based on the source
 * code of OAuthParameters to work around this issue.
 *
 * Note that, normally, we would write a superclass which extends
 * OAuthParameters, but since OAuthParameters is declared as a final
 * class, we cannot do so here.
 */

private static final SecureRandom RANDOM = new SecureRandom();
public OAuthSigner signer;
public String callback;
public String consumerKey;
public String nonce;
public String realm;
public String signature;
public String signatureMethod;
public String timestamp;
public String token;
public String verifier;
public String version;

private static final PercentEscaper ESCAPER =
    new PercentEscaper("-_.~", false);

public void computeNonce() {
    nonce = Long.toHexString(Math.abs(RANDOM.nextLong()));
}

public void computeTimestamp() {
    timestamp = Long.toString(System.currentTimeMillis() / 1000);
}

public void computeSignature(String requestMethod, GenericUrl requestUrl,
  HttpContent httpContent)
      throws GeneralSecurityException {
  OAuthSigner signer = this.signer;
  String signatureMethod = this.signatureMethod = signer.getSignatureMethod();

  TreeMap<String, String> parameters = new TreeMap<String, String>();

  // Include all OAuth values in the signature
  putParameterIfValueNotNull(parameters, "oauth_callback", callback);
  putParameterIfValueNotNull(parameters, "oauth_consumer_key", consumerKey);
  putParameterIfValueNotNull(parameters, "oauth_nonce", nonce);
  putParameterIfValueNotNull(parameters, "oauth_signature_method",
      signatureMethod);
  putParameterIfValueNotNull(parameters, "oauth_timestamp", timestamp);
  putParameterIfValueNotNull(parameters, "oauth_token", token);
  putParameterIfValueNotNull(parameters, "oauth_verifier", verifier);
  putParameterIfValueNotNull(parameters, "oauth_version", version);
```

```java
    // Include URL query parameters
    for (Map.Entry<String, Object> fieldEntry : requestUrl.entrySet()) {
        Object value = fieldEntry.getValue();
        if (value != null) {
            String name = fieldEntry.getKey();
            if (value instanceof Collection<?>) {
                for (Object repeatedValue : (Collection<?>) value) {
                    putParameter(parameters, name, repeatedValue);
                }
            } else {
                putParameter(parameters, name, value);
            }
        }
    }

    // Include postdata parameters (added in our implementation)
    if (httpContent != null && httpContent instanceof UrlEncodedContent) {
        @SuppressWarnings("unchecked")
        Map<String, Object> data = (Map<String, Object>)
            ((UrlEncodedContent)httpContent).getData();
        for (Map.Entry<String, Object> dataEntry : data.entrySet()) {
            Object value = dataEntry.getValue();
            if (value != null) {
                String name = dataEntry.getKey();
                if (value instanceof Collection<?>) {
                    for (Object repeatedValue : (Collection<?>) value) {
                        putParameter(parameters, name, repeatedValue);
                    }
                } else {
                    putParameter(parameters, name, value);
                }
            }
        }
    }

    // Normalize parameters
    StringBuilder parametersBuf = new StringBuilder();
    boolean first = true;
    for (Map.Entry<String, String> entry : parameters.entrySet()) {
        if (first) {
            first = false;
        } else {
            parametersBuf.append('&');
        }
        parametersBuf.append(entry.getKey());
        String value = entry.getValue();
        if (value != null) {
            parametersBuf.append('=').append(value);
        }
    }
    String normalizedParameters = parametersBuf.toString();

    // Normalize URL
    GenericUrl normalized = new GenericUrl();
    String scheme = requestUrl.getScheme();
```

```java
        normalized.setScheme(scheme);
        normalized.setHost(requestUrl.getHost());
        normalized.setPathParts(requestUrl.getPathParts());
        int port = requestUrl.getPort();
        if ("http".equals(scheme) && port == 80 ⊠ "https".equals(scheme)
                && port == 443) {
            port = -1;
        }
        normalized.setPort(port);
        String normalizedPath = normalized.build();

        // Construct signature base string
        StringBuilder buf = new StringBuilder();
        buf.append(escape(requestMethod)).append('&');
        buf.append(escape(normalizedPath)).append('&');
        buf.append(escape(normalizedParameters));
        String signatureBaseString = buf.toString();
        signature = signer.computeSignature(signatureBaseString);
    }

    public String getAuthorizationHeader() {
        StringBuilder buf = new StringBuilder("OAuth");
        appendParameter(buf, "realm", realm);
        appendParameter(buf, "oauth_callback", callback);
        appendParameter(buf, "oauth_consumer_key", consumerKey);
        appendParameter(buf, "oauth_nonce", nonce);
        appendParameter(buf, "oauth_signature", signature);
        appendParameter(buf, "oauth_signature_method", signatureMethod);
        appendParameter(buf, "oauth_timestamp", timestamp);
        appendParameter(buf, "oauth_token", token);
        appendParameter(buf, "oauth_verifier", verifier);
        appendParameter(buf, "oauth_version", version);
        return buf.substring(0, buf.length() - 1);
    }

    private void appendParameter(StringBuilder buf, String name, String value) {
        if (value != null) {
            buf.append(' ').append(escape(name)).append("=\"")
                    .append(escape(value)).append("\",");
        }
    }

    private void putParameterIfValueNotNull(TreeMap<String, String> parameters,
            String key, String value) {
        if (value != null) {
            putParameter(parameters, key, value);
        }
    }

    private void putParameter(TreeMap<String, String> parameters, String key,
            Object value) {
        parameters.put(escape(key),
                value == null ? null : escape(value.toString()));
    }
```

```
public static String escape(String value) {
    return ESCAPER.escape(value);
}

public void initialize(HttpRequest request) throws IOException {
    request.setInterceptor(this);
}

public void intercept(HttpRequest request) throws IOException {
    computeNonce();
    computeTimestamp();
    try {
        computeSignature(request.getRequestMethod(), request.getUrl(),
            request.getContent());
    } catch (GeneralSecurityException e) {
        IOException io = new IOException();
        io.initCause(e);
        throw io;
    }
    request.getHeaders().setAuthorization(getAuthorizationHeader());
}
}
```

Don't be too concerned about how this code works; it is basically the same as OAuthParameters, with the addition that it now also includes POST data to compute the signature.

Next, go back to the TwitterTest class and modify it as follows:

```
package com.twitter.api;

import java.util.HashMap;

public class TwitterTest {

    private static final String CONSUMER_KEY = "FILL IN YOUR API KEY";
    private static final String CONSUMER_SECRET = "FILL IN YOUR SECRET KEY";

    private static final String REQUEST_TOKEN_URL =
        "https://api.twitter.com/oauth/request_token";
    private static final String AUTHORIZE_URL =
        "https://api.twitter.com/oauth/authenticate";
    private static final String ACCESS_TOKEN_URL =
        "https://api.twitter.com/oauth/access_token";

    public static void main(String[] args) throws Exception {
        OAuthPostSignatureParametersProvider parametersProvider =
            new OAuthPostSignatureParametersProvider("twitter",
                CONSUMER_KEY, CONSUMER_SECRET,
                REQUEST_TOKEN_URL, AUTHORIZE_URL, ACCESS_TOKEN_URL,
                true);
        TwitterRESTClient client = new TwitterRESTClient(parametersProvider);

        String jsonResponse;
```

```
        System.out.println("----- Get user time line -----");
        jsonResponse = client.makeRequest("statuses/home_timeline.json");
        System.out.println(jsonResponse);

        System.out.println("----- Get user time line: 5 tweets -----");
        jsonResponse = client.makeRequest("statuses/home_timeline.json",
        new HashMap<String, String>() {{
            put("count", "5");
        }});
        System.out.println(jsonResponse);

        System.out.println("----- Get user WileyTech's timeline: 5 tweets -----");
        jsonResponse = client.makeRequest("statuses/user_timeline.json",
        new HashMap<String, String>() {{
            put("screen_name", "WileyTech");
            put("count", "5");
        }});
        System.out.println(jsonResponse);

        System.out.println("----- Post a tweet -----");
        jsonResponse = client.makeRequest("statuses/update.json", "POST",
        new HashMap<String, String>() {{
            put("status", "Posting this Tweet from Java!" +
                " [" + System.currentTimeMillis() + "]");
        }});
        System.out.println(jsonResponse);
    }

}
```

Again, don't forget to fill in your API keys. If all goes right, the first time you execute this code a browser window will open and ask you to authorize the app. Enter the PIN in the console, and the remainder of the code will execute. Try executing this code again, and the stored access code will be used:

```
----- Get user time line -----
[** HUGE JSON RESPONSE **]
----- Get user time line: 5 tweets -----
[** SHORTER JSON RESPONSE **]
----- Get user WileyTech's timeline: 5 tweets -----
[** DIFFERENT SET OF TWEETS**]
----- Post a tweet -----
{** JSON CONTAINING POSTED TWEET **}
```

Check your Twitter page. Notice that your tweet has been posted (a timestamp was added because Twitter does not allow you to post the same tweet again). See Figure 10-23.

If you're getting errors, it might be due to the following:

➤   Your access token might have been revoked. Try removing the text files under the tokens folder (you might need to refresh this folder in Eclipse) and trying again.

FIGURE 10-23

➤ You might be trying to post or request too many tweets in rapid succession. Twitter applied rate limiting to its services. Try again later.

➤ The parameters or endpoints might have changed (unlikely, as Twitter would assign a new version number). Check Twitter's documentation.

> **NOTE** *Note the shorthand notation used here to initialize an anonymous HashMap:*
>
> ```
> new HashMap<String, String>() {{
>     put("count", "5");
> }};
> ```
>
> *You can apply the same approach to initialize lists. Why the use of double braces ({{ and }}) here? The first set of braces creates a new anonymous inner class, extending the* HashMap *object. The second set of braces declares an "instance initializer" block that is run when the anonymous inner class is instantiated.*

The only thing left do is actually parse the received JSON. To do so, you'll be using another Google library called Google JSON, or GSON for short. You can find it at https://code.google.com/p/google-gson/. Installation is similar to what you've seen before—you download the latest version (here, google-gson-2.2.4-release.zip is used), extract the ZIP file, copy gson-2.2.4.jar to a folder in your Eclipse project (google-json is used here to keep in line with google-http), and add the library to the build path. Next, modify the TwitterTest class to look like this:

```java
package com.twitter.api;

import java.util.HashMap;

import com.google.gson.JsonArray;
import com.google.gson.JsonElement;
import com.google.gson.JsonParser;

public class TwitterTest {

    private static final String CONSUMER_KEY = "FILL IN YOUR API KEY";
    private static final String CONSUMER_SECRET = "FILL IN YOUR SECRET KEY";

    private static final String REQUEST_TOKEN_URL =
        "https://api.twitter.com/oauth/request_token";
    private static final String AUTHORIZE_URL =
        "https://api.twitter.com/oauth/authenticate";
    private static final String ACCESS_TOKEN_URL =
        "https://api.twitter.com/oauth/access_token";

    public static void main(String[] args) throws Exception {
        OAuthPostSignatureParametersProvider parametersProvider =
            new OAuthPostSignatureParametersProvider("twitter",
                CONSUMER_KEY, CONSUMER_SECRET,
                REQUEST_TOKEN_URL, AUTHORIZE_URL, ACCESS_TOKEN_URL,
                true);
        TwitterRESTClient client = new TwitterRESTClient(parametersProvider);

        String jsonResponse;

        System.out.println("----- Get user time line: 5 tweets -----");
        HashMap<String, String> data = new HashMap<>();
        Data.put("count", "5");
        jsonResponse = client.makeRequest("statuses/home_timeline.json",
            data);

        JsonParser jsonParser = new JsonParser();
        JsonElement jsonElement = jsonParser.parse(jsonResponse);
        JsonArray jsonArray = jsonElement.getAsJsonArray();

        for (JsonElement element : jsonArray)
            System.out.println(element.getAsJsonObject().get("text"));

    }

}
```

If you run this code, you'll now see the following, more user-friendly output (of course, your tweets will vary):

```
----- Get user time line: 5 tweets -----
```

```
"RT @wwwtxt: Hi, is there anyone out there on the net this Easter?
     I will be back again tomorrow if you miss me today. ?92APR"
"RT @BobVila: Here's something everyone can make! 5 Things to do with...
     Junk Mail! http://t.co/2qyTBJEkQX http://t.co/32ymeLUff9"
"RT @hari: How @reddit @Disqus @smittenkitchen are taming the 'Wild West'
     of online comments | http://t.co/I8f2FKJ694"
"RT @MDogGeist: so the wii-u is as old as the dreamcast when it was killed
     and the wii-u has sold less than half what the dreamcast did..."
"I've now been on twitter for half an hour or so, but I'm \"totally coding
     right now\" in my head. Procrastinators, unite!"
```

If you want, you can take some time to familiarize yourself with the GSON library, but its usage is relatively straightforward and can be derived quickly by using Eclipse's context pop-ups. You can also explore the Twitter REST service somewhat further to get out and post different information.

> **NOTE** One interesting way to use the Twitter REST service is through the `search/tweets.json` GET endpoint (this requires a single mandatory parameter, q, which contains the search query). You can use this, for example, to search for tweets users are posting about you or your company.

This concludes the section on accessing REST services. This section has covered a lot of ground, so feel free to go over the code again or experiment some more to get a feel for how everything works. Since REST has become so popular in recent years, you might want to explore the developer's section of your favorite productivity site or social network to see if they're offering something similar.

> **NOTE** These examples have been using a set of libraries and built-in classes to deal with HTTP communication and OAuth for you. However, many RESTful services also offer even higher-lever libraries (or third parties offer them), providing "bindings" to a number of languages, Java often among them. For Twitter, for instance, you can check out the `Twitter4J` library at `http://twitter4j.org/`, which offers a Java library to interact with Twitter's REST service. Methods and classes offered by such libraries are oftentimes more closely defined to the actual service (i.e., a method called `postTweet`), but since the goal here is to familiarize yourself with REST services in general, a more "pure" approach is applied.

You've now seen how to work with Java's built-in `HttpURLConnection` class to access RESTful services, as well as used Google's OAuth and HTTP client libraries to access more complex services. You've also seen how to parse XML and JSON.

As a final exercise, the next Try It Out shows how to access another REST service—Facebook.

TRY IT OUT Accessing Facebook

This exercise demonstrates how to use the REST service of Facebook. It assumes that you already have a Facebook account at `http://www.facebook.com`. Facebook developer's documentation can be found at `https://developers.facebook.com/`. Information on its REST API (which Facebook now calls the "Graph API") can be found at `https://developers.facebook.com/docs/graph-api/reference/`, and includes a list of all the resources you can access.

1. To access the Facebook Graph API, you'll first need to register as a developer. This can be done by navigating to `https://developers.facebook.com/` and selecting Register as a Developer under Apps in the upper menu.

2. Next, just as for Twitter, you need to create a set of keys under `https://developers.facebook.com/tools/accesstoken/`. Create a new app, give it a unique name, and select a category.

3. After creating your app, you'll be brought to your app's "Dashboard," which contains a wealth of information and settings to play with. See Figure 10-24.

FIGURE 10-24

4. Be sure to note your "App ID" and "App Secret" keys. Click + Add Platform, choose website, and enter `http://www.example.com` as the site URL, which you'll also use as a callback URL. Even if you're not the owner of this domain, it'll work fine to extract the callback URL (together with the access token) and copy it in your application. Don't forget to save your changes.

5. Facebook uses a complicated login flow with the possibility to modify many options and permissions, inspired by OAuth but not exactly the same. The page on manually building a login flow, found at `https://developers.facebook.com/docs/facebook-login/manually-build-a-login-flow`, provides more details if you're interested (there is a lot to read through).

6. Create a single class, called `FacebookTest`, using the following code:

```
package com.facebook.graph;

import java.awt.Desktop;
import java.io.BufferedReader;
import java.io.IOException;
import java.io.InputStreamReader;
import java.net.URI;
import java.net.URISyntaxException;
import java.util.HashMap;
```

```java
import java.util.Map;
import java.util.Map.Entry;

import com.google.api.client.http.GenericUrl;
import com.google.api.client.http.HttpRequest;
import com.google.api.client.http.HttpRequestFactory;
import com.google.api.client.http.HttpResponse;
import com.google.api.client.http.UrlEncodedContent;
import com.google.api.client.http.javanet.NetHttpTransport;

public class FacebookTest {
    public static final String CLIENT_ID = "300114530143039";
    public static final String CLIENT_SECRET = "55e0b30296331c05afa1542d7806122c";
    public static final String API_ENDPOINT_URL = "https://graph.facebook.com/";
    public static final String CALLBACK_URL = "http://www.example.com";

    public static void main(String[] args) {
        // Step 1: open browser and ask user to allow access: get user access token
        String userGrantAccessUrl = "https://www.facebook.com/dialog/oauth?" +
                "client_id=" + CLIENT_ID +
                "&redirect_uri=" + CALLBACK_URL +
                "&response_type=token";
        try {
            Desktop.getDesktop().browse(new URI(userGrantAccessUrl));
        } catch (IOException | URISyntaxException e) {}

        final String userAccessToken = getAccessToken();

        System.out.println("User access token: " + userAccessToken);

        // Step 2: get an app access token
        final String appGrantAccessToken = makeRequest("oauth/access_token", "GET",
                new HashMap<String, String>(){{
                    put("client_id", CLIENT_ID);
                    put("client_secret", CLIENT_SECRET);
                    put("grant_type", "client_credentials");
                }})
            .replace("access_token=", "");

        System.out.println("App access token: " + appGrantAccessToken);

        // Step 3: verify the user token with our app token
        String verificationResponse = makeRequest("debug_token", "GET",
                new HashMap<String, String>(){{
                    put("input_token", userAccessToken);
                    put("access_token", appGrantAccessToken);
                }});

        System.out.println("Status of token verification: " + verificationResponse);

        // Step 4: access the API
        // You'll need to provide the user access token with every request
        String userInformation = makeRequest("me", "GET",
                new HashMap<String, String>(){{
                    put("access_token", userAccessToken);
```

```java
            }});
        System.out.println("Here's some information about the user: ");
        System.out.println(userInformation);

    }

    private static String getAccessToken() {
        String accessToken = null;
        InputStreamReader converter = new InputStreamReader(System.in, "UTF-8");
        BufferedReader in = new BufferedReader(converter);
        while (accessToken == null) {
            System.out.println("Enter the access token from the callback URL:");
            try {
                accessToken = in.readLine();
            } catch (IOException e) {}
        }
        return accessToken;
    }

    private static String makeRequest(String operation, String method,
            Map<String, String> parameters) {
        NetHttpTransport transport = new NetHttpTransport();
        HttpRequestFactory factory;
        factory = transport.createRequestFactory();

        GenericUrl reqUrl = new GenericUrl(API_ENDPOINT_URL + operation);
        UrlEncodedContent content = null;
        if (parameters != null && method.equals("POST"))
            content = new UrlEncodedContent(parameters);
        if (parameters != null && method.equals("GET"))
            for (Entry<String, String> parameter : parameters.entrySet())
                reqUrl.put(parameter.getKey(), parameter.getValue());

        // If set, the access_token must be provided as a GET parameter
        // Even when we're making a POST request
        if (parameters != null && parameters.get("access_token") != null)
            reqUrl.put("access_token", parameters.get("access_token"));

        HttpRequest req = null;
        try {
            req = factory.buildRequest(method, reqUrl, content);
            HttpResponse resp = req.execute();
            if (resp.isSuccessStatusCode()) {
                return resp.parseAsString();
            } else {
                System.err.println("Request failed with status code: "
                    + resp.getStatusCode());
            }
        } catch (IOException e) {
            e.printStackTrace();
        }

        return null;
    }
}
```

7. Test the program. The first time you run this program, Facebook will ask you whether you want to give your app permission. Note that the default permissions do not allow you to post through your app. See Figure 10-25.

FIGURE 10-25

Next, Java will redirect you to the callback URL, which in this case is `http://www`
`.example.com`. See Figure 10-26.

Your Java program is waiting for you to provide the access token. This is the `ACCESS_TOKEN_`
`HERE` part of the callback URL: `http://www.example.com/#access_token=ACCESS_TOKEN_`
`HERE&expires_in=NUMBER`. Again, if you open the Facebook authorization page in your Java program (using a GUI and web browser component), you can "sniff out" this access token, but here, just manually copy and paste it into the Eclipse console.

Next, your program will continue with requesting an app access token and verifying the user access token with the app access token, using a similar `makeRequest` method as the one you used for your Twitter client. Once this final authorization step is finished, you can execute a real request, in this case requesting some information about the user who authorized the app (you). The final output should look like this:

```
Enter the access token from the callback URL:
    CAAEQ89v2Cz8BAEifGHPKiaTDZCGZAf1Uf5NaODOFKrC8kL1C5iYBsY4LLCmh6J8sGTuWCMdCOP
    faba9CEhJMweXofNMUp8W9skDOXGAZAimENwY3ZAebfEWx89ZAaxNCLL2PDi25X5mbUWoxD6dEiA
    9fxu16iZB7EVKj4vT4uoRaV4x4tofrgUWvulVZBnsgMYZD
User access token:
```

```
CAAEQ89v2Cz8BAEifGHPKiaTDZCGZAf1Uf5NaODOFKrC8kL1C5iYBsY4LLCmh6J8sGTuWCMdCOP
faba9CEhJMweXofNMUp8W9skDOXGAZAimENwY3ZAebfEWx89ZAaxNCLL2PDi25X5mbUWoxD6dEiA
9fxu16iZB7EVKj4vT4uoRaV4x4tofrgUWvulVZBnsgMYZD
```
App access token: 300114530143039|lhvmPn7r6HbmN4dj3LgAFgoisIk
Status of token verification:
```
{"data":{"app_id":"300114530143039","is_valid":true,"application":
"SeppeJavaClient","user_id":"507162275","expires_at":1398038400,
"scopes":["public_profile","basic_info","user_friends"]}}
```
Here's some information about the user:
{"id":"507162275",** ALL KINDS OF INFORMATION **}

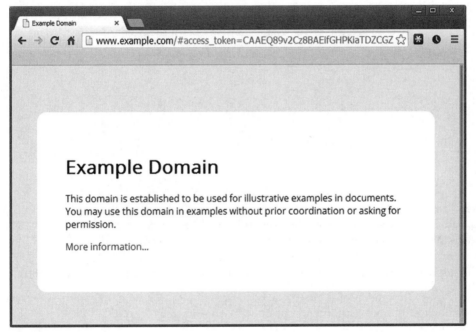

FIGURE 10-26

8. This exercise is meant to give you a taste of what's possible with Java and Facebook. Note that, just like for Twitter, there exists a `Facebook4J` library (`http://facebook4j.org/`) that makes this whole process a lot easier. Take a look if you want to invest more time in developing Java applications that interact with Facebook.

Screen Scraping

The last type of web service this chapter is going to discuss is not really a web service at all, but involves a technique called "screen scraping," used when you really, absolutely want to get some information out of a website, or when a website just didn't bother to provide a structured service based on SOAP or REST.

Let's say you're visiting an interesting page on Wikipedia about coffee varieties at `http://en.wikipedia.org/wiki/List_of_coffee_varieties`. You notice the list shown in Figure 10-27.

Variety	Arabica	Region(s)	Comments	Ref
Arusha	Arabica	Mount Meru in Tanzania, and Papua New Guinea	either a Typica variety or a French Mission.	[1]
Bergendal, Sidikalang	Arabica	Indonesia	Both are Typica varieties which survived the Leaf Rust Outbreak of the 1880s; most of the other Typica in Indonesia was destroyed.	
		Blue Mountains region of Jamaica. Also grown		

FIGURE 10-27

You'd like to extract this list for later use (perhaps to import into a database). You know you can copy and paste tables from websites into Excel, but where's the fun in that? You've already seen how to make HTTP requests to REST services interact with them, so why wouldn't it be possible to make HTTP requests to normal websites and parse the HTML page they give back? Sure, HTML contains a lot of formatting and is not a structured format such as XML or JSON, but it definitely seems possible.

This is exactly what screen scraping (also called data scraping or web scraping) does—it extracts data programmatically from output that's meant to be consumed by humans.

Depending on the type of data you want to extract, screen scraping can be more or less difficult to pull off. Some websites are structured in a complex way, make HTTP requests even after the main page has loaded (using JavaScript), or require certain cookies to be set (e.g., indicating that a user is logged in) before you can access pages. This section takes a look at screen scraping web pages both with and without cookie-based authentication. To screen scrape, you need to use yet another library in order to help parse and search through the received HTML pages. You certainly don't want to do this manually using Java's String manipulation methods.

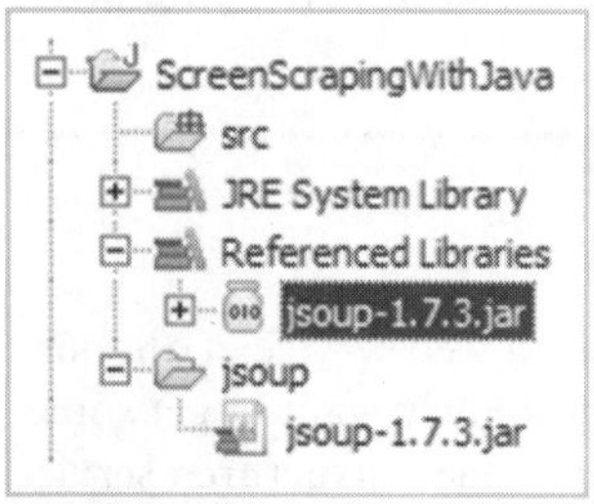

FIGURE 10-28

As always, start by setting up a new project in Eclipse, called `ScreenScrapingWithJava`. The library you will be using to do the HTML parsing is called `jsoup` and can be downloaded at `http://jsoup.org/download` (in this book version 1.7.3 is used). Simply download the core library JAR file and drag and copy it into an Eclipse folder within your project, named `jsoup`. Finally, right-click the JAR in Eclipse to add it to the build path. See Figure 10-28.

This is all you need to do to set up. Now take a look at how to extract data from a web page.

Screen Scraping Without Cookies

Create a class called `WikipediaGetter` with the following content:

```java
import java.io.IOException;
import java.util.ArrayList;
import java.util.List;

import org.jsoup.Jsoup;
import org.jsoup.nodes.Document;
import org.jsoup.nodes.Element;
import org.jsoup.select.Elements;

public class WikipediaGetter {
    public static void main(String[] args) throws IOException  {

        List<String[]> coffee = new ArrayList<String[]>();

        Document doc = Jsoup.connect(
            "http://en.wikipedia.org/wiki/List_of_coffee_varieties").get();

        Elements wikiTables = doc.select("table.wikitable");

        System.out.println(wikiTables.size() + " wikitables found");

        for (Element table : wikiTables) {
            if (table.html().contains("<th>Arabica</th>")) {
                // We've found our table!
                Elements rows = table.select("tr");
                for (Element row : rows) {
                    Elements cells = row.select("td");
                    if (cells.size() == 0)
                        continue;
                    String[] line = new String[cells.size()];
                    for (int i = 0; i < line.length; i++) {
                        line[i] = cells.get(i).text();
                    }
                    coffee.add(line);
                }
                break;
            }
        }

        for (String[] variety : coffee) {
            System.out.println("----- " + variety[0] + " -----");
            System.out.println("Arabica: " + variety[1]);
            System.out.println("Region(s): " + variety[2]);
            System.out.println("Comments: " + variety[3]);
        }
    }

}
```

This simple script does the following: it connects to the Wikipedia page using `jsoup`. Apart from being an excellent HTML parser, `jsoup` also provides user-friendly methods to perform HTTP requests, so you don't have to build your own `makeRequest` method around `HttpURLConnection`. Next, it fetches the HTML `table` elements with the `wikitable` class, searches until it finds the right table, and then loops through the `tr` and `td` elements to extract the contents of the tables.

If you're wondering how to know which element to fetch from the HTML structure, most browsers provide a way to inspect the source of each web page you view. See Figure 10-29.

FIGURE 10-29

To retrieve elements from the HTML tree, `jsoup` applies a selector method. Basic selectors include:

> `tagname`: Finds elements by the tag name, e.g., `table`

> `#id`: Finds elements based on ID, e.g., `#main-table`

> `.class`: Finds elements based on class name, e.g., `.wikitable`

➤ `[attribute]`: Finds elements with an attribute

➤ `[attribute=value]`: Finds elements whose attribute equals a value

Selectors can be combined to build more complex queries, e.g., `table.wikitable` could select all `table` elements with the class `wikitable`, or `table a` could find all link elements within a table. You can read more about selectors on the `jsoup` site.

Running your code will produce the following result:

```
2 wikitables found
----- Arusha -----
Arabica: Arabica
Region(s): Mount Meru in Tanzania, and Papua New Guinea
Comments: either a Typica variety or a French Mission.
----- Bergendal, Sidikalang -----
Arabica: Arabica
Region(s): Indonesia
Comments: Both are Typica varieties which survived the Leaf Rust Outbreak
    of the 1880s; most of the other Typica in Indonesia was destroyed.
** AND SO ON **
```

As you no doubt agree, screen scraping can oftentimes offer a very straightforward and simple method to extract data from web pages. However, screen scraping is generally regarded as an inelegant technique to be used only when no other mechanism for structured data exchange is available (such as REST or SOAP). The reasons for this are both technical and "ethical" in nature. First, web pages may change without notice, causing your screen scraping programs to break and require a great deal of maintenance. Second, it is not regarded good form to "hammer" websites with screen scraping programs. It makes thousands of requests to extract all data from the websites, which was originally meant for human consumption only. Therefore, always take care when screen scraping a website not to anger the website owner.

> **NOTE** *People sometimes build wrappers around websites that do not offer an official REST API based on screen scraping techniques, but rather a so-called "Evil API" that can be used by programmers to access a website in a programmatic manner. The reason such third-party tools are denoted as "evil" is due to the fact that the website owner does not intend or want programmers to access their resources in a programmatic manner.*

Screen Scraping with Cookies

Before showing you their content, websites frequently require your browser to send a set of cookies (small tokens of information) that were set by the website earlier to be able to identify you again. Recall that this was HTTP's way to work around its stateless nature. For instance, when you visit Twitter or Facebook in your browser and no cookie is sent with the request, the site will ask you to log in before continuing. Once you provide your username and password, the site will set a cookie to remember you in subsequent requests.

To see how this works, the next exercise accesses Twitter again, but this time using screen scraping techniques only. Create a class named `TwitterScraper` with the following source code:

```java
import java.io.IOException;
import java.util.HashMap;
import java.util.Map;

import org.jsoup.Connection;
import org.jsoup.Jsoup;
import org.jsoup.nodes.Document;
import org.jsoup.nodes.Element;

public class TwitterScraper {
    private static final Map<String, String> COOKIES =
        new HashMap<String, String>();
    private static final String USERNAME = "FILL IN YOUR USERNAME";
    private static final String PASSWORD = "FILL IN YOUR PASSWORD";

    public static void main(String[] args) throws IOException {
        System.out.println("Trying to log into Twitter...");
        boolean result = login(USERNAME, PASSWORD);

        System.out.println("Cookies are now:");
        System.out.println(COOKIES);

        if (!result) {
            System.out.println("Login failed! Try the following:");
            System.out.println("- Has the Twitter website changed?");
            System.out.println("- Are your username and password correct?");
            System.exit(0);
        }

        String username = getUsername();
        System.out.println("Your username is: "+username);

        String[] myStats = getStats(username);
        System.out.println("Your stats: ");
        System.out.println("- Tweets: "+myStats[0]);
        System.out.println("- Following: "+myStats[1]);
        System.out.println("- Followers: "+myStats[2]);

        String[] wileyStats = getStats("WileyTech");
        System.out.println("@WileyTech stats: ");
        System.out.println("- Tweets: "+wileyStats[0]);
        System.out.println("- Following: "+wileyStats[1]);
        System.out.println("- Followers: "+wileyStats[2]);
    }

    public static String[] getStats(String username) throws IOException {
        Connection connection = Jsoup.connect("https://twitter.com/"+username);
        // We do not need to be logged in to get stats
        Document result = connection.get();
        String[] stats = new String[3]; // tweets, following, followers
        try {
            Element statsTable = result.select("table.js-mini-profile-stats").get(0);
```

```
        stats[0] = statsTable.select(
            "a[data-element-term=tweet_stats]").text();
        stats[1] = statsTable.select(
            "a[data-element-term=following_stats]").text();
        stats[2] = statsTable.select(
            "a[data-element-term=follower_stats]").text();
    } catch (IndexOutOfBoundsException e) {
        // table.js-mini-profile-stats could not be found
        // Perhaps this user has enabled the new Twitter profile?
        Element statsTable = result.select("ul.ProfileNav-list").get(0);
        stats[0] = statsTable.select(
            "a[data-nav=tweets] span.ProfileNav-value").text();
        stats[1] = statsTable.select(
            "a[data-nav=following] span.ProfileNav-value").text();
        stats[2] = statsTable.select(
            "a[data-nav=followers] span.ProfileNav-value").text();
    }
    return stats;
}

public static String getUsername() throws IOException {
    Connection connection = Jsoup.connect("https://twitter.com")
            .cookies(COOKIES);
    Document result = connection.get();
    COOKIES.putAll(connection.response().cookies());
    return result.select("div[role=navigation] li.profile a.js-
        nav").attr("href").replace("/", "");
}

public static boolean login(String username, String password)
    throws IOException {
    COOKIES.clear(); // Clear all cookies
    // Request Twitter homepage to set first cookies and get token
    String authenticityToken = getAuthenticityToken();
    // Then login using a POST request
    Connection connection = Jsoup.connect("https://twitter.com/sessions")
            .data("session[username_or_email]", username)
            .data("session[password]", password)
            .data("remember_me", "1")
            .data("return_to_ssl", "true")
            .data("redirect_after_login", "/")
            .data("remember_me", "1")
            .data("authenticity_token", authenticityToken)
            .cookies(COOKIES);
    Document result = connection.post();
    COOKIES.putAll(connection.response().cookies());
    if (result.html().contains("action=\"https://twitter.com/sessions\"")) {
        // The sign-in form is still present in the result
        // The login was probably incorrect
        return false;
    }
    return true;
}

private static String getAuthenticityToken() throws IOException {
```

```
            // Request Twitter homepage and get token
            Connection initialConnection = Jsoup.connect("https://twitter.com/");
            Document initialResult = initialConnection.get();
            String authenticityToken = initialResult
                    .select("input[name=authenticity_token]").get(0).val();
            // Update cookies
            COOKIES.putAll(initialConnection.response().cookies());
            return authenticityToken;
        }

    }
```

This code is mostly similar to the one you saw previously, with the difference that you're now making POST requests, setting and sending cookies, and using more complex selectors. If you're wondering how you can figure out the names of the POST parameters to send along with the login request, these can be obtained by inspecting network traffic using the developer tools in any modern web browser (e.g., Firefox or Chrome). See Figure 10-30.

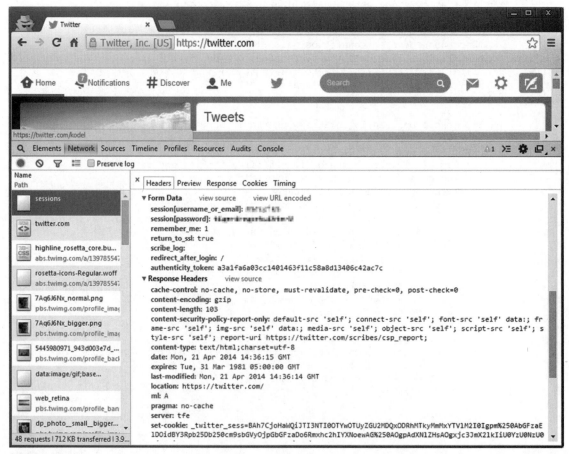

FIGURE 10-30

After executing this code (don't forget to fill in your username and password), you should receive something like the following output:

```
Trying to log into Twitter...
Cookies are now:
{twid="u=9807092", guest_id=v1%3A139809069245291074, remember_checked_on=1,
auth_token=0a5fe41724884eaab2e8b121e6ed74d6f74a2754,
_twitter_sess=BAh7CiIKZmxhc2hJQzonQWN0aW9uQ29udHJvbGxlcjo6Rmxhc2g6OkZsYXNo
%250ASGFzaHsABjoKQHVzZWR7ADoHaWQiJTRiM2IyN2VjMDZkZGMxZTVjNzc2MGI1%250AOTBh
NzAwN2U1Og9jcmVhdGVkX2F0bCsIZfeyhEUBOgxjc3JmX2lkIiUzMGQ2%250ANzNkMjQxNjRiN
TMzNDgzNzBjYTJiMDZjZWNhZjojJdXNlcmlcmkD9KSV--4244a4f3d399fab8a4eda1a3ad69e3f29
6a23c84, lang=en,
h=%7B%22tweet_id%22%3A%224565817081799972100%22%2C%22advertiser_id%22%3A%22
121336088%22%2C%22newer_tweet_id%22%3A%22458251425135734784%22%2C%22
older_tweet_id%22%3A%22458251414578270208%22%2C%22promoted_content%22%3A%7B%22
impression_id%22%3A%2242597fa3f64f6b16%22%2C%22disclosure_type%22%3A%22
promoted%22%2C%22disclosure_text%22%3A%22%22%7D%2C%22experiment_values%22%3A%7B%22
display.display_style%22%3A%22show_social_context%22%7D%7D}
Your username is: ** YOUR USERNAME **
Your stats:
- Tweets: 556
- Following: 377
- Followers: 143
@WileyTech stats:
- Tweets: 1 943
- Following: 897
- Followers: 3 832
```

CREATING YOUR OWN WEB SERVICES WITH JAVA

Now that you've seen how to access web services, you might be wondering how you can offer your own information over the web using Java. Java has excellent support for setting up web servers, services, and applications, but a full discussion of those is out of scope for a beginner's book.

Instead, this book will be using a simple framework—aptly named "Simple"—which can be downloaded from http://www.simpleframework.org/. Like always, create a new project in Eclipse (HTTPServer, for instance) and unzip the JAR file (simple-6.0.1.jar) to a folder in Eclipse (e.g., simple). Finally, add the JAR file to the build path.

Setting Up an HTTP Server

Create a class called HTTPServer with the following source code:

```java
import java.awt.Desktop;
import java.io.PrintStream;
import java.net.InetSocketAddress;
import java.net.SocketAddress;
import java.net.URI;

import org.simpleframework.http.Request;
```

```java
import org.simpleframework.http.Response;
import org.simpleframework.http.core.Container;
import org.simpleframework.http.core.ContainerSocketProcessor;
import org.simpleframework.transport.connect.Connection;
import org.simpleframework.transport.connect.SocketConnection;

public class HTTPServer implements Container {
    public void handle(Request request, Response response) {
        try {
            PrintStream body = response.getPrintStream();

            response.setValue("Content-Type", "text/plain");
            body.println("Hello there, you've requested: "+request.getPath());
            body.close();
        } catch (Exception e) {
            e.printStackTrace();
        }
    }

    public static void main(String[] list) throws Exception {
        // If you get an Address already in use: bind error, try changing the port
        int port = 880;

        Container container = new HTTPServer();
        ContainerSocketProcessor server = new ContainerSocketProcessor(container);
        Connection connection = new SocketConnection(server);
        SocketAddress address = new InetSocketAddress(port);
        connection.connect(address);

        Desktop.getDesktop().browse(new URI("http://127.0.0.1:" + port));

        System.out.println("Press ENTER to stop server...");
        System.in.read();

        connection.close();
        server.stop();

    }
}
```

Run the code. A web browser will open and connect you to a running HTTP server. Try modifying the URL (e.g., `http://127.0.0.1:880/test/me`) and note that the server changes its response accordingly. See Figure 10-31.

You can easily extend this class with what you've learned in the chapter on working with files to open and transmit HTML and other files stored on the server to the browser. The following class shows you how to do so:

```java
import java.awt.Desktop;
import java.io.OutputStream;
import java.io.PrintStream;
import java.net.InetSocketAddress;
import java.net.SocketAddress;
import java.net.URI;
import java.nio.file.Files;
```

```java
import java.nio.file.Path;
import java.nio.file.Paths;

import org.simpleframework.http.Request;
import org.simpleframework.http.Response;
import org.simpleframework.http.core.Container;
import org.simpleframework.http.core.ContainerSocketProcessor;
import org.simpleframework.transport.connect.Connection;
import org.simpleframework.transport.connect.SocketConnection;

public class HTTPServer implements Container {
    private static final int PORT = 880;
    private static final String ROOTDIR = "data";

    public void handle(Request request, Response response) {
        try {
            System.err.println(request.getPath());
            Path path = Paths.get(ROOTDIR + request.getPath());
            if (Files.exists(path) && Files.isRegularFile(path)) {
                OutputStream body = response.getOutputStream();
                byte[] data = Files.readAllBytes(path);
                body.write(data);
                body.close();
            } else {
                PrintStream body = response.getPrintStream();
                body.println("404 Not Found");
                body.close();
                response.setStatus(org.simpleframework.http.Status.NOT_FOUND);
            }

        } catch (Exception e) {
            e.printStackTrace();
        }
    }

    public static void main(String[] list) throws Exception {
        Container container = new HTTPServer();
        ContainerSocketProcessor server = new ContainerSocketProcessor(container);
        Connection connection = new SocketConnection(server);
        SocketAddress address = new InetSocketAddress(PORT);
        connection.connect(address);

        Desktop.getDesktop().browse(new URI("http://127.0.0.1:" + PORT));

        System.out.println("Press ENTER to stop server...");
        System.in.read();

        connection.close();
        server.stop();

    }
}
```

FIGURE 10-31

In your Eclipse project, create a new folder called `data`. In this folder, you can create or put files. For instance, try creating a file called `hello.htm` in your text editor with the content:

```
<html><body><h1>Hello!</h1></body></html>
```

Run the server (make sure to stop any running servers). Note the `404` error when opening `http://127.0.0.1:880/`. Now try accessing `http://127.0.0.1:880/hello.htm`; the web page shown in Figure 10-32 will appear.

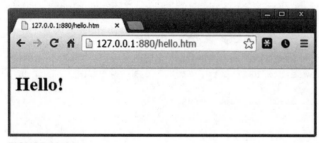

FIGURE 10-32

The `Simple` library is easy to extend with even more functionality (getting data the users enter in forms, for example). If you only need to provide information from Java to users via a web server, this should be enough to get started. Check out the documentation at `http://www.simpleframework.org/` for more information.

Providing REST Services

Just as with the JAX-WS library discussed earlier for SOAP, there exists an API for offering REST services called JAX-RS. Multiple implementations of this API exist, the most complete of which is called "Jersey." This library offers a complete package to offer and access REST services, but is somewhat complex to set up, so it will not be discussed further.

However, based on what you've seen so far, you know that a RESTful web service is nothing more than a structured URI scheme with a web server sending structured responses. As such, the `Simple` framework discussed in the previous section can also be leveraged to build a REST service. By combining what you've seen about databases, file IO, web services, and XML, you should be able to create your own REST services without much hassle.

For now, this chapter and the wonderful world of web services is left behind you. The chapter covered a lot of topics, ranging from networking, protocols, and HTTP to SOAP, REST, JSON and XML, and OAuth. Take some time to revisit some of the code you've seen, or feel free to explore on your own. As always, don't be afraid to search for help online whenever you get stuck. Web technologies can get very complex, but the good thing is that there is a large community of programmers trying to accomplish similar things, so you'll always find an answer if you encounter a problem.

In addition, this chapter—more so than others—has clearly illustrated the benefits of a rich library ecosystem as the one found for Java. To accomplish almost all of the tasks in this chapter, you've been using a third-party library handling a lot of the heavy lifting for you. Setting up an OAuth token exchange between a REST service still might not be as easy as you'd like, but think back on the small example on TCP/IP sockets in the beginning of this chapter and imagine having to write all other aspects of interacting with a web service on top of this. . . This illustrates another important point when programming in Java: don't be afraid to use existing libraries. As the old saying goes, buy the best, build the rest.

11

Designing Graphical Interfaces

WHAT YOU WILL LEARN IN THIS CHAPTER:

➤ The types of graphical user interface frameworks that exist in Java

➤ How you can make programs with a graphical user interface

➤ Understanding the containment hierarchy, layout managers, and events in a GUI context

➤ Using best practices when building graphical user interfaces

WROX.COM CODE DOWNLOADS FOR THIS CHAPTER

The wrox.com code downloads for this chapter are found at www.wrox.com/go/beginningjavaprogramming on the Download Code tab. The code is in the Chapter 11 download and individually named according to the names throughout the chapter.

Up until now, all the programs you've been working with throughout this book have been rather Spartan looking. Since most of the action happened on a command-line (or the Eclipse console), you might be wondering whether it is possible to give your programs a bit more visual flair, and, more importantly, make them more useful by means of adding some buttons or a textbox or two.

Luckily, Java provides a wide range of capabilities to work with graphical user interfaces—commonly abbreviated as GUIs—out of the box. Trying to come up with your own GUI classes from scratch would take you many years. This also means, however, that working with GUIs in Java is less straightforward than just dealing with input and output through the console, and constructing visual-rich programs will take up many more lines of code as well. As you might expect, all the components you'll need in order to build a nice-looking user interface will be implemented as classes. These classes adhere to Object-Oriented Programming principles, so you can find your way through them using the principles you've already learned.

COVERING THE BASICS OF GUIs IN JAVA

Java has been around for a while, so there are quite a number of GUI frameworks to choose from when you decide to start building your own user interfaces, both in the form of built-in as well as third-party libraries.

The reasons behind this are mostly historical, but are also influenced quite a bit by functional decisions. Some frameworks, for instance, will opt to keep as close as possible to the native look and feel of the operating system Java is running on, whereas others will try to go for a fancy, modern, or eccentric look. Some will focus on robustness or simplicity, whereas others will utilize advanced, performance-oriented functionalities such as hardware acceleration.

As a beginner's chapter on building GUIs with Java, things will be kept simple, using only built-in functionality without relying on third-party libraries or features that are too hard or complex to use. You'll note that unless you're building graphic-intensive programs, these components will serve just fine.

Highlighting the Built-In GUI Libraries

Before getting your feet wet with building your first GUI application, you need to get acquainted with some of the basics. You can start off with a short introduction, highlighting a bit more the architecture and history of Java's built-in GUI libraries.

Abstract Window Toolkit (AWT)

Back when Java was first released in 1995, Sun Microsystems provided a built-in library, called the Abstract Window Toolkit (AWT), to provide a standard widget toolkit (a widget is a typical GUI term used for a specific GUI component, such as a button or a check box) in the form of a thin layer above the native, underlying user interface, defined by the operating system. This meant that creating a button with AWT would call the routines of the underlying operating system as straightforwardly as possible to display the actual button, meaning that widgets created with AWT would look different depending on the actual operating system the Java program was running on; For example, OSX buttons look different than Windows buttons.

Although AWT is closely coupled to the underlying operating system (its components are called "heavyweight components" for that reason), the library itself is still enormous. It consists of no less than 12 packages, containing the collection of GUI widgets, classes to deal with GUI events (you will learn about events in the context of GUIs later), classes dealing with layout managers, interfaces to deal with input devices such as the mouse and keyboard, and even classes to handle the clipboard (copying and pasting) and drag-and-drop functionality.

Swing

Swing was originally developed to offer a more advanced set of GUI widgets compared to AWT. One goal was to offer a set of GUI components that would emulate the look and feel of the host operating system (as this was what users were familiar with) by default, but would also support a pluggable look-and-feel system that would allow applications to have a separate visual style.

In addition, Swing aimed to offer more components when compared to AWT, such as tabbed panels, lists, and scroll panes. Finally, unlike AWT widgets, Swing components are not implemented by relying on operating system–specific code. Instead, they are written entirely in Java and thus completely platform independent, so these widgets are referred to as being "lightweight." The notions of heavyweight and lightweight in this case indicate how the GUI components are implemented, rather than how they look or how complex they are.

> **NOTE** In fact, not all *Swing components are lightweight—there a few notable exceptions, but more on that later.*

One important aspect to keep in mind is that Swing is implemented, for the most part, as an extension of AWT. That is, every Swing top-level component (don't worry about what top-level means, you'll encounter this again in more detail soon) is implemented as a class extending an AWT counterpart, the difference being that the Swing components extend the AWT set in such a way that no native calls to the operating system are made anymore.

Since Swing draws the components itself (instead of relying on the operating system), it makes sense that there is some common set of functionality to draw basic 2D primitives (rectangles, lines, text, circles, and so on) on-screen. Indeed, this core functionality is provided by another set of libraries called "Java 2D," which, confusingly, is located under the `java.awt` package (the reason for this is that AWT already contained some form of basic graphic functionality, which was thus also extended).

Standard Widget Toolkit (SWT)

When people build GUIs in Java, they'll still almost always be using Swing to do so. Therefore, in this chapter, you'll focus most on this library. That said, however, there exists a number of additional GUI libraries as well, with the Standard Widget Toolkit (SWT) as a notable first example.

The origins of SWT date all the way back from when AWT was still in its infancy (and Swing still under development). The developers at IBM decided that AWT was too buggy and developed their own alternative, SWT. It is similar to AWT in the sense that its components are also heavyweight and thus also call native operating system routines to draw and display GUI components. However, SWT also offers some additional widgets using native code, in cases where native-platform GUI routines do not support the functionality required for SWT. In that way, SWT is a compromise between native performance and Swing's ease of use of.

It is interesting to note that SWT was originally conceived to support the development of VisualAge, an IDE made by IBM at the time. The company decided to eventually open-source the project, which then led to the development of Eclipse. That means Eclipse itself—the IDE used in this book—can be regarded as a prime example of SWT in action.

Does it make sense to use it yourself? In some cases, it might. When you are looking for a GUI toolkit that provides a sensible programming interface to access native widgets in a functional manner and with a more sensible structure and fallbacks than AWT, it might be interesting to give SWT a shot. If you care more about customization support and ease of use, and want a look and feel that appears similar on all platforms, Swing is probably better suited.

JavaFX

JavaFX is the "new kid" on the block concerning GUI toolkits, even though it has been around for quite some time by now. Its original goal was to offer a software platform for creating rich Internet and mobile applications, but is now geared toward replacing Swing as the standard GUI toolkit for Java, although Oracle will continue to offer both in the foreseeable future.

Note that JavaFX has been around since 2008, but it took a few years until the library was ready for use on non-Windows platforms. With the release of Java 8, JavaFX became an integral part of the JRE (and JDK), so that the latest version of JavaFX went from 2.2 to just simply JavaFX 8. These aspects form the main reason behind the lack of larger adoption of this GUI toolkit. Even though Oracle has been trying to put more effort behind the project in recent years, it can be argued that the time for a big breakthrough has passed, and even though the toolkit keeps improving, most people still stick to Swing as their default GUI toolkit today. Another reason why the framework is not yet as popular as it could be is because most of the GUI-related innovations these days tend to focus on web and mobile development, with standard desktop application development being more stabilized.

> **NOTE** *Speaking of platforms, Oracle—and Sun before them—has missed the boat somewhat regarding the creation of a GUI framework for Java on mobile platforms, i.e., iOS and Android. For Android, Google has driven a great deal of attention toward creating a nice-looking set of widgets (Android itself runs heavily on Java technology). Although Oracle had an internal prototype of JavaFX working on iOS and Android at one point, the code base was renamed and reworked significantly afterwards (called RoboVM on iOS). Even today, these mobile UI toolkits are considered experimental and not yet ready for prime time.*

Other Toolkits and Libraries

Apart from the ones you've just seen, there are a number of additional GUI toolkits and libraries as well. For instance, there are add-on libraries oriented toward extending Swing with additional helpful components, such as JGoodies or SwingX from SwingLabs, a library which also contains a number of Swing components. There also exist additional libraries that try to offer a complete solution, such as Apache Pivot, which is trying to position itself against JavaFX by offering a completely open-source package (parts of JavaFX are still proprietary). There's also Qt Jambi, a binding between the Qt GUI toolkit (that works across various platforms) and Java, as well as GTK-Java, which does the same for Java and the GTK GUI toolkit. Finally, as noted before, in case you might be interested in developing apps on Android later (which are written in Java), keep in mind that the platform comes with its own GUI toolkit and thus its own set of components and classes, although learning GUI libraries gets easier once you have seen one.

Choosing a GUI Library

In this section you've seen an overview of several GUI libraries, and by now you might be getting worried or overwhelmed by the number of choices offered. Which one is the best? Which one is easiest to learn? Which one should you go for?

For most of this chapter, you will continue with Swing. The reasons for this are because Swing is very robust, pretty easy to work with (as long as your GUIs don't need to be very complex), and well known by Java programmers, so you can easily find or get help. Remember that using Swing will always involve talking a little bit about AWT as well, which Swing extends.

Finally, keep in mind that some people who feel Swing is outdated will disagree with this choice; some would rather see Swing quietly disappear to be replaced with a more modern system—most likely, JavaFX. The reality, however, is that the multitude of projects in Java are, and continue to be, written with Swing. You certainly won't be left empty-handed regarding JavaFX, however. In the final parts of this chapter, you can take a look at setting up a small project with JavaFX, so you can get a feel for how everything works and decide yourself whether you want to continue with this UI toolkit and leave Swing behind.

Building with Containers and Components

You have already learned, generally, about many different GUI widget toolkits or GUI libraries offering a collection of GUI widgets, or GUI components, as they're called. Now what exactly is a GUI component? Basically, the GUI components determine the set of building blocks you can use to construct a user interface. They are the elementary, basic GUI entities. Think of a button, a text label, a textbox, and so on. In the Microsoft realm, GUI components are sometimes referred to as "controls," whereas other libraries prefer to use the term "widget." Just keep in mind, a GUI component is a widget is a control.

In Swing, every component has its own class, and all extend the base class `JComponent`, located under the `javax.swing` package. Why not take a look at some of them?

CLASS	USED AS	LOOKS LIKE
JButton	`JComponent component = new JButton("BUTTONS!");`	BUTTONS!
JLabel	`JComponent component =` `    new JLabel("A label");`	A label

JList	`JComponent component =`
	`    new JList<String>(`
	`        new String[]{`
	`            "---1---",`
	`            "---2---"`
	`    });`
		---1---
		---2---

JProgressBar	`JProgressBar component =`
	`    new JProgressBar(0, 100);`
	`component.setValue(20);`	

JScrollBar	`JComponent component =`
	`    new JScrollBar(`
	`        JScrollBar.HORIZONTAL,`
	`        50, 20, 1, 500);`
		◀ ▥ ▶

JSlider	`JComponent component =` `    new JSlider(0, 100, 33);`	
JSpinner	`JComponent component =` `    new JSpinner();`	0

continues

(continued)

CLASS	USED AS	LOOKS LIKE
JTextField	```JComponent component = new JTextField("Text field");```	Text field
JTextArea	```JComponent component = new JTextArea("Text area");```	Text area
JComboBox	```JComponent component = new JComboBox<String>(new String[]{ "---1---", "---2---" });```	---1--- ▼
JCheckBox	```JComponent component = new JCheckBox("Check boxes");```	☐ Check boxes
JRadioButton	```JComponent component = new JRadioButton("And radio buttons");```	◯ And radio buttons

Apart from components, there is also a second GUI element you should be aware of, called a "container." Containers hold components together in a specific layout and can also contain sub-containers. Therefore, a container can be seen as a special kind of component that holds other components and organizes them in a specific manner.

You should be aware of the following Swing container classes: `JApplet`, `JFrame`, `JDialog`, `JWindow`, and `JPanel`; all of them are derived from the AWT `java.awt.Container` class (which is subclassed in a number of AWT containers you can ignore, as you will only be using the Swing ones). You're probably getting anxious to start coding by now, so why not introduce one of the containers by means of a Try It Out?

TRY IT OUT   Writing Your First GUI Application

In this Try It Out, you will construct a simple GUI application using the `JFrame` container class.

1. As always, feel free to create a new project in Eclipse.

2. Create a class called `MyFirstFrame` with the following content:

```
import java.awt.BorderLayout;
import java.awt.Color;

import javax.swing.JButton;
import javax.swing.JFrame;
import javax.swing.JLabel;
import javax.swing.JPanel;

public class MyFirstFrame {
    public static void main(String[] args) {
        JFrame frame new JFrame();
```

```
                frame.setDefaultCloseOperation(JFrame.EXIT_ON_CLOSE);
                frame.setTitle("My First Frame");

                JPanel bluePanel = new JPanel();
                JPanel redPanel = new JPanel();

                JLabel label = new JLabel("<-- pick your side -->");

                frame.getContentPane().add(label, BorderLayout.CENTER);

                bluePanel.setBackground(Color.blue);
                redPanel.setBackground(Color.red);

                frame.getContentPane().add(bluePanel, BorderLayout.LINE_START);
                frame.getContentPane().add(redPanel, BorderLayout.LINE_END);

                JButton blueButton = new JButton("PICK BLUE TEAM");
                JButton redButton = new JButton("PICK RED TEAM");

                bluePanel.add(blueButton);
                redPanel.add(redButton);

                frame.pack();
                frame.setVisible(true);
        }
    }
```

3.   Run the project from Eclipse. You should see the window shown in Figure 11-1.

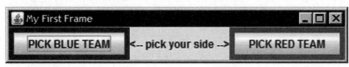

FIGURE 11-1

How It Works

This is how it works:

1.   The window you see is your actual JFrame, a container for other components or containers. The
     getContentPane() method gives you access to the actual container to which you can add() other
     components (or containers). Note the setTitle() method allows you to set the title, and the
     setDefaultCloseOperation() method allows you to specify what the Java program should do
     (in this case, stop completely) when the user closes this JFrame object.

2.   You also constructed two JPanel containers and set their background colors. They are added to the
     left and right sides of the JFrame content pane. The default layout for a JFrame content pane is a so-
     called border layout. Don't worry about this too much, as you will see layouts in more detail soon.

3.   Next, two buttons are created with different text labels, and they are added to the JPanels.

4.   Finally, calling the pack() method of JFrame ensures everything is laid out correctly and then
     shows the frame to the user.

5. Try resizing the window. What works and what does not? What could look better? Keep these aspects in mind for later.

6. Note that Java, by default, will pick a "look and feel" to match a cross-platform theme. You might have noted that the button Java shows looks nothing like a normal Windows button. If you want to select another Swing look, try adding the following code at the top of the `main` method:

```
try {
    UIManager.setLookAndFeel(UIManager.getSystemLookAndFeelClassName());
} catch (ClassNotFoundException | InstantiationException
        | IllegalAccessException | UnsupportedLookAndFeelException e) {
    e.printStackTrace();
}
```

(Eclipse will suggest which classes to import.) When you run the program again, you will see the window in Figure 11-2, which looks a lot more similar to your normal system environment.

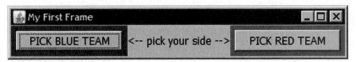

FIGURE 11-2

If you've followed along with the Try It Out (or just looked at the pictures), you might note that Swing will handle the look and feel of the buttons you've added to your window, but the window itself—its title bar; minimize, maximize, and close buttons; and border—still look as if they were drawn by the operating system. So what gives?

The explanation behind this is that there are four Swing components that are actually not lightweight and thus still drawn and displayed on-screen by calling an underlying operating system function. These are `JFrame`, `JDialog`, `JWindow`, and `JApplet`, which are all the container components that have some kind of border that's displayed in a window. Instead of Swing drawing these windows by itself (and thus also determining the look and feel of title bars and borders), it was decided to continue offloading this to the operating system, and that is why the actual window retains its look in this example.

> **NOTE** Actually, it is possible to define so-called "undecorated" windows in Swing, if you do want to draw your own custom controls for taking care of window management or apply custom borders. It is also possible to change the opacity (transparency) and shape of windows, so it is possible to make windows that look like whatever you want, although it requires some advanced usage of Swing and takes much more code than showing a standard looking window.

On another note, you might expect there to be a wealth of Swing look and feel to choose from, but in actuality, the number of high-quality "themes" out there is very limited. The main reason for this is that creating a complete look-and-feel package is very complex (especially when all components need to look good in all cases). You saw Nimbus mentioned (a SwingLabs project) as a notable exception. You can enable it by inserting the following code at the top of your `main` method:

```java
try {
    for (LookAndFeelInfo info : UIManager.getInstalledLookAndFeels()) {
        if ("Nimbus".equals(info.getName())) {
            UIManager.setLookAndFeel(info.getClassName());
            break;
        }
    }
} catch (Exception e) {
    // Nimbus not available, revert to system look and feel
    try {
        UIManager.setLookAndFeel(UIManager.getSystemLookAndFeelClassName());
    } catch (Exception ign) {}
}
```

(This snippet also shows you how to get a list of available look and feels.) The Nimbus look and feel looks like Figure 11-3 (using the "SwingSet" example provided by Oracle).

Feel free to use it in your own projects or just stick with the defaults.

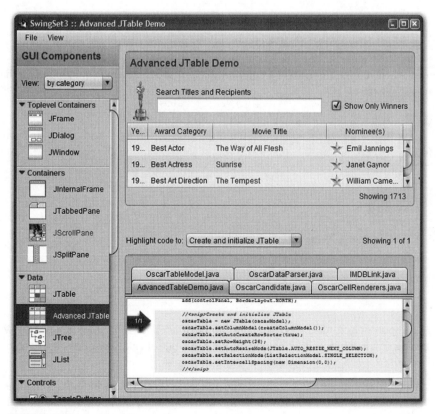

FIGURE 11-3

Looking at the Full Picture

You've now seen the differences between Swing components and containers and already utilized a handful of Swing classes. Earlier, you read that Swing extends the older and native AWT library. It therefore makes sense to take a step back and look at the whole class hierarchy to understand what exactly is going on, as the GUI hierarchy in Java can be somewhat confusing.

Start with the class tree representing only AWT objects, which will keep Swing out of the mix for now. You then end up with the GUI class hierarchy illustrated in Figure 11-4.

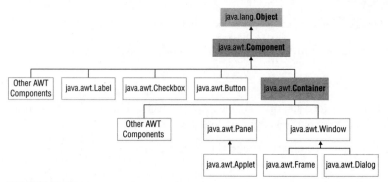

FIGURE 11-4

However, recall that you have been using J-classes (`JButton`, `JFrame`, and `JWindow`), that is, Swing classes. This means completely ignoring the AWT components and containers when making GUIs. Now see what happens when you ignore the AWT components and add the Swing components to the mix. This is illustrated in Figure 11-5.

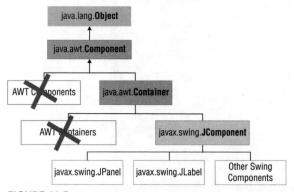

FIGURE 11-5

Note that each Swing component extends the `JComponent`, and that `JComponent` itself extends the AWT `Container` class, meaning that a `JButton` does not extend an AWT Button, a `JLabel` does not extend an AWT Label, and so on.

Now, where do Swing containers fit in? One of them, the `JPanel`, you can already find among the `JComponents`. However, the ones with a window border, namely `JFrame`, `JApplet`, `JDialog`, and `JWindow`, are missing. They are added to the class tree as shown in Figure 11-6.

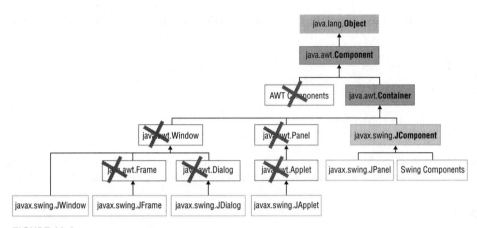

FIGURE 11-6

There they are. Note how things are a bit complicated (`JPanel` for instance does not extend the AWT Panel), but the `main` classes you'll be working with are all part of Swing, all starting with "J".

Annotating the class tree somewhat more, you finally get the full picture shown in Figure 11-7.

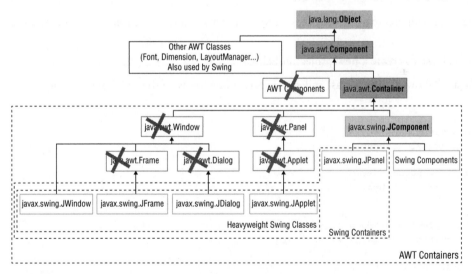

FIGURE 11-7

COMPARING LAYOUT MANAGERS

Now that you have a clear picture of the GUI class hierarchy, you are ready to move on to the next topic. Some of the general AWT classes that are reused in Swing represent layout managers. What is a layout manager? Basically, an object specifying the way components in a container should be laid out. Java offers a number of them out of the box, and you can combine these (by nesting containers inside each other) to create relatively intricate layouts.

Specifying a layout manager for a container is a simple operation. You just need to call the following method:

```
public void setLayout(LayoutManager manager)
```

For example:

```
JPanel redPanel = new JPanel();
redPanel.setLayout(new BorderLayout());
```

The questions then are which layout managers exist and what does each of them do? The following sections discuss each of the built-in layout managers in detail and provide examples of all of them.

FlowLayout

In a `FlowLayout`, all components will be arranged from left to right in the order that they are added. When a row is filled, a new row is started. Resizing the container or changing the width of the container programmatically thus changes the appearance. The `FlowLayout` is the default layout for `JPanel`.

TRY IT OUT Creating Flowing Panels

In this Try It Out, you will create a `JFrame`, set its layout manager to use a `FlowLayout`, and add some panels.

1. As always, feel free to create a new project in Eclipse.

2. Now make a rainbow. Create a class called `FlowLayoutFrame` with the following content:

```
import java.awt.Color;
import java.awt.Dimension;
import java.awt.FlowLayout;

import javax.swing.JFrame;
import javax.swing.JPanel;


public class FlowLayoutFrame {
    public static void main(String[] args) {
        JFrame frame = new JFrame();
        frame.setDefaultCloseOperation(JFrame.EXIT_ON_CLOSE);
        frame.setTitle("FlowLayout frame");

        frame.getContentPane().setLayout(new FlowLayout());

        frame.getContentPane().add(makePanel(Color.red));
        frame.getContentPane().add(makePanel(Color.orange));
        frame.getContentPane().add(makePanel(Color.green));
        frame.getContentPane().add(makePanel(Color.blue));
        frame.getContentPane().add(makePanel(new Color(75, 0, 130)));
        frame.getContentPane().add(makePanel(new Color(138, 43, 226)));

        frame.pack();
```

```
        frame.setVisible(true);
    }

    private static JPanel makePanel(Color color) {
        JPanel panel = new JPanel();
        panel.setBackground(color);
        return panel;
    }
}
```

3.   Run the project from Eclipse. You should see the window in Figure 11-8.

FIGURE 11-8

How It Works

This is how it works:

1.   In this class, a JFrame is created and given a title like before, but its layout manager is changed to be a FlowLayout. Then seven panels are added and colored with a rainbow pattern.

2.   Try resizing the window. Note how you cannot make the window smaller than its starting size. This is due to the fact that this is the minimum size for windows in Windows, and thus the layout manager has determined this to be the optimal size and has sized the panels accordingly as well, since none of them contain any components. Now say you would like to make your rainbow a bit bigger. You can do so by adding the following line to the `makePanel` method:

```
panel.setPreferredSize(new Dimension(100, 100));
```

3.   Run the program again; you will now see a bigger rainbow. Note that resizing the window shows the `FlowLayout` in action, as shown in Figure 11-9.

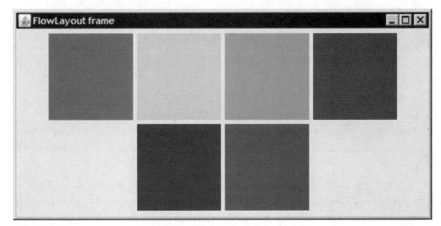

FIGURE 11-9

4. You might be wondering why you are using `setPreferredSize` instead of just `setSize`, which is also available as a method. This is because `setBounds` and `setSize` only have an effect when the layout manager of the container holding your components is set to `null`. This is a common mistake that throws many beginners off, especially since all containers have default layout managers and are thus not equal to `null`. By using `setPreferredSize`, you effectively signal to the layout manager: I would like this component to be this size, if you deem it possible.

The `FlowLayout` comes with three constructors. These are:

```
public FlowLayout();
public FlowLayout(int align);
public FlowLayout(int align, int hgap, int vgap);

// align: either FlowLayout.LEFT (or FlowLayout.LEADING),
//         FlowLayout.RIGHT (or FlowLayout.TRAILING),
//     or FlowLayout.CENTER

// hgap, vgap: horizontal/vertical gap between the components
```

ABOUT RIGHT-TO-LEFT ORIENTATION

Some languages, such as Arabic, are read from right to left, and operating systems include functionality to also make UI components appear in the correct reading order. In Java, it is also possible to change the reading orientation, and Swing will honor this setting as well—FlowLayout, for instance, will then order components from right to left. You can try this out with the following code snippet:

```java
import java.awt.ComponentOrientation;
import javax.swing.JFrame;

public class RightToLeft {
    public static void main(String[] args) {
        JFrame.setDefaultLookAndFeelDecorated(true);
        JFrame frame = new JFrame("Right to Left Frame");

        frame.setComponentOrientation(
            ComponentOrientation.RIGHT_TO_LEFT);

        frame.setSize(300, 300);
        frame.setDefaultCloseOperation(JFrame.DISPOSE_ON_CLOSE);
        frame.setVisible(true);
    }
}
```

BorderLayout

In a `BorderLayout`, a container is divided into five "zones," called North, South, West, East, and Center, in which components can be placed. You do not need to add components to all zones for a `BorderLayout` to work, as the components are allowed to stretch to fill available space.

The `BorderLayout` comes with two constructors. These are:

```
public BorderLayout();
public BorderLayout (int hgap, int vgap);

// hgap, vgap: horizontal/vertical gap between the components
```

Note that the `BorderLayout` is the default layout manager for the content pane of a windowed container (e.g., for a `JFrame`). You've already seen how it works in your first Try It Out for this chapter, but look at another example here.

TRY IT OUT   Experimenting with the BorderLayout

In this Try It Out, you create a `JFrame` to see how the `BorderLayout` layout manager works.

1. As always, feel free to create a new project in Eclipse when you want to. Create a class called `BorderLayoutFrame` with the following content:

```java
import java.awt.BorderLayout;

import javax.swing.JButton;
import javax.swing.JFrame;

public class BorderLayoutFrame {

    public static void main(String[] args) {
        JFrame frame = new JFrame();
        frame.setDefaultCloseOperation(JFrame.EXIT_ON_CLOSE);
        frame.setTitle("BorderLayout frame");

        /* Since the default layout manager for bordered containers is
         * already a BorderLayout, the following line is OPTIONAL here.
         */
        frame.getContentPane().setLayout(new BorderLayout());

        frame.getContentPane().add(new JButton("NORTH"),  BorderLayout.NORTH);
        // ... or BorderLayout.PAGE_START

        frame.getContentPane().add(new JButton("WEST"),   BorderLayout.WEST);
        // ... or BorderLayout.LINE_START

        frame.getContentPane().add(new JButton("EAST"),   BorderLayout.EAST);
        // ... or BorderLayout.LINE_END

        frame.getContentPane().add(new JButton("SOUTH"),  BorderLayout.SOUTH);
        // ... or BorderLayout.PAGE_END

        frame.getContentPane().add(new JButton("CENTER"), BorderLayout.CENTER);
        frame.pack();
        frame.setVisible(true);
    }
}
```

2. Run the project from Eclipse. You should see the window in Figure 11-10.

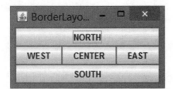

FIGURE 11-10

How It Works

This is how it works:

1. This class is similar to the previous one, but now a `BorderLayout` object is specified as the layout manager. This step is optional in the case of a `JFrame` container, because its default layout manager is already `BorderLayout`.

2. Components are now added to a specific position by specifying the location as the second argument of the `add` method.

3. Try resizing the window and see how the controls behave. Try removing a few of the buttons and see how the window reacts, as shown in Figure 11-11.

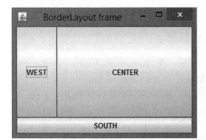

FIGURE 11-11

4. Try adding a call to `setPreferredSize` for one of the buttons. What happens? As you can see, `BorderLayout` has its own ideas about sizing components and does not adhere to your size hints. This does make the layout manager well suited to host nested `JPanels`, however (which then can be given their own separate layout manager in which you can lay out all components).

GridLayout

A `GridLayout` layout manager places components, as the name suggests, in a grid of cells. Each component will take up all the available space in its cell, and the dimensions of each cell are the same. When resizing containers with a `GridLayout` layout manager, the width and height of each cell will be resized accordingly.

A `GridLayout` layout manager can be constructed in two ways:

```
public GridLayout(int rows, int columns);
public GridLayout(int rows, int columns, int hgap, int vgap);

// rows, columns: number of rows and columns in the grid

// hgap, vgap: horizontal/vertical gap between the components
```

Note that when you specify 0 (zero) for the number of rows or columns (but not both), any number of components can be placed in the column or row, respectively (the actual non-zero value is then effectively ignored). When you specify both the number of rows and columns, the column value is also ignored. The number of components you add and the number of rows you have specified determine the real number of columns.

The following Try It Out shows an example.

TRY IT OUT   Creating the Useless Pocket Calculator

In this Try It Out, you create a `JFrame` to see how the `GridLayout` layout manager works. You also see how containers can be nested to create more complex layouts.

1.   As always, feel free to create a new project in Eclipse when you want to. Create a class called `GridLayoutFrame` with the following content:

```java
import java.awt.Container;
import java.awt.GridLayout;

import javax.swing.JButton;
import javax.swing.JFrame;

public class GridLayoutFrame {

    public static void main(String[] args) {
        JFrame frame = new JFrame();
        frame.setDefaultCloseOperation(JFrame.EXIT_ON_CLOSE);
        frame.setTitle("GridLayout frame");

        // 7 8 9 0
        // 4 5 6 C
        // 1 2 3 =
        // + - * /

        frame.getContentPane().setLayout(new GridLayout(4, 4));

        addButtons(frame.getContentPane(),
            "7", "8", "9", "0", "4", "5", "6", "C",
            "1", "2", "3", "=", "+", "-", "*", "/"
        );

        frame.pack();
        frame.setVisible(true);

    }
```

```
        private static void addButtons(Container contentPane, String ... strings) {
            for (String label : strings) {
                contentPane.add(new JButton(label));
            }
        }

    }
```

2. Run the project from Eclipse. You should see the window shown in Figure 11-12.

FIGURE 11-12

3. The buttons don't do anything (yet) and are pretty useless for now, but you can see already that you will need to add a textbox for any calculations. It is probably also apparent that it's not good to cram this into a single cell. It would be better to span this text the width of a whole row. Why not put your buttons in a `JPanel` and the textfield in the north position of the `BorderLayout` layout manager? Change your class to look like this:

```
import java.awt.BorderLayout;
import java.awt.Container;
import java.awt.GridLayout;

import javax.swing.JButton;
import javax.swing.JFrame;
import javax.swing.JPanel;
import javax.swing.JTextField;

public class GridLayoutFrame {

    public static void main(String[] args) {
        JFrame frame = new JFrame();
        frame.setDefaultCloseOperation(JFrame.EXIT_ON_CLOSE);
        frame.setTitle("GridLayout frame");

        JPanel buttonPanel = new JPanel();
        buttonPanel.setLayout(new GridLayout(4, 4));

        addButtons(buttonPanel,
            "7", "8", "9", "0", "4", "5", "6", "C",
```

```
                    "1", "2", "3", "=", "+", "-", "*", "/"
            );

            JTextField resultBox = new JTextField("*** BATTERY EMPTY ***");
            resultBox.setEditable(false); // Prevent user editing

            frame.getContentPane().add(buttonPanel, BorderLayout.CENTER);
            frame.getContentPane().add(resultBox, BorderLayout.NORTH);

            frame.pack();
            frame.setVisible(true);

        }


        private static void addButtons(Container contentPane, String... strings) {
            for (String label : strings) {
                contentPane.add(new JButton(label));
            }
        }
    }

}
```

The result will now look like Figure 11-13.

FIGURE 11-13

How It Works

This is how it works:

1. This class is similar to the previous one, but now you have specified a GridLayout object as the layout manager.

2. In the second version, a new JPanel container is constructed, and its layout manager is set to be a GridLayout. Then it is added to the center of the JFrame. A JTextField is then added in the north position. Note the use of the setEditable method to prevent users from typing in characters in the textbox.

GridBagLayout

The `GridBagLayout` layout manager is one of the most flexible and complex layout managers Java provides, while still being easy enough to use in a manual manner (`GroupLayout` and `SpringLayout` are even more flexible, but almost impossible to use by hand).

A `GridBagLayout` allows components to be placed in a grid of rows and columns, just like the `GridLayout` manager, but unlike `GridLayout`, cells in a `GridBagLayout` can have different widths and heights. In addition, it is possible for components to span across cells.

To arrange components, the `GridBagLayout` layout manager bases itself on the preferred sizes set for each component, as well as a series of so-called constraints, formulated by means of a `GridBagConstraints` object. Before you read more about these constraints, the following Try It Out introduces the `GridBagLayout` layout manager.

TRY IT OUT Creating the Pocket Calculator with GridBagLayout

In this Try It Out, you change your pocket calculator from the previous Try It Out to use `GridBagLayout` to demonstrate the added flexibility of this layout manager.

1. As always, feel free to create a new project in Eclipse when you want to. Create a class called `GridBagLayoutFrame` with the following content:

```java
import java.awt.GridBagConstraints;
import java.awt.GridBagLayout;
import java.awt.Insets;
import java.util.HashMap;
import java.util.Map;

import javax.swing.JButton;
import javax.swing.JFrame;
import javax.swing.JTextField;

public class GridBagLayoutFrame {

    public static void main(String[] args) {
        JFrame frame = new JFrame();
        frame.setDefaultCloseOperation(JFrame.EXIT_ON_CLOSE);
        frame.setTitle("GridLayout frame");

        frame.getContentPane().setLayout(new GridBagLayout());

        Map<String, JButton> buttons = makeButtons(
            "7", "8", "9", "0", "4", "5", "6", "C",
            "1", "2", "3", "=", "+", "-", "*", "/"
        );

        JTextField resultBox = new JTextField("*** BATTERY EMPTY ***");
        resultBox.setEditable(false);

        GridBagConstraints constraints = new GridBagConstraints();

        // Add number buttons
```

```
constraints.fill = GridBagConstraints.BOTH;
constraints.weightx = 1; constraints.weighty = 1;
constraints.fill = GridBagConstraints.BOTH;

// First row
constraints.gridy = 1;
constraints.gridx = 0;
frame.add(buttons.get("7"), constraints);
constraints.gridx = 1;
frame.add(buttons.get("8"), constraints);
constraints.gridx = 2;
frame.add(buttons.get("9"), constraints);
// Second row
constraints.gridy = 2;
constraints.gridx = 0;
frame.add(buttons.get("4"), constraints);
constraints.gridx = 1;
frame.add(buttons.get("5"), constraints);
constraints.gridx = 2;
frame.add(buttons.get("6"), constraints);
// Third row
constraints.gridy = 3;
constraints.gridx = 0;
frame.add(buttons.get("1"), constraints);
constraints.gridx = 1;
frame.add(buttons.get("2"), constraints);
constraints.gridx = 2;
frame.add(buttons.get("3"), constraints);

// Add text field on row above
constraints.gridy = 0;
constraints.gridx = 0;
constraints.gridwidth = 4;
constraints.anchor = GridBagConstraints.PAGE_START;
constraints.insets = new Insets(10, 4, 10, 4);
frame.add(resultBox, constraints);

// Add bottom buttons
constraints.gridy = 4;
constraints.gridwidth = 1;
constraints.anchor = GridBagConstraints.PAGE_END;
constraints.insets = new Insets(10, 0, 0, 0);
constraints.gridx = 0;
frame.add(buttons.get("+"), constraints);
constraints.gridx = 1;
frame.add(buttons.get("-"), constraints);
constraints.gridx = 2;
frame.add(buttons.get("*"), constraints);
constraints.gridx = 3;
frame.add(buttons.get("/"), constraints);

// Add buttons to the right
constraints.anchor = GridBagConstraints.LINE_END;
constraints.gridx = 3;
constraints.gridy = 1;
```

```
        constraints.insets = new Insets(0, 0, 0, 0);
        frame.add(buttons.get("0"), constraints);

        constraints.insets = new Insets(0, 10, 0, 0);
        constraints.gridy = 2;
        frame.add(buttons.get("C"), constraints);
        constraints.gridy = 3;
        frame.add(buttons.get("="), constraints);



        frame.pack();
        frame.setVisible(true);

    }


    private static Map<String, JButton> makeButtons(String... strings) {
        Map<String, JButton> buttons = new HashMap<>();
        for (String label : strings)
            buttons.put(label, new JButton(label));
        return buttons;
    }

}
```

2. Run the project from Eclipse. You should see the window in Figure 11-14.

3. Try resizing the window. Observe how the components stretch and behave.

FIGURE 11-14

How It Works

This is how it works:

1. This class is similar to the previous one, but a GridBagLayout object is now specified as the layout manager.

2. All components are added with the add method, as always, but they now specify a
GridBagConstraints object as the second argument, which the layout manager will use to lay out
all the components. The GridBagConstraints object is a simple container for a number of fields
(gridx, gridy, and so on), and the same object can be reused to position all components.

3. Try playing around with the constraints to guess what they do. Try changing some of them and observe
how they influence the look of the form. Try removing the weightx and weighty lines. What happens?

Now take a closer look at the fields in GridBagConstraints. You can set the following
GridBagConstraints instance variables:

➤ gridx and gridy: These integers specify the row and column of the cell where you want to
place the component. The upper leftmost cell has the position gridx=0 and gridy=0. You
can also set this to GridBagConstraints.RELATIVE to specify that a component should follow directly right of and/or under the component that was placed before.

➤ gridwidth and gridheight: These integers specify the number of columns and rows the
component spans. The default value for these is 1 (the component takes up a single cell). You
can set this to GridBagConstraints.REMAINDER to specify that the component should take
up all the remaining space in the row and/or column.

➤ fill: Used when the component's cell(s) span a larger area than the preferred size of the
component. When set to GridBagConstraints.NONE, the component's size will not be
stretched. When set to GridBagConstraints.HORIZONTAL, VERTICAL, or BOTH, the component's size will be stretched accordingly (try playing with these in the previous Try It Out).

➤ ipadx and ipady: These integers specify the internal padding of the component, with a default
value of 0. This determines how much space will be added to the size of the component.

➤ insets: Add a java.awt.Insets object here to specify the external padding of the component, i.e., the minimum amount of space between the component and the edges of the cell(s)
it resides in. By default, no external padding is used.

➤ anchor: This field determines where to place the component when the size of the component
is smaller than its cell(s). Valid values are GridBagConstraints.CENTER (the default), PAGE_
START, PAGE_END, LINE_START, LINE_END, FIRST_LINE_START (top-left corner), FIRST_
LINE_END (top-right corner), LAST_LINE_START (bottom-left corner), and LAST_LINE_END
(bottom-right corner). You can also use compass names (NORTH, NORTHEAST, and so on) if
you prefer, although those are considered to be deprecated.

➤ weightx and weighty: These two values determine how the layout manager should distrib-
ute space among the columns and rows, which is important for resizing behavior. The official
Javadocs mention that specifying weights "is an art that can have a significant impact on the
appearance of the components." In general, it is advisable to use either 0.0 or 1.0 as weights, and
use the numbers in between whenever necessary. Also important to know is that when you specify a weight of 0.0 (the default) for *all* components in the container, they will all clump together
in the center of the container. This is because the GridBagLayout will then put all extra space
between the edges of the container and the edges of the cell grid. Try removing the weightx and
weighty lines from the previous Try It Out and check this out for yourself.

CardLayout

The CardLayout layout manager is useful when you have two or more components (usually JPanel objects) that should share the same display space and when the user can choose which component should be shown.

Constructing it is very easy:

```
public CardLayout();
public CardLayout(int hgap, int vgap);

// hgap, vgap: horizontal/vertical gap between the components
```

The following Try It Out shows how it works.

TRY IT OUT Playing Your Cards Right with the CardLayout

In this Try It Out, you will get to see the CardLayout layout manager in use.

1. As always, feel free to create a new project in Eclipse when you want to. Create a class called CardLayoutFrame with the following content:

```java
import java.awt.BorderLayout;
import java.awt.CardLayout;
import java.awt.Color;
import java.awt.Dimension;
import java.awt.event.ItemEvent;
import java.awt.event.ItemListener;

import javax.swing.JComboBox;
import javax.swing.JFrame;
import javax.swing.JPanel;


public class CardLayoutFrame {
    public static void main(String[] args) {
        JFrame frame = new JFrame();
        frame.setDefaultCloseOperation(JFrame.EXIT_ON_CLOSE);
        frame.setTitle("CardLayout frame");


        JPanel cardPanel = new JPanel();
        cardPanel.setLayout(new CardLayout());
        cardPanel.setPreferredSize(new Dimension(300, 400));

        JPanel bluePanel = new JPanel();
        JPanel redPanel = new JPanel();
        bluePanel.setBackground(Color.blue);
        redPanel.setBackground(Color.red);

        cardPanel.add(bluePanel, "BLUE PANEL");
        cardPanel.add(redPanel, "RED PANEL");

        JPanel comboBoxPanel = new JPanel();
        String comboBoxItems[] = { "BLUE PANEL", "RED PANEL" };
```

```java
            JComboBox<String> cb = new JComboBox<>(comboBoxItems);
            cb.setEditable(false);
            cb.addItemListener(new ItemListener(){
                @Override
                public void itemStateChanged(ItemEvent evt) {
                    CardLayout cl = (CardLayout)(cardPanel.getLayout());
                    cl.show(cardPanel, (String)evt.getItem());
                }
            });
            comboBoxPanel.add(cb);

            frame.getContentPane().add(comboBoxPanel, BorderLayout.PAGE_START);
            frame.getContentPane().add(cardPanel, BorderLayout.CENTER);

            frame.pack();
            frame.setVisible(true);
        }
    }
```

2. Run the project from Eclipse. You should see the window in Figure 11-15.

FIGURE 11-15

3. Try selecting a different panel from the drop-down combobox. Notice how the blue panel changes to make room for the red one and vice versa.

4. You can also achieve the same effect by using a `JTabbedPane` Swing component instead of a `CardLayout` layout manager. The following class shows how:

```java
import java.awt.BorderLayout;
import java.awt.Color;
import java.awt.Dimension;
import javax.swing.JFrame;
import javax.swing.JPanel;
import javax.swing.JTabbedPane;


public class TabbedFrame {
    public static void main(String[] args) {
        JFrame frame = new JFrame();
        frame.setDefaultCloseOperation(JFrame.EXIT_ON_CLOSE);
        frame.setTitle("Tabbed frame");

        JTabbedPane cardTabs = new JTabbedPane();
        cardTabs.setPreferredSize(new Dimension(300, 400));

        JPanel bluePanel = new JPanel();
        JPanel redPanel = new JPanel();
        bluePanel.setBackground(Color.blue);
        redPanel.setBackground(Color.red);

        cardTabs.add(bluePanel, "BLUE PANEL");
        cardTabs.add(redPanel, "RED PANEL");

        frame.getContentPane().add(cardTabs, BorderLayout.CENTER);

        frame.pack();
        frame.setVisible(true);
    }
}
```

5. When you run the `JTabbedPane` version, you'll see Figure 11-16.

How It Works

This is how it works:

1. Note that the setup of this example is a bit more complicated than the previous ones. First of all, the layout manager for the content pane of the `JFrame` is unchanged (`BorderLayout`). Next, a new `JPanel` is created to store your "cards," and its layout manager is set to a `CardLayout` instance. Next, two colored cards (also `JPanel`s) are created and added to the `cardPanel`. The second argument of the `add` method, when using a `CardLayout`, should be a string identifier for this card.

FIGURE 11-16

2. Next, an additional panel is created to hold a JComboBox, which has the same strings used for the names of the panels ("BLUE PANEL" and "RED PANEL") included here as items. Some additional code adds an item listener, which is necessary to make the combobox actually do something when selecting an item. Don't worry about the details yet, as you will see much more about listeners when you read about GUI events. Just note for now that this code gets the CardLayout object from the cards JPanel and then instructs this layout manager to show a card in the cardPanel with a given string identifier.

3. The TabbedFrame version is somewhat simpler. Here, a single JTabbedPane component is set up and added to the JFrame. Now, you can directly add your two colored panels, and the JTabbedPane component handles everything else for you.

In the Try It Out, the most important line is the one that gets the CardLayout layout manager to show another card:

```
CardLayout cl = (CardLayout)(cardPanel.getLayout());
cl.show(cardPanel, (String)evt.getItem());
```

There are a few other helpful methods you can call for a CardLayout object:

➤ first (Container parentContainer): Show the first card of the container.

➤ next (Container parentContainer): Show the next card of the container or flip back to the first one when the end is reached.

➤ previous (Container parentContainer): Show the previous card or flip to the last one when the beginning is reached.

➤ last (Container parentContainer): Show the last card of the container.

➤ show (Container parentContainer, String name): Show the card that was added to the container with the given specific name (this is the one used in the Try It Out example).

In general, you'll not see the CardLayout used that often, especially since components such as JTabbedFrame allow you to accomplish the same with less boilerplate code (showing how many cards exist, handling switching between cards, and so on).

BoxLayout

BoxLayout is another layout manager that's relatively simple to use. Put simply, BoxLayout will stack components on top of each other or place them in a row. Therefore, you can think of it as a version of the FlowLayout layout manager, but with greater functionality.

There's only one constructor available:

```
public BoxLayout(Container target, int axis);
```

The target specifies for which container the layout should be performed, whereas the axis specifies whether you want components to be placed in a row or column by providing BoxLayout.LINE_AXIS or PAGE_AXIS.

One aspect you need to be aware of is that the BoxLayout constructor expects to get the container as an argument. Instead of writing the following:

```
myContainer.setLayout(new BoxLayout(BoxLayout.PAGE_AXIS));
```

You actually need to write the following:

```
myContainer.setLayout(new BoxLayout(myContainer, BoxLayout.PAGE_AXIS));
```

When laying out components, the BoxLayout will take the minimum, preferred, and maximum sizes into account. The layout manager will also adhere to the alignment of a component, which you can specify by passing Component.LEFT_ALIGNMENT, CENTER_ALIGNMENT, and so on, to the setAlignmentX and setAlignmentY methods of components. The following Try It Out introduces how everything works.

TRY IT OUT   Stacking Boxes with BoxLayout

In this Try It Out, you use the BoxLayout layout manager.

1. As always, feel free to create a new project in Eclipse when you want to. Create a class called BoxLayoutFrame with the following content:

```java
import java.awt.Color;
import java.awt.Component;
import java.awt.Dimension;

import javax.swing.BoxLayout;
import javax.swing.JFrame;
import javax.swing.JPanel;


public class BoxLayoutFrame {

    public static void main(String[] args) {
        JFrame frame = new JFrame();
        frame.setDefaultCloseOperation(JFrame.EXIT_ON_CLOSE);
        frame.setTitle("BoxLayout frame");

        frame.getContentPane().setLayout(
                new BoxLayout(frame.getContentPane(), BoxLayout.PAGE_AXIS));

        frame.getContentPane().add(makePanel(Color.red, 10,
                Component.CENTER_ALIGNMENT));
        frame.getContentPane().add(makePanel(Color.blue, 50,
                Component.LEFT_ALIGNMENT));
        frame.getContentPane().add(makePanel(Color.yellow, 100,
                Component.RIGHT_ALIGNMENT));
        frame.getContentPane().add(makePanel(Color.green, 200,
                Component.LEFT_ALIGNMENT));
```

```
        frame.getContentPane().add(makePanel(Color.pink, 500,
                Component.CENTER_ALIGNMENT));

        frame.pack();
        frame.setVisible(true);

    }

    private static JPanel makePanel(Color col, int w, float a) {
        JPanel panel = new JPanel();
        panel.setBackground(col);
        panel.setAlignmentX(a);
        panel.setPreferredSize(new Dimension(w, 50));
        panel.setMaximumSize(panel.getPreferredSize());
        panel.setMinimumSize(panel.getPreferredSize());
        return panel;
    }

}
```

2. Run the project from Eclipse. You should see the window in Figure 11-17.

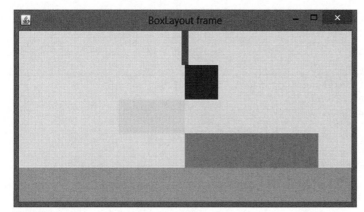

FIGURE 11-17

3. Observe what happens when you resize this window. A `BoxLayout` also allows you to create invisible "filler" components. Now modify this class to see how the filler components work:

```
import java.awt.Color;
import java.awt.Component;
import java.awt.Dimension;

import javax.swing.Box;
import javax.swing.BoxLayout;
import javax.swing.JFrame;
import javax.swing.JPanel;

public class BoxLayoutFrame {
```

```java
    public static void main(String[] args) {
        JFrame frame = new JFrame();
        frame.setDefaultCloseOperation(JFrame.EXIT_ON_CLOSE);
        frame.setTitle("BoxLayout frame");

        frame.getContentPane().setLayout(
                new BoxLayout(frame.getContentPane(), BoxLayout.PAGE_AXIS));

        frame.getContentPane().add(Box.createRigidArea(new Dimension(50,50)));
        frame.getContentPane().add(makePanel(Color.red, 10,
                Component.CENTER_ALIGNMENT));
        frame.getContentPane().add(Box.createVerticalGlue());
        frame.getContentPane().add(makePanel(Color.blue, 50,
                Component.LEFT_ALIGNMENT));
        frame.getContentPane().add(Box.createVerticalGlue());
        frame.getContentPane().add(makePanel(Color.yellow, 100,
                Component.RIGHT_ALIGNMENT));
        frame.getContentPane().add(Box.createVerticalGlue());
        frame.getContentPane().add(makePanel(Color.green, 200,
                Component.LEFT_ALIGNMENT));
        frame.getContentPane().add(Box.createVerticalGlue());
        frame.getContentPane().add(makePanel(Color.pink, 500,
                Component.CENTER_ALIGNMENT));

        frame.pack();
        frame.setVisible(true);

    }

    private static JPanel makePanel(Color col, int w, float a) {
        JPanel panel = new JPanel();
        panel.setBackground(col);
        panel.setAlignmentX(a);
        panel.setPreferredSize(new Dimension(w, 50));
        panel.setMaximumSize(panel.getPreferredSize());
        panel.setMinimumSize(panel.getPreferredSize());
        return panel;
    }

}
```

4.   Run the program again. Observe what happens when you resize the window now.

How It Works

This is how it works:

1.   The workings of this example should be easy to follow. First, the layout manager of the JFrame content pane is changed to a BoxLayout.

2.   Next, a number of panels are added. You set their background colors; minimum, maximum, and preferred sizes; and horizontal alignments using the makePanel method.

3.   Finally, in the second version of the class, Box.createRigidArea and Box.createVerticalGlue add rigid areas and glue between stacked components. The following section shows these options in more detail.

You saw in the Try It Out how to add glue and rigid areas, i.e. invisible components. You'll next consider these in a little more detail, but not before these general tips:

➤ Note how the alignment of a component can be set to a float value, meaning that you can also specify intermediate alignments between all the way to the left (0F), all the way to the right (1F), or a center alignment (0.5F). Try playing with this in the Try It Out.

➤ Note how the minimum and maximum sizes of the panels were set to be equal to the preferred size. If these are different values, or if you don't specify them all, the panel will be more flexible to stretch and fill any available space. When you're having trouble with components misbehaving in a `BoxLayout`, try checking their sizes.

➤ Now, concerning glue and rigid areas, there are three types of invisible components that can help you add space between components in a `BoxLayout`:

  ➤ A rigid area, created with `Box.createRigidArea(Dimension d)`: Use this when you want a fixed-size space between two components.

  ➤ Glue, created with `Box.createHorizontalGlue()` or `Box.createVerticalGlue()`: Use this to specify where excess space in a layout should go when resizing a window. Think of this component as some invisible elastic stretching glue between components. It still allows components to stick closely together, but will expand when stretched.

  ➤ A custom filler, created with new `Box.Filler(Dimension minimumSize, Dimension preferredSize, Dimension maximumSize)`: Use this to specify a component with whatever minimum, preferred, and maximum sizes you want. This is equal to creating some invisible `JPanel` with set sizes.

  ➤ A strut: Well, you read that there are three types of invisible components, but in actuality, there are four. A strut also provides a way to add filler, but the rigid area provides the same functionality and avoids some sizing issues in some cases, so that it is always better to use a rigid area instead of a strut.

  ➤ Finally, you can also add an invisible border to components to push them apart. We recommend against this solution, however, because you will end up adding glue or rigid areas anyway once you want to add a real border to your components.

GroupLayout and SpringLayout

The next two layout managers are placed in the same section, as they both offer a huge amount of flexibility, but are also incredibly hard to use. The reason behind this is that they were never meant to be used in a manual manner anyway.

The `GroupLayout` layout manager was originally developed to be used in combination with graphical GUI designers, such as the one provided in Netbeans (an IDE just like Eclipse). `GroupLayout` can still be used in a manual manner; the basic thing to know is that components are grouped hierarchically and groups are laid out either sequentially (one after another) or parallel (next to each other). On the other hand, the `SpringLayout` layout manager is even more complex, with the ability to emulate almost all features of the other layout managers. You can find online references showing you how to construct a `SpringLayout` by hand.

This book doesn't cover either of these layout managers in detail. This is because the other layout managers you have seen, `GridBagLayout` in particular, already allow you to build complex interfaces, especially once you start nesting containers and also throw smart components such as JTabbedFrame or JSplitPane in the mix. Later in this chapter, however, you'll get a quick tour of some visual GUI builders, which also allow you to see which kind of GroupLayout- or SpringLayout-based code these editors come up with.

Absolute Positioning (No Layout Manager)

Earlier in this chapter, you read that it is also possible to pass null as a layout manager to components. Doing so allows you to leave the positioning of components entirely up to you. Now explore this with a simple example in the following Try It Out.

TRY IT OUT Going Solo: Absolute Positioning Without a Layout Manager

In this Try It Out, you see how to lay out components manually, without using a layout manager.

1. As always, feel free to create a new project in Eclipse when you want to. Create a class called ManualLayoutFrame with the following content:

```java
import java.awt.Color;
import javax.swing.JFrame;
import javax.swing.JPanel;

public class ManualLayoutFrame {

    public static void main(String[] args) {
        JFrame frame = new JFrame();
        frame.setDefaultCloseOperation(JFrame.EXIT_ON_CLOSE);
        frame.setTitle("Manual layout frame");

        frame.getContentPane().setLayout(null);

        JPanel bluePanel = new JPanel(),
                redPanel = new JPanel(),
                greenPanel = new JPanel();
        bluePanel.setBackground(Color.blue);
        redPanel.setBackground(Color.red);
        greenPanel.setBackground(Color.green);

        bluePanel.setBounds(100, 100, 100, 100);
        redPanel.setBounds(50, 200, 400, 200);
        greenPanel.setBounds(150, 100, 50, 50);

        frame.add(bluePanel);
        frame.add(redPanel);
        frame.add(greenPanel);

        frame.pack();
        frame.setVisible(true);

        frame.setSize(500, 500);
    }

}
```

2. Run the project from Eclipse. You should see the window in Figure 11-18.

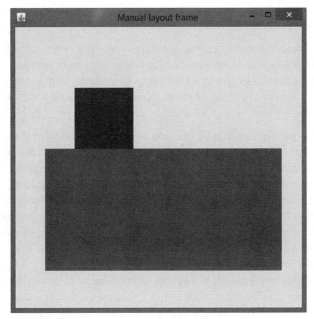

FIGURE 11-18

3. Observe what happens when you resize this window (there is no layout manager now to stretch things around). Also, try changing the order of the `add` method lines to make the green panel appear above the other ones (it is currently hidden).

How It Works

This is how it works:

1. The workings of this class should be easy to understand. The main things to note are the use of a `null` layout manager, as well as calling `setBounds` on the panels. Four dimensions are given: x-position, y-position, width, and height.

2. Finally, note the use of the `setSize` method here to size the `JFrame`, as there is now no layout manager that can make an informed guess based on the components contained in the `JFrame` container on which size to give the frame.

This concludes the overview on layout managers and how to use them. Take your time to play around with them and create some nested structures. Before moving on to the next big topic when dealing with GUIs—events—consider these helpful tips that help you when you lay out components.

➤ One of the problems beginners encounter when dealing with layout managers relates to the sizing of components. Remember that `setSize` and `setBounds` only work when a layout manager is not controlling your component. Since `JPanels` are controlled by a `FlowLayout`, by default, and bordered containers by a `BorderLayout`, this will never be the case by default.

➤ To specify sizes, you'll hence to resort to the `setMinimumSize`, `setPreferredSize`, and `setMaximumSize` methods. Try these first before trying something else.

➤ Sometimes, you'll want to add components while your program is running. You might encounter cases where your component does not appear. Occcassionally, you might note that the added component suddenly pops into view when resizing its containers. In that case, check out the `revalidate` and `repaint` methods of the component, which will force Java to draw it after adding it.

➤ You'll note that building GUIs is mostly a matter of creating components and adding them to each other. For these simple examples, it was easy to just put the complete GUI initialization in a `main` method and leave it at that. However, be aware that it is an easy mistake when building GUIs to suddenly forget everything about Object-Oriented Programming and end up with monster classes setting up a huge amount of GUI components. Thus, when building GUIs, always ask if you might be able to reuse certain parts, and keep in mind you can extend GUI classes just like you could any class! If you need a bold red label in many places of your program, why not construct an `ErrorLabel` that extends the `JLabel` class that already contains the right calls to set up the font and size, instead of always directly setting up a nice-looking `JLabel` every time you need it? If you need some kind of easy way to create forms row-by-row, consider creating a class-extending `JPanel` that uses a `GridBagLayout` together with some hand-rolled methods to make the GUI setup easier. In short, don't be afraid to abstract GUI aspects. Another even more important issue arising from putting logic and GUI-related code into the `main` method (the `main` method, in the examples above) is the fact that you might run into threading issues with Swing. The next section will explain in detail what this entails and how you can avoid such issues.

➤ Finally, when constructing GUIs, it is a nice idea to sketch out on paper first how your GUI should look, and derive some component/container tree out of it. Maybe the `JFrame` should contain two panels. One panel would contain a `JSplitPane`, with the left component a `JScrollPane` and the right component another panel. The layout manager would stack a number of different `JPanels`, each of which would contain certain buttons and labels. Sketch your ideas on paper first, and don't be afraid to put things into a separate `JPanel` (or even better, into a custom class-extending `JPanel`). It takes a little more work at first, but you'll be thankful later.

UNDERSTANDING EVENTS

All the GUI applications you've been building so far do not have any true functionality associated with them. Sure, you can add a `JButton` and even click it, but how do you make it actually do something? To add behavior to your graphical interfaces, you first need an introduction to the concept of events.

Introduction to Events

An event can be defined as a happening of something, an occurrence, meaning that something happened somewhere. In graphical user interfaces, events usually result from a user's action. For instance, the user clicks on a button, closes a window, resizes a window, selects an item in a combo-box, or even moves the mouse around inside a window.

When building console programs, there is a set sequence of actions, and the program will stop execution when it expects input from the user, and continues onward once it has received it. In graphical programs, the user can at any time do a number of things: type in a textbox, minimize a window, or click a button. All these actions by the user are called "events." Not only in Java, but in many other programming languages, there is usually an "event loop," which is a background task that constantly checks for any new event and responds accordingly. This type of program is said to be event-driven. In Java, you do not have to deal with this event loop directly, but you can plug into it so you can capture interesting events (a user clicked a button) and deal with them accordingly. This is done by creating so-called event listeners.

> **NOTE** Some programming languages make the concept of an "event loop" a core architectural construct. Node.js, for instance, has become popular as a JavaScript-based (not Java) programming framework that applies an event loop to the whole program, not just to the GUI.

Event Listeners

You've already learned that any user action within a GUI application will lead to some kind of event. By default, all of these events just happen, but to make useful applications, you'll need to define event listeners. These are objects that can receive a notification when a specific event of interest has happened. This is illustrated in the following Try It Out example.

TRY IT OUT Creating a BMI Calculator

In this Try It Out, you create a graphical Body Mass Index (BMI) calculator.

1. As always, feel free to create a new project in Eclipse when you want to. Create a class called BMICalculator with the following content:

```java
import java.awt.Dimension;

import javax.swing.Box;
import javax.swing.BoxLayout;
import javax.swing.JButton;
import javax.swing.JFrame;
import javax.swing.JLabel;
import javax.swing.JTextField;
import javax.swing.SwingUtilities;

public class BMICalculator extends JFrame {

    private final JTextField txtMass = new JTextField();
    private final JTextField txtHeight = new JTextField();
    private final JButton btnCalc = new JButton("Calculate BMI");
```

```java
public BMICalculator() {
    super();
    setDefaultCloseOperation(JFrame.EXIT_ON_CLOSE);
    setTitle("BMI Calculator");

    getContentPane().setLayout(
            new BoxLayout(getContentPane(), BoxLayout.PAGE_AXIS));

    txtMass.setPreferredSize(new Dimension(200,30));
    txtHeight.setPreferredSize(new Dimension(200,30));
    txtMass.setMaximumSize(txtMass.getPreferredSize());
    txtHeight.setMaximumSize(txtHeight.getPreferredSize());

    getContentPane().add(new JLabel("Your mass (kg):"));
    getContentPane().add(Box.createRigidArea(new Dimension(5,5)));
    getContentPane().add(txtMass);
    getContentPane().add(Box.createRigidArea(new Dimension(5,5)));

    getContentPane().add(Box.createVerticalGlue());

    getContentPane().add(new JLabel("Your height (cm):"));
    getContentPane().add(Box.createRigidArea(new Dimension(5,5)));
    getContentPane().add(txtHeight);
    getContentPane().add(Box.createRigidArea(new Dimension(5,5)));

    getContentPane().add(Box.createVerticalGlue());
    getContentPane().add(btnCalc);
    getContentPane().add(Box.createRigidArea(new Dimension(5,5)));


    pack();
    setVisible(true);
}

public static void main(String[] args) {
    SwingUtilities.invokeLater(new Runnable() {
        public void run() {
            new BMICalculator();
        }
    });
}
}
```

2. Run the project from Eclipse. You should see the window in Figure 11-19.

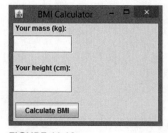

FIGURE 11-19

3. This is a good time to explore a bit and add some styling if you want to do so. Here's an example of something you can come up with:

```java
import java.awt.Color;
import java.awt.Dimension;
import java.awt.Font;
import java.awt.Insets;

import javax.swing.BorderFactory;
import javax.swing.Box;
import javax.swing.BoxLayout;
import javax.swing.JButton;
import javax.swing.JFrame;
import javax.swing.JLabel;
import javax.swing.JTextField;
import javax.swing.SwingUtilities;

public class BMICalculator extends JFrame {

    private final JTextField txtMass = makePrettyTextField();
    private final JTextField txtHeight = makePrettyTextField();
    private final JButton btnCalc = makePrettyButton("Calculate BMI");

    public BMICalculator() {
        super();
        setDefaultCloseOperation(JFrame.EXIT_ON_CLOSE);
        setTitle("BMI Calculator");


        getContentPane().setLayout(
                new BoxLayout(getContentPane(), BoxLayout.PAGE_AXIS));

        txtMass.setPreferredSize(new Dimension(200,30));
        txtHeight.setPreferredSize(new Dimension(200,30));
        txtMass.setMaximumSize(txtMass.getPreferredSize());
        txtHeight.setMaximumSize(txtHeight.getPreferredSize());

        getContentPane().setBackground(new Color(232, 240, 255));

        getContentPane().add(makePrettyLabel("Your mass (kg):"));
        getContentPane().add(Box.createRigidArea(new Dimension(5,5)));
        getContentPane().add(txtMass);
        getContentPane().add(Box.createRigidArea(new Dimension(5,5)));

        getContentPane().add(Box.createVerticalGlue());

        getContentPane().add(makePrettyLabel("Your height (cm):"));
        getContentPane().add(Box.createRigidArea(new Dimension(5,5)));
        getContentPane().add(txtHeight);
        getContentPane().add(Box.createRigidArea(new Dimension(5,5)));

        getContentPane().add(Box.createVerticalGlue());
        getContentPane().add(btnCalc);
        getContentPane().add(Box.createRigidArea(new Dimension(5,5)));
```

```
        pack();
        setVisible(true);
    }

    private JButton makePrettyButton(String title) {
        JButton button = new JButton(title);
        button.setFont(new Font(Font.SANS_SERIF, Font.PLAIN, 16));
        button.setBorder(BorderFactory.createRaisedBevelBorder());
        button.setBackground(Color.white);
        button.setForeground(new Color(53, 124, 255));
        return button;
    }

    private JTextField makePrettyTextField() {
        JTextField field = new JTextField();
        field.setFont(new Font(Font.SANS_SERIF, Font.ITALIC, 14));
        field.setHorizontalAlignment(JTextField.RIGHT);
        field.setBorder(BorderFactory.createLoweredBevelBorder());
        return field;
    }

    private JLabel makePrettyLabel(String title) {
        JLabel label = new JLabel(title);
        label.setFont(new Font(Font.SANS_SERIF, Font.BOLD, 14));
        label.setForeground(new Color(53, 124, 255));
        return label;
    }

    public static void main(String[] args) {
        SwingUtilities.invokeLater(new Runnable() {
            public void run() {
                new BMICalculator();
            }
        });
    }
}
```

4. To add a behavior to the Calculate button, change the class once again to look as follows:

```
import java.awt.Color;
import java.awt.Dimension;
import java.awt.Font;
import java.awt.event.ActionEvent;
import java.awt.event.ActionListener;

import javax.swing.BorderFactory;
import javax.swing.Box;
import javax.swing.BoxLayout;
import javax.swing.JButton;
import javax.swing.JFrame;
import javax.swing.JLabel;
import javax.swing.JOptionPane;
import javax.swing.JTextField;
import javax.swing.SwingUtilities;
```

```java
public class BMICalculator extends JFrame {

    private final JTextField txtMass = makePrettyTextField();
    private final JTextField txtHeight = makePrettyTextField();
    private final JButton btnCalc = makePrettyButton("Calculate BMI");

    private final BMICalculator self = this;

    public BMICalculator() {
        super();
        setDefaultCloseOperation(JFrame.EXIT_ON_CLOSE);
        setTitle("BMI Calculator");


        getContentPane().setLayout(
                new BoxLayout(getContentPane(), BoxLayout.PAGE_AXIS));

        txtMass.setPreferredSize(new Dimension(200,30));
        txtHeight.setPreferredSize(new Dimension(200,30));
        txtMass.setMaximumSize(txtMass.getPreferredSize());
        txtHeight.setMaximumSize(txtHeight.getPreferredSize());

        getContentPane().setBackground(new Color(232, 240, 255));

        getContentPane().add(makePrettyLabel("Your mass (kg):"));
        getContentPane().add(Box.createRigidArea(new Dimension(5,5)));
        getContentPane().add(txtMass);
        getContentPane().add(Box.createRigidArea(new Dimension(5,5)));

        getContentPane().add(Box.createVerticalGlue());

        getContentPane().add(makePrettyLabel("Your height (cm):"));
        getContentPane().add(Box.createRigidArea(new Dimension(5,5)));
        getContentPane().add(txtHeight);
        getContentPane().add(Box.createRigidArea(new Dimension(5,5)));

        getContentPane().add(Box.createVerticalGlue());
        getContentPane().add(btnCalc);
        getContentPane().add(Box.createRigidArea(new Dimension(5,5)));

        // Add BMI calculation
        btnCalc.addActionListener(new ActionListener() {
            @Override
            public void actionPerformed(ActionEvent arg0) {
                double mass;
                double height;
                try {
                    mass = Double.parseDouble(txtMass.getText());
                    height = Double.parseDouble(txtHeight.getText());
                } catch (NumberFormatException e) {
                    JOptionPane.showMessageDialog(self,
                            "Please enter a valid number for mass and height.",
                            "Input error",
                            JOptionPane.ERROR_MESSAGE);
```

```
                          return;
                      }
                      double result = calculateBMI(mass, height);
                      JOptionPane.showMessageDialog(self,
                              "Your BMI is: " + (Math.round(result*100.0)/100.0),
                              "Your BMI result",
                              JOptionPane.PLAIN_MESSAGE);
                  }
              });

          pack();
          setVisible(true);
      }

      protected double calculateBMI(double mass, double height) {
          return mass / Math.pow(height/100.0, 2.0);
      }

      private JButton makePrettyButton(String title) {
          JButton button = new JButton(title);
          button.setFont(new Font(Font.SANS_SERIF, Font.PLAIN, 16));
          button.setBorder(BorderFactory.createRaisedBevelBorder());
          button.setBackground(Color.white);
          button.setForeground(new Color(53, 124, 255));
          return button;
      }

      private JTextField makePrettyTextField() {
          JTextField field = new JTextField();
          field.setFont(new Font(Font.SANS_SERIF, Font.ITALIC, 14));
          field.setHorizontalAlignment(JTextField.RIGHT);
          field.setBorder(BorderFactory.createLoweredBevelBorder());
          return field;
      }

      private JLabel makePrettyLabel(String title) {
          JLabel label = new JLabel(title);
          label.setFont(new Font(Font.SANS_SERIF, Font.BOLD, 14));
          label.setForeground(new Color(53, 124, 255));
          return label;
      }

      public static void main(String[] args) {
          SwingUtilities.invokeLater(new Runnable() {
              public void run() {
                  new BMICalculator();
              }
          });
      }
  }
```

5. Try running the program and enter some numbers. Note that the button actually works, as shown in Figure 11-20.

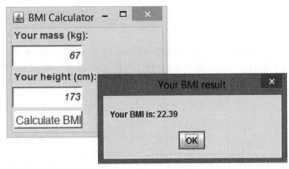

FIGURE 11-20

How It Works

This is how it works:

1. Instead of putting all the code in a single `main` method, like in the trivial examples before, now a proper class, extending `JFrame`, is created.

2. Note also the addition of the following pattern in the `main` method:

```
SwingUtilities.invokeLater(new Runnable() {
    public void run() {
        // Execute UI code here
    }
});
```

Using the static `invokeLater` method of the `SwingUtilities` class ensures that all UI-related code is executed on the Event Dispatch Thread. You'll see later on what this means exactly. For now, just keep this pattern in mind.

3. A set of methods is defined to create "pretty" text fields, buttons, and labels. Your definition of pretty might vary, so feel free to change and experiment with these methods.

4. Then the GUI is set up within the constructor of the class. A `BoxLayout` is used here, and all the components are stacked under each other.

5. The important code is located in the `addActionListener` method. As the name suggests, this method allows you to add a listener to your `btnCalc` button that's notified whenever an `ActionEvent` occurs. The listener itself is constructed by using an anonymous inner class (`new ActionListener() { . . . }`), a pattern that you will see occurring often for event listeners. This anonymous class needs to override and specify one method, `actionPerformed`, which will be called by the button whenever the user performs an action. In the case of a `JButton`, this means whenever the button is activated (clicked, focused on, and then Enter is pressed).

6. Inside the action listener, the mass and height are taken from the text fields, and a check is done to see if these fields contain invalid input (if they do, an error is displayed). To show messages, another Swing component called `JOptionPane` shows the message dialogs using a single static method. The first argument indicates the parent component of the message dialog to be shown, which in this case means the BMI Calculator. You cannot, however, just pass `this`, as `this`, in this context, would resolve to the anonymous `ActionListener` object, not to the `BMICalculator` object. Instead, use a

simple trick and define a final variable called `self`, which can be used in the anonymous inner class. This is another pattern you might see occurring often when creating event listeners.

7. It is always a good idea to separate logic code from interface code whenever you can. Therefore, the actual calculation of a BMI is properly separated into its own method: `calculateBMI`. The result is shown to the user with another message dialog.

SERIAL VERSION IDs

When following along with the Try It Out, you might have spotted an Eclipse warning saying that `BMICalculator` does not contain a serial version identifier. Eclipse will offer to generate a random one for you, which boils down to a line of code similar to this one being added to your class:

```
private static final long serialVersionUID = -8952857142790654268L;
```

Now what is this identifier and why is it useful? The reason behind this has to do with serialization (storing objects in a format that allows you to read them back out and initialize them as class instances again later). To make sure that the data of a stored object still matches a class definition (as this might have changed over time), Java also stores a special identifier that verifies that the object to be loaded back in still matches the identifier of the class. As such, as the name suggests, the `serialVersionUID` is mainly helpful for versioning reasons (an object with UID 100 will not be able to get instantiated to its class when the class definition is on version 101).

In most cases, Java can generate a `serialVersionUID` based on various aspects of the class at hand. However, it is recommended that all serializable classes explicitly declare `serialVersionUID` values, since the default `serialVersionUID` computation is sensitive to class details that may vary depending on compiler implementations. Since Swing components implement `Serializable` and because Eclipse cares about best practices, it asks you to specify a `serialVersionUID`.

Since it is unlikely that you will start serializing Swing components (they shouldn't contain important data anyway and should just concern themselves with UI), the best thing to do if you want to avoid these warnings is to use the default UID everywhere:

```
private static final long serialVersionUID = 1L;
```

You can also turn off these warning by navigating to Window, Preferences, Java ➤ Compiler ➤ Errors/Warnings and setting Serializable Class Without serialVersionUID to Ignore under Potential Programming Problems.

Now take a closer look to see how event listeners work. Swing components hold a collection of listener objects, which have registered themselves to be interested in being notified whenever an event occurs. For instance, for a `JButton`, you have seen how `ActionListener` objects can be registered using the `addActionListener` method. Note that the same listener can in theory be registered with multiple components.

> **NOTE** *By using the term event listener, you might expect the listening objects to be the active players in this setup, but actually, it is the event source (e.g., a button) that will notify its listeners when something interesting happens, by calling one of their methods. This listener-notifier setup is a typical programming pattern, commonly referred to as the observer pattern. The following chapter has much more information on Object-Oriented Programming patterns.*

Generally speaking, there are three ways you will see listener objects being defined and registered. First of all, for simple event listeners you know you'll only need with one particular component, it is common to define the listener directly as an anonymous inner class, like so:

```java
import java.awt.event.ActionEvent;
import java.awt.event.ActionListener;

import javax.swing.JButton;
import javax.swing.JFrame;
import javax.swing.JOptionPane;
import javax.swing.SwingUtilities;

public class ActionListenerExample extends JFrame {

    public ActionListenerExample() {
        super();
        setDefaultCloseOperation(JFrame.EXIT_ON_CLOSE);

        JButton btn = new JButton("Click Me!");

        btn.addActionListener(new ActionListener() {
            @Override
            public void actionPerformed(ActionEvent arg0) {
                JOptionPane.showMessageDialog(
                        null,
                        "You clicked me, nice!",
                        "Aw yeah!",
                        JOptionPane.PLAIN_MESSAGE);
            }
        });

        this.add(btn);

        pack();
        setVisible(true);
    }

    public static void main(String[] args) {
        SwingUtilities.invokeLater(new Runnable() {
            public void run() {
                new ActionListenerExample();
            }
        });
    }
}
```

The main benefit of this technique is that it is easy and simple, so it works well for simple components. The downside it that it leads quickly to messy-looking code, does not allow the same listener to be reused in multiple components, and will sometimes require you to do some variable hocus-pocus to access them in the inner class (remember the `self` variable from the Try It Out).

The second way will make the container component itself the event listener. This is helpful when you have multiple components to listen to and you already have a custom class for your container. In this case, you'll see the pattern `class Name extends JContainerName implements ListenerName` appearing, like in this example:

```
import java.awt.event.ActionEvent;
import java.awt.event.ActionListener;

import javax.swing.JButton;
import javax.swing.JFrame;
import javax.swing.JOptionPane;
import javax.swing.SwingUtilities;

public class ActionListenerExample extends JFrame implements ActionListener {

    public ActionListenerExample() {
        super();
        setDefaultCloseOperation(JFrame.EXIT_ON_CLOSE);

        JButton btn = new JButton("Click Me!");

        // The JFrame is now also the listener object
        btn.addActionListener(this);

        this.add(btn);

        pack();
        setVisible(true);
    }

    @Override
    public void actionPerformed(ActionEvent arg0) {
        JOptionPane.showMessageDialog(
                null,
                "You clicked me, nice!",
                "Aw yeah!",
                JOptionPane.PLAIN_MESSAGE);
    }

    public static void main(String[] args) {
        SwingUtilities.invokeLater(new Runnable() {
            public void run() {
                new ActionListenerExample();
            }
        });
    }
}
```

The upside of this approach is that it allows the class you already have as a container to act as a listener for its child components. The downside is that you need to add some extra code when you want to add a listener to multiple buttons, for instance, and need to know which button (not just that *a* button) was clicked. More about how to deal with this later.

Finally, you can also decide to keep the listener separated as much as possible by defining it in a new class:

```java
import javax.swing.JButton;
import javax.swing.JFrame;
import javax.swing.JOptionPane;
import javax.swing.SwingUtilities;

public class ActionListenerExample extends JFrame {

    public ActionListenerExample() {
        super();
        setDefaultCloseOperation(JFrame.EXIT_ON_CLOSE);

        JButton btn = new JButton("Click Me!");

        MySimpleButtonListener listener = new MySimpleButtonListener();
        btn.addActionListener(listener);

        this.add(btn);

        pack();
        setVisible(true);
    }

    public static void main(String[] args) {
        SwingUtilities.invokeLater(new Runnable() {
            public void run() {
                new ActionListenerExample();
            }
        });
    }
}

import java.awt.event.ActionEvent;
import java.awt.event.ActionListener;

public class MySimpleButtonListener implements ActionListener {

    @Override
    public void actionPerformed(ActionEvent arg0) {
        JOptionPane.showMessageDialog(
                null,
                "You clicked me, nice!",
                "Aw yeah!",
                JOptionPane.PLAIN_MESSAGE);
    }

}
```

Obviously, the advantage is that it becomes easy to reuse the same listener class (and instances, even) across different components. The downside is that this requires a little more effort to set up.

So far, you've only seen the `ActionListener` for a `JButton`. A wealth of other listeners exists as well. The general usage is always the same: construct a listener with the appropriate type using one of the three techniques seen previously, and then add it to a component using `addLISTENERTYPEListener`. A nonexhaustive list of some of the interesting listeners is included in the following table.

LISTENER (INTERFACE): METHOD TO ADD	CAN BE USED WITH: PURPOSE	METHOD(S) TO IMPLEMENT
Action Listener (`ActionListener`) - `addActionListener`	Fires `ActionEvent` when user performs primary action on component. Can be used with `JButton`, `JCheckBox`, `JComboBox`, `JRadioButton`, and `JTextField`.	`actionPerformed`: Code that reacts to the action.
Caret Listener (`CaretListener`) - `addCaretListener`	Fires `CaretEvent` whenever the caret (the cursor in a text field, for instance) moves or when the selection changes. Can be used with `JTextArea`, `JTextField`, and `JTextPane`.	`caretUpdate`: Code that reacts whenever caret is updated (is moved, the selection changes, text is inserted, and so on).
Change Listener (`ChangeListener`) - `addChangeListener`	Fires `ChangeEvent` whenever a component changes its state. Can be used with `JButton`, `JCheckBox`, `JProgressBar`, and `JRadioButton`. Also useful with `JSlider` and `JSpinner`, as these will fire events for the value of the slider or the spinner changes. These two components do not accept `ActionListeners`, so here you'll want to use Change Listeners.	`stateChanged`: Code that reacts to component changes.
Item Listener (`ItemListener`) - `addItemListener`	Fires `ItemEvent` whenever a state change occurs in the component's items. `JCheckBox`, `JComboBox`, and other components keep a list of items that accept this listener.	`itemStateChanged`: Code that reacts when state of items changes.

List Selection Listener (ListSelectionListener) - addListSelectionListener	Fires `ListSelectionEvent` when selection changes in the component's items. Only `JList` and `JTable` accept this listener.	`valueChanged`: Code that reacts when another item is selected from the component's items.
Window Listener (WindowListener) - addWindowListener	Fires `WindowEvent` when state changes occur in windowed components. `JDialog` and `JFrame` accept this listener.	`windowOpened`: Code that reacts when window has been shown for first time (in program's execution). `windowClosing`: Code that reacts when user requests the window to close. `windowClosed`: Code that reacts just after window has closed. `windowIconified` and `windowDeiconified`: Code that reacts when window is minimized or unminimized. `windowActivated` and `windowDeactivated`: Code that reacts when window is activated or deactivated. This method will not work with frames or dialogs, so you need to use the Window `FocusListener` here instead.
Window Focus Listener (WindowFocusListener) - addWindowFocusListener	Fires `WindowEvent` when a windowed component gains or loses focus. `JDialog` and `JFrame` accept this listener.	`windowGainedFocus` and `windowLostFocus`: Code that reacts when window gains or loses focus.
Window State Listener (WindowStateListener) - addWindowStateListener	Fires `WindowEvent` when the state of a windowed component changes, such as is maximized or minimized. `JDialog` and `JFrame` accept this listener.	`windowStateChanged`: Code that reacts when window is being (un)minimized, maximized, or returned to normal.
Component Listener (ComponentListener) - addComponentListener	Fires `ComponentEvent` when a component is hidden, moved, resized, or shown. All components accept this listener.	`componentHidden` and `componentShown`: Code that reacts when component is made invisible or visible. `componentMoved` and `componentResized`: Code that reacts when position or dimensions of component changes.

continues

(continued)

LISTENER (INTERFACE): METHOD TO ADD	CAN BE USED WITH: PURPOSE	METHOD(S) TO IMPLEMENT
Focus Listener (FocusListener) - addFocusListener	Fires FocusEvent when component loses or gains focus. All components accept this listener.	focusGained and focusLost: Code that reacts when component gains or loses focus.
Key Listener (KeyListener) - addKeyListener	Fires KeyEvent when user types on the keyboard and the component the listener is registered with has focus. All components accept this listener.	keyTyped: Code that reacts when user types a key (presses and releases a key). keyPressed and keyReleased: Code that reacts when user presses and releases a key.
Mouse Listener (MouseListener) - addMouseListener	Fires MouseEvent when the mouse pointer interacts with a component. All components accept this listener.	mouseClicked: Code that reacts when a user clicks a mouse button. mouseEntered and mouseExited: Code that reacts when the mouse pointer enters or exits a component. mousePressed and mouseReleased: Code that reacts when user presses and releases a mouse button.
Mouse Motion Listener (MouseMotionListener) - addMouseMotionListener	Fires MouseEvent when the mouse pointer is dragged or moved over a component. All components accept this listener.	mouseDragged: Code that reacts when a user moves the mouse while holding a mouse button down. mouseMoved: Code that reacts when a user moves the mouse.
Mouse Wheel Listener (MouseWheelListener) - addMouseWheelListener	Fires MouseWheelEvent when user scrolls the mouse wheel. All components accept this listener.	mouseWheelMoved: Code that reacts when the user moves the mouse wheel.
Mouse Adapter (MouseAdapter) - addMouseListener, addMouseMotionListener, addMouseWheelListener	Can be used to define all three mouse event listeners at the same time. Convenience class.	See three mouse event listeners above.

Don't worry if the amount of event types and listeners seems overwhelming for now (and this isn't even all of them). Just refer to this table when you encounter a need to add more behavior to your components. In most cases, using action listener should cover most of your needs.

That said, whichever listener you're using, you should still consider a few additional aspects. The first one relates to the event source—the component sending the event to the listeners. Earlier on, you read that in some cases you might want to determine exactly which button was clicked. For example, take the following base scenario:

```java
import java.awt.FlowLayout;
import java.awt.event.ActionEvent;
import java.awt.event.ActionListener;

import javax.swing.JButton;
import javax.swing.JFrame;
import javax.swing.JOptionPane;
import javax.swing.SwingUtilities;

public class ActionListenerExample extends JFrame implements ActionListener {
    public ActionListenerExample() {
        super();
        this.setLayout(new FlowLayout());
        setDefaultCloseOperation(JFrame.EXIT_ON_CLOSE);
        JButton btn1 = new JButton("Click Me!");
        JButton btn2 = new JButton("No, click me!");
        btn1.addActionListener(this);
        btn2.addActionListener(this);
        getContentPane().add(btn1);
        getContentPane().add(btn2);
        pack();
        setVisible(true);
    }

    @Override
    public void actionPerformed(ActionEvent ev) {
        JOptionPane.showMessageDialog(
            null,
            "You clicked a button!",
            "Aw yeah!",
            JOptionPane.PLAIN_MESSAGE);
    }

    public static void main(String[] args) {
        SwingUtilities.invokeLater(new Runnable() {
            public void run() {
                new ActionListenerExample();
            }
        });
    }
}
```

This class is comparable to the earlier example and acts as both a container and an action listener for two buttons. Now say you want to show a different message depending on which button was clicked.

The first way to do this is by changing the `actionPerformed` method as follows:

```java
@Override
public void actionPerformed(ActionEvent ev) {
```

```
    String message;
    if (((JButton)ev.getSource()).getText().equals("Click Me!"))
        message = "First button was clicked";
    else
        message = "Second button was clicked";

    JOptionPane.showMessageDialog(null,
            message, "Aw yeah!",
            JOptionPane.PLAIN_MESSAGE);
}
```

Of course, this is a terrible way to implement the desired functionality. Not only are you making an unsafe case (who says the source component will always be a button?), but you're also hardcoding some text that might later be changed. This does introduce an interesting method though: getSource(). This method allows you to get the source component for the incoming event. Why not directly use this method as is? You will need to make the two buttons class fields, however:

```
import java.awt.FlowLayout;
import java.awt.event.ActionEvent;
import java.awt.event.ActionListener;

import javax.swing.JButton;
import javax.swing.JFrame;
import javax.swing.JOptionPane;
import javax.swing.SwingUtilities;

public class ActionListenerExample extends JFrame implements ActionListener {
    private final JButton btn1 = new JButton("Click Me!");
    private final JButton btn2 = new JButton("No, click me!");

    public ActionListenerExample() {
        super();
        this.setLayout(new FlowLayout());
        setDefaultCloseOperation(JFrame.EXIT_ON_CLOSE);
        btn1.addActionListener(this);
        btn2.addActionListener(this);
        getContentPane().add(btn1);
        getContentPane().add(btn2);
        pack();
        setVisible(true);
    }

    @Override
    public void actionPerformed(ActionEvent ev) {
        String message = "";
        if (ev.getSource() == btn1)
            message = "First button was clicked";
        else if (ev.getSource() == btn2)
            message = "Second button was clicked";

        JOptionPane.showMessageDialog(null,
                message, "Aw yeah!",
                JOptionPane.PLAIN_MESSAGE);
```

```
        }

    public static void main(String[] args) {
        SwingUtilities.invokeLater(new Runnable() {
            public void run() {
                new ActionListenerExample();
            }
        });
    }
}
```

This is much better. There is, however, also another mechanism by which you can determine the correct action to take whenever an event is fired, that is by means of a so-called action command. This is especially useful when the same event source can lead to different behavior. The following example shows how action commands work. Pay particular attention to the use of the setActionCommand and getActionCommand methods.

```
import java.awt.Color;
import java.awt.FlowLayout;
import java.awt.event.ActionEvent;
import java.awt.event.ActionListener;

import javax.swing.JButton;
import javax.swing.JFrame;
import javax.swing.SwingUtilities;

public class DiscoLightsExample extends JFrame implements ActionListener {
    private final String ACTION_ON = "LIGHT ON";
    private final String ACTION_OFF = "LIGHT OFF";
    private final String ACTION_CYCLE = "CYCLE COLOR";

    private final Color[] COLORS = new Color[]{
            Color.white,
            Color.green,
            Color.red,
            Color.yellow,
            Color.orange,
            Color.pink
    };

    private int currentColor = 0;
    private boolean isLightOn = false;

    public DiscoLightsExample() {
        setTitle("Disco Light Party Frame");
        setLayout(new FlowLayout());
        setDefaultCloseOperation(JFrame.EXIT_ON_CLOSE);

        JButton btnOffOn = new JButton("Lights On");
        JButton btnColor = new JButton("Cycle Color");

        btnOffOn.setActionCommand(ACTION_ON);
        btnColor.setActionCommand(ACTION_CYCLE);

        btnOffOn.addActionListener(this);
```

```
            btnColor.addActionListener(this);
            getContentPane().add(btnOffOn);
            getContentPane().add(btnColor);
            pack();
            setVisible(true);
        }

        @Override
        public void actionPerformed(ActionEvent ev) {
            String action = ev.getActionCommand();
            System.err.println("Got action "+action);
            switch (action) {
            case ACTION_ON:
                isLightOn = true;
                getContentPane().setBackground(COLORS[currentColor]);
                ((JButton) ev.getSource()).setText("Lights Off");
                ((JButton) ev.getSource()).setActionCommand(ACTION_OFF);
                break;
            case ACTION_OFF:
                isLightOn = false;
                getContentPane().setBackground(Color.black);
                ((JButton) ev.getSource()).setText("Lights On");
                ((JButton) ev.getSource()).setActionCommand(ACTION_ON);
                break;
            case ACTION_CYCLE:
                if (isLightOn)
                    getContentPane().setBackground(COLORS[++currentColor
                        % COLORS.length]);
                break;
            }
        }

        public static void main(String[] args) {
            SwingUtilities.invokeLater(new Runnable() {
                public void run() {
                    new DiscoLightsExample();
                }
            });
        }
    }
```

On Threading and Swing

Finally, before moving on to the next section, there is one more important thing to highlight when working with event listeners—and indeed with UIs in general when using Swing. Recall that whenever you build a GUI with Java Swing, an event loop will start running in the background that will check for user actions and dispatch events to your listeners. To be more precise, all Swing event handling code runs on a special thread known as the Event Dispatch Thread. We won't talk in depth about threads in a beginner's book on programming, but in general, think about a thread as a unit of execution in a program. For instance, the following code snippet shows how two threads are created that will count from 1 to 10 in parallel:

```
public class CountingTask implements Runnable {
    private static int COUNTER = 0;
    private int threadId;

    public CountingTask() {
        threadId = ++COUNTER;
    }

    public void run() {
        for (int i = 1; i <= 10; i++) {
            System.out.println("Thread #"+threadId+" is at: "+i);
            try {
                // Rest a bit to give other threads a chance to work
                Thread.sleep(10);
            } catch (InterruptedException e) {
                e.printStackTrace();
            }
        }
    }

    public static void main(String[] args) {
        Thread thread1 = new Thread(new CountingTask());
        Thread thread2 = new Thread(new CountingTask());
        thread1.start();
        thread2.start();
    }
}
```

If you try to execute this code, you'll note that both threads' output lines will end up mixed on the console. This shows how threads can serve as a helpful way to define multiple work tasks within the same program. Note that your operating system is responsible for the actual allocation of CPU time to the various threads in your program. Even if you have only one CPU core, the operating system will make sure to divide calculation time so that each thread in all running programs on your computer get a chance to do their work, causing them to seemingly run in parallel. Note that running the code snippet above actually involves the creation of three threads: the main thread (all programs have one main thread, where the main method is invoked) and the two custom-defined ones.

Let's return to the discussion of the Event Dispatch Thread (EDT). This thread is started in the background (i.e., next to the main thread) to continually process events: button clicks, mouse clicks, and so on. Whenever you write code that makes changes to the GUI of a program, all this code *must* be executed in this Event Dispatch Thread as well. Updating visible components from other threads is the source of many common bugs in Java programs that use Swing. Note that this aspect is not specific to Swing; the same concept exists in other UI toolkits as well. To see how updating the UI outside the EDT can cause problems, take a look at the following code:

```
import javax.swing.DefaultListModel;
import javax.swing.JFrame;
import javax.swing.JList;


public class MultiThreadedFrame extends JFrame {
    public static final int LENGTH = 100;
```

```java
public static final JList<String> COMPONENT = new JList<>();

public class CountingTask implements Runnable {
    public void run() {
        for (int i = 1; i <= LENGTH; i++) {
            // Add an item
            ((DefaultListModel<String>) COMPONENT.getModel()).clear();
            ((DefaultListModel<String>)
                COMPONENT.getModel()).addElement("At: "+i);
            // Force component repaint
            COMPONENT.repaint();
            COMPONENT.invalidate();
            COMPONENT.repaint();
            // Sleep for a little to give other threads a chance
            try {
                Thread.sleep(1);
            } catch (InterruptedException e) {
                e.printStackTrace();
            }
        }
    }
}

public MultiThreadedFrame() {
    DefaultListModel<String> listModel = new DefaultListModel<>();
    COMPONENT.setModel(listModel);
    getContentPane().add(COMPONENT);
    pack();
    setSize(300,500);
    setVisible(true);

    // Increase the number of threads if problem does not appear
    for (int t = 0; t < 16; t++) {
        Thread thread = new Thread(new CountingTask());
        thread.start();
    }
}

public static void main(String[] args) {
    new MultiThreadedFrame();
}
}
```

When you run this code, you'll see a number of exceptions appearing in the console. Another undesired aspect of the code is that you'll (most likely) end up with multiple elements in your JList when the program stops running, even though you execute the clear() method before adding a new item in every thread. This is due to the fact that threads can run in parallel, meaning that two threads can add items right after they have both cleared the list.

> **NOTE** Some Swing components' methods are called "thread safe." However, this behavior has changed between Java versions before, so it is generally a good idea not to rely on thread-safe components. This also applies to JList.

You've already seen an important rule regarding the EDT, namely that all UI-related code should be run inside this thread. The way to do so is simple, namely by using the `SwingUtilities` helper class, which defines the following methods to help out with threading:

➤ `invokeLater(Runnable doRun)`: Executes `doRun.run()` asynchronously on the event dispatching thread.

➤ `invokeAndWait(Runnable doRun)`: Executes `doRun.run()` synchronously on the event dispatching thread, meaning that this method will wait until `doRun.run()` has completed.

➤ `isEventDispatchThread()`: Returns true if the current thread is the event dispatching thread.

In almost all cases, you'll use the `invokeLater` method to wrap UI-affecting code as follows:

```
SwingUtilities.invokeLater(new Runnable() {
    public void run() {
        // UI affecting code
    }
});
```

One particular place where it is important to use this method is in the `main` method of your programs, as it is guaranteed there that you will not yet be in the EDT (but instead in the initial main thread). Using `SwingUtilities`, you can rewrite the earlier example as follows:

```
import javax.swing.DefaultListModel;
import javax.swing.JFrame;
import javax.swing.JList;
import javax.swing.SwingUtilities;

public class MultiThreadedFrame extends JFrame {
    public static final int LENGTH = 100;
    public static final JList<String> COMPONENT = new JList<>();

    public class CountingTask implements Runnable {
        public void run() {
            for (int i = 1; i <= LENGTH; i++) {
                // Add an item
                ((DefaultListModel<String>) COMPONENT.getModel()).clear();
                ((DefaultListModel<String>)
                    COMPONENT.getModel()).addElement("At: "+i);
                // Force component repaint
                COMPONENT.repaint();
                COMPONENT.invalidate();
                COMPONENT.repaint();
                // Sleep for a little to give other threads a chance
                try {
                    Thread.sleep(1);
                } catch (InterruptedException e) {
                    e.printStackTrace();
                }
            }
        }
    }

    public MultiThreadedFrame() {
```

```
                DefaultListModel<String> listModel = new DefaultListModel<>();
                COMPONENT.setModel(listModel);
                getContentPane().add(COMPONENT);
                pack();
                setSize(300,500);
                setVisible(true);

                for (int t = 0; t < 16; t++) {
                    SwingUtilities.invokeLater(new CountingTask());
                }
        }

        public static void main(String[] args) {
            SwingUtilities.invokeLater(new Runnable() {
                public void run() { new MultiThreadedFrame(); }
            });
        }
    }
```

The fact that you must ensure all UI updating code is run on the EDT might seem like an annoying aspect of GUI programming at first, but there is a silver lining that relates to event listeners. Because the EDT is responsible for catching user-interface events and also passes these to any event listeners, any code that you execute inside an event listener will be run inside the EDT. This means that you do not need to use invokeLater, for instance, when running code inside the actionPerformed method of an ActionListener for a button, which, luckily, will also contain the multitude of UI-related code.

However, since this code is executed in the EDT, this means that, while the EDT is busy executing the event listeners, the event loop will block until all event listeners have finished what they need to do. Subsequent events will thus need to wait until they are handled, and since this can involve anything from button clicks to window resizes, this can quickly lead to unresponsive, sluggish interfaces when you stick too much calculation-heavy code in your event listeners. Again, this is illustrated with a simple example. Imagine you come up with the following beautiful progress-tracking interface to wrap around some heavy-duty code:

```
import java.awt.FlowLayout;
import java.awt.event.ActionEvent;
import java.awt.event.ActionListener;
import javax.swing.JButton;
import javax.swing.JFrame;
import javax.swing.JProgressBar;
import javax.swing.SwingUtilities;

public class ProgressTrackingFrame extends JFrame implements ActionListener {
    private boolean isRunning = false;
    private final JProgressBar bar = new JProgressBar(0, 100);
    private final JButton btn = new JButton("Start Calculation");

    public ProgressTrackingFrame() {
        super();
        setDefaultCloseOperation(JFrame.EXIT_ON_CLOSE);
        setTitle("Progress Tracker");
        setLayout(new FlowLayout());
        btn.addActionListener(this);
```

```
        add(bar);
        add(btn);
        pack();
        setVisible(true);
    }

    @Override
    public void actionPerformed(ActionEvent arg0) {
        if (isRunning) {
            // How to cancel here?
        } else {
            isRunning = true;
            btn.setText("Stop Calculation");
            long total = 1000000000;
            for (long i = 0; i < total; i++) {
                int perc = (int)
                        (i * (bar.getMaximum() - bar.getMinimum())
                                / total);
                bar.setValue(perc);
            }
        }
        isRunning = false;
        btn.setText("Start Calculation");
    }

    public static void main(String[] args) {
        SwingUtilities.invokeLater(new Runnable() {
            public void run() { new ProgressTrackingFrame(); }
        });
    }
}
```

Try running the program and starting the calculation. Unless you have a very fast machine, the loop will take some time to finish. Notice how the rest of the UI becomes frozen during the execution of the action listener. Try resizing the window. You'll note that this will lead to a garbled result that's typical for programs that do not redraw their UI anymore, as shown in Figure 11-21.

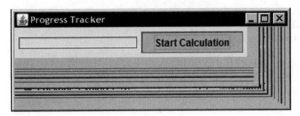

FIGURE 11-21

In some cases, Windows will notice that your program is not responding and might attempt to close it. Just wait a few more seconds, however, and you'll see that the program suddenly pops into life again and the event loop catches up to handle the other events. This is because the event listener includes heavy-duty code that is run inside the EDT.

Of course, you would like a way to improve things, and if possible, you'd also like to implement a way to cancel a running calculation.

Again, luckily, Swing already provides a mechanism to do this in a fairly simple manner, by means of the `SwingWorker` class. This class allows you to construct objects that represent some kind of background task. Here's how you can implement it. First of all, define a new class field like so:

```
private SwingWorker<Boolean, Integer> backgroundTask = null;
```

You can remove the `isRunning` field, as you'll no longer need it. Next, create a method to construct a background task for you:

```
public SwingWorker<Boolean, Integer> makeBackgroundTask(final long total) {

}
```

This method will construct a new `SwingWorker` anonymous inner class. You will need to provide two type parameters to this class. The first one represents the type of the final result value (you use a Boolean here). The second one represents the type of the intermediate result values (`Integer` is used here as these will be sent out to update the progress bar):

```
public SwingWorker<Boolean, Integer> makeBackgroundTask(final long total) {
    SwingWorker<Boolean, Integer> task = new SwingWorker<Boolean, Integer>(){
        @Override
        protected Boolean doInBackground() throws Exception {
            return true;
        }
    };
    return task;
}
```

The `doInBackground` method needs to be implemented and has to have your indicated final result type as a return type (Boolean). This method contains the work that will be performed in the background, so fill it up with your loop:

```
public SwingWorker<Boolean, Integer> makeBackgroundTask(final long total) {
    SwingWorker<Boolean, Integer> task = new SwingWorker<Boolean, Integer>(){
        @Override
        protected Boolean doInBackground() throws Exception {
            btn.setText("Stop Calculation");
            for (long i = 0; i < total; i++) {
                int perc = (int)
                        (i * (bar.getMaximum() - bar.getMinimum())
                            / total);
            }
            return true;
        }
    };
    return task;
}
```

Although you could still update the progress bar value inside this method, `SwingWorker` also provides a way to work with intermediate values in a better manner, by using its `publish` method. This method will queue intermediate results that can then be processed by a `process` method. You don't need to manually call the latter, as `SwingWorker` will determine when (based on time and results gathered) it is a good time to call this method:

```
public SwingWorker<Boolean, Integer> makeBackgroundTask(final long total) {
    SwingWorker<Boolean, Integer> task = new SwingWorker<Boolean, Integer>(){
        @Override
        protected Boolean doInBackground() throws Exception {
            btn.setText("Stop Calculation");
            for (long i = 0; i < total; i++) {
                int perc = (int)
                        (i * (bar.getMaximum() - bar.getMinimum())
                             / total);
                publish(perc);
            }
            return true;
        }
        @Override
        protected void process(List<Integer> percs) {
            for (int perc : percs)
                if (bar.getValue() < perc)
                    bar.setValue(perc);
        }
    };
    return task;
}
```

You can also use the `isCancelled` method to figure out whether your background task was cancelled from the outside. It is a good idea to check the result of this method as often as possible so a cancellation request can be dealt with as soon as possible, for instance in the deepest level of a loop:

```
public SwingWorker<Boolean, Integer> makeBackgroundTask(final long total) {
    SwingWorker<Boolean, Integer> task = new SwingWorker<Boolean, Integer>(){
        @Override
        protected Boolean doInBackground() throws Exception {
            btn.setText("Stop Calculation");
            for (long i = 0; i < total; i++) {
                if (isCancelled()) {
                    bar.setValue(0);
                    return false;
                }
                int perc = (int)
                        (i * (bar.getMaximum() - bar.getMinimum())
                             / total);
                publish(perc);
            }
            return true;
        }
        @Override
        protected void process(List<Integer> percs) {
            for (int perc : percs)
                if (bar.getValue() < perc)
                    bar.setValue(perc);
        }
```

```
        };
        return task;
    }
```

Finally, you can also override the `done` method to update your UI:

```java
public SwingWorker<Boolean, Integer> makeBackgroundTask(final long total) {
    SwingWorker<Boolean, Integer> task = new SwingWorker<Boolean, Integer>(){
        @Override
        protected Boolean doInBackground() throws Exception {
            btn.setText("Stop Calculation");
            for (long i = 0; i < total; i++) {
                if (isCancelled()) {
                    bar.setValue(0);
                    return false;
                }
                int perc = (int)
                        (i * (bar.getMaximum() - bar.getMinimum())
                                / total);
                publish(perc);
            }
            return true;
        }
        @Override
        protected void process(List<Integer> percs) {
            for (int perc : percs)
                if (bar.getValue() < perc)
                    bar.setValue(perc);
        }
        @Override
        public void done() {
            btn.setText("Start Calculation");
            backgroundTask = null;
        }
    };
    return task;
}
```

Next, the only thing left to do is to change your original action listener so it now sets up and executes your background task, using the `execute` method. Use the `cancel` method to send a cancellation request in case the user wants to cancel the calculation. The final result looks like this:

```java
import java.awt.FlowLayout;
import java.awt.event.ActionEvent;
import java.awt.event.ActionListener;
import java.util.List;

import javax.swing.JButton;
import javax.swing.JFrame;
import javax.swing.JProgressBar;
import javax.swing.SwingUtilities;
import javax.swing.SwingWorker;

public class ProgressTrackingFrame extends JFrame implements ActionListener {
    private final JProgressBar bar = new JProgressBar(0, 100);
    private final JButton btn = new JButton("Start Calculation");
```

```java
    private SwingWorker<Boolean, Integer> backgroundTask = null;

    public ProgressTrackingFrame() {
        super();
        setDefaultCloseOperation(JFrame.EXIT_ON_CLOSE);
        setTitle("Progress Tracker");
        setLayout(new FlowLayout());
        btn.addActionListener(this);
        add(bar);
        add(btn);
        pack();
        setVisible(true);
    }

    public SwingWorker<Boolean, Integer> makeBackgroundTask(final long total) {
        SwingWorker<Boolean, Integer> task = new SwingWorker<Boolean, Integer>(){
            @Override
            protected Boolean doInBackground() throws Exception {
                btn.setText("Stop Calculation");
                for (long i = 0; i < total; i++) {
                    if (isCancelled()) {
                        bar.setValue(0);
                        return false;
                    }
                    int perc = (int)
                            (i * (bar.getMaximum() - bar.getMinimum())
                                / total);
                    publish(perc);
                }
                return true;
            }
            @Override
            protected void process(List<Integer> percs) {
                for (int perc : percs)
                    if (bar.getValue() < perc)
                        bar.setValue(perc);
            }
            @Override
            public void done() {
                btn.setText("Start Calculation");
                backgroundTask = null;
            }
        };
        return task;
    }


    @Override
    public void actionPerformed(ActionEvent arg0) {
        if (backgroundTask == null) {
            backgroundTask = makeBackgroundTask(1000000000);
            backgroundTask.execute();
        } else {
            backgroundTask.cancel(true);
        }
```

```
        }

        public static void main(String[] args) {
            SwingUtilities.invokeLater(new Runnable() {
                public void run() { new ProgressTrackingFrame(); }
            });
        }
```

Try running the program again and observe what happens. Finally, it is good to know that you can also call get() and get(long timeout, TimeUnit unit) on a SwingWorker object to block until the background task has completed and you get the final result. In most cases, this blocking behavior is not what you want, and it is a better idea to have the done method of the worker call one of your objects to notify about the completion.

You've now seen all the important things you need to know about GUIs in Java. With a complex class hierarchy, a huge list of components and containers, layout managers that all have different behavior and a plethora of event listeners, building GUIs in Java can appear to be a daunting task at first. Don't be afraid to get started and build some simple interfaces. Check the online documentation and Eclipse's helpful autosuggest feature to get to know Swing's components and utilize them whenever you can. Exercise is key here, and this chapter has only outlined the basics. The final chapter in this book contains many case study examples that will have you building more realistic, complex graphical user interfaces, utilizing many of the available Swing components. Don't hesitate to have a look.

CLOSING TOPICS

This chapter closes with some additional topics related to the concept of GUIs.

Best Practices: Keeping Looks and Logic Separated

A first topic you'll read about relates to best practices when writing graphical user interfaces. Generally speaking, even after gaining knowledge of Object-Oriented Programming, beginners will find it relatively hard to keep domain logic separated from user-interface concerns. When you find yourself making monstrous user interfaces where buttons and text fields keep track of state, you'll know it is time for a change.

Ideally, you should be able to perform all your application logic using pure Java objects and without using any graphical user interface at all. Therefore, it is always a good idea to construct your core domain concepts first. Which concepts exist? What data needs to be stored? Which actions can be undertaken? Afterward, you can start building the GUI around all of this. As a challenge, consider creating a "console" version for your applications as an alternative to the graphical one. How hard would it be? Where are the main root issues? Here lies the opportunity for solid refactoring.

The next chapter talks more about patterns, and you will get acquainted with a very helpful pattern when building GUI-driven applications: the model-view-controller pattern.

Although separating your logic from UI is a must, it is also a good idea to keep your UI as architecturally sound as possible. Many of the examples you've seen in this chapter already reflect a natural progress in UI architecture, starting with sticking everything in a main method (bad) to creating custom UI classes (good), from creating huge event listeners in inner classes (bad) to separating them into separate classes and even into background tasks (good), from trying to make UIs as hierarchically flat as possible and fighting with layout managers (bad) to accepting the fact that you might want to create another JPanel, or perhaps a separate custom class extending JPanel and nesting this in a reusable manner (good). Writing GUIs in Java is by no means easy. It is oftentimes cumbersome, boring even. You want to focus on the core concepts of your program, and that involves a lot of boilerplate code. However, architectural decisions you make at the beginning might end up saving you a lot of time and headache later.

Let's Draw: Defining Custom Draw Behavior

It's already been stated that Swing components handle all drawing behavior by themselves, which is why they can look similar on each platform they're run on. You saw before how to work with different look and feels inside Swing, but you might also be interested in knowing whether you can override or extend rendering behavior of components.

The answer is that indeed, you can. All Swing components (JComponent) come with the following built-in methods:

➤ public void paint(Graphics g): Paints the component, its border, and its children by calling these methods:

  ➤ protected void paintComponent(Graphics g)

  ➤ protected void paintBorder(Graphics g)

  ➤ protected void paintChildren(Graphics g)

The Graphics object that's passed along can be regarded as a general surface area on which Java can draw, representing the geometric area of the component that will need to be painted.

To show this off, the following Try It Out will lead you through a simple painting application, which is also a good opportunity to show off a mouse listener and show another helpful component, the JFileChooser.

TRY IT OUT Making a Paint Application with Custom-Painted Components

In this Try It Out, you create a simple painting application by overriding the default painting behavior of a component.

1. As always, feel free to create a new project in Eclipse when you want to. Create a class called SimplePaint with the following content as a bare bones starting point:

```
import javax.swing.JFrame;
import javax.swing.SwingUtilities;

public class SimplePaint extends JFrame {
    public SimplePaint() {
        super();
        setDefaultCloseOperation(JFrame.EXIT_ON_CLOSE);
        setTitle("Simple Paint");


        pack();
```

```
            setVisible(true);
        }
        public static void main(String[] args) {
            SwingUtilities.invokeLater(new Runnable() {
                public void run() { new SimplePaint(); }
            });
        }
    }
```

2. Start out by adding some menu items to your JFrame. In fact, a JFrame comes with built-in functionality to set up a menu bar. You just need to construct a menu first:

```
import java.awt.event.ActionEvent;
import java.awt.event.ActionListener;

import javax.swing.JFrame;
import javax.swing.JMenu;
import javax.swing.JMenuBar;
import javax.swing.JMenuItem;

public class SimplePaint extends JFrame implements ActionListener {
    private final String ACTION_NEW = "New Image";
    private final String ACTION_LOAD = "Load Image";
    private final String ACTION_SAVE = "Save Image";

    public SimplePaint() {
        super();
        setDefaultCloseOperation(JFrame.EXIT_ON_CLOSE);
        setTitle("Simple Paint");

        initMenu();

        pack();
        setVisible(true);
    }

    private void initMenu() {
        JMenuBar menuBar = new JMenuBar();
        JMenu menu = new JMenu("File");
        JMenuItem mnuNew = new JMenuItem(ACTION_NEW);
        JMenuItem mnuLoad = new JMenuItem(ACTION_LOAD);
        JMenuItem mnuSave = new JMenuItem(ACTION_SAVE);
        mnuNew.setActionCommand(ACTION_NEW);
        mnuLoad.setActionCommand(ACTION_LOAD);
        mnuSave.setActionCommand(ACTION_SAVE);
        mnuNew.addActionListener(this);
        mnuLoad.addActionListener(this);
        mnuSave.addActionListener(this);
        menu.add(mnuNew);
        menu.add(mnuLoad);
        menu.add(mnuSave);
        menuBar.add(menu);
        this.setJMenuBar(menuBar);
    }
```

```
    @Override
    public void actionPerformed(ActionEvent ev) {

    }

    public static void main(String[] args) {
        SwingUtilities.invokeLater(new Runnable() {
            public void run() { new SimplePaint(); }
        });
    }
}
```

3. Feel free to run the program in between steps and check the result. You should get something like Figure 11-22.

FIGURE 11-22

Next, create a custom panel, that is, a panel with some custom paint code:

```
import java.awt.Color;
import java.awt.Dimension;
import java.awt.Graphics;
import java.awt.Point;
import java.awt.event.MouseAdapter;
import java.awt.event.MouseEvent;
import java.util.Collection;
import java.util.HashSet;
import java.util.Set;

import javax.swing.JPanel;

public class SimplePaintPanel extends JPanel {
    private final Set<Point> blackPixels = new HashSet<Point>();
    private final int brushSize;

    private int mouseButtonDown = 0;
```

```java
    public SimplePaintPanel() {
        this(5, new HashSet<Point>());
    }

    public SimplePaintPanel(Set<Point> blackPixels) {
        this(5, blackPixels);
    }

    public SimplePaintPanel(int brushSize, Set<Point> blackPixels) {
        this.setPreferredSize(new Dimension(300, 300));
        this.brushSize = brushSize;
        this.blackPixels.addAll(blackPixels);
        final SimplePaintPanel self = this;

        MouseAdapter mouseAdapter = new MouseAdapter() {
            @Override
            public void mouseDragged(MouseEvent ev) {
                if (self.mouseButtonDown == 1)
                    self.blackPixels.addAll(getPixelsAround(ev.getPoint()));
                else if (self.mouseButtonDown == 3)
                    self.blackPixels.removeAll(getPixelsAround(ev.getPoint()));
                self.invalidate();
                self.repaint();
            }

            @Override
            public void mousePressed(MouseEvent ev) {
                self.mouseButtonDown = ev.getButton();
            }
        };
        this.addMouseMotionListener(mouseAdapter);
        this.addMouseListener(mouseAdapter);

    }

    public void paint(Graphics g) {
        int w = this.getWidth();
        int h = this.getHeight();
        g.setColor(Color.white);
        g.fillRect(0, 0, w, h);
        g.setColor(Color.black);
        for (Point point : blackPixels)
            g.drawRect(point.x, point.y, 1, 1);

    }

    private Collection<? extends Point> getPixelsAround(Point point) {
        Set<Point> points = new HashSet<>();
        for (int x = point.x - brushSize; x < point.x + brushSize; x++)
            for (int y = point.y - brushSize; y < point.y + brushSize; y++)
                points.add(new Point(x, y));
        return points;
    }
```

4. Next, add this custom component to your JFrame:

```java
import java.awt.event.ActionEvent;
```

```java
import java.awt.event.ActionListener;

import javax.swing.JFrame;
import javax.swing.JMenu;
import javax.swing.JMenuBar;
import javax.swing.JMenuItem;

public class SimplePaint extends JFrame implements ActionListener {
    private final String ACTION_NEW = "New Image";
    private final String ACTION_LOAD = "Load Image";
    private final String ACTION_SAVE = "Save Image";

    private final SimplePaintPanel paintPanel = new SimplePaintPanel();

    public SimplePaint() {
        super();
        setDefaultCloseOperation(JFrame.EXIT_ON_CLOSE);
        setTitle("Simple Paint");

        initMenu();
        this.getContentPane().add(paintPanel);

        pack();
        setVisible(true);
    }

    private void initMenu() {
        JMenuBar menuBar = new JMenuBar();
        JMenu menu = new JMenu("File");
        JMenuItem mnuNew = new JMenuItem(ACTION_NEW);
        JMenuItem mnuLoad = new JMenuItem(ACTION_LOAD);
        JMenuItem mnuSave = new JMenuItem(ACTION_SAVE);
        mnuNew.setActionCommand(ACTION_NEW);
        mnuLoad.setActionCommand(ACTION_LOAD);
        mnuSave.setActionCommand(ACTION_SAVE);
        mnuNew.addActionListener(this);
        mnuLoad.addActionListener(this);
        mnuSave.addActionListener(this);
        menu.add(mnuNew);
        menu.add(mnuLoad);
        menu.add(mnuSave);
        menuBar.add(menu);
        this.setJMenuBar(menuBar);
    }

    @Override
    public void actionPerformed(ActionEvent ev) {

    }

    public static void main(String[] args) {
        SwingUtilities.invokeLater(new Runnable() {
            public void run() { new SimplePaint(); }
        });
    }
}
```

5. Try running the program again. Try dragging the mouse using the left and right mouse buttons. Although the implementation is horribly inefficient, the concept works, as shown in Figure 11-23.

FIGURE 11-23

6. Now continue by making the menu work. To do so, first make some modifications to your `SimplePaintPanel`, adding/changing the following methods:

```java
// Inside the mouseAdapter:
@Override
public void mouseDragged(MouseEvent ev) {
    if (mouseButtonDown == 1)
        addPixels(getPixelsAround(ev.getPoint()));
    else if (mouseButtonDown == 3)
        removePixels(getPixelsAround(ev.getPoint()));
}

// Add the following methods:
public void clear() {
    this.blackPixels.clear();
    this.invalidate();
    this.repaint();
}

public void addPixels(Collection<? extends Point> blackPixels) {
    this.blackPixels.addAll(blackPixels);
    this.invalidate();
    this.repaint();
}

public void removePixels(Collection<? extends Point> blackPixels) {
```

```
        this.blackPixels.removeAll(blackPixels);
        this.invalidate();
        this.repaint();
    }

    public boolean isPixel(Point blackPixel) {
        return this.blackPixels.contains(blackPixel);
    }

    // Change this method:
    private Collection<? extends Point> getPixelsAround(Point point) {
        Set<Point> points = new HashSet<>();
        for (int x = point.x - brushSize; x < point.x + brushSize; x++)
            for (int y = point.y - brushSize; y < point.y + brushSize; y++)
                points.add(new Point(x, y));
        return points;
    }
```

7. Making the New menu work then becomes a simple manner of filling up the `actionPerformed` method in the `SimplePaint` class like so:

```
@Override
public void actionPerformed(ActionEvent ev) {
    switch (ev.getActionCommand()) {
    case ACTION_NEW:
        paintPanel.clear();
        break;
    }
}
```

8. Next up is the ability to load images. Some tricks are used to convert everything to black and white, but you could theoretically show the image as is if you want to (try this out later by yourself if you want to take up the challenge):

```
@Override
public void actionPerformed(ActionEvent ev) {
    switch (ev.getActionCommand()) {
    case ACTION_NEW:
        paintPanel.clear();
        break;
    case ACTION_LOAD:
        doLoadImage();
        break;
    }
}

private void doLoadImage() {
    JFileChooser fileChooser = new JFileChooser();
    fileChooser.setFileSelectionMode(JFileChooser.FILES_ONLY);
    int result = fileChooser.showOpenDialog(this);
    if (result != JFileChooser.APPROVE_OPTION)
        return;
    BufferedImage image;
    File openFile = fileChooser.getSelectedFile();
```

```
    try (FileInputStream fis = new FileInputStream(openFile)) {
        image = ImageIO.read(fis);
    } catch (IOException e) {
        return;
    }
    if (image == null)
        return;
    paintPanel.clear();
    Set<Point> blackPixels = new HashSet<Point>();
    for (int x = 0; x < image.getWidth(); x++) {
        for (int y = 0; y < image.getHeight(); y++) {
            Color c = new Color(image.getRGB(x, y));
            if ((c.getBlue() < 128 || c.getRed() < 128 || c.getGreen() < 128)
                    && c.getAlpha() == 255) {
                blackPixels.add(new Point(x, y));
            }
        }
    }
    paintPanel.addPixels(blackPixels);
}
```

9. Try loading the project again and loading an image, as shown in Figure 11-24.

FIGURE 11-24

10. Finally, you can add the ability to save images:

```
@Override
public void actionPerformed(ActionEvent ev) {
    switch (ev.getActionCommand()) {
    case ACTION_NEW:
        paintPanel.clear();
```

```
                break;
            case ACTION_LOAD:
                doLoadImage();
                break;
            case ACTION_SAVE:
                doSaveImage();
                break;
        }
    }

    private void doSaveImage() {
        JFileChooser fileChooser = new JFileChooser();
        fileChooser.setFileSelectionMode(JFileChooser.FILES_ONLY);
        int result = fileChooser.showSaveDialog(this);
        if (result != JFileChooser.APPROVE_OPTION)
            return;
        File saveFile = fileChooser.getSelectedFile();
        if (!saveFile.getAbsolutePath().toLowerCase().endsWith(".png"))
            saveFile = new File(saveFile.getAbsolutePath() + ".png");
        BufferedImage image = new BufferedImage(
                paintPanel.getSize().width,
                paintPanel.getSize().height,
                BufferedImage.TYPE_INT_RGB);
        for (int x = 0; x < image.getWidth(); x++) {
            for (int y = 0; y < image.getHeight(); y++) {
                image.setRGB(x, y, Color.white.getRGB());
                if (paintPanel.isPixel(new Point(x, y))) {
                    image.setRGB(x, y, Color.black.getRGB());
                }
            }
        }
        try {
            ImageIO.write(image, "png", saveFile);
        } catch (IOException e) {
            return;
        }
    }
}
```

This approach works just as well, as shown in Figure 11-25.

Here is the full code for the two classes once more for convenience:

```
import java.awt.Color;
import java.awt.Point;
import java.awt.event.ActionEvent;
import java.awt.event.ActionListener;
import java.awt.image.BufferedImage;
import java.io.File;
import java.io.FileInputStream;
import java.io.IOException;
import java.util.HashSet;
import java.util.Set;
import javax.imageio.ImageIO;
import javax.swing.JFileChooser;
import javax.swing.JFrame;
```

```java
import javax.swing.JMenu;
import javax.swing.JMenuBar;
import javax.swing.JMenuItem;
import javax.swing.SwingUtilities;

public class SimplePaint extends JFrame implements ActionListener {
    private final String ACTION_NEW = "New Image";
    private final String ACTION_LOAD = "Load Image";
    private final String ACTION_SAVE = "Save Image";

    private final SimplePaintPanel paintPanel = new SimplePaintPanel();

    public SimplePaint() {
        super();
        setDefaultCloseOperation(JFrame.EXIT_ON_CLOSE);
        setTitle("Simple Paint");

        initMenu();
        this.getContentPane().add(paintPanel);

        pack();
        setVisible(true);
    }

    private void initMenu() {
        JMenuBar menuBar = new JMenuBar();
        JMenu menu = new JMenu("File");
        JMenuItem mnuNew = new JMenuItem(ACTION_NEW);
        JMenuItem mnuLoad = new JMenuItem(ACTION_LOAD);
        JMenuItem mnuSave = new JMenuItem(ACTION_SAVE);
        mnuNew.setActionCommand(ACTION_NEW);
        mnuLoad.setActionCommand(ACTION_LOAD);
        mnuSave.setActionCommand(ACTION_SAVE);
        mnuNew.addActionListener(this);
        mnuLoad.addActionListener(this);
        mnuSave.addActionListener(this);
        menu.add(mnuNew);
        menu.add(mnuLoad);
        menu.add(mnuSave);
        menuBar.add(menu);
        this.setJMenuBar(menuBar);
    }

    @Override
    public void actionPerformed(ActionEvent ev) {
        switch (ev.getActionCommand()) {
        case ACTION_NEW:
            paintPanel.clear();
            break;
        case ACTION_LOAD:
            doLoadImage();
            break;
        case ACTION_SAVE:
            doSaveImage();
            break;
        }
```

```
    }

    private void doSaveImage() {
        JFileChooser fileChooser = new JFileChooser();
        fileChooser.setFileSelectionMode(JFileChooser.FILES_ONLY);
        int result = fileChooser.showSaveDialog(this);
        if (result != JFileChooser.APPROVE_OPTION)
            return;
        File saveFile = fileChooser.getSelectedFile();
        if (!saveFile.getAbsolutePath().toLowerCase().endsWith(".png"))
            saveFile = new File(saveFile.getAbsolutePath() + ".png");
        BufferedImage image = new BufferedImage(
                paintPanel.getSize().width,
                paintPanel.getSize().height,
                BufferedImage.TYPE_INT_RGB);
        for (int x = 0; x < image.getWidth(); x++) {
            for (int y = 0; y < image.getHeight(); y++) {
                image.setRGB(x, y, Color.white.getRGB());
                if (paintPanel.isPixel(new Point(x, y))) {
                    image.setRGB(x, y, Color.black.getRGB());
                }
            }
        }
        try {
            ImageIO.write(image, "png", saveFile);
        } catch (IOException e) {
            return;
        }
    }

    private void doLoadImage() {
        JFileChooser fileChooser = new JFileChooser();
        fileChooser.setFileSelectionMode(JFileChooser.FILES_ONLY);
        int result = fileChooser.showOpenDialog(this);
        if (result != JFileChooser.APPROVE_OPTION)
            return;
        BufferedImage image;
        File openFile = fileChooser.getSelectedFile();
        try (FileInputStream fis = new FileInputStream(openFile)) {
            image = ImageIO.read(fis);
        } catch (IOException e) {
            return;
        }
        if (image == null)
            return;
        paintPanel.clear();
        Set<Point> blackPixels = new HashSet<Point>();
        for (int x = 0; x < image.getWidth(); x++) {
            for (int y = 0; y < image.getHeight(); y++) {
                Color c = new Color(image.getRGB(x, y));
                if ((c.getBlue() < 128 || c.getRed() < 128 || c.getGreen() < 128)
                        && c.getAlpha() == 255) {
                    blackPixels.add(new Point(x, y));
                }
            }
        }
```

```java
            paintPanel.addPixels(blackPixels);
        }

    public static void main(String[] args) {
        SwingUtilities.invokeLater(new Runnable() {
            public void run() { new SimplePaint(); }
        });
    }
}

import java.awt.Color;
import java.awt.Dimension;
import java.awt.Graphics;
import java.awt.Point;
import java.awt.event.MouseAdapter;
import java.awt.event.MouseEvent;
import java.util.Collection;
import java.util.HashSet;
import java.util.Set;
import javax.swing.JPanel;

public class SimplePaintPanel extends JPanel {
    private final Set<Point> blackPixels = new HashSet<Point>();
    private final int brushSize;

    private int mouseButtonDown = 0;

    public SimplePaintPanel() {
        this(5, new HashSet<Point>());
    }

    public SimplePaintPanel(Set<Point> blackPixels) {
        this(5, blackPixels);
    }

    public SimplePaintPanel(int brushSize, Set<Point> blackPixels) {
        this.setPreferredSize(new Dimension(300, 300));
        this.brushSize = brushSize;
        this.blackPixels.addAll(blackPixels);
        final SimplePaintPanel self = this;

        MouseAdapter mouseAdapter = new MouseAdapter() {
            @Override
            public void mouseDragged(MouseEvent ev) {
                if (mouseButtonDown == 1)
                    addPixels(getPixelsAround(ev.getPoint()));
                else if (mouseButtonDown == 3)
                    removePixels(getPixelsAround(ev.getPoint()));
            }

            @Override
            public void mousePressed(MouseEvent ev) {
                self.mouseButtonDown = ev.getButton();
            }
        };
        this.addMouseMotionListener(mouseAdapter);
```

```
            this.addMouseListener(mouseAdapter);
        }

        public void paint(Graphics g) {
            int w = this.getWidth();
            int h = this.getHeight();
            g.setColor(Color.white);
            g.fillRect(0, 0, w, h);
            g.setColor(Color.black);
            for (Point point : blackPixels)
                g.drawRect(point.x, point.y, 1, 1);

        }

        public void clear() {
            this.blackPixels.clear();
            this.invalidate();
            this.repaint();
        }

        public void addPixels(Collection<? extends Point> blackPixels) {
            this.blackPixels.addAll(blackPixels);
            this.invalidate();
            this.repaint();
        }

        public void removePixels(Collection<? extends Point> blackPixels) {
            this.blackPixels.removeAll(blackPixels);
            this.invalidate();
            this.repaint();
        }

        public boolean isPixel(Point blackPixel) {
            return this.blackPixels.contains(blackPixel);
        }

        private Collection<? extends Point> getPixelsAround(Point point) {
            Set<Point> points = new HashSet<>();
            for (int x = point.x - brushSize; x < point.x + brushSize; x++)
                for (int y = point.y - brushSize; y < point.y + brushSize; y++)
                    points.add(new Point(x, y));
            return points;
        }
```

How It Works

This is how it works:

1. There is a lot going on in this small project. Start by taking a look at the SimplePaint class. The JFrame is set up just like before; a SimplePaintPanel component is added to the content pane, and the initMenu() is called to initialize the menu bar.

2. The initMenu() shows you how you can set up menus with Swing. Note that JFrame has a dedicated area to place menu bars, which you can set and get using the setJMenuBar and getJMenuBar methods. Here, a single File menu entry was created, and three menu items were placed under it.

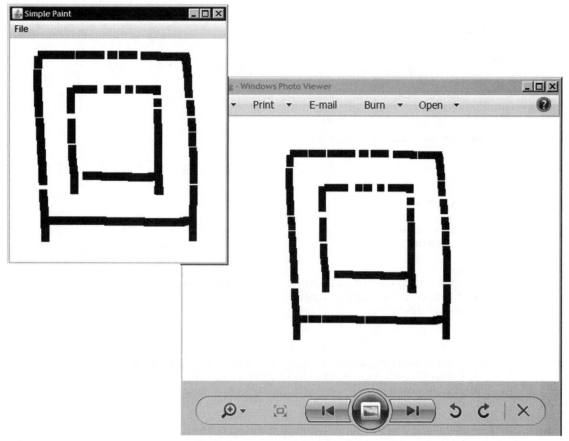

FIGURE 11-25

> **NOTE** *The Swing menu components are used here.* Menu, MenuBar, MenuItem, setMenuBar, *and* getMenuBar *also exist, but these correspond to the AWT components, which should be considered outdated. The naming is somewhat confusing, but that's the way it is.*

3. You will have noted that it is possible to assign action listeners to menu items. In this project, the SimplePaint class acts as a listener for all menu items as well. The actionPerformed method then determines which method to call based on the action command.

4. The New menu item performs a simple operation and just calls the clear method on the paint panel.

5. Loading an image is a bit more convoluted. First, a JFileChooser is constructed (you could also make this a class field; go ahead and try this if you want) and configured so users can only select

files. Next, the `showOpenDialog` method is called to display an Open File dialog. `JFileChooser` also has a lot of additional options you can configure, such as filtering which files to show. The result of this method is an integer determining whether the user selected a file or cancelled the dialog, or an error occurred. Next, the `getSelectedFile` method retrieves your file. Note that `JFileChooser` still utilizes the legacy `File` class. Next, a built-in utility class called `ImageIO` does the heavy lifting regarding reading image files. This class reads in common file formats, such as PNG, JPG, BMP, and GIF files, and returns a `BufferedImage` object to store the image data. Next, it iterates over all pixels in the image and applies a simple trick to determine whether the pixel color should be converted to a black pixel. Dark colors are converted to black, whereas light colors are not; that is what the `if ((c.getBlue() < 128 || c.getRed() < 128 || c.getGreen() < 128) && c.getAlpha() == 255)` line does. Once all the black pixels are gathered, the `paintPanel` object is instructed to add them.

6. The `save` method works similarly. Here, a fresh image is constructed with the width and height equal to the current width and height of the paint panel. Next, it loops over each pixel again and sets them to black when necessary. Note that some additional logic is applied to make the filename selected with `showSaveDialog` end in `.png`, as there is no way to force the `JFileChooser` to do this for you. (This is because file extensions are just a convention to tell the operating system what the default program should be to open files ending in a particular suffix. There is nothing preventing you from saving a PNG image as `image.txt` and opening it with an image editor afterward.)

7. Now take a look at the `SimplePaintPanel` class. This class extends `JPanel` and implements a mouse and mouse motion event listener by using the `MouseAdapter` class.

8. The mouse-related methods that are implemented are `mouseDragged` and `mousePressed`. The latter determines which button (left or right) is being pressed. When the mouse is dragged, it looks at the mouse button currently being pressed and determines whether black pixels should be added or removed. You might wonder why you can't just use `ev.getButton()` in the `mouseDragged` method to determine which mouse button is being pressed. The reason for this is that this will always return 0, as `getButton()` only returns the button number when the state has changed. Since you keep holding down the mouse button whilst dragging, no button state is changing. You can, however, use `SwingUtilities.isLeftMouseButton(ev)` instead, which will work, but here things were done manually to show off how the mouse event listener works as well.

9. The second interesting aspect to note is the custom `paint` method for this class. First, the whole panel surface is filled out with white, after which a pixel is drawn for each point in the `blackPixels` set.

10. Finally, it is important to know that you should tell Java when "my surface has changed; you should draw me again." This is what is done with the `invalidate` method. A `repaint` call is placed right after this to instruct Java to redraw the component (which will have Java make a call to the `paint` method).

11. You will notice this yourself when drawing quickly; the drawing code is horribly inefficient. There are many reasons for this. First, working with a set of pixels is not ideal, especially not for larger images. Second, Swing components were never really designed to perform high-speed drawing updates, which is what is done here while dragging. In a real painting application, you need to look for better-suited drawing components (those exist). That said, this example helps to explain various concepts, and custom drawing code can still be helpful whenever you know components will not need to be redrawn continuously.

If you want to try to improve this simple painting application (this is a great starter project with the right amount of challenges), here are some suggestions:

➤ Try using background tasks. Perhaps you don't need to call for a repaint every time the mouse is moved while dragged; perhaps you can postpone the redraw until the movement has settled down?

➤ Similarly, instead of adding a set of pixels based on every point the mouse touches while dragging, you can also poll less aggressively and draw line segments between two points the mouse has been. This solves the problem of gaps while drawing quickly, but makes it harder to draw smooth curves when moving quickly.

➤ Try exploring the `java.awt.Canvas` component. This component has been specifically designed for custom free-form drawing.

➤ Finally, you can add a panel with some buttons, such as to select colors and so on. In this case, you might want to drop the set of black pixels and work directly on and with the painting surface. You can also try using a `BufferedImage` to store your image data directly (and more efficiently).

Visual GUI Designers: Making Life Easy?

Earlier in this chapter, you learned that the `GroupLayout` and `SpringLayout` layout managers were originally designed to be used in combination with visual GUI designers. So what are these exactly?

Eclipse, by default, does not come with a visual GUI designer, but you can install one by selecting Install New Software from the Help menu and searching for the WindowBuilder packages, as shown in Figure 11-26.

> **NOTE** To make WindowBuilder understand Swing components, you will also need to search for the "Swing Designer" packages and install these as well.

Once the new package is installed (and you restart Eclipse), try creating a new class. Right-click it in the Package Explorer and select Open With ➤ WindowBuilder Editor. From this editor, you can switch between a Source and Design tab, as shown in Figure 11-27.

When you switch to the Design tab, WindowBuilder will complain about the fact that it cannot figure out that this is a GUI class. No worries; just modify the class to make it a `JFrame`:

```
import javax.swing.JFrame;

public class WindowBuilderExample extends JFrame {
    public WindowBuilderExample() {
    }
}
```

Open the Design tab once more (select Reparse when nothing appears). You will be presented with the screen shown in Figure 11-28.

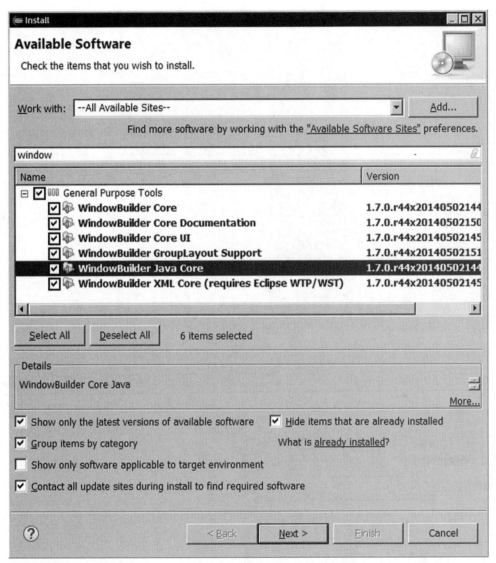

FIGURE 11-26

FIGURE 11-27

Here, you can drag and drop components and layouts to your `JFrame`. Figure 11-29 shows an example after five minutes of tinkering.

Note the row of buttons at the top of the designer view, including the one that allows you to quickly test a preview of your component in Figure 11-30.

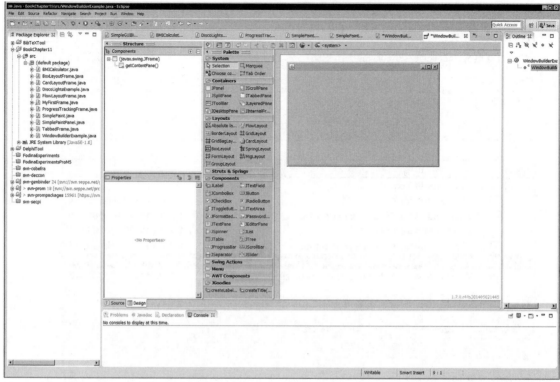

FIGURE 11-28

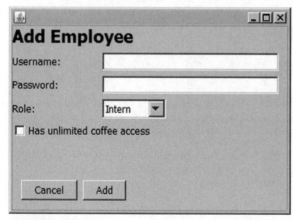

FIGURE 11-29

FIGURE 11-30

Once you're done prototyping, you can switch back to the source view and check out the generated code:

```java
import javax.swing.JFrame;
import javax.swing.GroupLayout;
import javax.swing.GroupLayout.Alignment;
import javax.swing.JLabel;
import java.awt.Font;
import javax.swing.LayoutStyle.ComponentPlacement;
import javax.swing.JTextField;
import javax.swing.JComboBox;
import javax.swing.DefaultComboBoxModel;
import javax.swing.JCheckBox;
import javax.swing.JButton;
import java.awt.event.ActionListener;
import java.awt.event.ActionEvent;

public class WindowBuilderExample extends JFrame {
    private JTextField textField;
    private JTextField textField_1;
    public WindowBuilderExample() {

        JLabel lblAddEmployee = new JLabel("Add Employee");
        lblAddEmployee.setFont(new Font("Tahoma", Font.BOLD, 22));

        JLabel lblUsername = new JLabel("Username:");

        textField = new JTextField();
        textField.setColumns(10);

        JLabel lblPassword = new JLabel("Password:");

        textField_1 = new JTextField();
        textField_1.setColumns(10);

        JLabel lblRole = new JLabel("Role:");

        JComboBox comboBox = new JComboBox();
        comboBox.setModel(new DefaultComboBoxModel(
            new String[] {"Intern", "Employee", "Manager"}));

        JCheckBox chckbxHasUnlimitedCoffee =
            new JCheckBox("Has unlimited coffee access");

        JButton btnCancel = new JButton("Cancel");

        JButton btnAdd = new JButton("Add");
        btnAdd.addActionListener(new ActionListener() {
            public void actionPerformed(ActionEvent arg0) {
            }
        });
        GroupLayout groupLayout = new GroupLayout(getContentPane());
        groupLayout.setHorizontalGroup(
        groupLayout.createParallelGroup(Alignment.LEADING)
        .addGroup(groupLayout.createSequentialGroup()
        .addGroup(groupLayout.createParallelGroup(Alignment.LEADING)
```

```
            .addComponent(lblAddEmployee)
            .addGroup(groupLayout.createSequentialGroup()
            .addGroup(groupLayout.createParallelGroup(Alignment.LEADING)
            .addComponent(lblUsername)
            .addComponent(lblPassword)
            .addComponent(lblRole))
            .addGap(54)
            .addGroup(groupLayout.createParallelGroup(Alignment.LEADING)
            .addComponent(comboBox, GroupLayout.PREFERRED_SIZE,
                GroupLayout.DEFAULT_SIZE, GroupLayout.PREFERRED_SIZE)
            .addComponent(textField, GroupLayout.DEFAULT_SIZE,
                229, Short.MAX_VALUE)
            .addComponent(textField_1, GroupLayout.DEFAULT_SIZE,
                229, Short.MAX_VALUE)))
            .addComponent(chckbxHasUnlimitedCoffee)
            .addGroup(groupLayout.createSequentialGroup()
            .addContainerGap()
            .addComponent(btnCancel)
            .addPreferredGap(ComponentPlacement.RELATED)
            .addComponent(btnAdd))
            .addContainerGap())
            );
            groupLayout.setVerticalGroup(
            groupLayout.createParallelGroup(Alignment.LEADING)
            .addGroup(groupLayout.createSequentialGroup()
            .addComponent(lblAddEmployee)
            .addPreferredGap(ComponentPlacement.RELATED)
            .addGroup(groupLayout.createParallelGroup(Alignment.BASELINE)
            .addComponent(lblUsername)
            .addComponent(textField, GroupLayout.PREFERRED_SIZE,
                GroupLayout.DEFAULT_SIZE, GroupLayout.PREFERRED_SIZE))
            .addPreferredGap(ComponentPlacement.RELATED)
            .addGroup(groupLayout.createParallelGroup(Alignment.BASELINE)
            .addComponent(lblPassword)
            .addComponent(textField_1, GroupLayout.PREFERRED_SIZE,
                GroupLayout.DEFAULT_SIZE, GroupLayout.PREFERRED_SIZE))
            .addPreferredGap(ComponentPlacement.RELATED)
            .addGroup(groupLayout.createParallelGroup(Alignment.BASELINE)
            .addComponent(lblRole)
            .addComponent(comboBox, GroupLayout.PREFERRED_SIZE,
                GroupLayout.DEFAULT_SIZE, GroupLayout.PREFERRED_SIZE))
            .addPreferredGap(ComponentPlacement.RELATED)
            .addComponent(chckbxHasUnlimitedCoffee)
            .addPreferredGap(ComponentPlacement.RELATED, 49, Short.MAX_VALUE)
            .addGroup(groupLayout.createParallelGroup(Alignment.BASELINE)
            .addComponent(btnCancel)
            .addComponent(btnAdd))
            .addContainerGap())
            );
            getContentPane().setLayout(groupLayout);
        }
    }
```

Well, the result certainly looks complicated. WindowBuilder will do its best to anticipate your further code and will make components such as textfields and class fields so you can access them from other methods and objects when needed (to get and set text). By default, listeners are inlined with anonymous inner classes, but you can change this to real listener objects as well. Be careful when changing around too many things, though, as WindowBuilder might then not be able to convert your changes to a GUI layout it understands. This immediately illustrates both the advantages and disadvantages of visual GUI designers. They provide a great, easy method to quickly prototype a GUI (image building the GUI above by hand), but can lose their head once you start making too many custom changes.

In general, especially when you're starting out, you are advised not to fall into the luring trap of visual designers promising rapid development. If you can construct your GUI with some nimble nested components and simple layout managers, then by all means go ahead. If you do need to build complex forms and don't want to waste time laying out everything by hand, WindowBuilder provides a great alternative. The designer is also a helpful way to get acquainted quickly with unfamiliar components.

Finally, it is worth noting that you can also download other plug-ins to make WindowBuilder aware of GUI toolkits other than AWT/Swing, such as SWT. Other IDEs (Netbeans especially) also come with great visual designers, and there are some commercial ones as well (Jvider, JFormDesigner, and others).

JavaFX: The Road Ahead?

Swing has been around for a long time, and although the toolkit is immensely robust, it is starting to show its age. You have seen this already when talking about custom painting, or when taking a look at some of the . . . less nice-looking look and feels. With high-resolution retina displays, smartphones, tablets, rich Internet applications, and hardware-accelerated desktop compositors, the Java community started to desire a more modern UI toolkit. JavaFX was kickstarted to answer this need, and the UI toolkit has been around since 2008. With the release of Java 8, JavaFX became an integral part of the JRE (and JDK), so that the latest version of JavaFX went from 2.2 to simply JavaFX 8.

Sadly, this beginner book can't go into depth on all aspects of JavaFX, but when you are familiar with Swing, switching to JavaFX, should you want to, doesn't pose too many hurdles. Answering the question whether you should use JavaFX is not so straightforward. If you're itching to use the latest and greatest, then by all means go ahead. Keep in mind, however, that the community surrounding JavaFX is still young, so it will be much easier to find Swing-related libraries, support, and help when you need it. Finally, the multitude of GUIs in Java were built and are still being built with Swing, so if you're looking to apply your skills in a real-life setting, you still need to be acquainted with Swing.

The chapter concludes with two example projects built with JavaFX. In the first example, you'll learn how to build the BMI calculator again. If you're following along, you can just copy the old `BMICalculator` class and throw out anything that has to do with AWT or Swing. You'll also see a few things commented out so you don't forget to deal with them later:

```
public class BMICalculatorFX {

    //private final JTextField txtMass = makePrettyTextField();
    //private final JTextField txtHeight = makePrettyTextField();
    //private final JButton btnCalc = makePrettyButton("Calculate BMI");

    public BMICalculatorFX() {
        /*
        btnCalc.addActionListener(new ActionListener() {
```

```
                    @Override
                    public void actionPerformed(ActionEvent arg0) {
                        double mass;
                        double height;
                        try {
                            mass = Double.parseDouble(txtMass.getText());
                            height = Double.parseDouble(txtHeight.getText());
                        } catch (NumberFormatException e) {
                            JOptionPane.showMessageDialog(self,
                                    "Please enter a valid number for mass and height.",
                                    "Input error",
                                    JOptionPane.ERROR_MESSAGE);
                            return;
                        }
                        double result = calculateBMI(mass, height);
                        JOptionPane.showMessageDialog(self,
                                "Your BMI is: " + (Math.round(result*100.0)/100.0),
                                "Your BMI result",
                                JOptionPane.PLAIN_MESSAGE);
                    }
                });
                */
            }

            protected double calculateBMI(double mass, double height) {
                return mass / Math.pow(height/100.0, 2.0);
            }


            public static void main(String[] args) {
                SwingUtilities.invokeLater(new Runnable() {
                    public void run() { new BMICalculatorFX(); }
                });
            }
        }
```

The first thing to do is to figure out a way to show a simple window using JavaFX. In JavaFX, the main actor is called an *application*, and it can manage and show various *stages*. For this simple JavaFX application, this leads to the following:

```
import javafx.application.Application;
import javafx.scene.Group;
import javafx.scene.Scene;
import javafx.stage.Stage;

public class BMICalculatorFX extends Application {

    //private final JTextField txtMass = makePrettyTextField();
    //private final JTextField txtHeight = makePrettyTextField();
    //private final JButton btnCalc = makePrettyButton("Calculate BMI");

    public BMICalculatorFX() {
        /*
        btnCalc.addActionListener(new ActionListener() {
            @Override
```

```
            public void actionPerformed(ActionEvent arg0) {
                double mass;
                double height;
                try {
                    mass = Double.parseDouble(txtMass.getText());
                    height = Double.parseDouble(txtHeight.getText());
                } catch (NumberFormatException e) {
                    JOptionPane.showMessageDialog(self,
                            "Please enter a valid number for mass and height.",
                            "Input error",
                            JOptionPane.ERROR_MESSAGE);
                    return;
                }
                double result = calculateBMI(mass, height);
                JOptionPane.showMessageDialog(self,
                        "Your BMI is: " + (Math.round(result*100.0)/100.0),
                        "Your BMI result",
                        JOptionPane.PLAIN_MESSAGE);
            }
        });
        */
    }

    @Override
    public void start(Stage stage) throws Exception {
        Scene scene = new Scene(new Group());
        stage.setTitle("JavaFX BMI Calculator");
        stage.setScene(scene);
        stage.sizeToScene();
        stage.show();
    }

    protected double calculateBMI(double mass, double height) {
        return mass / Math.pow(height/100.0, 2.0);
    }

        public static void main(String[] args) {
        Application.launch(args);
    }
}
```

Note that Eclipse will complain about your JavaFX imports. The reason for this is that they are only part of Oracle's JRE and other Java implementations might not support this. To solve this warning, right-click your project in the Package Explorer, select Build Path followed by Configure Build Path. In the window that opens, navigate to the Libraries tab and expand the entry for JRE System Library. Select Access Rules and click Edit. Next, add an access rule to make `javafx/**` accessible, as illustrated in Figure 11-31.

Press OK. Your build path window should now look like Figure 11-32.

Press OK again. Your project will recompile and the errors should disappear.

You can try running the project now. A window will appear, but it seems to contain absolutely nothing, which is not surprising seeing that you set up an empty scene for the stage:

```
Scene scene = new Scene(new Group());
```

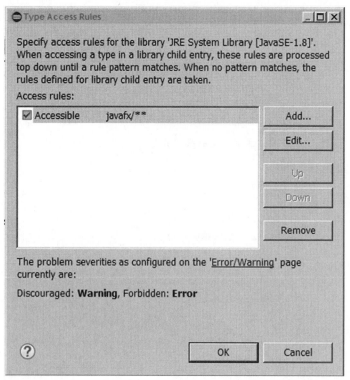

FIGURE 11-31

Now you can fill this scene with some actors. Just as with Swing, JavaFX also has several layout managers you can use. A simple VBox layout is used here:

```
import javafx.application.Application;
import javafx.scene.Group;
import javafx.scene.Scene;
import javafx.scene.control.Button;
import javafx.scene.control.Label;
import javafx.scene.control.TextField;
import javafx.scene.layout.VBox;
import javafx.scene.text.Font;
import javafx.stage.Stage;

public class BMICalculatorFX extends Application {

    private final TextField txtMass = new TextField();
    private final TextField txtHeight = new TextField();
    private final Button btnCalc = new Button("Calculate BMI");

    public BMICalculatorFX() {
        /*
        btnCalc.addActionListener(new ActionListener() {
            @Override
            public void actionPerformed(ActionEvent arg0) {
```

```java
            double mass;
            double height;
            try {
                mass = Double.parseDouble(txtMass.getText());
                height = Double.parseDouble(txtHeight.getText());
            } catch (NumberFormatException e) {
                JOptionPane.showMessageDialog(self,
                        "Please enter a valid number for mass and height.",
                        "Input error",
                        JOptionPane.ERROR_MESSAGE);
                return;
            }
            double result = calculateBMI(mass, height);
            JOptionPane.showMessageDialog(self,
                    "Your BMI is: " + (Math.round(result*100.0)/100.0),
                    "Your BMI result",
                    JOptionPane.PLAIN_MESSAGE);
        }
    });
    */
}

@Override
public void start(Stage stage) throws Exception {
    VBox vbox = new VBox(10);

    Label lblTitle = new Label("BMI Calculator");
    lblTitle.setFont(Font.font(18));
    vbox.getChildren().add(lblTitle);

    vbox.getChildren().add(new Label("Your mass (kg):"));
    vbox.getChildren().add(txtMass);

    vbox.getChildren().add(new Label("Your height (cm):"));
    vbox.getChildren().add(txtHeight);

    vbox.getChildren().add(btnCalc);

    Scene scene = new Scene(new Group(vbox));

    stage.setTitle("JavaFX BMI Calculator");
    stage.setScene(scene);
    stage.sizeToScene();
    stage.show();
}

protected double calculateBMI(double mass, double height) {
    return mass / Math.pow(height/100.0, 2.0);
}


public static void main(String[] args) {
    Application.launch(args);
}
}
```

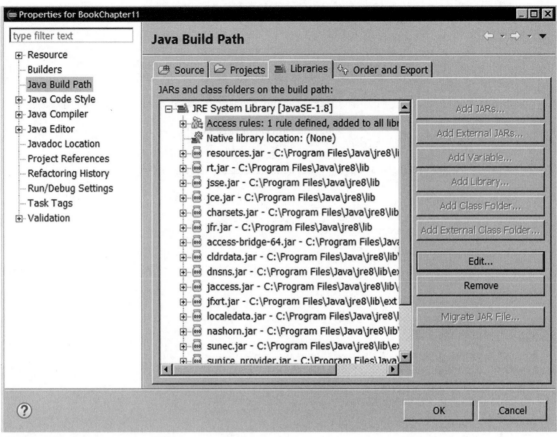

FIGURE 11-32

You'll notice that the basic concepts are not so different from Swing. Running your project now provides the beautifully crafted window shown in Figure 11-33.

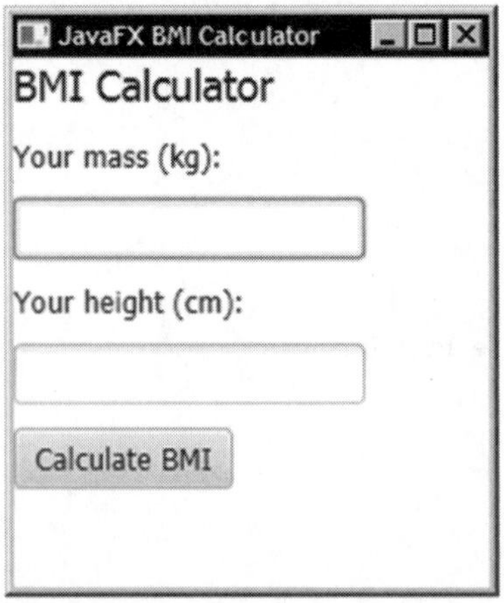

FIGURE 11-33

Next, you'll need to add an action handler to the button. Again, the basic concepts are the same—you need to catch interesting UI events and respond to them:

```java
import javafx.application.Application;
import javafx.event.ActionEvent;
import javafx.event.EventHandler;
import javafx.scene.Group;
import javafx.scene.Scene;
import javafx.scene.control.Button;
import javafx.scene.control.Label;
import javafx.scene.control.TextField;
import javafx.scene.layout.VBox;
import javafx.scene.text.Font;
import javafx.stage.Stage;
import javafx.geometry.Pos;
import javafx.scene.layout.HBox;
import javafx.stage.Modality;
import javafx.stage.StageStyle;

public class BMICalculatorFX extends Application {

    private Stage stage;
    private final TextField txtMass = new TextField();
    private final TextField txtHeight = new TextField();
    private final Button btnCalc = new Button("Calculate BMI");

    @Override
    public void start(Stage stage) throws Exception {
        this.stage = stage;

        VBox vbox = new VBox(10);

        Label lblTitle = new Label("BMI Calculator");
        lblTitle.setFont(Font.font(18));
        vbox.getChildren().add(lblTitle);

        vbox.getChildren().add(new Label("Your mass (kg):"));
        vbox.getChildren().add(txtMass);

        vbox.getChildren().add(new Label("Your height (cm):"));
        vbox.getChildren().add(txtHeight);

        vbox.getChildren().add(btnCalc);

        btnCalc.setOnAction(new EventHandler<ActionEvent>() {
            @Override
            public void handle(ActionEvent ev) {
                double mass;
                double height;
                try {
                    mass = Double.parseDouble(txtMass.getText());
                    height = Double.parseDouble(txtHeight.getText());
                } catch (NumberFormatException e) {
                    showMessage("Check your input.", "Error in number input");
```

```
                        return;
                    }
                    double result = calculateBMI(mass, height);
                    showMessage("Your BMI is: " +
                        (Math.round(result*100.0)/100.0), "Your BMI result");
                }
            });

        Scene scene = new Scene(new Group(vbox));
        stage.setTitle("JavaFX BMI Calculator");
        stage.setScene(scene);
        stage.sizeToScene();
        stage.show();
    }

    protected double calculateBMI(double mass, double height) {
        return mass / Math.pow(height/100.0, 2.0);
    }


    public static void main(String[] args) {
        Application.launch(args);
    }

    public void showMessage(final String message, final String title) {
        final Stage dialog = new Stage(StageStyle.UTILITY);
        dialog.setTitle(title);
        dialog.setResizable(false);
        dialog.initModality(Modality.WINDOW_MODAL);
        dialog.initOwner(this.stage);

        VBox vbox = new VBox(2);
        HBox pane = new HBox(10);

        dialog.setScene(new Scene(vbox));
        vbox.setAlignment(Pos.CENTER);

        vbox.getChildren().add(pane);
        pane.getChildren().add(new Label(message));
        Button btn = new Button("OK");
        btn.setOnAction(new EventHandler<ActionEvent>() {
                @Override
                public void handle(ActionEvent e) {
                    dialog.close();
                }
            });
        pane.getChildren().add(btn);
        dialog.showAndWait();
    }
}
```

Note that JavaFX does not provide a built-in method to show dialogs (this might be included in future Java updates, though). Here, a simple showMessage method was added that constructs a new stage window to show a message with an OK button. The end result looks like Figure 11-34.

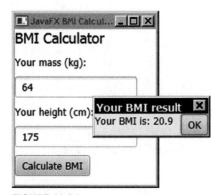

FIGURE 11-34

As of now, you might appreciate the cleaner coding style and look of JavaFX, but still wonder what the big deal is. Earlier, you read that JavaFX hardware accelerated graphics to allow for more spectacular graphical applications as well. The following and final example (adapted from an Oracle tutorial) shows this in action:

```java
import static java.lang.Math.random;

import javafx.animation.Animation;
import javafx.animation.KeyFrame;
import javafx.animation.KeyValue;
import javafx.animation.Timeline;
import javafx.application.Application;
import javafx.scene.Group;
import javafx.scene.Node;
import javafx.scene.Scene;
import javafx.scene.effect.BlendMode;
import javafx.scene.effect.BoxBlur;
import javafx.scene.paint.Color;
import javafx.scene.paint.CycleMethod;
import javafx.scene.paint.LinearGradient;
import javafx.scene.paint.Stop;
import javafx.scene.shape.Circle;
import javafx.scene.shape.Rectangle;
import javafx.scene.shape.StrokeType;
import javafx.stage.Stage;
import javafx.util.Duration;

public class ScreenSaver extends Application {

    public static void main(String[] args) {
        launch(args);
    }

    @Override
    public void start(Stage primaryStage) {
        Group root = new Group();
        Scene scene = new Scene(root, 800, 600, Color.WHITE);
        primaryStage.setScene(scene);
```

```java
Group circles = new Group();
for (int i = 0; i < 500; i++) {
    Circle circle = new Circle(30, Color.web("black", 0.10));
    circle.setStrokeType(StrokeType.OUTSIDE);
    circle.setStroke(Color.web("black", 0.15));
    circle.setStrokeWidth(2);
    circles.getChildren().add(circle);
}

Rectangle colors = new Rectangle(scene.getWidth(), scene.getHeight(),
        new LinearGradient(0f, 1f, 1f, 0f, true, CycleMethod.REPEAT,
                new Stop[]{
                        new Stop(0, Color.web("#f8bd55")),
                        new Stop(0.14, Color.web("#c0fe56")),
                        new Stop(0.28, Color.web("#5dfbc1")),
                        new Stop(0.43, Color.web("#64c2f8")),
                        new Stop(0.57, Color.web("#be4af7")),
                        new Stop(0.71, Color.web("#ed5fc2")),
                        new Stop(0.85, Color.web("#ef504c")),
                        new Stop(1, Color.web("#f2660f"))}
        ));
colors.widthProperty().bind(scene.widthProperty());
colors.heightProperty().bind(scene.heightProperty());
Group blendModeGroup = new Group(
        new Group(
            new Rectangle(scene.getWidth(), scene.getHeight(),
                    Color.WHITE), circles), colors);
colors.setBlendMode(BlendMode.OVERLAY);
root.getChildren().add(blendModeGroup);
circles.setEffect(new BoxBlur(10, 10, 3));
Timeline timeline = new Timeline();
for (Node circle : circles.getChildren()) {
  timeline.getKeyFrames().addAll(
    new KeyFrame(Duration.ZERO,
    new KeyValue(circle.translateXProperty(),
        random() * scene.getWidth()),
    new KeyValue(circle.translateYProperty(),
        random() * scene.getHeight())),
    new KeyFrame(new Duration(60000),
    new KeyValue(circle.translateXProperty(),
        random() * scene.getWidth()),
    new KeyValue(circle.translateYProperty(),
        random() * scene.getHeight())));
}
timeline.setCycleCount(Animation.INDEFINITE);
timeline.play();

primaryStage.show();
    }
}
```

Feel free to daydream while JavaFX shows its graphical prowess in Figure 11-35.

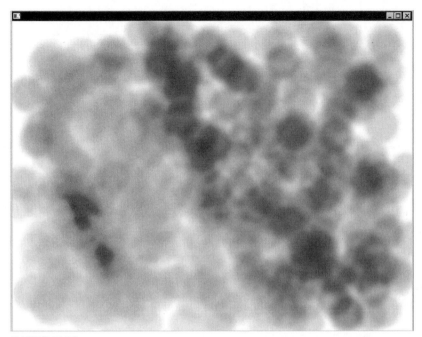

FIGURE 11-35

This concludes the chapter on building graphical interfaces. This has been a lengthy one, and even now, many Swing (and JavaFX) components remain worth taking a closer look at. As such, don't hesitate to get started building your own GUIs and exploring the Javadocs to hone your skills. Make sure to keep the best practices listed in this chapter in mind—keep logic and looks separated and structure your UI code in a neat manner.

Speaking of best practices, the following chapter will be completely devoted to these, as you delve into the topic of Object-Oriented Programming patterns. It covers best practices to solve common architectural challenges and structure your applications in the best maintainable and understandable way possible, something that will become immensely important as your applications start growing in size and complexity.

12

Using Object-Oriented Patterns

WHAT YOU WILL LEARN IN THIS CHAPTER:

➤   What programming patterns are and why they are useful

➤   How can object-oriented patterns be applied to structure applications

➤   Which libraries, frameworks, and best practices are commonly used in Java programming

WROX.COM CODE DOWNLOADS FOR THIS CHAPTER

The wrox.com code downloads for this chapter are found at www.wrox.com/go/ beginningjavaprogramming on the Download Code tab. The code is in the Chapter 12 download and individually named according to the names throughout the chapter.

Congratulations, you've reached the last chapter. The primary goal behind this chapter is to combine all the knowledge you've gained throughout this book and to show you how all the various pieces—control flow, input and output, class inheritance, and so on—come together to construct a complete application.

Since many aspiring programmers find it hard to start from a blank sheet and maintain order and structure in their applications, we aim to reach the goals listed above with a chapter on so-called programming patterns. This chapter will teach you a number of best practices and solutions for common problems you'll encounter when creating object-oriented applications with Java. As such, this chapter starts with a general introduction on programming patterns, before delving deeper into the patterns. Finally, the chapter ends with a brief overview of some third-party libraries that you may find useful when starting new projects.

INTRODUCTION TO PATTERNS

The concept of the design pattern is well known in the area of software engineering. Many definitions for "pattern" exist, but broadly speaking, a pattern is a *general applicable and reusable solution* that solves frequently occurring problems and architectural challenges in software design. In other words, a pattern provides a description on how to solve a particular problem, which is applicable in many situations.

Interestingly, the notion of a pattern did not originate in the realm of programming or software engineering, but as an architectural concept. In 1977, Christopher Alexander put forth the idea of capturing architectural design principles as reusable descriptions, formulated in his work, *A Pattern Language: Towns, Buildings, Construction.* He stated that "each pattern describes a problem that occurs over and over again in our environment and then describes the core of the solution to that problem in such a way that you can use this solution a million times over without ever doing it the same way twice." Then, in 1987, Kent Beck and Ward Cunningham started experimenting with the idea of applying patterns to programming and presented their results at object-oriented software engineering conferences. From that moment onward, software and programming "design patterns" have been popular in computer science.

The big surge in interest, however, followed the publication of the book *Design Patterns: Elements of Reusable Object-Oriented Software* in 1994 by Gamma, Helm, Johnson, and Vlissides, commonly referred to as the "Gang of Four." The book describes 23 design patterns for use in object-oriented software projects and has become highly influential in the field of software engineering. So much so that it is incredibly hard to find a mid- to large-scale Java, C++, Smalltalk, or other Object-Oriented Programming language-based project that doesn't contain one of these design patterns.

Remember that a pattern defines a concrete solution, meaning that you should be able to use a pattern repeatedly once the reference is given, and the solution must be applicable in lots of different situations. To describe and write down these patterns, many different forms have been proposed, ranging from free-form, narrative texts to structured forms containing well-defined sections (the Gang of Four books, for instance, applies a very structured form). In addition, a repository or catalogue should also be structured in such a way that specific patterns can be easily and quickly retrieved. To facilitate this, patterns are often structured in so-called pattern languages or pattern groups: a set of patterns aiming to solve the same general problem.

The "Gang of Four" book structures patterns as being Creational, Structural, or Behavioral. Creational patterns deal with object creation mechanisms, as the basic form of object creation could result in design problems or added complexity to the design. Structural patterns ease the design by identifying a simple way to realize relationships between entities. Behavioral patterns identify common communication patterns between objects to increase flexibility in carrying out this communication.

OBJECT-ORIENTED PATTERNS

This section takes you through a handful of the original Gang of Four design patterns. It's presented in a relaxed style, where instead of providing the pattern in a very strict and structured form (you can read the original book for that), you see how the pattern works, how you can spot it in real-life projects, how you can use it yourself, and then common pitfalls you should watch out for. Don't expect that all patterns will immediately be useful to you as a beginner, but you'll note that you will feel a natural tendency toward them as you become more experienced.

This book adopts the same structure and naming as the Gang of Four, dividing the patterns into Creational, Structural, and Behavioral categories. Keep in mind that the focus here is on how each pattern works and behaves in Java. The goal here is to show you the patterns that also teach you how to make architectural design choices and how each choice allows certain freedoms and takes away others. This section doesn't copy the description of the original patterns verbatim, as this would not offer much value.

Creational Patterns

Creational patterns deal with object creation. Instead of creating objects directly, these patterns offer more flexibility in terms of deciding which objects need to be created in a given case, meaning that they offer alternatives for the following standard creation procedure in Java, as you've seen throughout this book:

```
House myHouse = new House();
```

Here, the singleton, static utility class, service provider (this pattern is not mentioned in the Gang of Four book but is closely related to the singleton pattern), factory, and abstract factory patterns are covered. The builder and prototype creational patterns are not discussed, as both of them are less commonly applied in Java.

Singleton Pattern and Static Utility Class

Let's start with one of the most controversial object-oriented patterns, the singleton pattern. (We'll address the reasons behind its controversy later on.) The Gang of Four summarizes a design pattern as follows:

Ensure a class has instance and provide a global point of access to that instance.

This pattern is useful whenever exactly one object is needed to coordinate certain actions. In Java, an easy way to define a singleton class is as follows:

```java
public class Singleton {
    private static final Singleton INSTANCE = new Singleton();

    private Singleton() {}

    public static Singleton getInstance() {
        return INSTANCE;
    }

    // Other public methods follow here
}
```

You call the singleton's methods as follows:

```java
Singleton.getInstance().theSingletonMethod();
```

Note the different aspects at play here. First of all, the static final field is immediately initialized to contain the single `singleton` object (which cannot be changed afterward due to being final). Second, direct instantiation of objects is prohibited by making the constructor private. Third, the single instance is accessed calling the public static `getInstance()` method.

This way of defining a `singleton` class is called "eager initialization," as the single instance gets created no matter whether it will be used during the execution of the program. The alternative, called "lazy initialization," first sets the `INSTANCE` (nonfinal, then) field to null and initializes it the first time the `getInstance()` method is called. Using this approach, however, can introduce subtle bugs in multithreaded Java programs (where multiple tasks are executed in parallel) if not implemented correctly, so it is not advisable.

Another interesting, less-used way to define a `singleton` in Java is by using an `enum` type:

```java
public enum Singleton {
    INSTANCE;

    // Other public methods follow here
}
```

This method is preferred by some, as it takes advantage of Java's guarantee that `enum` values are instantiated only once in a Java program, are globally accessible, and are instantiated lazily without potential issues regarding multithreading. You use the `singleton` enum as follows:

```java
Singleton.INSTANCE.theSingletonMethod();
```

Now that you know how the `singleton` pattern works, it is time for a word of advice: this pattern is one of the most overused and badly used design patterns out there. The reason for this is easy to see: the singleton pattern provides an easy way out whenever you want to introduce global variables or state in your program. Why is this a bad thing? By allowing global state in your program, you allow any other parts of your program to access and modify this at any time, making these programs very hard to test and debug when something goes wrong (who modified the singleton in a bad manner?).

In many real-life cases, less experienced programmers will resort to using singletons whenever they feel that they need a "manager" class to store some centralized information, perform some centralized task, or babysit other objects. For example, take a look at the following extreme case:

```java
public class Account {
    private String name;
    private double amount;

    public String getName() {
        return name;
    }

    public double getAmount() {
        return amount;
    }

    public void setName(String name) {
        this.name = name;
```

```
        }

        public void setAmount(double amount) {
            this.amount = amount;
        }
    }


public class AccountManager {
    public Account createAccount(String name, double startFunds) {
        Account account = new Account();
        account.setName(name);
        account.setAmount(startFunds);
        return account;
    }
    public boolean isOverdrawn(Account account) {
        return account.getAmount() < 0;
    }
    public void addFunds(Account account, double amount) {
        account.setAmount(account.getAmount() + amount);
    }
}
```

This example can look a bit silly—rightly so—although note that there exist many cases of code with such anti-object-oriented design once you look behind the curtain. In cases such as these, it's easy to imagine that AccountManager should be a singleton. Any account will need a manager, and how many managers do you need? Of course, the correct answer is not one, but none. You can resolve this problem like so:

```
public class Account {
    private String name;
    private double amount;

    public Account(String name) {
        this(name, 0);
    }

    public Account(String name, double startAmount) {
        this.name = name;
        this.amount = startAmount;
    }

    public boolean isOverdrawn() {
        return this.amount < 0;
    }

    public void addFunds(double amount) {
        this.amount += amount;
    }

    public String getName() {
        return name;
    }
```

```
public double getAmount() {
    return amount;
}

}
```

You can use the `Account` class as is to encapsulate the data and the behavior, which has to do with the concept of an account. This is exactly what Object-Oriented Programming is about. Poorly designed `singleton` classes are oftentimes "helpers" or "utility" classes that add functionality to other classes. If possible, just move that behavior to the class itself.

> **NOTE** *This misuse of the singleton is captured in the so-called "god object" anti-pattern. Just as patterns recommend best practices, anti-patterns indicate commonly made mistakes and depict bad design decisions. A god object is a centralized object that contains and does too many things. It shows up in all other places of the codebase and becomes too tightly coupled to the other code.*

There are cases, however, where the use of singletons is helpful. A big insight lies in the fact that the singleton pattern solves two problems at once:

➤ Limits a class to a single instance.

➤ Provides a global point of access to an instance.

In Java, you should look at both requirements separately. If you want to limit a class to a single instance, this doesn't mean you want to allow every other object out there to access this instance. In those cases, providing a public, global point of access is a weak architectural decision. How, then, do you allow only one creation of a class? Like so:

```
public class Singleton {
    private static boolean CREATED = false;

    public Singleton() {
        if (CREATED)
            throw new RuntimeException(
                "Class "+this.getClass()+" can only be created once");
        CREATED = true;
    }

    // Other methods follow here

    public static void main(String args[]) {
        Singleton one = new Singleton();
        Singleton two = new Singleton();
    }
}
```

The `singleton` class can now be constructed at any time in any place, but will throw an error if you try to construct it more than once. This code ensures single instantiation, but does not dictate how the class is used (i.e., not a global point of access). This is a simple mechanism that's somewhat underused.

Providing a global point of access to an instance is the second and often the main reason that singletons are used. This concept makes it easy to reach for an object that's utilized in many places, but sometimes in places where you don't want it to be used. So what options are there to keep things organized?

In some cases, you can choose to pass in the object you need as an argument to the methods that need it. However, it can be argued that many objects don't fit well in the argument list of a method. For instance, when every method that's added to a log file also has a Log object in its argument list, things get messy quickly.

> **NOTE** *In many cases, singletons pop up for things that have to be used and accessed throughout a codebase. Logging is a traditional example. This concept is called "cross-cutting concerns," and an alternative programming paradigm—aspect-oriented programming—was designed to address these concerns. Libraries exist to bring aspect-oriented features to Java, but their use is not very widespread. Refactoring your code and trying to keep things as neat as possible is the preferred way to go.*

For "global" objects that only have to be accessed by a class and its subclasses, it is a good idea to make the singleton object a field of the superclass, together with a private method such as getObjectOfInterest(). The subclasses derived from the superclass then have access to the object they need, without the object being accessible to other classes and their instances.

For global classes that offer a set of utility functions, consider making the class and all its methods static to build a "static utility class." In many cases, this is a better approach and one you'll see in many Java programs. Many third-party libraries offer classes ending in "Utils" (FileUtils, StringUtils, and so on), and they contain nothing else but public static helper methods. Although these methods are also globally accessible, the class itself does not contain any state. Naturally, this point only holds when you do *not* define static variables in the helper class that's being modified by the methods. The only reason why static utility classes should contain static fields is to define helpful constants (such as the static double PI variable in the Math class). If you do decide to create a static utility class, however, always keep in mind the earlier example, and try to encapsulate as much behavior as possible in the appropriate classes themselves whenever possible (no AccountUtils!).

STATIC UTILITY CLASS OR SINGLETON?

You might be wondering what the difference is between the following two ways to define a singleton class in Java:

```java
// As a static utility class:
public class Singleton {
    private static int A = 0;
    public static int get() {
        return A;
```

continues

continued

```
        }
        public static void set(int a) {
            A = a;
        }
    }

    // A single instance of a class:
    public class Singleton {
        private static final Singleton INSTANCE = new Singleton();
        private int A;
        private Singleton() {
            A = 0;
        }
        public static Singleton getInstance() {
            return INSTANCE;
        }
        public int get() {
            return A;
        }
        public void set(int a) {
            A = a;
        }
    }
```

Ignoring the fact that using static variables to keep state is not good practice, both of these classes seem to achieve the same end, although there is a subtle difference. Consider a `Logger singleton` class with a `log(String message)` method. Imagine that, at first, this method just shows a message on the console, but later on, you want to add functionality to log a file and retain the ability to choose at runtime which of the two implementations to use. With a static utility class, you would have to resort to a check in the `log` method to see which path of execution to follow. If the singleton contains more methods, the check has to be added to every method, reducing maintainability and introducing redundancy. With the non-static `singleton` object, you can make the log method abstract and create two subclasses—`ConsoleLogger` and `FileLogger`. You can then determine the right object to assign as the instance, without modifying any other code. The second way is thus better practice from an Object-Oriented Programming viewpoint. That said, remember that whenever you are defining a utility class without its own state and thus holding a collection of simple utility functions, it is better to define it as a static class.

To conclude this discussion on the singleton pattern, consider the following guidelines:

➤ Always check whether you actually need a separate class or whether the behavior belongs in an existing class.

➤ When you need a globally accessible list of utility methods, use a static utility class without modeling any state (static variables that are being changed by the class methods).

➤ When you do need a single instance of a class, think about whether the instance also has to be globally accessible.

➤ If you do need a single instance of a class and it has to be globally accessible, you can use the full singleton pattern. Always be wary of this option, and make sure you've exhausted the other options mentioned here first.

As discussed, most singletons offer some general "helper" methods or provide a global centralized service for use in the rest of the application, such as a logging functionality. To avoid having a global collection of singleton objects, it is a good idea to group your singletons under a service provider, as described in the next pattern.

Service Provider Pattern and Null Object Pattern

Let's say you have a service offering logging functionality that needs to be called throughout all parts of your code. Perhaps you should implement it as a static utility class, as you've seen previously:

```
LoggingUtils.logMessage("Something bad happened", LoggingUtils.PRIORITY_HIGH);
```

Or perhaps create a singleton:

```
Logger.getInstance().logMessage("Something bad happened", Logger.PRIORITY_HIGH);
```

Disregarding the fact that this approach introduces some nasty global objects in the project, you still have the problem that these objects are very tightly coupled with the rest of the code. What if at one point you want to introduce a second logging system and decide which one to use at runtime?

The service provider pattern can help, because it allows you to keep a "registry" of services and swap them in and out at runtime. This is illustrated in the logging example. Imagine you have a `Logger` interface and two concrete implementing classes, `ConsoleLogger` and `EmailLogger` (an `AbstractLogger` can be defined here as well, for instance to hold the different priority level constants). Your service locator would then look like this:

```
public class ServiceProvider {
    private static final ServiceLocator INSTANCE = new ServiceLocator();
    private ServiceLocator() {}

    private Logger logger;

    public static ServiceLocator getInstance() {
        return INSTANCE;
    }

    private Logger getLogger() {
        return logger;
    }

    private void setLogger(Logger logger) {
        this.logger = logger;
    }
}
```

The service locator has some interesting benefits. First, it is not possible to change the service implementation at runtime. Second, the service provider is a singleton, but the services don't have to be. You can still prevent multiple instantiation, but instead of making five singletons globally accessible, everything can now go through one single locator. Third, adding services is just a simple manner of adding a field and the getter and setter methods.

In essence, the service provider pattern is a combination of a singleton and strategy pattern (as you'll see later).

One thing that you do need to consider, however, is remembering to set all services. When you forget to call the `setLogger` method in this example, for instance, the `ServiceProvider` will return `null`. There are several ways around this. You can manually check in your code to see if a provider returns `null`, you can force initialization by accepting a `Logger` object in the `ServiceProvider` constructor, or you can just initialize the service to a default one. Finally, you can also apply another pattern, the null object pattern, to solve this issue.

The basic idea of the null object is that instead of returning null, a special object returning the same interface as the desired object is returned, but with an implementation that does nothing. In the logging example, a `NullLogger` would look like this:

```
public class NullLogger implements Logger {
    public void logMessage(String message, int PRIORITY_LEVEL) {
        // Do nothing
    }
}
```

As you can see, this service implements all expected methods, but does not actually do anything. Now, when you default to this service in your provider class, the calling code doesn't have to handle nulls.

> **NOTE** The discussion on the null object pattern is also related to another commonly observed best practice, namely the fact that it is always better—whenever possible—to have functions return empty collections (collections containing zero elements) instead of a `null` value. A common reason why programmers choose to return `null` in the first place is to signal to the calling code that some kind of error occurred (the collection could not be retrieved or constructed), which is different from a successful execution returning an empty collection. In this case (signaling errors), the better practice is to rely on exceptions, which can be caught and handled accordingly by calling code. Following this practice will help greatly to avoid null pointer exceptions (e.g., by calling the `size()` method on a `null` object).

(Abstract) Factory Pattern

The factory pattern is another commonly applied creational pattern. It's summarized as follows: *Defer instantiation of a class to subclasses.*

In other words, the factory pattern provides an interface for creating an object, while providing different implementations for the creation of that object.

As an example, suppose you have an abstract class called `Account`, subclassed to `NormalAccount` and `VIPAccount`. Maybe the `VIPAccount` gets a bonus on creation, or a bonus every time funds are added, but the exact details of the implementation are not important.

Instead of directly using these objects as is, the factory pattern abstracts away the creation of them by defining separate creation methods that can be overridden. For the account example, the factory pattern can thus be implemented as follows:

```
public class AccountFactory {
    public Account createAccount(String name, double amount) {
        return new NormalAccount(name, amount);
    }
}

public class VIPAccountFactory extends AccountFactory {
    public Account createAccount(String name, double amount) {
        return new VIPAccount(name, amount);
    }
}
```

In other parts of the code, either of the following can be defined:

```
AccountFactory factory = new AccountFactory();
```

Or:

```
AccountFactory factory = new VIPAccountFactory();
```

Either one can call the same `createAccount` method to create the appropriate account.

Note that you can also choose to implement the factory methods directly in the account classes as static methods, making the constructor of the class private. This is another pattern that shows up a lot in Java projects.

Again, in other cases, different factory classes implement a single interface class. Sometimes, all factory classes subclass an abstract factory superclass (this is specifically referred to as the "abstract factory pattern") to encapsulate multiple related creation methods. Consider, for example, the abstract factory class `FurnitureFactory`, which provides abstract definitions for `createChair()` and `createTable()`, among others. This abstract factory can then be subclassed to the concrete `WoodFurnitureFactory` and `PlasticFurnitureFactory` classes, which would each create corresponding objects (`WoodChair`, `PlasticTable`, and so on), all of which are also subclasses of abstract `Chair` and `Table` classes. The benefit from using this pattern lies in the fact that all remaining code using these factories can work with the abstract `Chair` and `Table` classes, instead of the specific version the factory created. This approach retains more levels of abstraction.

Another reason that factory classes are often applied is to create a centralized location to keep a list of all created objects. For instance, you might opt to keep a list of all created accounts in the `AccountFactory` class and provide methods to easily retrieve a specific account later on. This is fine in some cases, but just as with the singleton pattern, you should take care not to construct overloaded factory classes containing too much behavior and logic. On a similar note, you might encounter factory objects that are also singletons. When this happens, keep an eye out for possible ways to restructure and streamline the affected code.

Structural Patterns

Structural patterns concern how classes and objects are structured, mainly how inheritance and interfaces should be applied to design, or redesign, object-oriented architectures in useful ways.

Most of these patterns involve wrapping of some kind, i.e., creating classes that contain instances of other classes or subclass other classes. Such patterns often show up in cases when code is being refactored or when complex classes are wrapped in simpler ones.

The adapter, bridge, decorator, façade, and composite patterns are discussed here. The type pattern, which is not explicitly mentioned in the Gang of Four book, but deals with an interesting and useful aspect of Object-Oriented Programming, is also included here as an explicit pattern. The structural proxy and flyweight patterns are not addressed, as their use cases are less relevant for beginners (feel free to look them up, however).

Adapter Pattern

The goal of the adapter pattern is to make classes with incompatible interfaces work together, as illustrated here. Imagine a world with two printer companies. One is called Ink4Ever and has a class somewhere in its driver code that looks like this:

```
public class InkjetPrinter {
    public void print(Document d, int nrCopies) {
        // Print code here
    }
    public void printDuplicate(Document d, int nrCopies) {
        // Print code here
    }
}
```

The second printer company, called MajorLaser, has a driver class like this:

```
public class LaserPrinter {
    public void print(Document d, boolean printDuplicate) {
        // Print code here
    }
}
```

After many years of fierce competition, the two companies merge to form a new entity, called Ink&Laser. The programmers start working on exciting new printer software, with the final task of creating a unified driver that can work with laser and inkjet printers.

The team decides it would be best to use the following single method throughout the codebase:

```
public void print(Document d, int nrCopies, boolean printDuplicate)
```

The question now is how to implement this approach so that it works with the inkjet and laser printer drivers, as they do not agree on their method signatures. One of the programmers suggests just merging the two legacy printers into a new, unified driver, like so:

```
public class UnifiedPrinter {
    public void print(Document d, int nrCopies, boolean printDuplicate) {
```

```
            if (isLaser()) {
                for (int copy = 1; copy <= nrCopies; copy++)
                    printLaser(d, printDuplicate);
            } else {
                if (printDuplicate)
                    printInkjetDuplicate(d, nrCopies);
                else
                    printInkjet(d, nrCopies);
            }
        }

        public void printInkjet(Document d, int nrCopies) {
            // Print code here
        }

        public void printInkjetDuplicate(Document d, int nrCopies) {
            // Print code here
        }

        public void printLaser(Document d, boolean printDuplicate) {
            // Print code here
        }

        public boolean isLaser() {
            // Figure out whether this is a laser printer or not
            return true;
        }
    }
```

At first, this seems like a smart idea, but the project manager disapproves. "This won't do," he tells his team, "It is far too hard to merge the two classes into a single one, what with the similarly named variables and all. Even more important, what are we going to do once we start supporting a third type of printer? This is not the object-oriented way to do things." The programmers are rubbing their heads. What would be the right way to implement this correctly? Starting purely from an object-oriented perspective, a natural place to start is by defining a `Printer` interface containing the method signature that all printer drivers should support:

```
public interface Printer {
    public void print(Document d, int nrCopies, boolean printDuplicate);
}
```

Next, `InkjetPrinter` and `LaserPrinter` can be renamed `LegacyInkjetPrinter` and `LegacyLaserPrinter`, and two new classes can be defined:

```
public class LaserPrinter implements Printer {

    public LegacyLaserPrinter printer = new LegacyLaserPrinter();

    @Override
    public void print(Document d, int nrCopies, boolean printDuplicate) {
        for (int copy = 1; copy <= nrCopies; copy++)
            printer.print(d, printDuplicate);
    }
```

```
    }

    public class InkjetPrinter implements Printer {

        public LegacyInkjetPrinter printer = new LegacyInkjetPrinter();

        @Override
        public void print(Document d, int nrCopies, boolean printDuplicate) {
            if (printDuplicate)
                printer.print(d, nrCopies);
            else
                printer.print(d, nrCopies);
        }
    }
```

Note how `LegacyInkjetPrinter` and `LegacyLaserPrinter` are now contained as instances in the adapter classes `InkjetPrinter` and `LaserPrinter`. This is exactly what this pattern is about: wrapping instances of incompatible classes in adapters. Note that the `Printer` interface can now be used everywhere in the code to pass around printer objects.

> **NOTE** *Of course, you still need to decide whether to use an* `InkjetPrinter` *or* `LaserPrinter` *class at construction. Since this is a creation issue, you might want to use the factory pattern to construct the appropriate object, based on the hardware configuration detected on the computer.*

Finally, note that there is another variant of this pattern where a new class is created that extends all original legacy classes. As you've seen before, multiple inheritance is not possible in Java, although one way to apply this pattern would be if all legacy classes also have associated interfaces. The new class can then implement all these interfaces.

Bridge Pattern

Next up is the bridge pattern. This pattern is sometimes confused with the adapter pattern, the reason being that the bridge pattern uses the adapter pattern, but goes a step further. It not only keeps flexibility in the implementation (e.g., to choose which printer class to use, all implementing the interface `Printer`), but also allows greater abstraction. Say you have the `Printer` interface and `InkjetPrinter` and `LaserPrinter` as implementing classes, perhaps still using the legacy classes. The key point to remember is that you have an interface and different implementations of this interface.

Now, an additional abstraction is added on top of the implementations, a class that will sit between the client code and the implementations. That is a bridging class. In the example, this class might be called `AbstractPrintSpooler`:

```
    public abstract class AbstractPrintSpooler {
        private Printer printer;

        public AbstractPrintSpooler(Printer printer) {
            this.printer = printer;
```

```
    }

    public void print(Document d, int nrCopies, boolean printDuplicate) {
        printer.print(d, nrCopies, printDuplicate);
    }
}
```

Note how this class reimplements all the methods from the original `Printer` interface and passes on every command to the contained `Printer` instance (again, this is an example of the adapter pattern). Instead of using the `Printer` interface in your client code, you now use `AbstractPrintSpooler`, however. Note that you can also decide to have `AbstractPrintSpooler` implement the `Printer` interface (this forces the abstraction to also implement all methods from the implementation) and to make the class nonabstract if you want to use it as is (which is also perfectly valid). All things considered, it does seem that the `AbstractPrintSpooler` class is adding nothing of value, so then why would you add another layer of abstraction? The reason is that you can now add concrete subclasses of this abstraction. Imagine for example a `GreenPrintSpooler` like so:

```
public class GreenPrintSpooler extends AbstractPrintSpooler {
    public GreenPrintSpooler(Printer printer) {
        super(printer);
    }
    public void print(Document d, int nrCopies, boolean printDuplicate) {
        printDuplicate = true;   // Force to print duplicates
        d.setToBlackAndWhite(); // Convert document to black and white
        print(d, nrCopies, printDuplicate);
    }
}
```

A concrete implementation of your spooler has now been created that will convert all documents to black and white and force the duplicate option to true before passing on the `print` command to the implementation. The benefits of this pattern should become clear to you now: bridges are helpful whenever an extra layer of abstraction is needed on top of something else. For example, whether to print green is a separate decision on top of the printer model being used.

Decorator Pattern

The decorator pattern also bears similarities to the adapter pattern. It allows you to add behavior to a single instance of a class without adding this behavior to all instances of the same class (as you would end up with through normal subclassing).

This pattern is commonly used in GUI programming, so it makes sense to include an example from this context. Imagine you have created a `Window` class to display fancy GUI windows. Now let's say you want to create a particular variant of these windows that cannot be minimized and needs to stay on-screen. You can simply create a `NaggingWindow` class that extends the `Window` class and adds behavior to disable the minimize button. Imagine that, sometime later, you also encounter a need to add scrollbars to some of your windows. No problem, as you can just create a `ScrollableWindow` class to do this. However, what about windows that should not be minimized and also need scrollbars? One solution might be to add a `NaggingScrollableWindow` class, but as windows get more and more features, this would quickly lead to a soup of redundant subclasses. One solution is to merge everything in the single `Window` class, but this would lead to a single, horribly confusing and lengthy class with many methods, such as `setHasScrollbars(boolean b)`. This solution also does not seem like the proper object-oriented way to program things.

Luckily, the decorator pattern can help. This pattern resembles the bridge pattern in that it contains both a combination of interfaces and abstract classes. For this example, you would need the following:

➤ `interface Window`: Contains all the method signatures windows need to support, such as `setTitle(String title)`.

➤ `class NormalWindow implements Window`: The class implementing the bare-bones window.

➤ `abstract class WindowDecorator implements Window`: The abstract decorator class. Just as with the bridge pattern, this class contains an instance of a `Window` object, as well as methods for all methods the `Window` interface defines. In the abstract calls, all method calls are passed to the `Window` object (this is called delegation).

➤ `class NaggingWindowDecorator extends WindowDecorator` and other decorators: These classes define the behavior you want to add on top of another object. These classes will override all methods that need to be extended, in most cases also involving a call to the original superclass method, which delegates to the `Window` object (`super.setTitle(title)`).

Once you put all of this in place, the complete code for the example above would look as follows. Note that the code sample below makes some "quick and dirty" shortcuts to get the point across, mainly by reusing the JFrame component in our window classes instead of writing a UI widget library from scratch.

```java
import javax.swing.JFrame;
public interface Window {
    public void setTitle(String title);
    public void addPanel(String message);
    public JFrame getJFrame();
}


import javax.swing.BoxLayout;
import javax.swing.JFrame;
import javax.swing.JLabel;
import javax.swing.JPanel;
import javax.swing.JScrollPane;
public class NormalWindow implements Window {
    private final JFrame jFrame;
    private final JPanel mainPane;
    public NormalWindow() {
        this.jFrame = new JFrame();
        this.jFrame.setDefaultCloseOperation(JFrame.DISPOSE_ON_CLOSE);
        // We allow ourselves to cheat here by first setting up a scrollpane
        // as the content pane for every window, with scroll bars hidden
        // Decorators are then free to re-enable these
        this.mainPane = new JPanel();
        this.mainPane.setLayout(new BoxLayout(this.mainPane, BoxLayout.PAGE_AXIS));
        JScrollPane scrollPane = new JScrollPane(mainPane,
```

```
                    JScrollPane.VERTICAL_SCROLLBAR_NEVER,
                    JScrollPane.HORIZONTAL_SCROLLBAR_NEVER);
            this.jFrame.setContentPane(scrollPane);
            this.jFrame.pack();
            this.jFrame.setSize(300, 400);
            this.jFrame.setVisible(true);
        }
        public void setTitle(String title) {
            jFrame.setTitle(title);
        }
        public void addPanel(String message) {
            JPanel pane = new JPanel();
            pane.add(new JLabel(message));
            mainPane.add(pane);
        }
        public JFrame getJFrame() {
            return jFrame;
        }
}


import javax.swing.JFrame;
public abstract class WindowDecorator implements Window {
    private final Window window;
    public WindowDecorator(Window window) {
        this.window = window;
    }
    public void setTitle(String title) {
        window.setTitle(title);
    }
    public void addPanel(String message) {
        window.addPanel(message);
    }
    public JFrame getJFrame() {
        return window.getJFrame();
    }
    public Window getWindow() {
        return window;
    }
}


import java.awt.event.WindowAdapter;
import java.awt.event.WindowEvent;
import javax.swing.JFrame;
public class NaggingWindowDecorator extends WindowDecorator {
    public NaggingWindowDecorator(Window window) {
        super(window);
        // Add a simple message just to show the decorator is working:
        getWindow().addPanel("Decorated with NaggingWindowDecorator");
        getWindow().getJFrame().setAlwaysOnTop(true);
        getWindow().getJFrame().setResizable(false);
        // The code below will prevent users from minimizing the window
        // by immediately re-opening minimized windows
        // In a real life context, you'd of course resort to the full suite
```

```
                // of Swing components as we've seen before, i.e. using JDialog
                getWindow().getJFrame().addWindowListener(new WindowAdapter() {
                    @Override
                    public void windowClosing(WindowEvent we) {
                    }
                    // The following will prevent minimizing
                    @Override
                    public void windowIconified(WindowEvent we) {
                        getWindow().getJFrame().setState(JFrame.NORMAL);
                    }
                });
        }
    }

    import javax.swing.JScrollPane;
    public class ScrollingWindowDecorator extends WindowDecorator {
        public ScrollingWindowDecorator(Window window) {
            super(window);
            // Add a simple message just to show the decorator is working:
            getWindow().addPanel("Decorated with ScrollingWindowDecorator");
            ((JScrollPane)
              getWindow().getJFrame().getContentPane()).setHorizontalScrollBarPolicy(
                  JScrollPane.HORIZONTAL_SCROLLBAR_ALWAYS);
            ((JScrollPane)
              getWindow().getJFrame().getContentPane()).setVerticalScrollBarPolicy(
                  JScrollPane.VERTICAL_SCROLLBAR_ALWAYS);
        }
    }

    public class WindowTester {
        public static void main(String[] args) {
            Window decoratedWindow1 = new NaggingWindowDecorator(new NormalWindow());
            Window decoratedWindow2 = new ScrollingWindowDecorator(new
              NaggingWindowDecorator(new NormalWindow()));
        }
    }
```

Note that this pattern shares a lot of similarities with the bridge pattern. The difference is that in this pattern, you continue to use the interface (`Window`) to define objects and the abstract class has to implement this interface as well. In the bridge pattern, the abstract class can (but does not have to) implement the defined interface and will be used in the client code (`AbstractPrintSpool` is used instead of the `Printer` interface).

Façade Pattern

The façade pattern also deals with wrapping objects and shares similarities with the adapter pattern. Again, it is related to the previous patterns:

➤ The adapter pattern converts the interface to the one the client code is expecting.

➤ The bridge pattern adds a layer of abstraction between the client code and implementations of an interface.

➤ The decorator pattern allows the addition and combination of behavioral extensions to an original interface.

➤ The façade pattern aims to provide a simplified interface around a collection of other interfaces.

The façade pattern is like the adapter pattern on steroids: the façade class will contain an instance of every class it wraps in order to provide a unified and simpler interface for the client code that needs it. For example, let's say you have a class to search for flights between two locations and a class to search for hotels between two locations. Instead of using these two classes as is in your code, it might be a good idea to define a third class (`TripPlanner`) that wraps around these two classes in order to find a list of suitable flights and hotels for a given set of locations and time period. The client can then use this façade class, which adds an extra layer of decoupling.

> **NOTE** *A word of warning for all these "wrapping" patterns. Note that all these patterns connect the wrapped class to their wrappers, meaning that if changes are made to the wrapped subsystems, all adapters, bridges, decorators, facades, and proxies might need to be changed and updated as well. Therefore, don't go too far when connecting classes together by wrapping them up around each other.*

Composite Pattern

The last structural pattern discussed in this chapter is less about wrapping around objects and more about grouping objects together. Luckily, the description of this pattern is easy to understand:

Allows a group of objects to be treated like a single object.

Basically, following the composite pattern boils down to implementing your own collection class, which is subject to the same methods as the members of that collection. This pattern is pretty interesting since it is easy to understand in essence, but there are multiple ways to implement it, all with their advantages and disadvantages.

This idea is illustrated with a simple example. Imagine you're programming an application for the human resources department. The department oversees a number of employees—project managers and programmers. You need to keep track of their names and salaries. As such, you set out to create the following class:

```
public class Employee {
    private String name;
    private double salary;
    private boolean manager;

    public Employee(String name, double salary, boolean manager) {
        this.name = name;
        this.salary = salary;
        this.manager = manager;
    }
```

```
    public String getName() {
        return name;
    }

    public double getSalary() {
        return salary;
    }

    public boolean isManager() {
        return manager;
    }
}
```

You discuss your progress with the HR team. They congratulate you on your work, but the team head mentions the following: "Sorry, I totally forgot to mention this—I thought this would be clear—but managers need to be able to oversee other employees, managers, or programmers, whereas programmers cannot."

No problem, you think, I'll just add a list to the Employee class to keep track of employees overseen by other employees:

```
public class Employee {
    private List<Employee> employees;
    private String name;
    private double salary;
    private boolean manager;

    public Employee(String name, double salary, boolean manager) {
        this.employees = new ArrayList<>();
        this.name = name;
        this.salary = salary;
        this.manager = manager;
    }

    public void addEmployee(Employee employee) {
        if (isManager())
            employees.add(employee);
    }

    public void removeEmployee(Employee employee) {
        if (isManager())
            employees.remove(employee);
    }

    public Employee getEmployee(int i) {
        return employees.get(i);
    }

    public int getNrEmployees() {
        return employees.size();
    }

    public String getName() {
```

```
        return name;
    }

    public double getSalary() {
        return salary;
    }

    public boolean isManager() {
        return manager;
    }
}
```

You discuss your changes with the team head. "Great," you're told, "this is exactly what we need!" Throughout the following months, the HR department requests more and more features. "We forgot to mention, we also want to keep track of the languages a programmer knows. Oh, and for managers, we want to keep track of the number of years they have been working at the company. Oh, and we also have a third type of employee that we want to add. . ." You keep expanding and changing your Employee class, and all is well in the world, right? Not so much. By now, your object-oriented senses should start tingling. The right approach to tackle this problem is to add an abstraction by creating separate Employee, Manager, and Programmer classes, like so:

```java
import java.util.ArrayList;
import java.util.List;

public abstract class Employee {
    private List<Employee> employees;
    private String name;
    private double salary;

    public Employee(String name, double salary) {
        this.employees = new ArrayList<>();
        this.name = name;
        this.salary = salary;
    }

    public void addEmployee(Employee employee) {
        employees.add(employee);
    }

    public void removeEmployee(Employee employee) {
        employees.remove(employee);
    }

    public Employee getEmployee(int i) {
        return employees.get(i);
    }

    public int getNrEmployees() {
        return employees.size();
    }

    public String getName() {
        return name;
    }
}
```

```java
        public double getSalary() {
            return salary;
        }
    }

public class Manager extends Employee {
    public Manager(String name, double salary) {
        super(name, salary);
    }
}

public class Programmer extends Employee {
    public Programmer(String name, double salary) {
        super(name, salary);
    }

    @Override
    public void addEmployee(Employee employee) {
        // Consider throwing an exception here
    }

    @Override
    public void removeEmployee(Employee employee) {

    }

    @Override
    public Employee getEmployee(int i) {
        return null;
    }

    @Override
    public int getNrEmployees() {
        return 0;
    }
}
```

Much better! Now every concept has its own class. Note how this immediately gives you a way to implement the composite pattern. You now have an easy way to treat a group of employees the same way as a single employee. The composite pattern makes it very easy to model a "has a" relation, which is particularly helpful when you want to model a tree structure, such as in this example.

To see why this is so helpful, look at the next simple example program, which shows the organizational structure starting from a particular employee:

```java
public class HRExample {
    public static void main(String args[]) {
        Employee programmerAimee = new Programmer("Aimee", 16000);
        Employee programmerBart = new Programmer("Bart", 15000);
        Employee programmerSeppe = new Programmer("Seppe", 14000);

        Employee managerJane = new Manager("Jane", 30000);
        Employee managerWiley = new Manager("Wiley", 35000);

        managerWiley.addEmployee(managerJane);
        managerWiley.addEmployee(programmerBart);
```

```
            managerJane.addEmployee(programmerAimee);
            managerJane.addEmployee(programmerSeppe);

            showOrganigram(managerWiley);
        }

        public static void showOrganigram(Employee e) {
            showOrganigram(e, 1);
        }

        private static void showOrganigram(Employee e, int level) {
            // Recursive function, show employee
            System.out.format("%"+(level*2)+"s - %s, " +
                "earning %s", "", e.getName(), e.getSalary());
            if (e.getNrEmployees() > 0)
                System.out.format(" manages %s employees:", e.getNrEmployees());
            System.out.println();
            for (int i = 0; i < e.getNrEmployees(); i++) {
                showOrganigram(e.getEmployee(i), level+1);
            }
        }
    }
}
```

Running this code prints the following:

```
 - Wiley, earning 35000.0 manages 2 employees:
   - Jane, earning 30000.0 manages 2 employees:
     - Aimee, earning 16000.0
     - Seppe, earning 14000.0
   - Bart, earning 15000.0
```

Here you can see the benefits of the composite pattern in action. In the recursive function, you don't need to pay attention to the differences among a programmer, manager, and groups of employees, as you can apply the same methods on all of them, using the single, abstract `Employee` class.

Note that there is also a second way to model a composite pattern: by having both the composite objects (the objects containing a list) and the member objects (objects without a list) implement a component interface that defines the operations that should be possible on both of them. It would use the following structure:

```
public interface Component {
    public void method1();
    public void method2();
    // ...
}

public class Member implements Component {
    @Override
    public void method1() {/*...*/}
    @Override
    public void method2() {/*...*/}

    // Other methods
}
```

```java
public class Group implements Component {
    @Override
    public void method1() {/*...*/}
    @Override
    public void method2() {/*...*/}

    public void addMember(Member member) {/*...*/}
    public void removeMember(Member member) {/*...*/}
    public Member getMember(int i) {/*...*/}
    public int nrMembers() {/*...*/}

    // Other methods
}
```

This implementation can be useful when the member and group nodes do not share any behavior other than a particular set of methods defined in the interface, or when you explicitly want to prevent executing list methods (`addMember`, `removeMember` ...) on the member objects. Note that it is also possible to combine the two approaches by defining an interface, an abstract class that implements the interface, and subclasses.

THE INTERFACE-ABSTRACT COMBO

This is a good point in the chapter to mention a particularly curious pattern that you might see in large, heavily "architected" codebases: the combination of an abstract class and an interface.

These classes will often be scattered across different packages, so you need to go on a hunt to find the code you're looking for in the dependency tree. For instance, an interface class might be named `IPerson`, `PersonInterface`, or just `Person`, and be located in the `com.bigcompany.models.hr` package, or perhaps in `com.bigcompany.models.hr.interface`. The abstract class implementing this interface might be named `AbstractPerson`, `PersonImpl`, `PersonImplementation`, or `Person`, and be located in `com.bigcompany.models.hr` or `com.bigcompany.models.hr.impl`, perhaps. The subclasses extending the abstract class are then named `NormalPerson` and `VIPPerson`, or `NormalPersonImpl` and `VIPPersonImpl`, and are located in `com.bigcompany.models.hr` or `com.bigcompany.models.hr.impl`...

What is going on here? In terms of, naming, different programmers prefer different strategies, but in general, an interface defines a contract that the implementations should adhere to. This immediately provides a good heuristic for deciding between an interface and an abstract class: a person is a noun. Normal persons and VIP persons are always, by definition, people. Starting with an abstract class makes more sense in this case. An abstract class describes all the subclasses.

The interface describes what the implementing classes should be able to *do*. Consider the `Comparable` built-in interface in Java, which describes the implementations that should add a method that allows you to compare one object of the implementing class to another object of that class. Maybe this applies to all persons as well (comparing alphabetically based on name, for instance), or maybe this only applies to some subclasses of a person, for example, `VIPPerson`. With subclassing, you describe a hierarchy of inherited behavior. With interfaces, you describe a set of behavior that can be implemented by classes.

So why would it make sense to apply both? First of all, using this approach allows a certain freedom. For instance, when you use and pass around the *interface* in your client code, you can later define a second abstract class (with descendants) that also implements this interface. These two sets of hierarchies can then differ from each other, but since they both implement the same interface, your client code will continue to work as normal, for both abstract classes and all their descendants, without you having to perform heavy refactoring. However, this doesn't mean that you should go out of your way to always define an interface and an abstract class. If you find yourself adding all the methods in the abstract class as signatures to the interface, the added benefit of the interface itself is little, especially since there is no immediate desire to create a second abstract class implementing that interface. Even if such a desire did arise, it is likely that you could refactor your current class tree to add the new abstract class as a subclass of the existing abstract class, since they appear to share so much behavior anyway.

The best thing to do is pick either an abstract class (a class *is* a...) or an interface (a class *can do*...) and refactor only when a need arises.

One particular real-life scenario you have seen before uses the decorator pattern, where the abstract class and its descendants contain most of the shared code and implement an interface (in simple cases, the abstract hierarchy can be replaced with a single class). The decorator classes can then form a second hierarchy of abstract classes and descendants (or can also be implemented as a collection of unrelated classes in simple cases), and also implement the interface. The interface then provides signatures for the functionality the decorators can tweak. Figures 12-1 through 12-4 provide a schematic overview of these cases.

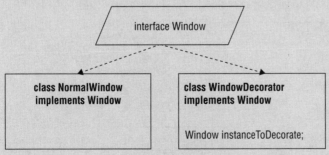

Simplest case: shared interface, two concrete classes

FIGURE 12-1

continues

continued

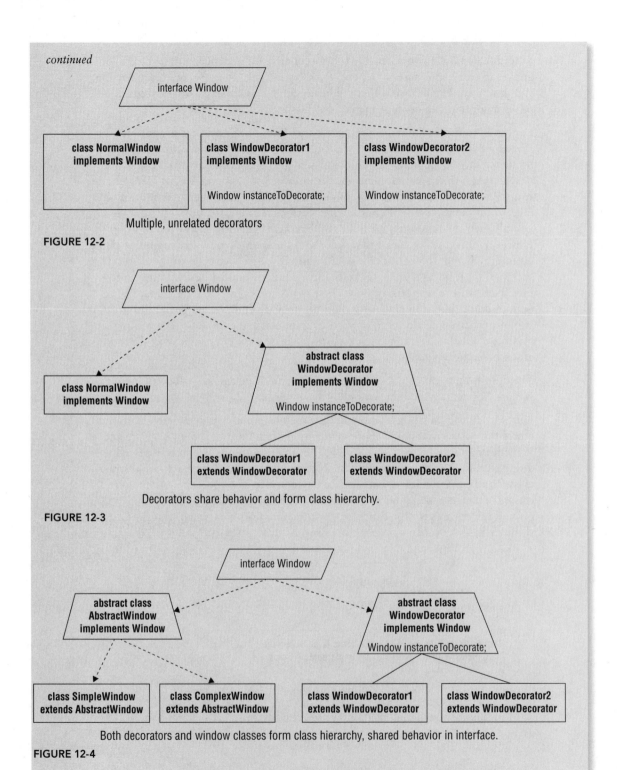

Multiple, unrelated decorators

FIGURE 12-2

Decorators share behavior and form class hierarchy.

FIGURE 12-3

Both decorators and window classes form class hierarchy, shared behavior in interface.

FIGURE 12-4

Type Pattern and Role Pattern

The last structural pattern covered in this chapter is not explicitly mentioned as such by the Gang of Four, but captures a powerful concept that's worth explaining on its own.

The idea is that you will create a level of abstraction above the classes and instances, meaning the concept of a class is made into a class itself. Each instance of that class, that is, each object, then represents a different class.

This idea might seem a bit confusing at first. Imagine you're programming an application to manage various kinds of products. Like a good object-oriented programmer, you start out by defining an abstract `Product` class and then define concrete subclasses: `Book`, `Movie`, `Music`, and so on. As time progresses, maybe your product tree becomes more and more complex, and you end up having more and more subclasses.

Your program is starting to become hard to maintain, with this gigantic product class tree that keeps growing. This is the typical object-oriented issue, right? Indeed, subclassing defines an "is a" relationship, but it's only one way of establishing this conceptual relationship.

You decide to sit back and think about your problem some more. At a basic level, you're trying to solve a simple concept. You have a set of products you want to manage and that share some particular attributes and behavior. Each product is of a certain type, a certain class, in your code. What if you tried to create a class for a class? A class conceptualizing the product type? You set out to try this idea:

```java
import java.util.Set;

public class ProductType {
    private String name;
    private Set<String> properties;

    public ProductType(String name, Set<String> properties) {
        this.name = name;
        this.properties = properties;
    }

    public String getName() {
        return name;
    }

    public Set<String> getProperties() {
        return properties;
    }
}

import java.util.HashMap;
import java.util.Map;

public class Product {
    private double price;
    private String name;
    private ProductType type;
    private Map<String, Object> typeProperties;
```

```java
    public Product(String name, double price, ProductType type) {
        this.name = name;
        this.price = price;
        this.type = type;
        this.typeProperties = new HashMap<>();
        for (String property : type.getProperties())
            this.typeProperties.put(property, null);
    }

    public double getPrice() {
        return price;
    }

    public String getName() {
        return name;
    }

    public void setProperty(String property, Object value) {
        validateProperty(property);
        typeProperties.put(property, value);
    }

    public Object getProperty(String property) {
        validateProperty(property);
        return typeProperties.get(property);
    }

    private void validateProperty(String property) {
        if (!typeProperties.containsKey(property))
            throw new IllegalArgumentException("Property "+property
                    +" not valid for type: "+type.getName());
    }
}
```

Next, you try it:

```java
import java.util.HashSet;

public class TypeTest {
    public static void main(String[] args) {
        ProductType musicType = new ProductType("Music",
                new HashSet<String>());
        ProductType movieType = new ProductType("Movie",
                new HashSet<String>());

        // Set some properties for books:
        ProductType bookType = new ProductType("Book",
                new HashSet<String>(){{
                    add("title");
                    add("author");
                    add("pages");
                }});

        Product someMusic = new Product("A music track", 0.99, musicType);

        Product aBook = new Product("My book", 44.99, bookType);
```

```
        aBook.setProperty("title", aBook.getName());
        aBook.setProperty("author", "Aimee, Bart and Seppe");
        aBook.setProperty("pages", 540);

        System.out.println("Book title: "+aBook.getProperty("title"));
        System.out.println("Book author: "+aBook.getProperty("author"));
        System.out.println("Book pages: "+aBook.getProperty("pages"));
    }
}
```

Congratulations, you've just implemented the first principle of Object-Oriented Programming (classes and objects) in an object-oriented manner, albeit a bit awkwardly. Your properties are currently all objects and will need to be typecast to be used in a meaningful way. It's also hard to know which properties a certain type has (this could be fixed by adding a method returning all properties). Also, this system does not support inheritance. Again, this could also be done by getting clever and determining that `ProductType` objects can have a "parent" `ProductType`. If a property is set to `null`, a product type can then ask a parent (if set) to see if they have a value for a particular property, which is the basics of data inheritance. You might also want to modify your `ProductType` class so it works more like a real constructor, which you could do by adding the following method:

```
public Product createProduct(String name, double price) {
    return new Product(name, price, this);
}
```

Which can be used like so:

```
Product someMusic = musicType.createProduct("A music track", 0.99);
Product aBook = bookType.createProduct("My book", 44.99);
```

Exciting, no? Using this pattern also has the added benefit that product types can be created and destroyed while the program is running, without requiring that you fire up Eclipse, define some new subclasses, compile everything, and ship it out. Just ask the users which properties the new type should have and you're golden. You could even allow users to save a list of product type definitions to a file, which can be loaded back in.

In fact, using this pattern, you can also go a step further than Java allows. Think about the following ideas, for instance:

➤ Allow the type of an object to change. With normal subclassing, this would not be possible (and rightly so!). If this is allowed, this pattern is sometimes called a role pattern. Imagine your program is managing employees who can be managers or programmers. You might want to create `Employee`, `Manager`, and `Programmer` classes, the latter two subclassing `Employee`. But what if an employee's role changes? Then modeling these concepts as a subclass is not a good idea, and you're better off with classes for `Employee`, `EmployeeRole` (abstract), `ManagerRole` (concrete subclass), and `ProgrammerRole` (concrete subclass), and then adding methods to `Employee` to set and get its role. What if roles can be defined at runtime as well? Then you need to resort to the type pattern explained here.

➤ Allow an object to have multiple types or roles, by keeping a list of types.

➤ Allow multiple inheritance, by allowing a type to have a list of parent types. What this means in practice is for you to determine.

In conclusion, the type pattern is a very powerful one, and it allows you to create your own object-oriented paradigm inside an existing one (object-oriented inception). Some warning, however—you will have noticed that this pattern is especially useful when you're dealing with shared *data*, that is, a list of properties for product types.

Note that this pattern's implementation will change a bit when you know up front what the set of properties will be. In that case, just implement this as follows:

➤ The fields you want to change at runtime can be implemented as fields in the class (`Product`, for instance). Fields that are not necessary for a certain product can be set to `null`.

➤ The fields that are determined by the type are implemented as fields in the type class and set at construction or by setters (e.g., in `ProductType`). Getters are added to the original class (`Product`) to fetch information from the type class (`ProductType`), or the type object is directly exposed (`getProductType()` in `Product`).

Note that all of this still has to do with data. When you also want to dynamically construct *behavior*, things get much more difficult. You're then better off resorting to subclasses, or you can apply the strategy pattern (which you'll see later) to dynamically assign another object to your type class from which a method will be called to execute some behavior. As a simple teaser, consider, for example, that you want to implement a method that calculates a discounted price. Sadly, the way this discount is calculated can differ for each product type. In this case, you need to get a bit clever when assigning properties and their values. Why not go a step further as well? The product manager above was basically assuming that all fields in a product type are non-static, non-final, public, and uninitialized. You can change your type class and allow for static final properties that are all public:

```java
import java.util.HashMap;
import java.util.Map;

public class ProductType {
    private String name;

    private Map<String, Object> staticProperties;
    private Map<String, Object> instanceProperties;

    public ProductType(String name) {
        this.name = name;
        this.staticProperties = new HashMap<>();
        this.instanceProperties = new HashMap<>();
    }

    public Product createProduct(String name, double price) {
        return new Product(name, price, this);
    }

    public String getName() {
        return name;
    }

    public void addStaticProperty(String name, Object value) {
        staticProperties.put(name, value);
    }
```

```java
    public void removeStaticProperty(String name, Object value) {
        staticProperties.remove(name);
    }

    public void addInstanceProperty(String name, Object value) {
        instanceProperties.put(name, value);
    }

    public void removeInstanceProperty(String name, Object value) {
        instanceProperties.remove(name);
    }

    public boolean isInstanceProperty(String name) {
        return instanceProperties.containsKey(name);
    }

    public boolean isStaticProperty(String name) {
        return staticProperties.containsKey(name);
    }

    public Object getStaticProperty(String name) {
        return staticProperties.get(name);
    }

    public Object getInstanceProperty(String name) {
        return instanceProperties.get(name);
    }

}
```

NOTE If you're up for a challenge, try making a general type class supporting static, instance, public, private, and final fields. In addition, try creating a `Typeable` interface that any class can implement and then add your custom typing functionality on top of it.

Next, rework the `Product` class:

```java
import java.util.HashMap;
import java.util.Map;

public class Product {
    private double price;
    private String name;
    private ProductType type;
    private Map<String, Object> instanceProperties;

    public Product(String name, double price, ProductType type) {
        this.name = name;
        this.price = price;
        this.type = type;
        this.instanceProperties = new HashMap<>();
    }
```

```java
    public double getPrice() {
        return price;
    }

    public String getName() {
        return name;
    }

    public void setProperty(String property, Object value) {
        validateProperty(property);
        instanceProperties.put(property, value);
    }

    public Object getProperty(String property) {
        validateProperty(property);
        if (!instanceProperties.containsKey(property)) {
            // Get the default initialized property from the type
            return type.getInstanceProperty(property);
        }

        return instanceProperties.get(property);
    }

    public Object getStaticProperty(String property) {
        if (!type.isStaticProperty(property))
            throw new IllegalArgumentException("Static property "+property+
                    " not valid for type: "+type.getName());
        return type.getStaticProperty(property);

    }

    private void validateProperty(String property) {
        if (!type.isInstanceProperty(property))
            throw new IllegalArgumentException("Property "+property+
                    " not valid for type: "+type.getName());
    }
}
```

Your main class will then look like this:

```java
public class TypeTest {
    public static void main(String[] args) {
        // Product types now have a discount calculator field...
        BookDiscountCalculator bookDiscounter = new BookDiscountCalculator();

        ProductType bookType = new ProductType("Book");
        bookType.addInstanceProperty("title", null);
        bookType.addInstanceProperty("author", null);
        bookType.addInstanceProperty("pages", 0);
        bookType.addStaticProperty("discountCalculator", bookDiscounter);

        Product aBook = bookType.createProduct("My book", 44.99);
        aBook.setProperty("title", aBook.getName());
        aBook.setProperty("author", "Aimee, Bart and Seppe");
        aBook.setProperty("pages", 540);
```

```java
        Product anotherBook = bookType.createProduct("My second book", 244.99);
        anotherBook.setProperty("title", anotherBook.getName());
        anotherBook.setProperty("author", "Patternicus");
        anotherBook.setProperty("pages", 800);

        showBook(aBook);
        showBook(anotherBook);
    }

    public static void showBook(Product bookProduct) {
        System.out.format("Book '%s' from '%s' (%s pages) costs '%s' " +
            "--> after discount = %s%n",
                bookProduct.getProperty("title"),
                bookProduct.getProperty("author"),
                bookProduct.getProperty("pages"),
                bookProduct.getPrice(),
                ((BookDiscountCalculator) bookProduct
                    .getStaticProperty("discountCalculator"))
                        .getDiscountedPrice(bookProduct.getPrice())
        );
    }

    public static interface DiscountCalculator {
        public double getDiscountedPrice(double originalPrice);
    }

    public static class BookDiscountCalculator implements DiscountCalculator {
        @Override
        public double getDiscountedPrice(double originalPrice) {
            return Math.max(10, originalPrice * 0.60 - 10);
        }
    }
}
```

Note how it is now possible to define a discount calculator for each product type.

> **NOTE** *If you've been following along closely throughout this book, you might remember that Java defines the concept of a class as an actual class, as* `java.lang.Class`. *Couldn't you just use that to make your classes at runtime, programmatically? Sadly, no. The constructor for this class* class *is not visible. The following will not work:*
>
> ```java
> Class myClass = new Class();
> ```
>
> *If you want to get clever, you can use Java's reflection capabilities together with a custom class loader to construct classes on the fly. If you want to see this approach in action, the most basic proof of concept looks like this:*
>
> ```java
> import java.net.URL;
> import java.net.URLClassLoader;
> import java.nio.file.Files;
> import java.nio.file.Path;
> import java.nio.file.Paths;
> ```
>
> *continues*

continued

```java
import javax.tools.JavaCompiler;
import javax.tools.ToolProvider;


public class ClassMaker {
    public static void main(String[] args) throws Exception {
        String source = "public class Test { "
            + "static { System.out.println(
                \"A new class enters this life!\"); } "
            "public Test() { "
            + "     System.out.println(
                \"Wow! Who has created me?\");"
            + "}"
            + "}";

    Path sourceDir = Files.createTempDirectory("_javaTest");
    Path sourceFile = Paths.get(sourceDir + "/Test.java");
    Files.write(sourceFile, source.getBytes());

    System.out.println("Compiling: "+sourceFile.toString());

    JavaCompiler compiler = ToolProvider.getSystemJavaCompiler();
    if (compiler == null) {
        System.out.println(
            "Could not get compiler. Are you running with JDK?");
        System.exit(1);
    }

    compiler.run(null, null, null, sourceFile.toString());

    System.out.println("Making class...");

    URLClassLoader classLoader = URLClassLoader.newInstance(
        new URL[] {
            sourceDir.toUri().toURL()
        });
    Class<?> cls = Class.forName("Test", true, classLoader);
    Object instance = cls.newInstance();

    System.out.println("Compiled a new class: "+cls);
    System.out.println("Created its instance: "+instance);
    }
}
```

Note that you must run this code with the JDK, which will then produce something like this:

```
Compiling: C:\Users\n11093\AppData\Local\Temp\
    _javaTest560570871985698759\Test.java
Making class...
```

```
            A new class enters this life!
            Wow! Who has created me?
            Compiled a new class: class Test
            Created its instance: Test@79dd63b4
```

Truly a Frankenstein-inspired class. If you think this is cheating by requiring the JDK, note that the Eclipse developers have managed to implement a Java compilation library on top of the JRE, which you could use here instead. There's also the BCEL (Byte Code Engineering Library). Finally, if you know the methods a class should have beforehand (as was the case in the previous example), you can start with an interface and then rely only on reflection to do the rest for you, without a class loader or compilation. Again, this is too advanced to discuss in full here (in fact, this is already very deep in Java's internals at this point). Finally, it's interesting to know that some developers have applied this concept toward creating software solutions that allow you to change a Java program while it is running, without having to stop it. Look up "hot code replace" if you wish to learn more about this.

Behavioral Patterns

Behavioral patterns are concerned with organizing communication between objects in an efficient and clean manner.

Here, the chain-of-responsibility, observer (and model-view-controller), iterator, visitor, template, and strategy patterns are covered. The command, interpreter, mediator, and state patterns are not discussed as they are less commonly used. They are interesting and very useful in particular cases, but deal less with architecture-related object-oriented programs and are therefore less suitable for a beginner's tour.

Chain-of-Responsibility Pattern

The chain-of-responsibility pattern describes a method that organizes objects in a chain. This is useful when certain commands are handled by different objects, each of them passing the command to the next object in the chain.

A simple example to illustrate this pattern is through a logging system. Imagine that an abstract `Logger` class is defined like so:

```java
public abstract class Logger {
    private Logger nextLoggerInChain;
    public void setNext(Logger logger) {
        nextLoggerInChain = logger;
    }

    public void logMessage(String message) {
        performLogging(message);
```

```
        // Pass command to next link in chain:
        if (nextLoggerInChain != null)
            nextLoggerInChain.logMessage(message);
    }

    // Method to be extended by subclasses
    abstract protected void performLogging(String message);
}
```

Separate subclasses, such as `ConsoleLogger`, `DatabaseLogger`, `FileLogger`, and so on, log messages to a related target and pass the message to the next link in the chain. An example `main` method might look like this:

```
public static void main(String[] args) {
    Logger consoleLogger = new ConsoleLogger();
    Logger emailLogger = new EmailLogger();
    Logger databaseLogger = new DatabaseLogger();

    consoleLogger.setNext(emailLogger);
    emailLogger.setNext(databaseLogger);

    // Send a message down the chain:
    consoleLogger.logMessage("Log this message");
}
```

The chain-of-responsibility pattern is somewhat underappreciated in practice. In most cases, you'll see examples like this one being solved by an implementation of the observer pattern (which you'll see next). However, the chain-of-responsibility pattern is still mentioned here, for two reasons. The first one is that this pattern also defines an order of responsibility. For a logging system, this is not important, but for other systems, it can be useful to establish an ordering, with the first objects in the chain getting a chance to handle the incoming message or object (and potentially modify it) before passing it on. The second reason entails this "passing on" behavior. In most cases where this pattern is useful, you'll code it in such a way that an object in the chain will only pass on an incoming object when the current link is unable to do anything useful with it. Once a link that can handle the incoming object is found, the processing stops there.

Observer Pattern and Model-View-Controller Pattern

The observer pattern describes a framework in which a particular object (the subject) maintains a list of dependents (observers) and notifies them of any important changes.

In Java, this pattern can be implemented in different ways. The first one is by using Java's built-in `java.util.Observable` class and the `java.util.Observer` interface. `Observable` defines the following methods your classes can override:

➤   `void addObserver(Observer o)`

➤   `void deleteObserver(Observer o)`

➤   `void deleteObservers()`

➤   `int countObservers()`

➤ protected void clearChanged()

➤ boolean hasChanged()

➤ void notifyObservers()

➤ void notifyObservers(Object arg)

➤ protected void setChanged()

The Observer interface defines only one method—void update(Observable o, Object arg)—which will be called by the subject. This is illustrated with an example. Say you are building an application to fetch stock quotes. At one point, you realize that other applications might want to plug in to your code to register an interest to be notified whenever you pull in a new stock quote. You decide to make the relevant class in your code Observable:

```java
import java.util.Observable;

// Observable class (the subject)
public class StockTicker extends Observable {
    public void updateStock() {
        // Stock retrieving code here
        // At the end, we get a Quote object, which we pass to our observers
        Quote latestStockQuote = ...;

        notifyObservers(latestStockQuote);
    }
}
```

Note the notifyObservers call. Observers can now be implemented as a class like so:

```java
import java.util.Observable;
import java.util.Observer;

public class StockObserver implements Observer {
    @Override
    public void update(Observable sender, Object receivedObject) {
        Quote quote = (Quote) receivedObject;

        // Do something interesting with the quote here
    }

}
```

Before getting updates from the subject, observers have to register themselves, like so:

```java
public static void main(String[] args) {
    StockTicker ticker = new StockTicker();

    StockObserver observer = new StockObserver();

    ticker.addObserver(observer);
    // Add other observers
}
```

The observer pattern encapsulates a simple but powerful concept that can greatly extend your programs. The observer pattern isn't implemented by using `java.util.Observable` class and `java.util.Observer` in many real-life cases, but rather is implemented in the form of a hand-rolled approach where one class keeps a list of objects it needs to "notify" in some way whenever something interesting happens. The reasons for this stem mainly from the fact that programmers sometimes want to get creative with their use of notification methods, want to keep a list of multiple types of observers, or are hindered by the fact that `Observable` is an abstract class that needs to be extended, preventing classes from extending from another abstract class. Don't worry, though, the pattern and the basic idea behind it are the same.

In fact, it seems that many built-in parts of Java are hampered by this issue, since many classes (especially those dealing with GUIs) prefer to go for a hand-rolled approach. In the Java world, people often refer to the observer pattern as the listener pattern (observers are called listeners in that case). The basic pattern is like this:

➤   The subject class keeps a list of registered listeners and is free to extend its own abstract classes.

➤   The listeners all implement an interface defining the "notification" methods.

➤   When something interesting happens to the subject, it goes through its list of listeners and calls the appropriate notification method.

A perfect way to illustrate this is by building a simple GUI application. As the subject, a simple `JFrame` is used here:

```
import javax.swing.JFrame;

public class GUIListenerExample {
    public static void main(String[] args) {
        // Create our subject
        JFrame frame = new JFrame();
        frame.setSize(400, 400);
        frame.setDefaultCloseOperation(JFrame.EXIT_ON_CLOSE);

        // Create our listener
        MyMouseListener listener = new MyMouseListener();

        // Register
        frame.addMouseListener(listener);

        // Go
        frame.setVisible(true);
    }
}
```

Note that `javax.swing.JFrame` extends `java.awt.Frame` and thus has nothing to do with `Observable`. The listener is created as follows:

```
import java.awt.event.MouseEvent;
import java.awt.event.MouseListener;

import javax.swing.JOptionPane;
```

```
public class MyMouseListener implements MouseListener {
    @Override
    public void mouseClicked(MouseEvent e) {
        JOptionPane.showMessageDialog(null, "You clicked the mouse!");
    }
    @Override
    public void mouseEntered(MouseEvent e) {}
    @Override
    public void mouseExited(MouseEvent e) {}
    @Override
    public void mousePressed(MouseEvent e) {}
    @Override
    public void mouseReleased(MouseEvent e) {}
}
```

This produces the mesmerizing application shown in Figure 12-5.

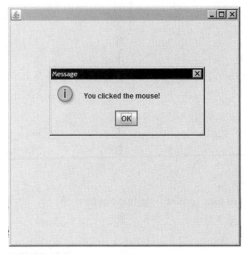

FIGURE 12-5

Note that nothing prevents you from implementing similar listener systems in your own applications. All you need is an interface and subjects that know how to register and notify them. Note that—as you've seen in the chapter dealing with GUI applications—you can also create one-shot throwaway listeners, like so:

```
import java.awt.event.MouseEvent;
import java.awt.event.MouseListener;

import javax.swing.JFrame;
import javax.swing.JOptionPane;


public class GUIListenerExample {
    public static void main(String[] args) {
        // Create our subject
        JFrame frame = new JFrame();
```

```
        frame.setSize(400, 400);
        frame.setDefaultCloseOperation(JFrame.EXIT_ON_CLOSE);

        // Create our listener
        MouseListener listener = new MouseListener(){
            public void mouseClicked(MouseEvent e) {
                JOptionPane.showMessageDialog(null, "You clicked the mouse!");
            }
            public void mouseEntered(MouseEvent e) {}
            public void mouseExited(MouseEvent e) {}
            public void mousePressed(MouseEvent e) {}
            public void mouseReleased(MouseEvent e) {}
        };

        // Register
        frame.addMouseListener(listener);

        // Go
        frame.setVisible(true);
    }
}
```

In some other cases, you'll see the subject acting as its own listener (GUIListenerExample extends
JFrame implements MouseListener):

```
import java.awt.event.MouseEvent;
import java.awt.event.MouseListener;

import javax.swing.JFrame;
import javax.swing.JOptionPane;

public class GUIListenerExample extends JFrame implements MouseListener {
    public GUIListenerExample() {
        this.addMouseListener(this);
    }

    public void mouseClicked(MouseEvent e) {
        JOptionPane.showMessageDialog(null, "You clicked the mouse!");
    }
    public void mouseEntered(MouseEvent e) {}
    public void mouseExited(MouseEvent e) {}
    public void mousePressed(MouseEvent e) {}
    public void mouseReleased(MouseEvent e) {}

    public static void main(String[] args) {
        // Create our subject
        JFrame frame = new GUIListenerExample();
        frame.setSize(400, 400);
        frame.setDefaultCloseOperation(JFrame.EXIT_ON_CLOSE);

        // Go
        frame.setVisible(true);
    }

}
```

Without a doubt, the observer pattern is one of the most useful patterns out there, especially since it forms the cornerstone of another pattern: model-view-controller. You were introduced to this pattern in the previous chapter on GUIs. Basically, a model-view-controller architecture expresses the fact that every program should be separated in three loosely coupled parts:

➤ The model as the central component containing the problem domain (accounts, users, and so on). This part should be completely independent from the user interface in the sense that the interface cannot directly manipulate the model.

➤ The controller is the component that sends commands to the model to manipulate it.

➤ The view is the interface through which the users get an output representation.

This description is a bit hand-wavy, so it is illustrated here with a simple example. Say you want to create a program to deal with checking accounts and you want to put a fancy GUI on top of it. You could start by building a simple window and just keep adding lists and variables until you have everything stuffed in a single ball of code spaghetti, but this is not the object-oriented way to do things. Instead, you start building the core problem domain and think about the classes that matter. In this case, that would be an account. You may recall this example from earlier:

```java
public class Account {
    private String name;
    private double amount;

    public Account(String name) {
        this(name, 0);
    }

    public Account(String name, double startAmount) {
        this.name = name;
        this.amount = startAmount;
    }

    public boolean isOverdrawn() {
        return this.amount < 0;
    }

    public void addFunds(double amount) {
        this.amount += amount;
    }

    public String getName() {
        return name;
    }

    public double getAmount() {
        return amount;
    }
}
```

Next up, you want to create a GUI to manage your account objects. You could start adding windows to this class, but again, this does not seem like the right way to do it. Instead, you decide to start with a new class:

```java
import java.awt.FlowLayout;
import java.awt.event.ActionEvent;
import java.awt.event.ActionListener;

import javax.swing.JButton;
import javax.swing.JFrame;
import javax.swing.JTextField;

public class AccountWindow extends JFrame {
    private JTextField funds, add;
    private JButton addButton;

    public AccountWindow() {
        this.setSize(400, 120);
        this.setDefaultCloseOperation(JFrame.EXIT_ON_CLOSE);
        this.setLayout(new FlowLayout());

        funds = new JTextField(30);
        add = new JTextField(30);
        addButton = new JButton("Add funds");

        funds.setEditable(false);
        addButton.addActionListener(new ActionListener() {
            @Override
            public void actionPerformed(ActionEvent arg0) {
                // Add funds here
            }
        });

        this.add(funds);
        this.add(add);
        this.add(addButton);
    }
}
```

The interface is Spartan-looking for now, but it will do, as shown in Figure 12-6.

FIGURE 12-6

A bigger question on your mind is how to fill in the "Add Funds" box. You want to keep your model and view as separate as possible, and thus avoid passing an Account object to this view. This is where the controller comes in. You start out by defining your controller:

```java
import javax.swing.JFrame;


public class AccountController {
```

```
    private Account model;
    private AccountWindow view;

    public AccountController(Account model, AccountWindow view) {
        this.model = model;
        this.view = view;
    }

    public void addFunds(double amount) {
        model.addFunds(amount);
        view.updateView(model.getAmount());
    }

    public static void main(String args[]) {
        Account myAccount = new Account("AimeeBartSeppe Ltd.", 3000);
        AccountWindow myView = new AccountWindow();

        AccountController controller = new AccountController(myAccount, myView);
        myView.setController(controller);
        myView.updateView(myAccount.getAmount());

        myView.setDefaultCloseOperation(JFrame.EXIT_ON_CLOSE);
        myView.setVisible(true);
    }
}
```

And modify the view accordingly:

```
import java.awt.FlowLayout;
import java.awt.event.ActionEvent;
import java.awt.event.ActionListener;

import javax.swing.JButton;
import javax.swing.JFrame;
import javax.swing.JTextField;

public class AccountWindow extends JFrame {
    private JTextField funds, add;
    private JButton addButton;
    private AccountController controller;

    public AccountWindow() {
        this.setSize(400, 120);
        this.setDefaultCloseOperation(JFrame.EXIT_ON_CLOSE);
        this.setLayout(new FlowLayout());

        funds = new JTextField(30);
        add = new JTextField(30);
        addButton = new JButton("Add funds");

        funds.setEditable(false);
        addButton.addActionListener(new ActionListener() {
            @Override
            public void actionPerformed(ActionEvent arg0) {
                if (controller != null)
```

```
                        controller.addFunds(Double.parseDouble(add.getText()));
                }
        });

        this.add(funds);
        this.add(add);
        this.add(addButton);
    }

    public void updateView(double funds) {
        this.funds.setText("Your funds: "+funds);
        this.add.setText("");
    }

    public void setController(AccountController controller) {
        this.controller = controller;
    }

}
```

You pat yourself on the back. Well done, the view can now call actions in the controller, which modifies its models and sends back updates to the view.

Still, you can't help but feel there's something missing... Most beginner programmers who want to decouple models and UI will end up with a solution resembling something you've just seen. Although the model is now completely unaware of the user interface that might exist (good!), the problem still remains that the controller is calling methods in the view and the view is calling methods in the controller, creating a problem where both need to be explicitly aware of one another.

Luckily, thanks to the observer pattern, there is a way to improve this situation. The basic idea is this: controllers will act as listeners in that they will be notified by the view and then can manipulate their models. The views will also act as listeners; they will be notified by the models but will not be able to manipulate them directly. The models finally act as subjects that notify interested parties, including the listening views.

One aspect of this idea has already been implemented, in a way. That is, the setController method basically registers the controller as a listener in the view. However, there is a smarter way to do this. Since you need to listen for UI events coming from the view, why not define the controller as an UI listener? Second, the controller is now allowed to call methods in the view, serving as an intermediator between the data stored in the models and how it is represented in the views. A better way to do this is to change your model to allow listeners.

So, start again with the Account class. You need to add the ability to notify view listeners. There are several ways to do this:

➤   A registerView method that just sets a single view listener.

➤   A hand-rolled listener solution that keeps a list of views.

➤   A hand-rolled listener solution that keeps a list of objects implementing a self-made AccountListener interface.

➤   Using the built-in Observable and Observer class and interface.

In order to make your program future-proof, go for the most flexible route. Start with defining an `AccountListener` interface:

```java
public interface AccountListener {
    public void notifyFundsChanged(double newAmount);
}
```

Next up, modify your model to accept `AccountListeners`:

```java
import java.util.ArrayList;
import java.util.List;

public class Account {
    private List<AccountListener> listeners;
    private String name;
    private double amount;

    public Account(String name) {
        this(name, 0);
    }

    public Account(String name, double startAmount) {
        this.name = name;
        this.amount = startAmount;
        this.listeners = new ArrayList<>();
    }

    public boolean isOverdrawn() {
        return this.amount < 0;
    }

    public void addFunds(double amount) {
        this.amount += amount;
        for (AccountListener listener : listeners)
            listener.notifyFundsChanged(getAmount());
    }

    public String getName() {
        return name;
    }

    public double getAmount() {
        return amount;
    }

    public void addAccountListener(AccountListener listener) {
        listeners.add(listener);
    }

    public void removeAccountListener(AccountListener listener) {
        listeners.remove(listener);
    }

    public void removeAllAccountListeners() {
```

```
            listeners.clear();
        }
    }
```

Next, change your view to behave as a listener. You also need to modify the view to accept listening controllers. In most cases, every view will have a single listening controller, so you can just keep this as a field instead of a list. Also, the controller object is used directly instead of defined as a separate listening interface (you can try to define an AccountViewListener and work from there if you want).

```
import java.awt.FlowLayout;
import java.awt.event.ActionEvent;
import java.awt.event.ActionListener;

import javax.swing.JButton;
import javax.swing.JFrame;
import javax.swing.JTextField;

public class AccountWindow extends JFrame implements AccountListener,
    ActionListener {
    private JTextField funds, add;
    private JButton addButton;
    private AccountController controller;

    public AccountWindow() {
        this.setSize(400, 120);
        this.setDefaultCloseOperation(JFrame.EXIT_ON_CLOSE);
        this.setLayout(new FlowLayout());

        funds = new JTextField(30);
        funds.setEditable(false);

        add = new JTextField(30);

        addButton = new JButton("Add funds");
        addButton.addActionListener(this);

        this.add(funds);
        this.add(add);
        this.add(addButton);
    }

    @Override
    public void notifyFundsChanged(double newAmount) {
        this.funds.setText("Your funds: "+newAmount);
        this.add.setText("");
    }

    public void registerController(AccountController controller) {
        this.controller = controller;
    }

    @Override
    public void actionPerformed(ActionEvent e) {
```

```
                controller.notifyAddFunds(Double.parseDouble(add.getText()));
        }
    }
```

Finally, your controller should be reworked:

```
    import javax.swing.JFrame;


    public class AccountController {
        private Account model;

        public AccountController(Account model, AccountWindow view) {
            this.model = model;
        }

        public static void main(String args[]) {
            Account myAccount = new Account("AimeeBartSeppe Ltd.", 3000);
            AccountWindow myView = new AccountWindow();

            AccountController controller = new AccountController(myAccount, myView);

            // Register controller and view
            // (This can also be done in controller constructor)
            myView.registerController(controller);
            myAccount.addAccountListener(myView);

            myView.setDefaultCloseOperation(JFrame.EXIT_ON_CLOSE);
            myView.setVisible(true);
        }
        public void notifyAddFunds(double amount) {
            model.addFunds(amount);
        }
    }
```

Note that, technically, the controller does not need to be aware of the view anymore, so you can remove the view field from the controller class. You can also remove it from the constructor, but depending on your preference, you can also let the controller handle its registration and register the view in the model, so that you can decide to keep it in.

When you run this application, you'll see that it behaves exactly the same as before.

> **NOTE** Well… almost exactly. Notice that the `funds` field stays empty until you add some funds. How would you solve this issue while adhering to the model-view-controller principles? Purists would argue that it would be best to add an `notifyControllerRegistered` method to the controller that can be called by the view. The controller would then call a `refreshListeners` method in the
>
> *continues*

> *continued*
>
> *model, which in turn would notify all the listening views to update their states. If this looks like a roundabout way of doing things, don't feel too bad; some implementations prefer to pass the controller to a view's constructor, so that it can be immediately registered and the controller can be notified immediately after the UI is set up. Some implementations allow views to be registered with controllers so that the controller can update their state directly, as you've seen before. In practice, all of these approaches are fine. The key reasoning behind the model-view-controller pattern is to establish a clear separation among data, data manipulation, and data representation. In other words, never mix UI code with data-handling code.*

Before continuing with the next pattern, you may want to read the sidebar about the so-called "lapsed listener" problem.

LAPSED LISTENERS

The observer pattern is a very helpful one, but it comes with a tricky issue that can pose problems in larger applications and cause memory leaks with long-running applications (applications taking up more and more memory until they crash).

The problem is this: let's say that you have a large application and the user decides to close the window of the account. The `AccountWindow` object is thrown away, and the user returns to an overview screen of all accounts. (By the way, if you feel up for it, try expanding the previous example to work with lists of accounts in a model-view-controller paradigm instead of just one account. Which classes do you need to add and which do you need to change?) So far so good, except that the window is still registered as a listener of the account object, which is still being kept around. This prevents the garbage collector from removing the window object from memory. In fact, the account object will just continue to notify the (hidden) window object for eternity. When an account is opened again in the UI, the programmer creates a new view object, so that over time, more and more objects are created and remain stuck as listeners.

The solution is simple: make sure to deregister all listeners when it is time to close them. Note that this is one of the few times when it makes sense to override `Object.finalize()`:

```
@Override
public void finalize() {
    // Deregister this listener
    super.finalize(); // Perform rest of finalization
}
```

However, this is easier said than done, since a listener… listens. It cannot shout to its subjects, "Hey, I'm about to get deleted; please deregister me from your lists." You need to make sure that this listener is deregistered when it's destroyed. A good way to do this is to have the view send a notification to the controller ("I've been closed, goodbye…") so that the controller can proceed to deregister the listener from the relevant views.

Another, more advanced, way of solving this issue is to work with so-called "weak references." These specify a reference to an object (a listener), but allow the garbage collector to kick in once all normal references are gone. In Java, this functionality is provided by the `WeakReference` built-in class, but it is best to explicitly program deregistration in your code. After all, that is why `removeListener` methods are provided.

Iterator Pattern

The next pattern discussed is also built in to Java itself, although contrary to the observer pattern, the iterator pattern is much more useable.

The design goal behind an iterator is to traverse through and access a container's elements, for instance, looping through members in a Java `List` object. Why is this concept so earth-shattering, you might ask. After all, if you have a collection, it makes sense that you can loop through its members. True, but the iterator pattern decouples the way a container is looped over from the container. For instance, the most logical iterator for a list would loop through members by index, but you might prefer to loop through members in reverse order, or random order, or sorted alphabetically first.

In Java, two interfaces exist to apply this pattern. `Iterable` is implemented by collections that can be looped over, and they subsequently implement a method (`iterator()`) to return an object implementing the `Iterator` interface. This is done with the methods `hasNext()`, `next()`, and `remove()`.

All collections in Java extend `Iterable`, meaning that you can get an iterator from every collection class. The following examples illustrates how you can loop over a list using an iterator:

```java
import java.util.ArrayList;
import java.util.Iterator;
import java.util.List;


public class IteratorTest {
    public static void main(String[] args) {
        List<String> list = new ArrayList<>();
        list.add("Bart");
        list.add("Aimee");
        list.add("Seppe");

        Iterator<String> iterator = list.iterator();
        while (iterator.hasNext()) {
```

```
            String name = iterator.next();
            System.out.println(name);
            if (name.startsWith("A")) {
                iterator.remove();
                System.out.println(" ... removed");
            }
        }
    }
}
```

What if you want to create a list returning a backward looping iterator? Just extend the built-in
List class, extending the iterator() method to return your own iterator. If you want to create a
list that can return both iterators, it's easiest to extend the List class with a separate method, as is
done in the following snippet:

```
import java.util.ArrayList;
import java.util.Iterator;
import java.util.List;

public class IteratorTest {
    public static void main(String[] args) {
        BackwardsList<String> list = new BackwardsList<>();
        list.add("Bart");
        list.add("Aimee");
        list.add("Seppe");

        Iterator<String> iterator = list.getBackwardsIterator();
        while (iterator.hasNext()) {
            String name = iterator.next();
            System.out.println(name);
            if (name.startsWith("A")) {
                iterator.remove();
                System.out.println(" ... removed");
            }
        }
    }

    public static class BackwardsList<T> extends ArrayList<T> {
        public Iterator<T> getBackwardsIterator() {
            final List<T> arrayList = this;
            Iterator<T> iterator = new Iterator<T>() {
                private int currentIndex = arrayList.size()-1;
                @Override
                public boolean hasNext() {
                    return currentIndex >= 0;
                }
                @Override
                public T next() {
                    return arrayList.get(currentIndex--);
                }
                @Override
                public void remove() {
                    arrayList.remove(currentIndex+1);
                }
```

```
        };
        return iterator;
    }
  }
}
```

Visitor Pattern

Just as with the chain-of-responsibility pattern you've seen before, the visitor pattern is a little bit more advanced and its benefits might not immediately be clear when programming smaller applications.

The main goal of a visitor pattern is to separate a certain algorithm (some code) from the data structure it operates on. Or, more practically speaking, the visitor pattern allows methods to be added to a related set of classes without having to modify the classes themselves.

Again, let's dive immediately into an example. Let's say you're creating a book management system. You decide to start from an abstract class and extend it to some concrete classes:

```
public abstract class Book {
    private String title;
    // ...
}

public class NonFictionBook extends Book {
    // ...
}

public class FictionBook extends Book {
    // ...
}

public class AudioBook extends Book {
    // ...
}
```

So far, so good. Now let's say at some point you have a list of books you're keeping track of:

```
public class VisitorTest {
    public static void main(String[] args) {
        Book[] books = new Book[]{
                new AudioBook(), new FictionBook(), new FictionBook(),
                new NonFictionBook(), new AudioBook(), new NonFictionBook()
        };

    }
}
```

Okay, now you want to sort this collection of books into three lists, one for each concrete class of books. Simple, you think; you can just write the following:

```
import java.util.ArrayList;
import java.util.List;
```

```
public class VisitorTest {
    public static void main(String[] args) {
        Book[] books = new Book[]{
                new AudioBook(), new FictionBook(), new FictionBook(),
                new NonFictionBook(), new AudioBook(), new NonFictionBook()
        };
        List<AudioBook> audioBooks = new ArrayList<>();
        List<FictionBook> fictionBooks = new ArrayList<>();
        List<NonFictionBook> nonFictionBooks = new ArrayList<>();

        for (Book book : books) {
            if (book instanceof AudioBook)
                audioBooks.add((AudioBook) book);
            else if(book instanceof FictionBook)
                fictionBooks.add((FictionBook) book);
            else if(book instanceof NonFictionBook)
                nonFictionBooks.add((NonFictionBook) book);
        }

        System.out.println("Nr. audio books: "+audioBooks.size());
        System.out.println("Nr. fiction books: "+fictionBooks.size());
        System.out.println("Nr. non-fiction books: "+nonFictionBooks.size());
    }
}
```

However, there are a number of problems with this code. It's kind of ugly looking with all the type-casting going on, and you realize that adding new types of books will require you to do a search for all places where you do something like this.

Luckily, the visitor pattern can help you separate your algorithm (categorizing a list of books in separate lists) from the data structure (the abstract class and its dependents). How? First of all, you define an interface for a "visitor," in this case, someone who can visit books like so:

```
public interface BookVisitor {
    public void visit(AudioBook book);
    public void visit(FictionBook book);
    public void visit(NonFictionBook book);
}
```

Next, add a method to your Book class so that it can accept visitors, as well as to all the concrete classes:

```
public abstract class Book {
    private String title;
    // ...

    abstract public void accept(BookVisitor visitor);
}


public class FictionBook extends Book {
    @Override
    public void accept(BookVisitor visitor) {
```

```
            visitor.visit(this);
        }
    }


public class AudioBook extends Book {
    @Override
    public void accept(BookVisitor visitor) {
        visitor.visit(this);
    }
}


public class NonFictionBook extends Book {
    @Override
    public void accept(BookVisitor visitor) {
        visitor.visit(this);
    }
}
```

You might be thinking there is no difference between this and the previous strategy, since both require you to override the accept methods. However, since the concrete class extends the abstract class, Eclipse will throw a warning in case you forget to implement this method in your new concrete class, and consequently will throw a warning to implement this in your interface as well. In short, there's no risk of forgetting anything in this case.

Finally, you need to define the visitor implementation:

```
import java.util.ArrayList;
import java.util.List;


public class CategorizingBookVisitor implements BookVisitor {

    private List<AudioBook> audioBooks;
    private List<FictionBook> fictionBooks;
    private List<NonFictionBook> nonFictionBooks;

    public CategorizingBookVisitor() {
        this.audioBooks = new ArrayList<>();
        this.fictionBooks = new ArrayList<>();
        this.nonFictionBooks = new ArrayList<>();
    }

    @Override
    public void visit(AudioBook book) {
        audioBooks.add(book);
    }

    @Override
    public void visit(FictionBook book) {
        fictionBooks.add(book);
    }
```

```
        @Override
        public void visit(NonFictionBook book) {
            nonFictionBooks.add(book);
        }

        public List<AudioBook> getAudioBooks() {
            return audioBooks;
        }

        public List<FictionBook> getFictionBooks() {
            return fictionBooks;
        }

        public List<NonFictionBook> getNonFictionBooks() {
            return nonFictionBooks;
        }
    }
```

The main program code now becomes a simple and elegant affair:

```
public class VisitorTest {
    public static void main(String[] args) {
        Book[] books = new Book[]{
                new AudioBook(), new FictionBook(), new FictionBook(),
                new NonFictionBook(), new AudioBook(), new NonFictionBook()
        };

        CategorizingBookVisitor visitor = new CategorizingBookVisitor();
        for (Book book : books)
            book.accept(visitor); // Accept the visitor

        System.out.println("Nr. audio books: "+visitor.getAudioBooks().size());
        System.out.println("Nr. fiction books: "+visitor.getFictionBooks().size());
        System.out.println("Nr. non-fiction books:
            "+visitor.getNonFictionBooks().size());
    }
}
```

The workings of the visitor pattern should be pretty clear by now. Consider the visitor to be an object ringing a doorbell at another object's house. By calling the `accept` method, the object opens the door and lets the visitor in.

Template Method Pattern

The last two patterns to be discussed are easy to understand and make you think, "Of course, this definitely seems like the normal way to do this." Nevertheless, it is worthwhile to explicitly discuss them, because they are easy to overlook in practice if you haven't encountered them before.

The template method pattern defines a general structure of a piece of code in a so-called template method, where some particular steps are kept abstract, left to the concrete subclasses to implement. This pattern is particularly useful when you know the general structure of a piece of code, but want to keep the internals flexible.

This can be illustrated with a simple example. Let's say you've written some code to get a list of expenses your company has incurred from a database, which you store in a `List<Expense>` object. You know that management will want to run different kinds of statistics on this list of expenses. What is the total sum of all expenses? How many different receiving companies are involved? How many products of a certain type were purchased? And so on. In any case, you realize that the general structure of all these questions is the same: you loop through the list, do something with every expense, and present the result. As such, you could make this type of template method:

```java
import java.util.List;

public abstract class ExpenseListCalculator {
    public final double calculate(List<Expense> expenses) {
        initialize();
        for (Expense expense : expenses) {
            handle(expense);
        }
        return getResult();
    }

    protected abstract void initialize();
    protected abstract void handle(Expense expense);
    protected abstract double getResult();
}
```

Calculating the total sum of all expenses would now look like this:

```java
public class ExpenseTotalSumCalculator extends ExpenseListCalculator {

    private double total;

    @Override
    protected void initialize() {
        total = 0;
    }

    @Override
    protected void handle(Expense expense) {
        total += expense.getTotalPrice();
    }

    @Override
    protected double getResult() {
        return total;
    }

}
```

Finding the amount of expense lines related to a given product is similarly easy:

```java
public class ExpenseProductCountCalculator extends ExpenseListCalculator {

    private double count;
    private String product;
```

```
        public ExpenseProductCountCalculator(String productToFind) {
            this.product = productToFind;
        }

        @Override
        protected void initialize() {
            count = 0;
        }

        @Override
        protected void handle(Expense expense) {
            if (expense.getProduct().equals(product))
                count++;
        }

        @Override
        protected double getResult() {
            return count;
        }

    }
```

The benefit of using this pattern comes not only from the fact that you can now easily create new implementations for a general algorithm, but you will also able to work with all these algorithms in a general manner, using the abstract class. You could now, for instance, easily define a list of `ExpenseListCalculator` objects that should be executed one by one and added to a report.

Strategy Pattern

The strategy pattern also deals with generalizing algorithms, but here, the focus is on selecting a particular algorithm at runtime, instead of algorithms extending a general template.

To see how this works, let's say you have a `customer` class. You want to add a method in order to send notification messages to this user. Depending on the user's preferences, they can be notified by text message, email, or Twitter. You want to avoid adding a bunch of `notifySMS`, `notifyEmail`, and `notifyTwitter` methods, which look ugly and are hard to maintain later on. There should be a better, object-oriented way to do this.

You realize that all these ways of notifying a customer can be regarded as different notification strategies, and thus get to work. First, you define a general interface:

```
public interface NotifyStrategy {
    public void notify(Customer customer, String message);
}
```

The `customer` class looks something like this:

```
public class Customer {
    private NotifyStrategy notificationPreference;

    public Customer(NotifyStrategy notificationPreference) {
        this.notificationPreference = notificationPreference;
    }
```

```
    // ...

    public void notify (String message) {
        notificationPreference.notify(this, message);
    }
}
```

An implementation of the notification strategy then looks like this:

```
public class EmailNotifyStrategy implements NotifyStrategy {

    @Override
    public void notify(Customer customer, String message) {
        // Send mail to customer.getEmail();

        System.out.println("Sending an email: "+message);
    }
}
```

You can test the program like so:

```
public class StrategyTest {
    public static void main(String[] args) {
        EmailNotifyStrategy emailNotifier = new EmailNotifyStrategy();

        Customer a = new Customer(emailNotifier);
        Customer b = new Customer(emailNotifier);

        a.notify("Your product has shipped!");
    }
}
```

This concludes the tour of the creational, structural, and behavioral design patterns. It is easy to feel overwhelmed by these concepts, especially if you're a newbie. Some of these patterns might look confusing, and some of them might look so nicely designed that you want to use them right away. Be careful not to overuse them.

Most of the patterns that were discussed deal, ultimately, with abstracting concepts and algorithms into more classes and objects. Most programmers will go through an "abstraction vision quest" sometime in their career, looking roughly like this:

1. Beginner programmers don't care too much about patterns and architecture. Their programs are small. They take care to put every concept into an appropriate class, but things stay manageable and nimble.

2. As programmers undertake bigger and bigger projects, they become at one point annoyed by a problem that one of the patterns tries to solve. Why do I have to keep adding subclasses to define product types? Maybe I should think at a higher level? What if I make a product type itself a class? Programmers start looking into design patterns, and suddenly, they seem like the perfect solution to all their problems.

3. Programmers are so happy with their use of patterns and the elegance they bring along, they start "thinking" ahead and start working out beautiful, elegant, and abstract architectures for their new projects.

4. At some point, everything breaks down again. Programmers undertake new projects with an inherent need to create decorators, observers, and some factories thrown in as well. At this point, you'll see the dreaded interface-abstract-concrete class combo showing up for every concept that needs to be defined. It is a grandiose architecture, but somehow, the joy is lost.

5. And so, at some point, programmers try hard not to over-engineer everything. Yes, big software architectures are impressive, but for simple projects, simplicity also brings elegance.

The main takeaway is that you should keep things as simple as possible. What is important to remember is that you should always keep an eye out for things that can be improved as your projects grow. Starting out small is awesome to keep things moving along, but when it's time to finally fix that hard-to-maintain issue, it's nice to keep the things you've learned in this chapter in the back of your mind.

HELPFUL LIBRARIES

It's impossible to list all libraries here, so the most common ones are included here for your reference. The main reason why we discuss these here—in a chapter on patterns and best practices—is because the Java ecosphere thrives mainly thanks to the great amount of excellent, well-known, and reliable libraries that have been built by the community throughout the years. Therefore, the old advice to "buy the best, build the rest" seems like a fitting inspiration (especially when "buy" means "get for free" in this context) for this closing best practice, which is to make use of helpful libraries. You might even end up loving some of them so much that you'll include them by default on the build paths of all your projects.

Apache Commons

The Commons is an Apache open-source project dedicated to building reusable Java components. In short, you could describe this as the project that adds the missing batteries to Java.

In actuality, this project does not encompass one library, but is split into a series of packages. Not all of them are as useful, but the following ones are worth checking out:

➤ Apache Commons Collections: Provides a replacement for Java's collection types. It is more efficient, more expandable, and easier to garbage collect.

➤ Apache Commons CSV: Useful when dealing with CSV files.

➤ Apache Commons Exec: Useful when you want to start and manage other programs from Java.

➤ Apache Commons IO: By far the most widely used commons library, mainly due to its `FileUtils` utility class, which adds a lot of static utility functions to deal with common file handling operations in a sensible manner. One downside is that, for compatibility reasons, `File` objects are used everywhere, instead of the NIO `Path`.

➤ Apache Commons Lang: Adds functionality to Java's language core. Useful additions include a better `Math` class and better String operation methods.

➤ Apache Commons Logging: Adds a thin bridge between your program and many other logging libraries.

➤ Apache Commons Math: Adds many mathematical and statistics components not available in Java by default.

See `http://commons.apache.org/`.

Google Guava

Another collection of libraries, Guava is used by Google in all its Java projects. The most important features include:

➤ Replacement for Java's default collections, making them faster and better. This was the initial idea for the creation of Guava, back when it was called "Google-collections" (you'll see this library popping up, but it is outdated and replaced by Guava).

➤ Tools to avoid `NullPointerExceptions`.

➤ Tools to add preconditions to methods.

➤ Tools to simplify other common tasks, such as writing a `toString()` method.

➤ Tools to efficiently manipulate strings.

➤ Tools to deal with I/O.

➤ Mathematical library.

➤ Tools to write parallel programs.

Note that there is a high degree of overlap regarding the objectives and content of Google Guava and Apache Commons, so it's best to stick with the same project if you can.

See `https://code.google.com/p/guava-libraries/`.

Trove

The Trove library provides yet another high-speed replacement for collection types. The reason for so many implementations stems from the fact that collections often form the cornerstone of every algorithm in Java, and it thus makes sense to keep these nimble and fast.

Trove is popular in some areas (some computer science researchers prefer it), but if you're already using Apache Commons or Google Guava, there's no need to add Trove for any particular reason. Just use the Commons Collections or Guava Collections.

See `http://trove.starlight-systems.com/`.

Colt

This is another library used by computer scientists aiming to add high-performance scientific computing functionality (linear algebra, statistics, fast multidimensional arrays, and others). In most cases, the functionality offered by Commons Math or Guava's math classes should suffice, but you might see this library pop up in a number of very intensive applications.

See `http://acs.lbl.gov/ACSSoftware/colt/`.

Lombok

Lombok aims to provide a set of features that simplifies the development of Java programs. It includes functionality to avoid having to write getters and setters manually, or to create a "data" object in a very straightforward manner. Its website shows the following example:

```
import lombok.AccessLevel;
import lombok.Setter;
import lombok.Data;

@Data public class DataExample {
  private final String name;
  @Setter(AccessLevel.PACKAGE) private int age;
  private double score;
  private String[] tags;
}
```

This code will automatically create getters, setters, `equals`, `hashCode`, and `toString`.

See `http://projectlombok.org/`.

OpenCSV

Just like the Apache Commons CSV library (see "Apache Commons" above), this is another well-maintained library for dealing with CSV files. Using this library can be more ideal in projects where you only desire to add functionality to read and write CSV files, without requiring any other libraries from the Apache Commons project. Including the OpenCSV library is then a simple matter of including one JAR file in your build path.

Reading a CSV files then becomes as easy as writing the following:

```
// Read csvfile using comma separator (,), double quote quote character ("),
// and skip the first 1 line(s)
CSVReader reader = new CSVReader(new FileReader("csvfile.csv"), ',', '"', 1);
String [] nextLine;
while ((nextLine = reader.readNext()) != null) {
    // Do something with nextLine here
}
```

See `http://opencsv.sourceforge.net/`.

HTML and JSON Libraries

These are libraries to parse HTML and deal with JSON data. Refer back to Chapter 10 of this book, which deals with web sources.

See the following libraries:

- `http://jsoup.org/` (jsoup)
- `http://jackson.codehaus.org/` (Jackson)
- `https://code.google.com/p/google-gson/` (Google-gson)

Hibernate and Other JPA-Compliant Libraries

These are libraries that work with persistent data. See Chapter 9 of this book on databases.

See `http://hibernate.org/` (Hibernate).

Joda-Time

This is a library that essentially fixes Java's date and time classes. It is extremely useful if you're stuck with an older Java version.

The library was so well written that the author of Joda-Time was contacted by Oracle to lead the development of the Java 8 `java.time` classes. So make sure you use those instead of `java.util.Date` when you can.

In case you cannot yet use Java 8 in one of your projects, see `http://www.joda.org/joda-time/` to download the library.

Charting Libraries

Many charting libraries exist in Java for making 2D and 3D plots. They differ in terms of flexibility, ease-of-use, and license used.

See the following:

- `http://www.jfree.org/jfreechart/` (JFreeChart)
- `https://code.google.com/p/charts4j/` (charts4j)
- `http://trac.erichseifert.de/gral/` (GRAL)
- `http://freecode.com/projects/jchartlib` (JChartLib)
- `http://jzy3d.org/` (Jzy3d)
- `http://jchart2d.sourceforge.net/` (JChart2D)
- `http://docs.oracle.com/javase/8/javafx/user-interface-tutorial/charts.htm#JFXUI577` (charts with JavaFX)

3D Graphics Libraries

These libraries provide bindings from Java to OpenGL and related APIs to use hardware-accelerated graphics in your projects—useful if you're developing graphic-intensive programs.

See the following:

➤ `http://jogamp.org/` (JogAmp)

➤ `http://www.lwjgl.org/` (LWJGL, geared toward game engine development)

➤ `http://env3d.org/beta/` (Env3D)

➤ `http://www.jpct.net/` (jPCT)

➤ `http://www.oracle.com/technetwork/java/javase/tech/index-jsp-138252.html` (Java 3D, which is outdated; replaced by JavaFX at this point)

➤ `http://docs.oracle.com/javase/8/javase-clienttechnologies.htm` (JavaFX)

Financial Libraries

These libraries offer financial quantitative algorithms and trading algorithms.

See the following

➤ `http://www.jquantlib.org/en/latest/` (JQuantLib, derived from QuantLib—`http://quantlib.org/index.shtml`—which also offers bindings to Java but is written in C++.)

➤ `http://finmath.net/java/` (FinMath)

➤ `https://code.google.com/p/maygard/` (Maygard)

➤ `http://www.javaquant.net/finalgo.html` (Java Quant)

➤ `http://www.eclipsetrader.org/` (EclipseTrader)

INDEX

application layer, OSI model, 356
applications
  applets, 20
  debugging, 6–7, 195–210
  Java beans, 21
  maintenance, 8–9
  object-oriented programming. *See* object-oriented programming
  programming process, 2–5
  servlets, 20
  standalone, 19–20
  structured programming, 9
  testing
    JUnit tests, 210–219
    principles, 7–8
  writing
    BMI calculator example, 497–504
    Eclipse example, 53–59
    GUI example, 468–470
    networked example, 356–360
    Notepad example, 43–46
    paint example, 526–540
argument passing, 109–115
arithmetic operators, 30–31
ArithmeticException, 176
ArrayIndexOutOfBoundsException, 186
ArrayList class, 121
arrays, 34–37
Arrays class, 126
arrow flowchart symbol, 3
ASCII (American Standard Code for Information Interchange), 264–265
aspect-oriented programming, 563
assertions, JUnit tests, 212
assignment operators, 30–31
AudioBook class, 609
AudioInputStream class, 281
autoboxing, 64, 125–126
AWT (Abstract Window Toolkit), 464

B

/b (backspace) escape character, 29
backslash (//) escape character, 29

backspace (/b) escape character, 29
@Before annotation, 211–212
@BeforeClass annotation, 211–212
behavioral patterns, 591–614
  chain-of-responsibility, 591–592
  iterator, 605–607
  model-view-controller, 597–604
  observer, 592–604
  strategy, 612–614
  template method, 610–612
  visitor, 607–610
beta testing, 8
BigDecimal class, 118
BigInteger class, 118
binary files, 263–265
binding, 244–245
bitwise operators, 31–32
black box strategy, 8
blank final variables, 83, 97–98
BMI (Body Mass Index) calculator, creating, 497–504
BMI example program
  comments, 24–26
  creating, 497–504, 546–555
  data types, 27–39
  identifiers, 22
  Java language structure, 21–22
  keywords, 22–23
  methods, 23–24
  naming conventions, 26
  overview, 2–5
  variables, 23
Book class, 223–224
Boolean operators, 32–33
bootstrap class loader, 17–18
BorderLayout layout manager, 476–478
BorderLayoutFrame class, 477–478
boxing, 64
BoxLayout layout manager, 489–493
BoxLayoutFrame class, 490–493
brackets ({ }), 22
branching, 135
break keyword, 157–158, 163–164
BreakLoop class, 165–168, 165–168

J

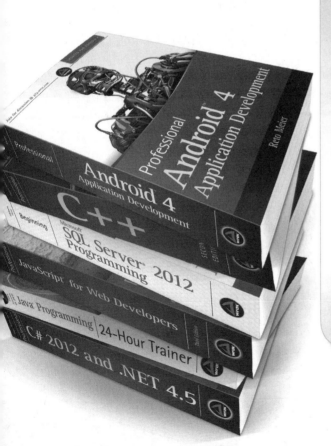